THE CONCEPT OF NATURE
IN NINETEENTH-CENTURY
ENGLISH POETRY

The Concept of Nature
in Nineteenth-Century
English Poetry

BY

JOSEPH WARREN BEACH

PAGEANT BOOK COMPANY
New York
1956

Copyright 1956 by Joseph Warren Beach

Published by Pageant Book Company
59 Fourth Avenue, New York 3, N. Y.

Library of Congress Catalog Card Number: 56-13061

Printed in U. S. A. by Noble Offset Printers, Inc,
400 Lafayette Street, New York City

* * *

Man gehorcht ihren Gesetzen, auch wenn man ihnen widerstrebt; man wirkt mit ihr, auch wenn man gegen sie wirken will . . . Sie hat keine Sprache noch Rede; aber sie schafft Zungen und Herzen, durch die sie fühlt und spricht.

—Goethe, *Fragment über die Natur*

* * *

ACKNOWLEDGMENTS

My acknowledgments to various publishing houses and authors for permission to quote from copyright works are made in the notes in connection with the passages quoted. Considerable portions of this book were read in early stages by my colleagues Dr. Alburey Castell and Dr. Mary Shaw. To both of these philosophical friends I am beholden for valuable suggestions; and while neither of them may be held responsible for any mistakes I may have made, I wish to express my thanks to them for their generous helpfulness.

INTRODUCTORY NOTE 1956

THE text of this volume is an exact reproduction of that published by the Macmillan Company in 1936. A few minor misprints in that text are here indicated in an errata slip. If I were to undertake a revision of this book, I would naturally take note of the relevant literature published during the twenty years' interval. The most notable contribution of more recent scholars is that of Jane Worthington, who, in *Wordsworth's Reading of Roman Prose* (Yale University Press, 1946), has shown how many features of Wordsworth's cosmic philosophy, as well as of his ethical system, were present in Roman Stoic writers with whom he was acquainted, and especially in Cicero and Seneca. The Stoic writers should be taken into account, along with English, French and German writers of the seventeenth and eighteenth centuries, as sources of the complex of ideas that entered into the poetic concept of nature here considered. I will also mention my article on "Reason and Nature in Wordsworth," which appeared in *The Journal of the History of Ideas,* I: 335-351 (June, 1940), in which I cite Cicero among the Stoics, as well as St. Thomas Aquinas, Henry More, Richard Hooker, Samuel Clarke, Grotius, Bolingbroke, and other modern writers, as among those who developed the concept of Right Reason, closely associated by Wordsworth with Nature in his ethical philosophy. This article was written mainly as a reply to numerous critics of the New Humanist school, who had attacked Wordsworth's "romanticism" for the "unsoundness" of his ethical position; my aim was to indicate how well the poet fitted in to an older and more "classical" humanist tradition.

ERRATA

p.29, in the title from D'Holbach, for Systeme, read Systéme

p.47, 1.25, for so, read as

p.80, 1.27, for Godheart's, read Godhead's

p.97, 1.12, for effect, read affect

p.120, 1.3, for vérifiable, read vérifiables

p.163, 1.9, for feroit, read ferois

p.193, 1.17, for sais, read sait

p.195, 1.20 (in the French quotation), for principles, read principes

p.200, 1.18, for or, read of

p.217, 1.10, for constant, read constante

p.257, 1.15 (in the Greek quotation), for T, read T'

p.284, 1.1, for Der, read Das

p.294, 1.1, for sanft,e read sanftem

p.330, 11.5-6, for Shelling, read Schelling

p.352, 1.17, for eine, read einer

p.562, 1.5, for économique, read économiques

CONTENTS

ix

PART TWO

TRANSCENDENTALISM

PART THREE

THE VICTORIANS

PART FOUR

DISAPPEARANCE OF THE CONCEPT OF NATURE

THE CONCEPT OF NATURE
IN NINETEENTH-CENTURY
ENGLISH POETRY

And what is gout? It is a provision of Nature to purify the blood of old men, and to purge the deep parts of the body. Such, at least, is the language of Hippocrates.

—Sydenham, *Medical Observations*

* * *

They learned to identify this mysterious bene-factor with the delight that is bred among the solitary rocks. . . .

—Shelley, *The Assassins*

CHAPTER I

INTRODUCTION AND CONCLUSION

FOR nearly two centuries it was a fashion among poets to sing the praises of abstract nature in terms that to our own critical spirit seem extravagant and often well-nigh ridiculous. And yet these romantic poets were in general men of strong and cultivated intelligence and unusual subtlety of mind. What they wrote, it is reasonable to suppose, cannot have been sheer nonsense. Indeed, we continue to read their nature-poetry with deep sympathy and an emotional response which we cannot altogether repudiate, however apologetic we may feel about it in our more rationalistic moods. This romantic nature-poetry marks, I believe, a significant chapter in human thought. It had its roots deep in the religious and scientific movements of the modern world. It did not run its course entirely without effect. And the nostalgic delight with which we return to it today gives evidence of emotional attitudes which we have shared and have not even yet entirely outgrown.

This book is the outcome of a long-standing desire to gain a clearer comprehension of the philosophical concept of nature as it appears in certain English poets of the nineteenth century. I have wished to see whether I could express, a little more precisely than I ever had done, what—besides brooks and birds—was meant by some favorite poet—Wordsworth or Meredith—when he talked of "nature." And I wished to see what connection could be found between this way of speaking in the poets and the general movement of thought in the period covered. I realize more and more acutely how broad and difficult is the field I have undertaken to explore, how far my study is from being exhaustive or comprehensive. But the general lines do seem to me tolerably clear; in my own mind I have arrived at certain conclusions that appear reasonably obvious on a survey of the whole field. And the reader will be able to follow the discussions of individual authors and understand the general bearing of them much better if I begin with a summary statement of these conclusions.

Summary Statement of Conclusions:

Science and Religion in the Concept of Nature

English and American poets of the eighteenth and nineteenth centuries, as well as European poets of the same period, were fond of personifying Nature—or the virtually equivalent Earth—using the term as an abstraction so as to cover not merely the individual phenomena but also the principle that was supposed to underlie them all. Most often this use of the word nature grew out of the poets' desire to associate the "beauteous forms" of the out-of-doors world with the laws and order of the universe, reinforcing the esthetic pleasure derivable from these beauteous forms with the philosophical notion of order and unity, and vice versa. In the more enthusiastic of these poets, it was assumed that the order of the universe is purposive, harmonious and, taken in the large, benevolent towards man and the other sensitive creatures. This was assumed to be inherently so in the nature of things, or—more often —it was considered as being such by the providential design of a good and intelligent deity. The two views are not always sharply distinguishable, but run over into one another; though it is sufficiently clear that the religious view is the more primary and is latently present in the other even when not recognized.

It is to be observed, however, that this concept of a harmonious and purposive nature was most often held by writers who were not orthodox Christians; that, however religious it might be in its essence, it carried more or less of a latent protest against the prevailing dogmatic religion. These writers were likely to be, in some sense of the words, deists or pantheists, rather than theists, and free-thinkers rather than strict Christian believers. Their sympathies were more with natural theology than with supernatural religion; they tended to conceive of God as a divine "principle" immanent in the universe—in process of realization there—rather than as a person who by his fiat created the universe out of nothing and who continues to determine its course by individual acts of volition. In rare cases, even, the nature-poets were professed atheists, especially in the period of their writing when they most used the term nature; thus insisting even more strongly on the elimination from the concept of nature of the dogmatic tenets of theistic religion. It was the disposition of these writers to stress the elements in the concept of nature derived from science at the expense of those derived from religion. But they continued to take for granted that nature is somehow "good"—an idea which could not have been derived from science pure and simple. And so the emotional tone of their view was tinged with religious assumptions or assumptions drawn from a metaphysic rooted in religion.

The general concept of nature described above was a synthesis of elements derived from science and religion: the scientific notion of regular and universal laws, the religious notion of divine providence. These two notions were fused into one by the metaphysical notion—equally supported by contemporary religion and science—of natural phenomena as purposive in action and adapted to one another and to the general designs of the cosmos. Historically considered, the faith based on this concept of nature amounted, for the literary mind, to a kind of substitute for the Christian religion. It was Christianity freed from various superstitious, irrational and, so to speak, parochial elements, and yet retaining enough emotional force to satisfy man's craving for a moral and intelligible universe. That it did actually constitute such a substitute religion is shown by the fact that the poets who harbored this conception were almost invariably not "fundamentalists," and by the fact, roughly true in a general survey, that their enthusiasm for nature was in almost inverse ratio to the hold of Christian dogma upon them.

The human mind cannot suddenly pass with ease and comfort from any form of faith to agnosticism or unbelief. It instinctively provides itself with means for easing off the emotional strain of such a transition. It provides philosophical bridges from faith to unfaith. And such a bridge was the romantic cult of nature, considered in the large. It made possible the passage without too great emotional strain from medieval Christian faith to the scientific positivism which tends to dominate cultivated minds to-day.

And while originally the concept of nature was equally compounded of religious and scientific elements, the fact that nature
served as a substitute for many of the articles of theistic religion
gave to it in effect—in comparison with orthodox Christianity—an
anti-religious cast. The word naturalism has consequently come
to have anti-religious connotations; and, roughly speaking, the degree of naturalism in any literary product is the degree of its
progress toward scientific positivism. But still the word nature
kept a strong tincture from its religious origins. One could not be a
"worshiper of nature" without retaining much of the sentiment
of religion, and without making, consciously or tacitly, assumptions which are in essence religious. Such was the assurance of the
purposiveness and benevolence of nature which continued to prevail among poets of the nineteenth century, some of whom were
militantly anti-Christian in their tone. As for their doctrine of
"progress," while this seems to have had its origin in thinkers
whose fetish was science rather than religion,[1] it came to prevail
with poets, like Tennyson, whose sympathies were more with religion than science; and the notion of progress lost much of its
force with the fading out of the religious assumptions of purposiveness and benevolence.

Nature, God, Man

Throughout this study, two frequently recurring themes are
the relation of nature to God, and the relation of man's spirit to
God and nature. The disposition to substitute nature for God is
the mark of naturalism, and is more or less present in the most
characteristic nature poets. This is partly grounded in the scientific
desire to stress the regularity of natural law and eliminate the arbitrary and irrational from the process of the universe. But the
concept of God as the original spiritual substance, the guarantee of
rationality, purposiveness and benevolence—it is this which makes
nature worthy of the enthusiasm of its devotees; and this spiritual
principle, latent or overt, is never altogether absent from any
philosophical nature-poetry.

Scientific method as such is incapable of providing this spiritual
principle in nature; there is always implied in any such conception

a metaphysic incompatible with pure materialism—a metaphysic in which the ultimate reality of things is spiritual. But since the mere scientific faculty is incapable of apprehending this ultimate reality, it becomes one of the concerns of romantic poets to discover and characterize a faculty competent to "see into the life of things." It was the search for this "higher" faculty which led them at length into some form of mysticism. But this very mysticism, which at first supported their enthusiasm for nature, tended in the long run to undermine it; the religious element in time largely expelled the naturalistic.

With regard to man as a psychical being, one great problem of nature-poetry is the genesis of his spiritual faculties. Nature-poets loved to think of man as the child of nature, intimately communing with her, subject to her laws like all other creatures, acting upon the instincts by her implanted in him, and drawing from her the very mind and spirit by which he conducts his rational and moral life. But poets unacquainted with the theory of organic evolution, and some of those acquainted with it, found too difficult of solution the problem of how man, a conscious and thinking being, possessed of an autonomous will, could have drawn his conscious and self-activating spirit from the automatic processes of will-less and unthinking nature. Many a stout vessel of naturalism went to pieces on this shoal; and it was only on the tides of evolutionism that later poets felt they had safely brought their spiritual cargoes into port. In the end it was found less difficult to derive man's spiritual faculties from nature than to regard the order of nature as benevolent and purposive. But sober reflection soon discounted this one-sided gain. It was of small advantage to derive man's spirit from nature if she was to be regarded herself as inhumanly cruel and immoral.

In the poetic concept of nature the elements derived from science and religion were maintained in a kind of equilibrium by the mediation of metaphysics. But it was at best a precarious and unstable equilibrium, which forever tended to break down with the overweight of one or other of the elements. In the romantic period it was the preponderance of the religious element that caused the break-down; in the Victorian period, that of the scientific element. Between these two break-downs there were two fairly successful attempts to restore the balance—one under the influence of transcendentalism, the other under that of evolutionary positivism. But no metaphysic has proved subtle enough to keep these rival forces pulling together, which is necessary if the concept of nature is to be maintained in a form that will content the poetic mind.

The Present Status of Nature

In twentieth-century poetry the term and concept of nature have virtually ceased to appear. One main reason for this is that the religious elements in the concept—purposiveness, benevolence, etc. —are no longer assumed to be true, and so the word nature has lost most of its emotional force. Moreover, the strain of animism, inheritance from the primitive mind, which persists, in however refined and rationalized a form, in the romantic concept of nature, has not been able to withstand the impact of modern critical thought. But the acute suffering of many earnest souls—a state of malaise which is almost universally manifest in contemporary literature—shows how great a loss they have suffered in giving up the inspiring concept of nature. This is not great enough, however, to compel critical minds to maintain a notion which has been equally repudiated by religion and science.

One of the hardest things for man to bear is spiritual isolation. The sense that he stands alone in the universe goes terribly against his gregarious sentiments. He is so frail and ineffectual a being, his experience and achievement fall so far short of what his ranging imagination conceives and his impetuous heart demands! He has an overpowering impulse to construct a system which will enable him to feel that he does not stand alone but is intimately associated with some force or group infinitely more powerful and significant than himself. In religion he may feel himself thus intimately associated with God and with other holy beings—the community of saints. With the waning of religious faith he grasps at nature—at the great benevolent order of things in which every individual is provided for in the harmonious plan of the whole; which speaks to him through every lovely and sublime object, and in whose eternal flux, while he may be lost, he is yet not ineffectual or without significance. The heart of nature-poetry is the sense a man has of his identity with the other manifestations of this living force, and with the living force itself—his envelopment by and absorption in nature. It is thus that he penetrates deeply into the comforting warmth and mystery of things. A Freudian would infallibly interpret this impulse as a reflection of childlike man's craving to return into his mother's womb. And this way of regarding the phenomenon is at least helpful in characterizing the feeling-tone of nature-poetry. Some such sentiment is at the root of the matter. But man as an intellectual and moral being finds many ways of rationalizing his impulse. The romantic concept of nature provides for men's demand that they shall have moral significance. As part of the race of men, one has especial importance in the eyes of nature; one's children will carry on the blessed saga and his virtues will bloom in far-off ages.

It is hard to comprehend how, with no increase of religious faith, the poets—spokesmen of man's emotions and aspirations—should have so completely given up this consoling concept of nature after no more than two centuries' trial. And we can have no more striking evidence of the critical force of the scientific spirit in modern times than that it should so soon have sapped and broken down the structure of poetic thought which it did so much to build up.

Poetry at the present time—our literature as a whole—is in desperate straits for something to take the place of religion or nature as a means of relieving man's intolerable burden of loneliness. There are some slight indications that a sense of social solidarity—class solidarity or the solidarity of a classless race—is what most alluringly offers itself. The theme which was treated by Shelley, by Whitman, by Swinburne and Meredith, in connection with nature, is here and there being taken up, a trifle feebly, and in complete dissociation from nature, by poets of a socializing tendency. It is perhaps particularly significant that the most promising of these socializing poets should be among those who show, in one way or another, the influence of T. S. Eliot. Of all modern poets there is none more absolutely free from any tincture of nature-faith than Eliot, heir to the "humanist" tradition of Babbitt and More. In this tradition, naturalism was repudiated as laying its

stress on the lower, or animal, elements in human nature. Moreover, Eliot draws his main inspiration from a period antedating the
mystic marriage of science and religion which produced the hy-
brid, nature. And so, in the present bankruptcy of nature, Eliot
returns to the faith of the church. But for his followers, it seems,
the faith of the church shares in the bankruptcy of nature. And
their only hope lies in such a reconstruction of society that the
individual man may actually realize his solidarity with his fellows.
In so far as these poets are Marxians, their line may perhaps be
traced to Hegel; but Hegel's nature has completely faded out of
their "dialectic." Contemporary poets, if questioned, would doubtless agree that the "nature" of transcendentalism was the transient
flower of a bourgeois ideology.

Scope of This Study

The limitation of this study to the nineteenth century is a matter of convenience. Even if I were well enough at home in the
earlier period to speak with any authority, the inclusion of
eighteenth-century writers in more than incidental fashion would
enlarge the work beyond all practical bounds. I refer in a footnote
to some of the notable scholars who have written on the concept of
nature in eighteenth-century literature.[2] And even in the nineteenth
century my study of so large a subject must obviously be partial
and selective.

My project is to study a number of nineteenth-century English
poets, chosen for their importance in illustrating the main aspects
of our subject, the philosophical concept of nature. But I permit
myself the luxury of straying beyond the limits of English poetry
in certain cases where the game is particularly tempting. One German poet—Goethe—is so exceptionally significant and various in his
treatment of the subject—he has so much incidental light to throw
on the problems of the English writers, and is so fascinating in
himself—that I could not keep him out. The same thing is true of
the prose-writer, Carlyle, outstanding in the imaginative literature
of transcendentalism, and of the two American poets, Emerson and
Whitman, notable transcendentalists in their treatment of nature,
and intimately related in thought to the English writers of the

period. I have finally thought it worth while to make a survey of contemporary poetry, in order to verify my conclusion that the philosophical concept of nature has almost entirely disappeared, and to furnish materials for judging of the reasons for its disappearance. In the chapters devoted to this survey, I have included two representative Irish poets, and have treated the Americans on equal terms with the English because of their equal interest and their perhaps even paramount significance in relation to our theme.

In the course of my discussion I frequently compare the ideas and expressions of one poet with those of another poet or philosophical writer. But neither as between poets nor as between philosophers and poets is it my primary concern to trace direct influences and borrowings. My effort being to come as near as possible to an understanding of certain terms as used in periods now historical, I summon the expressions of one writer to throw light on those of another. My main intention in the case of Wordsworth, for example, is to get as nearly as possible at his precise meaning; and in quoting from writers of the seventeenth and eighteenth centuries, my object is not so much to determine the particular source for his thought as to indicate *the kind of thing which probably made up the historical background of his thought,* and may help us to approximate an understanding of it. Naturally, I confine myself mainly to writers whom a given poet was known to have read, or with whom there is a fair likelihood that he was acquainted. In the case of Wordsworth, indications are particularly scant as to the authors with whom he was familiar in the formative period of his thinking. But we do have a list of the books which made up his library at the time of his death. And in making my citations mainly from these books, or from books for other reasons probably known to him, my object is to center attention on writing that was most likely to have influenced him, and to avoid too great extravagance of guessing. With other writers I have limited myself more strictly to sources known to have been familiar to them. But even where my comparisons are speculative, they are not necessarily without point. The thought of any given period is something "in the air," and frequently a mere analogue may be as illuminating as an authentic source.

The influence of the classics on the modern concept of nature is an important subject of study in itself. And whenever it is made, it may serve to correct an impression here and there. But I venture to guess that, in this matter, nine-tenths of the influence from the classics was exerted indirectly through modern writers who refer to them or pass on their opinions without acknowledgment. The three or four most important texts from Virgil and Pliny, Lucretius and Cicero, would be found repeated often enough by the English divines and philosophers to dispense the English poets from the necessity of hunting them down in the original; and even Plato and Plotinus were more familiar through Cudworth, Berkeley, Thomas Taylor, etc., than through the original Greek texts. As for "platonism" taken broadly, it had long before Wordsworth and Shelley become an integral part of the English literary tradition.

Outline of the Chapters

My study begins with a chapter illustrating the sensitiveness of romantic poets to the "beauteous forms" of nature, and their disposition to refer to nature in extravagantly "honorific" terms. This suggests the presence of implications going far beyond anything justified by the mere esthetic charm of nature, and leads to a study of the metaphysical concept of "universal nature"—in the romantic poets generally and more particularly in Wordsworth.

Prominent in Wordsworth is the idea of a universal nature, a "spirit of nature" or "soul of all the worlds"—an active principle sufficient to account for the animated and purposive behavior of things and so avoid the stigma of a purely mechanistic philosophy. I find it most likely that this concept of Wordsworth is grounded mainly in English natural theology of the seventeenth and eighteenth centuries, strongly supported as that was by the scientific theories of Newton, and given a decidedly "platonic" cast by writers like Cudworth, Henry More, Shaftesbury and Berkeley. Among other possible influences in shaping this concept were the pantheism of Spinoza, the materialism of writers like Priestley, and the world-soul theories of foreign writers like Schelling relayed to Wordsworth through Coleridge. The imaginative association of this universal nature, or spirit of nature, with country life and the beauties of natural scenery had been made by Shaftesbury and established as a tradition by certain of the eighteenth-century poets.

Wordsworth took for granted the purposiveness, harmony, benevolence of nature; and here he was in agreement with nearly all schools of eighteenth-century thought, atheist, deist and Christian. Nature was associated in his mind with innocence and unworldliness, and he believed that men could learn much from nature in regard to a happy and normal way of life. In his earlier poetry there was, I believe, a more strongly naturalistic trend than was to be found in writers on natural theology; and this may possibly be referred to the influence of writers like d'Holbach and Godwin, and almost certainly to that of Hartley. In this naturalism, Wordsworth was in marked contrast to poets like Cowper, Blake and Coleridge. His tendency was, in this period, to lay his emphasis more on nature than on God, and to assume that man's spiritual faculties were developed (if not actually originated) by natural means during a man's lifetime. The problem of the origin of man's mind (or spirit), however, was too difficult of solution by reference merely to nature: a growing dualism shows itself in Wordsworth's emphasis on imagination as a spiritual faculty necessary to the reading of nature, and he ended by virtually giving up nature and deriving man's spirit directly "from God, who is our home."

Shelley, under the influence of Godwin and French naturalistic thinkers, began as an atheist and a militant necessarian, attributing to nature whatever, even in man's moral life, religious writers attributed to God. His naturalism and necessarianism persist, in somewhat modified form, through most of his more philosophical poetry; and in "Prometheus Unbound," which reflects so much of contemporary scientific speculation, his naturalism strongly colors his faith in social revolution and the emancipation of man's spirit from religious and political despotism. But Shelley had also a predilection for idealistic metaphysics, which was confirmed by his readings in Plato and (probably) Plotinus. He was aware of the epistemological problems inherent in the relation between "subject" and "object" in human knowledge; and this was the rock on which his naturalism largely went to pieces. In "Adonais" we see him vainly striving to reconcile his naturalism with the neoplatonic concept of the "descent of the soul" and its return "to the burning fountain whence it came." And in "Prometheus" he falls into manifold confusions as he endeavors to render various scientific concepts in the language of neoplatonism and to interpret his earthy paradise in terms of the "platonic" concept of eternity.

Shelley, while he was seemingly well acquainted with the work of Erasmus Darwin, was unaffected by the notion, elaborately developed by Darwin, that man's spirit may be the product of natural evolution. Darwin believed in the natural origin of species, and carried his evolutionary bias into his theory of the genesis and development of mind. Some glimmering of this notion seems to have visited Goethe, and is one of the things that makes him interesting in relation to our study. Along with Goethe's romantic and pantheistic conception of nature went a strongly naturalistic bent, which was reinforced by his scientific studies, and prevented him from falling into mysticism and transcendentalism, except as these may be implied in the feeling-tone of his nature-poetry.

In the prose speculations of Carlyle and Coleridge, post-Kantian idealism begins to play an important part in the conception of nature. Carlyle supported his romantic conception of the divineness of nature with the idealism of Fichte and Novalis; and Coleridge tried to correct the naturalistic tendencies of his time with (among other things) the idealism of Schelling. In Coleridge German transcendentalism served progressively to enforce his Christian orthodoxy. In Carlyle the transcendental element tended to fade out in his later, pragmatic interpretation of the "laws of nature" as manifested in history. Carlyle's philosophy of nature, while it was anything but scientific in spirit, probably helped to "ease a severe transition" for many earnest minds, enabling them to pass without too great shock from a supernatural to a natural view of the world.

The importance of Coleridge's philosophy for our study lies in his influence on Emerson. Coleridge's scale-of-being theory of life was one of the factors which made it easier for Emerson to accept the scientific theory of evolution; but Coleridge's idealism and his *a priorism* in the interpretation of science were factors tending to prevent Emerson from drawing fruitful naturalistic conclusions from his evolutionism. The central thought of Emerson's nature-poetry is the oneness of man with the divine process of the world: if man can only realize this oneness of his spirit with the divine spirit, which remains the same through all change, he may be freed from his desolating sense of being "orphan and defrauded."

The romantic concept of nature appears full-blown in Whitman. His temperamental optimism was supported by the teachings of Emerson and by what he could assimilate of German idealism—especially that of Hegel—which assured him of the identity of objective nature with the divine creative process of thought. Whitman carried further than any other poet the logic of transcendentalism—that if the divine principle is immanent in all things, there is nothing that is not holy. This fell in with his democratic sentiment, and made it possible for him to celebrate the body equally with the spirit, and to include evil and death in his "lesson of acceptance"; it made him seem more naturalistic than he was.

In Arnold, Tennyson and Browning, there is a marked falling off of romantic enthusiasm for nature. Arnold is equally hostile to supernaturalism and to romantic naturalism. Tennyson, while deeply interested in science, is very suspicious of naturalistic interpretations, and very clear that nature must be supplemented by the religious belief in God and immortality. He takes little stock in natural religion and its teleology. His version of evolution makes much of the notion of progress and little of the notion of the origin of species from lower forms. The position of Browning is similar to Tennyson's, though he is less afflicted with doubts and less disturbed by the tendencies of current science.

The enthusiasm for nature and naturalism is strong again in Swinburne and Meredith, who both warmly espouse evolution. The earthly origin of man is associated in Swinburne with his revolutionary spirit, his Shelleyan passion for emancipating man from religious and political tyranny. In Meredith, evolutionism is made the basis of a naturalistic ethics; among all the poets it is he who most earnestly strives to show how man is spiritually child of earth. Meredith means to be a positivist; and he has managed to divest the concept of nature of most of its supernatural and transcendental character. But it is still bathed in a religious feeling-tone; his faith is subtly motivated by certain of the primary religious sentiments.

With Hardy romantic naturism is in full retreat. Thoroughly impregnated with the deterministic spirit of modern science, and with no trace of teleology, he finds nature hostile rather than favorable to man. The evolutionary development of consciousness is a flaw rather than a merit in the scheme of things; for it lays man open to spiritual tortures not greatly shared by the inferior creatures. The conduct of the world is in the hands of an Immanent Will, which is neither conscious nor purposive nor benevolent.

During the last fifty years there have arisen few poets fired with enthusiasm for abstract nature. In writers like Bridges and Yeats and Noyes there is a weakly platonism, going at times with evolutionism; a vague cult of beauty largely takes the place of the romantic worship of nature. In the most recent and characteristic poets, nature—word and concept—has virtually disappeared. Poetry has ceased to occupy itself with the cosmic problems dear to the Romantics and Victorians. Nature, no longer assumed to be purposive and benevolent to man, has ceased to be a word to conjure with. And for the emotional effect formerly associated with nature, the poet must turn elsewhere.

Our entire study, then, presents the picture of a brave and massive effort of the human spirit doomed to failure in the end. It takes on, shall we say, the aspect of a heroic tragedy, of which the protagonist is the poetic concept of nature, shown in triumph and then defeat.

Complicating Factors:

Golden Age

Our subject is really more complicated than appears in the foregoing summary. Especially in the romantic period, readers familiar with the literature of the subject will realize that I have left out of account, or but slightly stressed, several elements somewhat affecting the concept of nature. I have done this purposely in order not too greatly to confuse the reader at the outset, and because certain of these elements count for little in the study which follows, and do not greatly affect the conclusions to which it leads. The following sections I have placed at the end of this introduction as a kind of appendix. They will interest the professional scholar more than the general reader, and may well be omitted by the latter, at any rate for the present. They are considerations of interest to anyone wishing to get a notion of the great variety of meanings attaching to the word nature in the romantic period—the numerous connotations which tend to color it and to justify a poet in his feeling about it.

One such meaning, or connotation, of the word nature is that illustrated at length by Professor Fairchild in his study of *The Noble Savage*. The general notion of nature in the romantic period was greatly affected by the disposition, early manifest in European literature, to associate the word nature with a state of life untouched by human arts and institutions. This disposition is apparent, for example, in the widely diffused legend of the Golden Age—a time when men, fresh from the lap of Mother Nature, and obeying the good and happy impulses implanted by her in their bosoms, lived an innocent and blessed life. This legend of the Golden Age readily joined with the notion that the savage, or primitive, man is in many ways superior to the sophisticated product of a corrupt civilization, and that many of our ills may be cured by a return to something like the savage state. This doctrine was particularly rife in the eighteenth century. It is often associated with the name of Rousseau as its great apostle; though Professor Fairchild, following in the steps of Professor Lovejoy, has shown that Rousseau held it in extremely modified form, and that, indeed, he really exhibits the reaction against this sort of primitivism as strongly as he does the primitivism itself.[3] However that may be, it is clear that the concept of nature held by romantic poets like Wordsworth and Southey was somewhat colored by this primitivism. Mr. Fairchild shows that Wordsworth's celebration of the child and the peasant as beings particularly free from worldly taint and particularly wise in their natural way is closely analogous to the similar interpretation of the "noble savage." And he makes it clear that, in romantic poets, there generally clung to the word nature some faint aroma of the Arcadian Golden Age.

Ordre Naturel

What literary historians do not always sufficiently recognize is that this conception of a primitive natural order is no purely literary and mythical invention but is intimately bound up with legal and economic theory of a much more serious stripe. The economic doctrines of the French Physiocrats were based on the assumption of a benevolent and harmonious *ordre naturel*, which stands opposed to the *ordre positif* actually embodied in existing human laws and arrangements; and their efforts to free commerce and industry from the hampering restrictions of taxation, feudal privilege, etc., were motivated by this ideal of the *ordre naturel*—expressed by Montesquieu in the *Esprit des lois*, by Quesnay in his *Droit naturel*, and in many works on political economy, as well as in the more "literary" writings of Rousseau. This theory of nature has its part to play in the work of Adam Smith among English economists; and it was doubtless partly as a political economist that John Stuart Mill repudiated nature in favor of man's humane ideal as indicated below in Chapter V. This eighteenth-century theory of nature had its august progenitors in Roman jurisprudence and scholastic philosophy.[4] In Aquinas's famous classification of laws into eternal, natural, human and divine, natural law is that part of the divine plan of the universe which can be grasped by man and which enables him to distinguish good from evil, and Aquinas held that human law should be based on natural law. Here again, in Aquinas's synthesis of the teachings of the Bible and Aristotle, we find that the concept of nature is the joint production of theology and "science." So that even where the poets allow their imaginations to run riot in a legend of the Golden Age, we may assume that they were being indirectly affected by more serious currents of thought.

In their recent monumental study of *Primitivism and Related Ideas in Antiquity*, Professors Lovejoy and Boas have shown how the disposition to set up the primitive condition of man as a social and ethical standard is related to the concept of nature as a norm. "Primitivism . . . is closely related throughout most of its history to the assumption that correctness in opinion and excellence in individual conduct or in the constitution of society consists in conformity to some standard or norm expressed by the term 'nature' or its derivatives." [5] This statement is illustrated by a classified list of the many diverse meanings attached to the phrase, "state of nature," [6] and an account of the development of meanings for the Greek word for nature (φύσις),[7] leading to an explanation of how the two main forms of primitivism are related to this concept of nature.

By virtue of its (probably) original signification, 'nature' suggested the condition in which human society existed at its genesis; if, then, that which is 'by nature' is *eo ipso* the best or the normal condition, the primeval state of man must have been his normal and best state. But this implication was greatly re-enforced by the sense of 'nature' as that which is not made by man, not due to his contrivance, and the associated assumption that 'nature'—as a quasi-divine power—does all things better than man. Cultural as well as chronological primitivism thus seemed to be in accord with the norm of 'nature'; all man's alterations of or additions to the 'natural' order of things are changes for the worse.[8]

The culmination of "cultural primitivism" in classical antiquity is shown in the stoic ideal of a hard and simple life. The simple life is naturally often associated in classical literature with life in the country, and so there is ample precedent in the classics for that association of rural nature with virtue which Wordsworth found in eighteenth-century poets like Beattie and Cowper. In the mind of a poet like Wordsworth, his love of rural nature for its beauty came to be associated not merely with the metaphysical concept of universal nature but also with the ethical concept of nature as a norm for human conduct and opinion. And while this latter concept is of secondary importance in our present study, it should be kept in mind as generally implied in references to nature by romantic poets, serving to reinforce and give moral dignity to the general idea of "nature." It makes it easier for the poet to associate the laws of nature (in the scientific sense) with the moral laws (in the ethical sense), which latter were likewise referred to nature as their sanction and original.

Anti-Rationalism

Another consideration, developed by Fairchild, has to do with the effect produced on the poets' minds by the destructive analysis of knowledge carried on by Berkeley and Hume. The upshot of these metaphysical operations was to throw doubt on the power of the understanding (or reason) to arrive at a knowledge of reality. "Starting out in the rationalistic faith that the truth about mind could be discovered by the mind, it seemed at last to discover a truth about mind which discredited the same rationalistic faith which had motivated its quest." [9] The result was to throw the thinker back more on what we may broadly call intuition for the interpretation of spiritual truth. And this gave a less rationalistic cast to the word nature. Nature, interpreted by intuition, came to be in a sense a rival to reason or understanding as a means for apprehending spiritual truth. And the "return to nature" at times implied the virtual abandonment of reason in favor of some "higher" —some more mystical—faculty.

In this connection, it is pointed out that, with several of the romantic poets, the "return to nature" was synchronous with a repudiation of Godwin's theories in *Political Justice*. The moral philosophy which Wordsworth found inadequate for reaching final conclusions was the philosophy of men like Godwin, in all probability that of Godwin himself, who relied upon reason almost exclusively not merely for the determination of truth, but also for bringing men to just and reasonable practices in social life, and so for the rapid amelioration of human conditions. In their reaction against Godwinism, the romantic poets tended to make their appeal to the "heart," to the "imagination," and even to what Wordsworth calls in "The Excursion" the "Imaginative Will." Having in mind the distinction made by Kant between the Understanding and the "higher" Reason (*Verstand* and *Vernunft*), and the use made of this distinction by Fichte, Schelling and other German idealists, and taking his cue from the studies of Professor Gingerich, Fairchild applies the term transcendentalism to this anti-rationalistic tendency of the English poets. And since this is, broadly speaking, in contrast to the tendency of the pseudo-classicists to make much of reason and common sense, he builds upon it his very interesting definition of romanticism.

Romanticism is the endeavor, in the face of growing factual obstacles, to achieve, to retain, or to justify that illusioned view of the universe and of human life which is produced by an imaginative fusion of the familiar and the strange, the known and the unknown, the real and the ideal, the finite and the infinite, the material and the spiritual, the natural and the supernatural.[10]

It follows from this conception of romanticism that the romantic (the transcendentalist) "values the world which is created by his imaginative will more highly than the world of which his senses bring him their crudely literal reports." [11] And Mr. Fairchild dwells on the anti-scientific and non-rationalistic cast of their thought. "Wordsworth's view of nature is essentially non-rationalistic." [12] "The romanticists were moving from a more or less scientific to a more or less religious conception of nature." [13] One instance of this general trend is Wordsworth's pantheism.

In its broad lines this view is, I believe, correct and illuminating. But it would be very easy to misplace the emphasis and fall into radical misconceptions. To begin with "transcendentalism," there is no objection to the use of this term providing one does not assume that the manifestations in question are the outgrowth of the German school of idealism. The only one of the major romantic poets who was clearly familiar with, and affected by, the thought of Kant, Fichte, Schelling, etc., was Coleridge; and in his case this influence is most important in his prose works, beginning with *Biographia Literaria* (1817) and the second edition of *The Friend* (1818). Coleridge apart, it is later, in the prose writings of Carlyle and Emerson, and in the poetry of Emerson and Whitman, that one finds unmistakable traces of German transcendentalism. It is not traceable in the most pantheistic of Coleridge's poems, dating from 1795 and 1796. The "transcendental" influences in Shelley are rather "platonic" than German. As for Wordsworth, it has yet to be shown that he was not writing mainly in the tradition of English poetry of the eighteenth century and English theology of the seventeenth and eighteenth centuries. One main outcome of my essays on Wordsworth is to reaffirm this truth.

Particular caution is needed in reference to the broad characterization of romantic poetry as anti-scientific. In Chapter V, I shall have occasion to discuss Wordsworth's attitude toward science, and to show that he had no antagonism to scientific studies, though he deprecated the mechanistic tendency of some scientists who were incapable of viewing the universe in the large, and who took no account of the animating and motivating force behind all natural phenomena. In Chapter III, I shall endeavor to show that Wordsworth's metaphysical concept of nature was largely supported by Newtonian physics as interpreted by Newton himself and by some notable theologians of his time. As for Coleridge, he was not merely widely read in several of the natural sciences (being a pupil of the German physiologist, Blumenbach), but considered himself an authority in this field, and a chief apostle of the correct (the transcendental, and, as he contended, the platonic and Baconian) method of interpreting science (see Chapter XI). In Chapter VII, I shall show how deeply Shelley was impregnated with scientific theory—not merely with that associated with the Newtonian view of the universe, but with contemporary theories in chemistry, electricity, geology, astronomy, etc.; and how the very "transcendentalism" of "Prometheus Unbound" is tied up with the conceptions of natural science. Here of course I make use of the findings of Professor Grabo in *A Newton among Poets*, and "*Prometheus Unbound*"; *an Interpretation*,[14] which appeared later than Mr. Fairchild's studies. My general contention is that the metaphysical concept of nature is the joint construction of science, philosophy and religion, and is not dependent for its main force on Arcadian sentiment or on supernaturalism.

As for Wordsworth's "pantheism," it certainly owes more to the poetic imagination than to the dry deism of natural theology. Being, however, a derivative from deism—that is, from natural theology—it is a manifestation of the "naturalistic" trend in religion which so largely grew out of scientific speculation. And, in its effort to place God within his works rather than outside them, pantheism may be regarded as still more naturalistic than its parent, deism. This is evident not merely in Wordsworth but in the many romantic poets of the eighteenth century who showed a pantheistic trend. So that here again it is somewhat misleading to characterize the "religion of nature" as anti-scientific.

It is, however, broadly true, as Whitehead has emphasized in his *Science and the Modern World*,[15] that the romantic movement generally was in reaction against the type of rationalism which tended to reduce man and the world to machines. This type of rationalism was represented by those writers, especially in France, who gave its tone to the "age of reason," whose somewhat crass materialism is based in a partial reading of Newtonian physics and of the sensational psychology of Locke. It is characterized by its superficial view of the problems of epistemology, and by an exaggerated confidence in the power of common-sense reason (that is, of the scientific process of analysis and logical deduction) to give a satisfactory account of the ultimate nature of things. It is almost the opposite pole to the rationalism of Leibniz and Spinoza, which assumes the essentially "rational" or spiritual character of the universe.

The eighteenth-century rationalism in question is reflected in the necessarianism of Godwin in *Political Justice*. In quite another sense, Godwin's rationalism consists in a naïve confidence in plain reason as a driving power in human affairs (hence his "perfectibilism"), and in his own extremely simplified political scheme. Against both these forms of rationalism Coleridge was certainly in reaction. Wordsworth does not seem to have been badly bitten with necessarianism, and did not greatly need to react against it. Against a general mechanistic philosophy he does seem to have been in reaction; but at the very same time he was clinging to the "sensationalism" of Hartley's psychology, endeavoring to build his conception of the human spirit on "nature and the language of the sense." His turning from Godwin to "nature" was a turning from a glib and shallow social philosopher to the world of beautiful forms which he had long been used to associate with the rational power of the universe (as conceived by the religious philosophers). Nature was for him—

> . . . a Power
> That is the visible quality and shape
> And image of right reason . . .[16]

In my fifth chapter I shall indicate a possible source for this phrase, "right reason," in the theology of the early eighteenth century.

This supernal Reason, certainly, Wordsworth assumed to be enthroned in the very fabric of nature. It was an assumption explicit or implied in any of the theological writers he is likely to have perused. But he was so impressed with the failure of certain contemporary moral philosophers to arrive at the grounds of right and wrong by the exercise of cold "reason" that he felt obliged to have recourse to the inspirations of nature (as interpreted by the heart).

> One impulse from a vernal wood
> May teach you more of man,
> Of moral evil and of good,
> Than all the sages can.[17]

One moment of the "feeling" inspired by a spring day might have more to give him "than years of toiling reason." [18]

One recalls Pascal: "Le cœur a ses raisons que la raison ne connaît pas." But if one must have a philosophical sanction for Wordsworth's appeal to feeling, I have suggested, in Chapter V, that the most plausible sanction can be found in Rousseau. And so Wordsworth is brought well into line with the sentimental bias of romanticism. There is no doubt that he held some special insight requisite for him who was to see into the life of nature. Such insight was a gift of nature's own bestowal. In later years it takes on more the aspect of a special faculty distinct from reason, and he labors to give it a philosophical cast, under the influence perhaps of Spinoza or the Germans. But whether in 1798 (the year of "Tintern Abbey") his nature-philosophy is strictly to be called transcendental, or even anti-rationalistic, is open to doubt.

In his thought-provoking study of Coleridge on the Imagination (1935), Professor I. A. Richards suggests that the psychology underlying Coleridge's theory anticipated modern developments in its way of regarding the mind as a self-realizing activity—as an organic unity rather than a bundle of separate faculties. In his famous and often cloudy distinction between Understanding (eighteenth-century common sense) and Reason (the "higher" faculty; the reason of seventeenth-century divines)—a distinction suggested by the Kantian discrimination of *Verstand* and *Vernunft* —Understanding is "theory," Reason "the entire operation of the mind" (p. 138). Perhaps some such distinction may be implied in Wordsworth's thought. When he was disparaging mere "reason" (understanding), he was disparaging the effort to arrive at fundamental moral truth by some "scientific" faculty narrowly conceived (that "false secondary power by which we multiply distinctions")—that is, by the mere analysis of phenomena into their component elements. In his appeal to the heart, the imagination, and in some cases to "nature," he was perhaps vaguely recommending that "the entire operation of the mind" be brought to bear on the determination of "final things." On this distinction, or something like it, I have occasion to touch in Chapter IV, under the rubric, "The Failure of Wordsworth's Naturalism," and in Chapter V, under "Science, Moral and Physical"; in the one case in connection with certain theories of Professor Stallknecht, in the other in connection with Rousseau's distinction between sensitive and intellectual reason.

But all this terminology bristles with ambiguities. One suspects that, in both Coleridge and Wordsworth, their thinking may have led in two quite different directions. In their effort to restore its unity to the mind they may have been forward-looking, "modern." But the terms they used had a tendency to confuse them, and they fell into that very dichotomy of the mind which they were trying to avoid. Coleridge's Reason, Wordsworth's Imagination tended to establish themselves as separate, mystical faculties, "higher" than plain understanding and overruling its decisions, as Fichte's *Glaube* overruled the findings of his *Wissen*. The layman treads dimly among these high philosophical abstractions. But he simplifies as best he can. And for him what it comes to is that, in the end, these poets preferred a religious to a scientific interpretation of the universe.

The Transcendental Drift

It is here that the matter of dates takes on its importance. In several of the romantic poets there is to be traced a distinct conflict between the naturalistic and the "transcendental" elements, and an appreciable progress from the more naturalistic to the more transcendental phase during the period of their writing. Wordsworth and Shelley tried to be naturalistic and succeeded but indifferently in keeping to the position with which they started. The scientific philosophy of their day was insufficient to meet certain difficulties in psychology and epistemology which were inherent in their naturalistic ways of conceiving the world and the human spirit. Wordsworth turned orthodox; Shelley drifted towards "platonism"; Coleridge built up an elaborate and (he thought) systematic transcendental apparatus for the defense of Christian theology. In this sense it is true that "the romanticists were moving from a more or less scientific to a more or less religious conception of nature." But I think it would be more exact to say that they were moving from a more or less scientific conception of nature to a religious position which left but little room for any effective concept of nature.

In Coleridge's case, his transcendentalism meant the total abandonment of "the religion of nature"; in the case of Wordsworth and Shelley, the growing mystical tendency meant the gradual fading of nature out of the picture. It is only for the later poets, Emerson and Whitman, that German idealism made it possible to give a thoroughly transcendental interpretation of nature, and so maintain the "religion of nature." In Meredith, science is dominant again in the form of evolutionism. In the great monuments of nature-poetry of the romantic period—in Wordsworth and Goethe —the "religion of nature" was still strongly impregnated with naturalistic elements drawn from science.

Emphasis and Perspective

In my account of Wordsworth's and Shelley's naturalism, a reader acquainted with Professor Gingerich's *Essays in the Romantic Poets* [19] and other recent works dealing with their philosophy may be conscious of a certain foreshortening in the parts concerned with the *failure* of their naturalism, their gradual and steady recession from the naturalistic position. This process has been traced in fine detail, among others, by Mr. Gingerich, who shows how the poets' concern with "the human mind, its self-contained and constituent energies, its active, transcendental powers" gained ground over their interest in "external nature and sensation and the language of the sense." My chapter on "Shelley's 'Platonism'" makes no pretense to a comprehensive treatment of that subject, which has received much attention from recent writers [20] and would require a large volume in itself. My intention in the chapter in question is, in the fewest possible words, to remind the reader of what came to be a paramount element in Shelley's thinking and dreaming, an element which it is difficult to reconcile with his original naturalism and which tended to replace it.

It will readily be understood how the general scope and intention of my study involves such an emphasis on the naturalistic rather than the transcendental aspect of the romantic poets. In later poets like Emerson and Whitman, on the other hand, the more technical (the German) transcendentalism which enabled them to maintain a close alliance between nature and the human mind involves a greater relative emphasis on the transcendental factor.

Again, the scope of this study is such as to require very little consideration of the social and political aspects of "nature" to which scholars like Fairchild, Lovejoy and Tinker rightly devote so much attention, of the social and moral aspects to which such disproportionate and exclusive attention was given by the late Professor Babbitt. In a book so long as this is bound to be, the reader will surely be grateful for all possible eliminations that may tend to reduce its inordinate bulk.

PART ONE

THE ROMANTIC PERIOD

Après avoir fixé le sens que l'on doit attacher au mot *Nature*, je crois devoir avertir le Lecteur, une fois pour toutes, que lorsque, dans le cours de cet ouvrage, je dis que la nature produit un effet, je ne prétends point personnifier cette nature, qui est un être abstrait.

D'Holbach, *Systeme de la Nature*

* * *

One impulse from a vernal wood
May teach you more of man,
Of moral evil and of good
Than all the sages can.

Wordsworth, *The Tables Turned*

CHAPTER II

THE FORMS OF NATURE

THE praise of nature was so much in vogue with poets in the 1780's that Cowper felt impelled to distinguish between his own "most sincere" and "genuine" raptures and those perfunctory feelings "conjured up" by more conventional poets "to serve occasions of poetic pomp." [1] Some special merit attaches to anyone sensitive to nature. The poets agreed that nature (whatever this word means) is a refining and purifying influence, which tends to produce beautiful souls. Thus Akenside celebrates the man—

> Whose candid bosom the refining love
> Of Nature warms . . . [2]

Lessing says, "There is no doubt that the spirit of man is made gentler by studying Nature." [3]

The refining influence of nature is a constant theme with Wordsworth. It is, one might say, the central motif of "The Prelude," in his account of his own spiritual development. In the famous passage addressed to the "Wisdom and Spirit of the Universe," Wordsworth congratulates himself that, in his childhood, the "passions that build up the human soul" were intertwined,

> Not with the mean and vulgar works of Man;
> But with high objects, with enduring things,
> With life and nature; purifying thus
> The elements of feeling and of thought . . . [4]

In "The Prelude" and in the preface to *Lyrical Ballads,* he states his intention of taking for his poetic theme the heart of man "as found among the best of those who live . . . in Nature's presence." [5] Wordsworth's most extreme, as well as most charmingly imaginative, rendering of this notion is his lyric, "Three Years She Grew in Sun and Shower," in which personified nature speaks, and promises to impress her own beauty of form and spirit on the country girl whom she has undertaken to fashion into a lady of her own.

It has not always been a matter of course that nature is something to be indiscriminately praised, or an influence uniformly making for fineness of character. It is not so to-day for many minds approaching the subject in a cool critical spirit. And in considering the whole-hearted way in which romantic poets expressed their devotion to nature, we must take into account the complexity of meanings attaching to the term, and how, in the poet's mind, the various meanings insensibly supported and reinforced one another.

A Thing of Beauty

In its humblest and commonest sense, nature refers to the "beauteous forms" [6] of the external world, as distinguished from man and his works. Nature is "the common countenance of earth and sky";[7] it is "all that we behold from this green earth." [8] It is, to begin with, whatever delights the eye with its beauty and animation, whatever charms the fancy and distracts the mind. Among the romantic poets, none represents better this phase of nature-poetry than Keats, in such pieces as "Sleep and Poetry" or in the famous opening lines of "Endymion." No one is happier than he in his review of "Nature's gentle doings"; no one brings such nosegays of charming and variegated items, crushing together into one fistful so many samples of "the poetry of earth." And we know from Keats the simple and all-sufficient justification of nature in this sense—"A thing of beauty is a joy forever." In this sense nature means flowers, birds, brooks, breezes and moonlit glades. This is what Coleridge calls "Nature in the grove"; and that he has in mind a relatively simple type of nature-love is clear from the context in which he brings the phrase in—

> Even like a Lady vowed and dedicate
> To something more than Nature in the grove . . .[9]

This sort of thing is universal in poetry, as it is well-nigh universal in human experience. It would be to apply almost too dignified a word to call it esthetic. The love of color in flowers, of coolness in the breeze, the surrender to moonlight enchantment: these may be sheer animal reactions. Or, on a higher level of psychology, they may be no more than the reminder of our own high spirits or the soft abandonments of love.

In Keats, of course, the esthetic reference is generally wider, and in all imaginative poets this stage of nature-love passes over insensibly into something much higher, esthetically and humanly. The passage from one stage to another is shown, for example, in Wordsworth's sonnet to Sleep.

> A flock of sheep that leisurely pass by,
> One after one; the sound of rain, and bees
> Murmuring; the fall of rivers, winds and seas,
> Smooth fields, white sheets of water, and pure sky.

There are two ways in which these lines illustrate a higher stage of nature-poetry. The several items here passed in review are all chosen to fall in with a particular imaginative tone, suitable to the poet's aim of putting himself to sleep with soothing images. They are all "in keeping." Moreover, they are items not merely of natural beauty in general, but more specifically of the beauty of landscape. Nature is taken in a wider embrace, including a sense of the physiognomy of the earth.

Certain of the eighteenth-century poets are unmatched for this way of dealing with nature. The sort of landscape that Wordsworth sketches in the first part of "Tintern Abbey" is anticipated by many exquisite descriptions in Thomson and Cowper. And for perfectness of "keeping," together with economy of stroke and delicacy of music, there is perhaps nothing in Wordsworth or Shelley to compare with Collins's "Ode to Evening," and particularly the stanzas of landscape evocation ending:

> But when chill blustering winds, or driving rain
> Forbid my willing feet, be mine the hut
> That from the mountain's side,
> Views wilds, and swelling floods,

And hamlets brown, and dim-discovered spires;
And hears their simple bell, and marks o'er all
    Thy dewy fingers draw
    The gradual dusky veil.

But exquisite as this is in its imaginative constructiveness, and discreetly romantic too in its emotional tone, it does not advance us greatly in our understanding of the concept of nature. The word nature is not used, and there is no suggestion here of the peculiar emotional or philosophic implications of this word. This is English landscape rendered with sensitive feeling and taste. But the attitude is too purely esthetic to suggest either the passionate or the worshipful feeling of the true romantic nature-poets. This is scenery, and the subject for museful contemplation, but it is not what Byron calls "Nature's realms of worship, earth and air." [10]

Wild Nature: Byron

The romantic poets, sooner or later, make much of the wild aspects of nature, and very often just because they are wild—that is, unmarked by the impress of man and his difficult and onerous society. The poet, sensitive and shrinking soul, loves to escape from the heat and pressure of humanity, and so from himself as a social being, and to lose himself in the freedom of lonely places.

I live not in myself, but I become
Portion of that around me; and to me
High mountains are a feeling, but the hum
Of human cities torture: I can see
Nothing to loathe in nature, save to be
A link reluctant in a fleshly chain,
Class'd among creatures, when the soul can flee,
And with the sky, the peak, the heaving plain
Of ocean or the stars, mingle, and not in vain. [11]

Here the word nature is used in a comprehensive sense to include man and the external world together as a part of universal life. But the other sense is implicit in the sharp opposition of wild nature to the artificial world of cities and the fleshly chain. This opposition is formally stated in a very similar stanza from the same "Childe Harold."

> There is a pleasure in the pathless woods,
> There is a rapture on the lonely shore,
> There is society where none intrudes,
> By the deep Sea, and music in its roar:
> I love not Man the less, but Nature more,
> From these our interviews, in which I steal
> From all I may be or have been before,
> To mingle with the Universe, and feel
> What I can ne'er express, yet cannot all conceal.[12]

These illustrations of the romantic passion for the wild and sublime aspects of nature I have taken purposely from Byron, since I wish to come by due stages to the more philosophical interpretation of nature, and of all the great romantic poets save Landor, Byron is the one who has the least tincture of the philosophical, the "transcendental." In this he is the most "classical" of them all, partaking so little of the platonic sophistications of romantic thought, and apprehending it deeply neither on the scientific nor the religious side. It is true that, with his eloquent boldness of rhetoric, he has popularized the sentiment associated with the philosophy of nature,—a sentiment which he may have taken over from Shelley, or from Wordsworth—of whom Shelley presumably gave him some understanding. So that in "Childe Harold" due tribute is paid to the "stars, which are the poetry of heaven," which are "a beauty and a mystery." And he mentions even—

> . . . the feeling infinite, so felt
> In solitude where we are *least* alone;
> A truth which through our being then doth melt
> And purifies from self . . .[13]

But for any fine and philosophic sense of the sublimities of nature we must go to Wordsworth (as in "The Prelude") or to Shelley (as in "Mont Blanc" and "Prometheus Unbound").

Byron speaks, like the other romantics, of the book of nature.[14] But he does not imply, like many of them, that it is a book of wisdom, that there is actually something to be learnt from it. It is simply a "tome" that speaks more congenially to the heart of his hero than those written in the English language, since it speaks directly to his mood and passion. The honorific implication comes in in this way. Byron's heroes are men of more exalted—if often of less socially virtuous—character than the common run of the human herd. They are not subdued to the meanness, the petty hypocrisies, and the mere sheepish cowardice of ordinary men. Their passions are clear and elemental. So that not merely do they crave release from the constraints of ordinary society; but they find the types of, the match for, their own passions in the elemental forces of nature.

There is also in Byron something of the Arcadian and primitivistic tradition. The heroes of his oriental romances have often much of the rude simplicity and essential innocence of the Noble Savage. The idyll of Haidée in "Don Juan" brings in the romantic love which goes along with this same tradition. In his association with Haidée, a maiden untainted by the artificial and corrupt conventions of society and civilization, Don Juan is restored to innocent and "natural" passion.

Byron is romantic in his exaltation of passion. He is romantic in his stress upon the wild and elemental in nature. And, most of all, he is romantic in his craving to identify himself with, to lose himself in, these wild and elemental forces. This is, however, pretty largely confined to feeling, and implies in him very little of an intellectual conception of nature, on either the religious or the scientific side.

Nature and the "World"

Thus far I have tried to confine the concept of nature to the objects and phases of the external world, as distinguished from man and his works. This qualifying or defining phrase we can hardly do without. For the very use of the word nature—unless it is made explicitly more comprehensive—carries with it an opposition between what is natural and what is artificial. Most simply nature signifies in the poets the out-of-doors world as opposed to the indoor world, the country as opposed to town.

The poet's preference of country to town may be quite simple and unphilosophical. We prefer the country because flowers bloom there more freely, the birds sing there, the fields smell of hay, the waters flow more clear, and the landscape leads the eye pleasantly into blue distances. But the preference of country to town is seldom as simple as this. It is almost invariably tinged with some sense of merit attaching to it, grounded in ethical or religious considerations. The country is nature more obviously than the town because it is the world as it came unspoiled from the hands of the Great Artificer; whereas in town the aspect of things is defaced by the works of man, so often perverse and degraded. These poets seldom stop to think that a grassy meadow or a plowed field is the evidence of man's work; and a minster spire rising above tree-tops is felt to be an integral part of God's nature. So that nature generally suggests the opposition between God's world and man's. "God made the country, and man made the town."

By the same token, nature suggests the opposition between the natural and the artificial—that which is natural being the order of things before it is modified by the ingenuity (and often the perverseness) of man. It is clear that Wordsworth discovers more of nature among peasants than among townsmen. Their passions, he finds, are more simple, less confused, and more profound—better subject for poetry, and giving more promise of an ideal social condition in the future. Their social feelings have not been tainted with commercialism; their families not broken up by the industrial revolution.[15] And whoever has the choice of living where he will is wise to choose the country, because he will come under the beneficial influence of nature and be more open to her teaching.

Professor Fairchild has shown that in some poets, like Southey, Wordsworth's doctrine of the "educative value of scenery" is found in association with the legend of the noble savage and the primitivistic tradition.[16] But this is only a phase of Southey's thinking. And in their recommendations of life in the country none of the "Lakists," and few of the eighteenth-century poets whom they admired, were recommending the abandonment of civilization or the fruits of humane culture. Thus Cowper says most explicitly that, while "in cities foul example on most minds begets its likeness," and the virtues seldom thrive there, yet—

> ... true worth and virtue in the mild
> And genial soil of cultivated life
> Thrive most ...[17]

There is no thought here of preferring the wilderness of the noble savage to the civilized countryside of England. Nor could such a thought have had weight with the later poet, whose most admired models were Shakespeare, Spenser and Milton. What Wordsworth had in mind was the reduction of some of the complexities of urban life, and the sacrifice of vanity and worldly ambition to an ideal of strenuous intellectual and purified spiritual life. "Plain living and high thinking" [18] was what nature in the country signified to him.

Among the eighteenth-century poets admired by Wordsworth who celebrated communion with nature as an antidote to worldliness, were William Cowper and James Beattie. Cowper's "Task" is full of this theme. But it is found in even more concentrated form in Beattie's "The Minstrel; or, the Progress of Genius." This poem was particularly admired by Dorothy Wordsworth, who found in the person of the minstrel a close resemblance to the young poet, her brother. This humble shepherdswain, whose life was so simple, whose taste so free from the vulgarity of ordinary boyhood, his fancy so fertile, who was such an enthusiast for nature and solitude, and whose tranquil mind was so free from worldly ambition, she found to be a perfect type of William Wordsworth.[19] The direct teaching of the poem is that a solitary life with nature fosters gentle virtues,[20] and saves one from skepticism in opinion and sensualism in conduct.

> O Nature, how in every charm supreme!
>
> . . . .
>
> Blest be the day I 'scaped the wrangling crew,
> From Pyrrho's maze, and Epicurus' sty;
> And held high converse with the godlike few,
> Who to th' enraptured heart, and ear, and eye,
> Teach beauty, virtue, truth, and love, and melody.[21]

In courtly life, treachery prevails, and ruthless ambition.[22] Men are—

> Lured by toys that captivate the throng;
> To herd in cabinets and camps . . .[23]

It is only in the frame of nature that one can have "the calm, contented mind"; only there can one win back one's faith in human nature.

> Restore those tranquil days, that saw me still
> Well pleased with all, but most with humankind;
> When Fancy roamed through Nature's works at will,
> Unchecked by cold distrust, and uninformed by ill.[24]

In all this there is a close association between the gentle and humane virtues and the exercise of poetic fancy. Virtue seems to go with imagination, and both with country life. This is the implied teaching of Wordsworth's famous sonnet.

> The world is too much with us; late and soon,
> Getting and spending we lay waste our powers:
> Little we see in Nature that is ours;
> We have given our hearts away, a sordid boon . . .

We have lost our faculty for seeing nature with the imagination, as the pagans saw it, who, when they looked on the ocean, had sight of Proteus rising from the sea, or heard old Triton blow his wreathèd horn. And while Wordsworth does not say so in this place in so many words, we know that he has in mind more than the "pleasures of the imagination"; we know that in his mind the lover of nature is already the man who has turned his back on the more vulgar of worldly ambitions, and has chosen instead "plain living and high thinking."

The implication is stated more explicitly in the following passage from "The Excursion."

> For, the Man—
> Who, in this spirit, communes with the Forms
> Of nature, who with understanding heart
> Both knows and loves such objects as excite
> No morbid passions, no disquietude,

No vengeance, and no hatred—needs must feel
The joy of that pure principle of love
So deeply that, unsatisfied with aught
Less pure and exquisite, he cannot choose
But seek for objects of a kindred love
In fellow-natures and a kindred joy.[25]

Here complications begin to multiply. There are more or less fused together in this passage at least two distinct views of nature, —the one obvious enough and easy to accept at its face value, the other involving far-reaching assumptions or distinctions which need to be made clear. Natural scenery does readily lend itself to pure esthetic enjoyment. It pleases the senses and, in its various and subtle combinations of form and color, invites to the exercise of the more complex processes of esthetic composition and discrimination. And, so far as the appeal to the emotions is concerned, it has a fairly neutral or at least not too exciting effect. A secluded landscape may broadly be said to consist of "objects that excite no morbid passions." This is one obvious reason why gentle philosophic poets prefer country views to the streets of cities. The streets of cities are more apt to arouse morbid feelings and disquietude, being full of so many objects associated with our ambitions, anxieties, jealousies and ill-regulated passions. The city-dweller at least is likely to resort to the country for relief from the pressure of his worldly concerns.

These considerations are developed at length in Cowper's "Task,"—a philosophic poem in many ways more nearly anticipating the tone of "The Excursion" than any other.

God made the country, and man made the town.
What wonder then that health and virtue, gifts
That can alone make sweet the bitter draught
That life holds out to all, should most abound
And least be threaten'd in the fields and groves? [26]

The "bless'd seclusion from a jarring world" enjoyed by one engaged in rural occupations brings peace and freedom from the gross temptations of city life.[27] Domestic life in the country is

"friendly to the best pursuits of man, friendly to thought, to virtue, and to peace." [28] As for the esthetic offerings of the country,

> But are not wholesome airs, though unperfumed
> By roses, and clear suns, though scarcely felt;
> And groves, if inharmonious, yet secure
> From clamour, and whose very silence charms;
> To be preferr'd to smoke, to the eclipse
> That metropolitan volcanoes make,
> Whose Stygian throats breathe darkness all day long;
> And to the stir of Commerce driving slow,
> And thundering loud, with his ten thousand wheels? [29]

Cowper also welcomes country retreats as freeing one from the
constant reminders of national wars and injustices.

> O for a lodge in some vast wilderness,
> Some boundless contiguity of shade,
> Where rumour of oppression and deceit,
> Of unsuccessful or successful war,
> Might never reach me more.[30]

One is frequently reminded in the poems of Cowper that he was
"a stricken deer that left the herd," [31] and that his flight from life
—for such in his case his country seclusion may fairly be described
as being—had something of the morbid about it. Or rather it was
a wise therapeutic measure for the treatment of a sick mind. The
psychical weakness which caused him to go out of his head every
time he tried to measure his strength against that of others in the
practical pursuits of life made it necessary for him to withdraw
from scenes suggestive of this distracting rivalry. His religious
mania made it necessary for him to close his eyes upon the crass
reminders of evil rampant in private and public life. Wordsworth,
on the other hand, was normally sound of mind. Living in the
country, he need not hesitate to read in the newspapers of the dis-
tressing political events of his day. It had perhaps never occurred
to him to engage in practical pursuits, though, with his family connections, he had once thought of the Church. His call from the
first had been to the prophetic mission of poet. But for him too,

nature and country seclusion served positively for the stimulation of his intellectual and moral life; and negatively, they served to eliminate certain of the complexities, the worldly temptations, and too distracting reminders of ugliness and evil, thus leaving his imagination more free to deal in the "beautiful idealisms of moral excellence" which (according to Shelley) are the concern of poets.[32]

Nature as "Principle of Love"

But Wordsworth goes far beyond this consideration. He finds in the "forms" of nature a "pure principle of love" and joy so prevailing that one who feels it is impelled to seek for objects of a kindred love and joy in his fellows. The love and joy in nature extend themselves to his relations with human beings, thereby making the nature-lover a more humane and sociable being. But how is it that one finds this love and joy in nature? To answer this question carries us far beyond any meaning of nature that we have thus far considered, into realms scientific, religious, metaphysical. The pleasure which the poet takes in the mere "beauteous forms" of the outdoor world is reinforced by many assumptions drawn from his study and reflection on the "order of nature" as conceived by scientists, on the "universal order" as interpreted by philosophers and theologians. Whatever he has to say about the simplest features of scenery—about "fountains, meadows, hills, and groves" —is insensibly tinged with emotional associations drawn from these large speculations. As Professor Fairchild has expressed it:

To a large group of romanticists, of whom Wordsworth is the great example, scenery provided the best evidence of what the universe fundamentally is . . . Thus wild and semi-wild scenery became a body of symbols representing the romantic ideal of nature. And since the symbol often looms as large as the thing it symbolizes, "nature" was often, for practical purposes, taken as synonymous with "scenery"; although just as great abstractions loom up behind religious images, so behind "natural objects" hovered the universal spirit which gave those objects their value. With Wordsworth, love of external nature sometimes causes the symbol to absorb the thing symbolized, so that trees and mountains seem to have a power of their own, an efficacy such as might be ascribed by a devout Catholic to a religious image.[33]

In the four chapters that follow I shall try to indicate the main lines of thought that underlie and are generally more or less implied in Wordsworth's often extravagant and almost always fervent references to nature. If I lay my main emphasis on Wordsworth, it is because he is universally recognized as the most important and most characteristic of nature-poets in English. Frequent parallels with other poets of his day will show that his views in general were not peculiar to him, though he may have built up the doctrine of nature into a more elaborate structure and written more persuasively about it. Most of what he has to say of nature is not even new, but was anticipated by many eighteenth-century poets with whom he was acquainted. Thus on the side of religion alone, it is worth while reminding ourselves that Young had urged:

> Read Nature; Nature is a friend to truth;
> Nature is Christian; preaches to mankind;
> And bids dead matter aid us in our creed.[34]

Bowles had written of the "sense of quiet gladness" which in summer steals—

> From quiet nooks, and feels itself expand
> Amid the works of Nature, to the Power
> That made them.[35]

Cowper found a "natural supernaturalism" like Carlyle's in the course of the seasons.

> What prodigies can power divine perform
> More grand than it produces year by year,
> And all in sight of inattentive man?
> Familiar with th' effect, we slight the cause;
> And in the constancy of nature's course,
> The regular return of genial months,
> And renovation of a faded world,
> See naught to wonder at.
>
> . . . .
>
> All we behold is miracle; but, seen
> So duly, all is miracle in vain.[36]

The above references to nature are rather more conventionally religious than Wordsworth's in the most famous passages of his nature-poetry. He often shows a greater metaphysical subtlety than any of the poets just quoted; and sometimes he shows a disposition to avoid the direct religious reference and even to approximate the non-religious tone of "naturalism." But where he is most metaphysical, and where he is most naturalistic, some religious assumption, some strain of religious feeling is apt to be implied in what he has to say of nature. And this is a direct inheritance from eighteenth-century poetry.

Wordsworth was a man of strong and subtle intelligence, and we may generally take for granted that, in his often extreme and puzzling statements, he was never talking sheer nonsense. But he was not a systematic philosopher. He was writing as a poet, and we must make due allowance for the figurative character of his language and the ardent warmth of poetic expression. Still more, we must have in mind the great variation in sense in his use of the word nature, and his disposition to make two different meanings of the word equivalent in use. This is of course the point at which faulty reasoning is likely to appear and the poet is apt to deceive himself. At any rate, it is the point where we, who are not approaching the subject as poets, must supply the distinctions which the poet slurred over in his preference for analogy and identification. Again, we must make allowance in any poet of Wordsworth's time for the confidence with which he makes philosophic assumptions which we to-day are quite unable to make. In most cases, there is nothing peculiar in his making these assumptions; they were made pretty generally by contemporary thinkers of every stripe of opinion. Wordsworth is not more important for his individual force and charm than he is for his representative character in the history of English thought.

CHAPTER III

THE METAPHYSICAL CONCEPT OF NATURE

A MOST interesting aspect of Wordsworth's concept of nature, and central to our whole discussion, is his metaphysical notion of the spirit or soul of the universe. While this idea is rather widely diffused through his nature-poetry, it is most nearly expressed with philosophical explicitness in some half-dozen passages occurring in "Tintern Abbey," "The Prelude" and "The Excursion." The first and most famous passage is from "Tintern Abbey" (1798). This poem is entirely devoted to a statement of the reasons why the poet is a worshiper of nature,

> A lover of the meadows and the woods,
> And mountains, and of all that we behold
> From this green earth. . . .

After listing the benefits of nature to him in the way of pleasure, of consolation, of "tranquil restoration," and of moral culture, he arrives as the culminating gift of all.

> And I have felt
> A presence that disturbs me with the joy
> Of elevated thoughts; a sense sublime
> Of something far more deeply interfused,
> Whose dwelling is the light of setting suns,
> And the round ocean and the living air,
> And the blue sky, and in the mind of man;
> A motion and a spirit that impels
> All thinking things, all objects of all thought,
> And rolls through all things.

Thus, speaking apparently of nature itself in its most generalized sense, Wordsworth refers to it, or "something" inherent in it, as "a motion and a *spirit* that impels all thinking things, all objects of all thought."

The second passage is from a poem written in Germany in 1799, entitled "Influence of Natural Objects in Calling Forth and Strengthening the Imagination in Boyhood and Early Youth." This poem was incorporated in the first book of "The Prelude." It begins thus:

> Wisdom and Spirit of the universe!
> Thou Soul that art the Eternity of thought!
> And giv'st to forms and images a breath
> And everlasting motion! [1]

Here Spirit and Soul are words applied interchangeably to whatever it is in the universe that gives "to forms and images a breath and everlasting motion." There are several other passages in "The Prelude" in which the Soul of Nature is invoked or referred to.

> From Nature and her overflowing soul
> I had receiv'd so much that all my thoughts
> Were steep'd in feeling . . .[2]
>   .   .   .   .
> . . . my mind hath look'd
> Upon the speaking face of earth and heaven
> As her prime Teacher, intercourse with man
> Establish'd by the sovereign Intellect,
> Who through that bodily Image hath diffus'd
> A soul divine which we participate,
> A deathless spirit.[3]
>   .   .   .   .
> Oh! soul of Nature, excellent and fair,
> That didst rejoice with me, with whom I too
> Rejoiced, through early youth . . .[4]
>   .   .   .   .
> Oh! Soul of Nature! that dost overflow
> With passion and with life, what feeble men
> Walk on this earth! [5]

The final passage which I shall here cite in illustration of Wordsworth's concept is from the beginning of the ninth book of "The Excursion," which poem was published in 1814.

> "To every form of being is assigned,"
> Thus calmly spake the venerable Sage,
> "An *active* Principle:—howe'er removed
> From sense and observation, it subsists
> In all things, in all natures; in the stars
> Of azure heaven, the unenduring clouds,
> In flower and tree, in every pebbly stone
> That paves the brooks, the stationary rocks,
> The moving waters, and the invisible air.
> Whate'er exists hath properties that spread
> Beyond itself communicating good,
> A simple blessing, or with evil mixed;
> Spirit that knows no insulated spot,
> No chasm, no solitude; from link to link
> It circulates, the Soul of all the worlds."

Certain of the passages quoted—especially some of those from "The Prelude"—it might be possible to dismiss with the statement that Wordsworth is merely using figurative language. Nature being personified, the poet's instinct is to lend her a soul. It is obvious, however, that in the passages from "Tintern Abbey," from "Influence of Natural Objects," and from "The Excursion," Wordsworth is endeavoring to express himself, so nearly as possible, in accurate philosophical language; that whether clear or confused, consistent or inconsistent, there is implied a notion of the fundamental character of the natural process which is more than poetical. Nature is here conceived of, not merely as the order of things, the norm of conduct, the expression of benevolent design, but more specifically as the animating or activating principle of all things in the universe—not merely of living things, but of all phenomena.

In the development of this concept of nature, which more or less ruled for over a century in English poetry, I am going to suggest that an important part may have been played by the speculations of Ralph Cudworth in *The True Intellectual System of the*

Universe (1678), of his contemporary, Henry More, the Cambridge platonist, and of eighteenth-century platonists like Berkeley (in *Siris*). Along with these went the theological speculations of Newton in connection with the theory of gravitation, as set forth by the scientist himself, and further elaborated by Bentley, Clarke, and many other theological writers. Another strain was brought in by Shaftesbury's *Characteristics,* as shown in considerable detail for eighteenth-century poetry by Professor Moore in his two articles. Still another strain was brought in by the sensationalist and associationist philosophers, Hobbes, Locke, Hartley, etc., with modifications and corrections by Berkeley, Hume, etc., and political applications by Godwin. But this has reference less to the metaphysical concept of nature than to psychology, epistemology, the relation between man and the world of sense. Some account must be taken of the direct influence of Plato and Plotinus; of Spinoza, Leibniz, Rousseau, and possibly of Kant and the German idealists. But here again, it is not mainly the metaphysical concept of nature which is involved, but some other philosophical problem like that of the nature of reality or of the faculties by which truth may best be apprehended, and these questions are not primary in this chapter. For later poets, as I hope to show, the influence of German transcendentalism is important in shaping their concept of nature. I shall speak of the influence of French materialist writers on Shelley; but that is a separate consideration. In the early romantic period, the native English tradition is, I am inclined to think, nearly sufficient for our needs.

With regard to Wordsworth's acquaintance with writers mentioned in the following discussion, I refer the reader to the notes.[6]

The Animating Principle

The conception of nature as the animating principle of the universe is dominant in Goethe, who, as we shall see in the chapter devoted to the German poet, makes more of the mere *energy* of nature than most poets do. Nature as the animating principle of things is the subject of much eighteenth-century poetry, such as the passage in Cowper's "Table Talk" beginning,

> Nature, exerting an unwearied power,
> Forms, opens, and gives scent to every flower . . .[7]

But Cowper's view is merely figurative and poetical, as is made more evident by his introducing mythical Naiads along with actual flowers and birds. There is perhaps nothing more philosophical here, or more peculiar to the romantic period, than in Chaucer's reference to nature in the prologue to the "Canterbury Tales,"

> And smale foules maken melodye,
> So priketh hem natur in hir corages.

Nor is there implied any of the specific romantic philosophy of nature in Coleridge's lines, beginning,

> All Nature seems at work. Slugs leave their lair—
> The bees are stirring—birds are on the wing . . .[8]

More philosophical, and specifically romantic, are the words that Southey puts in the mouth of Joan of Arc:

> I saw the eternal energy pervade
> The boundless range of nature . . .[9]

But the reference which follows soon after to him "who formed this goodly frame of things" brings the thought back to a more conventionally religious level. Nature is given her full romantic rôle in Shelley's invocation to her—along with earth and heaven— in "The Revolt of Islam":

> O Earth! O Heaven!
> And thou, dread Nature, which to every deed,
> And all that lives or is to be hath given . . .[10]

This is definitely the philosophic concept, since it takes into account the need to explain the existence of whatever is, or at least hypostatizes nature as a principle or concept distinct from the individual beings whom it animates. This is still more evident in Coleridge's—

> All-conscious Presence of the Universe!
> Nature's vast ever-acting Energy! [11]

But Coleridge goes rather beyond Wordsworth's apparent intention, since he is here explicitly invoking the divine being in his anxiety to avoid any taint of materialism or pantheism. The vast ever-acting Energy of Nature, he wishes it distinctly understood, is none other than God himself. So he declares in another early poem, "Religious Musings," where he calls God "Him Nature's essence, mind, and energy." Coleridge seems never to have fallen into the romantic fashion of hypostatizing nature as a distinct principle. Nature, in his view, may describe, but it never explains anything. To explain anything in the universe we must have recourse to the fundamental and ultimate idea of God. This is involved in Coleridge's idealism—his belief that mind or reason is necessary to existence. In this respect he is in contrast to the prevailing philosophic temper of Goethe, Wordsworth and Shelley, who—in certain characteristic moods—are inclined to do without the idea of God, unless compelled to bring it back in order to guard against some materialistic misconception of their view. That, as I shall try to show later, is probably related to their more scientific temper, their disposition to a monistic interpretation of life.

Goethe, as I have said, loves particularly to think of nature in terms of energy, animation, perpetual movement and change. As he writes in a letter to a friend in 1831: "Die Natur wirkt ewig lebendig, überflüssig und verschwenderisch, damit das Unendliche immer gegenwärtig sei, weil nichts verharren kann." [12] Shelley is fond of the words power and strength to indicate the activating principle of the universe without specifically referring to it in religious terms.

> The secret strength of things
> Which governs thought, and to the infinite dome
> Of heaven is as a law . . . [13]
>
> . . . .
>
> The awful shadow of some unseen Power
> Floats tho' unseen among us. . . . [14]

So Wordsworth—

> . . . the blessed power that rolls
> About, above, below . . .[15]

But none of these poets is able to keep the concept of nature completely neutral, completely free from the terminology of metaphysical idealism and religion. Being poets, as well as heirs to an idealistic tradition, they are not able to do without the words *spirit* and *soul* in referring to this animating or activating principle of the world. In "Eins und Alles," Goethe must address himself to the World-Soul (*Weltseele*), perhaps influenced by the title of one of Schelling's volumes of *Naturphilosophie*. In his poem, "Weltseele," he finds it helpful, like Coleridge in his "Religious Musings," to employ imagery taken from the Leibnizian spiritual system of monads. In "Faust" it is the Earth-Spirit that weaves the Godhead's living garment on his loom of perpetual action. Indeed, Goethe is always ready to interchange the terms nature and God, by way of emphasizing the essentially spiritual character of the universal process.

Shelley, who tends to avoid the term and notion, God, still makes free use, in his most atheistical work, of the words soul and spirit. In "Queen Mab" he speaks of "Nature's Soul," and more than once apostrophizes the Spirit of Nature. And again, less figuratively, he writes:

> Throughout these infinite orbs of mingling light,
> Of which yon earth is one, is wide diffused
> A spirit of activity and life,
> That knows no term, cessation, or decay . . .[16]

And so Wordsworth finds himself as it were constrained to the use of these same words soul and spirit. In "Tintern Abbey," where he seems to have made a particular effort to express himself in terms free from specifically theological implications, he has "a motion and a spirit that impels all thinking things, all objects of all thought." First he wrote "motion." But this word was too mechanistic in its implications. It suggests an impulse passively received from without, and he wishes to suggest the dynamic, vital, or self-activating character of nature. And so he adds "spirit." This seems to be what he wishes to convey in the passage quoted from "The Excursion."

> To every Form of being is assigned
> An *active* Principle . . .
> . . . . it subsists
> In all things, in all natures . . .

The same thought Wordsworth expresses, in somewhat less philosophical language, in "The Old Cumberland Beggar," one of the *Lyrical Ballads*, where he declares that, even in "the meanest of created things," there is found—

> . . . a spirit and a pulse of good,
> A life and soul, to every mode of being
> Inseparably linked.

It is most likely that Wordsworth was endeavoring to free his view from the imputation of mechanistic materialism. Nature, he wishes to say, is not a mere succession of mechanical impulses conveyed from one dead atom to another, from one inert body to another. Every particle of nature—even stones and water and air —has in itself a spring of activity, of spontaneous movement. All natural beings, whether or not conscious spirits, "thinking things," yet partake somehow of the essence of spirit, or at least of life. Thus he would steer clear, on the one hand, of a world which has no need of spirit at all, a *méchanique céleste*—of which he could not conceive—and, on the other hand, of a world set going by spirit but purely mechanical itself. What he required was a world with the God *in* it, a universe impregnated with spirit.

What Wordsworth seems to mean in general in this passage from "The Excursion" is something like what Coleridge had in mind in his early poem, "The Eolian Harp." Coleridge, on a lovely summer evening in the country, has been exalted to a visionary apprehension of the unity of all life in nature, including man and his inner world.

O! the one life within us and abroad,
Which meets all motion and becomes its soul,
A light in sound, a sound-like power in light,
Rhythm in all thought, and joyance everywhere . . .

This is much the spirit and attitude of Wordsworth in his "Lines Written in Early Spring." But it is more strictly metaphysical in its suggestion of how the "one life" which manifests itself equally in the spiritual and the physical worlds ("within us and abroad") "meets all motion and becomes its soul." There is possibly a suggestion here of Berkeleian idealism, and also (in "the one life within us and abroad") a suggestion of Spinoza. We are reminded of the fact noted by M. Legouis in *The Early Life of William Wordsworth* that, in the early days of his friendship with Wordsworth, Coleridge was a fervent admirer of Spinoza and "spoke enthusiastically of Spinoza's formulas concerning God-Nature." [17]

Further along in the poem Coleridge makes another effort to state in philosophical terms his feeling of the ideal unity of nature.

And what if all of animated nature
Be but organic harps diversely framed,
That tremble into thought, as o'er them sweeps
Plastic and vast, one intellectual breeze,
At once the Soul of each, and God of all?

But the poet immediately repudiates this suggestion as smacking of the bold and dangerous views of the *philosophes*. He has indeed saved his nature from any taint of materialism—of the mechanical —by making it all share in the spiritual (intellectual) essence of the deity. But to make the creature share at all in the essence of deity is to skirt the shores of pantheism or other blasphemy.

Nor would Wordsworth have expressed himself in quite these terms, though he was much less nervous about the theological implications of his thought—being less aware perhaps of the theological pitfalls that lay to right and left of his path. But, at the same time, he was less strongly inclined to idealism in metaphysics, or less inclined to metaphysics at all. So that he would not so naturally have spoken of an intellectual breeze, nor have represented his "nature" as trembling into thought. The point with him was that it was *animated*, having an active being, and capable of propagating the impulses of the universal soul. The idea of the universal soul is here in Coleridge, and that and the "plastic" sweep of the intellectual breeze are what lead me to cite this passage in connection with Wordsworth. They serve to introduce a rather long discussion of certain speculations on the character of nature, in seventeenth- and eighteenth-century writers, which have their light to throw on the nature-poetry of Wordsworth's time.

Plastic Nature: Cudworth

The word plastic is worth dwelling on. It was a word considerably used by poets and philosophers in earlier times for expressing some power, found working in nature, which enables it to carry on its operations. In his "Religious Musings," in a passage probably reminiscent of Leibniz (among others), Coleridge refers to the spirits who carry out the commands of God in the conduct of the universe.

> . . . ye of plastic power that interfused
> Roll through the grosser and material mass
> In organizing surge! Holies of God!
> And what if monads of the infinite mind?

It is likely enough, by the way, that two of Wordsworth's expressions in the famous "Tintern Abbey" passage are reminiscent of expressions of his intimate friend Coleridge here: his "something far more deeply interfused," and his "rolls through all things." We shall see later how different a tone Wordsworth gives to these expressions, what a different range of associations they imply. Shelley's use of the word plastic in "Adonais," again, may be reminiscent of both passages cited from Coleridge, as well as of the "spirit that impels" in "Tintern Abbey." Shelley's indebtedness to both Coleridge and Wordsworth goes into innumerable minute points of expression. In "Adonais"—

> . . . . while the one Spirit's plastic stress
> Sweeps through the dull, dense world, compelling there
> All new successions to the forms they wear . . .

The word also appears frequently in eighteenth-century nature-poetry. In Akenside's "Pleasures of the Imagination," it is the Sovereign Spirit of the world (clearly identified with the deity platonically conceived) who is described in the act of creation.

> To spread around him that primeval joy
> Which filled himself, he raised his plastic arm,
> And sounded through the hollow depth of space
> The strong, creative mandate.[18]

And behind all the romantic poets, it is worth remembering, lies Pope and the best-known philosophical poem in the English language, the "Essay on Man." The relevant passage occurs at the beginning of the third Epistle.

> Here then we rest: "The Universal Cause
> Acts to one end, but acts by various laws."
>   . . . .
> Look round our World; behold the chain of Love
> Combining all below and all above.
> See plastic Nature working to this end,
> The single atoms each to other tend . . .
>   . . . .
> See Matter next, with various life endu'd,
> Press to one centre still, the general Good.
>   . . . .
> Nothing is foreign; Parts relate to whole;
> One all-extending, all-preserving Soul
> Connects each being, greatest with the least;
> Made Beast in aid of man, and Man of Beast . . .

This passage of Pope I have quoted thus at length because, along with Coleridge's plastic Nature, it has so many other points suggestive of thoughts in Wordsworth's "Excursion" passage: the universal Soul, the continuity of part with part (Wordsworth says: "properties that spread beyond itself communicating good"). These side-issues, however, we will leave for the time, and limit our consideration to "plastic Nature." And indeed we have implied here, in these lame and shallow verses of Pope, the whole problem that gave rise to the use of the word plastic in connection with nature. How are we to make the connection between the great original spirit and conceiver of the universe—the divine *numen*—and the natural laws and operations by which his will is carried out? To the line, "One all-extending, all-preserving Soul," Warburton appends the following footnote: "Which, in the language of Sir Isaac Newton, is, *Deus omnipraesens est, non per virtutem solam, sed etiam per substantiam: nam virtus sine substantia subsistere non potest.* Newt. Princ. Schol. gen. sub fin."

Whether Pope—or, for that matter, his inspirer, Bolingbroke—was capable of fully understanding the metaphysical distinction here made, may be a matter of doubt. But behind the whole of Pope's argument there does lurk obscurely the metaphysical and theological problem, or cluster of related problems: How can a mere mechanical force (*virtus*) be conceived of as acting towards an intelligible end? How can the whole universe of mechanical forces be conceived of at all without reference to an underlying substance (*substantia*), or ultimate basis of existence, of which they are the manifestations, and by virtue of which they have being?

These we might designate as the ultimate problems. But once granting the existence of the absolute being, or spiritual substance of the universe, the question arises as to how his will and thought are carried out or translated in the particulars of nature, so that mechanical operations have direction as if intelligent, and make for ends as if designed. Perhaps this question would not arise at all if the conception of the absolute being were of purely metaphysical origin, and completely free from the religious notions of the personal and the supernatural. For then the absolute being would be simply a term for characterizing the operations of the universe as having unity and intelligible direction, or at least having such a character as makes them conform to our notions of unity and direction; and each least operation and manifestation of nature would partake of the character of the whole. But very seldom is the notion of the absolute being so confined to purely metaphysical terms. And in particular, wherever the words God, deity, divine, are used for designating the absolute being, something of the less critical religious conception of deity is almost certain to color the thought. The question will arise as to the agency by which the will of the supreme being is carried out. And where there is some degree of philosophical subtlety, there is a natural reluctance, as Cudworth says, "in all the Protean Transformations of Nature . . . to bring God upon the stage, with his Miraculous extraordinary Power, perpetually at every turn." But how then, without the particular intervention of God at every turn, explain the regularity, the direction, the shaping power, of natural forces? For that natural forces have a shaping power, a drive and directive faculty, is what is implied in the use of the word plastic in reference to nature.

The term plastic was at one time widely used in the natural sciences. Lyell refers to its unwarranted use in geology and accuses Lamarck of resorting to a notion equally inadmissible in the objective science of biology.

When Lamarck talks of 'the efforts of internal sentiment,' 'the influence of subtle fluids,' and 'acts of organization,' as causes whereby animals and plants may acquire *new organs*, he substitutes names for things; and, with a disregard to the strict rules of induction, resorts to fictions, as ideal as the 'plastic virtue,' and other phantoms, of the geologists of the middle ages.[19]

Coleridge was much more hospitable to the notion of a plastic virtue as applied in biology and physiology, though not indeed with any reference to the origin of species. Thus he refers in *The Friend* to "Professor Blumenbach's *Bildungstrieb*, the *vis plastica*, or *vis vitae formatrix* of the elder physiologists, and the life or living principle of John Hunter." [20] This concept of plastic virtue in plant life is made use of by Henry Brooke in his platonic poem, "Universal Beauty," in explaining the activities of roots.

> *Their Figures*, pliant to some plastic SKILL,
> Alike, obsequious to its secret WILL;
> With *pointed Cone* the yielding Strata *pass:*
> Or here, *accumulate* their bulbous Mass . . .[21]

But we are concerned with the word in a sense more comprehensive than as applied in biology. And it was frequently used in a way to cover both the scientific and more strictly metaphysical concepts. Thus Maupertuis, in his *Système de la Nature*, refers to the notion of plastic natures, along with an alternative system for explaining natural phenomena.

Les uns ont imaginé des *Natures plastiques*, qui sans intelligence et sans matière exécutent dans l'Univers tout ce que la matière et l'intelligence pourroient exécuter. Les autres ont introduit des sub-stances intelligentes, des *Génies*, ou des Démons, pour mouvoir les astres, et pourvoir à la production des animaux, des plantes, et de tous les corps organisés.[22]

Again, George Cheyne, in his *Philosophical Principles of Religion*, which Wordsworth had in the 1705 edition, lumps the concept of plastic virtue together with various and sundry metaphysical notions.

That there is no such Thing as a *Universal Created Soul* animating this vast System according to *Plato*, or any *Substantial Forms* according to *Aristotle*, nor any omniscient *Radical Heat* according to *Hippocrates*, nor any *Plastick Virtue* according to *Scaliger*, nor any *Hylarchick Principle* according to *Henry Moor*, is evident from the following considerations. . . .[23]

And Coleridge, in an early letter, in discussing the problem of the origin and nature of life, makes the following observation: "Monro believes in a *plastic, immaterial nature, all-pervading.*

And what if all of animated nature
Be but organic harps, etc." [23a]

A most elaborate exposition of the theory of plastic natures is given by Ralph Cudworth in his *True Intellectual System of the Universe*, in the course of his monumental confutation of atheism. Cudworth is convinced that Democritean "atomism" is a philo-sophical instrument necessary for explaining the operations of nature; but at the same time he is a determined opponent of any form of pure materialism, or atheism—that is, of any system which undertakes to account for the ultimate origin and direction of the universe on a purely mechanical basis. The communication of impulse from atom to atom in accordance with the laws of physics, in an unbroken chain of material phenomena—such is the process of nature. But no material atoms—nor any chain of them—can possibly explain, or give rise to, what we find in the universe —intelligence, purpose, direction—let alone force itself, and the origination of force, movement and direction. Still less can any concourse of material atoms, of themselves, *organize* themselves, form themselves into animal organisms, induce in themselves sensibility and the higher processes of the intellect. In order to account for these we must turn to the original intelligent substance, which is God.

But, on the other hand, in this atomic process of the universe, we do find the manifestation of all these non-material attributes and faculties. The universe does conduct itself with intelligence, purpose, direction. Atomic matter is organized into animal and even spiritual forms by some plastic or shaping power. And the universe is endowed with this plastic nature by the supreme intellectual being, whose instrument it is. This is the alternative to supposing that every obscurest operation of nature is carried out by the immediate particular direction of God. As Cudworth expressed it:

That every thing in Nature should be done Immediately by God himself; this, as according to Vulgar Apprehension, it would render Divine Providence Operose, Sollicitous and Distractious, and thereby make the Belief of it to be entertained with greater difficulty, and give advantage to Atheists; so in the Judgment of the Writer *De Mundo*, it is not so Decorous in respect to God neither, that he should αὐτουργεῖν ἅπαντα, set his own Hand, as it were, to every Work, and immediately do all the Meanest and Triflingest things himself Drudgingly, without making use of any Inferior and Subordinate Instruments.[24]

Accordingly, Cudworth assigns all this drudgery to the "plastic nature." It is thus that he sums up his long exposition of the subject, defining the Plastick Nature.

It is a certain *Lower Life* than the *Animal*, which acts *Regularly* and *Artificially*, according to the direction of *Mind* and *Understanding*, *Reason* and *Wisdom*, for *Ends*, or in Order to *Good*, though it self do not know the Reason of what it does, nor is *Master* of that Wisdom according to which it acts, but only a *Servant* to it, and *Drudging Executioner* of the same; it operating *Fatally* and *Sympathetically*, according to *Laws* and *Commands*, prescribed to it by a *Perfect Intellect*, and imprest upon it; and which is either a *Lower* Faculty of some *Conscious Soul;* or else an Inferiour kind of Life or *Soul* by it self; but essentially depending upon a *Higher Intellect*.[25]

This plastic nature may be conceived of in a theistic or an atheistical fashion. In its atheistical form it constitutes the system of hylozoism, which, as Cudworth explains, is the direct opposite of atomism. For whereas atomism regards matter as consisting merely of extended resisting bulk, without life or cogitation, hylozoism regards matter, down to the smallest atom, as having life essentially belonging to it, though without any animal sense or reflexive knowledge, "as if life, and matter or extended bulk, were but two incomplete and inadequate conceptions, of one and the same substance, called body." [26] Thus matter is able of itself to form itself artificially and even to organize itself into sensible, nay, reasoning creatures; which makes unnecessary the assumption of an incorporeal soul in men, or even of any Deity in the universe to explain its regularity.

For Cudworth this atheistical hylozoism is a manifest paradox, or contradiction in terms. It can only be held by persons with a strong prepossession against a belief in God, "which to such is the highest of all paradoxes imaginable, and the most affrightful Bugbear." For persons so minded, I suppose, his own assumption of an "incorporeal substance" is but a means of escaping one paradox, or contradiction in terms, by recourse to another more abstruse and beyond the test of experience. Meantime, what a layman would like to know, in regard to this interesting hylozoist view, is whether the contradiction in terms which Cudworth finds in it might not conceivably be resolved by a more exact definition of terms, or by a more happy choice of terms to begin with.

Cudworth is not quite clear whether he holds the platonic (or neoplatonic) doctrine of a general mundane soul, and if so just what relation the plastic nature bears to this soul of the universe. In one place he says that, even if there were no mundane soul, yet there might be a plastic nature depending on the deity.[27] He says that, according to Aristotle, the plastic nature is either part of some mundane soul, or at least some inferior principle, depending on such a soul.[28] The platonists hold, he says, "that there is a plastic nature lodged in all particular souls of animals, brutes, and men, and also that there is a general plastic or spermatic principle of the whole universe distinct from their higher mundane soul, though subordinate to it, and dependent upon it." [29]

If then Wordsworth read in Cudworth of an active principle in all nature, he would have found here to his hand his "soul of all the worlds." And if Wordsworth's soul of all the worlds seems, on first reading, to bear a somewhat confused relation to the particular soul (or active principle) of each particular "Form of being," his view is at any rate less complicated than that of the "platonists," which involves at least four distinct stages in the hierarchy of souls: the particular souls of animals, brutes, and men; the general spermatic principle of the whole universe; the higher mundane soul; and the deity from whom depends the mundane.

There is to our apprehensions something quaint and fantastic in Cudworth's notions, derived from the theology of his own and the philosophy of earlier times. But it is a real metaphysical problem that he was attacking, the same problem that Plato solved with his definition of soul as "a movement that can move itself." [30] He was trying so to conceive the operations of nature as to get around the difficulties inherent in a mechanical system. He was trying to show how mere passive matter can be self-moved and moved towards rational ends—to introduce the dynamic principle which was not furnished by the atomic theory itself nor by the mechanics of contemporary science. And at the same time he wished not to resort to the hypothesis that the divine spirit is personally interfering at each stage of the process to give the necessary push. The word plastic is simply another word for self-acting, self-shaping, or possessed of independent life. But he was bound by an inescapable dualism inherent in the absolute distinction between matter and spirit. Consequently, he could not accept the assumption of the hylozoic heresy, that all matter, as such, has a "life, perception, and self-active power in it" capable of forming itself to the best advantage, making of itself sun and planet, organizing itself into animal forms, and even advancing "into all the acts of reason and understanding of men." [31] Such life and self-active power nature has only by allowance from the supreme spirit, whose servant it is.

But self-active power is what he needs to find in nature, or, as he several times calls it, in Wordsworth's very phrase, an "active Principle." Strato, he says, while denying the deity, was by so much ahead of Democritus that he did postulate such an "Active Principle and Cause of Motion."

Democritus his *Nature* was nothing but the *Fortuitous Motion* of Matter, but *Strato's Nature* was an *Inward Plastick Life* in the several parts of Matter, whereby they could Artificially frame themselves to the best advantage, according to their several Capabilities, without any Conscious or Reflexive Knowledge.[32]

Similarly he finds that Empedocles made friendship and discord to be "the *Active Principle* and *Immediate Operator* in this Lower World," not understanding by this two substantial principles in the world, as some suppose, "but only a *Plastick Nature*, as *Aristotle* in sundry places intimates." [33]

The Spirit of Nature: Henry More

The concept of plastic nature appears in Henry More under the guise of the spirit of nature, or the soul of the world. This subject is extensively gone into in the third book of More's treatise on *The Immortality of the Soul*. More's most precise and comprehensive definition of the Spirit of Nature is found in Chap. XII, section 1 (Book III).

The Spirit of Nature, therefore, according to that notion I have of it, is, *A substance incorporeal, but without Sense and Animadversion, pervading the whole Matter of the Universe, and exercising a Plastical power therein, according to the sundry predispositions and occasions in the parts it works upon, raising such* Phaenomena *in the World, by directing the parts of the Matter and their Motion, as cannot be resolved into mere Mechanical powers.*

Henry More's spirit of nature, then, is essentially the same as Cudworth's plastic nature. It is an incorporeal "substance" or "principle," which has the power of shaping the matter of the universe and directing its motion, and producing phenomena which cannot be accounted for on mere mechanical grounds. It has, therefore, the powers of a spirit and acts like a spirit, but has not the "sense and animadversion" of the human or divine spirit, or even of animal souls. On this point he is not quite certain. It is difficult to attribute to this spirit of nature the shaping powers of a spirit without endowing it with any of the familiar faculties of spirits as we know them. But he is at least sure that the spirit of nature does not possess the highest faculties of the human soul— reason and free will.

That the *Spirit of Nature* hath Life, and that both *Plastical* and *Omniform*, I dare more confidently to aver; but as to Sense and Animadversion, I hold it a more rash business to determine anything either negatively or affirmatively. But that it is devoid of Reason and Free Will is with me an establish'd Point.[34]

Like Cudworth's plastic nature, More's spirit of nature receives its powers from the deity, and is indeed "the Vicarious power of God" and "the great Quartermaster-General of Divine Providence." [35]

If I rightly understand More, the spirit of nature is identical with the platonic Soul of the World,[36] unless by calling it "the inferior Soul of the World," [37] he means to suggest, like Cudworth for his plastic nature, that it is a general soul of the world subordinate to, or dependent on, the higher Mundane Soul. More than once, however, he calls it "the Universal Soul of the World." [38] Like Cudworth he has this Soul of the World work through and manifest itself in the particular souls of living beings. After giving an account of some otherwise quite unexplainable phenomena, More asks:

What remains therefore but the *Universal Soul of the World*, or *Spirit of Nature*, that can do these feats? who, *Vertumnus*-like, is ready to change his own activity and the yielding Matter into any mode and shape indifferently, as occasion engages him, and so to prepare an edifice, at least the more rude strokes and delineaments thereof, for any Specifick Soul whatsoever, and in any place where the Matter will yield to his operations. But the time of the arrival thither of the particular guest it is intended for, though we cannot say how soon it is, yet we may be sure it is not later than a clear discovery of *Sensation*, as well as *Vegetation* and *Organization* in the Matter.[39]

Thus the specific soul of each animal is made possible by the general soul of the world, and is as it were an expression of this general soul, just as the active principle of "each form of being" in Wordsworth is an expression of, a parcel of, the Soul of all the Worlds, which "circulates" everywhere. The suggestion that the soul of the world can thus exert its plastic power only "where the Matter will yield to His operations" reminds us of Shelley's conception of "the dull dense world" through which sweeps "the one Spirit's plastic stress," and the similar thought in Coleridge. In all three cases the notion may well go back to Plotinus.[40]

More's conception is much less subtle, or strictly metaphysical in character, than Cudworth's. He is not primarily concerned with the problem of material phenomena shaping themselves, as if by conscious design, for rational ends. His spirit of nature is more like a formula for explaining, in scientific or pseudo-scientific phenomena, whatever seemed incapable of being explained on natural grounds. Such is the sympathetic sounding of violin strings tuned in unison on separate instruments, the attraction of the lodestone, the falling of a stone to the earth (not explainable on the grounds of pure mechanical motion), and the movement of the earth in its vortex (as set forth by Descartes). Such are the natural instincts of animals impelling them to acts which are for the good of the species—as the spider's spinning of her web, and the similar performances of bees, birds, silk-worms. Such again, in his fantastic world of pseudo-science, is the impression made on the foetus of the unborn child by the mother's imaginings or frights; or the passage of the souls of men into the shapes of cats, pigeons, weasels, or of other men, where "whatever hurt befalls them, in these *Astral* bodies, the same is inflicted upon their *Terrestrial*, lying in the meantime in their beds, or on the ground." [41] These phenomena, which he finds well authenticated in the works of the best writers, can only be accounted for on the assumption that, in the case of the mother's imaginings, "the deeply-impassionated Fancy of the Mother snatches away *the Spirit of Nature* into consent";[42] in the case of the injuries received by men when their souls are absent in astral bodies, that *"the Spirit of Nature* is snatch'd into consent with the Imagination of the Souls in these *Astral bodies,* or *Aiery* vehicles." [43]

More's spirit of nature is, indeed, a sort of hodge-podge of several distinct entities—the ethereal spirits appealed to by scientists of his time for explaining various phenomena of physics, the animal spirits by which they explained certain operations of the human body (neither of these properly speaking incorporeal spirits); the celestial and infernal personages and the spirits of the elements, of medieval demonology, corresponding to similar concepts in Greek philosophy. Altogether his spirit of nature, or soul of the world, is a crude sort of conception compared with Cudworth's essentially metaphysical principle of the plastic nature.

But partly for that very reason, it was still better adapted to impress the popular (and poetic) imagination and bear its part in building up the nature-philosophy which reached its refined culmination in the poems of Wordsworth and Shelley. The extreme variety of manifestations of this vaguely conceived "spirit" as he represented them was such as to make it a very convenient concept for poets who wished to include all of nature under a single mysterious and inspiring term. Thus the spirit of nature would account for the life of the vegetable world: " 'tis exceeding rational that all *Plants* and *Flowers* of all sorts (in which we have no argument to prove there is any particular Soul) should be the effects of this *Universal Soul of the World* . . . For there is one Soul ready everywhere to pursue the advantages of prepared Matter." [44] Like Wordsworth's "something far more deeply interfused," this spirit of nature "penetrating even all things is never idle." [45]

More does not, so far as I have observed, insist like Cudworth on its being an *"active* principle." But what is perhaps even more important for the poetic imagination, it is a *vital* one. Referring to the various modifications brought about in matter by mechanical motion, he insists that the immediate director of such motion is the Spirit of Nature, "since the Universal Motion of all the Matter of the World is *Vital,* and not *Mechanical,* unless it be by Accident." [46] Thus he provides, what the romantic poets so greatly craved, a non-mechanical spirit to be the animating principle of all nature.

Early Criticism of the Concept of Nature

The concept of Cudworth and More, concerning a plastic nature, a spirit of nature, or soul of the world, as distinct from God, did not go without protest on the part of seventeenth- and eighteenth-century writers, some of whom were probably known to Wordsworth and Coleridge. Thus Stillingfleet, in his *Origines Sacrae* (1662), expressly repudiates More's notion of a distinct spirit of nature.[47] He is followed in this by Sir Matthew Hale, the Lord Chief Justice, a writer praised by Cowper for his deep spiritual discernment. In his *Primitive Origination of Mankind* (1667), Hale objects both to the conception of a separate *Anima Mundi* and to that, sometimes held by the ancients, of the identity of the *Anima Mundi* with the Deity.[48] He is protesting, at one and the same time, against pantheism and against the unnecessary assumption of an *anima mundi*.

Hale has, in one place, a rather thorough logical analysis of the entire concept of nature as some distinct principle in the universe capable of solving the problems of causation, etc. He has been arguing against the "fortuitous" atomism of Democritus and Epicurus, and then he turns to the school of the "platonists."

Ask another sort of Philosophers for their Solution of it, they will tell you that Nature is the Cause, and a sufficient Solution of all these things: But what is that Nature, where is it, is it the nature or disposition of things themselves? Then it explicates it no otherwise but thus, That things have this excellency and order, because it is their nature to be so, or, that they are so because they are so. But if by Nature they mean some separate Existence, what then is it? Is it a Body or Spirit, is it a reasonable, an intelligent Being, or is it a surd and stupid Existence, or else is it a Law or Rule self-subsisting? If it be a reasonable, intelligent Existence, we differ but only *de nomine;* that which I call God they will call Nature, at least unless they suppose it an inferiour intelligent Being, and then the difficulty is only made somewhat more; that a subordinate intelligent Being was able to produce such Effects which appear to all Men to be Works of the greatest Power and Wisdom imaginable.[49]

Thus, lawyer-like, he exposes some of the logical dilemmas in which theorists like Cudworth and More are landed by the supposition of a Nature distinct from the Deity. He goes on to show that Nature can be a Law only as it represents an intelligent Agent working through it. And then he distinguishes the two main acceptations in which the word may be used.

1. As it signifies that *Principium activum* that gave every thing its Being; and thus it imports no other than Almighty God, that Supreme Intelligent Being, though improperly called Nature; viz. *Natura naturans.*

2. As it imports the Things or Effects principated or effected by this Intelligent active Principle, or the Effects or Creatures of God, or *Natura naturata . . .*[50]

This passage is interesting in two ways in connection with the romantic poets. In the first place, there appears here, both in Latin and in English, the phrase used by Wordsworth in "The Excursion," *active Principle*, and in a context suited to throw light upon his meaning. Again, Hale employs the scholastic distinction between *Natura naturans* and *Natura naturata* several times referred to by Coleridge in his philosophical writings; and, like Coleridge after him, he expressly condemns as illegitimate the first acceptation of the word Nature, as signifying any power distinct from the divine. Nature, he finds, is a totally inadequate substitute for the Deity as an originating cause of things. This opinion is stated by him even more distinctly and impressively in his later work, *A Discourse of the Knowledge of God and of Ourselves* (1688).[51]

But the strongest and most well-reasoned protest against the loose employment of the word nature to signify some independent power or principle was that of Robert Boyle, the great physical scientist, in his *Free Inquiry into the Vulgar Notion of Nature* (1686). His protest is all the more impressive for being made on three distinct grounds—religious, metaphysical and scientific. His metaphysical argument is very similar to Hale's. On religious grounds he objects to this "vulgar" notion of Nature—

For, it seems to detract from the honour of the great author and governor of the world; that men should ascribe most of the admirable things to be met with in it, not to him but to a certain nature, which themselves do not well know what to make of. 'Tis true, many confess that this nature is a thing of his establishing, and subordinate to him; but, tho' they own it, when they are ask'd the question, yet there are several who seldom or never regarded any higher cause. And whoever takes notice of their way of ascribing things to nature, may easily discern, that, whatever the words sometimes are, the agency of God is little in their thoughts . . .[52]

In discussing the views of Aristotle and the Peripatetics, Boyle says:

Whence 'twill not be difficult to perceive, that, if they do not quite exclude God; yet, as they leave him no interest in the first formation of the universe, so they leave him but little in the administration of the parts it consists of, especially in such as are sublunary. Instead, therefore, of the true God, they have substituted, for us, a kind of Goddess, with the title of nature; upon whom they look as the immediate agent and director in all excellent productions, and ascribe to her the praise and glory of them.[53]

This passage is particularly interesting in connection with a similar protest of Coleridge's against Aristotle's practical assumption of a Goddess Nature. It is found in a footnote to his *Aids to Reflection,* in connection with the distinction between *natura naturans* and *natura naturata,* to which I have referred above in the discussion of Hale.

It has in its consequences proved no trifling evil to the Christian world, that Aristotle's Definitions of Nature are grounded on the petty and rather rhetorical than philosophical Antithesis of Nature to Art—a conception inadequate to the demand even of *his* philosophy. Hence in the progress of his reasoning, he confounds the *natura naturata* (that is, the sum total of the facts and phænomena of the Senses) with an hypothetical *natura naturans,* a *Goddess* Nature, that has no better claim to a place in any sober system of Natural Philosophy than the Goddess *Multitudo;* yet to which Aristotle not rarely gives the name and attributes of the Supreme Being. The result was, that the idea of God thus identified with this hypothetical *Nature* becomes itself but an *hypothesis,* or at best but a precarious inference from incommensurate premises and on disputable principles; while in 6ther passages, God is confounded with (and everywhere, in Aristotle's *genuine* works, *included in*) the Universe: which most grievous error it is the great and characteristic merit of Plato to have avoided and denounced.[54]

Thus it will be seen that Coleridge ranged himself stoutly on the side of Stillingfleet, Hale, and Boyle, in their protest against the Cudworth-More hypothesis of a "principle call'd nature." [55] It is possible that Coleridge's reference to Aristotle's Goddess Nature is an echo of the same reference in Boyle. It is also not impossible that, in making his distinction between *natura naturans* and *natura naturata*, he may have been affected by Hale. The paradox of the case is that, in ranging himself against Cudworth and More (on the side of Plato and the angels), he is ranging himself against the two seventeenth-century writers most indebted to Plato and the platonists.

In Boyle, the strongest argument against the independent "principle" of nature is drawn from scientific considerations. He was impressed with the confusion introduced in scientific thought by the large number of senses in which the word nature was currently used; and in order to avoid ambiguity, he recommended various simple substitutes for the word in most of its uses. He found that scientific literature was full of vulgar axioms in regard to this "principle," which, on examination, would not hold water: such as, that nature always takes the shortest way, that nature abhors a vacuum, that nature never fails of her end, that nature cures disease. Most important of all is his contention that, given the atomic theory, the known laws of motion, and the intelligent being that set them going and directed them, the phenomena of the world are adequately accounted for without recourse to the independent principle of nature.

Supposing the common matter of all bodies to have been at first divided into innumerable minute parts by the wise author of things, and these parts to have been so dispos'd, as to form the world as it now is; and, supposing the universal laws of motion, among the parts of matter, to have been establish'd, and several conventions of particles contrived into the seminal principles of various things; all which may be effected by the mere motion of matter, skillfully guided at the beginning of the world; supposing all this, together with God's ordinary and general concourse, which we very reasonably may; I see not, why the same phenomena, that we now observe in the world, should not be produc'd, without taking in any such powerful and intelligent being, distinct from God, as nature is represented to be . . .[56]

He considers at length the causes for recovery from disease, and concludes that, in general, when we recover from, as when we succumb to, disease, it is because of conditions affecting the diseased body such as can be objectively studied, and not because of the mysterious working of a separate principle called Nature. "Many things, therefore, that are commonly ascrib'd to nature, may be better ascribed to the mechanism of the universe, and the human body." [57]

Boyle, then, does his best to get rid of the concept of nature as some power distinct from God on the one hand and the mechanical operation of the laws of motion on the other. But nature is far too convenient a word to be dispensed with altogether, and he frequently uses it himself. Thus, in his *Inquiry into the Final Causes of Natural Things,* he speaks of the instinct given by nature to certain insects,[58] and of what nature has or has not given to flies in the way of visual organs.[59] His own definition of nature, however, is such as to get rid of most of the mystic and occult associations of the terms spirit, or soul of nature, or plastic nature. Nature is, he says, "*the aggregate of the bodies that make up the world, in its present state, considered as a principle, by virtue of which they act and suffer, according to the laws of motion, prescribed by the author of things.*" [60] The element of the mystic or occult has thus retired into the phrase "considered as a principle," and that other inescapable phrase "prescribed by the author of things." There is nothing left of the sheer medievalism of More and Cudworth. For this physicist the *anima mundi* has gone into the discard.

Anima Mundi: Berkeley

It is far from having gone altogether into the discard for poets and metaphysicians. But more and more the disposition is to identify the *anima mundi* with the author of things, rather than to consider it as a distinct entity or principle. Thus platonism in the eighteenth century tends to take on a deistical or pantheistic cast. In 1711 the poet Henry Needler wrote an open letter on the Cause of Natural Effects, in which he expressed the view that "all those regular Effects, which we observe to be produced [in Nature] ought to be immediately attributed to [God], as the true *Anima Mundi* or *Active Principle* of Nature." [61] He goes on to show how utterly unqualified matter is to be the author of what passes in nature. And this being so—

There remain only created Intelligent Beings to be consider'd: Unless it should be imagin'd, that some Immaterial and Active, tho' *Unintelligent* Being, may Actuate Nature. But an Unintelligent Being, however Active and Immaterial, (supposing such a *Chimaera* possible,) cou'd never be qualified to govern Nature, because, being *Unintelligent*, it wou'd not be capable of receiving any Laws, nor of regulating itself by them, any more than Matter it self.[62]

This is a decisive repudiation of the independent spirit of nature which is plastic in power and at the same time wanting in "sense and animadversion."

That this notion was not so easily scotched, however, is shown by the fact that, so late as 1780, Richard Price finds it necessary, in a letter to Lord Monboddo, to state that he dissents from Cudworth's view of "plastic Natures," though agreeing with him and Plato, with Newton and Clarke, in his general view of nature. His view of nature is perfectly sober and orthodox, indeed, and quite different from Cudworth's on this point.

And that *Nature* to which atheists ascribe all things, and which they say contains in itself a principle of order, I consider as only the Divine Agency and Wisdom preserving, conducting, and governing all things according to certain fixed rules or laws.[63]

Lord Monboddo himself held a view much more like that of Cudworth and More, involving whatever is most complicated and fantastic in the views of the neoplatonists.[64]

Much more likely than Monboddo to have influenced Wordsworth and the early Coleridge is Bishop Berkeley, who devotes a large part of his *Siris* (1744) to a consideration of the *anima mundi*, or "universal spirit author of life and motion." [65] The word nature plays a very minor rôle in Berkeley's discussion; and he does not, I believe, employ the term, the spirit of nature. But the *anima mundi* is with him almost a synonym for nature. "Nature seems to be not otherwise distinguished from the anima mundi, than as life is from soul, and, upon the principles of the oldest philosophers, may not improperly or incongruously be styled the life of the world." [66] Berkeley is thoroughly familiar with "the learned doctor Cudworth," to whom he several times refers. Like Cudworth, he is concerned to show that no motion, nor any of the phenomena described by scientists, is adequately to be accounted for on mere mechanical grounds.[67] The various so-called laws of motion, etc., are to be regarded "only as rules or methods observed in the productions (sic) of natural effects, the efficient and final causes whereof are not of mechanical consideration." [68]

Berkeley seems to like to consider the universal spirit, which gives effect in the world to the intellectual decrees of God, in terms of some particularly rarefied sort of fire or light, the two words being more or less interchangeable in his use. This, in the world as a whole, is analogous to the working of the animal spirit in the human body.

In the human body the mind orders and moves the limbs: but the animal spirit is supposed the immediate physical cause of their motion. So likewise in the mundane system, a mind presides, but the immediate, mechanical, or instrumental cause, that moves or animates all its parts, is the pure elementary fire or spirit of the world. The more fine and subtile part or spirit is supposed to receive the impressions of the first mover, and communicate them to the grosser sensible parts of this world.[69]

This pure elementary fire or spirit of the world serves all the purposes of More's "spirit of nature" and Cudworth's "plastic nature." And it is, Berkeley would have us know, a concept held in common by the "Pythagoreans, Platonics and Stoics."

There is according to those philosophers a life infused throughout all things: the πῦρ νοερὸν, πῦρ τεχνικὸν, an intellectual or artificial fire, an inward principle, animal spirit, or natural life producing and forming within as art doth without, regulating, moderating and reconciling the various motions, qualities and parts of this mundane system. By virtue of this life the great masses are held together in their orderly courses, as well as the minutest particles governed in their natural motions, according to the several laws of attraction, gravity, electricity, magnetism, and the rest. It is this gives instincts, teaches the spider her web, and the bee her honey. This it is that directs the roots of plants to draw forth juices from the earth, and the leaves and cortical vessels to separate and attract such particles of air, and elementary fire, as suit their respective natures.[70]

Much of the confusion of More's conception is found in Berkeley's. At times this "intellectual or artificial fire" is, like Cudworth's plastic nature, a metaphysical device for avoiding the pitfalls of materialism—an active principle that accounts for the origin of motion, and enables matter to organize itself and to act intelligently for rational ends. This conception is expressed in the passage just quoted when Berkeley speaks of it, in platonic terms, as "producing and forming within as art doth without." The same thought is expressed in another place.

The phænomena of light, animal spirit, muscular motion, fermentation, vegetation, and other natural operations, seem to require nothing more than the intellectual and artificial fire of Heraclitus, Hippocrates, the Stoics, and other ancients. . . . The Stoics held that fire comprehended and included the spermatic reasons or forms (λόγους σπερματικοὺς) of all natural things.[71]

According to this view, the intellectual fire has a status very like that of the platonic "forms" or "ideas," representing the intellectual or rational equivalent of mere mechanical rules or scientific phenomena. But the conception of this intellectual fire is gradually made to grow out of a long pseudo-scientific discussion of the physical properties of air, fire, heat, light (all rather confused together). The whole operation has much the character of a conjurer's trick. When the fire which is the spirit of the world first makes its appearance (in connection with the Bishop's hobby of tar-water), it is anything but a spermatic reason or form. It is frankly an "inferior instrumental cause"—on a plane, one feels, with electricity or the animal spirits.

The order and course of things, and the experiments we daily make, shew there is a mind that governs and actuates this mundane system, as the proper real agent and cause. And that the inferior instrumental cause is pure aether, fire, or the substance of light which is applied and determined by an infinite mind in the macrocosm or universe, with unlimited power and according to stated rules; as it is in the microcosm, with limited power and skill by the human mind.[72]

One is not aware of the moment when fire ceases to be a material element and instrumental cause and turns into a spermatic reason or form. This magic transformation is made more easy by the ambiguity attaching to the word spirit in the science and philosophy of the period. Now spirit is simply a more subtile form of some subtile element like air or fire; and now it is an incorporeal essence, not subject to the disabilities of matter. The animal spirit is material, and nothing better than "the immediate physical cause" of certain motions. But the spirit of the world is an intellectual principle capable of "producing and forming within as art doth without."

It is natural, with so much ambiguity attaching to the character of this *anima mundi*, that considerable uncertainty should attach to the relation it bears to the purely rational and incorporeal prime mover. Berkeley is well aware that many of the ancients identified the soul of the world with God himself. He does not seem ready to take any very decided stand in this matter. He is content to point out that the several schools of ancient thought agreed on the universality and orderliness of the world-soul.

Thus much the schools of Plato and Pythagoras seem agreed in, to wit, that the soul of the world whether having a distinct mind of its own, or directed by a superior mind doth embrace all its parts by an invisible and indissoluble chain, and preserve them ever well adjusted, and in good order.[73]

He is sympathetic enough towards the pantheistic view to defend it several times against the charge of being atheistical.

If we suppose, that one and the same mind is the universal principle of order and harmony throughout the world, containing and connecting all its parts, and giving unity to the system, there seems to be nothing atheistical or impious in this supposition.[74]

The thing of prime importance is to demonstrate the inadequacy of merely mechanical explanations. Berkeley brings his well-known views on the ideality of matter, of motion in itself, of space, to bear on the problem. And his chief insistence is that, however we conceive of the spirit of the world, we must conceive of it as essentially intellectual or governed by mind.

Now whether the νοῦς be abstracted from the sensible world, and considered by itself, as distinct from, and presiding over the created system, or whether the whole universe, including mind together with the mundane. body, is conceived to be God, and the creatures to be partial manifestations of the divine essence, there is no atheism in either case, whatever misconceptions there may be; so long as mind or intellect is understood to preside over, govern, and conduct the whole frame of things.[75]

There are several minor points, to be mentioned later, in which Wordsworth might well have been influenced by Berkeley's discussion in *Siris*. In general, his indulgent attitude towards pantheistic views was such as would favorably impress Coleridge in the period of "The Eolian Harp" and Wordsworth in the period of "Tintern Abbey" and "The Prelude." The high esteem in which Berkeley was held for his metaphysical acumen and religious spirit and the great show he makes of scientific learning would give weight to his view of nature as a spirit of the world. It is reasonable to suppose that he had a strong influence on romantic nature-poetry in general; and that his conception of the spirit of the world may have affected even the atheist that Shelley considered himself at the time of writing "Queen Mab."

It is clear from the above survey that the philosophers here considered were divided into two main camps, according as they held that the active principle in nature was or was not something distinct from the intelligent first cause of all things. Among those who held that the active principle was not some entity distinct from the first cause, there was a division, too, between those who held that the active principle was none other than the first cause himself, who was constantly present and operating in all phenomena, and those who held that the active principle was simply an expression of the order originally prescribed by the first cause but now left to work automatically in accordance with his original prescription. Whatever view was held, its defender was inclined to call his opponent an atheist. But the one thing upon which they all agreed was that the universe could not be the fortuitous result of atoms in motion, but that an *active principle* was required to explain the regularity of its operations, the design and purposiveness evident in the parts and the whole.

The Active Principle: Newton

This insistence on an active principle in nature was not a mere vagary of metaphysicians. The notion was supported by the authority of the greatest of English scientists, who considered it essential, on simple scientific grounds, in order to account for many otherwise unaccountable phenomena.[75a] Of the several books in which Wordsworth may have made acquaintance with Newton's views, two of the most likely are Rohault's *Physica* (with Clarke's notes), 1697, and Bentley's *Sermons Preached at Boyle's Lecture* (1692). One of the most difficult problems of mechanics was to explain not merely the original cause of motion but also the preservation in the universe of the same quantity of motion against the loss of it in the operations of nature. Rohault, in his exposition of Descartes' theories, makes the point that, both for the origination of motion and for its preservation, it is necessary to have recourse to the power of God.

But because it is not the Part of a Philosopher to make him working Miracles every Moment, and to have perpetual Recourse to his Power, we shall take it for granted, that when he created the Matter of this World, he impressed a certain quantity of Motion upon the Parts of it, and that afterwards, by the common Course of his Providence, he hindred Things from returning into their original *Nothing*, and preserved always the same quantity of Motion, so that what remains for us to do, is only to enquire into other Circumstances of Motion, and to examine Second or Natural Causes.[76]

To this passage Clarke appends a footnote with quotations from Newton's *Optics*. The following is Newton's explanation of how the same quantity of motion is preserved.

If it be asked how Motion, which is thus perpetually lost, should be perpetually regained. The Answer is: That it is regained by certain *active principles*, such as are the *Cause of Gravity*, by which Planets and Comets keep their Motions in their Orbs, and Bodies acquire great Motion in falling. *The Cause of Fermentation*, by which the Heart and

Blood of Animals are kept in perpetual Motion and Heat; the inward
Parts of the earth are constantly warmed, and in some Places grow
very hot . . . and the Sun continues violently hot and lucid, and warms
all Things by his Light; (and the *Cause of Electricity* whereby Bodies
restore themselves to their former Figures; all which Causes shall be
treated of in their proper Places). For we meet with very little Motion
in the World, besides what is owing to these active Principles.[77]

Whether Wordsworth had read and meditated these passages in
Samuel Clarke's Latin version is a question we cannot answer. But
that he had been impressed with this problem of the preservation
of the original "quantity of matter" in the universe, and had felt
the need for an active principle (or spirit) for its solution seems
to me clearly indicated in the verses quoted from the Influence
of Natural Objects":

> Wisdom and Spirit of the universe!
> Thou Soul, that art the Eternity of thought!
> And giv'st to forms and images a breath
> And *everlasting motion!*

Wordsworth might have found in Bentley a more formal treatment of the metaphysical implications of the problem of attraction. It is thus that Bentley outlines his argument to refute the
Epicurean theory of a universe formed through the fortuitous concourse of atoms in motion.

(1) That by common motion (without attraction) the dissevered
particles of the chaos could never compose the world, could never
convene into such great compact masses as the planets now are, nor
either acquire or continue such motions as the planets now have.
(2) That such a mutual gravitation or spontaneous attraction can
neither be inherent and essential to matter, nor ever supervene to it,
unless impressed and infused into it by a divine power.
(3) That though we should allow such attraction to be natural and
essential to all matter, yet the atoms of a chaos could never so convene
by it as to form the present system; or, if they could form it, it could
neither acquire such motions, nor continue permanent in this state,
without the power and providence of a divine being.

. . . .

'Tis utterly inconceivable, that inanimate brute matter, without the
mediation of some immaterial being, should operate upon and affect

other matter without mutual contact; that distant bodies should act upon each other through a *vacuum*, without the intervention of something else, by and through which the action may be conveyed from one to the other . . .[78]

In composing this sermon Bentley was working on the basis of Newton's *Principia;* and he was in correspondence with Newton himself in regard to the various arguments used. There is little here that is not supported by the spirit, and even by the letter, of Newton's expressed views. This is particularly true of the last paragraph, in which Bentley is grappling with the vexed problem of attraction at a distance. In reference to this matter Newton writes in his third letter to Bentley:

It is inconceivable, that inanimate brute matter should, without the mediation of something else, which is not material, operate on and affect other matter without mutual contact, as it must be, if gravitation, in the sense of Epicurus, be essential and inherent in it. And this is one reason why I desired you would not ascribe innate gravity to me . . . Gravity must be caused by an agent acting constantly according to certain laws; but whether this agent be material or immaterial, I have left to the consideration of my readers.[79]

"Thou dost preserve the stars from wrong"

Whether the agent of gravity be material or immaterial Newton does not expressly pronounce in his letter to Bentley. But that it is directly controlled by the deity, if not indeed the very action of the deity, is clear from many passages in his works. For gravity, like the other manifestations of physical nature, gives clear evidence of that purposiveness which is the sign-manual of God. The following is a partial quotation of a passage from Newton's *Optics* cited by Clarke in his notes to Rohault. Newton is illustrating his thesis that the world was deliberately planned by God.

For while Comets move in very excentrick Orbs in all manner of Positions, blind Fate could never make all the Planets move one and the same way in Orbs concentrick . . . Such a wonderful Uniformity in the Planetary System must be allowed the Effect of Choice. And so must the Uniformity in the Bodies of Animals, they having generally a right and a left Side shaped alike, and on either Side of their Bodies, two Legs behind, and either two Arms, or two Legs, or two Wings before upon their Shoulders . . . And the Instinct of Brutes and Insects can be the Effect of nothing else than the Wisdom and Skill of a powerful everlasting Agent, who being in all Places, is more able by his Will to move Bodies within his boundless uniform *Sensorium*, and thereby to form and reform the Parts of the Universe, than we are by our Will to move the Parts of our own Bodies.[80]

The most striking instances of design noted by Newton are naturally the motions of the planets—the exact adjustment of their masses (and so their gravitating powers), their distances from the sun, and their velocities, so that they may follow just the orbits which they do. Newton has a good deal to say, in his letters to Bentley, of the elaborate contrivance shown by God in arranging all these things so harmoniously. One thing of particular interest is the planned combination of gravity and a projectile motion necessary to keep the planets in their orbits. This is graphically explained by Clarke in his notes to Rohault.

It now appears from the most exact Observations of the Phaenomena of the celestial Motions, that [the planets] are so placed in the free and open Spaces, as to revolve about certain Centers by a Force compounded of Gravity, and a *Projectile Motion in straight Lines*, which were impressed upon them by God at the Beginning; viz. the larger Planets about the Sun, and the Satellites or Moons about their own Planets; I shall explain the whole of this in a few Words.

Because all Matter gravitates towards all Matter, in a certain proportion to the Quantity and Distance . . . And because the Body of the Sun is much larger than all the Planets put together; it is manifest that if all the Planets were at rest in their proper Places, they would by their own Gravity be carried directly into the Sun.

Now because the Case was thus, and all the Planets *gravitated* towards the Sun, God impressed upon them *a projectile Motion in straight Lines* also; in such manner, as to be perpetually pull'd back from the straight Lines, and kept from flying off from their Orbs, and at the same time to be perpetually urged on by that *projectile Motion*, lest they should fall into the Sun by the Force of their Gravitation: So that by these two Forces acting together, they must necessarily be carried in some curved Line about the Sun; just as a Stone turned about in a Sling by being perpetually hindred by the String from flying off, all the while that it endeavours to recede from the Center by its projectile Motion, describes a Circle.[81]

This divinely planned combination of gravity with projectile motion (or transverse motion, as he calls it) is explained by Newton in his second letter to Bentley, and is set forth more elaborately by Bentley himself in his seventh Boyle sermon.

But, finally, if we should grant that these circular revolutions could be naturally attained, or, if they will, that this very individual world, in its present posture and motion, was actually formed out of chaos by mechanical causes, yet it requires a divine power and providence to have preserved it so long in the present state and condition. For what are the causes that preserve the system of our sun and his planets, so that the planets continue to move in the same orbs, neither receding from the sun, nor approaching nearer to him? We have shown that a transverse impulse impressed upon the planets retains them in their several orbs, that they are not drawn down toward the sun. And again, their gravitating powers so incline them towards the sun, that they are not carried upwards beyond their due distance from him. These two great agents, a transverse impulse and gravity, are the secondary causes, under God, that maintain the system of sun and planets.[82]

In considerations like these we have, perhaps, the clue to certain expressions of Wordsworth which were a great puzzle to the clear-headed and literal-minded Jeffrey. They occur in his "Ode to Duty" (1805). Wordsworth there tells us that he has grown tired of "uncharted freedom" in following his own impulses, and longs to place himself under the strict guidance of duty—"Stern Law-giver," "Stern Daughter of the Voice of God." Duty may be stern, but she also wears "the Godheart's most benignant grace."

> Flowers laugh before thee on their beds
> And fragrance in thy footing treads;
> Thou dost preserve the stars from wrong;
> And the most ancient heavens, through Thee,
> are fresh and strong.

What Jeffrey could not get through his head was Wordsworth's imaginative identification here of the moral law of God with his physical law, expressed in gravitation and the other laws of motion. In the last analysis, Wordsworth says, the duty which governs man's conduct goes back to the same divine fiat as the laws which govern and preserve the heavens. A similar association between the moral law and the wonders of the starry heavens is found in a famous passage in Kant.[83] But Kant does not *identify* the two as Wordsworth seems to do; and while he refers to the periodical movements of the planets, he does not attribute them to the moral law as a cause, nor has his imagery any of the peculiar vividness of Wordsworth's. Wordsworth's imagery and thought may both be traced, I think, to the speculations of Newton and his theological expositors on the workings of providence in the planetary world.

This doctrine has two aspects, reflected in the two lines of Wordsworth. First, "Thou dost preserve the stars from wrong." Clarke and Bentley both explain how the combination of the two forces prevents the planets from flying out of their orbits or falling into the sun, either of which contingencies would involve serious "wrong" to the stars. It is also, according to Newton, the divine law which prevents "the fixed stars from falling upon one another." [84] This thought turns up in some variation in practically every treatise on natural theology throughout the following century. Thus Foster:

I mention, therefore, as an instance of wisdom forever adorable by man, the *position* of the *sun,* so as to dispense its light and heat, regularly and in the most exact proportions, to its dependent planetary worlds; and the *situation* of the planets themselves, as to the degree of their *proximity* to, or *distance* from, the sun; without which, in all probability, according to the demonstrable laws of *gravity,* the *lesser* might not only have been disturbed in their course, but have started from their orbits, and have reduced the solar system to a wild and uninhabitable chaos.[85]

Still more significant, perhaps, for its possible influence on Wordsworth, is the expression of this thought in Shaftesbury's *Characteristics.* In the course of a rhapsodic address to the sun—rather suggestive, by the way, of Manfred's address to the sun in Byron's poem—he speaks thus of the relation of the planets to the sun in their circling motion.

Towards him they seem to tend, with prone descent, as to their centre, but happily controlled still by another impulse, they keep their heavenly order; and in just numbers and exactest measure, go the eter-

nal rounds. But, O thou who art the author and modifier of these various motions! O sovereign and sole mover, by whose high art the rolling
spheres are governed, and those stupendous bodies of our world hold
their unrelenting courses! . . . Thus powerfully are the systems held
entire, and *kept from fatal interfering.*[86]

Still another passage of similar import is that in which Berkeley
explains the operations of the "intellectual fire" which constitutes
the spirit or life of the world.

By virtue of this life the great masses are held together in their
orderly courses, as well as the minutest particles governed in their
natural motions, according to the several laws of attraction, gravity,
electricity, magnetism, and the rest.[87]

The eighteenth-century poets are full of the wonders of providence shown in the guidance of the planetary world. James Thomson sings in his "Seasons" of the hand that *impels,* as it first
launched and constantly rules the whole system,[88] thus reminding
us of Wordsworth's "motion and a spirit that impels . . ." Again,
Thomson sings of the attractive force of the sun, by which, as by a
chain indissolubly bound, the "system rolls entire." [89] Edward
Young, in his "Night Thoughts," anticipates Wordsworth in at
least comparing the law of man's heart with that of the heavens.
Man's angry heart, he says, if correctly viewed, will be found "As
rightly set as are the starry spheres." [90] Erasmus Darwin says of
Nature's Lord:

> He gives and guides the sun's attractive force,
> And steers the planets in their silver course.[91]

Henry Brooke wonders at the power that keeps the planets each
revolving in its own magick Circle, and compares the force of
gravitation to a Charm or Spell that binds the atoms together in
universal Wedlock.[92]

One special aspect of this matter is the thought of what might
happen if God should at any time withdraw himself from the
system which is kept going only by his presence. Thus Stillingfleet:

What is once in its being, I grant, will continue till some greater
force than itself put it out of being; but withal I add, that God's with-

drawing his conservation is so great a force, as must needs put that being, which had its existence from his power, out of the condition it was in by it . . . This is the case of all beings which come from an infinite power: their subsistence depends on a continual emanation of the same power which gave them being; and when once this is withdrawn, all those beings which were produced by this power must needs relapse into nothing . . . The most exquisite mechanism cannot put an engine beyond the necessity of being looked after. Can we then think this dull, inactive matter, by the force of its first motion, should be able still to produce the effects seen in the world, and to keep it from tumbling, at least by degrees, into its pristine chaos? [93]

This thought is developed by Cowley in his "Davideis," with a picturesque enumeration of the "wrongs" that would come to the world if God should withdraw his presence. If God were absent,

> . . . the Elements League wou'd cease,
> And all thy Creatures break thy Nature's Peace.
> The Sun wou'd stop his Course, or gallop back,
> The Stars drop out, the Poles themselves wou'd crack.[94]

Stillingfleet's notion of God's conservation of the great force of the universe suggests the other element in Wordsworth's thought, represented by the second line, "And the most ancient heavens, through Thee, are fresh and strong." Not merely does God's providence preserve the stars from wrong; it preserves the system of the universe from running down, from losing its force and growing stale. The ancient philosophers had their notion of the incorruptibility of the heavenly bodies, of which Wordsworth may have read in Plato's "Timaeus" or in some of his seventeenth-century divines. What chiefly concerns the moderns, the Newtonians, is the perpetual conservation of the energy by which the heavenly bodies are kept in motion. Bentley refers to the millions of years during which the heavens have endured, and believes that "it requires a divine power and providence to have preserved [the system] so long in the present state and condition. . . . This *universal attraction or gravitation*," he insists, "is an incessant, regular, and uniform action, by certain and established laws . . . it cannot be destroyed, nor impaired, nor augmented by any thing . . ." [95] This aspect of the law of gravitation is dwelt upon by Clarke in his *Discourse Concerning the Being and Attributes of God* (sermons preached in 1704 and 1705).

That most universal Principle of *Gravitation* itself, the spring of almost all the great and regular inanimate Motions in the World, answering . . . not at all to the *Surfaces* of Bodies . . . but entirely to their *Solid Content;* cannot possibly be the Result of any Motion originally impressed on Matter, but must of Necessity be caused . . . by something which penetrates the very Solid Substance of all Bodies, and continually puts forth in them a Force or Power entirely different from that by which Matter acts on Matter. Which is, by the way, an evident Demonstration, not only of the world's being *made originally* by a Supreme Intelligent Cause; but moreover that it depends every Moment on some Superior Being, for the *Preservation* of its Frame; and that all the great Motions in it are caused by *some* immaterial Power, not having *originally* impressed a *certain Quantity of Motion* upon Matter, but *perpetually* and actually exerting itself in every Part of the World. Which *Preserving and Governing Power* . . .[96]

"Something far more deeply interfused"

In the above quotation from Clarke, light is thrown on Wordsworth not merely by the notion of the preserving power that keeps the heavens fresh and strong. There is also the notion of the power of gravitation as something intimately diffused through matter, and no mere force of surface impact. It works not upon the surface of bodies but through their solid content. It is "something which penetrates the very Solid Substance of all Bodies." This is strongly suggestive of Wordsworth's "something far more deeply interfused," whose dwelling is . . . everywhere in nature.

In Foster, the conception is found in connection with that of the eternal omnipresence of the deity, and of an *active power diffused* throughout the whole system.

His essential being, therefore, if it was *once* co-existent with the universe . . . must continue *immutably* so: and there can need no other evidence of the *past*, and *present*, and *future*, and *eternal omnipresence* of the DEITY. We may however add, that the principle of *gravitation*, which is a law that obtains in all matter, and what unites and holds together the vast fabric of the material world, as it cannot be accounted for from any *mechanical* powers known in nature, and supposes therefore an *active power*, not affecting merely the surface, but penetrating to the very *center* of material beings, and diffused throughout the *whole system;* this wonderful principle, I say, affords not only the clearest evidence of the attribute of GOD, which we are now considering, but also, a strong presumption of his *immediate interposition*, and *influence*, in supporting the frame and order of the material world, in every part, and instant, of its duration.[97]

This conception of God as an infinitely extended spirit, omnipresent and co-extensive with space, and therefore adequate to account for such a subtle penetrating force as gravity, is likewise found in George Cheyne. In his first chapter, Cheyne has been elaborating his notion of the analogy between the human machine and the great machine of the universe. And then he adds:

Again, as the *spiritual* Part of the human Compound, is intimately present with, presides over, actuates and enlivens the whole and each Part of the Body; so the *Infinite Creator* and *Governour* of the *Universe* is co-extended with Infinite Space, is intimately present with every single Point of its Dimensions, presides over the Whole and all its Parts, maintains their Being and their first imprest *Energy*.[98]

This conception of God Cheyne may well have found in any one of a dozen writers on metaphysics and theology. But the pronouncement which is most likely of all to have impressed the religious-minded doctor of medicine was that of Newton. It is in his famous Scholium, added in the second edition of the *Principia* (1713), that Newton asserts of the deity that he actually constitutes space and time.

He is eternal and infinite, omnipotent and omniscient; that is, his duration reaches from eternity to eternity; his presence from infinity to infinity; he governs all things and knows all things that can be done. He is not eternity or infinity, but eternal and infinite; he is not duration or space, but he endures and is present. He endures forever and is everywhere present; and *by existing always and everywhere, he constitutes duration and space . . .*[99]

Wordsworth may very well have been acquainted with this famous statement of Newton. Or he may have read in Rohault Newton's account of the way this everlasting Agent manipulates the parts of the world in his Sensorium—this one "who, being in all places, is more able by his Will to move Bodies in his boundless uniform *Sensorium,* and thereby to form and reform the Parts of the Universe, than we are by our Will to move the Parts of our own Bodies." Newton goes on to make clear that God is not the Soul of the universe any more than man's soul is the soul of the things he perceives in his place of sensation. "The Organs of Sense are not for enabling the Soul to perceive the Species of Things in its Sensorium, but only for conveying them thither; and God has no need for such Organs, he being everywhere present to the things themselves." [100]

Besides the authority of physical science, Wordsworth had that of Plato and the platonists for his notion of a soul (or something) deeply interfused throughout the whole of nature. He was probably acquainted with the account given in the Timaeus of how God disposed the soul and body of the universe.

And in the centre he put the soul, which he diffused throughout the body, making it also to be the exterior environment of it. . . . Now when the Creator had framed the soul according to his will, he formed within her the corporeal universe, and brought the two together and united them centre to centre. The soul, interfused everywhere from the centre to the circumference of heaven, of which also she is the external envelopment, herself turning in herself, began a divine beginning of never-ceasing and rational life, life enduring throughout all time.[101]

Wordsworth was also almost certainly acquainted with Shaftesbury's deistic version of this concept of the universal diffusion of a divine soul. Only in Shaftesbury it is the soul of the supreme being himself, and not an intermediary world-soul, that is thus diffused. It is through our reason or thought, according to Shaftesbury, that we become—

. . . conscious of that original and eternally existent thought whence we derive our own. And thus the assurance that we have of the existence of beings above our sense and of thee (the great exemplar of thy works) comes from thee, the all true and perfect, who hast thus communicated thyself more immediately to us, so as in some manner to inhabit within our souls, thou who art original soul, diffusive, vital in all, inspiriting the whole.[102]

Here Shaftesbury speaks of the diffusion of the divine soul through the souls of men; but just below, referring to the planetary system, addressing the deity he asks: "How hast thou animated these moving worlds? what spirit or soul infused?" [103] And some pages earlier, following Plato's insistence that mind precedes and governs body, he quotes Virgil, translating thus:

> The active mind, infused through all the space,
> Unites and mingles with the mighty mass;
> Hence men and beasts.[104]

The platonic notion of something diffused throughout the universe ("a soul," "a pellucid and shining nature," "an occult fire or light or spirit") is frequently mentioned by Berkeley in *Siris,* where Wordsworth may very possibly have found it.[105]

"The Eternity of Thought"

Note should be taken of the metaphysical idealism implied in the above quotations from Shaftesbury. Just before the lines from Virgil, he informs us that the poet, in proper "order of precedency gives thought the upperhand. He makes mind originally to have governed body, not body mind." [106] In this he agrees with Plato, who states in the Timaeus, that God "made the soul in origin and excellence prior to and older than the body, to be the ruler and mistress, of whom the body was to be the subject." [107] The same "precedency" of thought seems to be implied in Wordsworth's lines from "The Influence of Natural Objects":

> Wisdom and Spirit of the universe!
> Thou Soul, that art the Eternity of thought!
> And giv'st to forms and images a breath
> And everlasting motion!

This idealism, like Plato's, distinguishes between the eternity of thought and the temporal character of phenomena. Wordsworth may well have read in the Timaeus the passage in which the distinction is drawn between that which is always in the same state and that which is merely in process of becoming.

First then . . . we must make a distinction and ask, What is that which always is and has no becoming; and what is that which is always becoming and never is? That which is apprehended by intelligence and reason is always in the same state; but that which is conceived by opinion with the help of sensation and without reason, is always in a process of becoming and perishing and never really is.[108]

How fully Wordsworth may have taken in the metaphysical implications of the Timaeus and its bearing on the doctrine of "ideas" as the eternally real entities, it is hard to know. But there is certainly a strong suggestion of this doctrine (as generally understood) in his statement that the "soul, that is the eternity of thought," gives "to forms and images a breath," as if he were saying that forms and images have their reality from the eternal "thought" which informs them. Here again, it is worth reminding ourselves that Shaftesbury, wondering over the mysterious "principle of sense and thought," and its still more mysterious relation to motion and matter, declares that "thought we own pre-eminent, and confess the realest of beings." [109]

In any case, Wordsworth is strongly impressed with the need for an appeal to eternity from the imperfections of time, an appeal in which metaphysics is brought in to the aid of moral faith in the universe. This is particularly evident in certain parts of "The Prelude" written much later than that quoted above. In one of them the poet is describing the bewildering and awfully beautiful scenery of an alpine chasm. And of the waterfalls, the crags and mutually thwarting winds and unfettered clouds, tumult and peace, darkness and light, he says, they—

> Were all the workings of one mind, the features
> Of the same face, blossoms upon one tree,
> Characters of the great Apocalypse,
> The types and symbols of Eternity,
> Of first, and last, and midst, and without end.[110]

In this and similar passages we seem to have a fusion of the Biblical concept of eternal God and the platonic concept of time and eternity. This is the account given in the Timaeus:

Now the nature of the ideal being was everlasting, but to bestow this attribute in its fulness upon a creature was impossible. Wherefore he resolved to have a moving image of eternity, and when he set in order the heaven, he made this image eternal but moving according to number, while eternity itself rests in unity; and this image we call time.[111]

Days and nights and months and years, Plato goes on to say, are parts of time, as are past and future; but none of these can be predicated of the eternal essence.

For they are motions, but that which is immovably the same cannot become older or younger, nor is subject at all to any of those states which affect moving and sensible things and of which generation is the cause.

This distinction between those things which are motions and the eternal essence which is immovably the same may have its light to throw on Wordsworth's "Upholder of the tranquil soul," who—

> . . . from the centre of Eternity
> All finite motions overruling, lives
> In glory immutable.[112]

In all these passages is manifest a certain weariness of time and change,—a weariness which is at the heart of much philosophy. The notion of the immutability of the supreme essence is closely akin to the notion of peace as the supreme ideal for human life. And it is precisely peace which, ten years later, in "The Excursion," Wordsworth finds at the core of things. He there describes the murmurings of a sea-shell held to the ear of a child, and then adds:

> Even such a shell the universe itself
> Is to the ear of Faith; and there are times,
> I doubt not, when to you it doth impart
> Authentic tidings of invisible things;
> Of ebb and flow, and ever-during power;
> And central peace, subsisting at the heart
> Of endless agitation.[113]

The Esthetic Synthesis: Shaftesbury

But here indeed we have got beyond the concept of nature into a distinctly religious realm, the realm of Faith. All but the first of the passages cited in the last section date from 1804 or later—from a period when Wordsworth's philosophy of nature was taking on a more religious cast. We are not yet ready to discuss the relation which the concept of God bears to the concept of nature in Wordsworth's philosophy. What we have now to consider is how a synthesis was made, in the poetic imagination, of the metaphysical concept of nature (as the universe known to science) and the esthetic concept of nature (comprising the beautiful forms found in the external world).

It was not Wordsworth who first made this synthesis. Perhaps the first English writer to fuse together the various meanings of nature in a single philosophic and imaginative system, with the tone and spirit we now call romantic, was Anthony Ashley Cooper, third Earl of Shaftesbury, in his *Characteristics* (1711). And one can even cite a particular passage in the dialogue of "The Moralists," which forms a part of that work, as likely to have served as model for eighteenth-century nature-poetry, including Wordsworth's "Tintern Abbey." Here it is that an English writer definitely takes his start with a romantic enthusiasm for the beauties of rural nature, and rises directly from this to the concept of nature as the unified system of all natural phenomena, and thence to that of the divine being who is its animating principle and the source of its beauty and goodness. This is found in the form of a prose-poem or rhapsodic hymn pronounced by Theocles.

Ye fields and woods, my refuge from the toilsome world of business, receive me in your quiet sanctuaries, and favour my retreat and thoughtful solitude. Ye verdant plains, how gladly I salute ye! Hail all ye blissful mansions! known seats! majestic beauties of this earth, and all ye rural powers and graces! Blessed be ye chaste abodes of happiest mortals, who here in peaceful innocence enjoy a life unenvied, though divine; whilst with its blessed tranquility it affords a happy leisure and retreat for man, who, made for contemplation, and to search his own and other natures, may here best meditate the cause of things, and, placed amidst the various scenes of Nature, may nearer view her works.

O glorious nature! supremely fair and sovereignly good! all-loving and all-lovely, all-divine! whose looks are so becoming and of such infinite grace; whose study brings such wisdom, and whose contemplation such delight; whose every single work affords an ampler scene, and is a nobler spectacle than all which ever art presented. O mighty Nature! wise substitute of Providence! impowered creatress! Or thou impowering Deity, supreme creator! Thee I invoke and thee alone adore. To thee this solitude, this place, these rural meditations are sacred; whilst thus inspired with harmony of thought, though unconfined by words, and in loose numbers, I sing of Nature's order in created beings, and celebrate the beauties which resolve in thee, the source and principle of all beauty and perfection.[114]

It would be too confusing at this point to bring in all the articles of Shaftesbury's nature-creed: his persuasion that the order of the world is good and guarantees the goodness of every individual life if taken in its connection with the whole: [115] that virtue is natural and to men's interest,[116] and happiness is derived from having the natural affections,[117] so that the private interest and good of each man works towards the general good.[118] The important matter for our present discussion is that Shaftesbury insists on the unity of all natural objects in "a system of all things, and a Universal Nature";[119] that he associates his love for the beauties of rural nature with this Universal Nature; and finally that he identifies the animating principle of universal nature with the deity. It is also important to note that this deistic nature-philosophy is given a decidedly platonic tinge by several features especially exploited in this culminating part of "The Moralists." One of these is the association of the "impowering Deity" with the One of platonic philosophy.[120] Another is the conception of all beauty in nature as a reflection of the ideal beauty, as well as the identification of beauty and goodness.[121] But most important of all the platonic elements, taking Shaftesbury in his relation to the poets who followed, is his representation of the "all-true and perfect" one, "the sovereign Genius and first Beauty," as "Original SOUL, diffusive, vital in all, inspiriting the whole." [122]

Eighteenth century poetry is full of the sort of deistic platonism given currency by Shaftesbury. Thus Thomson, in his "Seasons" (1726–1730), addresses the deity as "Source of Beings, Universal Soul of Heaven and earth, Essential Presence." [123] Again he asks:

What is this *mighty Breath*, ye curious, say,
That, in a powerful language, felt not heard,
Instructs the fowls of heaven; and through their breast
These arts of love diffuses? What, but God?
Inspiring God! who, boundless Spirit all,
And unremitting Energy, pervades,
Adjusts, sustains, and agitates the whole.[124]

And again he declares that Reason up-traces, from the dreary void,

> The chain of causes and effects to HIM,
> The world-producing ESSENCE, who alone
> Possesses being. . . .[125]

Mark Akenside, in "The Pleasures of the Imagination" (1744), expresses himself in more platonic terms. In the beginning, he says; ere the sun or moon were seen,

> Ere mountains, woods, or streams adorned the globe,
> Or Wisdom taught the sons of men her lore;
> Then lived the Eternal One: then, deep-retired
> In his unfathomed essence, viewed at large
> The uncreated images of things;
> The radiant sun, the moon's nocturnal lamp,
> The mountains, woods, and streams, the rolling globe,
> And Wisdom's form celestial. From the first
> Of days, on them this love divine he fixed,
> His admiration; till in time complete,
> What he admired and loved, his vital smile
> Unfolded into being.[126]

And again he describes how the Sovereign Spirit created the world with his plastic arm.

> Straight arose
> Those heavenly orbs, the glad abodes of life,
> Effusive kindled by his breath divine
> Through endless forms of being. Each inhaled
> From him its portion of the vital flame,
> In measure such, that, from the wide complex
> Of coexistent orders, one might rise,—
> One order, all-involving and entire.[127]

Still more platonic or neoplatonic in cast are the expressions of
Henry Brooke in his "Universal Beauty" (1735).

> Thro' various Worlds, still varying Species range,
> While Order knits, and beautifies by Change;
> While from th' *Unchangeable*, the *One*, the *Wise*,
> Still changing, endless Emanations rise,
> Of Substance, *duplicate*, or *triple*, *mixt*,
> *Single*, *ambiguous*, or *free*, or *fixt*,
> From Those array'd in Heav'ns resplendent Robes,
> To the Brute Essence on Terrestrial Globes. . . .
>
> .   .   .   .
>
> Thus Beauty, mimick'd in our humbler Strains,
> *Illustrious*, thro' the World's great Poem *reigns*.
> The ONE grows sundry by creative Pow'r;
> Th' ETERNAL's found in each revolving Hour;
> Th' IMMENSE appears in ev'ry Point of Space;
> Th' UNCHANGEABLE in Nature's varying Face;
> Th' INVISIBLE conspicuous to our Mind;
> And DEITY in ev'ry Atom shrin'd;
> From whence exults the animated Clod,
> And smiling Features speak the PARENT GOD.[128]

Henry Brooke is, like Erasmus Darwin, a standing reply to
critics who complain that poets have neglected the possibilities of
science as subject-matter for poetry. If Brooke and Darwin are to-
day poets known only to scholars, if they have made no effectual
impression on the imaginative and emotional life of England, it is
not because they failed to make the effort to poetize science. It is
either because they were not men of sufficient genius to make the
necessary appeal to our humanity, or because the scientific facts
they set forth were too technical, and had not yet been assimilated
to the familiar body of men's thought. These facts were not yet
"manifestly and palpably material to us as enjoying and suffering
beings"—which is the condition indicated by Wordsworth, in his
Preface to *Lyrical Ballads*, for the poetic use of the matter of science. Brooke's whole poem is a demonstration of divine providence
from the data of the material and moral world—from the system
of the heavens, from physics, and psychology, from meteorology

and geology, from plant-life, from anatomy and physiology, and from the manifold evidence of design in the lower animal world. I have already referred to his speculations on gravity and the movements of the planets.

Spirit Material or Immaterial?

One curious feature of Brooke's physics is the effort to make of a subtile airy element the animating soul of the universe, considered in its material aspect.

> The *subtile Mass* its copious Mantle *spreads*,
> Its Mantle wove of elemental Threads;
> *Thelastick Flue* of fluctuating Air,
> *Transfus'd invisible, enfolds* the Sphere;
> With Poinance delicate, pervades the Whole
> It's *Ear, Eye, Breath*, and *animating Soul* . . .[129]

This "subtile mass" and pervading "elastic flue of fluctuating air" corresponds to a conception of Newton's. It corresponds to the more materialistic representation of his "active principle," which, in the *Principia*, seems to accompany, like a mechanical variant, the religious explanation of several kinds of attraction.

And now we might add something concerning a certain most subtle spirit which pervades and lies hid in all gross bodies; by the force and action of which spirit the particles of bodies mutually attract one another at near distances, and cohere if contiguous; and electric bodies operate to greater distances, as well repelling as attracting the neighbouring corpuscles; and light is emitted, reflected, refracted, inflected, and heats bodies; and all sensation is excited, and the members of animal bodies move at the command of the will, namely by the vibrations of this spirit, mutually propagated along the solid filaments of the nerves, from the outward organs of sense to the brain, and from the brain into the muscles. But these are things that cannot be explained in few words, nor are we furnished with that sufficiency of experiments which is required to an accurate determination and demonstration of the laws by which this electric and elastic spirit operates.[130]

Did Newton conceive this ethereal medium or spirit as material or immaterial? According to Burtt, it is impossible to answer this question categorically. "The fact is, Newton's positivism was powerful enough to prevent his carrying his speculations very far in this direction." [131] The important thing is that this ethereal spirit is an alternative in his explanations to the "active principles," and that sometimes he abandons the one and the other in favor of the still more comprehensive notion of the will of God; since in any case he knows that, if we carry secondary causes back far enough, we come to the first cause, "which certainly is not mechanical." [132]

This uncertainty of Newton's may serve to remind us that the word spirit, though generally used by seventeenth- and eighteenth-century divines as denoting an immaterial being, sharply distinguished from matter by its peculiar properties, was not invariably so used either by divines or scientific writers; that there often clings to it something of its ancient and still popular use as denoting a subtile *matter*. Wordsworth had in his library Locke's *Letters to Stillingfleet* (Bishop of Worcester), 1697 and 1699, in which Locke defends his assertion, in the *Essay*, that the spirit in us that thinks may conceivably be a material substance; since "it is not much more remote from our comprehension to conceive that God can, if he pleases, superadd to our idea of matter a faculty of thinking, than that he should superadd to it another substance, with a faculty of thinking." [133] Locke explains that he has great authorities for using the word spirit for a thinking substance, without excluding materiality from it. He shows that Virgil, in the Aeneid, and Cicero in the Tusculan Questions, understand soul to be a *subtile matter*, "which might come under the name of *aura*, or of *ignis*, or *æther*, and this soul they both of them called *spiritus*." [134] He believes that the Scripture, in calling God a spirit, does mean that he is a "spiritual immaterial substance." "But this hinders not, but that if God, that infinite, omnipotent, and perfectly immaterial Spirit, should please to give to a system of very subtile matter, sense and motion, it might with propriety of speech be called spirit, though materiality were not excluded out of its complex idea." [135]

This is merely a speculation with Locke, who thinks it much more probable that the thinking substance in us is immaterial. More radical, and even startling, is the position of Joseph Priestley, "the philosophic Priestley," as Wordsworth calls him in his "Letter to the Bishop of Landaff" (1793). In his *Disquisitions relating to Matter and Spirit* (1777), Priestley declares himself a materialist and undertakes to prove that materialism is not inconsistent with the doctrines of Christian revelation. He brings a multitude of citations from classic antiquity, from the Church Fathers, from popular usage, etc., to show that, until quite recent times, the word spirit did not imply immateriality but was associated with some very subtle material substance. He shows that the "modern" conception of spirit as an immaterial substance having no relation to space and time introduces great difficulties, especially with regard to the relations of matter and spirit to one another. He believes that the property of impenetrability has been wrongly ascribed to matter; that matter consists of "*physical points* only, endued with powers of attraction and repulsion, taking place at different distances, that is, surrounded with various spheres of attraction and repulsion." [136]

This remarkable theory of matter, which, in a rough way, anticipates concepts of physics which have come to prevail a century or more after Priestley's time, he makes the basis for a still more remarkable metaphysical theory, viz. that matter and spirit are essentially *one substance;* that there is nothing in man "possessed of other properties besides such as may be superadded to those of *attraction* and *repulsion,* which we have found to belong to matter, or what may be consistent with those properties." [137] Accordingly, he finds fault with Locke for unnecessarily multiplying causes, when he "contends, that, for any thing we know to the contrary, the faculty of thinking may be a property of the body," and yet thinks "it more probable that this faculty inhered in a different substance, viz. an immaterial soul." [138] And he finds fault likewise with Hartley for assuming a something intermediate between the soul and the gross body, "which he distinguishes by the name of the *infinitesimal elementary body.*" This he finds particularly vexatious in Dr. Hartley, "who ascribes so much to matter, and so little to any thing immaterial in man (nothing but the faculty of simple *perception*)." [139]

In the first one of his introductory essays to *Hartley's Theory of the Human Mind* (1775),[140] Priestley has occasion, in connection with Hartley's theory of vibrations, to reiterate much of this materialistic view of the human spirit. Hartley's theory of vibrations he shows to have a purely materialistic basis, except for the assumption of the power of perception in the mind. "So that if it were possible that matter could be endued with this property, *immateriality*, as far as it has been supposed to belong to man, would be excluded altogether." [141] And he proceeds to sum up his own theory of materialism.

> I am rather inclined to think that, though the subject is beyond our comprehension at present, man does not consist of two principles, so essentially different from one another as *matter* and *spirit*, which are always described as having not one common property, by means of which they can effect or act upon each other; the one occupying space, and the other not only not occupying the least imaginable portion of space, but incapable of bearing relation to it; insomuch that, properly speaking, my mind is no more, *in my body*, than it is in the moon. I rather think that the whole man is of some *uniform composition*, and that the property of *perception*, as well as other powers that are termed *mental*, is the result (whether necessary or not) of such an organical structure as that of the brain.[142]

It is clear that Priestley derived from Hartley's system conclusions even more materialistic—and, in the broad sense of the word, behavioristic—than even Hartley himself. One thing should be borne in mind, however: Priestley valiantly labors to keep his theories consistent with the doctrines of revealed Christianity. He carries his materialistic assumptions to their extreme conclusion in the view that the deity himself is not to be conceived of as a strictly immaterial being. But that, he argues, is consistent with orthodoxy, and with the pronouncements of the early Church Fathers. His materialism he shows to be compatible with the doctrine of the resurrection. And while his conception of spirit is consistently materialistic, and necessitarian, he does not wish it to be considered as mechanistic. Thinking matter is still *thinking* matter. And as for the problem of self-activation, he holds that that is no more difficult on a materialistic, than on an immaterialistic, hypothesis.

> Of the *beginning of motion, or action*, we must sit down with acknowledging, that we have, in reality, no conception at all, and the

difficulty is by no means removed, or in the smallest degree lessened, by shifting it from *matter* to *mind*. Mr. Locke very justly observes, that "it is as hard to conceive self-motion in a created immaterial, as in a created material being, consider it how we will." [143]

In trying to determine what connotations the word spirit carried for Wordsworth, it is also worth while taking into account the views of Erasmus Darwin. This poet enjoyed so great a celebrity in England in the last decade of the eighteenth century and the first decade of the nineteenth that Coleridge, who had little admiration for him, called him in 1802 "the first literary character in Europe." [144] His *Zoönomia* and *The Botanic Garden* are referred to by Wordsworth's brother Christopher in his diary in 1793 in terms showing how important a figure he was in the university world.[145] It has generally been assumed that Wordsworth was well acquainted with *The Botanic Garden* (1791), and that his style in certain early poems was greatly influenced by Darwin. In one of his footnotes to that poem Darwin discusses the relation between matter and spirit. After a reference to Pythagoras' idea of the transmigration of spirit, he says:

Other philosophers have supposed, that there are two different materials or essences, which fill the universe. One of these, which has the power of commencing or producing motion, is called the spirit; the other, which has the power of receiving and of communicating motion, but not of beginning it, is called matter. The former of these is supposed to be diffused through all space, filling up the interstices of the suns and planets, and constituting the gravitation of the sidereal bodies, the attractions of chemistry, with the spirit of vegetation, and of animation. The latter occupies comparatively but small space, constituting the solid parts of the suns and planets, and their atmospheres. Hence these philosophers have supposed, that both matter and spirit are equally immortal and unperishable; and that on the dissolution of vegetable or animal organization, the matter returns to the general mass of matter; and the spirit to the general mass of spirit, to enter again into new combinations, according to the original idea of Pythagoras.[146]

According to this conception, spirit, though distinguished from matter by its activity in originating motion, has at least thus much of materiality that it occupies space and so presumably has extension. It has indeed little in common with the spirit of ordinary

religious views, there being no suggestion that it is rational or intelligent in character. It is simply—what it was so largely, but not
altogether, in Henry More—a theoretical invention for getting
round the supposed passivity of matter and so accounting for
phenomena like gravitation, chemical attraction, vegetation and
animation. The essential materialism of this conception of spirit
becomes more manifest in Darwin's *Temple of Nature* (1803),
in which the "spirit of animation" is invoked for explaining the
contraction of the fibres which constitute the muscles and organs
of sense. "The spirit of animation," says Darwin in a note, "is the
immediate cause of the contraction of the animal fibres, it resides
in the brain and nerves, and is liable to general or spatial diminution
or accumulation." [147] In general, then, spirit plays a rôle in Darwin
broadly analogous to that played by the active principle in Wordsworth.

Weltseele

For the concept of nature as a universal spirit there were, as we
have seen, plentiful materials in the main tradition of English
poetry and philosophical thought. It is not necessary to seek for
suggestions of such a concept outside the English tradition. But
still we cannot ignore the fact that, in the year 1798, there was
published in Germany Schelling's treatise on the world-soul (*Von
der Weltseele*); and that Coleridge had, probably from that very
year, some knowledge of the thought of Schelling as well as of
other German idealist philosophers. Every one assumes that Wordsworth would have heard a great deal of philosophical talk from
his intimate friend, and it is extremely probable that the concept of
a "world-soul," derived from English sources, was confirmed in
his mind by the appearance of it in the very title of the German
book. This is made all the more likely from the circumstance that
Schelling's concept of nature had a distinctly pantheistic cast,
which would have attracted both Coleridge and Wordsworth at
the time of its first appearance, however much it may have repelled them—and especially Coleridge—at a later period.

What I call the pantheistic cast of Schelling's thought is especially evident in the introductory essay to *Von der Weltseele*.

Schelling takes particular satisfaction in conceiving of nature as a single unified whole, in which God is everywhere present as "the One in this totality." His nature is thought of not as distinct from God, not as "the product of an incomprehensible creation, but as this creation itself"; not as "merely the appearance or revelation of the eternal, but rather at the same time this Eternal itself." Thus he feels that he has to do not with something "supernatural or outside of nature," but with the immediate and the "only real," "to which we ourselves belong and in which we exist." Such a philosophy breaks down the opposition between immanence and transcendence, and all flows together in one "God-filled world."

Der Zweck der erhabensten Wissenschaft kann nur dieser seyn; die Wirklichkeit, im strengsten Sinne die Wirklichkeit, die Gegenwart, das lebendige Da-seyn eines Gottes im Ganzen der Dinge und im Einzelnen darzuthun. . . . Es ist eine Totalität der Dinge, sowie das Ewige ist; aber Gott ist als das Eine in dieser Totalität; dieses Eine in Allem ist erkennbar in jedem Theil der Materie, alles lebt nur in ihm. . . . Hier handelt es sich nicht mehr von einer ausser- oder übernatürlichen Sache, sondern von dem unmittelbar-Nahen, dem allein-Wirklichen, zu dem wir selbst mit gehören und in dem wir sind. . . . Und wann wird endlich eingesehen werden, dass gegen diese Wissenschaft, welche wir lehren und deutlich erkennen, Immanenz und Transcendenz völlig und gleich leere Worte sind, da sie eben selbst diesen Gegensatz aufhebt, und in ihr alles zusammenfliesst zu Einer Gott-erfüllten Welt? . . . Von allem, was Vernunft als ewige Folge von dem Wesen Gottes erkennt, ist in der Natur nicht allein der Abdruck, sondern die wirkliche Geschichte selbst enthalten. Die Natur ist nicht bloss Produkt einer unbegreiflichen Schöpfung, sondern diese Schöpfung selbst; nicht nur die Erscheinung oder Offenbarung des Ewigen, vielmehr zugleich eben dieses Ewige selbst.[148]

Schelling made considerable pretensions to an understanding of physical science (electricity, magnetism, chemistry), and handled it with a cavalier boldness only possible, in his time, to a German transcendentalist. And for many years, Coleridge was fascinated by his queer mixture of science and metaphysics, and drew upon it freely in his own writings. He was drawing on it thus in the very years when he had come to condemn Schelling's philosophy as tainted with "gross materialism," and was discouraging the study of Schelling by his disciples.[149] But it is probable that, in the years

when Wordsworth was writing "The Prelude," his friend was full
of allusions to the writer who had brought such formidable scientific knowledge to the defense of idealism. As for Wordsworth,
this science would certainly have been over his head, as it was indeed too fantastic to make an appeal to his sturdy realistic mind.
But he might well have been impressed with the fact that a German
scientific writer had compiled a treatise on the "world-soul."
Wordsworth's specific references to the "Soul" of the universe or
of nature, it will be observed, date from a period later than "Tintern Abbey"; beginning with the "Influence of Natural Objects"
which was written in Germany in 1799.

Giordano Bruno was another philosopher, much admired by
Coleridge, in whose system the world-soul had its part to play; and
his world-soul was such as to appeal to Coleridge by virtue of its
strongly idealistic and, as we now say, "vitalistic" cast. An account
of this world-soul is found in the second dialogue of his treatise,
Della causa, principio, ed uno.[150] The world-soul here appears as
another name for the "universal Intellect" which "directs nature to
produce the various species as is fitting." By the Pythagoreans, says
Bruno, this universal intellect is called the "moving spirit and pro-
pelling power of the universe." By the platonists it is called the
"worldbuilder." According to the Magi it is this intellect which
"impregnates matter with all its forms"; and by its guidance and
ordering, things produce themselves in such orderly system "as cannot be attributed to chance, nor to any principles which cannot
consciously distinguish or arrange." It is variously described by Or-
pheus, Empedocles and Plotinus, but all in the same sense. Bruno
himself, or his mouthpiece in the dialogue, calls it "the inner artificer, because it forms and shapes material objects from within, as
from within the seed or the root is sent forth and unfolded the
trunk, and from within the trunk are put forth the branches, from
within the branches the finished twigs, and from within the twigs
unfurl the buds, and there within are woven like nerves, leaves,
flowers and fruits . . ." This artificer is not bound to a single part
of matter, "but operates continually throughout the whole." In
Bruno the world-soul is more clearly distinguished from the
"divine" spirit than in Schelling. It is a necessary intermediary between the divine spirit and the particular spirits which animate

particular things. But, as in Schelling's philosophy, it is "the true efficient cause, not so much extrinsic as even intrinsic, of all natural things."

If then Wordsworth heard Bruno referred to by Coleridge, he might well have been confirmed in his idea of a universal spirit or world-soul, conceived in distinctly non-mechanistic terms, and having decided affinities with Cudworth's plastic nature and More's spirit of nature.

Any discussion of Spinoza with his friend Coleridge would have tended to give a somewhat more pantheistic coloring to Wordsworth's concept of nature. Coleridge, in his early talk about Spinoza, gave the following concentrated definition of his views: "Each thing has a life of its own, and we are all one life." [151] If Wordsworth consulted the *Ethics* he would have found nature and God referred to as alternative terms for the same rational principle.[152] If this knowledge of Spinoza was derived from English books of metaphysics and divinity, he would have found him associated with "atheism." Berkeley, in *Siris*, refers to him as an example of "modern atheism," along with Hobbes and Collins.[153] Clarke has a considerable analysis of the false reasoning by which Spinoza establishes his atheistical position. He begins his discussion as follows:

Spinoza, the most celebrated Patron of Atheism in our Time, who taught that there is no Difference of Substances, but that the Whole and Every Part of the Material World is a Necessarily-Existing Being; and that there is no other God, but the Universe . . .[154]

As footnotes to his discussion Clarke appends many citations from Spinoza in the Latin. Arguments against heresy are notoriously dangerous, in that they so often infect the reader with unorthodox views to which he might never have been exposed. If Wordsworth's concept of nature was affected by the views of Spinoza as relayed through English divines, he may easily have been attracted by that very identification of God with nature against which the theologians directed their artillery.

Whether Spinoza ever referred to nature as the world-soul I do not know. But Bayle, in his article on Spinoza in the *Dictionnaire*,

refers to "le dogme qui a été si commun parmi les anciens de
l'âme du monde" as the kernel of Spinoza's philosophy.[155] Again,
d'Holbach writes, in his *Système de la Nature*, of "cette âme du
monde, cette énergie de la nature, ce principe actif que les hommes
personnifièrent, séparèrent par abstraction, ornèrent, tantôt d'at-
tributs imaginaires, tantôt de qualités empruntées de leur essence
propre." [156] It is in connection with Shelley that Helene Richter
cites these references by French writers to the doctrine of the
"world-soul." But it is not entirely impossible that Wordsworth
should have come upon this idea in d'Holbach, whose *Système* was
in his library. D'Holbach, the materialist and atheist, mentions this
notion in disparagement, as an example of man's anthropomorphic
tendency—his disposition to personify nature and read into it all
sorts of qualities associated with his anthropomorphic God. But this
does not preclude the possibility that Wordsworth might have been
impressed by finding the world-soul in d'Holbach, along with that
other magic phrase of nature-philosophy, the "active principle." [157]

Another possible source for Wordsworth's concept of the universal spirit of nature (as for Shelley's), and one nearer to the
platonic originals, is Thomas Taylor's exposition of Plotinus. If
Wordsworth could not, like Coleridge, read Plotinus in the original,
he may have read Taylor in his *Five Books of Plotinus*, London
1794; or some of the ideas of Plotinus may have been relayed to
him by Coleridge. In his commentary on "Nature, Contemplation,
and the One," Taylor says:

[Nature] subsists between soul and corporeal powers; for a
medium of this kind is necessary, in order to connect soul, which has a
self-motive essence, with body, which is entirely alter-motive, or moved
by another. . . . Nature . . . is the last of the causes which fabricate
this corporeal and sensible world, bounds the progressions of incorporeal essences, and is full of reasons and powers through which she
governs mundane affairs. . . . In short, nature is the one life of the
world, through which, as a root, all bodies, celestial and sublunary,
wholes and parts, blossom into existence.[158]

It may be worth mentioning in this connection that Paracelsus
taught the existence of a single ruling spirit of the universe, as well
as of many elemental spirits, each one of which constitutes the

soul, or life-giving force, of some created thing.[159] This view has particular relevance to Shelley, who was early acquainted with Paracelsus, and who, there is reason to believe, made some use of his cosmology in "Prometheus Unbound," and may have been affected by him, at least imaginatively, in his way of conceiving the universal spirit referred to in "Queen Mab."

Summary of this Chapter

Throughout this chapter I have refrained from attempting a precise statement of Wordsworth's metaphysical concept of nature. It is perhaps impossible to frame any such precise statement. It is very difficult to make sure of the main trend of his views, except in so far as it was broadly "dynamic"; and we are not yet ready to close with this problem. But we have some of the materials out of which, or the like of which, his metaphysical concept was presumably constructed.

It is of course doubtful how far Wordsworth was aware of the precise metaphysical implications of his concept of nature or of the literary sources from which it was drawn. And along with the possible sources discussed in this chapter, we must take into account the more obvious influence of ways of thinking and speaking drawn from the Bible, from popular theological discussion, and from the classical poets. Thus the word spirit must often have been associated in the poet's imagination with the Holy Spirit of the New Testament. When Wordsworth writes in "The Prelude":

> The Spirit of Nature was upon me there;
> The Soul of Beauty and enduring Life
> Vouchsafed her inspiration . . .[160]

the first line suggests the way in which religious people speak of the Holy Spirit as being laid upon some man of God; while the following lines join certain platonic associations to those derived from the thought of divine inspiration.

Again, the word spirit sometimes carries with it a half-thought at least of those spiritual beings which, in fairy lore and classical mythology, are fancied as occupying and animating springs and trees. Thus in "Nutting" (1799), the boy who had wantonly defaced the hazel thicket, after his moment of exultation, felt a sense of pain when he beheld "the silent trees, and saw the intruding sky." And the poet draws the moral.

> Then, dearest Maiden, move along these shades
> In gentleness of heart; with gentle hand
> Touch—for there is a spirit in the woods.

Here Wordsworth's fancy has conjured up a tutelary divinity such as peopled the world of Greek mythology. Such a fanciful use of the word spirit, while it may not help to define the intellectual concept expressed in the phrase, "the spirit of nature," may serve to remind us of the strain of animism to be found in many of these intellectual formulations. It would be interesting to inquire how far the primitive mind continues to operate, disguised, in the most rational systems of refined philosophy.

Coming then to more strictly philosophical formulations: it is not unlikely that the "active Principle" which, in "The Excursion," Wordsworth finds present in "every form of being," is a concept more or less reminiscent of Cudworth's "plastic nature"; it is found associated, like Cudworth's plastic nature, with the concept of "the Soul of all the worlds," and involves, like Cudworth's concept, an effort to escape from a mechanistic view of natural processes, and account for their teleological action. It is also not improbable that Wordsworth's "spirit" or "soul" of nature is reminiscent of, or goes back ultimately to, More's concept of a "Spirit of Nature" or "Universal Soul of the World," which is plastical like Cudworth's and which serves to explain many specific operations in the natural world that are otherwise not to be accounted for. The active principle is directly associated with "the Soul of all the worlds" in the passage from "The Excursion"; and in "The Old Cumberland Beggar," it is evidently the same active principle which Wordsworth characterizes as—

> . . . a spirit and a pulse of good,
> A life and soul, to every mode of being
> Inseparably linked.

More's concept is, like Cudworth's, strongly anti-mechanistic in character, though it is more confused with pseudo-scientific considerations. If we may distinguish between two closely related aspects of this common tendency, we may say that Cudworth's concept is the more "dynamic" and More's the more "vitalistic."

This concept of a distinct spirit of nature or *anima mundi* was strong enough to survive the attacks of Stillingfleet, Hale, Boyle, etc., and to make its reappearance in Berkeley, Monboddo, and doubtless in many other eighteenth-century writers. Berkeley is perhaps the 'one of them most likely to have been known to Wordsworth; but the probability is that the general concept was widespread in eighteenth-century literature, philosophic and imaginative, and that Wordsworth might have taken it out of "the air." In Berkeley and Monboddo, as in Cudworth and More, the entire concept owes much to the Pythagoreans, the platonists, and other classical schools of thought. This is likewise true of the corresponding concept in Bruno, in Paracelsus, and in Schelling, who was in some degree a disciple of Bruno; in Boyle's interpretation of Spinoza, in Taylor's interpretation of Plotinus, and in d'Holbach's satiric reference to the world-soul. So that if Coleridge, Wordsworth and Shelley were influenced by any of these writers, they were moving actually in the platonic tradition.

It would appear that Wordsworth joins with a universal spirit of nature the notion of each individual part of nature as having assigned to it, or inseparably linked with it, an active principle, a life and soul peculiar to itself. I think it impossible to determine whether Wordsworth means merely that the animating principle or soul of all the worlds is operative within each particular creature or division of nature, or whether his language is meant for something more than figurative, and he actually agrees with Cudworth, More, Bruno, Paracelsus, and many of the ancients, that the peculiar spirits of creatures and things are distinct from, though dependent on, the world-soul. In Cudworth the situation is very complicated.

Besides this *General Plastick Nature* of the Universe, and those *Particular Plastick Powers* in the *Souls of Animals*, it is not impossible but that there may be other Plastick Natures also (as certain Lower Lives, or Vegetative Souls) in some Greater Parts of the Universe; all of them depending, if not upon some higher Conscious Soul, yet at least upon a Perfect Intellect, presiding over the whole.[161]

It is thus quite natural for Cudworth to speak not merely of a plastic nature, but also, in the plural, of plastic "natures." And so in Wordsworth, the active principle is assigned to "every form of being"; it "subsists in all things, in all natures."

In Wordsworth's treatment of this subject, there is a reminder of the monads of Leibniz, as there is likewise of his theory of the ascending and descending scale-of-beings in the universe, and of the *plenum formarum*. In "The Excursion," after speaking of the several "natures" to which his actual principle is assigned, he turns to the general world-soul in which they have their being together.

> Spirit that knows no insulated spot,
> No chasm, no solitude; from link to link
> It circulates, the Soul of all the worlds.

There is some likeness here to the conception of Pope in the "Essay on Man." And still further light is thrown on Wordsworth's lines by a passage in *Siris* in which Berkeley declares that "there is no chasm in nature." He is speaking of the teachings of Iamblichus.

And he teacheth, what is also a received notion of the Pythagoreans and Platonics, that there is no chasm in nature, but a chain or scale of beings rising by gentle uninterrupted gradations from the lowest to the highest, each nature being informed and perfected by the participation of a higher.[162]

In my fifth chapter I shall have something to say of the bearing of the *plenum formarum* on the idea of a perfect and beneficent universe. How far Wordsworth took literally his conception of separate "natures" or modes of being, in which the active Principle appears as an individual spirit, we cannot tell. But his language and imagery in all this matter do suggest that his notion of a universal spirit of nature is derived from authors that make much of these inferior spirits, and that, refined as it is in his more modern mind, there may yet cling to his conception something of the medieval quaintness of Cudworth and More, as indeed it clung to the conceptions of Berkeley in *Siris*.

It is extremely likely that Wordsworth's notion of an active principle was reinforced by the speculations of Newton and his theological expounders, who again found it impossible to explain all the operations of nature on purely mechanical grounds. Wordsworth's concept of a force (by him imaginatively identified with duty) which "preserves the stars from wrong" has many anticipations in Newton, in the theological writers and the poets; it is most often associated with the will of God, manifested in gravity and other physical forces. Again, the notion of attraction as a force diffused throughout matter and penetrating into its mass (a force conceived of physically as an "active principle," and theologically sometimes as God himself constituting space and so present to matter everywhere) is reflected in Wordsworth's "something far more deeply interfused."

There is, in many of Wordsworth's expressions, a tinge of "platonic idealism," derived not improbably both from Plato himself and from various English platonists, especially from Shaftesbury and certain of the eighteenth-century poets. Shaftesbury is particularly important as having made perhaps the first striking esthetic synthesis of the love of rural nature with the scientific concept of universal nature, the first striking imaginative statement of how one rises from a contemplation of the beauties of natural scenery, through the concept of universal nature, to a knowledge of the supreme being as the soul diffused through the whole.

Among the writers who may have influenced Wordsworth, there was a division of opinion as to whether the spirit of universal nature (variously designated) is to be conceived of as an entity distinct from the supreme being and created by him, or as a mere emanation or expression of the divine power. Most of the natural theologians and platonizing deists were of the latter opinion. None of the writers considered held the atheistical position of Lucretius, whose nature is altogether independent of the divine power. And while Wordsworth was acquainted with the *De rerum naturae*,[163] there is no reason to suppose that for him the concept of nature ever ruled out some sort of God as the ultimate moving power of the universe. In his more naturalistic moments he may have tended to think, like Spinoza, of *deus sive natura,* or simply to leave God out of the picture. In his theological moments he insists that nature's self is "the breath of God,"

> Who through that bodily image hath diffused
> A soul divine which we participate,
> A deathless spirit.[164]

The point on which all the writers referred to in this chapter were agreed, and in which Wordsworth concurred, was that nature is animated by an active and spiritual principle, since it cannot be accounted for on purely mechanical grounds. For most of them the word spirit implies an immaterial essence. But there was some vagueness on this point in Newton. Locke admitted that the thinking substance in man *may* be conceived of as material; and Priestley insisted that it *was* so, going so far as to assert that there is no essential difference between matter and spirit except that spirit has certain added properties not found in unthinking matter. In Darwin's less philosophic theory, spirit, while technically distinguished from matter, is essentially a material essence. One might even mistake Berkeley's intellectual and artificial fire, "the elementary fire or spirit of the world," for something very like an extremely subtile material element. At any rate, many such materialistic conceptions of spirit were in the air at the time Wordsworth wrote "Tintern Abbey," and should perhaps be taken into account in an effort to formulate the main trend of his nature-theory. One aspect of this problem I shall try to approach in the following chapter.

Chapter IV

WORDSWORTH'S NATURALISM

The most comprehensive document in Wordsworth's nature-theory at the period of *Lyrical Ballads* (1798) is "Tintern Abbey." There is one remarkable feature of this poem when compared with the philosophic nature-poetry of the eighteenth century referred to in the preceding chapter. Throughout the whole of the poem Wordsworth does not once name God or make a single unmistakable reference to the supreme being. He does indicate that his commerce with the beauties of nature leads him to mystic intuitions which we feel to be in the broad sense religious. He has felt

> A presence that disturbs me with the joy
> Of elevated thoughts . . .

The word "presence" is often associated with the deity or other spiritual beings. Thus in the ninth book of "The Prelude," written in 1804, Wordsworth refers to his lifelong subservience—

> To presences of God's mysterious power
> Made manifest in Nature's sovereignty.[1]

But here in "Tintern Abbey," the reference is left, as it were, deliberately vague; and whatever elevating and consoling effect his mystical experience may have had upon him is referred to nothing more specifically religious than "nature and the language of the sense."

In the eighteenth-century poets of a philosophic turn, the concept of universal nature occurs most frequently in close association with the concept of the first cause, the supreme being, clearly identified with God. And if this is true of Thomson, Akenside,

110

Brooke—quoted in the last chapter—how much more so of a poet like Cowper, who had no indulgence for deism or other theological laxity.

Cowper, Blake, Coleridge

Cowper's "Task" (1785) is full of protest against all scientific study not illuminated by religious insight. Science is at the best a kind of solemn play to which it is a waste of precious time to devote one's life; and Cowper pities those who thus spend—

> The little wick of life's poor shallow lamp
> In playing tricks with nature, giving laws
> To distant worlds, and trifling in their own . . .[2]

It is true that he admires certain scientists who have used their knowledge to forward piety, among whom Newton ("childlike sage!") and Sir Matthew Hale stand out conspicuously. The true interpretation of nature is set forth in strict religious terms in the sixth book of "The Task."

> Some say that in the origin of things,
> When all creation started into birth,
> The infant elements received a law
> From which they swerved not since . . .
>
> .   .   .   .
>
> But how should matter occupy a charge,
> Dull as it is, and satisfy a law
> So vast in its demands, unless impell'd
> To ceaseless service by a ceaseless force,
> And under pressure of some conscious cause?
> The Lord of all, himself through all diffused,
> Sustains, and is the life of all that lives.
> Nature is but the name for an effect,
> Whose cause is God. He feeds the secret fire
> By which the mighty process is maintain'd . . .

Thus Cowper clears away all pantheistic nonsense about nature. And in order to make it perfectly clear that the God, whom he names as the cause of this effect which is nature, is the deity of Christian theology, he identifies him in these lines:

> One spirit—His,
> Who wore the platted thorn with bleeding brows,
> Rules universal nature. Not a flower
> But shows some touch in freckle, freak, or stain,
> Of his unrivall'd pencil.

Nothing could be further removed from the Calvinistic orthodoxy of Cowper than Blake's wild eccentric mysticism; yet these poets are at one in their condemnation of naturalism. Blake is an artist in most respects as opposite as possible to Wordsworth. Wordsworth begins with sober observation and record of what the eye sees; and if then he interprets, what he interprets is a reality brought him by the senses. With Blake the senses are felt to be treacherous and distorting instruments; and his reliance is on a two-fold—nay, a threefold, a fourfold vision of the truth. The interpretation of the phenomenal as not real in itself, but as mere shadow or symbol of reality; this is but the beginning of his mysticism. In his threefold vision appears "the apprehension of truth in a manner entirely supersensuous." Blake's own experience was "that man actually enjoys knowledge which by its nature cannot possibly have been acquired by means of the physical senses." "When he says 'Every thing possible to be believ'd is an image of truth,' he makes the widest statement of the doctrine that knowledge is the spirit's intuitive recognition of itself in the Universe, the perceiving spirit and the reality perceived being one." [3] It is in view of this threefold vision that the artist's function is interpreted; he is endowed with "Con- or Innate Science,"—a faculty of vision which he brings into the world with him, and which owes nothing to learning or imitation. This conception of the artist's function is the basis of Blake's criticism of Wordsworth's naturalism as a poet, to be found in Crabb Robinson's diary and letters. "Before spiritual enlightenment can come to the world it is necessary to annihilate those—

Who pretend to Poetry that they may destroy Imagination
By imitation of Nature's Images drawn from Remembrance." [4]

But even this threefold vision of the artist can apparently be transcended. There is the constant suggestion in Blake that in three-fold vision "the result is truth tempered to the weakness of the human soul, which is unable ordinarily to bear the strong light emanating from the Eternal. . . . We may perhaps define the difference between the two types of vision by saying that the artist is the recorder of a divine message, and so far reveals the nature of the Real: whereas the visionary of richer endowment becomes a conscious element of the Ideal, and enjoys the experience of immediately apprehending the homogeneity of all Being in Time and in Eternity." [5]

Blake is profoundly impressed with the illusoriness of Time and Space and of all that it brought to man through these modes of sensible perception. This distrust of the senses is developed notably in "Jerusalem" (1804).

The Visions of Eternity, by reason of narrowèd perceptions,
Are become weak Visions of Time and Space fix'd into furrows of
    death.
        .   .   .   .
Ah! weak and wide astray! Ah! shut in narrow doleful form,
Creeping in reptile flesh upon the bosom of the ground!
The Eye of Man, a little narrow orb clos'd up and dark,
Scarcely beholding the Great Light, conversing with the ground;
The Ear, a little shell, in small volutions shutting out
True Harmonies, and comprehending great as very small . . . [6]

It is because they proceed from the evidence of the senses and repudiate supersensuous knowledge that Blake is so violently opposed to the Deists—to Voltaire, Rousseau, Gibbon, Hume, and even to Newton:

Denying in private, mocking God and Eternal Life; and in Public
Collusion calling themselves Deists, Worshipping the Maternal
Humanity, calling it Nature and Natural Religion. [7]

Blake objects to the spiritual pride and blindness of Natural Religion and Natural Morality. He believes that man is innately depraved and in need of spiritual conversion. "Man is born a spectre or Satan, and is altogether an Evil, and requires a New Selfhood continually, and must continually be changed into his direct Contrary." [8] This is Blake's mature doctrine, and is even found in his "No Natural Religion" tractates (1788). It is curiously inconsistent with Blake's early antinomianism; but is more in keeping with his dominant philosophy, and follows logically from his mystical and super-idealistic metaphysics.

Blake is an isolated figure, having little influence on the literature of his time. He was out of the current of English thought in science and philosophy, and scarcely typical of the reigning nature-poetry. Coleridge was a figure of great influence, eagerly in touch with scientific and philosophical thought, and in some of his early nature-poetry was in the pantheistic eighteenth-century tradition. Some examples of his nature-poetry were given in the last chapter, taken especially from his very early "Eolian Harp" (1795). It is notable that, for the most part, Coleridge is less concerned with the phenomena of external nature than with man's soul and its relation to the spirit of God. Thus, in "The Destiny of Nations" (1796), he expresses himself in terms strongly reminiscent of Leibniz's *Monadology:*

> Others boldlier think
> That as one body seems the aggregate
> Of atoms numberless, each organized;
> So by a strange and dim similitude
> Infinite myriads of self-conscious minds
> Are one all-conscious Spirit, which informs
> With absolute ubiquity of thought
> (His one eternal self-affirming act!)
> All his involved Monads, that yet seem
> With various province and apt agency
> Each to pursue its own self-centering end.[9]

Similarly in "Religious Musings" (1796):

> 'Tis the sublime in man,
> Our noontide Majesty, to know ourselves
> Parts and proportions of one wonderous whole!
> This fraternises man, this constitutes
> Our charities and bearings. But 'tis God
> Diffused through all, that doth make all one whole.[10]

There is not so much here of the pantheistic, or deistic, note as in "The Eolian Harp," but even this sort of thing Coleridge avoids in his later poems, and his worship is reserved for such conventional objects as "the God in Nature." [11] In the "Hymn before Sunrise in the Vale of Chamouni" (1802), the terms in which he worships "Nature's God" are the simple terms of Old Testament theology.

Natural and Supernatural

With the poems of Thomson, Akenside and Cowper, as well as with those of Coleridge, Wordsworth was familiar. And yet, in writing his great nature-poem of 1798, he refrained, whether or not deliberately, from making the explicit association of nature with the deity which was so anxiously made by these other poets. Even the mild deism (or pantheism) of Thomson and Akenside is avoided by him, at least on the surface. This may have been for purely esthetic reasons—he may have wished to keep clear of the technically theological tone. Or he may have taken so for granted that the "something far more deeply interfused," the motion and spirit felt in nature, was an active principle bestowed on nature by God, that he felt it unnecessary to make the point explicit. Only six years later, in the fifth book of "The Prelude," [12] he was to refer to "Nature's self, which is the breath of God" and to speak of the Sovereign Intellect as having diffused through the face of earth and heaven—

> A soul divine which we participate,
> A deathless spirit. [13]

Nineteenth-century interpreters of Wordsworth (like Stopford Brooke) were inclined to consider his poems, down through "The Excursion," as representing a consistent body of doctrine. Ignoring differences of date and the progress of Wordsworth's thought, they read "Tintern Abbey" in the light of his expressions in "The Prelude." And they were unaware of the great difference in tone and view between the 1805–06 version of "The Prelude" and the revised version first published in 1850. Even to-day most readers are acquainted with this poem only in the 1850 revision, which is the form in which it appears in standard editions of his poems. In 1926 Professor de Selincourt published his edition of "The Prelude," setting the two texts side by side; and in his Introduction and Notes he made clear how greatly in his revision Wordsworth altered his expression in many passages so as to give a more Christian and orthodox tone to the whole. In attempting to reconstruct Wordsworth's views in the period covered by "The Prelude," it is obvious that we should prefer the testimony of the earlier version to that of the revision, made at a time when the poet, turned orthodox and conformist, was anxious not to offend the sensibilities of the faithful.

But according to more advanced opinion, even the testimony of the original version must be accepted with caution. All but the first two books of "The Prelude" were composed in 1804 and 1805, half a dozen years after "Tintern Abbey" and many more years subsequent to the period of his life of which the poem treats. His biographers are all agreed that his opinions had undergone very great changes in the interval, and in the judgment of his later biographers, he was inclined to color the record of earlier times with views which he entertained at the time of writing.

So that we cannot be confident that his conception of nature in "Tintern Abbey" is identical with that in "The Prelude"—that the earlier poem should be read in the light of the explicitly theistic tone of many passages in the later one. There is no reason to suppose that Wordsworth, in his moments of extremest unorthodoxy, was positively unreligious, or still less atheistical. And yet it is not improbable that in "Tintern Abbey" the absence of direct reference to the deity is symptomatic of a leaning towards a qualified naturalism.

With regard to deistic, or pantheistic, literature in general, we may say that it is unorthodox in its desire to substitute the natural for the supernatural, or to identify the two, or to lay the main stress on the natural. The divine, or supernatural, is conceived of as working invariably through the laws of nature, so that everything in the universe, both physical and moral, is explainable in terms of nature. This tendency is shown by Shaftesbury in his disposition to represent virtue as natural; and still more obviously in his concern that providence should be demonstrated from the natural order, without reference to revelation and without appeal to a system of rewards and punishments in the future life.[14] Again it is shown in his disparaging attitude towards miracles, which he considers not the best way of God's witnessing for himself.[15]

There were doubtless many contributing motives in the strong impulse of the eighteenth century thus to rule out the separate action of supernatural causes. Probably the most important of all such motives was the desire to conceive of a completely orderly universe—a universe simplified and made subject to rational inquiry—eliminating so far as possible arbitrary interferences, causes unrelated to the prevailing order and system. Thus in *Characteristics*, Philocles is represented, in the dialogue, as showing up, to an overzealous champion of miracles, how the latter plays into the hands of the atheists.

For whilst you are labouring to unhinge Nature, whilst you are searching heaven and earth for prodigies, and studying how to miraculise everything, you bring confusion on the world, you break its uniformity and destroy that admirable simplicity of order from whence the one infinite and perfect principle is known. Perpetual strifes, convulsions, violences, breach of laws, variation and unsteadiness of order, show either no control, or several uncontrolled and unsubordinate powers in Nature. We have before our eyes either the chaos and atoms of the atheists, or the magic and demons of the polytheists. Yet is this tumultuous system of the universe asserted with the highest zeal by some who would maintain a Deity.[16]

The above is the case for naturalism presented by a friend of religion. It is interesting to note that the word naturalist is applied to Philocles immediately after by his opponent.[17]

And when you, replied he, with your newly-espoused system, have brought all things to be as uniform, plain, regular, and simple as you wish, I suppose you will send your disciple to seek for Deity in mechanism; that is to say, in some exquisite system of self-governed matter. For what else is it you naturalists make of the world than a mere machine?

Nothing else, replied I, if to the machine you allow a mind. For in this case 'tis not a self-governed but a God-governed machine.[18]

The same desire to find perfect uniformity in nature, and to rule out the element of the arbitrary, is expressed, in much more uncompromising terms, and from an unreligious point of view, by d'Holbach in his *Système de la Nature* (1770).

La nature dans tous ses phénomènes agit nécessairement d'après l'essence qui lui est propre; tous les êtres qu'elle renferme, agissent nécessairement d'après leurs essences particulières . . . c'est ainsi que tout est lié dans l'univers; il n'est lui-même qu'une chaîne immense de causes et d'effets, qui sans cesse découlent les unes des autres. . . . Enfin nous sommes forcés d'avouer qu'il ne peut y avoir d'énergie indépendante, de cause isolée, d'action detachée dans une nature où tous les êtres agissent sans interruption les uns sur les autres, et qui n'est elle-même qu'un cercle éternel de mouvemens donnés et reçus suivant des loix nécessaires.[19]

There we have the demand for uniformity in its most "mechanical" and necessitarian form.

This is one of the books which may have influenced Wordsworth in the formation of his nature-philosophy. The "Système de la Nature, par M. Mirabaud, Londres 1781," was one of the items in the Rydal Mount catalogue. This book was published by d'Holbach in 1770 as by "M. Mirabaud," and continued to be put forth under that name. In 1809 Wordsworth referred disparagingly to this book, in his treatise on *The Convention of Cintra*, along with Condillac, Rousseau and Voltaire. It is in a passage in which he is arguing that Spain has nothing to fear from Jacobinism. For one thing "the pestilential philosophism of France" had made no progress in Spain.

A Spanish understanding is a hold too strong to give way to the meagre tactics of the 'Système de la Nature'; or to the pellets of logic which Condillac has cast in the foundry of national vanity, and tosses about at haphazard—self-persuaded that he is proceeding according to art. The Spaniards are a people with imagination: and the paradoxical reveries of Rousseau, and the flippancies of Voltaire, are plants which will not naturalise in the country of Calderon and Cervantes.[20]

That Wordsworth should speak scornfully of any author in 1809 is no proof that he may not to some degree have come under his influence in the years preceding 1798. In 1809 he had turned the great corner in his opinions both political and religious. From a lover of France and the Revolution he had turned anti-Jacobin and, we may well say, anti-Gallican. But there had been a time when he was touched with the breath of French "philosophism."

There was always doubtless something "meagre" about d'Holbach's "tactics." His unqualified atheism, his rigorous "behaviorism," his mechanical rationalism left no function for the mind, no scope for the feelings and the imagination. D'Holbach begins his first chapter with a warning against the error of attempting to distinguish between the physical and the moral man.

L'homme est un être purement physique; l'homme moral n'est que cet être physique considéré sous un certain point de vue, c'est-à-dire, relativement à quelques-unes de ses façons d'agir, dues à son organisation particulière. Mais cette organisation n'est-elle pas l'ouvrage de la nature? Les mouvemens ou façons d'agir dont elle est susceptible, ne sont-ils pas physiques? Ses actions visibles ainsi que les mouvemens invisibles excités dans son intérieur, qui viennent de sa volonté ou de sa pensée, sont également des effets naturels, des suites nécessaires de son méchanisme propre, et des impulsions qu'il reçoit des êtres dont il est entouré.[21]

Wordsworth may not have been unsympathetic, in the early period, to some form of necessarianism;[22] for this doctrine inclined one to look with indulgence on the defects of human nature, and generally involved the assumption that mankind are necessarily determined towards happiness. But necessarianism must have been much more palatable to him in its English guise, more "enthusiastic" in Godwin, more religious in Hartley and Priestley. And even these philosophers must have seemed to him "meagre" in their tactics compared with the rhapsodic Shaftesbury and the deistical poets. Yet one cannot help wondering whether there may not have been a moment when Wordsworth's mind responded to the simplifying rationalism of the philosophes.

In most of this French nature-philosophy there was a distinctly anti-clerical and even atheistic trend. These Frenchmen were particularly desirous of eliminating from their system the disturbing influence of theological ideas, as not subject to control and verification by objective methods. Thus Volney, in Les Ruines (1791), after his elaborate classification of the religions of the world, in all of which he was particularly impressed with the elements of the fantastic and irrational, but which had been the cause of endless wars and occasion for the tyranny of priests, concludes:

qu'il faut tracer une ligne de démarcation entre les objets vérifiable et ceux qui ne peuvent pas être vérifiés, et séparer d'une barrière inviolable, le monde des êtres fantastiques du monde des réalités; c'est-a-dire qu'il faut ôter tout effet civil aux opinions théologiques et religieuses.[23]

And d'Holbach often designates as "chimères" many of the dogmas of Christianity which are not conformable to experience and reason.

The position of d'Holbach and Volney is in marked contrast to that of another popular French philosopher writing a century earlier. Bayle, in his *Pensées diverses sur la comète* (1682), is equally desirous of extending the realm of natural law as far as possible; he allows that God works regularly through the laws of nature and the "enchaînement des causes secondes" and wishes in general to maintain natural law inviolate. Yet he insists that it is God who thus expresses his sovereign will, that he can perform miracles when he sees adequate occasion for it, and that, in any case, the regular action of the laws of nature does but show forth God's praise. Bayle is anxious to justify philosophy in its tendency to reduce nature to a system at the same time that he maintains the orthodox view of God's power.

Souffrez que je remarque par occasion l'injustice de ceux qui blâment la Philosophie, en ce qu'elle cherche des causes naturelles, où le Peuple veut à toute force qu'il n'y en ait point. Cela ne peut venir que d'un principe extrêmement faux, savoir, *que tout ce que l'on donne à la Nature est autant pris sur les droits de Dieu;* car en bonne Philosophie la Nature n'est autre chose que Dieu lui-même agissant, ou selon certaines loix qu'il a établies très librement, ou par l'application des Créatures qu'il a faites, et qu'il conserve. De sorte que les ouvrages de la Nature ne sont pas moins l'effet de la puissance de Dieu que les miracles et supposent une aussi grande puissance que les miracles; car il est tout aussi difficile de former un homme par la voye de génération que de resusciter un mort . . .[24]

Thus Bayle, wishing to keep on good terms with both religion and science, stigmatizes as extremely false the assumption that whatever one gives to nature is so much taken from the claims of God. Whether or not he was right in theory, history certainly shows that the notion he attacks is a popular one, shared by poets and theologians alike. Even the great mathematician Leibniz asserted, of Newton's deterministic physics, that he had robbed the deity of some of his most vital attributes and had sapped the foundations of natural religion.[25] Cowper says, in "The Task":

> God never meant that man should scale the heavens
> By strides of human wisdom. . . .
>
> .   .   .
>
>   Full often too
> Our wayward intellect, the more we learn
> Of nature, overlooks her Author more . . .[26]

William Paley, in his *Natural Theology* (1802), shows himself suspicious of writers who refer to nature in such a way as to seem to rule out the notion of a personal God. The personality of God is demonstrated by the evidences of contrivance in the universe.

> Amongst other things, [contrivance] proves the *personality* of the Deity, as distinguished from what is sometimes called nature, sometimes called a principle: which terms, in the mouths of those who use them philosophically, seem to be intended, to admit and to express an efficacy, but to exclude and to deny a personal agent. Now that which can contrive, which can design, must be a person. . . .[27]

On the whole, there was some reason for the view that those writers who tended to identify the natural with the supernatural, as well as those who substituted the natural for the supernatural, were showing a marked penchant for getting along altogether without the supernatural in their explanation of the universe.

Coleridge and Wordsworth

It was Coleridge, in the romantic period, who gave the most uncompromising account of the situation. There was a moment, in his own verse, when he was disposed to express himself in vaguely pantheistic terms. But there was relatively little of "naturalism" in this phase, and it was soon over. In his prose writings Coleridge took particular pains to deny the validity of the current conceptions of nature—which, he says, should be regarded as the direct antithesis of spirit.

I have attempted to fix the meaning of the words, Nature and Spirit, the one being the *antithesis* to the other: so that the most general and *negative* definition of Nature is, Whatever is not Spirit; and *vice versa* of Spirit, That which is not comprehended in Nature; or in the language of our elder divines, that which *transcends* Nature.[28]

There are several distinct philosophical reasons for making this sharp division between nature and spirit. One of these is the inadequacy of nature (cause and effect) to explain the *origin* of existence. The word origin, Coleridge declares,

. . . can never be applied to a mere *link* in a chain of effects, where each, indeed, stands in the relation of a *cause* to those that follow, but is at the same time the *effect* of all that precede. For in these cases the cause amounts to little more than an antecedent. At the utmost it means only a *conductor* of the causative influence; and the old axiom, *causa causae causa causati*, applies, with never-ending regress to each several link, up the whole chain of nature. But this *is* Nature; and no natural thing or act can be called originant, or be truly said to have an *origin* in any other. The moment we assume an origin in nature, a true *beginning*, an actual first—that moment we rise *above* nature, and are compelled to assume a *supernatural* power.[29]

Another reason for this sharp distinction between nature and spirit is the inadequacy of the conception of cause and effect to explain the autonomous character of spirit (involving will)—its independence of time and space. This involves considerations of both metaphysics and ethics.

I have already given one definition of Nature. Another, and differing from the former in words only, is this: Whatever is representable in the forms of Time and Space, is Nature. But whatever is comprehended in Time and Space, is included in the mechanism of Cause and Effect. And conversely, whatever, by whatever means, has its principle in itself, so far as to *originate* its actions, cannot be contemplated in any of the forms of Space and Time; it must, therefore, be considered as *Spirit* or *Spiritual* by a mind in that stage of its development which is here supposed, and which we have agreed to understand under the name of Morality, or the Moral State: for in this stage we are concerned only with the forming of *negative* conceptions, *negative* convictions; and by spiritual I do not pretend to determine *what* the WILL *is*, but what is is *not*—namely, that it is not Nature. And as no man who admits a Will at all (for we may safely presume that no man not meaning to speak figuratively, would call the shifting current of a stream the WILL of the river), will suppose it *below* Nature, we may safely add, that it is super-natural. . . .[30]

Coleridge is here reacting vehemently against the necessitarianism of writers like Godwin and Priestley. The concept of nature, being bound up with the mere ideal forms of space and time, and the merely mechanical "enchaînement des causes secondes," cannot account for its own origin, which must be outside the chain of cause and effect. It cannot account for the self-originating activities of spirit and will, and give a basis for morality, which implies freedom and responsibility in action.

Still further, Coleridge indicates—allying himself with the idealism of Berkeley and the Germans—the very nature which we behold with the bodily eye is in some sense the creation of our own minds, and dependent upon them for the character it bears. Thus in his famous ode, "Dejection" (1802), in speaking of the loss of his power for finding nature beautiful and joyous, he declares that this beauty and joyousness which, as a young man, he found in nature, was an emanation from his own soul.

> O Lady! we receive but what we give,
> And in our life alone does Nature live:
> Ours is her wedding garment, ours her shroud!
>   And would we ought behold of higher worth
> Than that inanimate cold world allowed
> To the poor loveless ever-anxious crowd,
>   Ah! from the soul itself must issue forth
> A light, a glory, a fair luminous cloud
>   Enveloping the Earth—
> And from the soul itself must there be sent
>   A sweet and potent voice, of its own birth,
> Of all sweet sounds the life and element.

Wordsworth was never so greatly disturbed, it seems, by these metaphysical scruples. He may never have held a purely mechanical view of nature; he may have naturally shared the traditional English craving for a spiritual or "dynamic" interpretation. But he does not seem to have taken so hard as Coleridge either the necessary sequence of cause and effect, nor the difficulty of reconciling our moral freedom with this hard and fast necessity. Time and space he would accept more simply as the natural forms for the manifestation of eternal law. He was temperamentally inclined to dwell not on the distinctness of "objective" and "subjective," of natural and supernatural, but on the oneness of the impulse in things which makes itself felt equally in the outward and the inward reality.

Moreover, at the time when he wrote "Tintern Abbey," he was, so far as we can make out, much less far advanced than Coleridge on the road of religious orthodoxy. M. Legouis points out that the French officer Beaupuy, under whose influence Wordsworth had fallen so deeply during his French sojourn, regarded religion as the enemy of liberty and progress, and that the same thing was true of William Matthews, "who, since Wordsworth's return to England, had been his most intimate friend and most regular correspondent." [31] M. Legouis reminds us further that for some years Wordsworth was one of Godwin's most fervent disciples, and that occasionally he sat under the preaching of the dissenting minister Joseph Fawcett, who "readily turned to Christian doctrine for arguments in defence of revolutionary ideas," but abandoned it "the moment he found himself in conflict with it, whether he desired to make a profession of determinism, or to glorify the intelligence, which he regarded as the source of virtue." [32] In 1796 Coleridge, in a letter to John Thelwall, described his friend Wordsworth as "a republican, and, at least, a semi-atheist." [33] This same John Thelwall was of the society at Alfoxden in 1797–98, engaged in many disputes with Coleridge on subjects political and religious. Thelwall was a dyed-in-the-wool democrat. "His ruling passion was a hatred of prejudices, amongst which he included religion. He seldom mentioned them without some sarcastic allusion." [34]

It is probable, as M. Legouis suggests, that Wordsworth, at this time, occupied a position somewhere between Coleridge and Thelwall. He was no doubt beginning to be influenced by Coleridge's mysticism. M. Legouis even suggests, with great plausibility, that

Wordsworth was strongly influenced, in his own nature-philos-ophy, by the notions expressed by Coleridge in poems like "The Eolian Harp" and "Religious Musings." But the naturalistic strain was strong in his thought and feeling. For him, accordingly, there was no difficulty in seeking within nature herself for clues to the ultimate motive-power of the universe. It was from the contempla-tion of external nature, from "nature and the language of the sense," that he received his "sense sublime of something far more deeply interfused."

There is a most interesting passage in *Aids to Reflection* in which Coleridge betrays a certain nervousness he felt in reading this pas-sage in "Tintern Abbey." He has been giving a review of the de-velopment of the mechanical philosophy in modern thought. When, he says, the Cartesian vortices had been expelled by New-ton:

Then the necessity of an active power, of positive forces present in the material universe, forced itself on the conviction. For a Law with-out a Lawgiver is a mere abstraction. . . . And what was the result? How was this necessity provided for? God himself—my hand trembles as I write! Rather, then, let me employ the word, which the religious feeling, in its perplexity, suggested as the substitute—the *Deity itself* was declared to be the real agent, the actual gravitating power! The law and the law-giver were identified. God (says Dr. Priestley) not only does, but *is* every thing. *Jupiter est quodcunque vides.* And thus a system, which commenced by excluding all life and immanent activity from the visible universe and evacuating the natural world of all nature, ended by substituting the Deity, and reducing the Creator to a mere anima mundi: a scheme which has no advantage over Spinosism but its inconsistency. . . . And what has been the consequence? An increasing unwillingness to contemplate the Supreme Being in his personal attri-butes: and thence a distaste to all the peculiar doctrines of the Christian Faith, the Trinity, the Incarnation of the Son of God, and Redemp-tion. . . . Many do I know, and yearly meet with, in whom a false and sickly *taste* co-operates with the prevailing fashion: many, who find the God of Abraham, Isaac, and Jacob, far too *real*, too substantial; who feel it more in harmony with their indefinite sensations

> To worship Nature in the hill and valley,
> Not knowing what they love;—

and (to use the language, but not the sense or purpose of the great poet of our age) would fain substitute for the Jehovah of their Bible

> A sense sublime
> Of something far more deeply interfused . . .[35]

Where there is smoke there is fire. If Coleridge in 1825 repudiates the notion that Wordsworth had succumbed to the prevailing taste, and would fain substitute a depersonalized "principle" for the personal God as the animating power in nature, it is doubtless because, in 1798, he greatly feared that this is what Wordsworth had done. And it seems fairly probable that this is just what, at that period, he was inclined to do.

Coleridge counted passionately on Wordsworth as the great philosophical poet of the age, and was able to interpret the poetic expressions of "Tintern Abbey" in the light of his own dualism. But Wordsworth's poems of this period do indicate, I believe, a fundamental opposition between his and Coleridge's approach to the world. They indicate a disposition to take one's start with natural phenomena, to read everything in the moral world in their light, and, while admitting, of course, the paramount importance of the spirit, to regard this as forming a part of "nature." In short, they show a tendency to rule out of consideration the concept of the supernatural. Wordsworth's imagination was steeped in eighteenth-century natural theology, which was the nurseling of seventeenth- and eighteenth-century science. He had been as deeply impressed as any other natural philosopher with the synthesis of physical laws made possible by Newton's formula. In "The Prelude" he mentions Newton with awed reverence. And even so late as the "Ode to Duty" he suggests the essential identity of law in the physical world with law in the moral world.

In "The Prelude" he lays great stress on nature as the seat of lawful order, and consequently suited to give moral instruction to man.

> . . . not in vain
> I had been taught to reverence a Power
> That is the very quality and shape
> And image of right reason, that matures
> Her processes by steadfast laws, gives birth
> To no impatient or fallacious hopes,
> No heat of passion or excessive zeal,

No vain conceits, provokes to no quick turns
Of self-applauding intellect, but lifts
The Being into magnanimity;
Holds up before the mind intoxicate
With present objects and the busy dance
Of things that pass away, a temperate show
Of objects that endure . . .[36]

In another most interesting passage of "The Prelude," Wordsworth signalizes the difference between himself and Coleridge, un-
derlining Coleridge's want of realism. This, he suggests, was caused
partly by his friend's enforced exile from nature in his childhood.

I have thought
Of Thee, thy learning, gorgeous eloquence,
And all the strength and plumage of thy Youth,
Thy subtle speculations, toils abstruse
Among the Schoolmen, and platonic forms
Of wild ideal pageantry, shap'd out
From things well-match'd, or ill, and words for things,
The self-created sustenance of a mind
Debarr'd from Nature's living images,
Compell'd to be a life unto itself,
And unrelentingly possess'd by thirst
Of greatness, love, and beauty.[37]

Thus, with the greatest admiration for the nobility of his friend's
spirit, Wordsworth considers that he has been led astray by the
verbalism of scholastic and "platonic" speculation, to the point of
substituting metaphysical notions for actual things.

The fundamental difference of mental habit between the two
poets is brought into striking relief by a remark of Coleridge's set
down in "Table Talk." Coleridge has been expressing his regret
that Wordsworth did not publish "The Prelude" before the inferior "Excursion." In "the plan laid out, and, I believe, partly
suggested by me," Wordsworth "was to treat man as man,—a subject of eye, ear, touch, and taste, in contact with external nature,
and *informing the senses from the mind, and not compounding a
mind out of the senses.*" [38] Now Coleridge's statement exactly reverses the order of things as carried out by Wordsworth. What he

mainly did in "The Prelude" was to compound a mind out of the senses, not inform the senses from the mind.

"Informing the senses from the mind" represents the idealism of Coleridge, which was radical, consistent and thorough-going. Derived first perhaps from Plato and the neoplatonists, nourished on the seventeenth-century English divines and upon Berkeley, it was triumphantly confirmed in his later years by Kant (as he understood him), by Fichte, Schelling and Hegel.[39] Wordsworth's idealism was partial and intermittent. In metaphysics, he was more or less of an idealist, instructed no doubt by Coleridge, by Plato and the seventeenth-century divines. That is, he seems to suggest that the universe is at bottom spiritual or rational, and that the process of nature must be interpreted as dynamic rather than mechanical. But in psychology he draws his inspiration, in his most representative period, from the school of English philosophy that derives from Locke, and that lays its stress on sensations as the basis of experience and so of the intellectual and spiritual life of man. As Mr. Beatty says, "There can be no manner of doubt that he approaches the problem of mind from the angle of Locke, basing his whole theory on the assumption that thought originates in experience, and that out of the product of sensation, or experience, ideas and the more complex forms of mentality are developed." [40] The only exception that I take to Mr. Beatty's statement is that he oversimplifies the situation—ignoring the elements of confusion or ambiguity in Wordsworth's theory, and the gradual shift of position that makes the doctrine of the "Intimations" ode so different (at least in emphasis) from that of "Tintern Abbey."

Associationism

Wordsworth's chief concern, both in "The Prelude" and in the nature-poems of 1798, was to show how the beautiful and noble objects of nature become associated in one's mind with esthetic and moral ideas: how by this means one's personal morale is improved, one's character is strengthened, one's attitude towards men is humanized, and one is enabled to "see into the life of things,"—that is, one is given insight into the spiritual governance of the universe. Professor Beatty has made it seem most probable that Wordsworth was guided in this inquiry by the associationist psychology of David Hartley, as well as by the associationist esthetics of Archibald Alison, and in general by the type of eighteenth-century philosophy that stems from Locke.

With regard to Wordsworth's acquaintance with Hartley, Mr. Beatty points out that the poet probably first took his Hartley on faith from Godwin, who avowedly based his work partly on Hartley; that Hartley was a writer in whom Coleridge was deeply interested at the period when he and Wordsworth were becoming friends, so much so that Coleridge named his first son after the psychologist, and described him in a poem of 1794-96 as—

> . . . he of mortal kind
> Wisest, he first who marked the ideal tribes
> Up the fine fibres through the sentient brain.[41]

Mr. Beatty further reminds us that in 1797 Lamb recommended to Coleridge a theme for a long poem to be taken from Hartley; that in 1798, at the time of his visit to Alfoxden, Hazlitt was deeply imbued with the opinions of Hartley; and that, in 1808, in a letter, Wordsworth "speaks of Hartley as one among the 'men of real power, who go before their age'; and exclaims, obviously referring to his own rediscovery of Hartley's book upon Man, 'How many years did it sleep in almost entire oblivion!' " [42] Finally, Mr. Beatty points out that Hartleian theories are developed not merely in Coleridge's "Religious Musings" but also in Samuel Rogers' famous "Pleasures of Memory." [43]

Leaving aside the theory of vibrations, which does not seem to have impressed Wordsworth, Hartley's leading doctrine is that our simpler ideas are sensations compounded, our more complex ideas are our simpler ideas compounded; that there is no such thing as innate ideas, but that, in the course of our lives, through association of pleasure or pain with certain experiences, we build up the higher sentiments. We build them up out of, ultimately, the simple elements offered by our sensations, and arrive at last at such complex ideal structures as imagination, ambition, self-interest, sympathy with our fellows, a feeling for God, and, as culmination of all, the moral sense.

While Wordsworth's poetical philosophy has not the coherence of Hartley's treatise, there are in "Tintern Abbey" and "The Prelude" many striking reminders of the conceptions and phraseology of Hartley. The general direction which Wordsworth follows is the same—from sensation to idea, and from idea to sentiment. And Hartley even furnishes the model for Wordsworth's famous scheme of three successive stages in the development of the poet's feeling for nature.[44]

What attracted Wordsworth to Hartley was, for one thing, the insistence on physical sensation as the starting point of the process of intellectual and moral development. This appealed to Wordsworth's realism, his disposition to refer to the world of the senses as the standard of reality, to work from the natural towards the spiritual. This is, by the way, one of the main elements of strength in his poetry—the frankly physical, nay physiological, character of his imagery. It appears, to give one instance, in the regularity with which the "heart," when referring to the emotions, is made to suggest the material organ which we carry in our breasts . . .

> . . . when the fretful stir
> Unprofitable, and the fever of the world,
> Have hung upon the beatings of my heart . . .

It is chiefly in the first book of "The Prelude" that we have a distinct statement of how the principle of association worked to build up the mental life of the poet out of the materials provided by the senses. Thus Wordsworth describes the process operating in him at the age of ten:

> Yes, I remember when the changeful earth,
> And twice five summers on my mind had stamped
> The faces of the moving year, even then
> I held unconscious intercourse with beauty
> Old as creation, drinking in a *pure*
> *Organic pleasure* from the silver wreaths
> Of curling mist, or from the level plain
> Of waters coloured by impending clouds.[45]

In the following verses he speaks of the peaceful mood induced by a view of the moon rising over the ocean. And then:

Thus oft amid those fits of vulgar joy
Which, through all seasons, on a child's pursuits
Are prompt attendants, 'mid that giddy bliss
Which, like a tempest, works along the blood
And is forgotten; even then I felt
Gleams like the flashing of a shield;—the earth
And common face of Nature spake to me
Rememberable things; sometimes, 'tis true,
By chance collisions and quaint accidents
(Like those ill-sorted unions, work supposed
Of evil-minded fairies), yet not vain
Nor profitless, if haply *they impressed*
Collateral objects and appearances,
Albeit lifeless then, and doomed to sleep
Until maturer seasons called them forth
To impregnate and to elevate the mind.
—And if the vulgar joy by its own weight
Wearied itself out of the memory,
The scenes which were a witness of that joy
Remained in their substantial lineaments
Depicted on the brain, and to the eye
Were visible, a daily sight; and thus
By the impressive discipline of fear,
By pleasure and repeated happiness,
So frequently repeated, and by force
Of *obscure feelings representative*
Of things forgotten, these same scenes so bright,
So beautiful, so majestic in themselves,
Though yet the day was distant, did become
Habitually dear, and all their forms
And changeful colours *by invisible links*
Were fastened to the affections.[46]

Thus Wordsworth indicates, in language half-technical, half-poetical, how the child's intercourse with beauty, whether conscious or unconscious, served to associate certain pure organic pleasures with certain scenes, impressing on his mind collateral objects and appearances, which were to remain lifeless or unconscious for years, but nevertheless linked invisibly to his affections by obscure feelings representative of things forgotten. It is in this way that, as he expresses it in his little poem on the rainbow, "the child is father of the man." [47]

Mr. Beatty lays appropriate stress on the prominence in Wordsworth's thought of reminiscence and retrospect. Whatever has once deeply impressed him becomes a permanent source of "feeding pleasures."

> The music in my heart I bore,
> Long after it was heard no more. [48]

The happy and salutary mood of the present is the source of the future mood.

> Some silent laws our hearts will make,
> Which they shall long obey:
> We for the year to come may take
> Our temper from today. [49]

In the twelfth book of "The Prelude," Wordsworth has a long discussion and illustration from his own experience of the permanent effect upon a man's spirit of certain particular moments of rich feeling connected with particular scenes.

> There are in our existence spots of time,
> That with distinct pre-eminence retain
> A renovating virtue, whence, depressed
> By false opinion and contentious thought,
> Or aught of heavier or more deadly weight,
> In trivial occupations, and the round
> Of ordinary intercourse, our minds
> Are nourished and invisibly repaired.
>
> .   .   .   .
>
> Such moments
> Are scattered everywhere, taking their date
> From our first childhood. [50]

Much that seems purely mystic in Wordsworth can be referred to this principle of association. The right and happy use of nature, he teaches, is with certain of her moods and forms to connect certain spiritual attitudes, and so to establish the connection that the one will infallibly call up the other. The train of association becomes habitual, and nature cannot fail to be "fostering nature" and to bring us "feeding pleasures." This is perhaps what he means to say in the following mediocre lines of "The Excursion":

> . . . by contemplating these Forms
> In the relations which they bear to man
> He shall discern, how, through the various means
> Which silently they yield, are multiplied
> The spiritual presences of absent things.[51]

Nature in this view is a sort of storage battery. In a long course of associating her forms with our own thoughts and attitudes, we charge her with forces, on which thereafter we may draw for inspiration and support.

In its general form, this notion is not peculiar to Hartley. Mr. Beatty has shown how Alison applied the doctrine of associationism to esthetics. It is thus that he sums up Alison's conclusion: "That the beauty and sublimity which are felt in the appearances of matter are to be ascribed to their expression of mind; or to their being the signs of those qualities of mind which are fitted, by the constitution of our nature, to affect us with pleasing or interesting emotion." [52] Mr. Beatty also quotes similar opinions from Rogers' Analysis of the first part of his "Pleasures of Memory" (1793).[53] In this case, however, he makes it perfectly clear that Rogers bases his views upon Hartley, even to the reproduction of the theory of vibrations.

How important Wordsworth considered the theory of associations is shown, for one thing, by his references to it in the 1800 Preface to Lyrical Ballads. He there tells us that his principal object in these poems is "to make the incidents of common life interesting by tracing in them . . . the primary laws of our nature: chiefly as far as regards the manner in which we associate ideas in a state of excitement." [54] Later on he shows how associationism is involved in the fact that each of his poems has a worthy purpose, though he may not always begin to write with a distinct purpose formally conceived.

For all good poetry is the spontaneous overflow of powerful feelings: but though this be true, poems to which any value can be attached, were never produced on any variety of subjects but by a man who being possessed of more than usual organic sensibility had also thought long and deeply. For our continued influxes of feeling are modified and directed by *our thoughts, which are indeed the representatives of all our past feelings;* and as by contemplating the relation of these general representatives to each other, we discover what is really important to men, so by the repetition and continuance of this act feelings connected with important subjects will be nourished, till at length, if we be originally possessed of much organic sensibility, such habits of mind will be produced that by obeying blindly and mechanically the impulses of those habits we shall describe objects and utter sentiments of such a nature and in such connection with each other, that the understanding of the being to whom we address ourselves, *if he be in a healthful state of association,* must be in some degree enlightened, his taste exalted, and his affections ameliorated.[55]

In his "experiments" in *Lyrical Ballads,* Wordsworth was undertaking to deal with "our elementary feelings," with "the essential passions of the heart," illustrating thereby "the primary laws of our nature; chiefly, as regards the manner in which we associate ideas in a state of excitement." These primary passions are the maternal passion, death as contemplated by the adult, the fraternal passion, moral passion, etc. It would seem that Wordsworth regarded the poems in *Lyrical Ballads* as more or less illustrative of the theory of associations. Mr. Beatty explains that it is according to this theory that we are to understand the restoration to a wholesome moral state of Peter Bell and of various characters in "The Excursion." "They receive a shock, or impulse which awakens in their minds the latent powers, and so opens up the avenue of association, so that the belated processes by which mature mind is built up out of sensations are begun. To use Wordsworth's own term, they are restored to 'a healthful state of association.' "[56]

Some vague connection with this theory is also shown by Mr. Beatty in Wordsworth's various classifications of his miscellaneous poems in later issues.[57] The classes have their order determined, among other things, by this principle: "the development of the individual in an order of time." And one reason for the classifications was to show clearly that as a whole the poems are "adjuncts to the Philosophical Poem, *The Recluse*." If Wordsworth showed some disposition to shift individual poems from one class to another, it was to make them conform better to his general plan. This plan, as Mr. Beatty undertakes to explain in detail, "is none other than that of a study of man's mind as he acquires knowledge by direct contact with reality and thus feels and acknowledges the vividness of sensation and emotion which accompany the vital knowledge which alone leads to wisdom. . . ." [58]

The first stage in experience, the beginning of each man's education, is the reception of impressions through the senses. This stage is emphasized in two lyrics of 1798, "Expostulation and Reply" and "Tables Turned." The first of these is particularly interesting in relation to the influence of the "sensational school" of philosophy on Wordsworth. In this poem, Wordsworth's friend Matthew—a person whom the poet describes in a note as "somewhat unreasonably attached to modern books of moral philosophy" —reproaches the poet with his neglect of book-lore, while he sits idle on his "old gray stone." And it is thus that the poet defends himself:

> The eye—it cannot choose but see;
> We cannot bid the ear be still;
> Our bodies feel, where'er they be,
> Against or with our will.

> Nor less we deem that there are Powers
> Which of themselves our minds impress;
> That we can feed this mind of ours
> In a wise passiveness.

> Think you, 'mid all this mighty sum
> Of things forever speaking,
> That nothing of itself will come,
> But we must still be seeking?

This poem and its companion piece have often been made the subject of grave criticism—as if the poet's recommendation of learning through the senses were a repudiation of the higher processes of thought and indeed of all active spiritual life. This must be judged an unreasonable interpretation of these poems, especially if they are taken in connection with his writing as a whole, or merely in connection with this one volume. What Wordsworth here asserts is simply that it is our senses which furnish us with the primary data out of which we build up our intellectual and moral life, and that from time to time it is well to return to the data of our senses for information and control upon our higher processes of thought.

Some readers may be misled by the mysterious reference to Powers which impress us of themselves, and to which we remain passive. These Powers are no mystic entities. *Powers* was a technical term of long standing in psychology. So far back as Sir Matthew Hale, at least, the distinction was current between the passive and the active powers of the mind.

> Now concerning *the Understanding*, it hath a *three-fold Power:*
> 1. A *Receptive or Passive Power*, whereby it takes in those Objects that are conveyed to it by an impression from without . . . Now without this receptive power, it were impossible for any knowledge to be in the Soul, because our Knowledge is not by Intuition, as the Divine Knowledge is, but by reception of the thing known, into the Soul. And hence it is plain, that all Knowledge is extrinsical to the Soul; for though it be *apta nata* to receive the species or object into it, yet without such reception it cannot actually know it.
> 2. A *Retentive* Power of the Object or Proposition received . . .
> 3. An *Active and Discursive* Power, whereby the Understanding is able to work upon those Objects thus received and retained and deduce Conclusions and Consequences from them . . . The Rule whereby this Active Power of the Understanding works, is that we call *Reason*, which is but a beam of the Divine Light, a part of the Image of God in Man . . .[59]

The same division of passive and active powers, with the omission of the intermediate retentive power, Mr. Beatty finds in another work much nearer to Wordsworth's time, and well known at least to Coleridge, Abraham Tucker's *Light of Nature Pursued*.

> These qualities [faculties] are called Powers in the writings of the studious, and distinguished into two kinds by the epithets of active and passive powers; both of which must concur in producing every alteration that happens, to wit, an active power in the agent to work the change and a passive in the recipient to undergo it. . . . Thus it appears

evidently that we are passive in sensation of every kind: but the matter is not quite so plain in the business of reflection, which the mind appears to carry on entirely upon its own fund without the aid of the body . . .[60]

Here it is more expressly asserted than in Hale that we are necessarily passive to sensations. If it be objected that in Tucker and Hale the powers are specifically identified with faculties of the mind itself, while in Wordsworth they seem to refer to something outside the mind which impresses itself upon it, we can find the word used in this latter sense in Locke's *Essay on the Human Understanding*.

Whatsoever the mind perceives in itself, or is the immediate object of perception, thought, or understanding, that I call *idea;* and the power to produce any idea in our mind, I call *quality* of the subject wherein that power is. Thus a snowball having the power to produce in us the ideas of white, cold, and round, the power to produce those ideas in us as they are in the snowball I call qualities . . . [61]
Most of the simple ideas that make up our complex ideas of substances, when truly considered, are only *powers*, however we are apt to take them for positive qualities. . . .[62]

As for the *passivity* of the mind to simple ideas, Mr. Beatty refers to another passage in Locke.

These simple ideas, the materials of all our knowledge, are suggested and furnished to the mind only by those two ways above mentioned, viz., sensation and reflection. When the understanding is once stored with these simple ideas, it has the power to repeat, compare, and unite them, even to an almost infinite variety, and so can make at pleasure new complex ideas. But it is not in the power of the most exalted wit or enlarged understanding, by any quickness or variety of thought, to *invent* or *frame* one new simple idea in the mind, not taken in by the ways before mentioned; nor can any force of the understanding *destroy* those that are there. . . .[63]

This same distinction between the passive and the active processes in the mind is found in Rousseau, in whom very likely it goes back to some of the English "sensationalist" school. Rousseau's account of simple and complex sensations is similar to

Locke's. Thus, in the second book of *Émile* (1762), which was one of the volumes in Wordsworth's library, he says:

> Une image peut être seule dans l'esprit qui se la représente; mais toute idée en suppose d'autres. Quand on imagine, on ne fait que voir; quand on conçoit, on compare. Nos sensations sont purement passives, au lieu que toutes nos perceptions ou idées naissent d'un principe actif qui juge.[64]

And again in the third book:

> Les idées simples ne sont que des sensations comparées. Il y a des jugements dans les simples sensations aussi bien que dans les sensations complexes, que j'appelle idées simples. Dans la sensation le jugement est purement passif, il affirme qu'on sent ce qu'on sent. Dans la perception ou idée, le jugement est actif; il rapproche, il compare, il détermine des rapports que le sens ne détermine pas.[65]

This distinction between passive and active operations of the mind is found in Rousseau associated with his recommendation for young children of a simple animal life in contact with "nature,"—which may very well have appealed to Wordsworth.

> Comme tout ce qui entre dans l'entendement humain y vient par les sens, la première raison de l'homme est une raison sensitive; c'est elle qui sert de base à la raison intellectuelle: nos premiers maîtres de philosophie sont nos pieds, nos mains, nos yeux.[66]

Thus, in accordance with Locke's famous dictum which traces all knowledge to sensation, Rousseau recommends that, in the earlier years, the child be left largely to his "sensitive reason," which serves as the basis of the "intellectual reason." The intellectual reason will come into its own in mature life.

It is in the light of this sturdy common-sense philosophy that Wordsworth insists in "Expostulation and Reply," as Mr. Beatty puts it, on "the necessity of allowing the senses to make their impression and to pay heed to them as the materials out of which all real knowledge is made." [67] Wordsworth knows, no one better, that our thought and our "affections" will carry us far beyond the mere materials furnished by our senses. But first we must begin with those materials; and we must often return to mere sense-impressions with a humble and wise passiveness, confident that they are possessed of powers that can of themselves impress and feed the mind. So far is he from Coleridge's program of informing the senses from the mind. In the poem that follows, Wordsworth further develops his position, representing the dangers of one method of so informing the senses from the mind—not to be sure Coleridge's "idealistic" method, but the opposite scientific method of "dissection" or analysis. But this is a consideration which would take us too far from the subject of our present discussion, and must be left for a later chapter.

More germane to our present subject is Wordsworth's account in "Tintern Abbey" of how far, starting with the materials furnished by the senses, we are carried by our thought and affections, through association of ideas. This poem illustrates particularly well the kind of transformation the psychological doctrine of Hartley undergoes under the wand of poetic imagination. Hartley, as a psychologist, is considering the entire range of sensations involved in our human experience as material out of which our ideas and sentiments are fabricated, whereas Wordsworth, poet-like, is chiefly concerned with the "beauteous forms" of nature as observed out-of-doors in the country. But this nature was the main source of sensations for the boy Wordsworth, and these "beauteous forms" are conceived of in terms of the physical sensations which they provoke, and which lead by due process of association to the operations of the "purer mind."

> But oft, in lonely rooms, and 'mid the din
> Of towns and cities, I have owed to them
> In hours of weariness, sensations sweet,
> Felt in the blood, and felt along the heart;
> And passing even into my purer mind,
> With tranquil restoration. . . .

He next goes on to show how the associated but "unremembered pleasure" may have affected his moral life, and then have brought him to that "blessed mood"—

In which the affections gently lead us on,—
Until, the breath of this corporeal frame
And even the motion of our human blood
Almost suspended, we are laid asleep
In body, and become a living soul:
While with an eye made quiet by the power
Of harmony, and the deep power of joy,
We see into the life of things.

Thus Wordsworth comes to the life of the spirit as the culminating and significant fact in human experience. But he does not forget that he has been led to this by nature—or otherwise, by the language of the sense.

. . . well pleased to recognise
In nature and the language of the sense,
The anchor of my purest thoughts, the nurse,
The guide, the guardian of my heart, and soul
Of all my moral being.

The Failure of Wordsworth's Naturalism

In one respect, and that a fundamental one, Wordsworth did not follow out the system of Hartley with perfect consistency. However it may have been in the period of "Tintern Abbey" and "Expostulation and Reply," the poet apparently could not get along without innate ideas, or something very like them. However much the sensations derived from nature might be assimilated to the substance of the mind and built up into the higher structures of thought and feeling, he could not quite account for this process without the intervention of some original impulse in the mind itself. There are many passages in "The Prelude," not to speak of later poems, in which he makes it clear that it was something in the poet's own spirit that enabled him to make the use he did of what he received from nature. For example, in describing his school-time and the spirit of religious love in which he walked with nature, he uses several different terms to characterize this native faculty of his, elsewhere called Imagination.

> But let this
> Be not forgotten, that I still retained
> My first creative sensibility;
> That by the regular action of the world
> My soul was unsubdued. A plastic power
> Abode with me . . .
>
>   An auxiliar light
> Came from my mind, which on the setting sun
> Bestowed new splendour . . .[68]

Again in the famous "spots of time" passage, in which he describes how the impression made by certain experiences serves to give added force to later experiences of the same kind, he states distinctly that—

> This efficacious spirit chiefly lurks
> Among those passages of life in which
> We have had deepest feeling that the mind
> Is lord and master, and that outward sense
> Is but the obedient servant of her will.[69]

And later:

>   So feeling comes in aid
> Of feeling, and diversity of strength
> Attends us, if but once we have been strong.
> Oh! mystery of Man, from what a depth
> Proceed thy honours! I am lost, but see
> In simple childhood, something of the base
> On which thy greatness stands, but this I feel,
> That *from thyself it is that thou must give,*
> *Else never canst receive.*[70]

Thus Wordsworth echoes, three years after, Coleridge's "we receive but what we give," and acknowledges—if I understand him rightly—that nature alone is insufficient to account for its own high ministry in human lives, that one must grant the original presence of a faculty in man by which he takes in the suggestions from nature and builds them up into the complicated structures of his spiritual life. It is by the collaboration of this native faculty with external nature that—

> . . . the mind of man becomes
> A thousand times more beautiful than the earth
> On which he dwells, above this frame of things
> .   .   .   .
> In beauty exalted, as it is itself
> Of substance and of fabric more divine.[71]

This collaboration between man's imaginative faculty and external nature was dimly adumbrated by Wordsworth in the earlier period, being suggested by the lines in "Tintern Abbey" in which he adapted an expression from Young—

> . . . all the mighty world
> Of eye and ear,—both what they half create,
> And what perceive.[72]

But it was not till "The Prelude" that he laid much stress on the active part taken by the mind itself in this operation.

The influence of Coleridge may have been an important factor in bringing about this modification of Wordsworth's view. Wordsworth may often and early have heard from Coleridge the sort of arguments against the Hartleian theory which he sets forth in the sixth and seventh chapters of *Biographia Literaria* (1817), and the closely related arguments of the eighth chapter against Descartes and Priestley and against "the hypothesis of Hylozoism." Coleridge shows how, on Hartley's theory, "the will, the reason, the judgment, and the understanding, instead of being the determining causes of association, must needs be represented as its creatures, and among its mechanical effects"; [73] how this mechanical materialism results in the "degradation of every fundamental idea in ethics or theology"; [74] how Hartley escapes these consequences in his own theological system by ignoring there the principles and results of his psychology; [75] and how all of Hartley's errors arise from "mistaking the conditions of a thing for its causes and essence; and the process by which we arrive at the knowledge of a faculty, for the faculty itself." [76] But the arguments which might be most effectively used against Hartleianism, though they seem to be directed more specifically against hylozoism in the place where they occur, are the following reflections borrowed from Schelling:

How the *esse* assumed as originally distinct from the *scire*, can ever unite itself with it; how *being* can transform itself into a *knowing*, becomes conceivable on one only condition; namely, if it can be shown that the *vis representativa*, or the Sentient, is itself a species of being, *i.e.*, either as a property or attribute, or as any hypostasis or self-subsistence. The former is indeed the assumption of materialism; a system which could not but be patronized by the philosopher, if only it actually performed what it promises. But how an affection from without can metamorphose itself into perception or will, the materialist has hitherto left not only as incomprehensible as he found it, but has aggravated it into a comprehensible absurdity. For, grant that an object from without could act upon the conscious self as on a con-substantial object; yet such an affection could only engender something homogeneous with itself. . . . In order to explain *thinking*, as a material phenomenon, it is necessary to refine matter into a mere modification of intelligence, with the twofold function of *appearing* and *perceiving*. Even so did Priestley in his controversy with Price. He stripped matter of all its material properties, substituted spiritual powers, and when we expected to find a body, behold, we had nothing but its ghost! the apparition of a defunct substance! [77]

As a matter of fact, while Hartley's system is indeed deterministic in its consequences, it is not materialistic in the full degree of Priestley's. For Hartley does assume a faculty of perception in the mind to begin with. [78] This indeed is one thing that Priestley reproaches him with, as well as the "infinitesimal elementary body" which he postulates as "intermediate between the soul and the gross body." [79] Hartley is so far from denying the existence of a something by which the sensations may be received that he more than once mentions the "sensitive soul, or principle" as a thing taken for granted without further explanation.[80] It is true, however, that he goes one step beyond Locke. To him it seems "that all the most complex ideas arise from sensation; and that reflection is not a distinct source, as Mr. Locke makes it." [81] In this respect, Hartley takes the same position as Condillac in his *Traité des Sen-*

sations (1854), at almost the same moment. It is perhaps curious that Wordsworth, who had been so much influenced by Hartley, should have referred to Condillac in such disparaging terms. But there is a considerable difference in tone between the two psychologists, and Condillac did not carry his account of the development of the human faculties into the same high regions of sentiment as Hartley. Again, Condillac was a Frenchman, and as early as 1802 Wordsworth had come to think of France as showing "equally a want of books and men." Moreover, we do not know in what terms Wordsworth would have referred to Hartley in the year 1809.

At any rate, there is this to be said about both Condillac and Hartley, that, whatever faculty is assumed for the reception of impressions from the senses, it is in the beginning passive to these impressions, and only through the gathered momentum of associations can it be said to manifest anything like autonomous activity. In Hartley there is some provision, in the long run, for the reciprocal action of "affections" like the imagination upon the sensations, so that these more spiritual entities or aggregates begin, like independent beings, to modify and remodel the original materials of experience. At this point it is worth quoting at length, from the Proposition headed: *To explain the Origin and Nature of the Passions in general.*

As sensation is the common foundation of all these [passions or affections] so each in its turn, when sufficiently generated, contributes to generate and model all the rest. We may conceive this to be done in the following manner. Let sensation generate imagination; then will sensation and imagination together generate ambition; sensation, imagination, and ambition, self-interest; sensation, imagination, ambition, and self-interest, sympathy . . . [etc.] *And, in an inverted order, imagination will new model sensation;* ambition, sensation and imagination; self-interest, sensation, imagination, and ambition; sympathy, sensation, imagination, ambition, and self-interest; theopathy, sensation, imagination, ambition, self-interest, and sympathy; and the moral sense, sensation, imagination, ambition, self-interest, sympathy, and theopathy; till at the last by the numerous reciprocal influences of all these upon each other, the passions arrive at that degree of complexness, which is observed in fact, and which makes them so difficult to be analyzed.[82]

There is really nothing here inconsistent with Hartley's theory of the—so to speak—automatic working of the law of association. These "affections," which act in so lively a fashion to "new model" sensation and one another, are not souls, personalities, "active principles," but merely bundles or "aggregates" of reactions become habitual. But to an imaginative reader this passage might suggest a very much more liberal interpretation of the autonomous working of soul, mind, imagination, or what not. And it is certain, as Mr. Beatty points out,[83] that Wordsworth lays much greater stress on the activity of the mind in the whole process of "brain-building" (to use Pater's phrase) than Hartley does. And in some of his accounts this activity of the mind seems to be operative from the very beginning, before there has properly been a chance for the emotional aggregates to have been built up. In the following passage, for example:

> Nor, sedulous as I have been to trace
> How Nature by extrinsic passion first
> Peopled the mind with forms sublime and fair,
> And made me love them, may I here omit
> How other pleasures have been mine, and joys
> Of subtler origin; how I have felt,
> Not seldom even in that tempestuous time,
> Those hallowed and pure motions of the sense
> Which seem, in their simplicity, to own
> An intellectual charm; that calm delight
> Which, if I err not, surely must belong
> To *those first-born affinities that fit*
> *Our new existence to existing things,*
> And, in our dawn of being, constitute
> The bond of union between life and joy.[84]

These first-born affinities, that fit our new existence to existing things, seem to imply more of an already constituted personality, or soul, present at the beginning, than is contemplated in Hartley's scheme. The idea of affinities between the individual and the universe occurs several times in Wordsworth. It is most distinctly stated perhaps in the concluding strophe of "The Recluse," where he proclaims—

How exquisitely the individual Mind
(And the progressive powers perhaps no less
Of the whole species) to the external World
Is fitted, and how exquisitely, too

. . . .

The external world is fitted to the Mind;
And the creation (by no lower name
Can it be called) which they with blended might
Accomplish . . .

This theme, though Wordsworth says it is but little heard of among men, is not, I think, a rare one among theological writers. It is, for example, the subject of the opening chapter of Hale's *Primitive Origination of Mankind*.

It is an admirable evidence of the Divine Wisdom and Providence, that there is that suitable accommodation and adaptation of all things in Nature, both to their own convenience and exigence, and to the governance, use, and exigence of one another . . . The instances thereof, that are suitable to the Design meant in this Discourse, shall be only these two, which I shall but shortly touch: 1. The admirable accommodation of the Sensible Faculty to the Objects of Sense, and of those Objects to it, and of both to the well-being of the Sensible Nature: 2. The admirable accommodation of the Intellectual Faculty in Man to Intellectual Objects, and of those Objects to it, and of both to the well-being of the Humane or Rational Nature.

Touching the former, the Sensible Nature in its complement and integrity hath five exterior powers or faculties, that are accommodated to all those motions or impressions of natural bodies, and their accidents which are useful to it; and by these five ports or gates all those impressions which are useful for the perception of the Sensible Nature are communicated to it . . . Is there such a motion or objectiveness of external Bodies which produceth light or colour, figure, vicinity, or distance? the Faculty of Sight is fitted to receive that impression or objectiveness, and that objectiveness fitted and accommodate to that Faculty . . . And so for the other Senses . . .

This doctrine of mutual accommodation of the faculties of man with the objects of his perception and thought, which is but one article in Hale's general creed of providential design in the universe, is naturally associated with a very different psychology and metaphysic from Hartley's. The emphasis is not on the *building up* of the human faculties out of the materials furnished by sensation, but on the interplay of two independent worlds, objective and subjective. And it goes, in Hale, with the assumption of the soul as an autonomous and active principle, still, after "six thousand years" of experience and observation, wrapped in a mystery far greater than that of any problem in physiology or anatomy.

We are certain that we have a vital, active Principle in us, by which we see, understand, remember, which we call the Soul. But whence that Soul comes, or how, and when, and in what manner it is united to the Body, how and in what manner it exerciseth its nobler acts of Intellection and Volition . . . these and many more difficulties, scarce explicable with any sufficient certainty, do occur in the little Shop of the Fabrick of Humane Nature.[85]

This brings us back again to the active principle referred to by Wordsworth in "The Excursion" and discussed in the preceding chapter. This principle was found by Wordsworth in "every Form of being," even inanimate, but more particularly in "the human Mind, its most apparent home." This location of the active principle both in external nature and in the human soul is found in George Cheyne. It is a "universal Principle," of which gravitation is a necessary and subordinate consequence.[86]

"The Prelude" is particularly full of references to the reciprocal action upon one another of outer and inner, in which there is a growing tendency to refer to the inner faculty in terms hardly consonant with the spirit of Hartley's psychology—

> A balance, an ennobling interchange
> Of action from without and from within;
> The excellence, pure function, and best power
> Both of the objects seen and eye that sees.[87]

Wordsworth tends more and more to refer to the active principle in the mind as the Imagination, not by any means with an invariable suggestion that this faculty is an aggregate of associated sensations, and to attribute to this poetic faculty an independent action much greater than anything associated with the imagination in Hartley.

Thus in the final book of "The Prelude": discussing the transfiguring power of moonlight upon a seaside landscape, he finds in this an analogy of the spiritual power of the imagination.

> The power, which all
> Acknowledge when thus moved, which Nature thus
> To bodily sense exhibits, is the express
> Resemblance of that glorious faculty
> That higher minds bear with them as their own.
> This is the very spirit in which they deal
> With the whole compass of the universe:
> They from their native selves can send abroad
> Kindred mutations; for themselves create
> A like existence; and, whene'er it dawns
> Created for them, catch it, or are caught
> By its inevitable mastery. . . .
>
> . . . .
>
> They build up greatest things
> From least suggestions; ever on the watch,
> Willing to work and to be wrought upon,
> They need not extraordinary calls
> To rouse them; in a world of life they live,
> By sensible impressions not enthralled,
> But by their quickening impulse made more prompt
> To hold fit converse with the spiritual world. . . .
>
> . . . .
>
> Such minds are truly from the Deity,
> For they are Powers; and hence the highest bliss
> That flesh can know is theirs—the consciousness
> Of Whom they are, habitually infused
> Through every image and through every thought,
> And all affections by communion raised
> From earth to heaven, from human to divine.[88]

This passage I have quoted from the 1850 version. In a number of slight points, the 1805-06 version more nearly approximates the Hartleian view; [89] which only goes to show that, as years went on, Wordsworth grew more and more independent of the associationist psychology.

Wordsworth's references to imagination and fancy suggest, more and more as he goes on, Coleridge's distinction (drawn from German philosophy) between reason and understanding. The reason is the higher faculty, and often associated by Coleridge with the will, which is the seat of our distinctively moral life. The imagination in both poets is roughly the poetical equivalent of this higher faculty of reason. Thus Wordsworth speaks in "The Excursion" of—

> ... principles of truth,
> Which the imaginative Will upholds
> In seats of wisdom, not to be approached
> By the inferior Faculty that moulds,
> With her minute and speculative pains,
> Opinion, ever changing! [90]

These lines follow on a long discussion, in which the speaker has commented sadly on the disposition of scientists in his time to study the universe in a narrowly analytical way—

> Viewing all objects unremittingly
> In disconnection dead and spiritless . . .[91]

and like Voltaire, making appeal "from higher judgment-seats" to lower. His use of the phrase "imaginative Will" shows the association in his mind of the esthetic faculty of imagination with the moral faculty, and the essential oneness of them both with the active principle of the soul.

Along with possible German influence shown in Wordsworth's growing insistence on the higher powers of the imagination, is the possibility, urged by Professor Stallknecht, that he was influenced by Spinoza's conception of the faculty of intuition. The following is Stallknecht's account of Spinoza's theory:

We may know objects (and the relations pertaining between them) . . . in one of three ways. We may apprehend them through mere experience without grasping the rationale of their activity or of their relations to other objects . . . Such knowledge is prone to error and confusion, for it is based upon no insight into the nature of the objects known, and is perforce superficial. But despite this, experience possesses a virtue that the second method of knowledge lacks, namely the warmth and vividness of that which we immediately sense. For the second mode of knowledge, which is called Reason, although infallible, deals only with the common properties of objects of which the theorems of geometry and the laws of physics are examples. . . . Such knowledge is abstract and gives us the rationale without the object, just as mere experience gives us the object without the rationale. Intuition, the third mode of knowledge, combines the good qualities of both mere experience and reason, giving us the object and the rationale inseparably united. Thus, in solving at a glance the proportion $2:4::3:x$, we combine the certainty of the rational demonstration with the familiar vividness of experience.[92]

It is this third faculty of intuition which leads to men's consciousness of their identification with the divine mind, and to the ecstatic contemplation of the divinity as the source of their highest joy, which Spinoza called the "Intellectual Love of God." Mr. Stallknecht cites a number of passages from the later books of "The Prelude" to illustrate the kinship of Wordsworth's later views with Spinoza's, and particularly the association of the imagination with the "intellectual love," the two being "each in each." He finds that Wordsworth's later conception of the imagination owes much to Spinoza's "intuition," and that this conception "answers the problems which Wordsworth's encounter with Godwinism had summoned to his mind."

In the first place he found in the imagination a *summum bonum* by which to judge the value of human actions. Thus he was no longer baffled in his search for a criterion of good and evil. . . . The problem of obligation was also solved. For coupled with understanding, the desires of the religious man are to be trusted. If he desires a way of life after he understands it, he may call that way of life good, thus his emotions are trustworthy.[93]

As Wordsworth grew older, however, Mr. Stallknecht holds, "the Spinozian morality ceased to give him entire satisfaction." He then turned to Kant, whose influence is traceable in the "Ode to Duty" and "The Excursion." We need not follow Mr. Stallknecht further in these speculations, which go somewhat beyond the range of our study; but content ourselves with noting that, whether

Wordsworth's later ethics was Kantian or Spinozistic, or neither of the two, his way of regarding nature came to be markedly at odds with his earlier Hartleian views.

In the Preface to the 1815 volume of his poems, there is an elaborate discussion of the imagination, in which it is distinguished from fancy. The definition of imagination is here made on strictly esthetic grounds. But even here, the extremely active powers of the imagination—"conferring additional properties upon an object, or abstracting from it some of those which it actually possesses," or modifying the images which are made use of—remind us how far Wordsworth has gone from the passive formation of trains of association involved in the Hartleian system. And considering how often, in "The Prelude" and elsewhere, the imagination is considered as something more than a mere esthetic faculty, rather as a spiritual faculty that enables its possessor to "see into the life of things," to intuit essential truth, we realize that Wordsworth was steadily moving away from the naturalism that is the note of "Tintern Abbey." Mr. Beatty distinguishes subtly and, I think, justly on the whole, between Coleridge's more radically transcendental and German interpretation of imagination and Wordsworth's continuing insistence on the (English) view of imagination as "simple truth to experience, to the real experience which we all know." [94] But still, the imagination is a faculty of the soul; the soul we bring with us into life with insights of its own. And after 1800 the stress is laid less on what the soul, or the imagination, receives from nature and more on what it confers upon nature.

"Intimations of Immortality"

The "Intimations" ode is hardly a nature poem at all in the sense in which "Tintern Abbey" is one. It was begun, as Mr. Beatty points out, on the twenty-seventh day of March, 1802, under the stress of Coleridge's gloom and despondency. "For Coleridge, to his own horror, was dying as a poet: that joy, which he and Wordsworth had proclaimed as the essential principle of the universe, had gone from his own heart; and he was in despair." The earlier stanzas of Wordsworth's ode set forth an experience very similar to that related of himself by Coleridge in his "Dejection" ode—the loss Wordsworth had suffered of "the glory and the dream" which as a child had invested for him the beauties of nature. The similarity of theme and the many verbal similarities make it extremely likely that one of the two poets was much influenced by the work of the other.[95] Mr. Beatty seems to think it was Wordsworth who was the borrower, but this view is disputed by later writers. In any case, before Wordsworth had completed his ode, Coleridge had written his. When Wordsworth took up his ode and completed it, he undertook to explain the loss of his youthful joy in nature, and introduced the notion of pre-existence.

> Our birth is but a sleep and a forgetting:
> The Soul that rises with us, our life's Star,
>   Hath had elsewhere its setting,
>   And cometh from afar:
>   Not in entire forgetfulness,
>   And not in utter nakedness,
> But trailing clouds of glory do we come
>   From God, who is our home. . . .

Wordsworth explained in his introductory note to the Ode that he was not taking this "shadowy" idea of pre-existence too seriously, regarding it not as an article of faith, but making the best use he could of it for his purpose as a poet. The point of view is none the less significant. Whether or not the individual soul has had an existence before the human birth, a man comes into this life endowed with a spiritual essence which is not from nature but from God. And it is this divine faculty which bestows upon natural objects the glory with which they shine to a child's imagination. Even the youth remains "Nature's priest" simply by virtue of his nearness to the divine source of inspiration. But the glory and the dream are the gift of the soul to nature, and they gradually die away, "and fade into the light of common day," as years remove the soul farther and farther from the original fount of glory.

So far then from nature's being the "nurse, the guide, the guardian" of the soul, as she was regarded in "Tintern Abbey," she is an agency for weaning the child's spirit from the thought of his spiritual origin. She is still referred to as a nurse, to be sure, but her action is described in very different terms.

> Earth fills her lap with pleasures of her own;
> Yearnings she hath in her own natural kind,
> And, even with something of a Mother's mind,
>   And no unworthy aim,
>   The homely Nurse doth all she can
> To make her Foster-child, her Inmate Man,
>   Forget the glories he hath known,
> And that imperial palace whence he came.

The poet goes on to describe how the visionary child is reduced to a commonplace man by imitating the various occupations of adults, and he expostulates with the child for bringing on his own slavery to the world.

> Full soon thy Soul shall have her earthly freight,
> And custom lie upon thee with a weight,
> Heavy as frost, and deep almost as life!

There were suggestions in "The Prelude" of this subdual of the spirit by "the regular action of the world," but there was, I think, nothing like this sharp antithesis between what man brings from God and what earth does to wean him away.

Most symptomatic of the altered point of view in the Ode is the mystical characterization of the infant mind which even Coleridge found it so hard to swallow:

> Thou best Philosopher, who yet dost keep
> Thy heritage, thou Eye among the blind, etc.

In "The Prelude" there is a very different account of the infant child, in which the whole stress is laid on what he receives from nature through the agency of his mother in the flesh.

>   . . . blest the Babe
> Nurs'd in his Mother's arms, the Babe who sleeps
> Upon his Mother's breast, who, when his soul
> Claims manifest kindred with an earthly soul,
> Doth gather passion from his Mother's eye!

Such feelings pass into his torpid life
Like an awakening breeze, and hence his mind
Even in the first trial of its powers
Is prompt and watchful, eager to combine
In one appearance all the elements
And parts of the same object, else detach'd
And loth to coalesce. Thus, day by day,
Subjected to the discipline of love,
His organs and recipient faculties
Are quicken'd, are more vigorous, his mind spreads,
Tenacious of the forms which it receives.
In one beloved presence, nay and more,
In that most apprehensive habitude
And those sensations which have been deriv'd
From this beloved Presence, there exists
A virtue which irradiates and exalts
All objects through all intercourse of sense.
No outcast he, bewilder'd and depress'd;
Along his infant veins are interfus'd
The gravitation and the filial bond
Of nature, that connect him with the world.
Emphatically such a Being lives,
An inmate of this *active* universe;
From nature largely he received; nor so
Is satisfied, but largely gives again,
For feeling has to him imparted strength,
And powerful in all sentiments of grief,
Of exultation, fear, and joy, his mind,
Creates, creator and receiver both,   ·
Working but in alliance with the works
Which it beholds.[96]

This passage I have given in its original form, written probably
in the year 1800. In its revised form, dating from much later, while
the direction of thought is similar, the passage is much briefer, and
several of the most characteristic associationist features are omitted.
It will be observed that, while the infant mind is represented as
"creator and receiver both," the act of creation, through his feelings of grief and joy, is accomplished in accordance with the strict
laws of associationist psychology. He is a living Being because he

is an inmate of this active universe. There is a world-wide difference between this realistic account of the flesh-and-blood relation
between the earthly mother and child and the famous passage in
the Ode about the child just come from God. Here we have the
notion of nature as fostering and to a large extent molding the
mind of man. In the Ode nature is shown as dulling and becloud-
ing the mind, or soul. The Ode is virtually a recantation of the
earlier doctrine of nature.

The new position becomes even clearer in the final stanzas of the
Ode, in which the poet develops the idea that the mature man has
not entirely lost the spiritual glory of the child, but that the earlier
experience has left a kind of spiritual deposit or residuum, to which
has now been added the special wisdom and humanity of the
"philosophic mind." The poet congratulates himself—

> That nature yet remembers
> What was so fugitive.

But when we come to examine what it is that nature remembers, it
proves to be not the "natural" but the spiritual—what Coleridge
would call the supernatural—elements in the child's experience:

> . . . those obstinate questionings
> Of sense and outward things;
> Fallings from us, vanishings;
> Blank misgivings of a Creature
> Moving about in worlds not realised,
> High instincts before which our mortal Nature
> Did tremble like a guilty Thing surprised. . . .

I think that Mr. Beatty is mistaken in trying to fit the "Intimations" Ode into the Hartleian theory. Coleridge certainly hailed it
in *The Friend* as the manifesto of a very different philosophy, and
cited it in support of a purely idealistic metaphysics. A large part
of it he quoted, including the lines just given, together with a sort
of philosophic gloss.

Disturbed as by the obscure quickening of an inward birth; made
restless by swarming thoughts . . . man sallies forth into nature—in na-

ture as in the shadows and reflections of a clear river, to discover the originals of the forms presented to him in his own intellect. Over these shadows, as if they were the substantial powers and presiding spirits of the stream, Narcissus-like, he hangs delighted; till finding nowhere a representative of *that free agency which yet is a fact of immediate consciousness* sanctioned and made fearfully significant by his prophetic conscience, he learns at last that what he seeks he has left behind, and but lengthens the distance as he prolongs the search. Under the tutorage of scientific analysis, haply first given him by express revelation (*e coelo descendit*, Γνῶθι σεαυτὸν) he separates the relations that are wholly the creatures of his own abstracting and comparing intellect, and at once discovers and recoils from the discovery, that the reality, the objective truth, of the objects he has been adoring, derives its whole and sole evidence from an obscure sensation, which he is alike unable to resist or to comprehend, *which compels him to contemplate as without and independent of himself what yet he could not contemplate at all, were it not a modification of his own being.*[97]

There is no such explicit statement of the idealistic position in Wordsworth's poem. But in general it does lend itself more readily to Coleridge's view of the soul as the originator of reality than to any view deriving from the "common-sense" school of philosophy. Altogether, the "Intimations" ode registers an almost complete abandonment of the Hartleian psychology. Our spiritual life is no longer regarded as the end-product of the process starting with simple sensations, but as the starting point of that process. A kind of spiritual wisdom is connate with us, shaping the objects of nature to conform with its intuitive knowledge, so that Wordsworth may be said here to imply something like the doctrine of innate ideas. Nature has largely been thrown overboard as the chief means of fostering and developing the soul, and Wordsworth has come round to something very like Coleridge's dualism. We are prepared for the conventional religious view of nature as the hinderer of the spiritual life expressed in Wordsworth's sonnet on Baptism (1822):

> Dear be the Church that, watching o'er the needs
> Of Infancy, provides a timely shower
> Whose virtue changes to a Christian Flower
> A Growth from sinful Nature's bed of weeds!

References to nature continue to be frequent throughout the later poems of Wordsworth. He continues to celebrate the effect of secluded country life in promoting unworldliness; he is no less persuaded than ever that the benevolence of God is everywhere manifested in nature; he believes that the spiritual life (and even Christian faith) may be assisted by the beauty of natural forms, provided faith is not "of sense the thrall." [98] But, as has been universally recognized, even by his most fervent and religious admirers, the heart has gone out of his nature-poetry. This later phase of Wordsworth's poetical philosophy has been traced in considerable detail by Professor Gingerich in his *Essays in the Romantic Poets*,[99] to which the reader may be referred for a fuller account than is here required. Wordsworth no longer calls himself, as in "Tintern Abbey," a "worshipper of Nature." His faith in nature seems to maintain itself mechanically on the momentum gained in his youth. It yields more and more to a theological faith, which tends to drain it of its strength. More than once he indulges in reservations and abatements. In "The Excursion," referring again to the rites of baptism, he reminds us—

> . . . that Man by nature lies
> Bedded for good and evil in a gulf
> Fearfully low . . .[100]

He seems to have quite forgotten the Hartleian psychology which makes so much, in the building up of the human spirit, of "the language of the sense." The "naturalism" has quite faded out of his concept of nature.

CHAPTER V

WORDSWORTH AND NATURE'S TEACHING

IF, AS I suppose, Wordsworth in 1806 had virtually abandoned the Hartleian form of naturalism in the "Intimations" ode, he had still in "The Excursion" (1814) a great deal to say about nature. He still had faith that man might learn much wisdom from the study of "nature." And, first of all, he held that nature was essentially benevolent, as he had held throughout his earlier periods of writing. A faith in nature's benevolence is inherent in nearly all nature-poetry up to the time of Hardy, and many different ways of regarding nature led to the same conclusion. Many different strains of thought might be present at the same time in Wordsworth's, all tending to reinforce the same faith in nature's essential goodness.

So widespread was the eighteenth-century persuasion that the natural order is an ideal one, whose arrangements are perfect, that it underlay whole systems of political economy and was assumed in many of the axioms of physics and medical science. The French Physiocrats took their name from the Greek words φύσις and κράτος, signifying, in this combination, the power of nature. They built on the theory that men in society are subject to natural laws in the same way as the physical elements, and that these natural laws must be followed by men if they are to gain their highest well-being. They could appeal, in support of this view, to the authority of Roman law and the philosophy of St. Thomas. This general concept of a natural order in society is shown by Lovejoy and Boas to have been widely prevalent among important writers of classical antiquity. In the seventeenth century Robert Boyle directed the force of his critical scientific spirit against the "vulgar notion of nature." He undertook to disprove the cheerful axioms that "nature never fails of her end," that she "always acts by the shortest ways," that "nature cures diseases," etc. But such axioms as these have continued to hold their ground in much popular scientific thought down to the present day; and the word nature is still heard on the tongues of physicians of a speculative turn. On every hand the poet would find assumed by the soberest thinkers this concept of a benevolent order of nature. And it would have been strange indeed if he had not associated this concept with the features of landscape which had been to him as a boy the source of so many "aching joys" and "dizzy raptures."

Necessarianism

The various forms of necessarianism to which Wordsworth may have been exposed were all equally optimistic. This is as true of the atheistic mechanism of d'Holbach and Volney as of the Christian associationism of Hartley and Priestley. Self-interest, working mechanically like the law of gravitation, works for man's happiness, since it works for a socially ordered state. D'Holbach remarks in the preface of his *Système de la Nature*:

L'homme n'est malheureux que parce qu'il méconnoît la Nature . . . Il voulut être Métaphysicien, avant d'être Physicien: il méprisa les réalités, pour méditer les chimères . . . Le but de cet Ouvrage est de ramener l'Homme à la Nature, de lui rendre la raison chère, de lui faire adorer la vertu, de dissiper les ombres qui lui cachent la seule voie propre à le conduire sûrement à la félicité.

Man is necessarily carried to his happiness because "man necessarily desires what is, or seems, contributory to his well-being" (utile à son bien-être).[1] If a man is apt to mistake what *seems* contributory for what *is* contributory to his well-being, that is the fault of a bad education, for which bad government is largely responsible.

In Hartley it is the associations established by pleasure and pain which necessarily lead man in the way of happiness. With him the way of happiness, of good, and of piety, is all one way.

Since God is the source of all good, and consequently must at last appear to be so, *i.e.* be associated with all our pleasures, it seems to follow, even from this proposition, that the idea of God, and of the ways by which his goodness and happiness are made manifest, must, at last, take place of, and absorb all other ideas, and he himself become, according to the language of the scriptures, *All in All*.[2]

Benevolence and generosity are necessarily developed in the natural operation of the law of association, because they give us the greatest pleasure.

Benevolence, in the limited sense, is nearly connected with sociality, and has the same sources. It has also a high degree of honour and esteem annexed to it, procures us many advantages and returns of kindness, both from the person obliged and others, and is most closely connected with the hope of reward in a future state, and with the pleasures of religion, and of self-approbation, or the moral sense. And the same things hold with respect to generosity in a much higher degree.[3]

In a discussion of the vexed problem of necessity and free will he finds the theory of free will as much beset with difficulties as that of necessity; and for a solution of the difficulties inherent in either theory he is obliged to resort to the universalist assumption that all souls shall be "restored" in the end.

If we suppose that all tends to happiness ultimately, this removes the difficulty so far as to produce acquiescence in the will of God and thankfulness to him; and that just as much upon the system of mechanism as that of free-will. . . . A parent who believes the doctrine of mechanism may, consistently with it, or rather must necessarily, in consequence of this belief, exhort his child. Therefore God, who is pleased to call himself our heavenly father, may do the same. And if we embrace the opinion of universal restoration, then all the exhortations contained both in the word and works of GOD, will produce their genuine effect, and concur to work in us dispositions fit to receive happiness ultimately.[4]

Before he had come under the influence of Hartley, Wordsworth had been to some extent a disciple of Godwin, according to the opinion of Harper, Legouis, Beatty, etc. In Godwin Wordsworth would have found the associationist utilitarianism of Hartley, without his religious piety; the necessarianism common to Hartley and the French philosophers; their common faith in education; the insistence of the French philosophers that only under a better system of government a better education is possible; their confidence that such a better system of government is being evolved; their faith in human Reason as the instrument that is gradually and infallibly bringing about the happiness of mankind. Godwin is strongly impregnated with the "perfectibilism" of Condorcet; and, like Condorcet, his optimism is based on his view of "the calm, the incessant, the rapid and auspicious progress which thought and reflection appear to be making in the world." [5]

Virtue and Benevolence Natural to Man

In so far as Wordsworth was subject to the influence of Shaftesbury, he must have held—what is the doctrine of "The Excursion" —that virtue means, in the long run, happiness, and that this is a law of *Nature*. In the *Inquiry concerning Virtue, or Merit*, which is the fourth of the treatises making up the *Characteristics,* Shaftesbury classifies the passions or affections that "govern the animal" as being:

1. The *natural Affections*, which lead to the good of the public.
2. or the *Self-affections*, which lead only to the good of the private.
3. or such as are neither of these; nor tending either to any good of the public or private; but contrary-wise: and which may therefore be justly styled *unnatural Affections* . . .[6]

Affections of the third sort are vicious and against the order of nature. Affections of the first two classes may be virtuous or vicious according to their intensity or degree and the balance maintained between them. Shaftesbury lays himself out to show "that to have the natural affections (such as are found in love, complacency, good-will, and in a sympathy with the kind or species) is to have the chief means and power of self-enjoyment: and that to want them is certain misery and ill." [7] After contrasting partial affection and "entire" affection so as to show the greater satisfactoriness of the latter, Shaftesbury says:

And if there be in Nature any such *original;* we may add, that the satisfaction which attends entire affection, is full and noble, in proportion to its final object, which contains all perfection; according to the sense of Theism above noted. For this, as has been shown, is the result of virtue. And to have this entire affection or integrity of mind, is *to live according to Nature*, and the dictates and rules of *supreme Wisdom*. This is morality, justice, piety, and natural religion.[8]

But the self-affections are also necessary to the good life. The essential is that they should be well balanced. But that being so, self-interest itself works for the general good.

Thus the Wisdom of what rules, and is first and chief in Nature, has made it to be according to the private interest and good of every one, to work towards the general good. . . . So that virtue, which of all excellences and beauties is the chief, and most amiable; that which is the prop and ornament of human affairs; which upholds communities, maintains union, friendship, and correspondence amongst men; that by which countries, as well as private families, flourish and are happy; and for want of which, everything comely, conspicuous, great and worthy, must perish and go to ruin; that single quality, thus beneficial to all society, and to mankind in general, is found equally a happiness and good to each creature in particular, and is that by which alone man can be happy, and without which he must be miserable.[9]

In Rousseau Wordsworth might have found a similar doctrine of the natural goodness of man. This doctrine is asserted over and over again in *Émile*. Man has a natural sense of right and wrong implanted in him by his conscience, and independently of reason. Rousseau speaks in *La Nouvelle Éloise* of "la douce voix de la Nature, qui réclame au fond de tous les coeurs contre une orgueilleuse philosophie." [10] In *Émile* he declares that he finds his ethical principles "au fond de mon coeur écrites par la Nature en caractères ineffaçables." [11] Moral goodness, he declares, is conformable to our nature.

Si la bonté morale est conforme à notre nature, l'homme ne sauroit être sain d'esprit ni bien consitué, qu'autant qu'il est bon. Si elle ne l'est pas et que l'homme soit méchant naturellement, il ne peut cesser de l'être sans se corrompre, et la bonté n'est en lui qu'un vice contre Nature.[12]

There is apparently some vagueness or confusion in Rousseau as to the relation between this natural goodness, which is a primitive passion of our hearts, and not within the gift of mere reason, and that love of self which is the source and principle of all the passions. The tone of Rousseau's sentiment makes him inapt to carry to its logical extreme the dominant French doctrine of self-interest.

Si c'en étoit ici le lieu, j'essayerois de montrer comment des premiers mouvements du coeur s'élèvent les premières voix de la conscience et comment des sentiments d'amour et de haine naissent les premières notions du bien et du mal: je feroit voir que *justice* et *bonté* ne sont point seulement des mots abstraits, de purs êtres moraux formés par l'entendement, mais de véritables affections de l'âme éclairée par la raison, et qui ne sont qu'un progrès ordonné de nos affections primitives; que, par la raison seule, indépendamment de la conscience, on ne peut établir aucune loi naturelle; et que tout le droit de la nature n'est qu'une chimère, s'il n'est fondée sur un besoin naturel au coeur humain.[13]

In his references to natural law and right of nature, I presume that Rousseau has in mind the theory of Hobbes or some one of his school as to the origin of government, and means to correct the notion that the law of nature could be established by the reason alone without the divine inspirations of conscience or the heart—a notion which shocks his religious sense. In Voltaire's poem on "La Loi naturelle," while the tone is very different from Rousseau's, the position is essentially the same. The law of nature is based on sentiments breathed into our hearts by God himself; and is but the expression in human conduct of a universal divine law existing independently of us.[14]

A similar position is taken by Bishop Parker. He objects strenuously to the "mechanical" psychology of Hobbes, to his view that the State of Nature is a state of war, and to his erection of a body of laws "that were never enacted by the Authority of a Legislator." According to Parker the state of nature is an expression of divine providence, and in order to believe in a state of nature one must first assume that there is a Sovereign Lord and Governor of the Universe. And so he arrives at the moral "rule of life" as signified by God to man "by the very Order and Frame of Nature." [15]

Samuel Clarke, in his *Discourse concerning the Being and Attributes of God* (delivered in 1704 and 1705), dwells on benevolence as an affection proper to the nature of man, in accordance with his doctrine of universal fitness.

> For if . . . there be a natural Difference between Good and Evil, and that which is Good is Fit and Reasonable, and that which is Evil is Unreasonable to be done; and that which is the greatest Good, is always the most Fit and Reasonable to be chosen: then, as the Goodness of God extends itself universally over all his Works through the whole Creation, by doing always what is absolutely best in the Whole; so every rational Creature *ought* in its Sphere and Station, according to its respective Powers and Faculties, to do all the Good it can to all its Fellow-creatures . . .[15a]

Further, Clarke argues, the obligation to benevolence may be deduced from the nature of man by considering the relations of parents to their children, to their kindred and friends, which require them to multiply affinities, "Till by Degrees the Affection of Single Persons becomes a Friendship of Families, and this enlarges itself to a Society of Towns and Cities and Nations, and terminates in the agreeing Community of all Mankind." These considerations lead Clarke to the assertion of his doctrine of Right Reason.

> And now this [eternal Rule of Equity] is That *right Reason*, which makes the principal Distinction between *Men* and *Beasts*. This is the *Law of Nature*, which (as *Cicero* excellently expresses it) is of Universal Extent, and everlasting Duration . . . which, being founded in the Reason and Nature of Things, did not then begin to be a Law, when it was first written and enacted by Men; but is of the same Original with the eternal Reasons or Proportions of Things, and the Perfections or Attributes of God himself.[16]

Clarke's doctrine of Right Reason is a somewhat transcendental version of Cumberland's in his *De legibus naturae* (1672). According to Cumberland, right reason is the means by which moral distinctions are apprehended; but by right reason he understands "merely the power of rising to general laws of nature from particular facts of experience." [17] This doctrine was more fully developed by Hartley, Mackintosh and later associationists. It is of interest in connection with that passage in "The Prelude" in which Wordsworth refers to Nature as—

> . . . a Power
> That is the visible quality and shape
> And image of right reason . . .[18]

Clarke's doctrine of natural benevolence is to be found also in Cumberland's argument against Hobbes. But the proponent of this doctrine who would be most likely to have affected Wordsworth is Godwin. It is developed in the tenth chapter of Book IV of *Political Justice* (1793), under the heading "Of Self-Love and Benevolence." Godwin is arguing against the typical French doctrine of self-love and in favor of "the practicability of disinterested action,"—the view held by Shaftesbury, Butler, Hutcheson and Hume.

A disposition to promote the benefit of another, my child, my friend, my relation, or my fellow being, is one of the passions; understanding by the term passion, a permanent and habitual tendency towards a certain course of action. It is of the same general nature as avarice, or the love of fame.[19]

It is true, Godwin points out, that this is not an original passion, but has its origin in self-interest, in that it gives one agreeable sensations. But what started as a means is converted into an end pursued for its own sake.

The good of my neighbor could not, in the first instance, have been chosen, but as the means of agreeable sensation. His cries, or the spectacle of his distress importune me, and I am irresistibly impelled to adopt means to remove this importunity. . . . Thus the good of our neighbor, like the possession of money, is originally pursued for the sake of its advantage to ourselves. But it is the nature of the passions speedily to convert what at first were means, into ends.[20]

And Godwin proceeds to dilate on the sublime emotions, the exalted pleasures, furnished us by the passion of benevolence.

Godwin considers that "great mischief has probably been done by those moralists, who think only of stimulating men to good deeds by considerations of frigid prudence and mercenary self-interest, and never apply themselves to excite one generous and magnanimous sentiment of our natures." One might point out that

Godwin has himself essentially espoused the doctrine of self-interest in deriving his passion of benevolence from the interested craving for agreeable sensations. But in this quarrel of the schools all parties come to the same conclusion—that virtue and benevolence are guaranteed to man by nature herself. This view Wordsworth would have found established by one line of thought or another in the theologians, the jurists, the associationist philosophers, or in the sentimental devotees of nature—Shaftesbury, Rousseau, Godwin.

Design in the Natural World

But Wordsworth would have found, in thoroughly orthodox writers, other grounds for his faith in the benevolence of nature. The chief reliance of natural religion in the seventeenth, eighteenth, and early nineteenth centuries, and the most constantly recurrent proof of the existence of God, was the evidence of design throughout nature. In Chapter III we have seen how Newton and the theologians found evidence of design in the disposition and movements of the heavenly bodies, which could not be explained simply by reference to known "efficient causes," but which must often be referred to "final causes" or the ends which God had in mind for them. This is but one instance in the natural world of what seventeenth- and eighteenth-century writers found to be true throughout nature, that it is designed, in the whole and in detail, to bring about the effects envisaged by divine wisdom.

In Wordsworth, while this assumption doubtless lurks more or less behind his poetry in all periods, the most explicit statement of it is found in "The Excursion," the one of his poems dealing largely with nature which falls within a period of his life when he was most orthodox in his religious views. It occurs in the long discourse addressed by the Wanderer to the unbelieving Solitary.

> These craggy regions, these chaotic wilds,
> Does that benignity pervade, that warms
> The mole contented with her darksome walk
> In the cold ground; and to the emmet gives
> Her foresight, and intelligence that makes
> The tiny creatures strong by social league;

Supports the generations, multiplies
Their tribes, till we behold a spacious plain
Or grassy bottom, all, with little hills—
Their labour, covered, as a lake with waves;
Thousands of cities in the desert places
Built up, of life, and food, and means of life! [21]

The Wanderer then goes on to speak of other communities, such as those of summer flies, and then of birds in flocks, where "more obviously the selfsame influence rules."

This general line of argument is to be found in many of the works of divinity listed in Wordsworth's library. In Hale it takes the form of insisting on the "adaptation of things of various and several Natures and Structures one to another, and all to some common End or Design." And Hale makes that comparison to a watch—all its parts in their fashion, functioning and mutual adaptation giving such unmistakable evidence of a conscious artist—which was to reappear so often in works of divinity, as for example in Paley's *Natural Theology* (1802).[22] In Stillingfleet the argument is drawn from Galen's exposition, in his *De usu partium*, of the specific adaptation of each organ and member of the body to its particular uses.

In the entrance of those books, Galen first shews the great variety of parts which is in several animals suitable to their several natures [horses' hoofs, etc.; lions' teeth and paws; etc., etc.]. Now that the configuration of parts is not the cause of the use of them afterwards, as the lion's paw of his courage . . . appears by this, because the young ones of the several kinds of animals, before their parts are grown up, strive to make the same use of them which the others do. . . . Afterwards he comes particularly to handle the several parts of man's body, and first begins with the hand; and shews in each part that it were impossible to have framed them with greater conveniency for their several uses than they have.[23]

And thus Stillingfleet goes on to show in detail, from Galen, just how each organ of the body is precisely adapted to its functions.

The writer who includes the greatest variety of instances of design is the scientist, Robert Boyle, in his *Inquiry into the Final Causes of Natural Things*. This discussion, bringing into one section numerous examples from astronomy, animal life, bird life, insect life, is perhaps the most fruitful quarry for the kind of argument that became so prominent in Paley, and in writers like Abraham Tucker ("Edward Search," *The Light of Nature Followed*, 1768–78), Bernardin de Saint-Pierre (*Études de la Nature*, 1784), and the authors of the Bridgewater Treatises of 1833. It was this type of argument that failed to impress Tennyson, as he records in "In Memoriam":

> I found him not in world or sun,
> Or eagle's wing, or insect's eye . . .

With regard to the argument for a deity derived from the regular motions of the planets and their adaptations to the needs of man, Boyle is not certain whether it is absolutely demonstrative. But certainly "there is nothing in that fabric unworthy a divine author: and the motions of the sun and stars may well allow us to think, that, among other purposes, they were made to illustrate the terrestrial globe, and bring heat and other benefits to the inhabitants of it." [24] And Boyle quotes from Newton the opinion that the situation of the several planets is an instance of divine wisdom and design.

Those planets, *says he*, have the greater density, *coeteris paribus*, which are placed nearest to the sun. Thus *Jupiter* is more dense than *Saturn*, and the earth more dense than *Jupiter*. For it was necessary to place the planets at different distances from the sun, that each might receive a greater or a less degree of his heat, according to its density. If our earth were placed in the orbit of Saturn, the water of it would be frozen up; and if in the orbit of Mercury, 'twould presently exhale in vapour.[25]

But Boyle finds much more convincing evidence of design in the formation and adjustment of animal bodies. I do not find any reference to "eagle's wing," though the bat's wing is given as a notable instance of design in the way of compensation.

Bats are esteem'd a contemptible sort of creature, yet they may afford us a considerable argument to our present purpose. For we have here an animal that flies like a bird, tho' it wants feathers, and has a fabric quite different from that of birds. And here too, we may observe the compensation that is made for parts that seem either deficient, or less advantageous, than those of the same denomination in other birds; as also the regard which the divine artist appears to have to the symmetry of parts in his animated works, and to their fitness to the places they are to frequent . . .[26]

Wordsworth's mole and his ants, or emmets, are both instanced by Boyle. "It is rational," he says, "from the manifest fitness of some things, to cosmical, or animal ends, to infer, that they were thereto ordained by an intelligent agent." He mentions the sagacity and government of bees, the provident industry of spiders, nature's provision for the propagation of animal species ("supports the generations, multiplies their tribes"). As for the foresight and intelligence of emmets—

Another obvious instance of the instinct that nature has given to some despicable insects, may be taken from ants: for 'tis known, that these little creatures do, in the summer, hoard up grains of corn against the winter.[27]

Coming now to the mole:

On the other hand, the deficiency observable in the eyes of some animals, compared to those of man, may be ascribed to the just contrivance of nature, that, on most occasions, declines doing what is unnecessary to the particular ends she aims at in the fabric of a part. Thus moles, being destin'd to live, for the most part, under ground, have the eyes so little, in proportion to their bodies, that 'tis commonly believ'd they have none at all; but tho' I have found the contrary, yet their eyes are very different from those of other four-footed beasts; which need not be wonder'd at, considering that nature design'd these creatures to live under ground, where sight is of no use, and where large eyes would be more expos'd to danger. . . .[28]

The eyes of the mole are given as one instance of the variation in the organs of sight according to the needs of different animals. And this brings us to Tennyson's "insect's eye." Says Boyle:

'Tis known that men, and most four-footed beasts, and birds, have several muscles belonging to their eyes, by help of which, they can turn them any way; and so obvert the organ of sense to the object. But nature, not having given that mobility to the eyes of flies, she, in recompense, furnishes them with a multitude of little protuberant parts, finely rang'd upon the convex of their large bulging eyes: so that by means of these little numerous studs, numberless rays of light are reflected from objects placed on either hand, above or beneath the level of the eye, and consequently fall upon that organ, to render the objects they come from, visible to the animal. . . .[29]

The tendency of the argument throughout this discussion is to show that each animal has organs fitted to its particular needs. This argument is taken up by Bentley in his Boyle's Lecture sermons [30] and made to apply particularly to man, and especially to the power of his eyes.

Secondly, we affirm, that our senses have that degree of perfection which is most fit and suitable to our estate and condition. For, though the *eye* were so piercing as to descry even opake and little objects some hundreds of leagues off, even that improvement of our sight would do us little service; it would be terminated by neighbouring hills and woods; or, in the largest and evenest plain, by the very convexity of the earth; unless we could always inhabit the tops of mountains and cliffs, or had wings too to fly aloft, when we had a mind to take a prospect. And if mankind had had wings (as perhaps some extravagant Atheist may think us deficient in that), all the world must have consented to clip them; or else the human race had been extinct before this time, nothing, upon that supposition, being safe from murder and rapine. Or, if the *eye* were so acute as to rival the finest microscopes, and to discern the smallest hair upon the leg of a gnat, it would be a curse, and not a blessing to us; it would make all things appear rugged and deformed, the most finely polished crystal would be uneven and rough; the sight of our own selves would affright us; the smoothest skin would be beset all over with ragged scales and bristly hairs; and besides, we could not see at one view above what is now the space of an inch, and it would take a considerable time to survey the then mountainous bulk of our own bodies.[31]

It has been suggested that in this passage is the germ, not merely of the acute eyesight of Gruldrig in *Gulliver's Travels*, but of the passage in the "Essay on Man" in which Pope tries to reconcile man to the particular organization that he has by representing that his inability to soar like birds or angels, and his not having the "microscopic eye" of insects, is an arrangement suited to his particular place in the scale of being.[32] Professor Lovejoy [33] believes the origin of Pope's thought to be a passage in William King's *De origine mali* (1702, English trans. 1731), in which that author explains why man has not wings:

'Tis plain that in his present circumstances he cannot have them, and that the use of them would be very mischievous to society; and yet the want of them exposes us to many inconveniences.

Pope's lines have a much closer resemblance to Bentley. Especially striking is their common supposition of an eye so acute as to rival the finest microscopes.

> Why has not Man a microscopic eye?
> For this plain reason, Man is not a Fly.

But this "microscopic eye" makes it most likely that both Pope and Bentley, and King too for that matter, drew their suggestion from Locke's *Essay concerning Human Understanding*. In Book II, Chap. 23, Locke has a long section devoted to the thesis that "the infinitely wise Contriver of us, and all things about us, hath fitted our senses, faculties, and organs, to the conveniences of life, and the business we have to do here." He mentions the inconvenience that results from our being removed "into parts of this air, not much higher than that we commonly breathe in," and suggests how intolerable we should find the noise "if our sense of hearing were but one thousand times quicker than it is." If a man's eyesight were one thousand or one hundred thousand times acuter than it is, nothing would appear the same to him as to other men, and he could not talk about objects of sight with other men. The tenderness of his vision might make him unable to bear bright sunshine, "or not so much as open day-light." Compare Pope's suggestion in regard to greater acuteness in the sense of smell:

> Or quick effluvia darting thro' the brain,
> Die of a rose in aromatic pain?

And if by the help of such *microscopical* eyes (if I may so call them) a man could penetrate farther than ordinary into the secret composition and radical texture of bodies, he would not make any great advantage by the change, as such an acute sight would not serve to conduct him to the market and exchange; if he could not see things he was to avoid at a convenient distance; nor distinguish things he had to do with, by those sensible qualities others do.[34]

In short, Locke concludes, God has made our senses "so as is best for us in our present condition." [35]

The adaptation of the eyes of various animals to their several conditions was a favorite topic of religious writers during the next century and a half. George Cheyne has an account of the special conformation of the eyes of fish, of land animals that seek their food close to the ground, of those that seek it on higher places, and those that seek it in the dark.[36] Paley has a special account of the conformation of a fish's eye so as to receive rays of light that have passed through water.[37] When Tennyson found not God in "eagle's wing, or insect's eye," he was going against the dominant tradition of two centuries of English thought.

Plenum Formarum

One of the chief arguments of Archbishop King for the goodness of the universe is derived from the concept of a graduated scale of beings descending from the highest of celestial creatures down through man and the lower animal and vegetable worlds. This concept is derived partly from observation of the animal world and partly from abstract metaphysical considerations. These last have been set forth by Professor Lovejoy in an article entitled "Optimism and Romanticism." [38] According to Mr. Lovejoy it was considered by many philosophers that, since every Platonic Idea has a valid claim to existence, there must be a perfect continuum of conceivable forms in the universe, a *plenum formarum*. This concept, Mr. Lovejoy points out, has its origin in the Timaeus, 29; it is the essential principle of the dialectic of neoplatonic emanationism; it was employed by Abelard and Thomas Aquinas among others. The existence of a *plenum formarum* or scale of beings is not merely positive evidence, in itself, of the goodness of God's universe. It serves as an answer to the objections of doubters founded on the defectiveness of man's faculties. This argument is thus formulated by Edmund Law, the translator of King's *De origine mali:*

From the supposition of a Scale of Being, gradually descending from perfection to nonentity, and complete in every intermediate rank and degree, we shall soon see the absurdity of such questions as these, Why was not man made more perfect? Why are not his faculties equal to those of angels? Since this is only asking why he was not placed in a quite different class of beings, when at the same time all other classes are supposed to be already full.[39]

This scale of being, running from the highest angelic intelligences down through man to the lowest forms of life, is found in Sir Matthew Hale, in George Cheyne, and other English writers; some of these will be considered in a later chapter in connection with Coleridge. The idea is found also in Locke, in a passage illustrating the thesis that *in things which sense cannot discover, analogy is the great rule of probability.* The following is a part of Locke's discussion:

Thus finding . . . that there is a gradual connexion of one with another, *without any great or discernible gaps between, in all that great variety of things we see in this world,* which are so closely linked together, that, in the several ranks of beings, it is not easy to discover the bound betwixt them; we have reason to be persuaded, that *by such gentle steps,* things ascend upwards in degrees of perfection. It is a hard matter to say where sensible and rational begin, and where insensible and irrational end; and who is there quick-sighted enough to determine precisely, which is the lowest species of living beings, and which the first of those who have no life? . . . Observing, I say, such gradual and gentle descents downwards in those parts of the creation that are beneath man, the rule of analogy may make it probable, that it is so also in things above us and our observation; and that there are several ranks of intelligent beings, excelling us in several degrees of perfection, ascending upwards towards the infinite perfection of the Creator, by gentle steps and differences, that are every one at no great distance from the next to it.[40]

The phrase italicized in the passage from Locke is what makes it significant in relation to the following passage from James Foster, taken from a chapter *Which treats of the goodness of God; and answers the principal Objections, which have been urged against it.*

Nay, if we suppose ... that there are not only in the highest, but in every other rank of beings, rising in regular gradation one above another, as many creatures as there would have been, if each of these orders had existed alone, the leaving out of any species of mere animals, whose pleasures exceed their pains, must subtract just so much from the universal happiness.

If there was really but one, and that the highest, order of beings only in the universe, this would leave *such a prodigious chasm* in nature, as reason must be astonished at, and could never justly account for: nay benevolence itself, as well as reason must be shocked, and start at the thought of it. Or if the chain of being was maintained, in every link, quite down to the race of man, why should he be excluded?—Is his nature incapable of happiness, or unfit for the enjoyment of it? Was there not happiness originally designed for it, adapted to its powers? ... Why then, I ask again, should man, in particular, be omitted in the scale of being? [41]

This solicitude to avoid any great gap, or prodigious chasm, in nature, as inconsistent with the notion of a rational and beneficent universe, is a prominent feature in the thought of Leibniz. Thus he reflects, in reference to the possibility that man might have been left out of the world, on account of his fragility:

Mais ce seroit apparement un défaut que quelques Philosophes d'autrefois auroient appellé *Vacuum formarum*, un vuide dans l'ordre des espèces.[42]

I have been thus particular in citing passages on this topic because of the light they may have to throw on certain lines of Wordsworth in "The Excursion," already quoted in the chapter on the Metaphysical Concept. They are in the passage dealing with the active Principle.

> Whate'er exists hath properties that spread
> Beyond itself, communicating good,
>
> .   .   .   .
>
> Spirit that knows no insulated spot,
> *No chasm*, no solitude; *from link to link*
> It circulates, the Soul of all the worlds.

Thus Wordsworth makes his own fusion of the two, or several, metaphysical notions—that of the active principle (together with that of the world-soul), and that of the chain of beings, in which there is no break, no *vacuum formarum*. Wherever he may have come upon these various notions, they are all found combined in Pope (with the possible exception of the active principle). The doctrine of the ideal fulness of the several classes is expressly stated by Pope:

> Where all must full or not coherent be,
> And all that rises, rise in due degree.[43]

In Pope, too, as in Wordsworth, and in the theologians, this doctrine is made contributory to that of the perfect goodness of the world.

> See Matter next, with various life endu'd,
> Press to one centre still, the gen'ral Good.

The chain of being—the figure implied in Wordsworth's phrase, "from link to link"—is a common notion among eighteenth-century poets, many of whom were most familiar to Wordsworth. It is in Henry Baker's "The Universe," where man is reminded that he is but "one single link in Nature's mighty chain." [44] It is in Thomson's "Summer" and "Autumn." Most interesting is the passage in Akenside's "Pleasures of the Imagination," where the notion of "the ascent of being" is combined with an explicit statement of the Leibnizian doctrine of the best possible of all worlds. Akenside is giving an account of the neoplatonic emanation of the world from the Sovereign Spirit.

> He too, beholding in the sacred light
> Of his essential reason all the shapes
> Of swift contingence, all successive ties
> Of action propagated, through the sum
> Of possible existence, he at once
> Down the long series of eventful time,
> So fixed the dates of being, so disposed
> To every living soul of every kind
> The field of motion and the hour of rest,
> That all conspired to his supreme design,—
> To universal good: with full accord

Answering the mighty model he had chose—
The best and fairest of unnumbered worlds
That lay from everlasting in the store
Of his divine conceptions. Nor content,
By one exertion of creating power,
His goodness to reveal; through every age,
Through every moment up the tract of time,
His parent hand, with ever new increase
Of happiness and virtue, has adorned
The *vast harmonious frame:* his parent hand,
From the mute shell-fish gasping on the shore
To men, to angels, to celestial minds
For ever leads the generations on
To higher scenes of being; while, supplied
From day to day with his enlivening breath,
Inferior orders in succession rise
To fill the void below.[45]

Universal Harmony, Universal Love

In the above quotation from Akenside I have italicized the phrase, "vast harmonious frame," by way of introduction to one special aspect of nature-philosophy. Every thing in nature is harmonious with every thing else. This is evident in the manifold adjustments of organ to function, or end, and in the manifold adaptations of the external world to human needs (as extensively set forth in such books as Abraham Tucker's *Light of Nature Followed,*[46] and still more extensively in William Derham's *Physico-Theology,* 1713). It is true on the broader principle of the *plenum formarum.* And it is true on the still broader and more speculative ground that the universe as a whole makes up one system, in which what may seem ill from a restricted point of view is seen to be good by reference to the design and intention of the whole:

All Discord, Harmony not understood;
All partial Evil, universal Good.[47]

This last is the doctrine of King and Law, and—what is more to the point in our discussion—it is the doctrine of Shaftesbury, who puts it thus explicitly:

Now, if the whole system of animals, together with that of vegetables, and all other things in this inferior world, be properly comprehended in one system of a globe or earth: and if again this globe or
earth itself appears to have a real dependence on something still beyond; as, for example, either on its sun, the galaxy, or its fellow-
planets; then it is in reality a part only of some other system. And if it
be allowed, that there is in like manner *a system of all things, and a universal Nature;* there can be no particular being or system which is not
either good or ill in that general one of the universe: for if it be insig-
nificant and of no use, it is a fault or imperfection, and consequently
ill in the general system.

Therefore if any being be wholly or really ill, it must be ill with respect to the universal system; and then the system of the universe is ill,
or imperfect. But if the ill of one private system be the good of others;
if it makes still to the good of the general system, (as when one creature lives by the destruction of another; one thing is generated from
the corruption of another; or one planetary system or vortex may swallow up another) then is *the ill of that private system no real ill in itself;*
any more than the pain of breeding teeth is ill, in a system or body
which is so constituted, that without this occasion of pain, it would suffer worse, by being defective.[48]

Shaftesbury frequently recurs to this concept of a universal system
in which the defects of individuals contribute to the perfection
of the whole.[49] In Part I, Section III of "The Moralists," he explains that, since the perfection of nature involves the regular
action of its universal laws, we cannot expect them to make exception in individual cases, and we must not regard it as an evil when,
in accordance with these laws, some puny animal falls over a preci-
pice and is destroyed. And the same principle justifies the destructive action of earthquakes, storms, pestilential blasts, etc., and even
the production of monstrous forms—"Nature still working as before, and not perversely or erroneously; not faintly or with feeble
endeavours; but o'erpowered by a superior rival, and by another
Nature's justly conquering force." [50]

Wordsworth in writing of nature was moved, more or less consciously, by the various considerations set forth in this chapter.
And, like other poets and philosophers, with an obstinate and religious determination to find design, order, and harmony everywhere in the universe, and to ignore everything that seems to con-
tradict this providential interpretation, it was inevitable that he

should find that Nature is "kind" and "kindly," [51] that she is "fostering Nature," [52] "holy Nature," [53] that one can safely trust oneself to her influences,[54] and that she teaches a "lesson deep of love." [55] Critics often write as if this were a peculiarly romantic view of nature, and an effect of the baleful influence of Rousseau. But the case of Pope is sufficient to show that it is perfectly consistent with the neoclassical temper. And we have seen that it is involved in the speculations of divines of various stripes of orthodoxy long before the appearance of Rousseau and Saint-Pierre.

In Wordsworth this conviction of the universal presence of love in nature is equally characteristic of his writing in phases as distinct from one another as those of "The Excursion" and *Lyrical Ballads*. His classic treatment of this theme is in the poem "To My Sister" (1798). On the first mild day of March Wordsworth invites his sister to put on her woodland dress and come out with him for a walk; they will drink in the love which is abroad in the air, and so prepare their spirits for the whole year that is to come.

> Love, now a universal birth,
> From heart to heart is stealing,
> From earth to man, from man to earth:
> —It is the hour of feeling.
>
> One moment now may give us more
> Than years of toiling reason:
> Our minds shall drink at every pore
> The spirit of the season.
>
> Some silent laws our hearts will make,
> Which they shall long obey:
> We for the year to come may take
> Our temper from to-day.
>
> And from the blessed power that rolls
> About, below, above,
> We'll frame the measure of our souls:
> They shall be tuned to love.

Here again we must take into account the imaginative synthesis made by Shaftesbury and the eighteenth-century poets of the mere esthetic beauty of the external world with the philosophic concept of universal nature. In our own day such a poem as this could hardly be written; or if so, only because the influence of Wordsworth still lingers in some minds that have resisted contemporary ways of thought. The almost complete decay of the nature-philosophy that gives support to Wordsworth's feeling—and particularly of the teleological interpretation of natural phenomena—has removed the whole support to the esthetic structure of romantic feeling. In Wordsworth's time, it was almost a matter of course to associate the springing of grass, the songs of mating birds, and the mild blandishment of spring sunshine with the whole system of natural theology. This synthesis of elements is present in James Thomson, a poet whom Wordsworth greatly admired. For him the cuckoo celebrates the same theme as Wordsworth's redbreast, "the symphony of spring," "the passion of the groves."

> When the first soul of love is sent abroad,
> Warm through the vital air, and on the heart
> Harmonious seizes, the gay troops begin,
> In gallant thought, to plume the painted wing . . .[56]

And from the mere vital activities of the creatures in spring, Thomson rises to the subject of man's moral life.

> Still let my song a nobler note assume,
> And sing the infusive force of Spring on man;
> When heaven and earth, as if contending, vie
> To raise his being and serene his soul.
> Can he forbear to join the general smile
> Of Nature? Can fierce passions vex his breast,
> While every gale is peace, and every grove
> Is melody? [57]

And behind the moral and esthetic view lies the larger philosophic concept of universal love.

> I cannot go
> Where UNIVERSAL LOVE not smiles around,
> Sustaining all yon orbs, and all their sons;

From seeming evil still educing good,
And better thence again, and better still,
In infinite progression.[58]

The Ministry of Pleasure

In another lyric, written at nearly the same time with "To My Sister," Wordsworth sets forth very simply his doctrine that it is chiefly through pleasure (otherwise joy) that nature develops man's character, and that pleasure is our normal state of being. In "Lines Written in Early Spring" it is the seeming pleasure taken by living things in their various activities which sets the poet brooding over the failure of men to realize their own capacities for joy.

The birds around me hopped and played,
Their thoughts I cannot measure:—
But the least motion which they made
It seemed a thrill of pleasure.

The budding twigs spread out their fan,
To catch the breezy air;
And I must think, do all I can,
That there was pleasure there.

If this belief from heaven be sent,
If such be Nature's holy plan,
Have I not reason to lament
What man has made of man?

Taken simply and normally, without grave critical examination, such poetry can hardly fail to delight a reader susceptible to the charm of mild spring weather and of animated life in the moment of returning vitality. When we begin to examine it in the cool light of reason a thousand questions present themselves, and we are in danger of making ourselves and the poet ridiculous with solemn objections and anxious apologies. We are apt to take too literally what may be no more than analogies and fanciful suggestions. But still, we have undertaken to make out what Wordsworth did mean

by nature, and we may as well push on with the inquiry, praying
that common sense may save us from the worst pitfalls in our path.

And first, with regard to the pleasure which Wordsworth discovers in the activities of animal and vegetable life. It is often difficult to determine how far this poet actually attributes to nature,
literally, those qualities and faculties which he describes in her. It
might be sufficient for his purpose that these qualities and faculties should *seem to the imagination* to be present in nature, should
be so constantly associated with certain objects as infallibly to work
upon the observer's imagination for his inspiration and instruction.
There are places where Wordsworth distinctly refers to this way
in which nature may affect man's mind for his profit. Thus in
"The Prelude" he refers to "Nature's secondary grace"—

> The charm more superficial that attends
> Her works, as they present to Fancy's choice
> Apt illustrations of the moral world,
> Caught at a glance, or traced with curious pains.[59]

But the tracing of these "apt illustrations" is, he says, the work of
Fancy. The faculty of Imagination probes deeper into "the life of
things." Wordsworth took very seriously—nay, solemnly—the
poetic faculty of imagination. It is not to be supposed that the
"moral" associations established in natural objects were so established in a purely fanciful and arbitrary way. They were more
than merely plausible likenesses, sufficient to hang his sentiment on.
In Wordsworth's account of the imagination, as in his account of
nature, there is a cloudy margin of uncertainty, an emotional daz-
zle, in which ambiguities thrive, in which it is not possible to distinguish sharply the bounds of scientific truth and of the heart's
desire. But Wordsworth strove for sobriety and precision of statement, and this is one thing that challenges the critic to such an examination as the present one. If the poet were not so conscientious
in his statements, we could let them go for flights of fancy. If he
were not in such deadly earnest, we need not question him so
closely. It is clear that the analogies discovered by his imagination between nature and spiritual truth have for him some depth

of meaning, some real validity for thought, some grounding in the essence of things.

This is shown in the distinction he draws in "The Prelude" between the serious work of the imagination and the more frivolous, arbitrary and unrealistic play of fancy.[60] It is shown in the cautious qualification with which, in Book II, he refers to his imaginative process of attributing the sentiment of being to every creature in the organic and inorganic worlds; he does not undertake to determine whether it was a mere act of association of ideas—the transference of his own enjoyments by sympathy to creatures who do not really share in them—or whether he had actually received a revelation of "things that really are." [61]

This brings us back to "Lines Written in Early Spring," with their earnest but qualified attribution of pleasure to plant and animal beings. The poet grants that he cannot measure the thoughts of birds; but their least motion "seemed" a thrill of pleasure. The movements of budding twigs has the same effect upon him. He tries to be scientific; but he must think, do all he can, that there was pleasure there. And the poem ends with a conclusion based upon an emotional assumption. *If* this interpretation of lower life is a revelation ("if this belief from heaven be sent"); *if* such be Nature's holy plan. . . . One cannot but be impressed with the modest sobriety of this expression of a poetic attitude, the evident desire to keep as close as possible to the literal truth. But for that very reason it calls for a more critical examination, and we are impelled to ask, how much sense does it make?

It is probable that Wordsworth meant seriously and literally to attribute pleasure to the budding twigs as well as to the birds at play. And in doing so he had the authority of a serious contemporary man of science, who had expressed the opinion that plants do probably have feelings and even ideas. In my "Note on Wordsworth's Reading" I refer to the poet's letter to Joseph Cottle, the year before this poem was written, requesting the loan of Erasmus Darwin's *Zoönomia*. In this work (1794-96), Darwin devotes an entire section to discussing the sensibility of plants. He first gives reasons for thinking that the stamens and pistils of flowers "shew evident marks of sensibility, not only from many of the stamens and some pistils approaching towards each other at the sea-

son of impregnation, but from many of them closing their petals
and calyxes during the cold parts of the day." [62] More than this, he
argues that "the vegetable world possesses some degree of voluntary powers." This appears, for one thing, "from their necessity to
sleep, which we have shewn in Sect. XVIII to consist in the temporary abolition of voluntary power." [63] He then shows that "the
associations of fibrous motions are observable in the vegetable
world, as well as in the animal." And from these and other analogies between vegetable and animal life he is led to ask whether
vegetables may not have actual ideas.

This leads us to a curious inquiry, whether vegetables have ideas of
external things? As all our ideas are originally received by our senses,
the question may be changed to, whether vegetables possess any organs
of sense?

He believes that they have at least four different kinds of sense,
in addition to that of "love."

Thus, besides a kind of taste at the extremities of their roots . . . for
the purpose of selecting their proper food: and besides different kinds
of irritability residing in the various glands, which separate honey, wax,
resin, and other juices from their blood; vegetable life seems to possess
an organ of sense to distinguish the variations of heat, another to distinguish the varying degrees of moisture, another of light, another of
touch, and probably another analogous to our sense of smell. To these
must be added the indubitable evidence of their passion of love, and I
think we may truly conclude, that they are furnished with a common
sensorium belonging to each bud, and that they must occasionally repeat those perceptions either in their dreams or waking hours, and consequently possess ideas of so many of the properties of the external
world, and of their own existence.[64]

Thus we see that Wordsworth's modest suggestion, in poetry,
that the twigs of plants may be endowed with sensibility is vastly
more conservative than the solemn prose speculations of Darwin,
who attributes to vegetable life not merely sensibility, but some degree of voluntary power and even of conscious thought. But leaving out of consideration the theories of Erasmus Darwin, who soon
fell into discredit and oblivion, how does Wordsworth's suggestion

look in the light of biological science since *The Origin of Species?*
I wonder whether, in point of fact, it has not more plausibility to-
day than at the time it was made; whether it would not be taken
more indulgently by a reader steeped in biological studies than by
one brought up on old-time metaphysics, mathematics, and classic
poetry. Are not biologists more inclined since Charles Darwin than
before to affirm the continuity of the life-process manifested
throughout the vegetable and animal worlds, and—in spite of distinctions and degrees—to assume some sort of radical identity
throughout? They may distinguish more carefully than Wordsworth between the irritability (contractility) of vegetable tissues
and the sensibility of animal life, which latter implies, certainly in
the more highly organized forms, a sensitiveness to pain and
pleasure.

But will they not agree that, from the turning of twigs to the
light, all the way up to man's conscious seeking for pleasure, there
is a continuous chain of functionally similar manifestations? This
view is confirmed by our knowledge that, in the animal world,
there are many degrees of sensitiveness to pain and pleasure, and
that in man's behavior the instinctive and the conscious are inex-
tricably interwoven and combined in varying proportions. The
point of identity throughout the entire chain is that the movement
in question, whether purely "mechanical," or instinctive, or made
with a consciousness of specific objectives, is by way of avoidance
of what is unfavorable and attraction to what is favorable to the
organism.

In the process of the building up of man's attitudes, Wordsworth, following the Hartleian psychology, makes much of pain
and pleasure as the directing forces. This theory Wordsworth
makes use of in the Preface to *Lyrical Ballads* in his defense of the
poet, who is subject to the necessity of producing immediate pleasure in the reader. This necessity, he says, need not be considered
as a degradation of the poet's art.

It is an acknowledgement of the beauty of the universe . . . It is a
homage paid to the native and naked dignity of man, to the grand elementary principle of pleasure, by which he knows, and feels, and lives,
and moves. We have no sympathy but what is propagated by pleasure:
I would not be misunderstood; but wherever we sympathise with pain it

will be found that the sympathy is produced and carried on by subtle combinations with pleasure. We have no knowledge, that is, no general principles drawn from the contemplation of particular facts, but what has been built up by pleasure, and exists in us by pleasure alone.[65]

This guidance by pleasure and pain, which operates in the development of man's moral life, Wordsworth doubtless takes as the clue to behavior in lower animal life as well, and something analogous he finds operating in the vegetable world.

But then, one asks, why in this poem does he speak of pleasure and not of pain? Any fair survey of the living world will bring to mind the enormous volume of pain involved,—a volume so vast and constant that we are unable to determine whether pain or pleasure predominates in the life of any organism. If nature's plan be a holy one, why can it not provide for pleasure without pain, or for such a predominance of pleasure over pain that we can be assured the one is but a minor incident to the production of the other? If one is seriously bent on discovering nature's plan, why shut one's eyes so resolutely on the innumerable evidences of her savagery, ruthlessness, indifference? Why not take into account, with Tennyson, "nature red in tooth and claw"?

Well, in this particular poem, the defender of Wordsworth might argue, he is describing a spring day, when the life-forces are triumphantly rising in every juicy stalk and every bird is a-quiver with the mating impulse. He has in view some favored English grove, where the periwinkle is encouraged to "trail its wreath," where the evidences of cut-throat competition are not so clear as in an African jungle, nor the blight of the elements laid upon life so obvious as in the deserts of Arabia.

But the critic is at once upon our backs. Why choose a spring day and a budding grove to illustrate nature's plan? Why not, like Thomas Hardy, choose winter in Durnover Field, the ground frozen to iron hardness, sky a dull gray, and birds vainly seeking food? Hardy is, it must be confessed, a somewhat lonely figure among nature-poets, and marks a distinct movement away from the romantic interpretation of nature. During the great periods of nature-poetry, the writers seem in a conspiracy to ignore her more sinister aspects and assume, without much question, that her plan is a holy one. And the reasons are many and complicated.

Some of them we have considered. The growing scientific view of nature as uniform and regular seemed to confirm the metaphysical assumption that she is rational and purposive, and these two assumptions played into the hands of a religious faith that her reason is spiritual and her ends benevolent. Proceeding on this explicit or tacit assumption, it was almost inevitable that poets should take their illustrations of nature's ways from either her genial or her sublime aspects. But even supposing that poets could free themselves from these philosophical assumptions—which are not so generally entertained today—there are still reasons why they should choose the more cheerful and exalting aspects of nature for exploitation.

Taking the case of Wordsworth's spring song, we might contend, for the poet, that pain and pleasure, while equally prominent in life, are not equally significant and rewarding concepts. In human psychology, he argues in the Preface, pain is subservient to pleasure as a determinant of feeling and thought.

I would not be misunderstood; but wherever we sympathize with pain it will be found that the sympathy is produced and carried on by subtle combinations with pleasure. We have no knowledge . . . but what has been built up by pleasure, and exists in us by pleasure alone. The Man of Science, the Chemist and Mathematician, whatever difficulties and disgusts they may have had to struggle with, know and feel this. However painful may be the objects with which the Anatomist's knowledge is connected, he feels that his knowledge is pleasure; and where he has no pleasure he has no knowledge.[66]

Applying this distinction more broadly to vital phenomena, we find that life may be jointly determined by the two types of stimulus; but the one type is negative, the other positive. The one warns us what to avoid, the other invites us down the road of destiny. The one states the limitations inherent in the conditions of living; the other suggests the possibilities, the potentialities, of life. The one tells us what life is not, or cannot be; the other what it is, or may be. While therefore the consideration of pain is valuable as a discipline, we must look to pleasure for the meaning, the positive values, of life. The specific character of living tissues is then most fruitfully defined, not by what they turn from, but what they turn *to*.

In "Lines Written in Early Spring," Wordsworth is asserting a literal kinship of man with plants and animals. The means by which "fostering" nature leads birds to function as birds he finds to be pleasure, the gratification of their instincts. Man too he knows to be a creature so organized as to realize his nature through the gratification of his instincts (and his higher powers); and such gratification is pleasure. He realizes how far man has fallen short of his capacity for such gratification. He might have done so much better by himself. But, through mental perversity, through the setting up of mistaken ideals, through a fault in calculation (all this we read into the poem)—through a failure to take his cue from nature (this is there without reading in), he has missed the good life, and the poet must grieve to think "what man has made of man."

And again, in defining nature's plan for man, he leaves out of account the pain which invariably accompanies the life-process, not merely because he regards pleasure as more positively defining the character of life, but also because—being a poet—he is concerned not so much with what life actually is, scientifically observed, as with what it may be if man will apply his thought and exercise his faculty of choice. Science impartially notes that nature is full of pleasure and pain; and may be made to say, without too much stretching of the facts, that living organisms thrive on pleasure. The poet, seizing on this hopeful aspect of things, reminds man that he is capable of pleasure in a high degree, and exhorts him to cultivate to the utmost the capacities with which nature has endowed him.[67]

Nature as a Norm of Conduct

In "Lines Written in Early Spring," the word nature is used, as it has very generally been used throughout the history of thought, as signifying the normal course of things, to which it is wise for man to submit as a matter of hygiene. Nature then is taken as a norm of conduct for man.

John Stuart Mill, in his powerful and clear-headed essay on Nature (written in the 1850's) makes strenuous objection to the error involved, as he believes, in thus making nature a norm of conduct. In his preliminary definitions of nature, he points out that the word may be used in two main senses: as signifying "all the powers existing in either the outer or the inner world and everything which takes place by means of those powers"; or else, "not every thing which happens, but only what takes place without the agency, or without the voluntary and intentional agency, of man." [68] In making nature the guide of our human conduct, we are taking it in the second sense; and this, Mill says, "the order of nature, in so far as unmodified by man, is such as no being, whose attributes are justice and benevolence, would have made, with the intention that his rational creatures should follow it as an example." [69] Mill gives a most impressive account of the ineptitudes and fiendish cruelties inherent in the order of nature. For any one who reads with an open mind he makes it clear that we cannot accept the order of nature as such, without modifications, as inherently benevolent or intelligent in its provision for justice in mortal affairs. He goes on to show how fallacious is the assumption that good invariably results from following our natural instincts or what we consider such. The final conclusion of Mill's argument is this:

The scheme of Nature regarded in its whole extent, cannot have had, for its sole or principal object, the good of human or other sentient beings. What good it brings to them, is mostly the result of their own exertions. Whatsoever, in nature, gives evidence of beneficent design, proves this beneficence to be armed only with limited power; and the duty of man is to co-operate with the beneficent powers, not by imitating but by perpetually striving to amend the course of nature—and bringing that part of it over which we can exercise control, more nearly into conformity with a high standard of justice and goodness.[70]

Mill's essay was an admirable corrective for some of the enthusiastic confusions of romantic poetry and natural theology. But Mill oversimplified the problem to a ridiculous degree, largely through his own Victorian bias in favor of sheer moral discipline, as well as through his false reduction of natural philosophy to mere theology. His program—to amend the course of nature—is at least as naïve and one-sided as the program of the poets—to follow nature. Nowhere in his essay does he suggest whence man derives the high standard of justice and goodness by reference to which he is to amend the course of nature. For a writer like Mill, who endeavors to get along entirely without the notion of distinctively supernatural powers, it would appear on the face of it that any moral standard must be derived, like everything else in human thought, from nature herself in some sense of the word. The distinction which he draws between the two concepts of nature is one very hard to maintain. Whatever happens, with or without the voluntary agency of man, falls under the more comprehensive category, as Mill himself points out.

In any case, this definition of nature as "whatever happens," or "all the powers existing in either the outer or the inner world," fails to do full justice to the philosophic concept of nature, which has in view not so much what happens or the powers which cause it to happen, as the *order* in which it happens, and apparently *must* happen. According to this conception, whatever happens with our voluntary agency, as well as without it, happens in accordance with an *order* of things. And the term nature is a reminder to man that nothing can be brought about in either the outer or the inner world which contravenes the established order of things.

But then, Mill might ask us, how can anything in the world be *unnatural*—how can any act of ours contravene the established order? Strictly speaking, of course, no real thing or act can lie outside the order of nature—except on the assumption of supernatural happenings, which is, I believe, inadmissible for Mill. But however it may be in theory, the distinction between natural and unnatural applies practically to the relation between human objectives and the means chosen for their realization. And the significance of this distinction lies in the fact that man, with some power of choice, is liable to error in the means chosen. Given his objectives, those means are natural which are rightly adapted to realize the objectives; for they conform to the order in which things happen in this world of which we are a part. The object of all science is to ascertain the order in which things come about, and seem bound to come about, in this universe. And the part of wisdom is, given man's objectives, to choose means for their realization which are actually conformable to the ascertained order of nature.

It is also possible that, in the choice of objectives themselves, man may go astray through ignorance of the order in which things are bound to happen in this world. Assuming that, in some sense, the general objective of all men is necessarily their own well-being, it is possible that men, through ignorance, may take for objective some conception of well-being which is simply not capable of realization, since it runs counter to the established order. The order of nature is bewilderingly complicated, and a man has to take into account a large number of interacting forces, and make a difficult and intricate calculation of the net result.

Thus—returning at length to Wordsworth—the poet, in "The Excursion," considers the case of his Solitary. This man, a typical victim of romantic egoism, melancholy and cynicism, has retired to a life of solitude, cutting himself off from humanity—both its tragic sufferings and its fortifying virtues—and sinking deeper and deeper into the bog of his own black thoughts. He does not even take advantage of the "natural" means of maintaining his physical and mental health. And here it is that Wordsworth uses the term nature in the simple sense of norm of conduct. He tells the Solitary not to study so late but to get up early in the morning and climb the mountain daily, and join too in the hunt of the "red deer."

> Take courage, and withdraw yourself from ways
> That run not parallel to nature's course.[71]

Thus the poet, like any doctor, uses the word nature as signifying the laws of health and the close relation between bodily and mental well-being.

At another point in the poem, he uses the word to signify the psychological conditions which, being violated, may result in bodily harm. The Wanderer is telling the story of a poor Magdalene whose lover has fled the country, and who has been set to nurse the child of another couple. She is not allowed to see her own child, and it dies in her absence. And now, whenever she has leave from her service, she goes to the graveyard to indulge her feeling of penitence and grief over the loss of her child. These visits, so necessary to her moral life, she has kept up in spite of their being forbidden by her employers. And so the latter, to enforce their commands, have confined her to the narrow bounds of their garden.

I failed not to remind them that they erred;
For holy Nature might not thus be crossed,
Thus wronged in woman's breast: in vain I pleaded—
But the green stalk of Ellen's life was snapped,
And the flower drooped....[72]

Wordsworth's point is that these employers, for all their good intentions, cut the girl off from an emotional indulgence which was all she had to live by and was consequently essential to her wellbeing, spiritual and physical. And, whether or not his psychological analysis was altogether right, he was justified, assuming it to be right, in using the word nature to signify the conditions necessary to her well-being.

There would be little point in multiplying examples of such use of the word nature, since it is not peculiar to Wordsworth, to poets, or to the Romantic period.

Science, Moral and Physical

The use of nature which we are here exemplifying has a vaguely medical—and so scientific—flavor. But while we have seen how much the speculations of science had probably entered in to form the general concept of nature which Wordsworth assumes, we have also seen that it is a science carefully guided by a religious metaphysic. Indeed, Wordsworth's control upon science—and upon all abstract thinking—is stricter than that. The mind may easily go wrong unless guided by what is called the heart or the imagination and amounts practically to spiritual insight or intuition. This spiritual insight is particularly fostered by communion with the beauty of the external world. And so the science—which enters so largely into the concept of nature—is in turn checked or "controlled" by the direct testimony of nature as esthetically (or sentimentally) apprehended. This is the doctrine of "The Tables Turned" (1798), pendant to "Expostulation and Reply," which latter poem was discussed in the preceding chapter. Wordsworth here continues the theme of "wise passiveness" to the influence of rural nature. Nature, he says, is a better teacher than books.

She has a world of ready wealth,
Our minds and hearts to bless—
Spontaneous wisdom breathed by health,
Truth breathed by cheerfulness.

One impulse from a vernal wood
May teach you more of man,
Of moral evil and of good,
Than all the sages can.

Such is the lore which nature brings;
Our meddling intellect
Mis-shapes the beauteous forms of things:—
We murder to dissect.

Enough of Science and of Art·
Close up those barren leaves;
Come forth, and bring with you a heart
That watches and receives.

It is not unlikely that Wordsworth was influenced in writing these lines by something he had read in Rousseau, or certain ideas of Rousseau which were "in the air" at the time. In the second book of *Émile* Rousseau dwells much on the value for young children of the knowledge that comes to them through their senses in the course of mere animal play. In this connection he makes the distinction (noted in the preceding chapter) between the sensitive reason and the intellectual reason, the former being the foundation of the latter. The sensitive reason is much more active in the child and natural to him; and it is not wise to try to force a too early development of the intellectual reason, which, if forced, will only result in a specious and artificial wisdom. It is on this account that Rousseau objects to the too early inculcation of book learning, which tends to make the child a parrot and a slave to the wisdom of others. A child should be encouraged to express himself in the physical movements and exercises in which he so naturally indulges.

Non-seulement ces exercices continuels, ainsi laissés à la seule direction de la nature, en fortifiant le corps, n'abrutissent point l'esprit; mais au contraire ils forment en nous la seule espèce de raison dont le pre-

mier âge est susceptible, et la plus nécessaire à quelque âge que ce
soit. . . .

Les premiers mouvements naturels de l'homme étant donc de se
mesurer avec tout ce qui l'environne, et d'éprouver dans chaque objet
qu'il aperçoit les qualités sensibles qui peuvent se rapporter à lui, sa première étude est une sorte de physique expérimentale relative à sa propre
conservation, et dont on le détourne par des études spéculatives avant
qu'il ait reconnu sa place ici-bas. . . . Comme tout ce qui entre dans l'entendement humain y vient par les sens, la première raison de l'homme
est une raison sensitive; c'est elle qui sert de base à la raison intellectuelle: nos premiers maîtres de philosophie sont nos pieds, nos mains,
nos yeux. Substituer des livres à tout cela, ce n'est pas nous apprendre
à raisonner, c'est nous apprendre à nous servir de la raison d'autrui;
c'est nous apprendre à beaucoup croire, et à ne jamais rien savoir.[73]

Rousseau more than once expresses his dislike for books taken as a
substitute for first-hand knowledge through experience. "Je hais
les livres; ils n'apprennent qu'à parler de ce qu'on ne sais pas." [74]

Wordsworth in "The Tables Turned" is not apparently considering the distinction thus drawn by Rousseau between childhood
and maturity, but is urging the need, at any period of life, for returning to the testimony of the "sensitive reason" in order to correct the often mistaken conclusions of the "intellectual reason,"
the "meddling intellect." He is not recommending—any more than
Rousseau—an abandonment of books and learning ("Science"),
but is simply urging a restoration of the balance between book-
learning and the direct inspirations of nature. He is also drawing a
distinction, which Rousseau has not here in mind, between the
legitimate and the illegitimate use of the intellectual reason; he is
suggesting that scientific study must be synthetic instead of merely
analytic. It is more than likely that the "Science" he has in mind
here is the moral philosophy [75] of writers like Godwin, against
whom—as has often been shown—he had been reacting vigorously
in the preceding years. This kind of moral science had proved inadequate, as he relates in "The Prelude," to relieve the disenchantment following on his great enthusiasm for the French Revolution.
At this period he made an earnest effort to "anatomize the frame of
social life" and to analyze the mind, so as "to establish in plain day
her titles and her honours." But quite in vain. For he was—

> . . . endlessly perplexed
> With impulse, motive, right and wrong, the ground
> Of obligation, what the rule and whence
> The sanction; till, demanding formal *proof*,
> And seeking it in everything, I lost
> All feeling of conviction, and, in fine,
> Sick, wearied out with contrarieties,
> Yielded up moral questions in despair.[76]

It was in this state of things that his sister Dorothy and country life brought him back "to those sweet counsels between head and heart," whence grew "genuine knowledge, fraught with peace." [77]

These counsels between head and heart are what Wordsworth is recommending in "The Tables Turned." The head uncounseled is a meddler; it has such a penchant for dissection, for taking things apart and leaving them dead! It is only when the elements of an experience are put together again and seen as a whole that they have anything significant to teach us. And therefore it is necessary, in all contacts with nature, to "bring with you a heart that watches and receives."

Here again it may be that Wordsworth was somewhat under the influence of Rousseau. At any rate he was showing himself similarly in rebellion against the dry reason of the *philosophes*,—that rebellion which is so distinctive and radical a feature of the romantic movement as a whole. In the "Profession de foi du vicaire savoyard," which forms a part of the fourth book of *Émile*, Rousseau presents a state of general doubt, and impossibility of arriving at conclusions by purely logical means, similar to that described by Wordsworth in "The Prelude." In such a discouraging state of mind, he realizes that philosophers can only multiply his doubts and that he must necessarily, in order to believe anything, take his interior light for guide.[78] Somewhat later in his discussion, while claiming for himself, as "an active and intelligent being," the "honor of thinking," he recognizes the danger of trusting too much to his mere intellectual reason.

J'oserai prétendre à l'honneur de penser. Je sais seulement que la vérité est dans les choses et non pas dans mon esprit qui les juge, et que moins je mets du mien dans les jugemens que j'en porte, plus je suis sûr d'approcher de la vérité: ainsi ma règle de me livrer au sentiment plus qu'à la raison, est confirmée par la raison même.[79]

"Hence my rule, to yield more to feeling than to reason, is confirmed by reason itself." In this opposition, feeling (sentiment) corresponds to "sensitive reason" and "reason itself" to "intellectual reason." Rousseau's sensitive reason (which is more passive) corresponds to Wordsworth's "heart that watches and receives." One moment of this faculty, under the right conditions, may give us more, as Wordsworth says in his lines "To My Sister," "than years of toiling reason." Toiling reason may be the more active and "intellectual" faculty; but on that very account is more liable to error. If we are deceived, it is not by nature but by ourselves. "Jamais la nature ne nous trompe; c'est toujours nous qui nous trompons." [80]

> Nature never did betray
> The *heart* that loved her . . .[81]

The heart is less apt to be betrayed because it is inspired more directly by the sensitive reason, which is nature's own language.

En suivant toujours ma méthode, je ne tire point ces règles [the principles of ethics] des principes d'une haute philosophie, mais je les trouve au fond de mon coeur écrites par la Nature en caractères ineffaçables.[82]

There is certainly some vagueness or confusion of thought in both Rousseau and Wordsworth. What they are both contending against is the philosophy of mere logical reason. The inspirations of the heart, sentiment, the interior light, which they refer to nature, are what Coleridge and the German idealists would call by some other name—such as intuition—and attribute to anything but nature. Rousseau, Wordsworth, Coleridge, and the German idealists are all equally arguing against the sufficiency of the *Understanding* (*Verstand*) as a guide to truth; but the surer guide, which Wordsworth and Rousseau find in "nature and the language of the sense," Coleridge and the Germans find in the Higher Reason (*Vernunft*), which comes not from nature (the language of the sense), but from some more direct, less fallible—ultimately some supernatural source.[83]

The confidence with which Wordsworth and Rousseau make their appeal to nature from the treacherous findings of the understanding or "intellectual reason" rests ultimately on a religious (but unorthodox) assumption—the assumption that man is naturally good. This is made explicit in Rousseau's *Émile,* as we have earlier seen.

A notable passage in "The Prelude" has its light to throw on this apparent disparagement of "Science" in "The Tables Turned." Here again what the poet has in mind is mainly moral science (or psychology), and he makes much clearer what he means in the earlier poem by saying, "We murder to dissect." Again, he refers primarily, not to anatomical but to psychological dissection. And what he disparages is not so much the dissection of the mind as the failure to recognize the unity of the mind which has thus been divided into its component elements. In the second book of "The Prelude," in acknowledging the greater expertness of Coleridge in the true science of psychology, he is confident of his friend's agreement on this point.

> . . . But who shall parcel out
> His intellect by geometric rules,
> Split like a province into round and square?
> Who knows the individual hour in which
> His habits were first sown even as a seed?
>
> . . . .
>
> . . . Thou, my Friend! art one
> More deeply read in thy own thoughts; to thee
> Science appears but what in truth she is,
> Not as our glory and our absolute boast,
> But as a succedaneum, and a prop
> To our infirmity. No officious slave
> Art thou to that false secondary power
> By which we multiply distinctions, then
> Deem that our puny boundaries are things
> That we perceive, and not that we have made.
> To thee, unblinded by these formal arts,
> The unity of all hath been revealed.[84]

That Wordsworth had no scorn for science as such is evident in the famous and eloquent passage in the Preface to *Lyrical Ballads*, where he says of poetry that it "is the breath and finer spirit of all knowledge; it is the impassioned expression which is in the countenance of all Science." He follows this with an explicit reference to various physical sciences, which, he holds, may become excellent subject-matter for poetic treatment whenever they are sufficiently humanized.

The remotest discoveries of the Chemist, the Botanist, or Mineralogist, will be as proper objects of the Poet's art as any upon which it can be employed, if the time should ever come when these things shall be familiar to us, and the relations under which they are contemplated by the followers of these respective Sciences shall be manifestly and palpably material to us as enjoying and suffering beings. If the time should ever come when what is now called Science, thus familiarised to men, shall be ready to put on, as it were, a form of flesh and blood, the Poet will lend his divine spirit to aid the transfiguration, and will welcome the Being thus produced as a dear and genuine inmate of the household of man.[85]

In "A Poet's Epitaph" (1799), there is a scornful reference to a physical scientist ("physician," "philosopher")—

> One that would peep and botanise
> Upon his mother's grave.

But no real scorn for science is manifest in this reference, which goes along with similar disparaging characterizations of a lawyer, a divine, a soldier, a moralist, and a public man ("statist"). Each one of these is an unsympathetic—because blind and heartless—representative of his profession—all of them set in contrast to the poet, who, weak and idle in comparison with these serious men, is praised for his humane feeling and unpretentious wisdom.

So far as I have observed, the only passage in Wordsworth which might properly be regarded as attacking the general scientific tendencies of his time is that in "The Excursion" where the Wanderer, having praised the Scotch religious reformers for their willingness to look "beyond their own poor natures and above," then

proceeds to ask whether contemporary science is to prove incapable
of the same largeness of view.

> "Now, shall our great Discoverers," he exclaimed,
> Raising his voice triumphantly, "obtain
> From sense and reason, less than these obtained,
> Though far misled? Shall men for whom our age
> Unbaffled powers of vision hath prepared,
> To explore the world without and world within,
> Be joyless as the blind? Ambitious spirits—
> Whom earth, at this late season, hath produced
> To regulate the moving spheres, and weigh
> The planets in the hollow of their hand;
> And they who rather dive than soar, whose pains
> Have solved the elements, or analysed
> The thinking principle—shall they in fact
> Prove a degraded Race? and what avails
> Renown, if their presumption make them such?
> Oh! there is laughter at their work in heaven!
> Inquire of ancient Wisdom; go, demand
> Of mighty Nature, if 'twas ever meant
> That we should pry far off yet be unraised;
> That we should pore, and dwindle as we pore,
> *Viewing all objects unremittingly,*
> *In disconnection dead and spiritless;*
> *And still dividing, and dividing still,*
> *Break down all grandeur*, still unsatisfied
> With the perverse attempt, while littleness
> May yet become more little; waging thus
> An impious warfare with the very life
> Of our own souls!" [86]

In this passage Wordsworth appeals directly from Science (the
short-sighted science of the *philosophes*) to mighty Nature. The
grandeur of the physical world itself, in natural scenery, is invoked
as an antidote to the little views of a "Voltaire." In similar spirit,
earlier in "The Excursion," he has represented the Wanderer as
supplementing his scientific studies with the beauty of external
nature. He studied—

. . . books that explain
The purer elements of truth involved
In lines and numbers, and, by charm severe,
(Especially perceived where nature droops
And feeling is suppressed) preserve the mind
Busy in solitude and poverty.

. . . .

Yet, still uppermost,
Nature was at his heart as if he felt,
Though yet he knew not how, a wasting power
In all things that from her sweet influence
Might tend to wean him. Therefore with her hues,
Her forms, and with the spirit of her forms,
He clothed the nakedness of austere truth.
While yet he lingered in the rudiments
Of science, and among her simplest laws,
His triangles—they were the stars of heaven,
The silent stars! [87]

Implicit Assumptions

Wordsworth does not seem to have been aware to what degree this nature to which he appealed against the false conclusions of science was an ideal construction built up on the basis of scientific theories. There was always a touch of the mystical about his concept of nature, as if it were something to be directly intuited by the imagination. He was not even aware, it seems to me, how many religious and metaphysical assumptions were involved in his faith in nature, and how religion and science worked together to reinforce the emotions which he felt in the presence of her beauteous forms, giving them a spiritual content not to be accounted for in terms of mere esthetics, still less in those of the organic pleasure derived by a healthy animal from movement in the open air. His extreme love of nature was partly the result of associations made habitual in a happy childhood amid country scenes. His conception of nature as something to be worshiped was an inheritance from eighteenth-century literature and sentiment. It was something taken for granted, not seeming to require demonstration or analysis. It was really a very complex construction of the mind, the result of long growth and the coming together of many discrete elements. It involved the scientific notion of nature as an integral whole governed in its operations by constant and uniform laws. It involved the half-metaphysical notion of an active or "spiritual" principle, sufficient to account for the origin of motion, for purposiveness, and for phenomena like gravitation, animation and consciousness. Above all it involved the religious notion of a providence working through the laws and purposiveness of nature with a benevolent view to the well-being of the whole and of mankind in particular.

All these ideas were involved, I take it, in the concept of universal nature which Wordsworth inherited from current eighteenth-century thought. But I do not suppose that he was often clearly conscious of the presence of all or many of these ideas in the background of his sentiment for nature. By what I have called the esthetic synthesis, this concept of universal nature had been intimately associated with the beauty and grandeur, with the peacefulness and stability, or various objects and forms of the visible world. This synthesis is already present in writers like Shaftesbury and many of the poets; but it appears in its intensest and most comprehensive form in Wordsworth. Any of the beauteous forms of nature is sufficient to arouse in him the sentiments appropriate to this range of ideas. It was not necessary for him, in order to feel these sentiments, to recapitulate the various intellectual assumptions involved. Indeed, I think he would have been surprised to learn how many such intellectual assumptions actually were involved. So completely had they been assimilated in his mind to the general concept of nature that they existed there in the form of sentiment rather than of thought. This is one reason why his nature-poetry is so acceptable as poetry. Philosophy appears in it in a guise suitable to the uses of imagination and emotion.

But for all that the philosophy is essential. Take away the intellectual assumptions which are the feeding source of Wordsworth's sentiment for nature, and you will see how fast the color fades from the sentiment itself. Already in Arnold and Tennyson, nature has ceased to be the object of reverent and heart-felt enthusiasm; for it has ceased to be the unmistakable manifestation of divine purposiveness and providence. In Hardy, nature has turned sinister, her teaching dubious or vile. In contemporary poetry, nature has become a box of toys, a stage-set for the puppet-passions of men, or a mere decorative arrangement in form and color. She began to lose her hold on poets' imaginations the moment she ceased to be the exponent of science, of metaphysics and of religion.

CHAPTER VI

NATURE IN WORDSWORTH: SUMMARY

IN THE poetry of Wordsworth, the pleasure taken in the forms of the natural world, especially in rural scenes, is almost invariably associated, more or less consciously, with the thought of universal nature conceived as an orderly system. The esthetic synthesis of Shaftesbury and of many eighteenth-century poets is in him continued and given greater volume, depth and variety of content. The mere imaginative pleasure taken in natural objects is reinforced by the conviction, shared by scientists and theologians alike, that nature, in the whole and in every detail, is the result of providential design. The order of nature may be taken by men as a norm of conduct. The well-being of men is provided for within the frame of nature. With men, as with the lower animals and vegetable organisms, natural impulses tend towards the well-being of the individual, and we are guided by the admonitions of pain and pleasure, especially the latter. Virtue is more natural to us than vice, providing us with greater and more lasting gratifications. Whatever defects are found in life in a narrow view are seen to be, or may be assumed to be, contributory to the general scheme of things and therefore good in the large view. Communion with nature in the country, where her forms have not been obscured by man's artificial inventions, is therefore beneficial to man, leading him as it does to reflection on her benevolent dispositions and harmonies. Wordsworth's preference of country to town, like that of many eighteenth-century poets, is probably somewhat colored by the romantic legend of a Golden Age, in which man's heart and manners were still natural, uncorrupted by institutions and ideas which had swerved from the simplicity of nature. Wordsworth's view of the child and the peasant as beings particularly close to nature and sharing in her wisdom is analogous to the romantic view of the savage, or primitive man, though Wordsworth does not seem to have taken much stock himself in this conception of the "noble savage."

In order to represent the operations of nature as a whole, to account for her (as-it-were) purposive and rational procedure, and to keep clear of the odium and the logical difficulties inherent in pure materialism, or mechanism, Wordsworth, following the lead of many philosophers, theologians and poets, conceives of nature as a spirit, a soul of things, an active principle. This view is given countenance by the speculations of Newton and of many theological expositors of his system. In Newton and in many other scientific and quasi-scientific writers, by the way, there is considerable confusion between two quite distinct conceptions of "spirit"—the scientific conception of a highly subtile form of matter—an animating fluid, a spirit of vegetation, of electricity, of attraction, etc.— and the abstract metaphysical notion of spirit as a "principle" accounting for motion, for all kinds of activity, and for the purposive and rational behavior of the universe. This confusion is to be found in such influential writers as Henry More and Bishop Berkeley, and is not relieved by the strain of platonism that runs through so much philosophy of the time. But this is not the whole story. Further confusion was brought into the matter by a third and distinct conception common in theology—the conception of a spirit as a disembodied "soul" or intelligence, an immaterial person.

It is extremely difficult—it is indeed impossible—to be certain in exactly what proportions these three ways of conceiving spirit entered into Wordsworth's concept of the "spirit of nature." Nothing makes one realize more acutely that we are dealing with a period already half lost in the mists of time than the impossibility of making sure of the exact views of Wordsworth and Shelley, in spite of the wealth of evidence available. I have the impression that both Wordsworth and Shelley are markedly more modern than philosophers like Cudworth and More, or even than Berkeley, notwithstanding the extreme originality and subtlety of mind of the Bishop of Cloyne. The mere passage of time, in less than a century, had made it impossible for these mere poets to fall into ways of expression which were entirely natural to the great philosopher. I am inclined to think that, in Wordsworth's concept of nature, the metaphysical way of conceiving spirit was decidedly dominant. And yet I suppose the romantic conception of nature would never have got itself established in poetry and philosophy if it had not been for the "scientific" and the religious uses of the word spirit which tended to reinforce, to give color and body to, the abstract and shadowy spirit of metaphysics. And it seems obvious that, in romantic use, the words spirit and nature have often a sensible tincture of primitive animism.

Another occasion for uncertainty is inherent in the relation of the spirit of nature to the deity, and in the various and shifting conceptions of deity which complicate the problem of this relation. In certain of the writers who may have influenced Wordsworth, this spirit of the universe is thought of as having its active and rational nature by delegation from the original divine intelligence. In others it is a mechanism set going by the divine intelligence at the beginning and now operating fatally in the grooves laid down by him. In others it is a perpetual emanation of the divine intelligence, who is everywhere present in its operations and so accountable for their rationality and purposiveness. In still others—certain of the French writers in particular—the deity is completely ruled out of the picture, and the machine of the universe works automatically. In general, these latter were not much troubled by the metaphysical scruples which—among other motives—led the more religious writers to refer the rationality of nature, in the last analysis, to the rationality of God. Or it was another set of metaphysical scruples which affected their thought.

There are suggestions in Wordsworth of all of the above-mentioned views, except perhaps that of a machine set going by God in the beginning and now operating fatally. But perhaps it is significant that, in the period of "Tintern Abbey," in his reference to the active principle of the universe, he does not have recourse to the deity in order to explain the goodness and purposiveness of nature. And what makes it significant is the prevalent fashion, in eighteenth-century poems of this character, of referring to nature in terms strongly marked with a kind of platonic deism. It seems possible that Wordsworth was still measurably under the influence of writers like d'Holbach and Godwin, and was desirous of avoiding any suggestion of supernaturalism. He wished perhaps to attribute to nature the self-active power of a non-materialistic philosophy without referring this power to any theological source. Nature seems to have with him at this period a more autonomous character than it has with Cudworth, Shaftesbury, Thomson, or even with Newton. If Wordsworth were more of a systematic philosopher, one might almost suspect that he had for the moment espoused the doctrine of hylozoism,—a doctrine repudiated by Cudworth with such gentle disparagement and by Coleridge with the greater vehemence befitting a time in which there was more danger of its prevailing. So that Wordsworth does perhaps bear out in "Tintern Abbey" the popular view deprecated by Bayle that "whatever one gives to nature is so much taken from the claims of God." His nature-philosophy derived much of its force and many of its characteristic features from theology and theological metaphysics. But it was trying hard to stand by itself as an independent system. It is at any rate true that the main period of Wordsworth's nature-poetry was that in which he was least dominated by the theological doctrines of Christianity. Nature may be regarded as then in very large measure a kind of substitute religion, which we may call the religion of naturalism.

A central problem of naturalism is the place of man and man's spirit in the system of nature. It was Wordsworth's earnest desire to establish man's close kinship with the nature which he revered.

> To her fair works did Nature link
> The human soul that through me ran. . . .

In this he was greatly helped by the associationist psychology, which enabled him to realize how man's spiritual life is built up out of the materials furnished by nature—sensations, as Hartley designates them; the fair forms of nature, as they show themselves to the poet. But even Hartley must start with the soul, in which this building-up process is carried on. Whence comes the soul, and what part does *it* play in the building-up process, are problems not faced by Hartley; the soul is conceived of as a passive recipient of sensations, or as a substance to be shaped by sensations and their derivative ideas. This appears to have been pretty much the situation with Wordsworth at first. But gradually the active part played by a man's own soul, or his creative faculty, the imagination, in shaping the materials offered by the senses, came to be more and more stressed by him.

Many factors doubtless contributed to bring about this radical change of emphasis in Wordsworth's thinking. Fully to explain it would be to give a complete account of Wordsworth's emotional and intellectual life, as this has been given by Professors Legouis and Harper, and more recently and variously by Garrod, Read, Fausset, Herford, Batho and Sperry.[1] The mere influence of Coleridge must be given a major place in the picture. The gradual reaction of Wordsworth against the ideals of the French Revolution, and against all things French, including the religion of reason, would be a factor of great and incalculable importance. This threw him back, in politics, religion and social philosophy, upon views less congenial with the naturalism which he had once espoused. His passion for English scenery lent a glamour to the time-hallowed institutions there enshrined. The very deepening of his patriotism tended to endear to him the national church and restore him more and more to religious orthodoxy. The influence of rationalists and anti-clericals like Godwin gave way to that of theological writers of a traditional stamp. The entire complex of his opinions and emotional reactions came to work against the assumptions of naturalism, just as with Swinburne and Meredith they worked in favor of them. Mr. Read has suggested, with no little plausibility, that his thwarted love-affair in France had wide and continuing reverberations in his intellectual life. He naturally came to distrust the inspirations of "nature," and to rely more and more on the prescriptive admonitions of Duty as voiced by religion. "Me this unchartered freedom tires." During the long period of disenchantment, when he had "given up moral questions in despair," he was compelled to a very vigorous effort of "compensation," sublimation and reconstruction of faith. He was led to have more reliance on various "transcendental" faculties,—on the heart, the intuition, the "higher reason," or on religious faith. It has been variously suggested that, under these circumstances, he was influenced by the philosophy of Rousseau, of Spinoza, of Kant; and it is obvious that he was strongly influenced by the element of "mysticism" which was never absent from Christian theology, even in the eighteenth century.

One result of this change of attitude was the increasing emphasis laid on the creative activity of the poetic imagination. And this brought to the fore a problem which he had scantily provided for in his earlier thinking—the origin of the human soul, of which the imagination is a constituent faculty. However much he might credit nature with a major part in the *education* of the spirit, he had not ruled out the important circumstance that the child comes into existence already possessed of a spirit susceptible of being educated. The soul may be the nurseling of nature, its ward and pupil; but it is not nature's child, but the child of God, "who is our home."

Thus Wordsworth, like so many reflective minds, like some of the greatest of professional philosophers, is a Janus-thinker, facing in two opposite directions. In his naturalist phase, he looks towards the scientific rationalism associated with the names of Newton and Locke. In his "transcendental" phase he looks towards religious intuitionism. His intuitionism serves as a check on his naturalism, and in the end largely replaces it. At his peak of poetic inspiration, represented by "Tintern Abbey," the two tendencies were maintained in equilibrium, and together gave its force to the romantic concept of nature. Ambiguous as this concept may have been—nay, by virtue of its very ambiguity—it was for Wordsworth a fairy wand by which he transformed "the common countenance of earth and sky" into a spiritual paradise, and the children of earth to spirits "trailing clouds of glory."

It is worth reminding ourselves that Wordsworth was seemingly altogether unaffected by the evolutionist views or leanings of his contemporaries, Erasmus Darwin and Goethe. The education of the spirit by nature was for him, as it was for Hartley, an affair confined to the life of the individual human being. It did not occur to him that the human race itself might be the product of a natural process of evolution. With later poets this idea played a larger part in their conception of how man is related to nature, and it enabled some of them, like Swinburne and Meredith, to maintain a naturalism which Wordsworth virtually abandoned. The theory of evolution will therefore be of considerable importance in most of the later chapters of this study. But the impulse given to philosophic nature-poetry by the theory of evolution was not lasting; it was not strong enough to withstand the withering effect of scientific realism. Nor did any of the evolutionary poets command a note as sweet, homely and inspiring as Wordsworth's. Wordsworth is, of all English poets, the one who gave the most impressive and the most emotionally satisfying account of man's relation to universal nature. This is partly due to his peculiar imaginative endowments; and partly to the fact that his poetry held in solution more of the philosophic ideas implied in the "worship of nature" than that of any other English poet, or held them more perfectly in solution.

It is probable that Wordsworth was not fully conscious how many ideas derived from religion and science, as well as from romantic tradition, underlay and gave color to his concept of nature. He was probably not aware of all the metaphysical considerations involved in his view of nature as a spirit or active principle; of the range of considerations involved in his "naturalism," or the precise reasons for his drift away from naturalism. Indeed, it is obvious both in "The Prelude" and "The Excursion" that he was scarcely aware of the radical change of thought involved in the marked, if gradual, change of emphasis in his poetry, by which nature yielded more and more to the constructions of orthodox religion. In the period of his writing when it is most stimulating and inspiring, this is doubtless partly due to the very fact that the intellectual ideas involved are implicit rather than explicit. They are not something that must be labored for and defended by an arduous exercise of the mind. They are something inherited, taken for granted, an element which he took in with the very air he breathed. So that, while his poetry belongs so largely to the category of the reflective, it has, at its best, the sureness, grace and buoyancy of movements and expressions that are instinctive rather than reasoned.

Chapter VII

SHELLEY'S NATURALISM·

THE word nature is much less frequent in Shelley than in Wordsworth. This is partly owing to the fact that he does not attempt,
like Wordsworth, to trace the influence of natural objects in the
development of his imagination. It is partly owing to the poetic
quality which led him, in his mature work, to employ symbolism
in places where Wordsworth used an abstract term. The entire
scenery of "Alastor" (1815) symbolizes that nature which, to the
over-sensitive soul of the poet, furnishes a refuge from the cruelty
and misunderstanding of the world, but which in the long run
proves his undoing. For Shelley brings to poetry a subtler spirit,
a more complicated feeling; he sounds, in this poem, a strong note
of romantic irony, and suggests that nature, whom he loves so
fanatically as "mother of this unfathomable world," may be a fatal
companion for a poet. In later poems—as well as in the earlier
"Queen Mab"—nature is shown in a less dubious light. In "Mont
Blanc" (1816) the sublime mountain symbolizes—

> . . . the secret strength of things
> Which governs thought, and to the infinite dome
> Of Heaven is as a law . . .

The west wind, in the famous "Ode" (1819), symbolizes the variegated power of natural phenomena and nature's promise of a world
reborn to a spirit desolated by the wintry bleakness of the present.
In "The Cloud" (1820) is symbolized the essential oneness of
nature amid her manifold changes of form. In the ode "To a Skylark" (1820) is symbolized the gladness of natural creatures who
are free from the "hate, and pride, and fear" which sadden and

cloud the spirit of man. In "Prometheus Unbound" (1818–19) there is no need for specific reference to abstract nature since she is represented by one of the leading characters in the allegory; and the physical operations of nature are visibly presented in the masque by Earth and Moon and Ocean and other personifications.

The natural scenery of Shelley has a quality very different from Wordsworth's. It is less realistic, less familiar. It is an imaginative composite of features taken from nature and put together in a pattern suitable to the poet's thought and mood. For this reason Shelley is often felt to be less a poet of nature than Wordsworth; he does not follow nature so faithfully, but compels her to ends of his own. In a sense, however, he is more of a nature-poet. For he readily passes beyond the visible shows of nature to the larger cosmic operations in which she manifests her power and direction. His view is less confined to the surface of the earth where man dwells, more free to follow the movements of cloud and tide and lightning; he visits the secret caves of the earth and circles the orbits of the planets. He is more prone to dwell on the forces and processes—electricity, gravity, light, heat, chemical force, vegetation—by which nature is constituted an entity for scientist and mathematician. The sensuous appeal is as rich and constant in Shelley as in Wordsworth; but it is on a different level of experience, less familiar, and calling for a greater stretch of imagination. In the esthetic synthesis of universal nature with individual "beauteous forms," the element of scientific theory is greater and more constant, though Shelley's symbolism often requires a gloss. And in a larger proportion of cases, the word nature with him obviously refers to the philosophical abstraction.

The Order of Nature

It may be considered unfortunate that the word nature is most frequently used, and the philosophy of nature most sharply defined, in an early and markedly inferior poem—"Queen Mab" (1813)—in which Shelley's imagination is thin and conventional, his language bald and feeble, and the "esthetic synthesis" most imperfectly brought about. But for all its crudeness, this poem does

include many important elements—some of them abiding elements
—in Shelley's philosophy of nature; in many ways it is a preliminary
sketch for what he did so magnificently half a dozen years later in
"Prometheus Unbound." And perhaps we should be grateful that
Shelley has left a document in which his ideas are so simply exposed
to the simplest apprehension.

There are many references in "Queen Mab" to the laws of
nature as conceived by science. Or rather the reference is to nature's
law, as conceived by eighteenth-century materialists, with their
penchant for generalizing and simplification, and their frequent
confusion of two distinct meanings of the word. The heavenly
bodies fulfill immutably "eternal nature's law." [1] Nature can be
relied on better than the Christian hell to deal out punishment to
wrong-doers.

> And all-sufficing nature can chastise
> Those who transgress her law. . . .[2]

One of the "laws" of nature for Shelley at this period was for men
to eat no animal food. The flesh of the lamb which man devoured,
"still avenging nature's broken law,"

> Kindled all putrid humours in his frame,
> All evil passions, and all vain belief. . . .[3]

Nature had evidently established vegetarianism as her "law."

It will be seen that Shelley carries even farther than Wordsworth the concept of nature as a norm of conduct for human
beings. The justice of man is but a feeble reflection—nay, often,
perversion—of the justice of nature. Yet Shelley holds, with Rousseau and to some degree with Wordsworth, that the justice of
nature may be found, if man will look candidly, in his own heart.

> Spirit of Nature! no.
> The pure diffusion of thy essence throbs
> Alike in every human heart.
> Thou, aye, erectest there
> Thy throne of power unappealable;

> Thou art the judge beneath whose nod
> Man's brief and frail authority
> Is powerless as the wind
> That passeth idly by.
> Thine the tribunal which surpasseth
> The show of human justice
> As God surpasses man.[4]

The poet Shelley does not tell us by what signs one may recognize the decrees of nature; but throughout the entire period of his writing he takes for granted that he can recognize them. In "The Revolt of Islam" (1817) he declares it to be—

> ... Nature's law divine that those
> Who grow together cannot choose but love,
> If faith or custom do not interpose ...[5]

In "The Cenci" (1819) the son of the Count considers that his father's crimes have freed him from the filial obligations which nature imposed upon him.

> "He has cast Nature off, which was his shield,
> And Nature casts him off, who is her shame."[6]

The Lord Chancellor who refused to Shelley the custody of his own children has overthrown "Nature's landmarks."[7] In "Prometheus Unbound" Shelley regards Truth, Liberty and Love as "Nature's sacred watchwords."[8]

The operations of the universe in its entirety are an expression of "Nature's unchanging harmony."[9] It is not by the decrees of nature that man is vicious and miserable. The youthful Shelley states more crudely than Rousseau, more crudely even than Godwin, the doctrine that it is false institutions that have corrupted the natural goodness of man.

> ... Nature!—no!
> Kings, priests, and statesmen blast the human flower
> Even in its tender bud.[10]

Nature is the eternal, the changeless element in the universe.[11] But it is inherent in her law to bring about the regeneration of a corrupt and ailing world. The fairy guide and prophet in "Queen Mab" assures the spirit of Ianthe that humanity will not be forever slavish and bloody.

> Now, to the scene I show, in silence turn,
> And read the blood-stained charter of all woe,
> Which nature soon, with recreating hand,
> Will blot in mercy from the book of earth.[12]

This work of regeneration will be brought about by man whenever he consents to be reunited with nature and work in concert with her law.

> How sweet a scene will earth become!
> Of purest spirits, a pure dwelling-place,
> Symphonious with the planetary spheres;
> When man, with changeless nature coalescing,
> Will undertake regeneration's work. . . .[13]

This bald and jejune statement in "Queen Mab" is of the utmost importance for the interpretation of Shelley's refined symbolism in "Prometheus Unbound." For the central allegory of that poem has to do with the regeneration of the world which is to come about when man (Prometheus) "coalesces" with changeless nature (Asia). It is true that Asia stands for much more than mere nature as conceived in "Queen Mab." She obviously stands for Love as well, and love conceived in a comprehensive platonic fashion. So that she may be said to represent, like Prometheus himself, one of the elements essential to an ideal humanity. But she is also associated in Shelley's allegory with the benevolent order of nature, from which it is possible for man to be temporarily divorced, but with which he must be reunited in order to secure his happiness and restore the world to its perfection.

The history of Shelley's naturalism is roughly parallel to that of Wordsworth's. Naturalism was at first even more dominant in Shelley's view; and it gradually tended to yield, as in Wordsworth, to a more mystical philosophy, made necessary largely by the difficult problems concerned with the nature and origin of the human spirit.

Shelley's naturalism was, in the beginning, of a much more extreme type than Wordsworth's. Wordsworth started with a sort of pantheism, derived mainly from current English poetry. Shelley started with a sort of atheism derived perhaps from current French philosophy. It is known that Shelley had been at an early age a diligent reader of Helvétius, d'Holbach, Condorcet, and Volney, as well as of the English Godwin; [14] and from some or all of these he may have derived the view of nature expressed with so much definiteness—so much baldness and prosiness indeed—in "Queen Mab."

In this poem the Fairy, who corresponds roughly to the didactic phantom of Volney's *Ruines*, conveys the Spirit of the girl Ianthe in his magic car into the midst of the astronomical heaven, which with its rolling and innumerable systems seems the most fitting temple for the "Spirit of Nature," though "not the lightest leaf that quivers to the passing breeze is less instinct with" this spirit.[15] It is clear that Shelley, like other poets of his day, was most deeply impressed, among the operations of nature, with those which came within the compass of Newton's synthesis. But he too was eager to extend the conception of immutable law beyond physics and astronomy into the realm of human life and morality. The Fairy and the Spirit enter a Hall of Spells—a place of instruction, in which the secrets of the future are to be revealed. Then approaching the parapet which separates the palace from the heavenly abysses—

> There, far as the remotest line
> That bounds imagination's flight,
>   Countless and unending orbs
> In mazy motion intermingled,
> Yet still fulfilled immutably
>   Eternal nature's law.
>   Above, below, around
>   The circling systems formed
>   A wilderness of harmony;
>   Each with undeviating aim,

> In eloquent silence, through the depths of space
>   Pursued its wondrous way.
>   . . . .
>
>   The Fairy pointed to the earth.
>   The spirit's intellectual eye
>   Its kindred beings recognized.
> The thronging thousands, to a passing view,
>   Seemed like an anthill's citizens.
>   How wonderful! that even
> The passions, prejudices, interests,
> That sway the meanest being, the weak touch
>   That moves the finest nerve,
>   And in one human brain
> Causes the faintest thought, becomes a link
>   In the great chain of nature.[16]

Necessarianism

The great chain of nature is a commonplace of eighteenth-century philosophy. The phrase occurs in d'Holbach, for one, a writer from whom Shelley quotes extensively in the notes to "Queen Mab." D'Holbach was bent on showing that man is himself the work of nature, subject to her laws, unable to extricate himself from their web, unable even to conceive getting clear from the cycle of natural law. In the first chapter of his *Système de la Nature*, d'Holbach points out what an error it is to try to distinguish between man as physical and man as a moral being. "Moral man is nothing but this physical being considered from a certain point of view," etc.[17] In a later chapter d'Holbach makes out that the moral activity of man is identical in essence with the physical activity of matter.

La conservation est donc le but commun vers lequel toutes les énergies, les forces, les facultés des êtres semblent continuellement dirigées. Les Physiciens ont nommé cette tendance ou direction, *gravitation sur soi;* Newton l'appelle *force d'inertie;* les Moralistes l'ont appellée dans l'homme *amour de soi;* qui n'est que la tendance à se conserver, le désir du bonheur, l'amour du bien-être et du plaisir, la promptitude à saisir tout ce qui paroît favorable à son être, et l'aversion marquées pour tout ce qui le trouble ou le menace; sentimens primitifs

et communs de tous les êtres de l'espèce humain, que toutes leurs
facultés s'efforcent de satisfaire, que toutes leurs passions, leurs volontés,
leurs actions ont continuellement pour objet et pour fin. Cette *gravitation sur soi* est donc une disposition nécessaire dans l'homme et dans
tous les êtres, qui par des moyens divers, tendent à persévérer dans
l'existence qu'ils ont reçue, tant que rien ne dérange l'ordre de leur
machine ou sa tendance primitive.[18]

A variant of this mechanical account of man's motivation is
found in Volney's *Ruines*, which is known to have had a strong
influence on several of Shelley's poems, and from which he quotes
in the notes to "Queen Mab." In Volney's fifth chapter, the wise
phantom instructs the author that there is no use in man's referring
his ills to fate, or to any obscure agents or mysterious causes.

Que l'homme connaisse ces lois! *qu'il comprenne la nature des êtres
qui l'environnent, et sa propre nature,* et il connaîtra les moteurs de sa
destinée; il saura quelles sont les causes de ses maux, et quelles peuvent
en être les remèdes. Quand la *puissance secrète* qui *anime l'univers*
forma le globe que l'homme habite, elle imprima aux êtres qui le compose des *propriétés essentielles* qui devinrent la *règle* de leurs mouvemens individuels, le lien de leurs rapports réciproques, la cause de
l'harmonie de l'ensemble; par-là, elle établit un ordre régulier de causes
et d'effets, de principes et de conséquences, lequel, *sous une apparence
de hasard,* gouverne l'univers et maintient l'équilibre du monde: ainsi,
elle attribua au feu le mouvement de l'activité. . . . elle ordonna à la
flamme de monter, à la pierre de descendre, à la plante de végéter; à
l'homme, *voulant l'exposer au choc* de tant d'êtres divers, et cependant
préserver sa vie fragile, elle lui donna la faculté *de sentir.* Par cette
faculté, toute action nuisible à son existence lui porta une sensation de
mal et de *douleur;* et toute action favorable, une sensation de *plaisir* et
de *bien-être.* Par ces sensations, l'homme, tantôt détourné de ce qui
blesse ses sens, et tantôt entrainé vers ce qui les flatte, a été *nécessité
d'aimer* et de *conserver sa vie.* Ainsi, *l'amour de soi, le désir du bien-
être, l'aversion de la douleur,* ont été les *lois essentielles et primordiales
imposés à l'homme par la NATURE même;* les lois que la puissance
ordonnatrice quelconque a établies pour le gouverner, et qui, semblables
à celles *du mouvement dans le monde physique,* sont devenues le principe
simple et fécond de *tout ce qui s'est passé dans le monde moral* . . .[19]

So Volney and d'Holbach bring in together two famous eighteenth-century doctrines—the doctrine of self-interest and that
of necessity in the moral world. The doctrine of self-interest

is particularly strong with the French writers, and is, I believe, logically essential to this way of explaining human motives. But it was repudiated or modified by Godwin and other English writers of this school; it plays no appreciable part, so far as I know, in the philosophy of Shelley; and therefore I will not pursue it further.

The doctrine of necessity is common to all these writers, French and English, including men so influential with the poets as Hartley, Godwin and Priestley. It is stated compactly by d'Holbach in the following terms:

La nécessité est la liaison infaillible et constant des causes avec leurs effets. Le feu brule nécessairement les matières combustibles qui sont placée dans la sphère de son action. L'homme désire nécessairement ce qui est, ou ce qui paroît, utile à son bien-être. La nature dans tous ces phénomènes agit nécessairement d'après l'essence qui lui est propre; tous les êtres qu'elle renferme, agissent nécessairement d'après leurs essences particulières; c'est par le mouvement que tout a des rapports avec ses parties et celles-ci avec le tout; c'est ainsi que tout est lié dans l'univers; il n'est lui-même qu'une chaîne immense de causes et d'effets, qui sans cesse découlent les unes des autres.[20]

With this one may compare the first sentence from Shelley's long note on Necessity: "He who asserts the doctrine of Necessity means that, contemplating the events which compose the moral and material universe, he beholds only an immense and uninterrupted chain of causes and effects, no one of which could occupy any other place than it does occupy, or act in any other place than it does act." [21]

This doctrine of necessity, working in the material and moral worlds, is stated in most uncompromising accents by Shelley in "Queen Mab." Necessity is there simply another name for the "Universal Spirit" or the "Spirit of Nature,"

> A spirit of activity and life,
> That knows no term, cessation, or decay.

It is "wide diffused" through the "infinite orbs of mingling light"; it guides the whirlwind, works through disease and health,

Rolls round the eternal universe, and shakes
Its undecaying battlements, presides,
Apportioning with irresistible law
The place each spring of its machine shall fill.

In a storm at sea, while to the eye of the mariner,

All seems unlinked contingency and chance:
No atom of this turbulence fulfils
A vague and unnecessitated task,
And acts but as it must and ought to act.
Even the minutest molecule of light
That in an April sunbeam's fleeting glow
Fulfils its destined though invisible work,
The universal Spirit guides; nor less,
When merciless ambition, or mad zeal,
Has led two hosts of dupes to battlefield,
That, blind, they there may dig each other's graves,
And call the sad work glory, does it rule
All passions: not a thought, a will, an act,
No working of the tyrant's moody mind,
Nor one misgiving of the slaves who boast
Their servitude, to hide the shame they feel,
Nor the events enchaining every will
That from the depths of unrecorded time
Have drawn all-influencing virtue, pass
Unrecognized, or unforeseen by thee,
Soul of the Universe! eternal spring
Of life and death. . . . etc.
Spirit of Nature! all-sufficing Power,
Necessity! thou mother of the world.[22]

To this passage Shelley appended two notes. The first is a citation from d'Holbach, in which the principle of necessity is illustrated by examples taken from the physical and the moral worlds.
These examples correspond to those given by Shelley, and doubtless represent the "source" of the entire passage in "Queen Mab."
The first example is that of a storm, in which not a single molecule
of dust or water was placed by chance, but "chaque molécule agit

précisément comme elle doit agir, et ne peut agir autrement qu'elle ne fait." The second example follows:

Dans les convulsions terribles qui agitent quelque-fois les sociétés politiques, et qui produisent souvent le renversement d'un empire, il n'y a pas une seule action, une seule parole, une seule pensée, une seule volonté, une seule passion dans les agens qui concourent à la révolution comme destructeurs ou comme victimes, qui ne soit nécessaire, qui n'agisse comme elle doit agir, qui n'opère infailliblement les effets qu'elle doit opérer, suivant la place qu'occupent ces agens dans ce tourbillon moral. Cela paroîtroit évident pour une intelligence qui sera en état de saisir et d'apprécier toutes les actions et réactions des esprits et des corps de ceux qui contribuent à cette révolution.[23]

The second and very long note of Shelley is an exposition of the philosophy of necessity, with an attempt to reconcile it with the action of the will and to indicate how it affects religious beliefs and the attitude towards good and evil. While there are some parts of this discussion that resemble views of d'Holbach, it may have been inspired by Priestley, Godwin or other popular English writers.

The word necessity ceases to be prominent in the finer poetry of Shelley's later years. And in the evolution of Shelley's thought, the deterministic implications tend to fade out of the idea of necessity even when the word is used. In "Prometheus Unbound" much stress is laid on the will as a determining factor in the moral world. As Shelley becomes confirmed in his faith that existence is spiritual in essence, it is no longer possible to conceive of necessity in materialistic terms. The paramount force in the universe is "eternal Love," the sole power not subject to "Fate, Occasion, Chance, and Change." This is the statement of the oracular Demogorgon, himself a refined symbol of Necessity. The Necessity he symbolizes takes on the character of Destiny as conceived by the Greek tragedians. It takes on, too, a platonic cast; for Demogorgon defines himself as Eternity. What he ushers in is "eternal Love," another platonic conception. The process of the world is, in "Prometheus," clearly conducted by moral forces; and the entire myth is more or less associated with the platonic doctrine of the One and the Many. The perfected state of man on earth which is ushered in by Demogorgon's destruction of Jupiter is associated with the timeless eternal state from which man has been separated by the conditions of mortality. The journey of Asia to the cave of Demogorgon is symbolic of the return of the soul, through the perturbations of mortal existence, back to the unconditioned state of pre-existence.

But the synthesis of Shelley's naturalism and his platonism is anything but perfectly accomplished. And in "Prometheus" we still find lingering traces of the earlier necessarian concept. There is one significant passage in particular—a passage left unexplained, so far as I know, by the commentators—which can best be understood in the light of this concept.

It is in the second scene of the second act. Asia and Panthea have been summoned by dreams to the cave of Demogorgon. They are passing through a dense and flowering forest, through which sounds the voluptuous music of amorous nightingales. The passage I am about to quote suggests that this forest of exquisite odorous flowers and bird-songs symbolizes the life of the senses and desire, the natural human life through which we make our way into the infinitude of the spirit. And then comes the passage in which it is stated clearly enough that the very desires of sense which we follow, or think we follow, of our own will, are but the impulsions of necessity driving us on to our destiny.

> There those enchanted eddies play
> 　　Of echoes, music-tongued, which draw,
> 　　By Demogorgon's mighty law,
> 　　With melting rapture, or sweet awe,
> All spirits on that secret way;
> 　　As inland boats are driven to Ocean
> Down streams made strong with mountain-thaw:
> 　　And first there comes a gentle sound
> 　　To those in talk or slumber bound,
> 　　And wakes the destined soft emotion,—
> Attracts, impels them; those who saw
> 　　Say from the breathing earth behind
> 　　There streams a plume-uplifting wind
> Which drives them on their path, while they
> 　　Believe their own swift wings and feet
> The sweet desires within obey . . .

Necessity, then, or nature, employs man's very desire for pleasure as the means of drawing or driving him on the path she wishes him to follow. This is the poetical way of expressing the hopeful utilitarian doctrine common to d'Holbach, Condorcet and Volney, to Hartley, Godwin, Erasmus Darwin and Bentham, that men become social and moral beings through the natural working of their desire to avoid pain and secure pleasure. They all believed more or less fervently in the necessary betterment of mankind by the pursuance of this natural law. Perhaps the neatest statement is that of Volney:

Cette amélioration devient un effet nécessaire des lois de la nature; car, par *la loi de la sensibilité*, l'homme tend aussi invinciblement à se rendre heureux, que *le feu à monter*, que la pierre à graviter, que l'eau *à se niveler*. Son obstacle est son *ignorance*, qui l'égare dans les moyens, qui le trompe sur les effets et les causes. A force d'expérience il s'éclairera; à force d'erreurs il se redressera; il deviendra sage et bon, *parce qu'il est de son intérêt de l'être*. . . .[24]

Shelley may well have supposed that, in "Prometheus," he had succeeded in reconciling the necessarian doctrine with the platonic concept of "eternal Love" as the moving power. To the critical reader the joining of the two conceptions appears imperfect. In the following chapter I give further evidence of the confusions resulting from his attempt to combine naturalistic with platonic views.

Necessity, Atheism, and the Animating Principle

The conception of necessity as the law of nature carries with it, for Shelley, as for many of the French philosophers, the corollary of atheism. Necessity is an "all-sufficing" Power because it rules out the notion of arbitrary and capricious interference, of anything which would confuse or interrupt the working of natural law. With Shelley the intellectual and the moral arguments for atheism were perhaps equally powerful. In "Queen Mab," as in "The Revolt of Islam" (1817), there are numerous references, in the tone of Volney, to the wars, the crime, the tyranny, and various other evils associated with religion and caused by it. But the intellectual reasons are equally strong, and are introduced in close connection with the moral ones. In "Queen Mab" the Spirit of Ianthe relates how her mother had taken her when an infant to see the burning of an atheist, and how when the child wept over the cruel scene her mother had comforted her.

> Weep not, child! cried my mother, for that man
> Has said, There is no God.

Whereupon the Fairy confirms this declaration of faith by reference to the testimony of Nature.

> There is no God!
> Nature confirms the faith his death-groan sealed:
> Let heaven and earth, let man's revolting race,
> His ceaseless generations tell their tale;
> Let every part depending on the chain
> That links it to the whole, point to the hand
> That grasps its term! let every seed that falls
> In silent eloquence unfold its store
> Of argument: infinity within,
> Infinity without, belie creation;
> The exterminable spirit it contains
> Is nature's only God; but human pride
> Is skilful to invent most serious names
> To hide its ignorance.[25]

Thus Shelley has made a curious reversal of the argument Coleridge uses to demonstrate the need for assuming a spirit beyond nature. Since each cause in the sequence is itself caused, reasons Coleridge, nothing in nature can be regarded as more than a link in a chain. "The moment we assume an origin in nature, a true *beginning*, an actual first—that moment we rise *above* nature, and are compelled to assume a *supernatural* power." Just so! reasons Shelley. But to assume a supernatural power is to assume something inconceivable. We cannot conceive of a hand grasping the chain at its beginning. All that we know is the chain of causes extending backward and forward *ad infinitum*. We cannot conceive of a link in the chain which was not itself caused; hence we cannot conceive creation. Men invent gods in their own evil image. But the only divinity in nature is "the exterminable spirit it contains." As Shelley expresses the matter in the note appended to this passage, taking his cue from Hume's famous exposition:

The only idea which we can form of causation is derivable from the constant conjunction of objects, and the consequent inference of one from the other. In a case where two propositions are diametrically opposite, the mind believes that which is least incomprehensible;—it is easier to suppose that the universe has existed from all eternity, than to conceive a being beyond its limits capable of creating it; if the mind sinks beneath the weight of one, is it an alleviation to increase the intolerability of the burthen?

. . . .

There certainly is a generative power which is effected by certain instruments: we cannot prove that it is inherent in these instruments; nor is the contrary hypothesis capable of demonstration: we admit that the generative power is incomprehensible; but to suppose that the same cause is produced by an eternal, omniscient, omnipotent being, leaves the cause in the same obscurity, but renders it more incomprehensible.[26]

The great interest of Shelley's argument in our discussion is that the idea of God is ruled out as being inconsistent with the idea of nature.[27]

Similar reasoning Shelley puts in the mouth of Cythna in "The Revolt of Islam." She is arguing against the peoples' vain notion of "some Power" that "builds for man in solitude."

> What is that Power? Ye mock yourselves, and give
>   A human heart to what ye cannot know:
> As if the cause of life could think and live!
>   'Twere as if man's own works should feel, and show
>   The hopes and fears and thoughts from which they flow,
> And he be like to them! [28]

We who think and live, Shelley argues, are by that very fact finite and limited, subject to the law of necessity. The cause of life itself must be outside all such limitations; it cannot therefore be a thinking and knowing creature; it cannot be what men call God. Shelley prefers to call it necessity.

In substituting the words Nature or Necessity for God, Shelley wished to emphasize his deterministic conception of the universe, especially strong in the earlier years of his writing, and to get rid of the theological connotations of the word God. He could not of course, any more than other nature poets, get rid of the notion of an active principle working in nature. For this active principle he has a variety of terms, such as "the universal Spirit" and the "spirit of activity and life." More frequent in the later poems is some variant of the word power. Thus in "The Revolt of Islam" we read:

> . . . we know not whence we live,
> Or why, or how, or what mute Power may give
> Their being to each plant and star and beast,
> Or even these thoughts.[29]

In the "Hymn to Intellectual Beauty" (1816),

> The awful shadow of some unseen Power
> Floats tho' unseen among us.

In this more platonic conception the active principle of the universe is represented in the terms of "intellectual Beauty," but it is the same universal Spirit of which Shelley speaks in "Queen Mab." And there is the same insistence that this unseen power is not the God of theology, but remains the mysterious force which animates nature and is to be interpreted only in terms of nature. Shelley speaks of his efforts as a youth to get an answer to the riddle in religious terms, and states categorically that no response is ever given to such vain questions.

> No voice from some sublimer world has ever
> To sage or poet these responses given—
> Therefore the names of Demon, Ghost, and Heaven,
> Remain the records of their vain endeavor . . .

In the same year with the "Hymn to Intellectual Beauty" he has another phrasing of the concept of the active principle as power. In his "Mont Blanc," he takes the snow capped mountain as a sym-

bol of that principle, or force, whatever it may be, that animates
the universe of material and spiritual beings.

> The secret strength of things
> Which governs thought, and to the infinite dome
> Of heaven is as a law, inhabits thee!

Whether or not he is here echoing Volney, he is using the exact
phrase which occurs in the passage quoted above, "*la puissance
secrète qui anime l'univers.*" [30] Note that Volney repeats the phrase,
with a variation, in the same passage: "les lois que la puissance
ordonnatrice quelconque a établies pour le gouverner" (the laws
which the legislative power, whatever it is, established to govern
man). Shelley is particularly fond of using the word Strength (or
Power) with the word "secret" or some equivalent, suggesting that
the animating principle of the universe is mysterious and unsound-
able. By Demogorgon's mighty law, the echoes draw "all spirits on
that secret way." We do not know "what mute Power" may give
their being to the various creatures of nature. It is "the awful
shadow of some unseen Power" that floats among us. In "The Revolt of Islam" Cythna speaks of—

> Necessity, whose sightless strength for ever
>   Evil with evil, good with good, must wind
> In bands of union which no power may sever.[31]

In "Alastor" the poet thus addresses nature:

> Mother of this unfathomable world!
> Favour my solemn song, for I have loved
> Thee ever, and thee only; I have watched
> Thy shadow, and the darkness of thy steps,
> And my heart ever gazes on the depths
> Of thy deep mysteries.[32]

It is curious how often these expressions, which have so strong
a flavor of the mysteries of religion, occur in passages where Shelley, like Volney, was most expressly repudiating the religious interpretation. They are the nature-poet's substitute for the mysteries

of religion. This is a not infrequent phenomenon. We have found it in the early poems of Wordsworth, and we shall find it in Emerson and Swinburne. At times, there is a startling resemblance between the phrasing of the nature-poet and the religious poet. Such is the passage in "Adonais" (1821), so strongly reminiscent of Coleridge:

> . . . he doth bear
> His part, while the one Spirit's plastic stress
> Sweeps through the dull, dense world, compelling there
> All new successions to the forms they wear. . . .[33]

But here, of course, the nature-poet has pretty much given way to the mystic platonist. Only there remains the word "compelling" to remind one of the lingering notion of Necessity.

Psychology: d'Holbach, Erasmus Darwin

It will be observed how definitely Shelley, in his early work, ranges man's moral life, along with the physical world, under the general rule of necessity. But, aside from certain suggestions that necessity works in motiving man through the beneficent effects of pleasurable desire, Shelley seems to have occupied himself very little with the problem of how man's psychical life is built up by natural means, and still less with the problem of how it might have originated within the chain of nature. He does not even go so far as d'Holbach in signalizing the probability that man is a production of the earth in temporal history. The nearest he seems to have come to a reference to this problem is in his note defending a vegetarian diet.

> The origin of man, like that of the universe of which he is a part, is enveloped in impenetrable mystery. His generations either had a beginning, or they had not. The weight of evidence in favour of these suppositions seems tolerably equal; and it is perfectly unimportant to the present argument which is assumed.[34]

There is a corresponding passage in d'Holbach, in which he says that the student of nature is free to assume that the human race was produced "either in time or from all eternity"; but that certain considerations favor the former view.

Cependant quelques réflexions semblent favoriser ou rendre plus probable l'hypothèse que l'homme est une production faite dans le tems, particulière au Globe que nous habitons, qui par conséquent ne peut dater que de la formation de ce globe lui-même, et qui est un résultat des loix particulières qui le dirigent.[35]

And d'Holbach proceeds to discuss how man, like other animals, conforms to the physical environment in which he finds himself; our earth having produced a considerable variety of living things in accordance with the variety of the climate.

Thus d'Holbach goes farther than Shelley in his speculations on the origin of the race. And in his speculations on the working of self-interest, of the natural instinct for "conservation" and the necessary impulse to seek happiness, he sketches vaguely an outline of human psychology within the frame of nature. The nearest Shelley comes to anything of this kind is his reference in a note to "Queen Mab" to Locke as having "traced all knowledge to sensation." [36]

This abstention of Shelley's is the more surprising in view of his acquaintance with Hartley and his apparently intimate acquaintance with Erasmus Darwin's *Temple of Nature* (1803). In this poem and the accompanying notes, Darwin, following in the footsteps of Locke and Hartley, has built up an elaborate theory of the origin of the human mind as a part of the general evolutionary process. This is contained mainly in the third canto of *The Temple of Nature*, entitled "Progress of the Mind," following on the account, in Canto I, of the spontaneous generation and natural evolution of life on the earth. A general outline of the whole process is first given.

> Immortal Guide! O now with accents kind
> Give to my ear the progress of the Mind.
> How loves and tastes and sympathies commence
> From evanescent notices of sense?
> How from the yielding touch and rolling eyes
> The piles immense of human science rise?—

>   With mind gigantic steps the puny Elf,
>   And weighs and measures all things but himself.

Then, more in detail, the poet exhibits the progressive development of the four "sensorial powers" of Irritation, Sensation, Volition and Association.

>   First the new actions of the excited sense,
>   Urged by appulses from without, commence;
>   With these exertions pain or pleasure springs,
>   And forms perceptions of external things.
>   Thus, when illumined by the solar beams,
>   Yon waving woods, green lawns, and sparkling streams,
>   In one bright point by rays converging lie
>   Plann'd on the moving tablet of the eye;
>   The mind obeys the silver goads of light,
>   And IRRITATION moves the nerves of sight.
>   These acts repeated rise from joys or pains,
>   And swell Imagination's flowing trains . . .
>   . . . .
>   Each passing form the pausing heart delights,
>   And young SENSATION every nerve excites.
>   Oft from sensation quick VOLITION springs,
>   When pleasure thrills us, or when anguish stings;
>   Hence Recollection calls with voice sublime
>   Immersed ideas from the wrecks of Time . . .
>   . . . .
>   Hence Reason's efforts good with ill contrast,
>   Compare the present, future, and the past . . .
>   . . . .
>   And last Suggestion's mystic power describes
>   Ideal hosts arranged in trains or tribes.
>   So when the Nymph with volant finger rings
>   Her dulcet harp, and shakes the sounding strings;
>   As with soft voice she trills the enamour'd song,
>   Successive notes, unwill'd, the strain prolong;
>   The transient trains ASSOCIATION steers,
>   And sweet vibrations charm the astonish'd ears.

In this Canto there follows an account of the fineness of sensation in brutes, and man's finer organ of touch, which results in his

sense of form and the consequent development of ideas. There is
an account of the development of language, with the intellectual
power consequent upon it, and of the development of reason in
man, resulting from his clear ideas and his power of recollection.

> Whence REASON's empire o'er the world presides,
> And man from brute, and man from man divides.

In these lines, according to Leopold Brandl, in his study of this
poem, Darwin made a great step forward in evolutionary theory
by interposing a link between man and the unreasoning brutes—
namely, a class of men of lower intellectual powers than those of
the present race.[37]

In the Additional Notes appended to the poem, Darwin develops
his theory of the animal and mental faculties in more scientific
language, agreeing with his earlier exposition in the prose treatise,
Zoönomia; or, The Laws of Organic Life (1794–96). In order
that the reader may appreciate how carefully Darwin worked out
his system, and on how strictly naturalistic, not to say materialistic
a basis, I will quote a considerable portion of his note on the Faculties of the Sensorium.

I. The fibres, which constitute the muscles and organs of sense,
possess a power of contraction. The circumstances attending the exertion of this power of contraction constitute the laws of animal motion,
as the circumstances attending the exertion of the power of attraction
constitute the laws of motion of inanimate matter.

II. The spirit of animation is the immediate cause of the contraction
of animal fibres, it resides in the brain and the nerves, and is liable to
general or spatial diminution or accumulation.

III. The stimulus of bodies external to the moving organ is the remote cause of the original contractions of animal fibres.

IV. A certain quantity of stimulus produces irritation, which is an
exertion of the spirit of animation exciting the fibres into contraction.

V. A certain quantity of contraction of animal fibres, if it be perceived at all, produces pleasure; a greater or less quantity of contraction, if it be perceived at all, produces pain; these constitute sensation.

VI. A certain quantity of sensation produces desire or aversion;
these constitute volition.

VII. All animal motions which have occurred at the same time, or in
immediate succession, become so connected, that when one of them is

reproduced, the other has a tendency to accompany or succeed it. When fibrous contractions succeed or accompany other fibrous contractions, the connexion is termed association; when fibrous contractions succeed sensorial motions, the connexion is termed causation; when fibrous and sensorial motions reciprocally introduce each other, it is termed catenation of animal motions.

VIII. These four faculties of the sensorium during their inactive state are termed irritability, sensibility, voluntarity, and associability; in their active state they are termed as above irritation, sensation, volition, association.

The rest of the note is a more specific indication of the physiology of these various operations in the sensorium, which is defined as—

. . . not only the medullary part of the brain, spinal marrow, nerves, organs of sense and muscles, but also at the same time that living principle, or spirit of animation, which resides throughout the body, without being cognizable to our senses except by its effects.

In this system of physiology and psychology, which doubtless owes much to Hartley, fibrous contractions seem to have taken the place of the Hartleian vibrations. In addition to this physiology of the mind, Darwin has a kind of social psychology, based in the physical relations of parenthood and sexual love, and in the perception of ideal beauty (arising from the sense of touch) and the impulse of imitation. Parental love (personified as Storgè) is the "first chain of society," giving rise to tender affections.[38] The second chain of society is sexual love, personified by Cupid and Psyche.[39] The third chain of society is ideal beauty, typified by Eros, beloved of Dione.[40] And the "great bond of society" is Christian morality, typified by the Seraph Sympathy, derived from imitation.[41]

This system of psychology is something unique in English poetry. The nearest approach to it is found perhaps in Bridges' "Testament of Love." Something roughly equivalent is implied in Meredith's celebration of the human spirit as the offspring of "blood and brain"; but Meredith does not attempt to give this view a scientific basis in physiology. I have paid so much attention to Darwin's system because of its theoretical interest, and also by way of signalizing the fact that so striking a theory was entirely ignored by Shelley, in spite of his acquaintance with the poem in which it appears. As for his reasons for thus ignoring it, we can only guess. It may be that it seemed to him too speculative, too little grounded in objective and tested knowledge, and that it lacked the validity of other scientific theories which he did borrow from Darwin. It may be that it seemed to him not to meet the real metaphysical difficulties presented by epistemology. It may be that already his readings in Plato and the neoplatonists had predisposed him against so purely materialistic an account of the origin of the human spirit, even though he could accept d'Holbach's materialistic conception of its manner of operation within the chain of necessity. Whatever the reasons, Darwin's theory of the evolution of mind did not "take" with Shelley, and this proved a circumstance of prime importance in the later development of his philosophy. It may partly account for the dominance of a "platonism" which did so much to vitiate his original naturalism.

"Prometheus Unbound"

The culmination of Shelley's naturalism is "Prometheus Unbound," and this in spite of the mystical platonism with which it is there associated. A profoundly naturalistic tendency is shown both in the particular scientific theories which are made so prominent and in the general philosophical doctrine of the poem. This doctrine is obviously naturalistic, in the manner of d'Holbach, Condorcet and Godwin, in its sharp contrast with orthodox Christian philosophy. The faith in human perfectibility upon this planet takes the place of the Christian doctrine of the fall of man and the whole scheme of redemption. An earthly millennium takes the place of the Christian heaven. The operation of destiny—mythical form of necessity—in bringing about this earthly millennium, takes the place of divine providence and the atonement. In the person of Prometheus, man wins his salvation by the exercise of his own will (under the dominion of necessity) and by the exertion of his own intellectual and moral faculties, which have been not so much helped as hindered hitherto by supernatural power. In a certain sense Prometheus takes the place of Christ as the savior of man;

but it is to be observed that he is man himself acting as his own savior.

In all interpretations of the poem, beginning with Mrs. Shelley's, Prometheus has been assumed to be a representation of humanity, or of some aspect of man—his mind or genius. Even Leigh Hunt's interpretation, expressed in the romantic idiom of the time, is but a variation on this. Prometheus, according to Hunt, is "a personification of the Benevolent Principle, subjected for a time to the Phantasm of Jupiter." [42] This Benevolent Principle constitutes, for Godwin, one of the most essential characteristics of humanity, and one which is destined to be of the utmost importance in bringing about the reign of justice and reason.

But while Prometheus is represented as working out his own salvation without supernatural aid, it is to be noted that, at the beginning of the poem, chained to his rock, he has been long separated from his beloved Asia, living in exile in her Indian vale, and that his release from torture and the blessed transformation of the world are coincident with his reunion with Asia. One chief clue to the meaning of the poem lies in the correct interpretation of this symbolic Asia. She has been variously interpreted as Nature,[43] as "the spirit of divine beauty and love," [44] as "the Idea of Beauty . . . the spirit of Nature . . . Love and Beauty." [45] And these multiple interpretations have been given authority by Mrs. Shelley's original interpretation of her as symbolizing "Venus and Nature." An examination of the poem makes it clear that Asia stands for all these related abstractions.

The association of beauty and love was familiar enough to Shelley in Plato and the neoplatonists, as well as in simple classical mythology. The association of Venus with nature was familiar to him in the opening lines of Lucretius, whom he read as a boy at Eton. Here Shelley had found the invocation to the goddess as "increase-giving Venus, who beneath the gliding signs of heaven fillest with thy presence the ship-carrying sea, the corn-bearing lands, since through thee every kind of living things is conceived, rises up and beholds the light of the sun." [46] And almost immediately afterward he read that "nature gives birth to all things and increase and nourishment." [47] Abstract nature and the mythical goddess of love he found associated in these terms:

Since thou then art sole mistress of the nature of things and without thee nothing rises up into the divine borders of light, nothing grows to be glad or lovely, fain would I have thee for a helpmate in writing the verses which I essay to pen on the nature of things . . .[48]

The spiritual significance of the identification of Asia with Venus (goddess of love and beauty) has been widely, though a trifle vaguely, appreciated from the beginning. Christian commentators have been glad to expound Shelley's doctrine that humanity is to be saved by love. But the poem has waited more than a hundred years for an interpreter who should make clear and definite the significance of her identification with nature. Professor Carl Grabo, in *A Newton among Poets* and *"Prometheus Unbound": an Interpretation*, has shown how much of the most exquisite and elusive imagery of "Prometheus" and other poems of Shelley was suggested by the writings of contemporary scientists, and how many of the leading ideas of "Prometheus" are derived from the observations and theories of men like Newton, Davy, Beccaria, and Erasmus Darwin. And most important of all is the light he throws by this means on the symbolic significance of Asia.

Mr. Grabo shows that Shelley was deeply indebted to the scientific speculations of Erasmus Darwin in the poetry and notes of *The Botanic Garden* and *The Temple of Nature*, and perhaps also in his *Zoönomia*. And he makes it seem highly probable that Shelley's account of the "uprise" of Asia from the sea is to be read in the light of Darwin's similar account of the emergence of Dione (Aphrodite) in *The Botanic Garden*, and his interpretation of this incident in the notes to *The Botanic Garden* and the text of *The Temple of Nature*. In the second act of "Prometheus" Panthea, addressing her sister Asia, recalls the circumstances of her first appearance.

> The Nereids tell
> That on the day when the clear hyaline
> Was cloven at thine uprise, and thou didst stand
> Within a veinèd shell, which floated on
> Over the calm floor of the crystal sea,
> Among the Aegean isles, and by the shores
> Which bear thy name,—love, like the atmosphere
> Of the sun's fire filling the living world,

Burst from thee, and illumined earth and heaven
And the deep ocean and the sunless caves
And all that dwells within them; till grief cast
Eclipse upon the soul from which it came.

The corresponding passage in *The Botanic Garden* I give only in part.

So young DIONE nursed beneath the waves,
And rock'd by Nereids in their coral caves,
Charm'd the blue sisterhood with playful wiles,
Lisp'd her sweet tones, and tried her tender smiles.
Then on her beryl throne by Tritons borne,
Bright rose the Goddess like the Star of morn;
When with soft fires the milky dawn he leads,
And wakes to light and love the laughing meads . . .[49]

Darwin has the following footnote on this passage:

There is an ancient gem representing Venus rising out of the ocean supported by two Tritons. . . . It is probable that this beautiful allegory was originally an hieroglyphic picture (before the invention of letters) descriptive of the formation of the earth from the ocean, which seems to have been the opinion of the most ancient philosophers.

In *The Temple of Nature* Darwin definitely associates this mythological incident with his theory of the evolution of organic life—which took its origin in the ocean and made its first great advances in the mud of the seashore.

ORGANIC LIFE beneath the shoreless waves
Was born and nurs'd in Ocean's pearly caves;
First forms minute, unseen by spheric glass,
Move on the mud, or pierce the watery mass;
These, as successive generations bloom,
New powers acquire, and larger limbs assume;
Whence countless groups of vegetation spring,
And breathing realms of fin, and feet, and wing.[50]

Darwin goes on to recount the evolution of oak, whale, lion, eagle, and man; he dwells on the evidence of shell and coral, on

the emergence of islands and continents; on the emigration of animals from the sea; on the natural history of "musquito," diodons,
beavers, remora. Then he comes to the hieroglyphic representation
of all this evolution in Egypt's rude designs.

> —So erst, as Egypt's rude designs explain,
> Rose young DIONE from the shoreless main;
> Type of organic Nature! source of bliss!
> Emerging Beauty from the vast abyss!
> Sublime on Chaos borne, the Goddess stood,
> And smiled enchantment on the troubled flood;
> The warring elements to peace restored,
> And young reflection wondered and adored.[51]

The prose comment is partly as follows:

> The Egyptian figure of Venus rising from the sea seems to have
> represented the Beauty of organic Nature; which the philosophers of
> that country, the magi, appear to have discovered to have been elevated
> by earth-quake from the primeval ocean.[52]

The more specifically evolutionary features of Darwin's theory
—his views on the origin of species—do not appear in Shelley so far
as I have observed. But it seems almost certain that he does mean
his Asia to stand—among other things—as "type of organic Nature,"
and perhaps, in one aspect, as type of the earth in particular. She
typifies in nature the same beneficent and increase-giving forces as
the classical Venus. And the blessed state of man follows, in Shelley's myth, on his re-alliance with the beneficent forces of nature
from which he has been shut off by the evil spells of Jupiter. Asia
typifies much more than natural love, to be sure, including in her
range of meanings all that Plato includes in his Uranian Venus,
with whom Shelley was so well acquainted. But the significant
thing for our present study is that she should represent, along with
the spiritual ideal of the Uranian Venus, the forces of the physical
universe.

That she does represent physical nature Mr. Grabo makes much
more likely by showing the relation which she bears in the poem
to the Spirit of the Earth. By citations too numerous to be detailed

here Mr. Grabo shows that the Spirit of the Earth is closely associated with, or typifies, the operations of atmospheric electricity
as they were understood by Beccaria and other writers of the
time. And this Spirit of the Earth has a particularly intimate relation to Asia, whom it calls mother, though its actual parentage is
unknown. It has been wont to come—

> Each leisure hour to drink the liquid light
> Out of her eyes, for which it said it thirsted
> As one bit by a dipsas . . .[53]

Mr. Grabo interprets plausibly as follows: "The atmospheric electricity derives from, renews itself from, the earth." In this phase of
the allegory, then, Asia represents the earth as the source of atmospheric electricity. And, as Mr. Grabo makes probable by several
citations, Shelley is identifying love on its physical side with electricity; and not merely that, but with energy, and with the spirit
of animation in organic life. In associating electricity with the
spirit of animation, Shelley was in line with the speculations of
Beccaria and other scientists of the time; even Davy, though he
"was cautious in ascribing an electrical character to the spirit of
animation," yet "believed the subject to be worthy investigation." [54]

As for Shelley's associating the spiritual operations of love with
the material operations of electricity, Mr. Grabo has made this
seem plausible by showing that Darwin advanced a theory of matter which identifies it with energy, the units of matter being "no
more than radiant points of force." [55] We have seen in an earlier
chapter that such a concept was held by Priestley; and it was taken
into account as possibly correct by Davy in his speculations.[56]
Grabo cites from Shelley's *Refutation of Deism*, a similar interpretation of matter as "immaterial."

Matter, such as we behold it, is not inert. It is infinitely active and
subtile. Light, electricity and magnetism are fluids not surpassed by
thought itself in tenuity and activity: like thought they are sometimes
the cause and sometimes the effect of motion; and, distinct as they are
from every other class of substances, with which we are acquainted,
seem to possess equal claims with thought to the unmeaning distinction
of immateriality.[57]

It is by reference to such a concept of matter, in which electricity plays a dominant rôle, that Mr. Grabo explains the puzzling description of the Spirit of the Earth in the fourth act of "Prometheus," in which it is represented by—

> Ten thousand orbs involving and involved,
> Purple and azure, white, green and golden,
> Sphere within sphere . . . etc.[58]

Readers will differ as to the demonstrative character of Mr. Grabo's argument; and many will prefer to leave this extraordinary passage as a mere tissue of fanciful invention on Shelley's part. But the more one studies Shelley, the more one realizes that very little in his poetry is purely fanciful, but that some subtle intellectual concept underlies his most curious metaphors. Without Mr. Grabo's interpretation much of the fourth act of "Prometheus" remains a rather wearisome riot of uncontrolled fancy. He has brought an imposing array of contemporary scientific lore to his interpretation. I believe we must give him the benefit of the doubt, and assume with him that nearly everything in Shelley's account of the Spirit of the Earth in Act IV conforms to his conception of it as an electrical force.

It would take too long to list the scientific theories—astronomical, geological, meteorological—to which, on Grabo's showing, Shelley has given embodiment in "Prometheus Unbound," and to indicate how they are related in his allegory to the moral regeneration of the world which is the theme of the poem. One does not feel certain how far we should assume in his doctrine an *identification* of moral and physical phenomena, or an assertion of the *interdependence* of the two series. Perhaps we are to regard them as merely analogous or parallel. But there are some instances in which they appear to be more than that. In his notes on "Queen Mab," Shelley expresses the view that the obliquity of the earth's axis—

> . . . will gradually diminish until the equator coincides with the ecliptic; the nights and days will then become more equal on the earth throughout the year, and probably the seasons also. There is no great extravagance in presuming that the progress of the perpendicularity of the poles may be as rapid as the progress of the intellect; or that there

should be a perfect identity between the moral and physical improvement of the human species.[59]

The result of this progress in perpendicularity will be a better climate and accordingly improved mentality for man. In this case the moral phenomena would seem to be a consequence of the physical.

A similar view seems to be expressed in "Prometheus," but with the terms reversed.

> In *Prometheus Unbound* earth and moon, after the liberation of Prometheus, became warm and habitable. Shelley depicts them as reliving their youth, his scientific authority being, presumably, Darwin, who believed that at one stage in the earth's history the climate was equable from pole to pole and there were no violent storms, a recollection of which time, lingering in the memory of the race, was the origin of the legend of the Garden of Eden.[60]

In this case the physical improvement seems to be represented as following upon the moral. Again, Grabo shows that Shelley associates the destructive phenomena of electricity with Jupiter and his reign of hate, while under the reign of Prometheus, electricity turns good, and lightning is man's slave; [61] that, further, the noxious gases (like nitrous oxide) turn sweet and wholesome in the millennial régime.[62] In Act III there are several passages describing the transformation of the material world which follows on the release of Prometheus and Asia's sounding of her horn. The Spirit of the Earth describes how, at this magic signal, "all things had put their evil nature off." [63] And Earth herself describes to Prometheus how, at the touch of his lips, the spirit of reviving life penetrated her mass, and—

> . . . Henceforth the many children fair
> Folded in my sustaining arms; all plants,
> All creeping forms, and insects rainbow-winged,
> And birds, and beasts, and fish, and human shapes,
> Which drew disease and pain from my wan bosom,
> Draining the poison of despair, shall take
> And interchange sweet nutriment; to me
> Shall they become like sister antelopes . . . etc.[64]

We are perhaps in danger of sometimes taking too literally the physical phenomena by means of which Shelley wished to symbolize a spiritual event—of assuming a factual connection where he wished to suggest a poetical analogy. Thus we may be inclined to read into his thought a transcendental or superstitious meaning which was not intended. But it does seem not unlikely that Shelley believed in something like an occult sympathy between the material and moral worlds. Such a view certainly seems implied in the note to "Queen Mab" cited in the next to the last paragraph. Such an occult sympathy between the material world and the human soul was held to exist by Henrik Steffens, the German geologist and disciple of Schelling.[65] There are traces of this conception in Wordsworth. How far literally it was held by Shelley in writing "Prometheus" it is hard to determine. But certainly he was greatly confirmed and heartened in his perfectibilist philosophy by numerous facts and hypotheses derived from contemporary science, which, if they do not literally *explain* the operations of the spirit, strikingly parallel and illustrate them. In the same way, later enthusiasts found in evolution an encouragement of their faith in human progress and illumination. The paradox of Shelley's case is that he should have summoned science to support a transcendental view of the natural order so little in harmony with the "modesty of nature," the strict sobriety of scientific method.

Of the "platonic" element in "Prometheus Unbound" I shall have something to say in the following chapter. Meantime some brief reference should be made to several features of the poem discussed in this chapter on which some light may be thrown by the "neoplatonic" speculations of Paracelsus. Miss Elizabeth Pierce Ebeling, in a manuscript thesis deposited in the University of Minnesota library,[66] has made it seem not improbable that Shelley was acquainted with Paracelsus, and that he drew from him many suggestions for the cosmology of "Prometheus." Among the doctrines of Paracelsus which have their counterpart in the poem is that of the guiding spirits (archeus) of the several heavenly bodies. The Spirit of the Earth in Shelley is, according to Miss Ebeling, such an archeus; and the various other living spirits which appear in the poem are likewise provided for in the system of Paracelsus.

Another leading idea of Paracelsus is that of the Evestrum, a sort of attendant spirit born with everything, uniting the created being with the eternal. It is the business of the Evestrum to regulate sleep, to reason, and to prefigure future events.[67]

. . . .

There are two kinds of Evestrum, mortal and immortal. The mortal Evestrum is "like a shadow on the wall. The shadow grows and originates with the body, and remains with it up to its ultimate matter. . . . Everything, animate and inanimate, sensible and insensible, has conjoined with it an Evestrum, just as everything casts a shadow." The eternal Evestra, on the other hand, are not born with individuals, have no beginning and no end. They consist of the Evestrum of comets, the Evestrum of impressions, and the Evestrum of miracles. . . . These Evestra . . . are the means by which celestial things operate, and "Gods by their Evestrum alone have wrought miracles." [68]

Miss Ebeling makes it seem very probable that Demogorgon has much of the character of a "prophetic Evestrum."

Again, as Miss Ebeling points out, the action of the Macrocosm, or universe, in the system of Paracelsus, resembles that of the Microcosm, man; [69] and this is in accordance with the transformation that comes over the physical universe with the spiritual liberation of Prometheus. So that the notion of an occult sympathy between the material universe and the human spirit may have had its original suggestion at the time when as a boy Shelley "pored over the reveries of Albertus Magnus and Paracelsus." [70]

It can hardly be supposed that in "Prometheus Unbound" Shelley took seriously, as philosophical truth, the "reveries" of a Renaissance astrologer and mystic. The spirits and Evestra of the poem are to be regarded in much the same light as the supernatural machinery of "The Rape of the Lock"—having in mind, to be sure, the deeper seriousness of Shelley's imagination and his faculty for reading a genuine moral significance into imagery drawn from the realms of myth and fancy. The mystical machinery of "Prometheus" does not cancel the naturalism of the poem, but rather serves to give it wings. Behind the machinery, it is true, there do lurk certain metaphysical assumptions, largely of "platonic" origin, which it is difficult to reconcile with the naturalistic point of view. Some of these will be discussed in the following chapter.

What is significant for us in the present discussion is that this romantic poet should have sought so earnestly to ground his views in the findings and the spirit of science. In the general action of the poem, certainly, his stress is laid on naturalistic rather than supernatural views of human destiny.

The fall of Jupiter signifies the liberation of man's mind from religious superstition, from ignorance and fear, as well as from political and ecclesiastical tyranny. Jupiter, as I conceive him, is a figure of comprehensive, if negative, significance. He is a kind of Everlasting No. He stands for the force of inertia in human affairs and the heart of man. He is much less substantially real a being than Prometheus or Asia, about as real as "error" in Christian Science philosophy. He is something which man allows himself to think and suffer, the rule of which is limited by man's sufferance, and which is destined to give way before the rule of man's intelligence and will. He stands for all that hampers the progress of civilization. And his downfall coincides with the union of Prometheus and Asia—signifying not merely humanity's espousal of love (in its ideal platonic sense), but also, it now seems likely, man's alliance with nature as explored and interpreted by science.

CHAPTER VIII

SHELLEY'S "PLATONISM"

IN THE main body of Shelley's poems, naturalism lives on most uneasy terms with a manner of thought which, for want of a more exact word, we may call "platonism." In making use of this word, I do not mean to determine how far the cast of thought involved derives directly from Plato, how far from the neoplatonists, and how far from the platonic tradition in English poetry. Still less would I dream of distinguishing in Plato between what he taught as his own doctrine and what he passed on as the doctrine of his master Socrates. Nor again do I pretend to determine, in general, how far the ideas expressed by Shelley represent a correct understanding of the meaning of Plato or the neoplatonists. Poets are often deeply influenced by philosophers whose tenets and methods of reasoning they but imperfectly comprehend. It is well known that there are certain notions and imaginative constructions current in English poetry which have their ultimate origin in the rigorous speculations of the Greek Academy, however much they may have been transformed by the literary mind. They are to be found, for example, in the four Hymns of Spenser. And while a scholar like W. L. Renwick [1] may point out many elements in Spenser which are derived rather from Ficino or Castiglione or other Renaissance writers than from Plato directly, and may indicate how far Spenser falls short of the logic and metaphysic of Plato, it is none the less acknowledged on all hands that Spenser's Hymns are in a tradition that goes back to Plato and is in some significant sense platonic.

Something of the same kind is true for Shelley. And, in tracing the fortunes of "nature" in his poetic art, it is necessary to make some reference to his "platonism" as an element that came in to modify his naturalism. The subject of Shelley's platonism is one that has not yet been thoroughly studied by competent scholars;[2] this study is bound to be made before many years, and my halting approximations will then be set right. Meantime, speaking roughly, I may point out what seem to me the two main concepts in which Shelley is influenced by the "platonic" tradition. The first is the concept of the soul as having "descended" from the realm of the Eternal and as destined to return to "the burning fountain whence it came." The second, the more important and inclusive concept, is that of the general or "eternal" *forms* (ideas, essences, abstractions, intelligibles) as in some sense the most real things in the universe, and of the natural world as having a sort of secondary reality, which it has in so far as it "partakes" of the essence of the eternal forms. This is a view as remote as possible from the ordinary assumptions of nature-philosophy; and it is the strange amalgam of two foreign bodies of thought which gives its peculiar stamp to Shelley's poetry from 1815 onwards. The influence of platonism is vaguely felt in "Alastor" (1815). It is more obvious in the "Hymn to Intellectual Beauty" and "Mont Blanc" (both 1816). It is still more strong in "Prometheus Unbound" (1818–19), "The Witch of Atlas" (1820), "Epipsychidion" and "Adonais" (both 1821).

Platonic views may have come to Shelley from many sources. Most important, along with the poetry of Spenser, were Plato himself, and very probably, Plotinus and Paracelsus. Adolf Droop, in his German dissertation on Shelley's reading, shows how often Shelley was busied with Plato, from his Eton days on.[3] He was acquainted with at least several of the dialogues (including the Phaedo and the Phaedrus), with the Republic, and with the Symposium, which he read with his master at Eton, and of which he made a beautiful translation in 1818. During his Oxford days with Hogg in 1810–11, they had "several of the publications of the learned and eccentric platonist, Thomas Taylor. In truth," as Hogg says, "it would be tedious to specify and describe all the reflected lights borrowed from the great luminary, the sun of the Academy, that illumined the path of two young students."[4] Hogg's phrasing suggests that, at this early period, Shelley's acquaintance with platonic doctrine was derived at least as much from "reflected lights" as from "the great luminary" himself. Among the works of Thomas Taylor were *Concerning the Beautiful, or a paraphrased translation from the Greek of Plotinus*, London 1787, *Five Books of Plotinus*, London 1794, and *Select Works of Plotinus*, London 1817. In several cases the thought and phrasing of his poems more closely resemble those of Plotinus, in Taylor's translation, or in Taylor's interpretation, than those of Plato himself; and there is, I think, a reasonable probability that from Taylor in the beginning the poet derived his main "platonic" inspiration.

"Hymn to Intellectual Beauty"

In his "Hymn to Intellectual Beauty," Shelley may have been influenced either by Plato's Symposium or by Plotinus's discourse on Beauty, or by both. In the Symposium the *locus classicus* is the passage in which are reported the sayings of the prophetess Diotima on the subject of love and beauty. He who aspires to love rightly, we are told, while choosing a single object of his love (a pupil for his instruction), should not forget that beauty is one and the same thing in all forms; he should consider that the beauty which is in souls is more excellent than that which is in outward form. I quote from Shelley's own translation:

The lover would then conduct his pupil to science, so that he might look upon the loveliness of wisdom; and that contemplating thus the universal beauty, no longer . . . would he unworthily and meanly enslave himself to the attractions of one form, nor one subject of discipline or science, but would turn towards the wide ocean of intellectual beauty, and from the sight of the lovely and majestic forms which it contains, would abundantly bring forth his conceptions in philosophy; until, strengthened and confirmed, he should at length steadily contemplate one science, which is the science of this universal beauty. . . . It is eternal, unproduced, indestructible; neither subject to increase or decay; not, like other things, partly beautiful and partly deformed; not at one time beautiful and at another time not; not beautiful in relation to one thing and deformed in relation to another. . . . Nor does it subsist in any other that lives or is, either in earth, or in heaven, or in any other place; but it is eternally uniform and consistent, and monoeidic with itself. All other things are beautiful through a participation of it, with this condition, that although they are subject to production and decay, it never becomes more or less, or endures any change.[5]

From very early days—even before his imagination had been engaged with the concept of nature (an abstraction largely from the laws of physical science)—Shelley had been familiar with the concept of a universal and ideal beauty,—a beauty above, and prior to, that of individual forms, being the beauty-in-idea on which all individual forms are modeled, and by participation in which alone these forms are beautiful; since it alone is original, eternal, "neither subject to increase or decay." And now, in this Hymn, he endeavors to make an imaginative synthesis of the "universal Spirit" of Nature, the "great Mother," the "mute Power," which he had celebrated in "Queen Mab," in "Alastor" and "The Revolt of Islam," with the intellectual concept of abstract beauty held by Plato.

Shelley had always been obsessed, like other philosophical poets, with the thought of "doubt, chance, and mutability" as shadows which dog the footsteps of mortals and characterize the phenomena of nature. He had expressed this sad thought in his stanzas on "Mutability" (1815). And now again he returns to it. He declares that no religious revelation has yet availed to sever—

> From all we hear and all we see,
> Doubt, chance, and mutability.
> Thy light alone, like mist o'er mountains driven,
> Or music by the night wind sent
> Through strings of some still instrument,
> Or moonlight on a midnight stream,
> Gives grace and truth to life's unquiet dream.

While the figures applied to the intellectual beauty are mostly such as to suggest tenuousness and inconstancy, these qualities are not meant to characterize the ideal beauty itself but merely the fleetingness of its appearances to mortals. Shelley really finds in Plato's abstract beauty a principle which, by its very abstraction from mortal conditions, transcends all change. "All other things are beautiful through participation of it, with this condition, that although they are subject to production and decay, it never becomes more or less, or endures any change." Shelley sees that mortals achieve an eternal status just in the degree to which they participate in this intellectual beauty.

> Love, Hope, and Self-esteem, like clouds depart
>   And come, for some uncertain moments lent.
> Man were immortal and omnipotent,
> Didst thou, unknown and awful as thou art,
> Keep with thy glorious train firm state within his heart.
>   Thou messenger of sympathies,
>   That wax and wane in lovers' eyes—
> Thou—that to human thought art nourishment,
>   Like darkness to a dying flame!
>   Depart not as thy shadow came,
>   Depart not—lest the grave should be,
> Like life and fear, a dark reality.

The power of this august spirit descended on the passive youth of the poet "like the truth of nature." Being more or less identified with the spirit of nature, this intellectual beauty utters what in "Prometheus Unbound" Shelley calls "Nature's sacred watchwords,"—Truth, Liberty, and Love.[6] Like Plato's supreme beauty, Shelley's "unseen Power" teaches love for more than an individual, so that the poet professes himself—

>   . . . one who worships thee,
>   And every form containing thee,
>   Whom, Spirit fair, thy spells did bind
>   To fear himself, and love all human kind.

If Shelley was acquainted with Plotinus's discourse on the Intellectual Beauty, he would find there an elaboration of Plato's concept. In the Hymn it is the intellectual beauty that "gives grace and *truth* to life's unquiet dream." It is particularly to be noted that, in Plotinus, emphasis is laid on the peculiar *reality* of this intellectual beauty, since it is the model on which all material beauty is formed, and is antecedent to it in the thought of the divine artist; and that, consequently, nature is clearly conceived as being secondary to the intellectual principle which constitutes the true wisdom and the real being of the universe.[7] The world of nature is a copy of the original world of Real Being which is Wisdom. "This second Kosmos at every point copies the archetype: it has life and being in copy, and has beauty as springing from that diviner world." [8]

This discourse on the Intellectual Beauty, being the eighth book of the fifth Ennead of Plotinus, was not, so far as I know, among the works translated by Taylor; and it is not very probable that Shelley was acquainted with it. It is much more likely that he had read Plotinus's treatise on Beauty, the sixth book of the first Ennead, Taylor's translation of which was accessible in editions of 1787 and 1792. And most of the leading ideas of the other treatise are present in this one. Great stress is here laid on the intellectual process (in Mackenna's translation, the Intellectual-Principle) as essential to the soul's beauty; the beauty here considered is the intellectual beauty of Plato's Symposium and Shelley's poem. Beauty and Good are virtually synonymous in Plotinus's treatment; so that Shelley would be following Plotinus in the strongly ethical tinge of his conception. To have communion with the absolute beauty the soul must mount into a supersensuous realm and become godlike.[9] As in the other treatise, the absolute beauty is here represented as having and bestowing reality (in Mackenna, "reality of Being").[10] And here, as everywhere in Plotinus, mere objects of sense are represented as "nothing more than images, vestiges and shadows" of the ideal beauty;[11] while base and deformed things are "things devoid of form," matter being by its nature "averse from the supervening irradiations of form."[12] For "it is by participation of species that we call every sensible object beautiful."[13]

There is even a suggestion of Shelley's imagery for characterizing the inconstancy of the manifestation of beauty in human experience, though in Plotinus the images are applied to the delusive beauty of matter, in which the ideal beauty is but imperfectly shadowed.[14] The parallel is more marked in a passage from Ennead III, book vi, quoted by Taylor in one of his supplementary notes. This passage is worth quoting, since, in Taylor's translation, it suggests so much of the characteristic imagery of Shelley's poems.

So that it is a phantom, neither abiding nor yet able to fly away; capable of no one denomination and possessing no power from intellect, but constituted in the defect and shade, as it were, of all real being. . . . And the apparent being which we meet with in its image is non-being, and as it were *a flying mockery*. So that the forms which appear in matter are merely ludicrous, *shadows falling upon shadow*, as in a mirror, where the position of a thing is different from its real situation; and which, though apparently full of forms, possesses nothing real and true—but imitations of being and *semblances flowing about a formless substance.*[15]

Whether or not Shelley was acquainted with this or any other work of Plotinus, he would have encountered very similar doctrine in Edmund Spenser. Thus in Spenser's "Hymn in Honour of Beautie" we have a poetic account of the Ideal archetype of beauty after which the "worlds great workmaister" patterns the individual forms of things.

> What time this worlds great workmaister did cast
> To make all things such as we now behold,
> It seemes that he before his eyes had plast
> A goodly Paterne, to whose perfect mould
> He fashioned them as comely as he could,
> That now so faire and seemely they appeare,
> As nought may be amended any wheare.
>
> That wondrous Paterne, wheresoere it bee,
> Whether in earth layd up is secret store,
> Or else in heaven, that no man may it see
> With sinful eyes, for feare it to deflore,
> Is perfect Beautie, which all men adore;
> Whose face and feature doth so much excell
> All mortal sence, that none the same may tell.
>
> Thereof as every earthly thing partakes
> Or more or lesse, by influence divine,
> So it more faire accordingly it makes,
> And the grosse matter of this earthly myne
> Which clotheth it thereafter doth refyne,
> Doing away the drosse which dims the light
> Of that faire beame which therein is empight.

Reality Ideal

Plato, Plotinus, Spenser, or other "platonist," it matters not: somehow Shelley had become imbued with a very different view of reality from that which refers it to nature as its origin and measure. It is a view of reality in which, on the contrary, nature is referred, for its origin and significance, to the world of reason, of forms or "ideas," of soul. This soul, these forms, are not regarded as a product of nature, the outcome of her laws, nor as mere abstractions or generalizations expressing the substance of the facts of nature. They are the original reality, of which the facts of nature are more or less shadowy reflections. One figurative image of this original reality in Shelley is his Witch of Atlas, whose beauty made—

> The bright world dim, and everything beside
> Seemed like the fleeting image of a shade.[16]

Another image is the idealized Emilia Viviani in "Epipsychidion":

> Veiled Glory of this lampless Universe!
> Thou Moon beyond the clouds! Thou living Form
> Among the Dead! Thou Star above the Storm!
> . . . .
> Thou Mirror
> In whom, as in the splendor of the Sun,
> All shapes look glorious which thou gazest on!

Still another platonic image for the original reality is Asia in "Prometheus," who is intellectual beauty at the same time that she is Nature and Venus or Love.

> Lamp of Earth! where'er thou movest
> Its dim shapes are clad with brightness . . .[17]

There is in the first act of "Prometheus" a curious representation of the platonic doctrine of the archetypes or Real Beings. Its special form is taken, according to Miss Ebeling, from Paracelsus' doctrine of the Evestra; and Professor Grabo refers it to a similar conception of Porphyry's set forth in Taylor's translation of Proclus.[18]

> For know there are two worlds of life and death:
> One that which thou beholdest; but the other
> Is underneath the grave, where do inhabit
> The shadows of all forms that think and live,

Till death unite them and they part no more;
Dreams and the light imaginings of men,
And all that faith creates or love desires,
Terrible, strange, sublime, and beauteous shapes.[19]

If these doubles of living beings are suggested by the Evestra of Paracelsus, as well as by the platonic archetypal forms, this would explain why the poet represents them as being "shadows" of the forms that live. It is more characteristic of Shelley to represent the living creatures as the "shadows" of the archetypal forms. In "The Witch of Atlas" mortal men are pictured as wandering unpiloted over the wild surface of an enchanted lake, while the immortal witch takes her way in the calm depths—

Where in bright bowers immortal forms abide
Beneath the weltering of the restless tide.[20]

In all the passages quoted the imagery is poetic. But behind the imaginative conceptions of Shelley and supporting them, in his finest poetry, lies a serious intellectual persuasion that the character of the universe is essentially ideal and spiritual. This goes along with an abiding distrust of the anthropomorphic views of popular religion, an abiding hatred for the spiritual tyranny and political despotism of the church. Thus he writes in 1822, in the full maturity of his thought:

I differ from Moore in thinking Christianity useful to the world; no man of sense can think it true. . . . I agree with him that the doctrines of the French, and Material Philosophy, are as false as they are pernicious, but still they are better than Christianity, inasmuch as anarchy is better than despotism. . . .[21]

What is important for us here is not the repudiation of Christianity but the repudiation of the French materialists. Since the period of "Queen Mab," Shelley had come to believe that in its ultimate (and original) nature the world is both rational and moral. It proceeds upon a Pattern—something analogous to the objective entertained by the human artist who works out his ideal in material forms. This pattern it is which gives shape and direction to the world.

This is the basis for Shelley's confidence in the ultimate triumph of Prometheus and Asia. They are working in conformity to the ideal pattern of the universe. Indeed, Asia is herself a symbolic representation of this ideal pattern. She is Nature—representative of the laws and processes of the material universe—and at the same time she is Love. And Love, as Demogorgon informs Asia, is the one thing in the universe not subject to "Fate, Time, Occasion, Chance, and Change." [22] Love is, in Shelley as in Plato, one of the terms used for describing the original pattern of the universe. It is possible that, in the passage from "Prometheus" just alluded to, Shelley had in mind the remarks of Agathon in the Symposium.

At the origin of things, as I have before said, many fearful deeds are reported to have been done among the Gods, on account of the dominion of Necessity. But as soon as this deity [Love] sprang forth from the desire which forever tends in the universe towards that which is lovely, then all blessings descended upon all living things, human and divine . . . Love is the divinity who creates peace among men, and calm upon the sea, the windless silence of storms, repose and sleep in sadness. . . . Yes, Love, who showers benignity upon the world, and before whose presence all harsh passions flee and perish. . . .[23]

This sounds very much like Shelley's description of the benign effects of Asia's return. The many fearful deeds done among the Gods under the dominion of necessity remind one of the reign of Jupiter in Shelley's poem. But the dominion of necessity gives way to "the desire which forever tends in the universe towards that which is lovely." Love, in short, is not subject to necessity. This is the view of Demogorgon.

Fate, Time, Occasion, Chance, and Change. To these
All things are subject but eternal Love.

It was perhaps Plato who helped Shelley to his solution—such as it was—of the problem of necessity. And it was unquestionably Plato and platonism which largely influenced him in his prevailing view of reality as spiritual in essence.

It would be a tedious and highly speculative business to account for, and trace, the process of Shelley's conversion to this view. In platonism there was doubtless something deeply congenial to Shelley's poetic temperament. But he was not without his strictly intellectual training in metaphysics. Droop shows that he was engaged with the Essays of Hume in the winter of 1810–11, and again in 1811, 1812, 1813; and that references to Hume are found in his writings in later years. He had examined "Hume's reasonings with respect to the non-existence of external things," and had doubtless been impressed with them. He had likewise busied himself with Berkeley's philosophy in 1811, 1813, 1817; and this influence may be traced in various philosophical essays of Shelley. In 1812 he was still unconvinced by Berkeley's reasoning. As he wrote to Godwin:

> I have read Berkeley, and the perusal of his arguments tended more than anything to convince me that immaterialism and other words of general usage, deriving all their force from predicates in non, were invented by the pride of philosophers to conceal their ignorance, even from themselves.[24]

In later years Shelley had more sympathy with the views of Berkeley. Helene Richter believes that in the course of time he became a convinced follower of Berkeley.[25] But for him the chief interpreter of the "intellectual philosophy" was Drummond. In the preface to "The Revolt of Islam," referring to the gloomy and misanthropic philosophy of the age, Shelley adds: "I ought to except Sir W. Drummond's *Academical Questions;* a volume of very acute and powerful metaphysical criticism." Professor Fairchild gives a sketch of the reasoning by which Drummond solves the problem involved in the opposition of necessity and free will by substituting "the sentiment of desire which prevails in our minds" for the free will, which he cannot admit.[26] Fairchild points out a similar doctrine in Spinoza, and suggests that Shelley settled the matter for himself by a combination of platonic theory with this Spinozistic speculation of Drummond's.[27]

The religious dilemma of necessity and free will may have had its part to play in bringing Shelley to the later position, though it is a question whether he ever properly came to grips with the problem.[28] But in his view of the nature of being, the rational analysis of the concept of being found in the platonists had doubtless been reinforced by the epistemological approach of English philosophers, with their destructive analysis of our mental processes considered as means of bringing us knowledge of the external world. In certain of his poems, the problem circles round the nature and origin of thought; and it is mainly there, in Shelley as in Wordsworth, that naturalism tends to break down under the urgency of an idealistic conception of the human mind or spirit.

"Subject" and "Object"

In several of the passages quoted from Shelley in the last chapter, "subjective" and "objective" (as we are now accustomed to call them)—or *internal* and *external* as he calls them—[29] are mentioned together as parallel products of the same creative principle, suggesting the "pantheistic" position of Spinoza and the earlier Wordsworth. The poet knows not "what mute Power may give"—

> Their being to each plant and star and beast,
>   Or even these thoughts.

The objective world and the mental world are creations of the same "universal Spirit" of nature, as in Wordsworth it is the same motion and spirit—

> . . . that impels
> All thinking things, all objects of all thought,
> And rolls through all things.

Again in Shelley it is "the secret strength of things"—

> Which governs thought, and to the infinite dome
> Of heaven is as a law.

This is strikingly reminiscent of Wordsworth's poetic identification, in the "Ode to Duty," of the moral law with the law of gravitation.

Shelley is fond of listing the phenomena of the universe so as to bring a variety of natural objects into the same picture with the activities of man,—all equally subject to change and decay.

The fields, the lakes, the forests, and the streams,
Ocean, and all the living things that dwell
Within the dædal earth. . . .

. . . .

The ways and works of men, their death and birth,
And that of him and all that his may be;
All things that breathe and move with toil and sound
Are born and die; revolve, subside, and swell.
Power dwells apart in its tranquillity
Remote, serene, and inaccessible. . . .[30]

Conscious man and unconscious forest and ocean are lumped together, in their helplessness and mutability, and set over against the constant and tranquil essence which he calls Power. Shelley has gone farther than Wordsworth in effacing the lines of demarcation between man and the other children of nature.

But still he is too much of a philosopher to overlook the distinction between "subjective" and "objective," between thought and things. Indeed, he has made as earnest an effort as Wordsworth to consider the mysterious relation between man's thought and the external universe which it mirrors. This is one of the main subjects of his musing in "Mont Blanc" (1816).

The everlasting universe of things
Flows through the mind, and rolls its rapid waves,
Now dark—now glittering—now reflecting gloom—
Now lending splendor, where from secret springs
The source of human thought its tribute brings
Of waters,—with a sound but half its own. . . .

That is, the mind is a channel through which flows the external universe of things. Owing to the limitations of this cavernous channel, the external reality is in gloom except where the fitful light of the outer world glitters on its surface. But there is also an interior light which illumines it, and an actual contribution to these waters flowing through the mind, where human thought, gushing forth from secret springs, brings its own tribute of waters. There is, one feels, a certain shadowiness or confusion in the imagery here—perhaps an actual confusion in the syntax. I am inclined to think that where Shelley speaks of these flowing waters as "lending splendor," he is referring not to the light of external reality, but to that shed by the mind itself. Shelley is much concerned, in one place or another, with the obscurity of the human mind. In a letter to Hogg in 1811, he exclaims over the strangeness and inconsistency of his own character, which constitutes even for him an insoluble mystery; he would like his friend to find the clue which "even the bewildered explorer of the cavern cannot reach." [31] Again in his fragmentary "Speculations on Metaphysics" (1815) he has the imagery both of the river and of the interior light. Here the river symbolizes the thought flowing from the springs of the mind itself rather than the universe of things flowing through the mind.

Thought can with difficulty visit the intricate and winding chambers which it inhabits. It is like a river whose rapid and perpetual stream flows outwards . . . The caverns of the mind are obscure, and shadowy; or pervaded with a lustre, beautifully bright indeed, but shining not beyond their portals. [32]

Some light may be thrown on Shelley's symbolism by Mary Shelley's account in *Valperga* of the cave of the human mind. [33] Certain powers sit as sentinels at the entrance, others in the vestibule, "still illumined by the light of day." Within, "excluded from the light of day, Conscience sits, who can see indeed, as an owl, in the dark." Beyond all this, "there is an inner cave, difficult of access, rude, strange and dangerous." Here abide the monstrous creatures which symbolize madness—the creations of the morbid imagination. "But it is here also that Poetry and Imagination live; it is here that Heroism, and Self-sacrifice, and the highest virtues dwell"—equally the interior creations of the mind, but these illuminated, as the morbid passions are not, by "an inborn light." This is essentially identical with the cave of the witch Poesy referred to in "Mont Blanc." And this "inborn light" is, I presume, the same as the "lustre" which pervades the caverns of the mind in "Speculations on Metaphysics" and the light which "lends splendor" to the waters of the universe flowing through the mind—in each case this "inborn light" is to be distinguished from the "glitter" thrown by the light of day, that is, by external reality. The two kinds of illumination are both essential to the mental experience of men. And, to vary the figure as Shelley varies it, the sound of "things" flowing through the mind is but half that made by these external things, and half lent by the flowing of the mind itself. The thought is similar to that found in many passages of Wordsworth, in which he indicates how man's feeling (or sensibility to impressions) doth—

> Create, creator and receiver both,
> Working but in alliance with the works
> Which it beholds.

Shelley goes on, in "Mont Blanc," to compare the passing of the universe of things through his mind to the flow of the torrent of Arve through its ravine. He is again reminded of the problem of his "own separate phantasy"—

> My own, my human mind, which passively
> Now renders and receives fast influencings,
> Holding an unremitting interchange
> With the clear universe of things around. . . .

And this leads him, by association of ideas, to a figure obviously suggested by Plato's cave of the mind, though Shelley is speaking of the cave of the witch Poesy.

> One legion of wild thoughts, whose wandering wings
> Now float above thy darkness, and now rest
> Where that or thou art no unbidden guest,
> In the still cave of the witch Poesy,
> Seeking among the shadows that pass by—
> Ghosts of all things that are—some shade of thee.

Scholars remind us that, in Plato, the distinction is between things as we know them (the shadows on the wall) and the archetypal "forms" (which throw the shadows).[34] In Shelley the distinction lies between "things" and the mind or thought that mirrors things. Between these he distinguishes clearly. And while they may be equally comprised in nature, while they may be co-ordi-

nately derived from the secret strength or Power, the problem is
bound to arise: how can mind or thought be derived from a power
which itself is not conscious or intelligent? That it is not conscious
or intelligent seems to be implied in frequent atheistic statements
of earlier poems.

>   What is that Power? Ye mock yourselves, and give
>   A human heart to what ye cannot know;
>   As if the cause of life could think and live!

That Shelley made essentially the same assumptions at the time of
writing "Mont Blanc" is indicated by the following circumstance.
It was written during a brief tour in the vale of Chamouni during
which he also wrote in the visitors' book at Montanvert the atheistic verse in Greek which Byron discovered there some weeks later
and thought fit, in his friend's best interests, to rub out:

>   Ειμι Φιλάνθρωπος δεμωκράτικος τ ἄθεος τε [35]

So far as I know Shelley never considered the problem of the
human mind from the genetic point of view. He never tried to
imagine how the mind might come into existence in the course of
nature. He did not even, like Wordsworth, adopt the Hartleian
notion of mind as built up out of the elements of sensation. He
largely took the mind for granted.

Eternal and Immortal: "Adonais"

What he did wrestle with was the relation of our moral life
to the Eternal, from which it comes, and to which it returns, as
he asserts in "Adonais." Even at this late date Shelley was trying
to combine the concept of nature with that of the eternal forms or
intelligibles. And here it was made particularly difficult by his preoccupation with death. However it may be with Plato in the
Phaedo and elsewhere, in Shelley the question of what becomes of
the human spirit after death tends to confuse the issues of platonism by bringing in the idea of immortality alongside the idea
of the eternal forms. The elegy is a highly conventional literary

genre, and Shelley, in writing of the death of a poet, is somewhat affected by the conventional religious notion that one is better off dead than alive.

> Peace, peace! he is not dead, he doth not sleep—
> He hath awakened from the dream of life—
> 'Tis we, who, lost in stormy visions, keep
> With phantoms an unprofitable strife. . . .

This is perfectly consistent with the views of Plato and Plotinus. It does not go very well with Shelley's lifelong doubt or questioning of the immortality of the soul. And one cannot be sure whether or not he is here giving in to the Christian and platonic faith in the soul's survival. Perhaps he is simply trying to render the platonic conception of the "reality" of the spirit in so far as it participates in the eternal beauty, or truth, or wisdom.

> Dust to the dust! but the pure spirit shall flow
> Back to the burning fountain whence it came,
> A portion of the Eternal, which must glow
> Through time and change, unquenchably the same. . . .

This is a very difficult concept to render in the imaginative terms of poetry, or in any terms satisfying to the heart save those of Christian theology. And these last Shelley is reluctant to use. He tries several different ways of expressing his thought, involving distinct conceptions of the poet's "immortality." First he develops the idea of the oneness with nature of the spirit that loves her.

> He is made one with Nature; there is heard
> His voice in all her music, from the moan
> Of thunder, to the song of night's sweet bird;
> He is a presence to be felt and known
> In darkness and in light, from herb and stone,
> Spreading itself where'er that Power may move
> Which has withdrawn his being to its own;
> Which wields the world with never-wearied love,
> Sustains it from beneath and kindles it above.

The author of "Endymion" and the "Ode to a Nightingale" is obviously in a greater degree one with nature than ordinary men, and through his poems has become "a presence to be felt and known" throughout her realm of beauty. But it is not obvious why he is more one with her being dead than while he was living and actively dealing with her. However that may be, he is made one with her. And then Shelley goes on to identify this "nature" with a spirit of more definitely platonic cast.

> He is a portion of the loveliness
> Which once he made more lovely; he doth bear
> His part, while the one Spirit's plastic stress
> Sweeps through the dull dense world, compelling there
> All new successions to the forms they wear,
> Torturing the unwilling dross that checks its flight
> To its own likeness, as each mass they bear;
> And bursting in its beauty and its might
> From trees and beasts and men into the Heaven's light.

Throughout this part of "Adonais" much of the imagery is what I have called platonic, whether or not it goes back directly to Plato. The "one Spirit's plastic stress" most nearly echoes certain lines of Coleridge quoted in Chapter III. The "dull dense world" which must be compelled into form suggests the "grosser and material mass" of Coleridge's poem, and they both suggest, as does "the unwilling dross" that checks the flight of the spirit, Spenser's platonic "Hymn in Honour of Beautie," from which I have already quoted. Spenser is concerned in this poem with the way in which physical beauty in a human being is stamped upon it by the soul.

> For when the soule, the which derived was,
> At first, out of that grave immortall Spright,
> By whom all live to love, whilome did pas
> Downe from the top of purest heavens hight
> To be embodied here, it then tooke light
> And lively spirits from that fayrest starre
> Which lights the world forth from his firie carre.

Which powre retayning still or more or lesse,
When she in fleshly seede is eft enraced,
Through every part she doth the same impresse,
According as the heavens have her graced,
And frames her house, in which she will be placed,
Fit for her selfe, adorning it with spoyle
Of th' heavenly riches which she robd erewhyle.

Thereof it comes that these faire soules, which have
The most resemblance to that heavenly light,
Frame to themselves most beautifull and brave
Their fleshly bowre, most fit for their delight,
And the *grosse matter* by a soveraine might
Tempers so trim that it may well be seene
A pallace fit for such a virgin Queene.

. . . .

Yet oft it falles that many a gentle mynd
Dwels in deformed tabernacle drownd,
Either by chaunce, against the course of kynd,
Or through *unaptness in the substance* fownd,
Which it assumed of some *stubborne grownd*,
That will not yield unto her formes direction,
But is deform'd with some foule imperfection.

This account of the soul's descent "from the top of purest
heavens hight" reminds one of passages of similar tenor in a work
with which Shelley may well have been acquainted in Thomas
Taylor's translation—Plotinus on the Descent of the Soul—as
well as in others of the *Five Books of Plotinus*.

Shelley, then, has gone considerably beyond the simpler conception of nature. But he comes back to the thought of nature at the
end of the stanza. The one Spirit bursts—

. . . in its beauty and its might
From trees and beasts and men into the Heaven's light.

It may be purely accidental, but this order of listing the forms of
animated life corresponds exactly with the order of appearance in
nature of the three forms of sensitivity found in living things.

So much for Shelley's effort to express the thought of the poet's

oneness with nature. He next proceeds to consider a quite independent way of conceiving his deathlessness. It is the one conception of immortality accepted by the positivists. Keats, says Shelley,
has joined what George Eliot calls—

> . . . the choir invisible
> Of those immortal dead who live again
> In minds made better by their presence. . . .[36]

Shelley's way of putting the matter is rather more poetic than
Eliot's.

> The splendors of the firmament of time
> May be eclipsed, but are extinguished not;
> Like stars to their appointed height they climb,
> And death is a low mist which cannot blot
> The brightness it may veil. When lofty thought
> Lifts a young heart above its mortal lair,
> And love and life contend in it for what
> Shall be its earthly doom, the dead live there
> And move like winds of light on dark and stormy air.

Among these illustrious dead who died young like Keats he mentions Chatterton, Sidney and Lucan. But they need not be persons
whose names have remained to us. They include—

> . . . many more, whose names on earth are dark,
> But whose transmitted effluence cannot die
> So long as fire outlives the parent spark.

This is a relatively simple thought, and one which is easily reconciled with the notion of the dead as superior to the living. An
early death adds luster to an illustrious name. Moreover, it takes
time for illustrious names to make themselves felt. This way of
viewing the deathlessness of Keats goes very well with Shelley's
notion that the poet, by losing his mortal life, has become "a portion of the Eternal."

But now Shelley turns his back altogether on these simple ideas
—oneness with nature, continued life through "transmitted efflu-

ence"—and soars into the realm of sheer platonism. He bids us come with him to Rome, to the peaceful graveyard where Keats lies, and consider how well he is rid of this troubled "dream of life," being now united with the one eternal being.

> The One remains, the many change and pass;
> Heaven's light forever shines, Earth's shadows fly;
> Life, like a dome of many-coloured glass,
> Stains the white radiance of Eternity,
> Until Death tramples it to fragments.—Die,
> If thou wouldst be with that which thou dost seek!
>
> . . . .
>
> That Light whose smile kindles the Universe,
> That Beauty in which all things work and move,
> That Benediction which the eclipsing Curse
> Of birth can quench not, that sustaining Love
> Which through the web of being blindly wove
> By man and beast and earth and air and sea,
> Burns bright or dim, as each are mirrors of
> The fire for which all thirst; now beams on me,
> Consuming the last clouds of cold mortality.
>
> . . . .
>
> I am borne darkly, fearfully afar:
> Whilst, beaming through the inmost veil of Heaven,
> The soul of Adonais, like a star,
> Beacons from the abode where the Eternal are.

The imagery employed by Shelley in this magnificent passage is partly original, but still more of it is traditional among "platonists." And behind the imagery is a system of philosophical concepts which may differ from thinker to thinker, and which in some writers take on greater complexity and a more fantastic character than in others, but which, for all that, have a certain consistency among themselves or belong in the same gamut of thought. So far as Shelley is concerned, his thought seems to me to find its most enlightening illustrations in Plotinus and Taylor's commentary on him.

The One and the Many

Most philosophers have been taken up with the problem of the One and the Many. It is closely related to the poet's problem of mutability. The poet is distressed with the change and decay inherent in all mortal experience and longs for a steadfast and eternal order conceived of as underlying all this confusion and disappointment—

> . . . an ever-fixed mark,
> That looks on tempests and is never shaken.

Shelley had already dealt with this problem in the "Hymn to Intellectual Beauty" and "Prometheus Unbound," where beauty and love are names for the steadfast and eternal thing beyond the reach of "doubt, chance, and mutability."

In metaphysics the classic statement of the problem was made by Parmenides in his poem on "Nature." Parmenides wished to distinguish between that which was universally existent, the ὄν, and that which was not universally existent, the μὴ ὄν. For him the ὄν, the unity of the universe, was real; the μὴ ὄν, its variety or particularity or plurality, was unreal or phenomenal. In Plotinus this distinction appears worked up in an elaborate and mystical theology. The One is that original, infinite, absolute cause of being, which, since it is the cause of all existence, is itself "above existence." From the One derives all that exists, in successive waves or stages of emanation, in which existence progressively gets farther and farther away from the original oneness. The first stage is the νοῦς, or Intellectual-Principle, which partakes both of the absolute being of the One and of thought, which enables it to set in motion the diversified existence of the later stages. The second stage is the soul, a link between the immaterial and the material. The soul may preserve its unity and remain in the νοῦς or it may participate in the corporeal world and be accordingly disintegrated. The term soul is applied either to the single world-soul, or to the innumerable individual souls which it embraces; and these individual souls have the same choice of being ruled by the νοῦς, or turning aside to the sensual and losing themselves in the finite.

It is the soul that, turning aside from the νοῦς, generates the material world, with its rich and bewildering variety of phenomena.

It appears to be a combination of logical and emotional compulsions which drives a Plotinus to push back ever farther from the multiple world of sense and thought to the absolute blank of the One. Whatever is material is subject to the ignominy of alteration, buffeted about by the winds of change. Whatever is multiple may be broken up and destroyed. Whatever thinks is subject to the contamination of the sensual objects of its thought. There is no point of rest or dignity until we arrive at the final essence of which we can predicate nothing save that it is above and antecedent to all that exists. This type of mind seems ridden with a perpetual nostalgia for an ultimate something untouched by any of the experiences which, in this world, distract and confuse us, or by any of the soilures of sense. It is a logical passion too: the passion to reduce many things to their common term, as having, somehow, greater validity than any of the separate items, and to reduce all common terms to their common term, until at length we arrive at the final abstraction of all abstractions.

Reduction every where takes place into that which is one, and in every thing there is a certain one, to which that thing is reduced; and this universe is reduced into a *one* prior to itself, but which is not simply *the one*, and this is the case until we arrive at that which is perfectly and simply one; and this is no longer referred to another. Indeed, by receiving *the one* of a tree, *the one* of a soul, and *the one* of the universe, we shall every where receive that which is most powerful and venerable; but if we receive *the one* of true beings, that is, the principle, fountain, and power of reality, shall we be diffident and suspect that it is nothing? Indeed it is no one of the natures of which it is the principle; and it is such that nothing can be predicated of its nature, neither being, nor essence, nor life; for it is incomprehensibly raised above these.[37]

Such is the tone of the mystical philosopher, wearied with motion and division, variety and struggle, with all that the common man calls reality, and sick for the ultimate stillness and oneness that lie beyond thought and beyond experience. Such was the spell which neoplatonism laid on Coleridge, the "inspired charity-boy" of Christ's Hospital.

How have I seen the casual passer through the Cloisters stand still, intranced with admiration . . . to hear thee unfold, in thy deep and sweet intonations, the mysteries of Jamblicus, or Plotinus (for even in those years thou waxedst not pale at such philosophic draughts). . . .[38]

This spell was laid, in his eighteenth year, on Shelley too, another sensitive spirit shrinking, like Coleridge, from the hard edges of reality. And when, in his Italian exile, he came to ponder the death of Keats, this spell was on him as he wrote of the dead poet:

> Envy and calumny and hate and pain,
> And that unrest which men miscall delight,
> Can touch him not and torture not again;
> From the contagion of the world's slow stain
> He is secure, and now can never mourn
> A heart grown cold, a head grown gray in vain. . . .

What he celebrates in the following is more than the mere peace of the grave. It is the peace of a soul returned again to "the burning fountain whence it came," after its descent into corporeal life. This image of the soul as fire derived from a burning fountain is used by Plotinus.

> . . . as if from universal fire one should be a vast and another a diminutive fire; while in the mean time all the various gradations would proceed from universal fire, or rather from that which is the source of this general fire.[39]

The terms in which Shelley characterizes the torturing sorrows of mortal life are such as might have been used by any poet who had keenly experienced them in his own person. But the general context of the passage indicates a specifically philosophical background for his thought. This background is perhaps best to be gathered from a reading of Plotinus on the Descent of the Soul and Taylor's commentary on it. It may be worth while, at least, to give two brief extracts, the one from Taylor's translation of Plotinus, and the other from his introductory essay.

> But our business at present is to speak of the human soul, which is reported to suffer every evil through its connection with body, and to

lead a miserable life, oppressed with sorrows and desires, with fears and other maladies; to which the body is a bond and a sepulchre, and the world a cavern and a den.[40]

Should it be again asked, why therefore partial souls descending into generation are filled with such material perturbation, and such numerous evils? We reply, that this takes place . . . through their vehement familiarity with body . . . through a disordered condition of being, naturally arising from the composition of dissimilar natures, viz. of the immortal and mortal, of the intellectual and that which is deprived of intellect, of the indivisible and that which is endued with interval; for all these become the cause of this mighty tumult and labour in the realms of generation. For *we pursue a flying mockery which is ever in motion;* and the soul indeed, by verging to a material life, *kindles a light in her dark tenement the body, but she herself becomes situated in obscurity;* and by giving life to the body, she destroys herself and her own intellect, in as great a degree as these are capable of receiving destruction. . . .[41]

Considering, for the moment, only the figures of speech in this last passage, the "flying mockery which is ever in motion" reminds one of Shelley's imagery in the "Hymn to Intellectual Beauty." As for the figure of light and obscurity, this is more or less present throughout the latter part of "Adonais." It may have gone back to Parmenides. But Shelley was familiar with it in Spenser, in Plato, and not improbably in Plotinus. It appears in the two following passages of Plotinus, together with figures suggestive of Shelley's "unwilling dross," his "contagion of the world's slow stain," and his figure of the material world as but the shadow or image of the ideal. The second passage reminds one of the song in celebration of Asia in the second act of "Prometheus Unbound."

Matter . . . opposing herself to soul, is illustrated by its divine light, yet is incapable of receiving that by which it is illustrated; for it cannot sustain the irradiations of soul though present, because, through its depravity, it is incapable of beholding a nature so pure and divine. But matter obscures by sordid mixture, and renders debile the light which emanates from soul: by opposing the waters of generation she occasions the soul's entrance into the rapid stream, and by this means renders her light, in itself vigorous and pure, polluted and feeble, like the faint glimmerings from a watch tower beheld in a storm; for if matter was never present the soul would never approach to generation; and this is the lapse of the soul, thus to descend into matter and become debilitated and impure. . . .[42]

Intellect indeed is beautiful, and the most beautiful of all things, being situated in a pure light and in a pure splendor, and comprehending in itself the nature of beings, of which indeed this our beautiful material world is but the shadow and image; but intellect, that true intelligible world, is situated in universal splendor, living in itself a blessed life, and containing nothing unintelligible, nothing dark, nothing without measure. . . .[43]

Shelley is presumably trying to conceive of the status of the dead poet in terms of the platonic doctrine of eternal "ideas,"—taking that doctrine in its traditional and literary form. But in doing so, he makes certain assertions which are in contradiction to the philosophy of nature that holds so important a place in his earlier poems. It is a large question whether Shelley took literally the doctrine of pre-existence logically implied in the concept of the descent of the soul, or even the corollary doctrine of the individual soul's survival of death.[44] But without such an assumption it is hard to attach any substantial prose meaning to the notion which dominates the last eighteen stanzas of "Adonais,"—the notion that by the fact of dying the poet has been made "a portion of the Eternal." One is a portion of the Eternal in so far as one participates in the supreme Beauty, the supreme Love. The supreme Beauty and Love are eternal abstract forms, not subject to the limitations of time and space. But no individual can participate in these eternal essences without existing; and one cannot exist without having been born. Such at least are the assumptions of any nature-philosophy,—of the philosophy implied in "Queen Mab," "The Revolt of Islam," the "Hymn to Intellectual Beauty," and "Prometheus Unbound." Having once come into existence and participated in the abstract principle of beauty or love, one does become a portion of the eternal, and in that sense enters into a timeless state unaffected by the event in time which we call death. But without a distinct assumption of the immortality of the soul it is hard to conceive in what sense a dead person has become any more a portion of the eternal than one still living and participating in it. It is perfectly simple and logical for Browning, with his Christian faith, to look for heaven to make up for the deficiencies of earth—

On the earth the broken arcs; in the heaven a perfect round.[45]

In Shelley this conception is a paradox, a confusion of thought, unless it means the recantation of his earlier faith.

Recent students of Shelley are in agreement that, in the last four years of his writing, he shows a growing disposition to espouse some form of faith in the immortality of the soul. They are also in agreement, however, that the immortality which he conceives is not the immortality of ordinary Christian faith, in which the human soul maintains its personal identity, but implies the surrender of those faculties which determine the identity of the individual and some kind of union with the absolute being, with "intellectual beauty" or ultimate reality, more or less like the nirvana of Indian philosophy. Here again arises the question why such union with the absolute being, with the eternal forms, is more accessible to the dead than the living. According to recent interpreters there is no satisfactory answer to this question to be found in Plato himself, but in the more elaborate systems of the neoplatonists, this superiority of the dead to the living is a corollary of the doctrine of the descent of the soul. In its pure state the soul is part and parcel with the One; but the One, in the impulse to variation, to realization or materialization, enters into the phenomenal existence of time. For the human soul this means entering into sensual life, which is subject to all the disabilities and humiliations described above. And since it is life which, "like a dome of many-coloured glass, stains the white radiance of Eternity," it is only through the gate of death that one can enter into this radiance.

It is quite conceivable that a naturalist should accept the strict platonic doctrine of eternal forms, and suppose that a human soul has its reality in the degree in which it participates in these abstract essences. And for the naturalist it would be easier to conceive of such participation for the living than for the dead. But this same naturalist would find it impossible to accept the neoplatonic doctrine, which for him would involve the paradox that the non-existent is somehow more real than the existent.

In "Adonais," accordingly, we must either take Shelley's representation of death as an effort to suggest, by poetic symbolism, by a kind of myth, the unsatisfactoriness and insufficiency of mortal life; or we must suppose that Shelley was unable to maintain the system by which he had endeavored to interpret all experience in terms of nature—that he had finally been forced, by the thought of death, to give in more or less to the idea of the supernatural. The weight of the evidence tends to support the latter supposition. His mysticism may be confused, but it is some form of idealistic mysticism which dominates his thinking from "Prometheus" on.

"Prometheus Unbound"

The contradictions between naturalism and platonism which appear in "Adonais" are even more marked and irreconcilable in "Prometheus Unbound." Professor Carl Grabo has recently undertaken, with great learning and plausibility, to interpret the philosophy of that poem, with especial regard to the interwoven strands of natural science and neoplatonism. He has thrown a world of light on Shelley's thought, which is shown to be a tissue of marvelous subtlety and ingenuity. But he has not succeeded in making the two strains of thought in Shelley live together on friendly terms.

On the one hand is the representation of earthly existence as shut away from the reality of heaven, that reality of the eternal One which lies behind the illusions of matter and the deceptions of sense.[46] Prometheus and Asia are, in many passages, types of the individual soul, unhappily separated from the sea of the universals, lost for a time in the illusions of sense, but returning again, by the grace of their divine destiny, to the eternal state of being; reversing the process of generation, floating down the stream of life backwards, to the state of pre-existence; or, in their journey to the cave of Demogorgon, returning to the timeless source both of material and spiritual being.[47] On the other hand, the main fable of the poem is concerned with the building up on earth of a state of perfected humanity, a collective society in which the individuals are so penetrated with the spirit of divine love that they live in complete harmony, acting as one person. In this main fable of the poem Prometheus symbolizes the race of man as a whole, the racial will of mankind, the over-soul of the race;[48] while Asia represents the life-giving forces of nature, the creative spirit in nature (as well as the creative Love), with which mankind must be reunited if it is to attain its ideal state of being. One meaning of this symbolism is that man will attain his perfection through his knowledge of natural science. This perfected state of mankind is several times described in terms which cannot be reconciled with the notion of a timeless platonic being. Man is to be—

> . . . the king
> Over himself; just, gentle, wise; but man
> Passionless—no, yet free from guilt or pain,
> Which were, for his will made or suffered them;
> Not yet exempt, though ruling them like slaves,
> From chance, and death, and mutability.[49]

Here is the most explicit statement that mankind, in this utopian state, is still beneath the rule of passion, of time (mutability), of temporal circumstance (chance), and death.

Shelley does apply the term Eternity to his utopian order, and makes use of platonic or neoplatonic notions to give carrying power to his thought. Jupiter is, in his mythology, not merely error and evil (creations of the mind, or will, of man), but also the temporal state, in which evil and error flourish; he is destined to be dethroned by the mysterious Demogorgon (symbol of destiny and eternity);[50] and upon his fall, the dead hours themselves "bear Time to his tomb in Eternity."[51] But, as Mr. Grabo acknowledges, the reader's mind refuses to identify the active social state of collective humanity with the neoplatonic conception of the eternal One in which all distinctions are merged, and in which morality itself ceases to have a meaning. There is of course a sense in which a human being, or a human society, that has subjected itself to the moral law, may be said to be living *sub specie æternitatis*, assuming that the universe is essentially moral in its nature. And it is also possible to think of humanity, having conceived a moral ideal, as making a perpetual approach to the realization of this ideal, approximating it, in the mathematical sense of the word, by infinite degrees. Perhaps this is one thing Shelley had in mind in describing the fall of Jupiter ("ever, forever down")[52] and in his account of the progress of the hours to Eternity. These concepts are both perfectly consistent with a thorough-going naturalism; but neither of them requires the elaborate apparatus of neoplatonic mysticism, nor any theory of the descent of the soul into generation or the three hypostases of the One.

Another confusion of Shelley's thought (if his myth is here to be taken seriously) is that involved in the physical transformation of the world which follows on the spiritual conversion of humanity. The assumption seems to be that the physical universe is sensitive to the ethical status of man, or that the mind of man, in its improvement, is capable of affecting the state of the physical universe. The climate is improved, the lower orders of animal life grow moral, and the very poisons lose their virulence. This quaint notion seems to be supported by a whole brace of disparate though superficially related conceptions. One of these is that the essential reality of the universe is intellectual or spiritual, and that physical phenomena are more or less deceptive and illusory. This concept is congenial to neoplatonism, and it had a certain fascination for the mind of Shelley in his later years. But it is in no way congenial to naturalism. To the naturalist it would seem, on the basis of this concept, that there is no real difference between good and bad in physical phenomena if they are both the illusory creations of thought, and that the transformation of the physical universe is nothing but a shadow-play in a shadow-world. But even if one subscribes to the mystical idealism of this view, there is no reason to suppose that the mind of man has any such extraordinary power over the physical universe,[53] which is presumably the creation of, and subject to, a more comprehensive intelligence than man's. Mr. Grabo suggests, in certain places, that Shelley means simply that, with the improvement of his intellect, man will be able to control the forces of nature through his knowledge of science. But such a plain view of things as that has no proper relation at all to the platonic concepts with which Shelley makes play.

But, according to Mr. Grabo, Shelley was making an effort to reconcile the Newtonian concept of energy with the platonic concept of the world as an emanation of divine intellect.

Newton's hypothesis that matter is one form of ether, the dregs of ether so to speak, reduces the universe to a manifestation of energy.

Matter is but energy in a lymphatic or frozen state and convertible back to its more active form. Ether, the mysterious fount of all energy, emanates from God and functions as light, electricity, and the spirit of animation. Everything exists, therefore, in God; but what this ether is, of which the universe consists, cannot be known save as it manifests itself in its works.[54]

Assuming this interpretation of Newton's views to be correct, it is at once obvious how alien all this is from the metaphysics of neoplatonism. There is no suggestion here that matter is unreal or illusory, or that time is unreal. God manifests himself in the operations of matter, or energy, and the operations of matter are conceivable only in time. There is no suggestion in Newton's sublime picture of the physical universe that the order of time is vicious and unsatisfactory; it is rather a prime condition for realizing the purposes of God. Still less is there any suggestion that the operations of matter are determined by the thought of man. If they are emanations of thought, it is the thought of the universal divine being.

Equally unsatisfactory is the appeal to Berkeley.

The Berkeleyan concept that all the universe is thought and the Newtonian concept that all the universe is energy are blent in Shelley's philosophy. Energy is thought or emanates from thought. Thought shapes those forms of energy which constitute the physical universe. Energy is electric and electricity is love, or, during the reign of Jupiter, hate; for energy may be misused for evil ends. In the Promethean day the forces of the physical world are beneficent because thought has become good and love is the sole principle of being.[55]

Here again is the confusion between the universe conceived in terms of thought, and the universe as the creation and toy of *man's* thinking. Berkeley never taught that man's thought is the creator of reality; and he would have been surprised, I think, to hear that the physical world may be recreated by the thought of man. It is true enough that, in man's own ethical world, everything depends on the cast of his mind and will; that in the measure in which love rules, an end is put to evil. The rule of Jupiter fades before the light of Asia. But here again it is hard to see how the forces of the physical world can be affected, except in so far as

man may learn to control them through his better acquaintance
with them, or in so far as he may control them to better ends. And
in any case, one does not see how their reality is affected one way
or another, nor how Eternity comes into the picture. The physical
forces when used for beneficent ends must still be conceived as
operating under the phases of time and space.

Again, Mr. Grabo endeavors to relate Shelley's platonism to his
vitalism. Even so early as "Queen Mab" he conceives of all matter
as animated and sentient.[56] And as he proceeds, he comes to think
of material and immaterial as indistinguishable, since matter is
essentially spiritual in nature. Mr. Grabo is inclined to think that
Shelley may have been affected by Erasmus Darwin's conception
of organic life as evolving by virtue of an inherent energy of its
own. One is reminded of the views of Lamarck and Samuel Butler,
and, Mr. Grabo suggests, of Bergson's "creative evolution." But
the very mention of Erasmus Darwin, of Lamarck and Butler, and
even of Bergson, assures us that there is nothing in this "vitalism"
which necessarily entails platonism of any stripe. It does not even
rule out some form of materialism, though it does seem to negate
the cruder forms of mechanism. The evolution of the universe,
whether it is conducted by mechanistic compulsion or the inherent
energy of its substance, does not imply the neoplatonic conception
of the universe as, in all its magnificent diversity, a remote illusory
emanation of the mind of a mindless One. Still less does it imply
that our human experience of the universe is essentially unreal and
vain, and that we can attain to reality only at the cost of returning
to the mindless One, to the state of pre-existence, beyond the illusions and deceptions of sense, where all distinctions are merged in
a mystic identity. Nor, finally, does it imply that the changing universe, which makes itself known under the modes of time and
space, can ever arrive at "reality" until it has ceased to operate
(and evolve) under those modes; nor that mankind, when in the
course of time it arrives at an ideal spiritual state, will cease to experience life under the modes of time and space or to have dealings with a universe in which "vitalism" and "dynamism" have
significance.

And then, finally, the confusion or inconsistency of thought
which Shelley manifests, in "Prometheus" as in "Adonais," on the

subject of immortality, grows out of his attempt to conceive, at times, of death as a state of the soul in which the spiritual meaning of life is to be enjoyed apart from the prime conditions of living. And this results very probably from an incomplete understanding of the platonic theory of the eternal "forms" under which all things manifest themselves, or from the incomplete assimilation of his naturalistic view of the world with the neoplatonic theory of the descent of the soul into generation.

Evolution of Shelley's Thought

It was perhaps in connection with the origin and destiny of the human spirit that the contradiction between Shelley's naturalism and his platonism came most sharply to light. The evolution of his attitude towards the human spirit is a natural one, especially when we take into account the then prevailing cast of scientific thought. Shelley was part and parcel of the Newtonian phase of thought, dominated by the idea of universal law. In "Queen Mab" he distinctly regarded the human spirit as controlled by the same natural laws as the operations of the physical universe. Such was the opinion of many writers with whom he was in sympathy because of their revolutionary views. But he soon began to speculate on the relation between the "universe of things" and the mind of man that mirrors this objective universe and interprets it in terms of conscious thought. Newtonian philosophy was helpless to suggest with any plausibility how spirit might be explained by the laws of matter and motion. There was indeed the Hartleian theory of ideas coming into being as compounded sensations, and the elaboration of this in Erasmus Darwin on the side of physiology. But we have seen how, in the long run, Hartley's system proved insufficient for the purposes of Wordsworth. And Shelley seems never to have taken to the views of Hartley or Darwin on this subject. So that he was even more fatally destined than Wordsworth to give in to the notion of spirit, of mind, as something taken for granted from the start, not so much independent of the material universe as sovereign over it and more real in essence.

From the beginning, indeed, Shelley's materialism was qualified by a disposition to regard matter itself as animated and sentient.

This vitalism gradually gave way, under the influence of Berkeleian and platonic views, to a broader conception of existence as essentially spiritual in nature. So that the mind of man took its place naturally in a comprehensive metaphysic as of one piece with the underlying reality of things.

This development was perhaps inherent in his poetic cast of mind, destined to come about as his temperamental bias asserted itself, and merely delayed by the revolutionary passion which led him at first to throw in his lot with the French materialists. This, however, taken alone, is too simple a view of the situation. Perhaps, if Shelley had lived two generations later, the specifically "platonic" development might never have taken place. He might have found in the theory of evolution, as developed and interpreted in the nineteenth century,[57] a pattern of thought enabling him to maintain the mind and spirit of man within the framework of nature. His constitutional idealism might, in such a case, have tempered the sharp winds of positivism and given the poetic concept of nature a new lease on life. But we need not pursue so wide a speculation nor inquire after the fate of nature had Shelley lived in the age of Meredith and Hardy instead of the age of Coleridge and Wordsworth.

CHAPTER IX

GOETHE

To MAINTAIN the mind and spirit of man within the framework of nature—this is what Goethe managed to do more consistently than any other poet of his time, and with more circumstance and plausibility. And this because of the objective and sensuous character of his imagination, supported as it was throughout his career by scientific studies. His naturalism was more steady and constant than either Wordsworth's or Shelley's, and with him it was a growing and not a waning element of his philosophy. It may not be possible to demonstrate any very great specific effect of his view of nature upon English writers. But the general quality of his mind made itself felt in a thousand subtle ways. And entirely irrespective of his influence, he seems to insist on being included in any study of the poetic concept of nature. The subtlety and force of his mind, the boldness and range of his imagination, give peculiar weight to whatever he has to say on this subject; and he takes his place with our own Wordsworth and Meredith among the most important of nature-poets in the modern world.

Comprehensive View of Nature

Goethe is no simple worshiper of nature. As a poet personifying her in her ever-varied aspects, and as a realist in his regard for plain truth, he has many references to nature as a power hostile to man or indifferent to his spiritual aims. These are, however, more frequent, I believe, in his earlier writings. In "Werther" (1774), the hero is divided between a view of universal nature (à la Shaftesbury) as a blessed harmony of all animate and inanimate things, and the opposed view of her as everywhere struggle, pain and de-

struction. Such are the emotions of a romantic sentimentalist finding in nature the reflection of his own moods.

In his "ode," "Das Göttliche" (1783), Goethe sets forth the
"humanistic" view that nature is unfeeling and indifferent, and
that only in the nobility and orderliness of man do we have a suggestion of those higher beings whose existence we surmise (*den
unbekannten höhern Wesen, die wir ahnen*). But this apparent contradiction of his more usual view of nature is hardly more than a
matter of terminology. The forces of external nature are indeed
indifferent to man. But Goethe does not mean to assert that man's
spiritual faculties are something which make him independent of
nature, and that his real kinship is with a supernatural world.
These "higher beings" are a figure of speech, or at most a classical
equivalent for the term God. And God, we know, was uniformly
regarded by Goethe, from the 1780's onward, in the pantheistic
fashion, and was to all intents and purposes indistinguishable from
universal nature. The basis of his view of the world is Spinoza's
deus sive natura. As he writes to Friedrich Jacobi in 1785, opposing Jacobi's supernaturalism: "Spinoza does not prove the existence
of God; existence *is* God. (*Spinoza beweist nicht das Dasein
Gottes, das Dasein ist Gott.*)" [1] The "divine" of "Das Göttliche"
is a conventional term for designating the spiritual nature of man.
But the spiritual nature of man, like everything about him, is a part
of universal nature.

This comprehensive view of nature as including man is very
distinctly set forth in the paragraphs of Goethe's "Fragment über
die Natur," an imaginative formulation of views dating from the
winter of 1781–82, the year when the poet began to be occupied
with a systematic study of the human skeleton. It is worth giving,
in literal translation, a considerable number of these pregnant paragraphs.[2]

Nature: we are surrounded and wrapped about by her—unable to
break loose from her, and unable to penetrate any deeper into her. . . .
She has thought and she reflects continually—only not like man but
like nature. She has kept to herself her own comprehensive meaning,
which no one can make out in her.
Men are all within her, and she within all. With all she plays a

friendly game; and the more you win from her, the better she likes it. . . .

Even that which is most unnatural is still nature. Whoso sees her not everywhere, sees her nowhere aright.

She loves herself and cleaves perpetually to herself with eyes and hearts innumerable. She has divided herself up in order to take pleasure in herself. Forever she lets new creatures grow up to take pleasure in her, craving insatiably to impart herself.

She spouts forth her creatures out of nothingness, and tells them not whence they come nor whither they go. They have simply to run. The way . . . she knows.

Her spectacle is ever new because she is forever creating new spectators. Life is her fairest invention, and death is her artist's device for having more life.

You obey her laws even when you strive against them; you work with her even when you mean to work against her.

She has no speech nor language; but she creates tongues and hearts, by means of which she feels and talks.

She is everything. She rewards herself and punishes herself, delights and tortures herself. She is rude and gentle, lovely and frightful, impotent and all-powerful. Every thing is perpetually present in her. Past and future she knows not. The present is to her eternity. Kind she is. I praise her and all her works. She is wise and silent. You will force no explanation from her, nor bully her into granting any favor that she gives not freely. Sly she is, but for a good end; and it is best not to take notice of her cunning.

She has set me here, and she will lead me forth. To her I trust myself. She may deal with me [as she likes]. She will not hate her own handiwork. . . . For everything she is to blame, and to her must credit be given for everything.

It seems that Goethe says here everything that can be said of abstract nature. The geniality of his imagination is matched by his sense for fact, and they are both matched by a kind of religious feeling of trust and reconciliation. Nature is the bundle of contradictions which we all find in human experience. "She is rude and gentle, lovely and frightful, weak and all-powerful." But this poet trusts himself to the natural order as others trust themselves to God; he accepts the order of things as being what he has to deal with and all that there is. He realizes that he can by no means get free from the order of nature, and that his very struggles to overcome her are activated by the force he has from her. He imagines, indeed, that nature takes pleasure in man's triumphs over her. For it is over one tendency in nature that he triumphs by virtue of some other tendency equally in her. In this, we find a striking anticipation of Meredith's "Earth and Man," as well as of Huxley's "game of chess." [3] Other paragraphs remind one of Swinburne's "Hertha" and Hardy's "The Mother Mourns."

"Weder Kern noch Schale"

Goethe did not like the materialistic cast of d'Holbach's *Système de la Nature*,[4] but there is much in his view to suggest that of the French philosopher. *"Wir sind von ihr umgeben und umschlungen —unvermögend, aus ihr herauszutreten, und unvermögend, tiefer in sie hineinzukommen."* This is very like d'Holbach's effort to show, in his first chapter, how man is himself the work of nature, unable to extricate himself from her web, unable even to conceive getting clear of the cycle of natural law. It is true that Goethe stops short of d'Holbach's somewhat naïve assertion that man is a purely physical being. He has no inclination to reduce things to so mechanical a basis, or to assert the absolute reign of necessity over men's actions.

Again, there is some reminder of d'Holbach in Goethe's realization that we can never get at the ultimate secrets of nature, though here again he does not express himself with atheistical rudeness. Man, says d'Holbach,

... wanted to push out beyond the visible world, to pass the limits of his sphere; and constant and repeated falls have warned him of the folly of the enterprise. He wanted to be a metaphysician before being a physicist; he despised realities in order to meditate on chimæras; he neglected experience to feed himself upon systems and conjectures.[5]

And Goethe declares repeatedly, in one way or another, that nature will vouchsafe no light on the questions whither and whence. *"Wir sollen nur laufen. Die Bahn kennt sie."* This point he makes even more clear in his letters of a later period. "Man need seek nothing behind the phenomena; they themselves are the teaching." He knows, indeed, that there is something behind the phenomena—in that he is a deeper thinker than d'Holbach—but it is forbidden to man to penetrate into this background of reality.

The highest to which man can attain is Wonder, and if the primary phenomenon (*Urphänomen*) arouses wonder in him, let him be content. A higher it cannot vouchsafe him, and he need not seek to find anything further behind—here is the limit.[6]

But he acknowledged that men are not content with this, but for the most part "are like children looking in a mirror, who turn it round to see what there is on the other side." [7]

This attitude of Goethe's, however, is by way of warning against our futile pretension of understanding intellectually what lies behind our natural experience. Spiritually—or effectually—we are in contact with what is deepest in nature by being in contact with the phenomenon. Specifically he is arguing against the supernatural view of Jacobi that "nature hides God." For himself he claims the "pure, deep, native and cultivated way of regarding things, which has taught me firmly to see God in nature, and nature in God." [8] Intellectually, one may not be able to state the inner meaning of nature; in effect, we are perpetually living with it. This is the burden of his little lyric, "Allerdings" (1820). It is his reply to the assertion of the physical scientist that no one can penetrate into the heart of nature.

> "*Glückselig! wem sie nur*
> *Die äussre Schale weist!*"
> Das hör' ich sechzig Jahre wiederholen,
> Ich fluche darauf, aber verstohlen;
> Sage mir tausend tausendmale:
> Alles giebt sie reichlich und gern;
> Natur hat weder Kern
> Noch Schale,
> Alles ist sie mit einemmale. . . .

"*Happy is he to whom she shows only the outer shell!*" That I have heard repeated sixty years. That view I curse, but secretly. I say to myself a thousand thousand times: Nature gives generously and willingly. Nature has neither kernel nor husk. She is everything all at the same time.

And again,

Wir denken: Ort für Ort
Sind wir im Innern.

We think that, wherever we are, we are at the heart of things.

Thus we have Tennyson's "Flower in the Crannied Wall" without the *if*.

> Flower in the crannied wall,
> I pluck you out of the crannies,
> I hold you here, root and all, in my hand,
> Little flower—but *if* I could understand
> What you are, root and all, and all in all,
> I should know what God and man is.

Goethe does not put the impossible condition. He does not seek to understand nature "root and all, and all in all." But even so he does know directly "what God and man is." He is content, like Meredith, to leave unput "the questions that sow not nor spin."

These questions he is content to leave unanswered because it is enough for him to realize his own oneness with, his personal participation in, the eternal divine process of nature. This mystical feeling of oneness with the *Weltall* is most completely expressed in his poem, "Eins und Alles" (1821), of which I quote the first two stanzas.

> Im Gränzenlosen sich zu finden,
> Wird gern der Einzelne verschwinden,
> Da löst sich aller Ueberdruss;
> Statt heissem Wünschen, wildem Wollen,
> Statt läst'gem Fordern, strengen Sollen,
> Sich aufzugeben, ist Genuss.

> Weltseele, komm uns zu durchdringen!
> Dann mit dem Weltgeist selbst zu ringen,
> Wird unsrer Kräfte Hochberuf.
> Theilnehmend führen gute Geister,
> Gelinde leitend, höchste Meister,
> Zu dem, der alles schafft und schuf.

If we leave out of account the figurative "good spirits"—perhaps an echo of the monadology of Leibniz, found also in Goethe's "Weltseele" (about 1804)—and the word "Weltseele," doubtless derived from Schelling—both of these more or less artificial accretions to Goethe's fundamental conception of nature—we have here the classic statement of Goethe's lifelong gospel of the acceptance of nature and of our inescapable part in it. We bear our part in any case, and our blessedness lies in the imaginative realization of our identity with the world-process. This we shall find to be the kernel of Emerson's nature-poetry. As for the goal of the process, Goethe has no suggestion of this. The process seems to be regarded as self-justifying.

There is a Heraclitean cast to the conception. The poet takes pleasure in contemplating the eternal movement or action: the πάντα χωρεῖ.

> Es soll sich regen, schaffend handeln,
> Erst sich gestalten, dann verwandeln;
> Nur scheinbar steht's Momente still.
> Das Ewige regt sich fort in allen;
> Denn alles muss in Nichts zerfallen,
> Wenn es im Seyn beharren will.

This joy in the mere activity of nature was present in the early "Fragment," in certain paragraphs which I did not earlier quote.

> There is in nature a perpetual life, becoming and activity; and yet she makes no progress. She is constantly transforming herself, and there is in her not a moment of rest. Of tarrying she has no conception, and she has laid her curse on standing still. . . . She gives wants to men because she loves activity. Strange how she brings about all this movement with so little effort. Each need is a boon. Quickly appeased, and quickly roused again. If she gives one thing more, it is a new spring of desire.

"Dauer im Wechsel"

This joy that Goethe takes in the thought of nature's eternal activity is a leading note in the famous song of the Erdgeist in "Faust." [9] It would be strange, indeed, for a poet, a philosopher and a moralist like Goethe not to be appalled and wearied at times with the notion of perpetual change, so that he longed to distinguish some element of fixity in all this movement. At the heart of eternal change there must be an eternal stillness—something which knows no variableness, neither shadow of turning. This mood is expressed in "Dauer im Wechsel" (first published in 1804). And Goethe's thought here has a slightly platonic cast. That which is abiding in the welter of change and reduction to the "element" is the ideal value and form provided by man's creative spirit:

> Den Gehalt in deinem Busen
> Und die Form in deinem Geist.

That Goethe does not mean to take a "humanistic" position hère and oppose the human spirit to the course of nature, is obvious, however, from the general tenor and direction of his thought, and particularly from the relation this piece bears to the others included in the section of poems entitled "Gott und Welt" (1827). If the poet finds content, or intrinsic value, in his heart and form in his mind, it is not because he has got beyond or outside of nature. This is, like everything else about him, a provision of nature itself. In the "Fragment" he says that nature rejoices in man's winning the game against her. The spiritual life of man is such a game, and the artist and philosopher in their creation are the crown of man's spiritual life, which is a part of the eternal process of nature. Goethe's effort to give a comprehensive view of man's make-up and its relation to eternal nature is found in the very late poem, "Vermächtnis" (1829).

In this somewhat obscure poem Goethe insists on the equal claims upon man of the conscience or moral law; the physical senses—which are to be trusted implicitly in observation, provided the understanding is alert; reason—which is the organ for synthesizing the observations of the senses, and enables us evanescent beings to participate in eternity; and the feeling which joins us to the small band of noble souls made up of philosophers and poets.

For our purposes the most significant passages are those in which he speaks of eternity and affirms the authority of the moral law in our breast. Within ourselves we find the moral "center" of the universe as the sun is the center of our solar system. "The independent conscience is the sun to your ethical day. *(Der selbstständige Ge-wissen ist Sonne deinem Sittentag.)*" This is part of the ancient wisdom to which man is to cleave; and for this truth we sons of earth have to thank the wise man who (paraphrasing freely) taught the earth and her sister planets to circle round the sun.

> Verdank' es, Erdensohn, dem Weisen,
> Der ihr die Sonne zu umkreisen
> Und dem Geschwister wies die Bahn.

Edouard von der Hellen, in his commentary on this passage, takes for granted that this is a reference to the Copernican theory. He cites from Goethe's *Geschichte der Farbenlehre* passages of high praise for Copernicus, especially for his great discovery that earth is not the middle point of the universe. Goethe himself, says the German editor, "was on his way, like Copernicus with the geo-centric error, to clear away the anthropocentric error, and indeed in his view of the world he drew the ethical consequences." [10]

There may be some question as to the interpretation of the adjective "independent" as applied to the conscience. But the context in this poem and the general course of Goethe's thought shows us the probable meaning. It is not that man's conscience is independent of nature, as the "humanistic" view would have it; but rather that it is independent of any supernatural or transcendental authority. The Copernican theory, in making the sun the center of the solar system, by the same stroke made man's own conscience the center of his moral life.

The other passage most to our purpose in "Vermächtnis" is one which throws light on the statement in "Dauer im Wechsel" that art shows us how to find "content in our bosom, form in our mind." Here it is man's reason which enables him to view things *sub specie æternitatis;* and it is the same reason that rejoices in the living process of nature.

> Vernunft sey überall zugegen,
> Wo Leben sich des Lebens freut.
> Dann ist Vergangenheit beständig,
> Das Künftige voraus lebendig,
> Der Augenblick ist Ewigkeit.

There are many parallel passages in Goethe. One of them is found in "Das Göttliche." Referring to the various unique faculties of man, Goethe says: "Man alone is capable of doing the impossible: he makes distinctions, chooses and judges; he can give duration to the instant."

> Nur allein der Mensch
> Vermag das Unmögliche:
> Er unterscheidet,
> Wählet und richtet;
> Er kann dem Augenblick
> Dauer verleihen.[11]

In this poem, as we have seen, Goethe does make a distinction between man, who is capable of justice and nobility, and nature, which is "indifferent." But this is not, we have seen, a constant and characteristic distinction with Goethe, as it is with Matthew Arnold. Otherwise we might suppose that Goethe regarded man's spirit as an organ for transcending nature and creating eternity in a world of mere mutability. But already, nearly ten years earlier, in "Künstlers Abendlied" (1775), Goethe had specifically named nature as the inspiration for the artistic faculty by which man does create his eternity. Here the artist appeals to nature to help him in the task, to which he feels incompetent, of shaping the conception after which he gropes.

Here it is the esthetic faculty in artistic expression, as in "Vermächtnis" it is reason, which enables man to fix his phenomenal experience in eternal form. The mind of man is capable of giving permanency to the past, of anticipating the future, and giving duration to the fleeting instant. In "Künstlers Abendlied," though in lighter tone, Goethe has expressed much the same thought as Keats in the "Ode on a Grecian Urn." And it is with the aid of nature that he is to enlarge his narrow experience into eternity.

Nature is here taken on her lighter side, that expressed in such lyrics as "Mailied." This is nature in her delightsome sensuous aspects—sunshine, flowers, and bird songs. It is an "impulse from a vernal wood" which Goethe here craves as means to enlarge his narrow being. The nature of "Vermächtnis" is the being which appeals to man's reason, the inspirer of Kepler and Copernicus, the principle of law and science. Such is the nature of the early "Fragment," and the aspect that occupies Goethe's imagination more and more during the period of his scientific studies. She is Mother Nature, who has begotten us men, and must be given credit for whatsoever we are.

The most interesting of all the suggestions of the "Fragment" is that nature has created man to be witness of her spectacle and give voice to her inarticulate thoughts. She is herself unconscious and unfeeling, the poet implies, but has created living beings who can feel and interpret for her. She is one and uniform, but has multiplied and diversified herself in her creatures.

Sie liebet sich selber und haftet ewig mit Augen und Herzen ohne Zahl an sich selbst. Sie hat sich auseinander gesetzt, um sich selbst zu geniessen. Immer lässt sie neue Geniesser erwachsen, unersättlich, sich mitzuteilen. . . . Ihr Schauspiel ist immer neu, weil sie immer neue Zuschauer schafft. . . . Sie hat keine Sprache noch Rede; aber sie schafft Zungen, durch die sie fühlt und spricht.

This is much more daring and modern than anything in Wordsworth or Shelley. There is indeed an approach to this conception in Shelley's "Hymn of Apollo," when he puts these words into the mouth of the god of song:

> I am the eye with which the Universe
>   Beholds itself and knows itself divine;
> All harmony of instrument or verse,
>   All prophecy, all medicine are mine,
> All light of Art or Nature;—to my song
> Victory and praise in its own right belong.

The difference between the two representations lies in the more purely figurative character of Shelley's imagery.[12] In some sense the universe beholds itself and knows itself divine—in poetry and the arts. But the god who presides over the arts is after all but a personification, and there is no suggestion at all of the mechanism by which this result is brought about. Goethe gives us something more conceivable and more in line with cosmic history. It is nature, the sum of the observed forces of the universe, that moves forward towards self-consciousness, and creates in living beings the organs by which consciousness may be had.

In view of later developments in Goethe's conception of nature, we may take this to be an imaginative anticipation of the idea of evolution. At least the concept appears less purely mythical if it is viewed in the light of our present persuasion that man's organs of sense, his power of speech, and the emotional and intellectual life associated with sense and speech are products of natural evolution.

Intimations of Evolution

In considering Goethe's poetic concept of nature it is important to bear in mind that he was, for more than fifty years, an enthusiastic and diligent student of the natural sciences—botany, osteology and comparative anatomy, the anatomy of insects, optics, and the science of color. He studied infusoria under the microscope. He published many scientific papers. During the month before his death in 1832, he prepared for the press the second of two papers in which he championed the evolutionary views of Geoffroy de Saint-Hilaire against the reactionary arguments of Cuvier. He was much more interested in this controversy over the interpretation of nature than in the revolution of 1830.[13]

Goethe's enthusiasm for the views of Saint-Hilaire is the enthusiasm of a naturalist for some one who has reached the goal towards which his own studies were tending. For more than thirty years, his own thought shows what I call "intimations" of organic evolution. So much so that he is sometimes regarded as one of the precursors of Lamarck and Darwin.

Almost from the beginning of his scientific studies he had been impressed with the close interrelation of all parts of nature, including man himself. In 1784 he wrote to a friend:

I have refrained from stating the conclusion, to which Herder has pointed in his Ideas, namely, that it is impossible to find the difference between man and animal in any particular feature. On the contrary, man is related to the animals in the closest manner. The agreement of the whole makes each creature what it is, and man is man by the form and nature of his upper jaw-bone as well as by those of the last joint of his little toe.[14]

Again he writes:

All operations which we observe, of whatever kind they may be, are bound together in the most constant fashion, and run over into one another.... These activities, from the lowest to the highest, from the falling of the roof-tile to the luminous spirit-glance which dawns upon you and which you share with others—all fall into an orderly relation to one another. We try to express the relation in the following series: accidental, mechanical, physical, chemical, organic, psychic, ethical, religious, creative.[15]

The theory of evolution is not necessarily implied in these statements. But two ideas are expressed which lead quite naturally to the theory of evolution, and which indeed post-Darwinian thought finds it very difficult to dissociate from evolution. One of them is the extremely close relation between man and the other animals. Goethe has not yet conceived of this as a blood-relation resulting from lineal descent. The other idea is the close relation of all forms of activity in the universe and their disposition in an ascending scale from what Goethe calls the accidental (zufällig), through the categories of the mechanical, the physical, the chemical, to the organic, and then upwards through the psychic, or conscious, to the various spiritual categories of the ethical, religious, creative (genial). It is a kind of Aristotelian scheme, which requires only the concept of genesis or transmutation to pass over into the evolutionary view.

Now the notion of some sort of scale of ascent in the organic world was common in Goethe's day, and does not necessarily accompany any theory of the "transmutation of species." In Schelling, Steffens and Coleridge, as we shall see in a later chapter, this scale is run down into the inorganic world and includes something corresponding to Goethe's categories of the physical and chemical. But, so far as Steffens and Coleridge were concerned, it is to be noted that this scale of beings goes along with a great deal of what we may call the mythology of science—theories so fantastic and speculative that we cannot seriously associate them with objective science and the theory of organic evolution. Moreover, Coleridge several times expressly repudiated the "bestial" theory, as he designated the type of evolution espoused by Erasmus Darwin.[16] And his scale of ascending categories is cut off sharp before it arrives at the psychic proper; since he held that there could be no thought of connection between the sensitivity of the lower animal world and the intellectual faculties of man. This opinion was shared by Lyell and set forth in his *Principles of Geology* (1830-33).[17] And all these circumstances serve to distinguish rather sharply the bookish *a priorism* of Coleridge's scientific outlook from the genuine objective naturalism of Goethe. Both of the ideas above mentioned are in him significant by virtue of his insistence on an organic relation between man and the physical nature in which he finds himself embedded, between the spiritual and material in nature.

Max Morris shows how, in the 1790's, Goethe passed gradually from the current eighteenth-century static conception of nature to that of a continuous state of change.[18] Goethe's own particular studies pointed in this direction. His theory of plant organs as all, except the root and stem, having the character of modified leaves, was set forth in his *Versuch, die Metamorphose der Pflanzen zu erklären* (1790). He is here occupied with the essentially Aristotelian concept of "form." The *Urbild*, or *Urpflanze*, is a type or epitome of what is common to all plants—"the original common characters, or, as we should say, the 'stem characters,' lying at the base of all forms." [19]

Professor Osborn implies that Goethe in this monograph teaches the doctrine of evolution. Morris holds the apparently more exact view that he merely points in that direction. But he says of Goethe's theory:

It operates in the field where lies the great problem of the living form; it breaks through the narrow circle of Linnaeus's botany, concerned merely with counting, classifying and labeling, and the question that is here raised—whence then the similarity of plant forms?—has since been answered by the doctrine of evolution.[20]

Again he shows how the further course of scientific thought was to supply what was wanting to Goethe's theory.

The common leaf-character of plant organs is explained by the processes of evolution and adaptation. The plant has in the course of enormous ages transformed what were originally similar parts into organs of distinct form and function, which now altogether evolve themselves from the same groundwork of organs (*Organanlage*). Goethe's observation then opens the widest prospect, but first only in the way of twilight—or dawning—surmise.[21]

So much for botany. Still more unmistakably leading Goethe in the way of evolution were his studies and theories in comparative anatomy—his observation of vestigial structures in man, his prediction of the discovery of premaxillary bones in man, his vertebrate theory of the skull, later reached independently by Oken. Here, as in his botanical studies, he was guided by the passion for discovering, behind the variety of organic forms, the ideal or universal type to which they all refer. As Morris says:

His goal is not to learn isolated facts, as in the collecting and classifying science of the Enlightenment, but to follow them back to the archetype (*bis zum Urphänomen*), that is, to the phenomenal fact purified of all that is accidental and peculiar in the particular case, since this is valid for us more than all particular cases falling within its scope, and by it we measure each one of these particular cases. "What is the general? The particular case. What is the particular? A million cases. (*Was ist das Allgemeine? Der einzelne Fall. Was ist das Besondere? Millionen Fälle.*)" [22]

It was thus the philosophic notion of the eternal Form beneath the variety of individual forms which guided Goethe in his scientific studies, and which in turn led to the evolutionary notion of changing forms. This idea began to clarify itself during the nineties. To quote Morris again:

His view of the world exhibits itself from the nineties on as a complex of phenomena in constant change evolving into greater completeness [of development]. . . . This idea secures poetic expression in the poem, "Dauer im Wechsel." Here appears, as the constant element in the evolution of all organic and inorganic forms, "der Gehalt in deinem Busen und die Form in deinem Geist." Taking his departure from this comprehensive view, Goethe recognizes that the animal species do not remain unchanged through successive generations, but adapt themselves to their environment and perpetually transform themselves. This thought is not found in the *Versuch über die Gestalt der Tiere* (1790), but emerges first in the *Versuch einer allegemeinen Vergleichungslehre*, dating from the beginning of the nineties, and is fully formulated in the *Vorträgen* of 1796. Here Goethe clearly expresses the idea of this *Urphänomen*, on which the later doctrine of evolution is based: "Thus much, then, we have gained, that we may assert without hesitation that all the more developed organic natures, including fish, amphibious animals, birds, mammals, and at the peak of the last-named, man, were formed upon one archetype, which only in its highly constant parts more or less wavers back and forth, but which still daily changes and modifies its form by propagation." [23]

Among other later suggestions of the evolutionary point of view in Goethe is the following remark made by him in conversation in 1809. There is here a strong suggestion of the view of man held by later evolutionists as being the culmination of an evolutionary process, with an upward direction, including the speculative notion that man in his present evolved state is himself a stage on the way to something "higher."

One might think of nature (said Goethe) as a gambler standing by a gaming-table and ceaselessly crying, "Double the stakes!"—that is, with what she has already won, continuing to play on happily to infinity, throughout the whole realm of her operation. Stone, beast, plant —after several such lucky throws her entire winnings are put back into the game. And who knows whether even the entire man is not a gambler's throw for higher stakes? [24]

The "Metamorphoses"

Most of Goethe's nature-poems to which I have referred date from the period of his most intensive scientific studies or later. He was much more deeply imbued with the spirit of science than either Wordsworth or Shelley; and the philosophic concepts expressed in his nature-poems are more obviously inspired by, and consonant with, scientific theories and assumptions. And—what is still more important—at the time when most of these poems were written he had already come to think rather familiarly in evolutionary terms, which was never true of Wordsworth or Shelley. So that he was not forced to give up objective nature, or drop her out of sight, in the interests of spirit—the subjective mirror and interpreter of nature. There are indeed a number of indications that he was inclined to think of our spiritual faculties as *derived* from nature. This view is already present in the "Fragment" of 1781–82, in the poetic statement that nature "has no speech nor language, but creates tongues and hearts through which to feel and speak." Such a statement impresses us as poetic or mythical, rather than as of the nature of scientific truth, largely because there is no hint here of evolution, of what we may call the mechanics of this miracle. This lack is somewhat supplied, if I rightly interpret them, by two poems written by Goethe in what I call his evolutionary period.

These two poems, "Die Metamorphose der Pflanzen" and "Metamorphose der Tiere," are the outcome of Goethe's project of writing poems on specifically scientific themes. This project was suggested to him by the indifferent reception given to his scientific papers by fellow scholars, as well as his own difficulty in writing a comprehensive treatise for the exhibition of his ideas.[25] He was led to think of employing his great and acknowledged gift as poet for the better propagation of his views. Thus he wrote "The Metamorphosis of Plants" in 1798, eight years after the prose treatise on the same subject. In sending this poem to a friend he wrote, "I have it in mind to compose a poem in the same style on the subject of the magnetic forces."[26] At about the same time he was discussing with Schiller "the possibility of giving an exhibition of nature-lore through the medium of poetry." And in the Annals for 1799, after mentioning several scientific topics that have interested him, he says, "Behind all these matters there swam before my soul's vision the idea of a great nature-poem."[27] Such a poem he never wrote. But he did compose, in about the year 1806, a companion-piece to the botanical poem of 1798, "The Metamorphosis of Animals."

The two poems which Goethe wrote in fulfilment of this project are interesting and finished works, mainly intellectual in appeal, rather than works of imaginative genius. They are somewhat stiff and conventionally classical in expression, lacking in the spontaneous warmth and elusive loveliness of his most famous lyrics. And his failure to carry out his larger program further illustrates the often observed difficulty of assimilating much of the detail of scientific knowledge to the stuff of poetry. If any modern poet should have been qualified to do this it was Goethe. But these two poems do form a significant commentary on his general poetic conception of nature, and remind us, in particular, how readily Goethe could refer the operations of the spirit to the general field of natural law.

The bulk of "The Metamorphosis of Plants" is devoted to an account of the transformation of the leaf into the other organs of the plant, culminating in the flower and the fruit. It is here presumably that Ruskin gets the imagery of his "marriage of the leaves," to which he gives such a simpering Victorian tone in *Fors Clavigera*.[28] The process of reproduction brings Goethe to his favorite conception of the oneness of eternal nature throughout all change. Then in the final lines he draws the general conclusion as to the ceaseless permutation of forms, and draws an analogy between the love-process in the plant and the development of the sentiments of love in man.

> O, gedenke denn auch, wie aus dem Keim der Bekanntschaft
>   Nach und nach in uns holde Gewohnheit entspross,
> Freundschaft sich mit Macht aus unserm Innern enthüllte,
>   Und wie Amor zuletzt Blüthen und Früchte gezeugt.
> Denke, wie mannichfach bald die, bald jene Gestalten,
>   Still entfaltend, Natur unsern Gefühlen geliehn!
> Freue dich auch des heutigen Tags! Die heilige Liebe
>   Strebt zu der höchsten Frucht gleicher Gesinnungen auf;
> Gleicher Ansicht der Dinge, damit in harmonischem Anschaun
>   Sich verbinde das Paar, finde die höhere Welt.

As the flowers (or love-organs) of the plant are derived by progressive modification from the original element, the leaf, so in man his social habits *(holde Gewohnheit)*, his sentiments of friendship and love—the identity of mental outlook of individuals making the harmony of love—all these spiritual faculties and manifestations are derived by natural evolution from the original "germ of acquaintanceship." It is perhaps no more than an analogy; but it places the evolution of sentiment in the same natural cycle as the evolution of flowers.

As in this poem Goethe makes the evolution of sentiment the culmination of the natural process, so in the "Metamorphosis of Animals" he puts at the peak of this process the conception of law as taught to man by nature, and carried over by him into the realms of ethics, esthetics and politics. In the next-to-the-last strophe he describes the impulse in nature to allow organic forms or species to develop at their own will, or capriciously, and how then this capricious impulse is checked by the set limits within which nature is obliged to work. This leads him, in the final strophe, to reflect on the beautiful balance in nature of freedom and law—a pregnant thought which man should ponder.

Dieser schöne Begriff von Macht und Schranken, von Willkür
Und Gesetz, von Freiheit und Maass, von beweglicher Ordnung,
Vorzug und Mangel, erfreue dich hoch: die heilige Muse
Bringt harmonisch ihn dir, mit sanfte Zwange belehrend.
Keinen höhern Begriff erringt der sittliche Denker,
Keinen der thätige Mann, der dichtende Künstler; der Herrscher,
Der verdient es zu seyn, erfreut nur durch ihn sich der Krone.
Freue dich, höchstes Geschöpf, der Natur, du fühlest dich fähig,
Ihr den höchsten Gedanken, zu dem sie schaffend sich aufschwang,
Nachzudenken. Hier stehe nun still und wende die Blicke
Rückwärts, prüfe, vergleiche, und nimm vom Munde der Muse,
Dass du schauest, nicht schwärmst, die liebliche volle Gewissheit.

It would be rash to assert that, in these poems, Goethe has in mind specifically the theory of the derivation of species from one another by progressive modification; still less that he is prepared to explain the mechanism of the process on the basis of mutations and the struggle for existence. In the case of the vegetable, what he is considering is the transformation of parts within an individual plant conformably to an inherent cycle of development. In the case of the animal world, he is considering mainly the way in which, in each species and in each individual, the several organs are developed to function according to nature's model for that species. What we might say is that, while he has not embodied in these poems the specific conception of biological evolution as worked out by nineteenth-century scientists, his whole conception implies a comprehensive evolutionary philosophy, which requires only the Darwinian hypothesis to give it substance and convincingness. In the "Metamorphosis of Animals" he represents nature as an impulse working in animal life towards certain ends and limited by certain conditions inherent in herself; and, what is still more significant, he represents her as, in the process of creation, soaring to higher and higher conceptions.

It is significant, too, that in these poems there is no suggestion of looking outside of nature for an interpretation of her meaning and origin. There is no reference to theological or teleological systems. In this connection we should have in mind a note of Goethe's from the nineties, in which he characterizes his method of study:

The way of regarding the natural product in itself, without reference to use or purpose, without reference to its first author, but simply as a living whole, which, just because it is living, includes cause and effect within itself, so that we can step up to it and demand a reckoning from it directly, and trust it to give us information on the nature of its own being.[29]

This is precisely the method pursued in the two "metamorphosis" poems. The muse is here simply the mouthpiece, passing on to man the lessons learned from a study of plant and animal life, without the help of revelation or *a priori* notions. And the constant assumption of the whole discussion is the self-sufficiency and self-subsistence of nature. What is most important to us in the whole affair is the suggestion that man's life of feeling and thought is included in this self-subsistent nature and an outcome of the evolutionary process. His sentiments are derived from nature much as the flowers are. And his intellectual constructions—his conceptions of law, of morality, his esthetic and political conceptions—are likewise derived from nature herself. At his intellectual highest, he is but "thinking after nature the most exalted thoughts to which she has attained in the progressive process of creation."

There is here no suggestion of the physical substance which, as pointed out by Huxley in his essay "On the Physical Basis of Life" (1868), is somehow involved in both the material and the spiritual activities of organisms. Let me recall to the reader the culminating and critical passage in Huxley's discussion.

It may seem a small thing to admit that the dull vital actions of a fungus, or a foraminifer, are the properties of their protoplasm, and are the direct results of the nature of the matter of which they are composed. But if, as I have endeavored to prove to you, their protoplasm is essentially identical with, and most readily converted into, that of any animal, I can discover no logical halting-place between the admission that such is the case, and the further concession that all vital action may, with equal propriety, be said to be the result of the molecular forces of the protoplasm which displays it. And if so, it must be true, in the same sense and to the same extent, that the thoughts to which I am now giving utterance, and your thoughts regarding them, are the expression of molecular changes in that matter of life which is the source of our other vital phenomena.

There is in Goethe, I presume, no such specification of a physical substance which, as it were, serves as a link between the activities of matter and spirit. But he does clearly conceive that connection, and range the manifestations of the universal activity in an ascending scale of categories. That he would have welcomed with enthusiasm Huxley's speculations based on the known properties of protoplasm, I think there can be no doubt. It would have been a perfect confirmation by observed fact of his philosophical belief in the oneness of natural phenomena, and of the derivation of spiritual phenomena from the same natural fountain as material.

Comparisons

This last, as he conceives it, is a bold and very modern view, going far beyond Wordsworth and Shelley. Wordsworth's timid Hartleianism gave way so readily to an essentially religious idealism! Shelley started with a strong conviction that man's spirit is bound up with matter "in the great chain of nature." But he was too much puzzled by the opposition between "subject" and "object" to maintain this view in its integrity. He found in evolution no hint as to how the human spirit may be thought of as derived from nature, and he tended to lose himself in a more platonic form of Wordsworth's doctrine.

Having in mind the time when he wrote, Goethe is far more naturalistic than Coleridge, Emerson or Whitman. Whatever acquaintance he may have had with German metaphysics, he did not fall into the popular form of idealism which led Emerson to speak of nature as "the externization of the soul," and which led both Emerson and Whitman to interpret all nature in terms of human ideals. So that his tentative evolutionism had more effect on his philosophy than that of men who lived in the period when evolution was defined and accepted.

This is true of him, likewise, in comparison with Tennyson and Browning. He was not led by religious qualms to look askance at nature and to erect a mystical dualism in order to save his spiritual aspirations from the destructive findings of science. It is the consistently scientific attitude of Goethe which most nearly anticipates the evolutionary naturalism of Meredith.

PART TWO

TRANSCENDENTALISM

What is Nature? An encyclopedical, systematic
Index or Plan of our Spirit.

—Novalis, *apud* Carlyle

* * *

Whatever satisfies souls is true. . . .

—Whitman

CHAPTER X

CARLYLE

THERE is one imaginative prose writer whose influence was so widespread, and who had so much to do with the dissemination among poets of the German romantic feeling for nature, that we cannot afford to pass him by without some brief consideration. Carlyle was eagerly read by poets like Emerson, Whitman, Meredith, and even, I believe, by Longfellow, and served particularly as a means of passing on to them in popular form certain elements in the thought of Goethe and of the German transcendental philosophers.

Carlyle indulged little in the description of natural scenery and outdoor life. But in his early essays on German literature, on Richter and Goethe, he gives a notion of the romantic tone of German writing about nature. And there is one glowing passage in *Sartor Resartus*, in which an account of wild mountain scenery is made the occasion to strike nearly every possible note of the romantic philosophy of nature. It is in the chapter on the Sorrows of Teufelsdröckh, and serves to exhibit the solace and elevation which nature may bring to the heart of sad and disenchanted mortals.

A hundred and a hundred savage peaks, in the last light of Day; all glowing, of gold and amethyst, like giant spirits of the wilderness; there in their silence, in their solitude, even as on the night when Noah's deluge first dried! Beautiful, nay solemn, was the sudden aspect to our Wanderer. He gazed over these stupendous masses with wonder, almost with longing desire; never till this hour had he known Nature, that she was One, that she was his Mother and divine. And as the ruddy glow was fading into clearness in the sky, and the Sun had now departed, a murmur of Eternity and Immensity, of Death and of Life, stole through his soul; and he felt as if Death and Life were one, as if the Earth were not dead, as if the Spirit of the Earth had its throne in that splendor, and his own spirit were therewith holding communion.[1]

It would perhaps be impossible to find assembled in so few words so many characteristic items of romantic nature-poetry. Wild and solitary mountains, like giant spirits; splendor of color, stupendous size, sunset; longing desire; the sentiment of wonder, of immensity, of eternity; the oneness of death and life. And as for nature hypostatized, the knowledge that she is one, that she is divine, that Earth is not dead, but alive; that she is the mother of lonely man, a spirit with whom he may hold communion.

Nature in Novalis

Teufelsdröckh, we know, is Carlyle. And while he has behind him Wordsworth and Coleridge, Shaftesbury and Pope, his poetical sentiments are supported by a set of philosophical ideas or "intuitions" which are largely German in origin and complexion. There is, not overwell assimilated, the idealism of Fichte, built upon Kant's repudiation of the sensationalism of Locke. Kant's and Fichte's positions are briefly stated in Carlyle's essay on the "State of German Literature" (1827); they are treated somewhat more at length in his essay on Novalis (1829); and are often alluded to in the whimsical terms of Teufelsdröckh's clothes philosophy.[2] Of Fichte Carlyle was particularly interested in *Ueber das Wesen des Gelehrten*. In Chapter XII, I show reason to think that he may also have read, among Fichte's popular philosophical treatises, *Die Bestimmung des Menschen*, and pondered Fichte's view of knowledge and faith as opposed ways of apprehending truth.[3] In his essay on Novalis, he gives a considerable account of that romantic "poet's" mystical views on nature, which, he says, are "perhaps partly the fruit of his Idealism."[4]

He first refers to Novalis's habit "of considering Nature rather in the concrete, not analytically and as a divisible aggregate, but as a self-subsistent universally connected whole." There is some analogy between Novalis's thought here and that of Wordsworth when he objects to the reliance of mechanical-minded scientists on "that false secondary power by which we multiply distinctions," and declares that in consulting only this faculty, "we murder to dissect." Novalis opposes to the "rude, intuitive poet" the scholastic who "annihilates all living Nature, to put an Artifice of Thoughts

(*Gedenkenkunststück*, literally Conjurer's trick of Thoughts) in its room. His aim is an infinite Automaton." In primeval days man's "mind had a peculiar unity, and only by Practice divided itself into separate faculties." This way of following out "the endless divisions of Nature" leads to very dubious results.

For Nature too remains, so far as we have yet come, ever a frightful Machine of Death: everywhere monstrous revolution, inexplicable vortices of movement; a kingdom of Devouring, of the maddest tyranny; a baleful Immense: the few light-points disclose but a so much the more appalling Night, and terrors of all sorts must palsy every observer.[5]

This is very much the style in which Carlyle makes Teufelsdröckh speak of nature at the time when he was at his spiritual nadir, bound by the iron law of necessity and guided only by the flickering light of his understanding.

Seen in this analytical way, says Novalis, nature is a monster hostile to man, which he must fight against and subdue. But then we come to the well of Freedom, which lies in our own souls, and there we sit and gaze.

The purer World lies even in us, in this Well. Here discloses itself the true meaning of the great, many-colored, complected Scene; and if full of these sights we return into Nature, all is well known to us, with certainty we distinguish every shape.[6]

No longer frightened by their fever dreams, by "this so-called Nature," which is "a Sport of the Mind, a waste Fantasy of their Dream," men begin to perceive "a high moral Order in the Universe"; they perceive that "the significance of the World is Reason." In order to become Master of Nature, man has but to honor it as "the Emblem of his own Spirit"; he has but to train his moral sense. For "Moral Action is that great and only Experiment, in which all riddles of the most manifold appearances explain themselves."

It is clear how this interpretation of nature goes with a popular idealist metaphysics. It is only by reference to his own moral standards that man is able to find the meaning of nature, to see it not as "dead, hostile Matter, but the veil and mysterious Garment of the Unseen." [7] Carlyle quotes a number of the apothegms or fragmentary sayings of Novalis, which express this view in picturesque poetic terms.

> Nature is an Æolian Harp, a musical instrument; whose tones again are keys to higher strings in us. . . . What is Nature? An encyclopedical, systematic Index or Plan of our Spirit.[8]

This last statement is startlingly like certain of Emerson's, which I quote in Chapter XI, in connection with the transcendental views of Coleridge, and which may have been suggested partly also by Novalis, known directly or through this essay of Carlyle's.

Transcendental Idealism

Novalis's metaphysical creed, Carlyle tells us, might safely enough "be classed under the head of Kantism, or German metaphysics generally." [9] More specifically, as he several times tells us, Novalis was a disciple and poetic interpreter of Fichte.[10] As for the doctrines of Kant, Carlyle points out that—

> . . . the organs of the Mind, what is called the Understanding, are of no less arbitrary, and, as it were, accidental character than those of the Body. Time and Space themselves are not external but internal entities: they have no outward existence, there is no Time and Space *out* of the mind; they are mere *forms* of man's spiritual being, laws under which his thinking nature is constituted to act.[11]

Again, he refers to the "Kantian" distinction between the lower and higher faculties of the mind, *Verstand* and *Vernunft*. These transcendentalists recognized "a higher faculty in man than Understanding . . . Reason *(Vernunft)*, the pure, ultimate light of our nature; wherein, as they assert, lies the foundation of all Poetry, Virtue, Religion." [12] It is clear that, for Carlyle, the separating activity of the mind which, according to Novalis, reduces nature to "dead, hostile Matter," corresponds to Kant's Understanding, and the moral faculty that restores the unity of things and makes us see that "the significance of the World is Reason," corresponds to the higher faculty which is the pure, ultimate light of our nature.

One result of this conception is to reduce matter to a mere phenomenon.

To a Transcendentalist, Matter has an existence, but only as a Phenomenon: were *we* not there, neither would it be there; it is a mere
Relation, or rather the result of a Relation between our living Souls
and the great First Cause; and depends for its apparent qualities on *our*
bodily and mental organs; having itself *no* intrinsic qualities: being, in
the common sense of that word, Nothing.[13]

Carlyle gives a sketch of Fichte's way of representing the phe-
nomenality, and at the same time the ideality, of nature.

There is, in fact, says Fichte, no Tree there; but only a manifestation
of Power from something which is *not I*. The same is true of material
Nature at large, of the whole visible Universe, with all its movements,
figures, accidents and qualities; all are impressions produced on *me* by
something *different from me*.[14]

Another version of this is given by Carlyle in his essay on the "State
of German Literature." And here he refers to Fichte's doctrine of
the Divine Idea, defined by Fichte in his lectures on *The Nature
of the Scholar.*

According to Fichte, there is a "Divine Idea" pervading the visible
Universe; which visible Universe is indeed but its symbol and sensible
manifestation, having in itself no meaning, or even true existence independent of it. To the mass of men this Divine Idea of the world lies
hidden; yet to discern it, to seize it, and live wholly in it, is the condition of all genuine virtue, knowledge, freedom; and the end, therefore,
of all spiritual effort in every age.[15]

In this view of the world, we may roughly distinguish the metaphysical and the religious elements. The metaphysical element consists in the notion that the world exists merely as sensible manifestation of the idea—that is, of thought or intelligence. This idealistic
view of reality is often suggested, in more or less figurative language, in *Sartor Resartus* (1833–34). Thus:

So that this so solid-seeming World, after all, were but an air-image,
our ME the only reality: and Nature, with its thousand-fold production and destruction, but the reflex of our own inward Force, the
"phantasy of our Dream" . . .[16]

All visible things are emblems; what thou seest is not there on its own account; strictly taken, is not there at all; Matter exists only spiritually, and to represent some Idea, and *body* it forth.[17]

For Matter, were it never so despicable, is Spirit, the manifestation of Spirit: were it never so honorable, can it be more? The thing Visible, nay the thing Imagined, the thing in any way conceived as Visible, what is it but a Garment, a Clothing of the higher, celestial Invisible, "unimaginable, formless, dark with excess of bright"? [18]

The same view of reality appears in the lectures *On Heroes, Hero-Worship, and the Heroic in History*, delivered in 1840.

They seem to have seen, these brave old Northmen, what Meditation has taught all men in all ages. That this world is after all but a show,—a phenomenon or appearance, no real thing. All deep souls see into that, —the Hindoo Mythologist, the German Philosopher,—the Shakespeare, the earnest Thinker, wherever he may be:
"We are such stuff as Dreams are made of!" [19]

And we find a dash of this idealism even in *The French Revolution* (1837).

But if the very Rocks and Rivers (as Metaphysic teaches) are, in strict language, *made* by those outward Senses of ours, how much more, by the Inward Sense, are all Phenomena of the spiritual kind: Dignities. Authorities, Holies, Unholies! [20]

This view of reality as the product of thought is supported in *Sartor Resartus* by the Kantian analysis of Time and Space as necessary forms of thought.[21] And metaphysical idealism passes over insensibly into its religious phase when the whole universe is conceived of as the manifestation not of our human thought but of the eternal thought of God—as a product of the Divine Idea. Thus Nature is not simply "the reflex of *our* inward Force," but, "what the Earth-Spirit in *Faust* names it, *the living visible Garment of God*." [22] And we see—

That this so solid-looking material world is, at bottom, in very deed, Nothing; is a visual and tactual Manifestation of God's power and presence,—a shadow hung out by Him on the bosom of the void Infinite; nothing more.[23]

As for ourselves, we too are manifestations of the same divine idea. "Who am I; what is this ME? A Voice, a Motion, an Appearance;—some embodied, visualized Idea in the Eternal Mind?" [24]

The exact relation of Carlyle's thought to that of his German sources is an intricate and highly technical subject, which has been threshed out by a succession of scholars. It is sufficient for our purposes here to give a brief summary of the findings of Professor Harrold, the latest and most comprehensive writer on this subject. According to Harrold, Carlyle's nature-philosophy is a rather free development of Goethe's notion of the world as the vesture of the spirit; a development in which certain doctrines of Kant, Fichte and Schelling were loosely applied under the inspiration of the mystical Novalis. Carlyle did not rightly understand the implications of Kant's distinction between Understanding and Reason as faculties that occupy themselves with quite distinct subject-matter; it was not Kant he was following in his representation of Understanding as a lower faculty than Reason and subservient to it, in ascribing to Reason a mystical significance and virtually identifying it with Faith. In all this Carlyle is more in line with the views of Jacobi, and his "version of Kant is substantially the transformation wrought by Coleridge." [25]

Again, Carlyle's account of Fichte's idealism, according to Harrold, is "a good popular account of Berkeley's doctrine." [26] But he did not thoroughly understand the idealism of either Berkeley or Fichte. "From Carlyle's point of view, nature is not, as for Berkeley, the creation by a Spirit *for* created spirits, but is the illusory fabric spun by our notions of time and space." [27] "Carlyle could not have agreed with Fichte that the only reality is thought. He seems never to have inquired into the Fichtean teaching that being means being conscious, that the universe is really an *idea*—the product of consciousness." [28] Carlyle seems rather to have supposed that time, space and matter are nothing but illusion. This was a false inference from Kant's doctrine of the *formal* nature of space and time. "Agreeing with Kant that space and time are ideal, that they have no absolute reality, Carlyle goes further and denies them any reality whatsoever." [29]

This view of the non-reality of the external world fell in with the widespread literary notion of the dream-like nature of the world and of life, which was early impressed on Carlyle's imagination by a famous passage from Shakespeare's "Tempest" and confirmed by Dugald Stewart's essay "On the Idealism of Berkeley." [30] It was also supported by an imperfect assimilation of Schelling's "philosophy of identity," with which Carlyle was superficially acquainted. "The forms of matter in the outer world, Schelling maintained, are symbolic in that they are analogous, step by step, with the processes of the inner life." [31] This notion of the symbolic nature of the world Carlyle was familiar with in Novalis and Goethe ("Alles Vergängliche ist nur ein Gleichniss"), and he may have met with it in Schiller.[32] It is expressed by Carlyle in his statement that nature is "the realized thought of God."

Natural Supernaturalism

Such was the quasi-religious metaphysic which Carlyle took up as a substitute for the lost orthodoxy of his childhood, and as a defense against Edinburgh materialistic rationalism.[33] His work is full of ironic protest against the mechanism of "cause-and-effect" philosophies,[34] against naturalism,[35] unbelief,[36] atheism,[37] and mere scientific rationalism.[38] His frequent insistence on the divineness of Nature [39] means not an espousal of the Christian dispensation but repudiation of a self-sufficient naturalism.

The same thing is true of his fondness for regarding the order of the world as supernatural, and his cult of wonder.

For Goethe, as for Shakespeare, the world lies all translucent, all *fusible* as we might call it, encircled with WONDER; the Natural in reality the Supernatural, for to the seer's eyes both become one.[40]

This is the burden of the chapter in *Sartor Resartus* entitled "Natural Supernaturalism." [41] Here Carlyle asserts that each phenomenon of the universe is a miracle—an incomprehensible wonder—and that only as the wonder wears off through our familiarity do we lose the sense of its religious character. Philosophy is "throughout but a continual battle against Custom; an ever-renewed effort to *transcend* the sphere of blind Custom, and so become Transcendental." [42] Space and Time and Civilization are among the prime miracles.

Sweep away the Illusion of Time; glance, if thou have eyes, from the near moving-cause to its far distant Mover: The stroke that came transmitted through a whole galaxy of elastic balls, was it less a stroke than if the last ball only had been struck, and sent flying? Oh, could I (with the Time-annihilating Hat) transport thee direct from the Beginnings to the Endings, how were thy eyesight unsealed, and thy heart set flaming in the Light-sea of celestial wonder! Then sawest thou that this fair Universe, were it in the meanest province thereof, is in very deed the star-domed City of God; that through every star, through every grass-blade, and most through every Living Soul, the glory of a present God still beams. But Nature, which is the Time-vesture of God, and reveals Him to the wise, hides Him from the foolish.[43]

This wondrous and miraculous character of the universe is developed at length in *Heroes and Hero-Worship;* and there, as in *Sartor Resartus,* wonder is asserted to be the basis of religious worship.

Nay surely, to the Atheistic Thinker, if such a one were possible, it must be a miracle too, this huge illimitable whirlwind of Force, which envelops us here; never-resting whirlwind, high as Immensity, old as Eternity. What is it? God's Creation, the religious people answer; it is the Almighty God's! Atheistic science babbles poorly of it, with scientific nomenclatures, experiments, and what not, as if it were a poor dead thing, to be bottled up in Leyden jars and sold over counters: but the natural sense of man, in all times, if he will honestly apply his sense, proclaims it to be a living thing,—ah, an unspeakable, godlike thing; towards which the best attitude for us, after never so much science, is awe, devout prostration and humility of soul; worship if not in words, then in silence.[44]

For the rest, as is natural to a man of this kind, he (Teufelsdröckh) deals much in the feeling of Wonder; insists on the necessity and high worth of universal Wonder; which he holds to be the only reasonable temper for a denizen of so singular a Planet as ours. "Wonder," says he, "is the basis of Worship: the reign of wonder is perennial, indestructible in Man; only at certain stages (as the present), it is, for some short season, a reign *in partibus infidelium.*" That progress of Science, which is to destroy Wonder, and in its stead substitute Mensuration and Numeration, finds small favor with Teufelsdröckh, much as he otherwise venerates these two latter processes.[45]

Carlyle's cult of wonder is full in the romantic tradition; and his interpretation of nature illustrates once again how almost inevitably romantic nature-philosophy is the accompaniment of unorthodoxy in religion. His theology is natural theology poetized by transcendentalism. His views are here in striking contrast with Newman's. The romantic spirit is not entirely wanting in Newman; but his attitude towards the religion of wonder serves to remind us with how much suspicion Christian orthodoxy looks on the romantic versions of transcendentalism. It is thus that Newman expresses himself in regard to Sir Robert Peel's notion that a knowledge of science naturally conduces to religion.

The truth is that the system of Nature is just as much connected with religion, where minds are not religious, as a watch or a steam-carriage. The material world, indeed, is infinitely more wonderful than any human contrivance; but *wonder is not religion, or we should be worshipping our railroads.* What the physical creation presents to us is a piece of machinery, and when men speak of a Divine Intelligence as its Author, this God of theirs is not the Living and True, unless the spring is the god of a watch, or steam the creator of the engine. Their idol, taken at advantage (though it is *not* an idol, for they do not worship it), is the animating principle of a vast and complicated system; it is subjected to laws, and it is connatural and co-extensive with matter. Well does Lord Brougham call it "the great architect of nature"; it is an instinct, or a soul of the world, or a vital power; it is not the Almighty God.[46]

There is much in this passage from Newman which Carlyle could have wholeheartedly indorsed. He had perhaps as little sympathy as Newman for the dry rationalism of natural theology. But he writes in a very different tone. It is certain that he sometimes incurs the suspicion of that pantheism at which Newman is here directing his sarcasm. His god is much more like the "animating principle" of a vast system than like the Living and True God of Christian theology. And his identification of worship with wonder is in sharp contrast to the attitude of Newman in the phrases which I have italicized. It is beyond question that Carlyle did much to dissolve in his transcendental solution the theological dogmas of Christianity.

At the same time his transcendentalism was of a kind to sap the foundations of any solid naturalism. The vague religiosity which is such a solvent of dogma is equally discouraging to the patient effort of the scientific mind bent on placing man in his natural setting, determining the conditions imposed upon him by the observed nature of things, and enabling him to utilize his knowledge of the world for the attainment of his ideals. Consider, for example, the romantic statement of his "idealism" in his early romance of *Wotton Reinfred*.

Is not all visible nature, all sensible existence, the symbol and vesture of the Invisible and Infinite? Is it not in these material shows of things that God, virtue, immortality are shadowed forth and made manifest to man? Material nature is a Fata-morgana, hanging in the air; a cloud-picture, but painted by the heavenly light; in itself it is air and nothingness, but behind it is the glory of the sun ... It is only the invisible that really *is*, but only the gifted sense that (sic) can of itself discern this reality! [47]

Such is the utterance of a character who is supposed to stand for Coleridge, the English interpreter of "Kantism." There is little comfort here for an earnest practical mind seeking a clue to the interpretation of knowledge and experience. The case for idealism is so grossly over-stated, or rather so misstated and missed. If material nature is such a Fata-morgana, common sense protests, how vague and insubstantial is the truth behind that paints it on the clouds! If the symbol of the Invisible is so tenuous and illusory, what suggestion can it offer of the reality which it stands for? What can one take hold of to guide one in this misty region? Where are the tests and controls of objective science? Where is the sober matching of fact with fact, the confident building up of knowledge from age to age? One does not feel that one has to do here with Wordsworth's Power (in Nature) "that is the visible quality and shape and image of right reason." One feels thrown back, by this dreamy mysticism, on fantasy and whim and wish-fulfilment.

And yet, with this poor opinion of the nature apprehended by our senses, and of the scheme of nature built by scientific speculation on the data of our senses, it is curious how infallibly Carlyle returns, in his historical writing, to the concept of nature as a clue to human behavior. This appeal to nature in history will be our subject in the following section.

Historical Pragmatism

We may distinguish roughly two periods in Carlyle's nature-philosophy. The first is the poetic, or transcendental period, comprising the essays on German Literature, *Wotton Reinfred* and *Sartor Resartus*. The second period—which comprises *Chartism* (1839), *Past and Present* (1843), *Latter-Day Pamphlets* (1850), and the *History of Frederick the Great of Prussia* (1858–65)—we might call the pragmatic. *On Heroes, Hero-Worship,* etc. (delivered as lectures in 1840), may be regarded as transitional, partaking largely of both the transcendental and the pragmatic view of nature. It is in the second period that Carlyle applies the term nature in his criticism of political and social institutions and his interpretation of history. Nature is here understood as the order of the universe as it manifests itself in history and human institutions; and we hear much of the laws of nature,[48] of the order of Nature,[49] Nature's regulations,[50] "Nature's appointments . . . which are truth." [51] The important thing for men is to conform to the laws of nature in whatever they undertake and institute; otherwise their politics are vain. They will have to find out what method of handling public affairs, for example, is in accordance with the eternal laws of nature.

If a Parliament, with suffrages and universal or any conceivable kind of suffrages, *is* the method, then certainly let us set about discovering the kind of suffrages, and rest no moment till we have got them. But it is possible a Parliament may not be the method! Possibly the inveterate notions of the English People may have settled it as the method, and the Everlasting Laws of Nature may have settled it as not the method! Not the whole method; not the method at all, if taken as the whole? If a Parliament with never such suffrages is *not* the method settled by this latter authority, then it will urgently behoove us to become aware of that fact, and to quit such method;—we may depend upon it, however unanimous *we* be, every step taken in that direction will, by the Eternal Law of things, be a step *from* improvement, not towards it.[52]

Alternative expressions for the laws of nature are the terms Reality,[53] Fact,[54] Truth,[55]—each of these terms associated with nature as an equivalent, or in a phrase like the following: "It was a Reality, direct from the great Heart of Nature once more." [56]

It might be supposed that whatever comes to pass in this world is within the order of nature, that it is a reality and a fact. But Carlyle seems to have in mind the distinction (drawn in our Chapter V) between nature as the sum of what comes to pass and nature as the order of things in conformity to which desired objectives may be attained. Whatever man does conformably to the order of nature in pursuing his objectives is covered by the terms Fact and Reality. When he tries to attain his objectives by ill-chosen means he is indulging in falsity. Thus nature dooms the man who will not work, since only by work can life be maintained. Human laws may be judged by reference to their efficiency.

Any law, however well meant as a law, which has become a bounty on unthrift, bastardy and beer-drinking, must be put an end to . . . He that will not work, and save according to his means, let him go else-whither; let him know that for *him* the Law has made no soft provision, but a hard and stern one; that by the Law of Nature, which the Law of England would vainly contend against in the long-run, *he* is doomed either to quit these habits, or miserably be extruded from this Earth, which is made on principles different from these.[57]

The great heroes in history are invariably characterized by Sincerity—that is, by the recognition of Facts in the order of nature. Thus Napoleon had the sincerity, the "instinct of Nature," which led him to follow the principle of *"la carrière ouverte aux talens*, the implements to him who can handle them," which had been so lamentably neglected in the artificial social system of the French monarchy.[58] But in his later tyrannical and imperialistic phase Napoleon "parted with Reality."

The compact, clear-seeing, decisive Italian nature of him, strong, genuine, which he once had, has enveloped itself, half-dissolved itself, in the turbid atmosphere of French fanfaronade. The world was not disposed to be trodden down underfoot; to be bound into masses, and built together, as *he* liked, for a pedestal to France and him: the world had quite other purposes in view! Napoleon's astonishment is extreme. But alas, what help now? He had gone that way of his; and Nature also had gone her way. Having once parted with Reality, he tumbles helpless into Vacuity; no rescue for him.[59]

Even more of this sincerity and instinct of nature was possessed by Cromwell and Frederick the Great. The latter in particular proved himself nature's man by the infallible efficiency with which he guided the affairs of Prussia, in an epoch which was chiefly characterized by lies—that is, by the show and vanity of kingship, the disposition to parade one's greatness, à la Louis XIV, instead of solidly being great. Carlyle has occasion to discuss a certain policy of Frederick's, the commutation of the *Ritterdienst*. In this he was opposed by a few ill-advised nobles. But, says Carlyle, "if your plan *is* just, and a bit of Nature's plan, persist in it like a law of Nature." [60]

At times it seems as if for Carlyle might makes right. In the long run, certainly, he believes that the right wins out in human affairs, that might is with the right.

Curious: in those days (of the French Revolution) when Hero-worship was the most incredible thing to every one, how it does come out nevertheless, and assert itself practically, in a way we all have to credit. Divine *right*, take it on the great scale, is found to mean divine *might* withal! While old false Formulas are getting trampled everywhere into destruction, new genuine Substances unexpectedly unfold themselves indestructible. [61]

For nature means order, and whoever puts order into human affairs has both right and might with him.

What is injustice? Another name for *dis*order, for unveracity, unreality; a thing which veracious created Nature, even because it is not Chaos and a waste-whirling baseless Phantasm, rejects and disowns. [62]

May we not say, moreover, while so many of our late Heroes have worked rather as revolutionary men, that nevertheless every Great Man, every genuine man, is by the nature of him a son of Order, not of Disorder? . . . His mission is Order; every man's is. He is here to make what was disorderly, chaotic, into a thing ruled, regular. He is the missionary of Order. Is not all work of man in this world a *making of Order?* [63]

This making of order is everywhere emphasized by Carlyle in his great heroes—in Napoleon, Cromwell, Frederick. And he is tolerant of any ruthlessness in brushing away "false formulas" on the part of a ruler who is genuinely making order in the state. Thus

when Cromwell arbitrarily interrupted Parliament in its projects
for a Reform Bill which promised to throw England back again
into disorder:

> Cromwell walked down to these refractory Members; interrupted
> them in that rapid speed of their Reform Bill;—ordered them to be-
> gone, and talk there no more.—Can we not forgive him? John Milton,
> who looked on it all near at hand, could applaud him. The Reality had
> swept the Formulas away before it.[64]

So we see, after all, that nature means for Carlyle something
more than the set of conditions to which we must conform if we
are to attain our objectives. Nature has objectives of her own;
and the chief of these is what Carlyle calls order. "Intellect, insight,
is the discernment of order in disorder; it is the discovery of the
will of Nature, of God's will . . ." [65]

Thus Carlyle makes Nature's will and God's will synonymous.
And it is here that we find the clue to such consistency as there is
between Carlyle's distrust of external nature in his transcendental
phase and his reliance on it in his pragmatic phase. Professor Harrold remarks that Carlyle "always wavered between a love of nature
as suffused with deity, and a rejection of her as a cloud on the otherwise dazzling face of Truth." [66] His identification of the will of
nature with God's will is reminiscent of a doctrine of Fichte, which,
while he did not perfectly comprehend it, served as a clue to him
in a wide range of speculations. This was Fichte's doctrine of the
Divine Idea, not as a reality lying behind and apart from the world
of sense, but as a moral principle progressively realizing itself, and
coming to actuality, in the finite world, in man, nature and history.
"This central doctrine of the dynamic revelation of a moral principle active in spite of, and by means of, time and matter will be
seen determining [Carlyle's] conception of time, nature, history, heroes, labor, society, ethics." [67]

The reason why Carlyle could find nature so much more real
in history than in the world of the senses and of physical science
is doubtless that history lends itself so much better to the manipula-
tions of a moral philosopher. History has not yet been made subject
to the tests and controls of an objective method; its facts may be
combined and interpreted more or less to suit one's taste. That was

certainly true of history in Carlyle's day. In history one could so much more easily escape from the net of determinism; one could so much more confidently give a religious interpretation of history, with so much less liability of being challenged and proved in error. History is a record of the doings of men, and lends itself more readily than physics and astronomy to a "humanistic" interpretation.

The Real Tendency of the World

Whatever its metaphysical basis, Carlyle's formula, identifying the will of nature with God's will, is not unlike that which Matthew Arnold somewhat later took over from Bishop Wilson— "reason and the will of God." And another of Carlyle's formulas is singularly like certain of Arnold's. Carlyle praises Mahomet for preaching that God's will is the best for us. Possessed of this belief, he says, man becomes—

. . . the high-priest of this Temple of a World. He is in harmony with the Decrees of the Author of this World; co-operating with them, not vainly withstanding them; I know, to this day, no better definition of Duty than that same. All that is *right* includes itself in this of co-operating with the real Tendency of the World: you succeed by this (the World's Tendency will succeed), you are good, and in the right course there.[68]

This real Tendency of the World with which it is man's duty to co-operate is very like "the natural current there is in human affairs," to which, Arnold says, culture directs our attention;[69] "the main stream of man's advance," which for more than two hundred years has moved towards Hellenism rather than Hebraism;[70] "the inevitable drive of events," of which the British Philistine has not an inkling;[71] "the natural and necessary stream of things," which is flowing in favor of the humanities.[72] Arnold's thought, again, is akin to Carlyle's when he defines God as "the Eternal not ourselves that makes for righteousness." [73]

Both Arnold and Carlyle are more indebted to secular than to religious thought in talking thus of the real Tendency of the World and the natural and necessary stream of things. But there is a vestige of Christian theology in their disposition to make the inevitable drive of events synonymous with the will of God. Carlyle's philosophy of nature, even in this pragmatic phase, is reminiscent of the time when there was "a divinity that shapes our ends." The religious tinge of his thinking grows fainter as he gets farther from his Christian and transcendental origins. But he still occasionally makes his equation between "the Everlasting Laws of Nature" and "a divine message, or eternal Regulation of the Universe." [74] Carlyle in his interpretation of politics and history makes a great show of being realistic and "hard-boiled." But the confidence with which he determines and approves the real Tendency of the World owes more to religious than to strictly naturalistic thought.

The final effect of Carlyle's philosophy was, however, the opposite to that intended. Like transcendentalism in general, while it was in reaction against the arid naturalism of the age of reason, it furnished a screen behind which the scattered forces of naturalism might reassemble. It satisfied the demands of religious sentiment at the same time that it sapped the foundations of religious dogma. It provided a temporary resting place for spirits wearied by the search for truth and not prepared to make a clean break with the past. In his philosophy of nature unconsciously he was doing his best—to use a phrase from Arnold—to "ease a severe transition," [75]— to make possible the passage from a supernatural to a natural reading of the world, and that with a minimum of "violent shocks" and "bitter pain."

Chapter XI

COLERIDGE, EMERSON, AND NATURALISM

When Emerson gave up the ministry of the gospel in 1832, he found himself looking earnestly for some other serious field to cultivate, some other subject on which he could preach without the hampering restrictions to which he had been subject in the church. And what he found was nature—the world of phenomena surveyed by science. The right interpretation of this world of phenomena was the main subject of his little treatise on *Nature*, published in 1836; it is the subject of innumerable references in his Journals over a long course of years; and occupies much of his attention in his essays, lectures and poems. His interest in natural science was greatly stimulated by his visit, in 1833, to the Museum of the *Jardin des Plantes* in Paris. Here he found before his very eyes the several animal forms graded from lowest to highest in the scale. How much he was impressed is shown by his entry in his Journal:

> The universe is a more amazing puzzle than ever, as you glance along this bewildering series of animated forms,—the hazy butterflies, the carved shells, the birds, beasts, fishes, insects, snakes, and the up-heaving principle of life everywhere incipient, in the very rock aping organized forms. Not a form so grotesque, so savage, nor so beautiful but is an expression of some property inherent in man the observer,— an occult relation between the very scorpions and man. I feel the centipede in me,—cayman, carp, eagle and fox. I am moved by strange sympathies; I say continually "I will be a naturalist." [1]

This passage has often been cited as evidence that Emerson was early converted to the modern scientific theory of evolution; and it certainly does bring up that interesting question. At the same time it brings up the more comprehensive problem of Emerson's general approach to scientific fact and theory. When he says that "not a form . . . but is an expression of some property inherent in man the observer," he implies, I believe, the "idealistic" interpretation of natural phenomena which is common to transcendentalists, and which he seems to have derived, in large part, from Coleridge. The influence of Coleridge upon him was, at any rate, so important at an early period of his thinking that it is worth special consideration.[2]

The present chapter will be concerned with rather technical matters which have a bearing on Emerson's poetical concept of nature. First of all I wish to indicate how much of his thought on the subject of nature grows out of Coleridge's exposition of the right method of scientific study—his conception of the "Idea" as the source of fruitful speculation and discovery. This *a priorism* which Emerson takes over from Coleridge has its main origin, I suggest, in German metaphysics, and is closely related to the form of transcendental idealism developed by Schelling. I wish then to indicate how this *a priorism* affects the type of evolutionism held by Coleridge in common with Schelling and his disciple Henrik Steffens, and how Emerson's concept of evolution was qualified by this same attitude of mind. In conclusion, I shall have some general remarks to make on Emerson's place in the naturalistic movement. We shall then be ready to take up, in the following chapter, Emerson's nature-poetry.

The "Idea" in Scientific Speculation

Emerson was familiar with Coleridge's *Aids to Reflection* from 1829 on; with *Biographia Literaria* from 1829 or 1835; with the treatise *On the Constitution of the Church and State* from 1834; with *Specimens of Table Talk* from 1835. But the book of Coleridge's which most deeply impressed him, from 1829 on, was *The Friend,* and in that book, the second section, consisting of "essays on the principles of method common to all investigations," particularly Essays V and XI.

This discussion of method in the second section of *The Friend*—consisting of essays first introduced in the 1818 edition of that work

—corresponds to, and is in large part identical with, Coleridge's discussion of this subject in his *Preliminary Treatise on Method*, contributed by him as a general introduction to the Encyclopædia Metropolitana in the same year 1818, and frequently reprinted separately.[3] The exposition in the *Preliminary Treatise* is in some points fuller, more systematic, and more easily intelligible, than that in *The Friend;* but, so far as I know, Emerson was not acquainted with the *Treatise*, and I shall confine my references to the form taken by the discussion in *The Friend*.

It is in Essay V that Coleridge begins his exposition of right method in scientific investigation. He points out that objects must be considered in their relations, and that there are two kinds of relations in which objects of mind may be contemplated, of which one is that of law. "In whatever science the relation of the parts to each other and to the whole is predetermined by a truth originating in the mind, and not abstracted or generalized from observation of the parts, there we affirm the presence of a law . . ." What Coleridge wishes to assert is the superior fruitfulness of the "synthetic" (rather than the "analytic") method, of the *a priori* (rather than the *a posteriori*). And he confirms his opinion by the authority of Plato.

The grand problem, the solution of which forms, according to Plato, the final object and distinctive character of philosophy, is this: for all that which exists conditionally (that is, the existence of which is inconceivable except under the condition of its dependency on some other as its antecedent) to find a ground that is unconditional and absolute, and thereby to reduce the aggregate of human knowledge to a system.[4]

Emerson was very much struck with this formula and, in his *Nature*, he repeats it literally and in the same connection—that of law as deduced from "a truth originating in the mind."

The philosopher, not less than the poet, postpones the apparent order and relations of things to the empire of thought. "The problem of philosophy," according to Plato, "is, for all that exists conditionally, to find a ground unconditioned and absolute." It proceeds on the faith that a law determines all phenomena, which being known, the phenomena can be predicted. That law, when in the mind, is an idea.[5]

Now, in attributing the above formula to Plato, Coleridge gives no reference. It happens that the formula appears, almost literally, in Kant's *Critique of Pure Reason*, as follows:

So sieht man wohl, der eigenthümliche Grundsatz der Vernunft überhaupt (im logischen Gebrauche) sei: zu dem bedingten Erkenntnisse des Verstandes das Unbedingte zu finden, womit die Einheit desselben vollendet wird.[6]

In Smith's translation:

Obviously the principle peculiar to reason in general, in its logical employment, is:—to find for the conditioned knowledge obtained through the understanding the unconditioned whereby its unity is brought to completion.[7]

Having in mind Coleridge's inaccuracy and his extreme want of candor in giving credit for his ideas, I venture to suggest that he has either forgotten that this is Kant's expression, or else that he found it more convenient to refer to the classic philosopher, by way of disguising the degree to which he was indebted to the Germans of his own day.

This formula is closely bound up with the main subject of Coleridge's discussion in these essays—the importance of "mental initiative" or "initiative thought" in scientific study. And this too, while his references are to Plato and Bacon, is a line of thought into which he had most probably been led by Kant and Schelling. The "momentous distinction" between reason and understanding found in *Aids to Reflection*—though it involves some misunderstanding of Kant's meaning—was probably suggested by a passage in the preface to Kant's *Critique*.[8] And it is not improbable that from certain phrases there used by Kant Coleridge derived his first suggestion for the notion, developed at length in *The Friend*, of the importance of "initiative thought" in scientific investigation, proceeding from "ideas" which are the subjective aspect of "laws." Coleridge insists that these laws cannot be "abstracted or generalized from observation of the parts,"—a notion derived perhaps from Kant's remark on the "true method" in geometry, "not to inspect the visible figure of the triangle, or to analyze the bare conception of it, and from this, as it were, to read off its properties, but to bring out what was necessarily implied in the conception that he (Thales) had himself formed *a priori*, and put into the figure, in the construction by which he presented it to himself." This again reminds one of Coleridge's statement about the relation of objects "pre-determined by a truth originating in the mind." As Kant has it, "reason has insight only into that which it produces after a plan of its own, and . . . it must itself lead the way with principles of judgment based upon fixed laws."

It is true that Coleridge finds this doctrine in Bacon (as well as Plato); and here he gives references and more or less pertinent quotations. But the very reference to Bacon he would have found in Kant's preface, together with an account of the relation between ideas (or laws) and experiments very like that which Coleridge gives as Bacon's.[8a] Here again, as in the case of Plato, Coleridge is very likely drawing a red herring across the trail of his German inspirations. And the notion which Emerson takes over so lightly from Coleridge—skimming the poetic cream off this milk of metaphysic—comes eventually from the "founder of the transcendental school." It is greatly transmogrified, to be sure!

But let us return to the passage taken by Emerson from Coleridge's fifth essay. Emerson's concluding sentence reads: "That law, when in the mind, is an idea." This notion of law as the objective form of idea is one which Emerson found repeated several times, in more technical and elaborated forms, in the succeeding chapters of *The Friend*, as well as in *Aids to Reflection*. Thus in a footnote to Essay X:

> The sense is, that the productive power, or *vis naturans*, which in the sensible world, or *natura naturata*, is what we mean by the word, nature, when we speak of the same as agent, is essentially one . . . In other words, idea and law are the subjective and objective poles of the same magnet, that is, of the same living and energizing reason. What an idea is in the subject, that is, in the mind, is a law in the object, that is, in nature.[9]

Again, in *Aids to Reflection*, as conclusion to an elaborate hocus-pocus of prothesis, thesis and antithesis, Coleridge states: "Thus an IDEA conceived as subsisting in an Object becomes a Law; and a LAW contemplated *subjectively* (in a mind) is an Idea." [10]

Returning now to Essay V, we find Coleridge announcing the "remarkable fact" that "the material world is found to obey the same laws as had been deduced independently from the reason," and inquiring, with Plato, into the "ground of the coincidence between reason and experience; or between the laws of matter and the ideas of the pure intellect." Again, he speaks later of the "principle of connection given by the mind [in scientific investigations], and sanctioned by the correspondency of nature"; and still again, he points out "how nature, or that which in nature itself is more than nature, seems to come forward in order to meet, to aid, and to reward every idea excited by a contemplation of her methods in the spirit of filial care," etc., etc. This notion of "the coincidence between reason and experience; or between the laws of matter and the ideas of the pure intellect" turns up in various forms in Emerson: as "that correspondence of the outward to the inward world of thought and emotions, by which it [external nature] is suited to express what we think"; as the "radical correspondence between visible things and human thoughts," and "that wonderful congruity which subsists between man and the world." [11]

The same thought is found in Schelling in phrases almost identical with those of Coleridge and Emerson—"the correspondency (or coincidence) of nature with the maxims of our reflective reason" (*die Uebereinstimmung der Natur mit den Maximen unserer reflectirenden Vernunft*).[12] Coleridge's whole discussion is in effect a defense of the deductive method pursued by pseudo-scientists like Schelling and Steffens. The notion of the relations of objects as "pre-determined by a truth originating in the mind," is inherent in the whole of Schelling's "Naturphilosophie," and derives from the central, the radical place in his transcendental system, of self-consciousness (*Selbstbewusstseyn*) from which, as a starting-point, he proceeds to deduce, *a priori*, his "construction of matter." Coleridge may have found also in Schelling enthusiastic reference to systematizing ideas as fruitful in scientific research.[13] Coleridge shares with Schelling his antipathy to mere hypothesis (arrived at inductively by abstraction or generalization "from observation of the parts"); and his faith in speculative physics, which proceeds *a priori* and by "intuition," as the soul of true experiment and the mother of all great discoveries. From men capable of this procedure Coleridge looks to have a demonstration of "an unbroken series of correspondencies in nature." Once again it appears likely that Emerson's thought, in so far as it is derived from Coleridge, goes back to German idealism.

Coleridge's pious defense of *a priorism* in science is continued in Essay VI. This essay is mainly devoted to illustrations of the futility of mere classification in science, unguided by "mental initiative" or "initiative thought." Coleridge's examples are chiefly drawn from botany, and it is the great classifier, Linnæus, who bears the brunt of his attack. Here Emerson follows him, brilliantly and somewhat recklessly condensing Coleridge's thought. In one passage in *Nature* he is discussing the need to establish a relation between the facts of science and the thought and interests of man.

And neither can man be understood without these objects, nor these objects without man. All the facts in natural history taken by themselves, have no value, but are barren, like a single sex. But marry it to human history, and it is full of life. Whole floras, all Linnæus' and Buffon's volumes, are dry catalogues of facts; but the most trivial of these facts, the habit of a plant, the organs, or work, or noise of an insect, applied to the illustration of a fact in intellectual philosophy, or in any way associated to human nature, affects us in the most lively and agreeable manner.[14]

Emerson's thought is more vague and less interesting philosophically than Coleridge's. Moreover, he makes the mistake of citing Buffon (famous for his creative imagination), along with Linnaeus, as an example of the barrenness of catalogues of facts without ideas. In other equally literary passages in *Nature* Emerson was closely following Coleridge's thought, though perhaps without quite completely taking it in.[15] Much more plain and sober was Emerson's disparagement of mere classification in the lecture given before the Boston Natural History Society in November 1833.[16]

In his same Essay VI Coleridge gives an example of how the pregnant idea may be at work in chemical experiment. It may be no more than chance, but it is curious that Emerson should in the same connection use Coleridge's very phrase, "the charm of chemistry." In Essay VII there is an instance given of the importance of the *a priori* element in mathematics.

A mathematical *theoria seu contemplatio* may . . . be perfect. For the mathematician can be certain that he has contemplated all that appertains to his proposition. The celebrated Euler, treating on some point respecting arches, makes this curious remark:—"All experience is in contradiction to this; *sed potius fidendum est analysi; i.e.* but this is no reason for doubting the analysis." The words sound paradoxical; but in truth mean no more than this, that the properties of space are not less certainly the properties of space because they can never be entirely transferred to material bodies.[17]

This striking instance of the paramountcy of the "idea" in its own realm was avidly seized on by Emerson, in his incautious exposition of "idealism," to illustrate how, "even in physics, the material is degraded before the spiritual," when "this feeble human being has penetrated the vast masses of nature with an informing soul, and recognized itself in their harmony, that is, seized their law."

The astronomer, the geometer, rely on their irrefragable analysis, and disdain the results of observation. The sublime remark of Euler on his law of arches, "This will be found contrary to all experience, yet is true"; has already transferred nature into the mind, and left matter like an outcast corpse.[18]

This is "transcendentalism" with a vengeance, and with a total lack of definition!

Another of Coleridge's instances of the pregnant idea in science was "the grand conception" of John Hunter—the definition of "life" which flitted before him more or less elusively all his days, until "in the astonishing preparations for his museum, he constructed it for scientific apprehension out of the unspoken alphabet of nature." [19] Emerson several times refers to the theories of John Hunter, echoing Coleridge. The point with them both seems to be that life is not to be regarded as a function or *creature* of the organs in which it acts, but rather as the animating principle of all organized forms. This dynamic theory of life is often expressed by Emerson, who follows Coleridge in taking what we now call the "vitalistic" (as opposed to the "mechanistic") point of view.

I have given a few of the more striking instances in which Coleridge influenced the thought of Emerson; all of them illustrating the need for the illuminating "idea" in the interpretation of scientific data. This was something like an obsession with Emerson over a long course of years, and is reflected in innumerable comments in his Journals and his published writings.

Emerson does not always seem to have grasped distinctly the metaphysical basis of this thought in Coleridge,—Schelling's doctrine of the identity of objective and subjective, and the essentially "ideal" (or intelligent) character of the world-process, which is a manifestation of thought.

Thus we have Emerson, in his essay on "Nature," jauntily echoing Coleridge's favorite distinction between *natura naturans* and *natura naturata*.[20] This distinction between the two aspects of nature (active and passive) is common enough in philosophy, beginning with Averroës, and might have been found by Coleridge in Giordano Bruno or Spinoza, or in the seventeenth-century divines, as well as in Bacon. But it is most probable that one of the passages in *The Friend* was written under the influence of Schelling and another under that of Kant.[21] Thus it seems that Emerson's poetic fantasia in his essay has its roots in a soil in which Kantian rationalism and Schellingesque transcendentalism were by Coleridge adroitly mixed with piety and platonism. But Emerson seems to have missed the metaphysical point of the distinction drawn by Coleridge. Coleridge is wishing to insist that the nature of materialists, conceived of as a series of mechanical impulses acting on inert bodies, is incapable of explaining itself, of originating itself, of acting intelligently and purposively. This is passive nature, *natura naturata*. The evolutions of this passive nature can only be understood by reference to a productive power or agency, *vis naturans, forma formans*, which acts through it. And this ultimate agency of nature is ideal or intelligent in character. "The productive power, which in nature acts as nature, is essentially one (that is, of one kind) with intelligence, which is in the human mind above nature." [22]

But while Emerson sometimes misses the metaphysical implications of what he takes over from Coleridge, the practical results are the same in the two thinkers—a sort of spiritual anthropomorphism in the interpretation of scientific data, a disposition not so much to be guided by the facts in building up theories, as to read a human (and religious) meaning into the facts. The theory of evolution is one of many such illuminating ideas; and the attitude of both Emerson and Coleridge towards this theory—their understanding of its meaning—is largely determined by this idealistic or anthropomorphic bias.

Transcendental Idealism

In reading *The Friend*, Emerson would come at length on the culminating Essay XI, with its long quotation from Wordsworth's "Intimations" ode and its statement of the central doctrine of idealistic metaphysics. Already there have been glimpses of this idealism. Emerson will have read of "truth, that must be found within us before it can be intelligibly reflected back on the mind from without." [23] But here in Essay XI he will have read more at length how—

Under the tutorage of scientific analysis, haply first given to him by express revelation (*E cœlo descendit*, γνῶθι σεαυτὸν), [man] separates the relations which are wholly creatures of his own abstracting and comparing intellect, and at once discovers and recoils from the discovery, that the reality, the objective truth, of the objects he has been adoring, derives its whole and sole evidence from an obscure sensation, which he is alike unable to resist or to comprehend, *which compels him to contemplate as without and independent of himself what yet he could not contemplate at all, were it not a modification of his own being*.[24]

Then follows the quotation from the "Intimations" (strophes vi and ix), and Coleridge goes on with his disquisition:

Long indeed will man strive to satisfy the inward querist with the phrase, laws of nature. But though the individual may rest content with the seemly metaphor, the race can not. If a law of nature be a mere generalization, it is included in the above as an act of the mind. But if it be other and more, and yet manifestable only in and to an intelligent spirit, *it must in act and substance be itself spiritual:* for things utterly heterogeneous can have no intercommunion. In order therefore to the recognition of himself in nature *man must first learn to comprehend nature in himself, and its laws in the ground of his own existence*.[25]

It is from expressions such as I have italicized above that Emerson probably had his first introduction to the German form of idealism. This was reinforced, no doubt, by neoplatonic notions, to which Emerson took with avidity, and by other inspirations from Swedenborg, from the East, and perhaps directly from Kant, Schelling, and others of the Germans. This idealism of Coleridge's is not, I believe, strict Kantian doctrine. Kant had carefully distinguished between *things in themselves* and *phenomena*—the former having perhaps an existence independent of our thinking, the latter indeed dependent for their character on what Coleridge calls "relations which are wholly creatures of our abstracting and comparing intellect." Wanting this distinction of Kant's, the idealism of Coleridge has often a rather loose and irresponsible character. It is, I think, from Schelling that he derives the notion that nature has "its laws in the ground of [man's] own existence." And it is this simplified form of idealism that Emerson echoes so often and with such a poetic disregard for definition and exactitude.

Thus in *Nature* we read, in the poet's "orphic song," that "the laws of [Man's] mind externized themselves into day and night, into the years and the seasons." Here again we read:

Each phenomenon has its roots in the faculties and affections of the mind . . . Nature is not fixed but fluid. Spirit alters, moulds, makes it . . . Build therefore your own world. As fast as you conform your life to the pure idea in your mind, that will unfold its great proportions.[26]

In his oration on "The Method of Nature," Emerson declares, in more philosophical terms:

In the divine order, intellect is primary; nature secondary; it is the memory of the mind. That which once existed in intellect as pure law, has now taken body as Nature. It existed already in the mind in solution; now, it has precipitated, and the bright sediment is the world.[27]

The same ideas appear in much later work, with no diminution of poetical extravagance in the phrasing. In his lecture on "Poetry and Imagination":

Chemistry, geology, hydraulics, are secondary science. The atomic theory is only an interior process *produced*, as geometers say, or the effect of a foregone metaphysical theory. Swedenborg saw gravity as

only an external of the irresistible attractions of affection and faith. . . .
The world realizes the mind. Better than images is seen through them
. . . The poet discovers that what men value as substances have a higher
value as symbols; that Nature is the immense shadow of man . . .[28]

In his essay on "Nature":

Nature is the incarnation of a thought, and turns to a thought again,
as ice becomes water and gas. The world is mind precipitated, and the
volatile essence is forever escaping again into the state of free thought.
Hence the virtue and pungency of the influence on the mind of natural
objects, whether inorganic or organized. Man imprisoned, man crystal-
lized, man vegetative, speaks to man impersonated.[29]

And in "The Poet," he says: "The Universe is the externization
of the soul." [30]

Emerson grows particularly reckless when echoing Coleridge's
distinction between understanding and reason, which he handles
with a looseness going far beyond anything possible to Coleridge.
He has been much impressed with Coleridge's derivation of understanding from the mere senses, which makes it unreliable and inferior. Thus in *Nature:*

To the senses and the unrenewed understanding, belongs a sort of
instinctive belief in the absolute existence of nature . . . The presence
of Reason mars this faith. The first effort of thought tends to relax this
despotism of the senses which binds us to nature as if we were a part
of it . . . The sensual man conforms thoughts to things; the poet conforms things to his thought . . . The Imagination may be defined to be
the use which the Reason makes of the material world . . . The advantage of the ideal theory over the popular faith is this, that it presents
the world in precisely that view which is most desirable to the mind.
It is, in fact, the view which Reason, both speculative and practical,
that is, philosophy and virtue, take.[31]

Note this incautious admission that idealism is to be preferred
because "it presents the world in precisely that view which is most
desirable to the mind." Emerson means of course much more than
the mind; he means the heart, the moral sense, the religious. He
means that the view in question is the one that he *likes best.* This
emotional bias is clearly operating everywhere in Coleridge's
thought, though he is much too shrewd to admit it. It is even

present in Kant, who does more or less admit it. Emerson is, especially in his prose, a poet of infinite charm and tonic quality. As for his philosophy of nature—as *philosophy*—must we not admit that it is, for the most part, a loose and popular rendering of Coleridge, who gives a loose and popular rendering of (mainly) Shelling, who—for all his magnificent show of dialectic—is no better than a Kant run wild?

Evolution and the Scale of Being

In considering Emerson's attitude towards evolution, his manner of interpreting this scientific theory, and the philosophical inferences drawn from it by him, we must have in mind the transcendental bias of his thought. We must consider also that his opinions were not shaped primarily by the great scientific writers, Buffon, Lamarck, Saint-Hilaire, and Darwin, but by a succession of second-rate, popular, and more or less dubious authorities. And the first of these was Coleridge.[32]

Much has been made, by literary critics, of passages in certain English poets—Coleridge, Tennyson, Browning, Emerson—which, long before the publication of *The Origin of Species*, suggest the doctrine of evolution. But a close examination will often show that these poets did not have in mind the theory of the "transmutation of species" (to use Lyell's term for it). What they had in mind was often merely the concept of a "graduated scale of being" in the organic world. This was a concept widely held by scientists and philosophers in the eighteenth century and earlier, many of whom had not a tincture of the modern evolutionary views. It was held by Leibniz, Locke, Berkeley and Kant, by Sir Matthew Hale, and other theological writers, by Lessing, Herder, Bonnet, Robinet, Buffon, Goethe, Lamarck—not to speak of the poets Pope, Akenside, and Thomson—associated, or not associated, with the "transmutation of species." It was held by Schelling and Steffens, and was taken over from them by Coleridge in his *Hints Towards the Formation of a More Comprehensive Theory of Life*, where he gives a highly elaborated account of the scale of being extending up through various stages of organized life to men. It is doubtful whether Emerson was acquainted with this work, which was not published till 1848. But he had certainly read several briefer essays of Coleridge's on the same theme: the Dialogue between Demosius and Mystes in *The Constitution of the Church and State* (1830), the "Monologue" on Life, published in *Fraser's Magazine* in November, 1835, a brief paragraph in *Specimens of Table Talk* (1835), and, above all, the following paragraph from *Aids to Reflection*, a book which Emerson read with close attention as early as 1829:

Every rank of creatures, as it ascends in the scale of creation, leaves death behind it or under it. The metal at its height of being seems a mute prophecy of the coming vegetation, into a mimic semblance of which it crystallizes. The blossom and flower, the acme of vegetable life, divides into correspondent organs with reciprocal functions, and by instinctive motions and approximations seems impatient of that fixture, by which it is differenced in kind from the flower-shaped Psyche, that flutters with free wing above it. And wonderfully in the insect realm doth irritability, the proper seat of instinct . . . typically rehearse the adaptive understanding, yes, and the moral affections and charities, of man . . . Thus all lower natures find their highest good in semblance and seekings of that which is higher and better. All things strive to ascend, and ascend in their striving. And shall man alone stoop? [33]

To the modern reader this sounds much like the evolutionary doctrine of Lamarck. But Coleridge means nothing of the sort. He is not talking of the origin of species. He more than once repudiated the notion that man is derived from any lower animal form, or that any animal species is derived from another. He is simply enunciating the traditional doctrine of the scale of being, which he might have found in such perfectly orthodox works as Matthew Hale's *Primitive Origination of Mankind* and Berkeley's *Siris*.

In considering this notion, we must always bear in mind that it may be held in several distinct ways. (1) It may be held in connection with the theory of the "transmutation of species," with the understanding that the "higher" forms have been derived from the lower by natural means such as those set forth by Lamarck and Darwin. (2) It may not imply evolution at all in this sense, but still be thought of as a series of events in chronological sequence; life being regarded historically as later in appearance than inorganic matter, and the higher forms of life as following the lower in a graduated scale of ascent. (3) It may not even imply chronological sequence, or take into account at all the question of successive appearance in time. The several orders of living beings are then ranged from lowest to highest as a matter of classification, by way of showing the *unity of plan* which runs through the whole of nature.

Lyell, in his *Principles of Geology* (1830–33), repudiates with almost equal firmness the first and second views listed above. He believes neither in the "evolution of one species out of another," nor in the chronological succession of higher and higher forms of being. The most that he admits is "the unity of plan that runs through" the system of vertebrated animals.[34] Browning, in "Paracelsus" (1835), admits the second and third views, including the unity of plan running from inorganic matter up to man's spiritual life and the historical sequence in this graduated ascent. This is apparently the position of Tennyson, too, in the canceled stanzas of "The Palace of Art" (1833).[35] There is nothing to show that these poets did not agree with Lyell in ascribing each new species to a particular act of creation, rather than assume a "transmutation of species."

In Schelling and Steffens and Coleridge the evolution of the successive stages of being is worked out in an elaborate systematic way. But they are writing not as scientists but as metaphysicians, proceeding *a priori* from the assumptions of a mystical idealism. The following is a very brief summary of the theory which they held in common. The life possessed by organized beings is really but a later step in a life-process already manifested in inorganic matter. Life is definable as a process of progressive "individuation." Metaphysically it is a manifestation of "unity in multeity." It is the result of the opposition of positive and negative forces, or "polarity." There are three grand ascending stages in organic life; characterized, respectively, by productivity (in plants), irritability (in insects), and sensibility (in higher animal forms). These three manifestations of organic life correspond to the three groups of material phenomena known as magnetism, electricity and chemical affinity. To understand these three material forces philosophically, one must make an analysis of the metaphysical concepts of time and space. For all life—all existence—is grounded in the "spiritual" laws of the mind. Such is, in summary, the set of views developed, rather obscurely and fragmentarily, in Coleridge's *Theory of Life*, and implied—some of them—in the other brief essays referred to above. It has been shown by the Swiss scholar, Heinrich Nidecker, that Coleridge took the entire theory from two works of Henrik Steffens, *Beiträge zur innern Naturgeschichte der Erde* (1801) and *Grundzüge der philosophischen Naturwissenschaft* (1806), and that his treatise contains many long passages literally translated from Steffens's *Beiträge*, as well as from Schelling's *Allgemeine Deduktion des dynamischen Processes* (1800).[36] I am inclined to think that Coleridge took hints for his treatise also from Schelling's *Ideen zu einer Philosophie der Natur* (1797) and *Erster Entwurf eines Systems der Naturphilosophie* (1799), and possibly also from his *Von der Weltseele* (1798).

Coleridge several times uses the words "evolution" and "evolve" in connection with the ascending progress of life. And Schelling and Steffens use both the French word "evolution" and the German "Entwicklung."[37] To the modern and non-transcendental mind these words, in these connections, inevitably imply the derivation of the higher forms of organic life from the lower, and ultimately (if we insist on thinking the matter through) the derivation of organic life from inorganic matter (abiogenesis, or *generatio æquivoca*). It is hard for us to understand, what apparently we must understand, that none of these men had in view, as necessary to their theory, any such historical process in which one species had its origin by modification from another. Schelling's and Steffens's "evolution," like Coleridge's, is a mere·logical, or conceptual, unfolding, or disinvolvement, of the lower category of being from the higher, or vice versa. Steffens states clearly, in his *Anthropologie* (1822):[38]

Wir nennen diese Thiere die niedrigern, nicht als wenn die höhern sich aus ihnen erzeugt hätten. So wie sie da sind, setzen sie eben so gewiss die ganze Organisation voraus, wie irgend ein Organ seines erscheinenden Thieres das Ganze voraussetzt.[39]

We call these animals the lower, not as if the higher ones had been begotten of them. By their very existence they imply inevitably the total range of organized beings, just as any organ of an animal that makes its appearance implies the totality of that animal.

This notion of the implication of the whole in the part is akin to the view of Coleridge, several times stated in the Dialogue of Demosius and Mystes, that the higher "powers" of life imply the lower, the lower imply the higher, and neither is even conceivable except in terms of the other. These statements in Coleridge are mystical and dogmatic; but in Schelling the positions are elaborately deduced *a priori* from the very nature of life as necessarily conceived by the mind. In the *Erster Entwurf* there is a subtle exposition of the "mutual determination of sensibility and irritability"; [40] and a main object of his in this work is to explain in detail the mutual involvement of the organic and the inorganic which Coleridge more or less dogmatically asserts.

The word "evolution" is used by these writers to signify that the life process is "dynamic"—the manifestation of a principle inherent in its least part, deriving from the essentially "ideal" nature of existence. A modern scientist may be strongly inclined to adopt a dynamic rather than a mechanical view of the universal process. But it is practically impossible for him to conceive of the passage from one order of organized being to another without thinking either of a special act of creation, or else of change, modification, transmutation, "historical transition,"—some one of the concepts implied in the ordinary use of the word "evolution." This incapacity of the scientist derives, perhaps, from the necessity under which he labors of thinking of natural events as following one another in time and bearing to one another the relation, if not of cause and effect, then at least of antecedent and consequent. But the transcendental philosopher does not labor under this disability, owing to his having raised himself somehow above the concept of time, and so above that of antecedent and consequent. Schelling, in discussing the "gradation of powers," as readily reads his scale downward as upward. Schelling and Coleridge, accordingly, in their published works, seldom touch remotely upon the scientific problem of evolution—whether, namely, the phases later in time are in some sense *derived* from the earlier phases, and by what means this derivation or transition is brought about. They move, as it were, on an altogether different plane of thought, where this consideration is irrelevant.

When, however, Coleridge does condescend to this objective

plane, he is perfectly explicit, like Steffens, in his repudiation of the evolutionary hypothesis. Thus Coleridge, in a letter to Wordsworth in 1815.[41] He is explaining why he is disappointed in "The Excursion." He had hoped that Wordsworth would "have exploded the absurd notion of Pope's 'Essay on Man,' Darwin, and all the countless believers even (strange to say) among Christians of man's having progressed from an ourang-outang state—so contrary to all history, to all religion, nay, to all possibility." Coleridge was curiously confused here on the subject of Pope, in whose poem there is no evolutionary implication so far as I can see. As in Coleridge's own system, so in Pope's, the infinite gradation of orders is simply a logical necessity, something "essential to th' amazing whole."

With Erasmus Darwin the case was different. In *The Temple of Nature* and *Zoönomia* he did teach the doctrine of spontaneous generation of life in the lowest organisms and the progressive development of higher forms of life. He did point out the likeness of human anatomy to that of four-footed animals and suggest that man may have taken his origin from a family of monkeys. He did outline the development of human faculties; he described the struggle for existence among animals and plants, and just missed the connection pointed out by his grandson between this struggle and the "survival of the fittest." "His view of the origin of adaptations or of design in Nature was thoroughly naturalistic, believing that adaptations had not been specially created, but that they had been naturally and gradually acquired by powers of development planted within the original organisms by the Creator." [42] In short, he was a thorough evolutionist. Moreover, Coleridge was under the mistaken impression that he was an atheist, which made him all the more ready to reject his views.

What these men could not stomach in evolution was the final conclusion to which it led, that man too, like the other species, is derived from lower forms of life. It contradicted their religious faith that man was created in the image of God and had fallen from his high estate. Schelling, in his *Vorlesungen über die Methode des akademischen Studiums* (1803), denies that man's primitive state was brutish and barbarous, and asserts that it was, on the contrary, a condition of high culture directly inspired by religion.[43] Coleridge was disappointed with Wordsworth for not having, in "The Excursion," affirmed the doctrine of the Fall of Man. The doctrine of the "ascent of man" was inconsistent with the persuasion of Coleridge that man's reason is a faculty quite distinct from any mental powers which he shares with the lower animals. It is interesting to note that in this persuasion the great English geologist agreed with Coleridge.

The superiority of man (says Lyell) depends not on those faculties and attributes which he shares in common with the inferior animals, but on his reason, by which he is distinguished from them. When it is said that the human race is of far higher dignity than were any pre-existing beings on the earth, it is the intellectual and moral attributes only of our race, not their animal, which are considered. . . . The sudden passage from an irrational to a rational animal is a phenomenon of a distinct kind from the passage from the more simple to the more perfect forms of animal organization and instinct. To pretend that this step, or rather leap, can be part of a regular series of changes in the animal world, is to strain analogy beyond all reasonable bounds.[44]

But Coleridge has left on record his rejection not merely of the animal origin of man but also of the transmutation of species in general—"since there is the same reason for asserting the progression of every other race of animal from some lower species as of the human race," and they are both equally "in contradiction to all experience." [45] So that we may be perfectly confident that in his various accounts of the "scale of being" he does not mean to imply anything like the modern scientific theory of evolution.

Emerson and Evolution

In forming his views on nature, Emerson started where Coleridge left off. He was subject to various influences under which Coleridge did not fall. Views and expressions which in Coleridge did not carry the modern evolutionary implication came in the end to carry this implication for Emerson. He must have read in *Table Talk* Coleridge's somewhat sentimental repudiation of the theory of man's descent from a lower animal form:

Look at that head of Cline, by Chantrey! Is that forehead, that nose, those temples, and that chin, akin to the monkey tribe? No, no. To a man of sensibility no argument could disprove the bestial theory so convincingly as a quiet contemplation of that fine bust.[46]

In the long run, however, Coleridge's condemnation of the "bestial theory" would make less impression than his account of how "the animal rises" in the "scale of being." And so was planted the seed of what in the end was to flower as the evolutionary faith. But it was a long time in flowering.

In 1830 Emerson read Lee's *Life of Cuvier;* but there he found no encouragement for the view that one species may be derived from another by "transmutation," and he noted rather ruefully, I think, that Cuvier took no stock in the Coleridgean "scale of beings." [47] In Dr. John Abernethy's lectures on Hunter's "theory of life," Emerson did find much made of the "concatenation" of animal forms.[48] But Abernethy was obviously troubled by his own inability to find more than esthetic significance in this concatenation. It never occurred to him to interpret it *genetically* by reference to the origin of species. Much the same position was occupied by Sir Charles Bell in his treatise on *The Hand, its Mechanism and Vital Endowments as Evincing Design* (1833), which was read by Emerson in the year of its publication.[49] Bell gives no countenance to evolutionary views. But he does present the view of a "progressive system" in nature, and that of "an anticipating or prospective intelligence"; and he has some notion of the immensities of time at nature's disposal for carrying on her operations. Emerson was greatly impressed with the examples given by Bell of the similarity of organs in animals of the most diverse kind and period. And he reproduced certain of these, together with the pious moral drawn by Bell, in a lecture delivered in Boston in December, 1833, on "The Relation of Man to the Globe." In this lecture he speaks of the fact—

. . . the most surprising, I may say the most sublime, that man is no upstart in the creation, but has been prophesied in nature for a thousand thousand ages before he appeared; that, from times incalculably remote, there has been a progressive preparation for him, an effort to produce him; the meaner creatures containing the elements of his structure and pointing at it from every side. . . . His limbs are only a more exquisite organization—say rather the finish—of the rudimental forms that have already been sweeping the sea and creeping in the mud; the brother of his hand is even now cleaving the Arctic sea in the fin of the whale, and innumerable ages since was pawing the marsh in the flipper of the saurian.[50]

This has often been cited as evidence that Emerson had accepted the theory of evolution. Such a conclusion is quite unwarranted. The thought is taken bodily from Bell, who does not dream of the evolutionary hypothesis. It is simply proof of "an anticipating or prospective intelligence" at work in nature. In 1834, Emerson refers in his Journal to the fact that "Dr. Darwin's work has lost all its consequence in the literary world." "Why?" he adds. "Not from Currie, nor from Brown. A dim, venerable public decides upon every work." [51] "Brown" is probably a reference to Thomas Brown, whose *Observations on the Zoönomia of Dr. Darwin* (Edinburgh, 1798) offers, according to Rees's *Cyclopedia* of 1819, "a complete refutation of the sophisms contained in" Darwin's work. The inference is that Emerson shared the opinion of the "dim, venerable public" on Darwin's evolutionary theory.

Even in *Nature* there is nothing specifically evolutionary. But in September, 1836, this work was published and off its author's hands. And what he has to say from now on is much more pertinent, from the scientific point of view. The reason for this is unmistakable. Emerson has been reading Lyell. There are several entries in the Journal and a highly significant passage in his lecture on "The Humanity of Science," delivered in December, all bearing testimony to the impression made by Lyell.[52] Most significant are the references to Geoffroy de Saint-Hilaire and Lamarck, whose evolutionary theories were set forth by Lyell in order to refute them. In the Journal and in his lecture Emerson gives a fanciful account of the "system of Lamarck." [53] One scholar somewhat uncritically speaks of the time "when Emerson lectured on evolution in 1836." [54] Judging by the outline of the lecture given by Cabot, this interpretation is unjustified. Emerson's subject was "the humanity of that spirit in which nature works," and Lamarck was offered merely as an example of the "tyrannical instinct" which impels the mind "to reduce all facts to a few laws, to one law." The utmost we can say is that in 1836 Emerson's imagination had been impressed with Lamarck's concept as an interesting scientific theory.

But once this seed was lodged in his mind, it was bound to sprout. Emerson had no such theological grounds as Coleridge for fighting shy of the "bestial theory." The doctrine of the fall of man meant nothing to him—on the contrary. His theology was of the most nebulous and accommodating order. As the years went on, he became more and more case-hardened by neoplatonism and every form of Oriental "idealism" against the assaults of any objective fact whatsoever. His mind was one in which contraries lived happily together in a sort of benign solution. That is the note of transcendentalism. He was exposed to scientific influences which Coleridge did not encounter. Moreover, was it not his own revered Coleridge who had first fired his imagination with the thought of an ascending scale of life, and even talked of how irritability was "evolved out of the growth," and sensibility out of irritability? A mere Emerson could not be expected to distinguish, like Coleridge, between a purely logical evolution and an actual "historical" process.

The transition from the scale-of-being phase of Emerson's thought to the strictly evolutionary phase was made by insensible degrees; and it is perhaps doubtful whether he himself was aware of what was taking place. In 1841, in his oration on "The Method of Nature," and in the poem, "Woodnotes," his expressions are a shade more evolutionary than in any earlier utterance. In 1844, in his essay on "Nature," he is several shades more evolutionary. In this year appeared that scandal-rousing book, *Vestiges of the Natural History of Creation*, probably written by Robert Chambers. This book contains the most elaborate statement and most plausible defense of the evolution theory that Emerson had ever encountered. But so familiar was this way of thought by then that it caused him neither shock nor excitement. The only thing that bothered him was the perfunctory piety with which the author tried to gild the pill for his religious readers.[55] From now on Emerson's Journal entries show a more marked evolutionary cast. Not long after the notice of the *Vestiges*, we have the most uncompromising declaration Emerson was ever to make that man is a child of earth:

The master can do his great deed, the desire of the world,—say to find his way between azote and oxygen, detect the scent of the new rock superposition, find the law of the curves,—because he has just come out of Nature, or from being a part of that thing. . . . He knows the laws of azote because just now he was azote. Man is only a piece of the universe made alive.[56]

The next book which deeply affected Emerson's views of nature was by a now forgotten writer, the German-American jurist, Johann Bernhard Stallo. It was apparently in 1849 that Emerson read Stallo's *General Principles of the Philosophy of Nature* (Boston, 1848).[57] Stallo had a vigorous philosophical mind, and gives, I think, an acceptable résumé of the systems of Schelling and Hegel, with some account of Kant and Fichte, and of "Oken's system of nature." From his book Emerson probably learned more of German metaphysics than from any other reading; it is from this time on that we have the most frequent references to Schelling and Hegel, as well as to Oken, Saint-Hilaire, and other evolutionary naturalists. The evolutionism that Emerson found in Stallo, however, was rather vague and transcendental. He writes in his Journal of "Schelling's *aperçu*" (the word is Stallo's) and its later forms in Oken, Hegel, etc.: "The idea was that the form or type became transparent in the actual forms of successive ages as presented in geology." [58] That is the nearest Emerson comes in these years to a statement of the theory of evolution.

In his direct quotations from Stallo there is one very interesting, if obscure, expression: "*The development of all individual forms will be spiral.*" [59] This is evidently the notion Emerson wished to express in the motto added to *Nature* in 1849:

> A subtle chain of countless rings
> The next unto the farthest brings
> . . . .
> And, striving to be man, the worm
> Mounts through all the spires of form.

But the main reflections of Emerson after reading Stallo are in line with his favorite notion of the creative Idea and his equally favorite "idealism."

The Origin of Species passed without notice. Either Emerson's attention was not drawn to this epoch-making book; or else, after Chambers and Stallo, it made no particular impression upon him. Beside the high and mystical discourse of German idealists, mere objective science was perhaps too dry for Emerson. In 1873 he notes: "Darwin's *Origin of Species* was published in 1859, but Stallo, in 1849, writes, 'animals are but foetal forms of man.'" [60] This oracular utterance is of more import to the Concord sage than the ranged and sifted evidence of natural selection.

The writing of Emerson which most strikingly suggests the theory of evolution is found in a lecture, first delivered in 1854, and brought to its final form in two lectures on "Poetry and Imagination" delivered in 1872. By the year 1854 he had been subjected to every important influence that was to mold his scientific outlook, and this is the sum of his philosophy of nature. The following passages are the most significant:

First innuendos, then broad hints, then smart taps are given, suggesting that nothing stands still in Nature but death; that the creation is on wheels, in transit, always passing into something else, streaming into something higher; that matter is not what it appears;—that chemistry can blow it all into gas. . . . The ends of all are moral, and therefore the beginnings are such. Thin or solid, everything is in flight. I believe this conviction makes the charm of chemistry,—that we have the same avoirdupois matter in an alembic, without a vestige of the old form; and in animal transformation not less, as in grub and fly, in egg and bird, in embryo and man; everything undressing and stealing away from its old into new form, and nothing fast but those invisible cords which we call laws, on which all is strung.

[Thought] has its own polarity. One of these vortices or self-directions of thought is the impulse to search resemblance, affinity, identity, in all its objects, and hence our science, from its rudest to its most refined theories.

The electric word pronounced by John Hunter a hundred years ago, *arrested and progressive development*, indicating the way upward from the invisible protoplasm to the highest organisms, gave the poetic key to Natural Science, of which the theories of Geoffroy Saint-Hilaire, of Oken, of Goethe, of Agassiz and Owen and Darwin in zoölogy and botany, are the fruits,—a hint whose power is not yet exhausted, showing unity and perfect order in physics.

The hardest chemist, the severest analyzer, scornful of all but dryest fact, is forced to keep the poetic curve of Nature, and his result is like a myth of Theocritus. All multiplicity rushes to be resolved into unity. Anatomy, osteology, exhibit arrested or progressive ascent in each kind, the lower pointing to the higher forms, the higher to the highest, from the fluid in an elastic sack, from radiate, mollusk, articulate, vertebrate, up to man; as if the whole animal world were only a Hunterian museum to exhibit the genesis of mankind.

Identity of law, perfect order in physics, perfect parallelism between the laws of Nature and the laws of thought exist. In botany we have the like, the poetic perception of metamorphosis,—that the same vegetable point or eye which is the unit of the plant can be transformed at pleasure into every part, as bract, leaf, petal, stamen, pistil or seed. . . .

. . . Natural objects, if individually described and out of connection, are not yet known, since they are really parts of a symmetrical universe, like words of a sentence; and if their true order is found, the poet can read their divine significance orderly as in a Bible. Each animal and vegetable form remembers the next inferior and predicts the next higher.[61]

These paragraphs illustrate extremely well the insensible degrees by which Emerson passed from the progressive-development phase of thought to the strictly evolutionary. In this lecture, Emerson's constant theme is the familiar one of identity of law in nature. There is very little here that cannot be paralleled in Coleridge's scale-of-being paragraph in *Aids to Reflection* or in the essays on method in *The Friend*. The only paragraphs in which the evolutionary implications are marked are the two beginning with "the electric word pronounced by John Hunter." There is nothing in Coleridge about the electric word, "arrested and progressive development." Nor apparently can it be found in Hunter.[62] In his Journals, however, Emerson refers to the phrase "arrested development" as occurring in *Vestiges of Creation*.[63] And indeed we do find in Chambers the words "arrested," "progressive," and "development," all used together in connection with old John Hunter. And his "grand conception" takes on, under Chambers' wand, evolutionary implications which it did not have for Hunter himself nor, certainly, for Coleridge.

Saint-Hilaire had taken on evolutionary implications in Lyell, which were reinforced by Chambers and Stallo. In the meantime, Emerson had come on the theories of Lorenz Oken, a follower of Schelling but a true evolutionist in a queer sort of way. He is particularly known for his theory of the origin of life in the *Urschleim*. Emerson's "fluid in an elastic sack" refers perhaps to the "infusoria," or microscopically minute bladders with a fluid content, which make up the primary sea-slime of Oken's theory.[64]

Of the other scientists in his list, the only certain evolutionist is Darwin. But Emerson now, presumably, read them all in the light of evolution,—the only light which, in the long run, makes sense out of their discoveries and classifications. The theory of evolution, like its predecessor and parent, the theory of progressive development, had now come to be the supreme example of what he had all along been seeking in natural history—"identity of law, perfect order in physics, perfect parallelism between the laws of nature and the laws of thought." The later theory completed the other, and was now indistinguishable from it. And in listing its proponents, he did not try to distinguish between those who prepared the ground for evolution and those who occupied its advanced position.

Emerson and Naturalism

It was Emerson's transcendentalism that made it possible for him to accept evolution without a qualm. His fluid theology put up none of the resistances that Coleridge's did to the "bestial theory." But it was also his transcendentalism that prevented him from drawing from evolution the conclusions that Swinburne and Meredith drew or making the applications which are made by all thorough-going naturalists. Whatever the origins of transcendentalism, it fed on what it found congenial, and confirmed itself by appeal to the neoplatonists, to Swedenborg, to the Indian and Persian sages. As he goes on, Emerson's idealism becomes more and more self-assured. The more he learns of natural history, the more certain he is that it is all a projection of the mind, an expression of the inherent moral purpose of the universe which is found in the human spirit.

Thus in the years following his reading of Stallo, we find him laying down propositions like this: "That Nature works after the same method as the human imagination. That Nature makes flowers, as the mind makes images. . . . That organic matter, and mind, got from the same law, so correspond." [65] On the basis of Stallo he distinguishes three eras in men's attitude toward nature: the Greek era, when they deified nature; the Christian, when they looked on nature as an evil; and the Modern, which began in reaction against "the too idealistic tendencies of the Christian period" —but "now the tendency is to marry mind to Nature, and to put Nature under the mind, convert the world into the instrument of Right Reason." [66]

This sounds very fine—converting the world into the instrument of Right Reason; but it appears in suspicious company, with the idea of putting nature "under the mind." What is involved here may be no more than a matter of emphasis. But it is true that Emerson almost invariably views nature all too blandly through the eyes of the "mind," reading it in the light of "innate ideas" and all the hoary preconceptions of "idealism." Almost never does it occur to him that the mind may have something to learn from nature, from the world which it finds given to it from without. This is the secret of his fondness for Swedenborg and Hegel, as well as Schelling, in this later period. In 1854 he writes, "This age is Swedenborg's" because of our determination to "repudiate the Hebrew ideas, and embrace the subjective philosophy of the Saxons, that *the soul makes its own world*." [67] As for Hegel, Emerson finds his form of evolutionism attractive because in it the "unfolding" is *an unfolding of nature from the mind*:

Nature is brute, but as this [ideal unity] animates it,—only a language, a noun, for the poet. Nature always the effect; Mind the flowing cause. . . . Mind contains the law; History is the slow and atomic unfolding . . . ever the ascending effort. . . . Natural Sciences have made great strides by means of Hegel's dogma, which put Nature, and thought, matter and spirit, in right relation, one the expression or externalization of the other.[68]

That Hegel's dogma had anything to do with the strides made by natural science is extremely doubtful. Science made its great strides, in the nineteenth century, as in the eighteenth, seventeenth, and sixteenth, by the cool and patient application of the inductive method, by bold experiment and hypothesis constantly controlled by observation. Science goes on under any metaphysic that will leave it alone. But it was an emotional necessity for Emerson to suppose that an idealistic metaphysic was essential to good science. This is the reason why he never rightly understood the implications of evolution—that man, being, as Emerson once boldly asserted, "only a piece of the universe made alive," has everything to learn from the universe, the world of things—about nature, about himself, his own mind, his moral being, and his very spirit. Emerson was so anxious to read ethical meanings into nature that he never stopped to inquire where man got these ethical concepts. He took for granted that they are somehow given *a priori:* eternally inherent in the intellectual system of the universe. He never glimpsed the idea that ethical concepts may be themselves the product of evolution, and that consequently, in appraising them, something may be learned by studying the conditions under which they came into being.

There can be no question of the historical importance of the transcendental movement. The transcendentalists were ethical and religious liberals; and their liberalism was a great solvent of dogma. Human nature being what it is, transcendentalism was an absolutely necessary step in the transition from supernaturalism to naturalism. Without it these religious and sensitive souls would have altogether foundered, and civilization would have suffered more damage than it has. Under cover of transcendentalism naturalism was enabled to make great advances. But the transcendentalists did not themselves develop the possibilities of naturalism. They approached things from the wrong side. They lost themselves in the fogs of mysticism. They followed after strange gods. In Emerson, to employ the electric word of John Hunter, naturalism suffered an "arrested development."

Chapter XII

EMERSON'S NATURE-POETRY

THE constant theme of Emerson's nature-poetry is the identity of being which runs through all the diverse forms of nature,—which identity of being is the identity of spirit. Nothing is isolated, but each fact exists in relation to the whole. Nothing is fixed, for the eternal spirit is passing through a ceaseless cycle of change.

Spiritual Identity of Being

There is a frequent suggestion of Goethe's titles, "Eins und Alles," "Dauer im Wechsel," "Weltseele"; and with the last of these poems Emerson was certainly acquainted. In the undated poem, "Pan," this theme of spiritual identity has a curious suggestion of Leibniz—the spiritual monads, the "fulgurations" of Deity in the Monadology—but Leibniz passed on through the medium of the poets, Goethe or Coleridge.[1] In "Xenophanes" (1834), Emerson develops the thought that "all things are of one pattern made," and universal nature, an infinite paroquet, continually repeats the same note. And other angles of the same theme are shown in "Hamatreya," "Bohemian Hymn," "Ode to Beauty."

But the classical expression of this theme in Emerson is his "Brahma" (1857). This poem is fine enough and important enough in its thought to be quoted entire.

> If the red slayer think he slays.
> Or if the slain think he is slain,
> They know not well the subtle ways
> I keep, and pass, and turn again.

Far or forgot to me is near;
 Shadow and sunlight are the same;
The vanished gods to me appear;
 And one to me are shame and fame.

They reckon ill who leave me out;
 When me they fly, I am the wings;
I am the doubter and the doubt,
 And I the hymn the Brahmin sings.

The strong gods pine for my abode,
 And pine in vain the sacred Seven;
But thou, meek lover of the good!
 Find me, and turn thy back on heaven.

Mr. Frederic Ives Carpenter, in his *Emerson and Asia*, has shown how, in this most fascinating of Emerson's poems, the images are taken, line by line, from the *Vishnu Purana*, the *Bhagavat Gita* and the *Katha Upanishad*.[2] But the central idea is one that was thoroughly familiar to Emerson from very early days, long before he was acquainted with these Indian books. It is a gem of many facets, this theme of identity of being. Now it is the unity of nature with God; now the unity of man with nature; and now it is his unity with the God that is nature's soul. And almost always it brings in the notion of eternal constancy in the midst of eternal flux. One of the earliest hints of the idea in Emerson is the *abrégé* in his Journal of Heraclitus' doctrine:

[Wisdom] consisted in discovering the law which governs all things. All nature is governed by constant laws. The phenomena themselves, which appear discordant, concur in the harmony of the whole. . . . Meanwhile all change. Attraction. Repulsion.[3]

In 1837 we have the following reflection:

Who shall define me as an Individual? I behold with awe and delight many illustrations of the One Universal Mind. I see my being imbedded in it; as a plant in the earth so I grow in God. I am only a form of him. He is in the soul of me. (Etc., etc.)[4]

In 1839, under the influence of his studies in natural history, Emerson brings science into the magic circle.

The perception of identity is a good mercury of the progress of the mind . . . The poet, the true naturalist . . . domesticates himself in nature with a sense of strict consanguinity. His own blood is in the rose and the apple-tree. The Cause of him is Cause of all. He is in the chain of magnetic, electric, geologic, meteorologic phenomena, and so he comes to live in nature and extend his being through all: then is true science.[5]

In the preceding chapter, several passages from Emerson's prose essays of a later date give striking illustration of this theme of identity, which reaches its witty culmination in "Brahma," and which is a basic feature of his nature-poetry proper.

"Woodnotes": the Esthetic Synthesis

The great comprehensive nature-poem of Emerson is "Woodnotes," of which the first part was printed in the *Dial* in 1840, the second part in 1841. Nearly every aspect of Emerson's feeling for nature is here represented; and here is shown particularly well the connection there is in Emerson's mind between nature-lore, the esthetic beauties of the woodland, the wholesomeness of rustic life, on the one hand, and on the other hand, the philosophical concept of universal nature and the religious concept of "the eternal Pan." In his way of assuming this connection between two complex sets of ideas Emerson is following in the tradition of Wordsworth and the great romantic poets.

The first part of the poem gives a portrait of a nature-lover, associated by most readers with the hermit of Walden, though it seems likely that a part of it was written before Emerson "knew Thoreau's gifts and experiences." [6] It is a picture of a nature-lover whose prized knowledge "seems fantastic to the rest" of the world; who was privy to secrets and sights not yielded by nature to the others; who roamed the deep woods of Maine, "content alike with man and beast"—for, "go where he will, the wise man is at home." Wherever he was, thanks to his great soul, "he was the heart of all the scene." And he could never be lost. For however trackless the thicket, he would find the water's bed and follow it down. This impossibility of being lost, for the true nature-lover, is made symbolic of a doctrine we have met before, in Wordsworth and Goethe,—the doctrine of the faithfulness of nature.

> For Nature ever faithful is
> To such as trust her faithfulness.
> When the forest shall mislead me,
> When the night and morning lie,
> When sea and land refuse to feed me,
> 'Twill be time enough to die;
> Then will yet my mother yield
> A pillow in her greenest field,
> Nor the June flowers scorn to cover
> The clay of their departed lover.

The first two lines remind one of Wordsworth's assurance, in "Tintern Abbey," that "Nature never did betray the heart that loved her." And we need have the less hesitancy in making the comparison in view of Emerson's wide acquaintance with Wordsworth and his known particular love for "Tintern Abbey."

In the second part, the poem becomes more philosophical. The opening strophes develop the typical romantic doctrine of the superior wholesomeness of life remote from cities and crowds.

> The rough and bearded forester
> Is better than the lord.

This persuasion is grounded, to begin with, in the familiar assumption that the rough life of the country disciplines and tempers the spirit, which is apt to degenerate under the self-indulgence of civil luxury. But there is a deeper feeling than this. There is the perception, half rational, half mystical, that man, being rooted in nature, loses his force and innocence when removed from his natural setting. The pine planted in a porcelain vase withers away, "the orphan of the forest." Man flourishes best amid the beauties of nature.

> Whoso walks in solitude
> And inhabiteth the wood,
> Choosing light, wave, rock and bird,
> Before the money-loving herd,
> Into that forester shall pass,
> From these companions, power and grace.

It is the teaching of Wordsworth's "Three Years She Grew in Sun and Shower." Like Wordsworth, Emerson assumes that innocence is the child of a retired life with nature; and there is an echo in the lines that follow of the English poet's ideal of "plain living and high thinking."

"Woodnotes": Universal Nature

But this is only the beginning of Emerson's teaching in "Woodnotes." The "nature" of the woodsman, the pioneer and the peasant is merely the outward husk and symbol of that universal nature which is spirit and destiny, and whose note is unity in multiplicity, constancy in change. And now the song of the pine-tree, uttering "the old oracles," goes on to blend the doctrine of Heraclitus and Xenophanes and Aristotle with the modern metaphysics of Schelling and Coleridge and Hegel, and with the natural science of Newton and Laplace, of Hunter and Buffon, Lamarck and Saint-Hilaire,—the science which is shortly to find expression in the work of Darwin.

> Hearken! Hearken!
> If thou wouldst know the mystic song
> Chanted when the sphere was young.
>
> . . . .
>
> To the open ear it sings
> Sweet the genesis of things,
> Of tendency through endless ages,
> Of star-dust and star-pilgrimages,
> Of rounded world, of space and time,
> Of the old flood's subsiding slime,
> Of chemic matter, force and form,
> Of poles and powers, cold, wet, and warm:

> The rushing metamorphosis
> Dissolving all that fixture is,
> Melts things that be to things that seem,
> And solid nature to a dream.

These oracles are, like all oracles, only for fit ears.

> These echoes are laden with tones
> Which only the pure can hear.

Emerson has the same persuasion as Wordsworth and Coleridge that the joy and wisdom of nature are only for the pure in heart. "The world is too much with us . . ." Nature is only to be apprehended by the philosophical imagination; this alone can read her inmost secret, which is harmony. This is the secret of nature's beauty—the harmonic relation of each part with the whole. Nature is a sequence of "lofty rhymes."

> For Nature beats in perfect tune,
> And rounds with rhyme her every rune . . .
> . . . .
> The wood is wiser far than thou;
> The wood and wave each other know
> Not unrelated, unaffied,
> But to each thought and thing allied,
> Is perfect Nature's every part,
> Rooted in the mighty Heart.

The thought of the last few lines is a favorite one with Emerson. Thus in *Nature:*

Herein is especially apprehended the unity of Nature,—the unity in variety,—which meets us everywhere . . . Xenophanes complained in his old age, that, look where he would, all things hastened back to Unity . . . The fable of Proteus has a cordial truth. A leaf, a drop, a crystal, a moment of time, is related to the whole, and partakes of the perfection of the whole. Each particle is a microcosm, and faithfully renders the likeness of the world.[7]

This last sentence has a striking resemblance to Schelling's statement that "every particle of matter must be for itself a copy of the entire universe" *(ein jeder Theil der Materie für sich Abdruck des ganzen Universum seyn muss)*.[8] The same thought might have been found by Emerson in many other writers—in Aristotle, in Leibniz, in Goethe. But I fancy that Emerson's thought in this particular connection is as near to Schelling's as to any other writer's. Emerson's notion of an informing soul of the universe, which is thought recognizing itself in the law and harmony of natural phenomena, might be an echo of Schelling. Thus Emerson, speaking in *Nature* of the charm of one of Plato's or Aristotle's definitions, and the analogous charm of the Antigone of Sophocles:

> It is, in both cases, that a spiritual life has been imparted to nature; that the solid seeming block of matter has been pervaded and dissolved by a thought; that this feeble human being has penetrated the vast masses of nature with an informing soul, and recognized itself in their harmony, that is, seized their law.[9]

And Schelling:

> Indem nach eine unvermeidlichen Nothwendigkeit das Band des Ganzes auch das Wesen des einzelnen Verbundenen ist, beseelt es dieses unmittelbar; Beseelung ist Einbildung des Ganzen in ein Einzelnes.[10]

What Emerson has to say in *Nature* of "the universal Being" and the "universal soul within or behind his individual life," [11] again reminds one of the "universal organism"—by Schelling more metaphysically defined—of which he says that "we recognize in it once more that being which the most ancient philosophy in surmise hailed as the *common soul of nature*." [12] While Emerson read German with difficulty, and the evidences are slight of his having any direct acquaintance with Schelling, it is not impossible that he may have plowed his way through portions of the German philosopher. He generally tried to read the men whom he found highly recommended by Coleridge.[13]

So far as his thought is concerned, the important thing to note is that, according to Emerson, it is *only by reference of the part to the whole in nature* that man can realize her beauty and his own share in it.

Man's Oneness with Nature

He goes on directly, in "Woodnotes," to describe the predicament of man when deprived of this realization and so cut off from the sources of his strength.

> But thou, poor child! unbound, unrhymed,
> Whence camest thou, misplaced, mistimed,
> Whence, O thou orphan and defrauded?
> Is thy land peeled, thy realm marauded?
> Who thee divorced, deceived and left?
> Thee of thy faith who hath bereft,
> And torn the ensigns from thy brow,
> And sunk the immortal eye so low?
>
> . . . .
>
> When thou shalt climb the mountain cliff,
> Or see the wide shore from thy skiff,
> To thee the horizon shall express
> But emptiness on emptiness;
> There lives no man of Nature's worth
> In the circle of the earth;
> And to thine eyes the vast skies fall,
> Dire and satirical,
> On clucking hens and prating fools,
> On thieves, on drudges and on dolls:
> And thou shalt say to the Most High,
> "Godhead! all this astronomy,
> And fate and practice and invention,
> Strong art and beautiful pretension,
> This radiant pomp of sun and star,
> Throes that were, and worlds that are,
> Behold! were in vain and in vain;—
> It cannot be,—I will look again.
> Surely now will the curtain rise,
> And earth's fit tenant me surprise;—
> But the curtain doth *not* rise,
> And Nature has miscarried wholly
> Into failure, into folly."

This—for Emerson—passionate passage, in which he anticipates Hardy's disillusionment with nature, not to mention Edna Millay's momentary desolation in "Renascence," brings us to the very heart of his—or indeed any—nature-philosophy, so far as the emotional motivation is concerned. The perennial appeal of the concept of nature to the poets is this: that it enables us men to maintain our sense that we are not "orphan and defrauded," that we are not "divorced, deceived," lonely and helpless in the universe. The sense of oneness with nature is more necessary in proportion as the poet has a weaker sense of the personal identity of God; and it is historically the emotional equivalent of the religious sense of oneness with—of sonship to—God. With a pantheist like Emerson, nature and God are virtually interchangeable terms, and so we find him now saying of the poet: he "domesticates himself in nature with a sense of strict consanguinity. His own blood is in the rose and the apple-tree"; or now saying of himself: "I see my being imbedded in the One Universal Mind; as a plant in the earth so I grow in God." And in either case the emotional urge is to put off all sense of homelessness and isolation.

The metaphysical aspect of this is the assertion of the identity of matter and spirit, objective and subjective—of the essentially spiritual, or ideal, character of the universe. This idealism in Emerson has been amply illustrated in the preceding chapter; but it is worth while giving a few more citations from his prose in order that the reader may appreciate the dense philosophical context for the simpler statements of the poet. In his essay on "The Over-Soul," Emerson has a notable passage in which he refers to the beatitude open to man in so far as he can realize his oneness with the spirit of the universe.

And this deep power in which we exist and whose beatitude is all accessible to us, is not only self-sufficing and perfect in every hour, but the act of seeing and the thing seen, the seer and the spectacle, the subject and the object are one.[14]

Here the emphasis is on the equivalence of objective and subjective. But behind the equivalence, or identity, of objective and subjective is the idealistic assumption of the more original or real character of the subjective. In "The Poet," Emerson writes:

The Universe is the externization of the soul . . . "The mighty heaven," said Proclus, "exhibits, in its transfigurations, clear images of the splendor of intellectual perceptions; being moved in conjunction with the unapparent periods of intellectual natures." [15]

It was emotionally essential to Emerson to believe that the external universe is one substance with the human soul (interpreter of the divine idea), and not something foreign to it and beyond the reach of its intuitions. In this connection there is a peculiarly intimate glimpse of Emerson's feeling in a Journal entry of 1839.

If, as Hedge thinks, I overlook great facts in stating the absolute laws of the soul; if, as he seems to represent it, the world is not a dualism, is not a bipolar unity, but is *two*, is Me and It, then is there the alien, the unknown, and all we have believed and chanted out of our deep instinctive hope is a pretty dream.[16]

This is a most unusual tone for Emerson to take. His utterances, even in the intimacy of his diary, are almost invariably cheerful and affirmative. Here for once we see him letting the shadow of a doubt fall across his spirit. He shudders at this sense of the alien, the unknown, as a child shudders at the dark when his mother leaves him for the night.

To exorcise this alien, this unknown, is, we may say, the emotional impulse of all philosophy; and the romantic movement may be regarded, on the side of philosophy, as the process of exorcising it through affirming the unity of ideal and real. In order to appreciate the metaphysical bias of romantic poetry it is worth while considering the tone of certain of the professional scientists and philosophers. There was Henrik Steffens, the Scandinavian geologist who became a German professor and developed his variation of Schelling's nature-philosophy. This is the sort of cry that Steffens utters, in his scarce-comprehensible jargon:

Eine tiefe Angst hat die Zeit ergriffen, gleichmässig zittert man vor der Unendlichkeit des Werdens im Endlichen und vor der Endlichkeit des Seyns im Unendlichen . . .

A deep anguish (or terror) has seized upon our times, and man trembles equally before the infinity of becoming in the finite and before the finiteness of being in the infinite . . .[17]

This anguish of spirit, says Steffens, is to be exorcised by another more philosophical view.

... und wem es gelungen ist, sich ihr eigen zu machen, der erkennt nicht nur jene Einheit der Dinge mit einer allgemeinen Einheit, sondern auch die mit ihr zugleich gegebene selige Einheit der Dinge mit sich selbst, durch welche die ewige Einheit, die ihnen innewohnt, und die nicht getheilt seyn kann, da die absolute Einheit sich nicht theilen lässt, als Eins gesetzt wird mit ihrem abgesonderten Daseyn, so dass sie durch ihr Werden sind und durch ihr Seyn werden.

And whoever succeeds in making this view his own, recognizes not merely that oneness of things with a universal Oneness, but also the blessed oneness of things with themselves which goes along with the other, by virtue of which the eternal Oneness which inhabits things, and which cannot be divided (since the absolute Oneness does not allow of division), is made one with their separated being, so that they exist through its becoming and through its existence they become (or come into being).[18]

Peacock Wit and Primal Mind

This anguish of the spirit gone astray in the universe is a note of literary men and philosophers alike. It is heard in Fichte's *Bestimmung des Menschen* when the disciple of philosophy has been taught to doubt the freedom of the will and the competence of knowledge to bring him truth. It is heard in the Introduction to Schelling's *Ideen zu einer Philosophie der Natur*; here the philosopher lays on the faculty of "mere reflection" the blame for our spiritual distress. This faculty has a deadening effect upon the spirit by virtue of its separating activity—the division which it works between man and the world. In this we recognize another version of Wordsworth's "false secondary power that multiplies distinctions."

Die *blosse* Reflexion also ist eine Geisteskrankheit des Menschen, noch dazu, wo sie sich in Herrschaft über den ganzen Menschen setzt, diejenige, welche sein höheres Daseyn im Keim, sein geistiges Leben, welches nur aus der Identität hervorgeht, in der Wurzel tödtet ... Ihr zertrennendes Geschäft erstreckt sich aber nicht nur auf die erscheinende Welt; indem sie von dieser das geistige Prinzip trennt, erfüllt sie die intellectuelle Welt mit Chimären, gegen welche, weil sie jenseits

aller Vernunft liegen, selbst kein Krieg möglich ist. Sie macht jene
Trennung zwischen dem Menschen und der Welt permanent, indem
sie die letzte als ein Ding an sich betrachtet, das weder Anschauung
noch Einbildungskraft, weder Verstand noch Vernunft zu erreichen
vermag.

Mere reflection is a sickness of the spirit of man, especially where it
lords it over the whole man,—a sickness which nips his higher being
in the bud, withers at the root his spiritual life, which is the product
of identity alone . . . Its separating activity extends not merely to
the world of appearances; in separating the spiritual principle from
this world of appearances, it fills the intellectual world with chimaeras,
against which it is not even possible to make war, since they lie beyond
all reason. It makes permanent that division between man and the
world, since it regards the latter as a thing in itself, which neither observation nor imagination, neither understanding nor reason, is capable
of reaching to.[19]

But this deadening effect of mere reflection, says Schelling, may be
offset by the intuitive realization of man's oneness with nature.

Solange ich selbst mit der Natur *identisch* bin, verstehe ich was eine
lebendige Natur ist so gut, als ich mein eigenes Leben verstehe;
begreife, wie dieses allgemeine Leben der Natur in den mannichfaltig-
sten Formen, in stufenmässigen Entwicklungen, in allmählichen An-
näherungen zur Freiheit sich offenbaret; sobald ich aber mich und mit
mir alles Ideale von der Natur trenne, bleibt mir nichts übrig als ein
todtes Object und ich höre auf, zu begreifen, wie ein *Leben ausser* mir
möglich sey.

So long as I myself am *identical* with Nature, I understand what a
living Nature is as well as I understand my own life; I comprehend
how this universal life reveals itself in the most various forms, in developments along the scale of being, in gradual approaches to freedom.
But as soon as I separate myself, and with me all ideal being, from
Nature, nothing is left to me but a dead object, and I cease to comprehend how *life* is possible *outside of me*.[20]

Emerson's cure for anguish and unfaith is likewise abjuring mere
reflection—"peacock wit"—in favor of some deeper source of inspiration and revelation—"the primal mind that blows in streams,
that breathes in wind." The passage in which he recommends this
renouncement of "peacock wit" is on the surface more in the man-

ner of Wordsworth than of Schelling. It is poetic rather than metaphysical in style. But underneath the poetry lurks the metaphysics. When man has addressed to the godhead his complaint that nature has miscarried into failure and folly, the pine-tree takes up again its oracular discourse.

> Alas! thine is the bankruptcy,
> Blessed Nature so to see.
> Come, lay thee in my soothing shade,
> And heal the hurts which sin has made.
> I see thee in the crowd alone;
> I will be thy companion.
> Quit thy friends, as the dead in doom,
> And build to them a final tomb . . .
>   . . . .
>
> Behind thee leave thy merchandise,
> Thy churches and thy charities;
> And leave thy peacock wit behind;
> Enough for thee the primal mind
> That flows in streams, that breathes in wind;
> Leave all thy pedant lore apart;
> God hid the whole world in thy heart.
> Love shuns the sage, the child it crowns,
> Gives all to them who all renounce.
> The rain comes when the wind calls;
> The river knows the way to the sea. . . .
>   . . . .
>
> And thou,—go burn thy wormy pages,—
> Shalt outsee seers, and outwit sages.

There is something of the New Testament in the adjuration to quit one's friends, to "leave all and follow" the spirit which speaks from the pine-tree. New England transcendentalism breathes strongly in the command to leave merchandise, churches and charities. Emerson's favorite among Wordsworth's poems was the "Ode"; and his celebration of the child in preference to the sage is reminiscent of Wordsworth's "mighty prophet! seer blest!" Both poets, of course, have scriptural allowance for this interpretation of the child. Wordsworth comes in again with the advice to leave behind "thy peacock wit" and rely upon the "primal mind." Here is Wordsworth's "wise passiveness"; here is the sweet lore of nature opposed to the "meddling intellect." And the scornful reference to "wormy pages" is in line with Wordsworth's counsel: "Close up those barren leaves."

Thus Emerson is full in the Wordsworthian tradition in deprecating "mere reflection" as a means of apprehending the spirit of nature. But it is to be observed that, since Wordsworth wrote his ballads of 1798, a current of thought had flowed from Germany to confirm this view and give it philosophical grounding. This current of thought came to Emerson through the channel of Coleridge's prose writings, through *Sartor Resartus* and other work of Carlyle; it came also perhaps through the writings of Victor Cousin, with which he was acquainted as early as 1835.[21] It is not impossible that he had gone to some of the original sources in Fichte and Schelling. It is therefore probable that behind the lines quoted from "Woodnotes" there lie considerations drawn from German transcendentalism which were not present, in the same form, in the mind of Wordsworth when he wrote his ballads.

Note that in Schelling's and Steffens's discussion of man's identity with nature, the relationship has a double aspect. The anguish in man's spirit is healed by the sense of his oneness with nature. But this is made possible by the interpretation of nature in terms of man's spirit—that is, in terms of the mind. "As soon as I separate myself, *and with me all ideal being*, from Nature, *nothing is left to me but a dead object*, and I cease to comprehend how life is possible outside of me." In this statement of Schelling we have the metaphor, so common in romantic writing, of the deadness of nature when not rightly interpreted and given ideal character by the mind of man. The metaphor of a dead nature is found in a famous passage of *Sartor Resartus*, in the chapter on the Everlasting No.

To me the Universe was all void of Life, of Purpose, of Volition, even of Hostility: it was one huge, dead, immeasurable Steam-engine, rolling on, in its dead indifference, to grind me limb from limb.[22]

While the discussion in *Sartor Resartus* is anything but close-knit and consecutive; while many elements, emotional and philosophical, are involved in the experience that brought Teufelsdröckh to this blackness of mood: the dominant element is the loss of his sense of moral freedom resulting from the mechanistic view of the world prevailing in scientific thought. It was the extension of the doctrine of necessity to the realm of moral conduct that reduced Teufelsdröckh to despair. It was the reaffirmation of moral freedom for man that restored him to a hopeful state of mind. Broadly speaking, the Everlasting No was a declaration of Necessity as including man and his moral life. The Everlasting Yea was a counter-assertion of the moral freedom of man.

Carlyle had gone through many discussions, especially in German literature, of the problem of necessity and free will. He had encountered various solutions of this problem, more or less grounded in Kant's distinction between Understanding and Reason. Among such solutions, the one which seems most likely to have impressed Carlyle was that of Fichte. Carlyle's reference to Fichte's theory of the Divine Idea [23] suggests that he had read Fichte's lectures on *The Nature of the Scholar*, in which that term is defined. And it is equally probable that he had read the eloquent and popular philosophical treatise, *Die Bestimmung des Menschen*, in which there are many phrases, attitudes and formulations suggestive of those in *Sartor Resartus*.

Fichte here relates how for him nature had, in moments of depression, seemed a dead inert mass; but with a change in his philosophical attitude, it had become again a living and meaningful universe. His treatise is divided into three books. In the first, entitled Doubt (*Zweifel*), he gives a simple exposition of the mechanistic view of the universe, which satisfies his mind, but leaves his heart desolate, since it deprives him of all sense of personal freedom. In the second book, a Socratic spirit leads the thinker through a destructive analysis of the process of acquiring knowledge (*Wissen*). He comes to the conclusion that knowledge can present him only with its own "picture-world," and nowise with the world of reality or truth lying beyond itself. As the Spirit admonishes him:

Die Realität, die du schon erblickt zu haben glaubtest, eine unabhängig von dir vorhandene Sinnenwelt, deren Sklav du zu werden fürchtetest, ist dir verschwunden; denn diese ganze Sinnenwelt entsteht nur durch das Wissen, und ist selbst unser Wissen; aber Wissen ist nicht Realität, eben darum, weil es Wissen ist . . . Wahrheit geben kann es nicht; denn es ist in sich selbst absolut leer. Nun suchst du denn doch etwas, ausser dem blossen Bilde liegendes Reelles—mit deinem guten Rechte, wie ich wohl weiss—und eine andere Realität, als die soeben vernichtete, wie ich gleichfalls weiss. Aber du würdest dich vergebens bemühen, sie durch dein Wissen, und aus deinem Wissen zu erschaffen, und mit deiner Erkenntniss zu umfassen. Hast du kein anderes Organ, sie zu ergreifen, so wirst du sie nimmer finden.

The reality, in which thou didst formerly believe,—a material world existing independently of thee, of which thou didst fear to become the slave,—has vanished; for this whole material world arises only through knowledge, and is itself our knowledge; but knowledge is not reality, just because it is knowledge . . . It cannot give us truth, for in itself it is absolutely empty. Thou dost now seek, and with good right as I well know, something real lying beyond mere appearance, another reality than that which has thus been annihilated. But in vain wouldst thou labour to create this reality by means of thy knowledge, or out of thy knowledge; or to embrace it by thy understanding. If thou hast no organ by which to apprehend it, thou wilt never find it.[24]

That there is such an organ for apprehending the reality beyond appearance is revealed in the following book, entitled Faith (*Glaube*). Faith is in this formulation the equivalent of Reason in Kantian metaphysics. And Faith proves to be the organ for apprehending ultimate reality because it is faith that announces to man his vocation, which is to act in accordance with the moral law. Thus Fichte's solution is the same as Carlyle's. Action, moral action, doing right, is the means by which man frees himself from the iron law of necessity and puts himself at one with the spiritual reality lying back of natural appearances. In Fichte, the opposition lies rather between doing and enjoying. But in both cases it is the moral sense which reveals the spiritual truth of the universe, and assures man of his freedom. And in Fichte as well as in Carlyle, this moral sense involves the renouncement of earthly pleasure; and the renouncement of earthly pleasure results in a new realization of the spiritual glory of the world.

Nachdem so mein Herz aller Begier nach dem Irdischen verschlossen ist, nachdem ich in der That für das Vergängliche gar kein Herz mehr habe, erscheint meinem Auge das Universum in einer verklärten Gestalt.

Now that my heart is closed against all desire for earthly things, now that I have no longer any sense for the transitory and perishable, the universe appears before my eyes clothed in a more glorious form.[25]

It is man's moral sense—his sense of the necessity for action—that reveals to him the true nature of the universe. It is chiefly through man that the Divine Idea manifests itself. Man and his moral sense are more central to Fichte's philosophy than to that of any of his contemporaries. He is somewhat suspicious of Schelling's emphasis on nature and sharply opposed to Rousseau's conception of nature. It is only a nature thoroughly interpenetrated with man's ethical assumptions which he will admit as a true subject of man's love and admiration. The reason why nature ceases to be foreign and hateful is simply that, rightly interpreted, it is found to be of one stuff with man's intellect and moral sense.

Die Natur, in welcher ich zu handeln habe, ist nicht ein fremdes, ohne Rücksicht auf mich zu Stande gebrachtes Wesen, in welches ich nie eindringen könnte. Sie ist durch meine eigenen Denkgesetze gebildet, und muss wohl mit denselben übereinstimmen; sie muss wohl mir überall durchaus durchsichtig, und erkennbar, und durchdringbar seyn bis in ihr Inneres. Sie drückt überall nichts aus als Verhältnisse und Beziehungen meiner selbst zu mir selbst, und so gewiss ich hoffen kann, mich selbst zu erkennen, so gewiss darf ich mir versprechen, sie zu erforschen. Suche ich nur, was ich zu suchen habe: ich werde finden; frage ich nur, wonach ich zu fragen habe: ich werde Antwort erhalten.

The Nature on which I have to act is not a foreign element, called into existence without reference to me, into which I cannot penetrate. It is moulded by my own laws of thought, and must be in harmony with them; it must be thoroughly transparent, knowable and penetrable to me, even to its inmost recesses. In all its phenomena it expresses nothing but the connexions and relations of my own being to myself; and as surely as I may hope to know myself, so surely may I expect to comprehend it. Let me seek only that which I ought to seek, and I shall find; let me ask only that which I ought to ask, and I shall receive an answer.[26]

In Emerson's "Woodnotes," the problem of necessity and free will seems not to be involved at all, at least on the surface. And it is curious how little part this problem plays in his speculations in general. In this he is like Wordsworth, and in contrast to Coleridge. The mechanistic view seems to have troubled Emerson so little at any time that he found it unnecessary to make noisy protestations of moral freedom.

But the opposition between Knowledge and Faith—between Understanding and Reason, or Intuition—does seem to be strongly present here, though expressed in poetic terms. It is nature interpreted by "peacock wit" that leaves man orphan and defrauded, and miscarries into failure, into folly. In order not to be something foreign and fearful, nature must be interpreted by the primal mind—by the heart. The heart is, with Emerson as with Wordsworth, the poetical equivalent of religious terms like Faith or metaphysical terms like Reason. And he is essentially offering the same prescription as Fichte when he cries:

> Leave all thy pedant lore apart;
> God hid the whole world in thy heart.

When he says that love "gives all to them who all renounce," it would seem that he is recommending more than the renunciation of "the world," or of selfish pleasure. To be sure, he remembers Carlyle's citation of Goethe: "Well did the wisest of our time write: 'It is only with Renunciation (*Entsagen*) that Life, properly speaking, can be said to begin.' " [27]

He remembers the gospel dictum: "He that loseth his life . . ." But he also has in mind the teaching of the transcendental philosophers, that it is not by "mere reflection," not by "knowledge" or the "understanding," that one can apprehend the spiritual reality of the universe.

The Eternal Pan

In the passage that follows, Emerson writes much in the spirit of Goethe. He takes the same delight as the German poet in the ceaseless evolution of natural forms and phases; and he rests in his doctrine of *Dauer im Wechsel*. Once rid of peacock wit and pedant lore, and back again to the inspirations of the primal mind, man is at liberty to realize his oneness with the spirit that moves in all things—or rather, as it seems, to lose his petty identity in the divine whole.

Hearken once more!
I will tell thee the mundane lore.
Older am I than thy numbers wot,
Change I may, but I pass not.

.   .   .   .

All the forms are fugitive,
But the substances survive.
Ever fresh the broad creation,
A divine improvisation,
From the heart of God proceeds,
A single will, a million deeds.
Once slept the world, an egg of stone,
And pulse, and sound, and light was none;
And God said, "Throb!" and there was motion
And the vast mass became vast ocean.
Onward and on, the eternal Pan,
Who layeth the world's incessant plan,
Halteth never in one shape,
But forever doth escape,
Like wave or flame, into new forms
Of gem, and air, of plants, and worms.
I that to-day am a pine,
Yesterday was a bundle of grass.

.   .   .   .

Unto every race and age
He emptieth the beverage . . .

.   .   .   .

The world is the ring of his spells,
And the play of his miracles.

.   .   .   .

As the bee through the garden ranges,
From world to world the godhead changes;
As the sheep go feeding in the waste,
From form to form He maketh haste . . .

In this dizzy flight of the imagination, a dozen philosophies meet and fuse. "Change I may, but I pass not" is Heraclitus and Goethe. The fugitive forms and stable substances are a platonic, or neoplatonic, reading of the modern scientific doctrine of metamorphosis—"So careless of the type she seems . . ." The divine improvisation is the song of the Erdgeist in "Faust" translated by Carlyle in *Sartor Resartus*. The play of miracles of "the eternal Pan" is Carlyle's "natural supernaturalism."

In what follows there are anticipations of Whitman (in the first two lines), of Meredith's "Earth and Man," of Swinburne's "Hertha." For this poem, dating from 1841, contains a pretty complete statement of the doctrine of "Brahma," and that before Emerson was acquainted with any of the Hindu sources of that poem.

> Alike to him the better, the worse,—
> The glowing angel, the outcast corse.
> Thou metest him by centuries,
> And lo! he passes like the breeze;
> Thou seek'st in globe and galaxy,
> He hides in pure transparency;
> Thou askest in fountains and in fires,
> He is the essence that inquires.
> He is the axis of the star;
> He is the sparkle of the spar;
> He is the heart of every creature;
> He is the meaning of each feature;
> And his mind is the sky,
> Than all it holds more deep, more high.

This is the final word of Emerson's nature-philosophy. Human littleness and insufficiency are lost in the thought of the eternal Pan, of which mortal men are but one phase like another. It relieves the strain on our individual conscience to realize how infinitesimal a part we play in the drama of the ages. Our anxious distinctions of good and evil grow vague and petty in the perspective of eternity. And at the same time our hearts are lifted up with the consciousness that we are part and parcel of the universal, the august and infallible Spirit.

Emerson and Meredith

Emerson stands between Wordsworth and Meredith, and has marked affinities with each of these nature-poets. But his emphasis is rather different from that of either. Meredith moves in the full tide of evolutionary faith and hopefulness. And he realizes, as Emerson does not to any marked degree, the moral implications of this theory of man's earthly derivation. A comparison of his "Woods of Westermain" with "Woodnotes" makes one realize how thoroughly ethical—and utilitarian—is Meredith's reading of earth where Emerson's is mystically religious, transcendental and imaginative. It is quite true, as Dr. Wahr has pointed out in his contrast of Emerson and Goethe,[28] that the American philosopher generally proceeds from a moral preconception. But his morality is puritanical in tradition and platonic in rationale. It is something mystically given from above. Whereas the morality of Meredith is conscientiously built up out of the materials offered by nature and life. Hence Meredith, while in some ways a thorny and repellent poet in comparison with Emerson, approaches nearer to the humanity, the earthy homeliness, of Wordsworth. And he is worldly somewhat as Goethe is worldly.

In many ways the likeness of Emerson and Meredith is greater than their difference. For both of them nature is rather a book of spiritual hieroglyphics than the volume of enchanting landscapes which it is—among other things—for Thomson and Wordsworth and Keats. In both cases the accent is somewhat sharp and crisp and wanting in the sensual charm of Milton and Shelley. The scent of both is more of resin than of rose-leaves. There are probably no two nineteenth-century poets more close akin in general imaginative quality than these two. There are many lines in Meredith that make one think of Emerson.

And "The Woods of Westermain" has much the same theme as "Woodnotes." In both the pinewoods are symbolical of a nature which is fundamentally benign, but is easily seen as "dire and satirical" by one who approaches it in the wrong spirit. With Emerson it is the worldly entanglements of friends and merchandise and peacock wit which make one see nature as miscarried into failure and folly, and it is through the "primal mind" that one must

realize one's identity with the eternal Pan. With Meredith it is
fear and distrust, it is the sensual hungers and shrinking of the
nerves, that fill nature with spectral terrors; you must look "with
the soul" to read her spiritual meaning.

> Enter these enchanted woods,
>   You who dare.
> Nothing harms beneath the leaves
> More than waves a swimmer cleaves.
> Toss your heart up with the lark,
> Foot at peace with mouse and worm,
>   Fair you fare.
> Only at a dread of dark
> Quaver and they quit their form:
> Thousand eyeballs under hoods
>   Have you by the hair.
> Enter these enchanted woods,
>   You who dare.

The notion of enchanted woods is common enough in romance,
and familiar to Meredith from the German folk-lore imbibed in his
school days. And I would not more than suggest a parallel here
with Emerson's picture of the pampered lord who cannot meet the
challenge of the woodland.

> He goes to my savage haunts
>   With his chariot and his care;
>   My twilight realm he disenchants,
>   And finds his prison there.

At any rate the thought is similar.

As to how well Meredith was read in Emerson's poetry there is
no evidence. That he had some acquaintance with his writings is
clear from the comparison he draws, in a letter of 1865, between
Carlyle the humorist and Emerson the philosopher.[29] It is a long
step from Emerson to Meredith, and there may be no direct connection between the poetry of the two men. But there is at least a
reasonable probability of such a connection. Emerson is one of the
two poets in English in whom the evolutionary note distinctly

anticipates Meredith. And it is pleasant to think of the American poet as a link in the chain between Wordsworth and Meredith.

Emerson and Wordsworth

As for Wordsworth, his influence on Emerson is obvious, in several ways noted above, especially under the head of the "esthetic synthesis." But the center of Wordsworth's philosophy is man, and he is primarily concerned with the way man has built up his spiritual life out of the inspirations of nature. He has a much more *human* point of view than Emerson; and while he is equally insistent on the paramountcy of the spirit, his view of nature is more realistic than Emerson's, much more down to the ground. While no breath of evolutionism has touched the earlier poet, he realizes more effectively than his better-informed follower how man is a child of earth.

Emerson, on the other hand, has a more philosophical cast of mind—or of imagination—than Wordsworth. He is more widely read in philosophy. His concept of universal nature is more sharply defined, and is enriched with colorings drawn from platonic and neoplatonic sources, from oriental philosophy and from German transcendentalism. His idealism is more insistent. His opposition of mind and heart seems to be more explicitly grounded than Wordsworth's in the philosophical distinction between understanding and reason, or knowledge and faith. He gives more dramatic expression to the emotional craving for oneness with nature, and to the sufferings of man when divorced from her. His conception of the universal process, the eternal Pan, has been fortified with considerations drawn from classical philosophy and from modern evolutionary science.

It is a nice speculation whether in Emerson the romantic concept of nature has gained or lost ground. Philosophically, I believe, it is somewhat enlarged and solidified. But the very transcendentalism which has given it this advantage at the same time has tended to reduce the element of "naturalism"; and naturalism, in Wordsworth and Shelley, was a considerable factor in deepening the concept of nature. But what gives nature its advantage in Wordsworth is the quality of his imagination, which has more body and poignancy than Emerson's, whether it has to do with "man, the heart of man, and human life," or with the natural setting of man's activities, or with the interchange between nature and man. It is Wordsworth and not Emerson who could say of the shepherd Michael:

> . . . he had been alone
> Amid the heart of many thousand mists,
> That came to him, and left him, on the heights.

It is Wordsworth who could say, of the effect of Michael's son upon the old man's feeling:

> . . . that from the boy there came
> Feelings and emanations—things which were
> Light to the sun and music to the wind;
> And that the old man's heart seemed born again.[30]

Brilliant as Emerson's imagination is on the philosophical side, the relative defect in his *sensibility* prevents him from having the importance of Wordsworth as an exponent of nature.

CHAPTER XIII

WHITMAN

THE poetic faith in nature perhaps nowhere appears more full-blown than in the poems of Whitman. Nowhere perhaps, in the range of poetry written in English, is the thought of nature more confidently called to the support and inspiration of the spirit. Whitman may be regarded as in some ways marking the culminating point in the romantic concept of nature.

This American poet was subject to innumerable influences tending to foster in him this romantic concept. Most of these it would be difficult or impossible to trace to particular literary sources, though one may be tolerably certain of the *sort of thing* he would have read and heard spoken of. This nature-doctrine was in the air, widely diffused in Whitman's America. What seems most probable is that in *Leaves of Grass* he was influenced by the idealistic interpretation of nature found in the writings of Emerson and in popular abstracts of the German philosophers—Kant, Fichte, Schelling and Hegel, and above all Hegel. But along with this, and earlier in time, was the influence of deism, of English natural theology, and the closely related influence of the concept of nature in revolutionary political and social thought—as in Rousseau's *Contrat Social*, Thomas Paine's *Common Sense*, and the American Declaration of Independence. In many ways Whitman has been compared to Rousseau; but I do not know whether he came directly under his influence as a writer. In one of the many notes he took preparatory to writing *Leaves of Grass* is an account of Rousseau's career, together with a characterization of the *Confessions* and the general statement that an American poet might read him but should never imitate him.[1] It is most likely that Whitman, like so many English poets, was influenced by Rousseau indirectly if at all, through ideas of his widely disseminated and present everywhere "in the air."

Whitman thought very highly of Thomas Paine and was well acquainted with an intimate friend of that revolutionary pamphleteer. In a public lecture in 1877 he referred to Paine as "the author of *Common Sense*." [2] In that book Whitman would find an account of the "natural" origin of government, in the association of small groups of persons under primitive conditions for their mutual freedom and security. Of such a simple and representative government Paine declares that it is approved by the "voice of nature." [3] Paine held the view, later set forth by Godwin and Herbert Spencer, that the less government the better, and this view he justified by reference to nature. [4] In his argument against monarchy, again, he appeals to nature. [5] In Whitman's poetry, as we shall see, the ideal of democracy was intimately associated with the idea of nature, and the idea of nature was penetrated with religious assumptions.

Whitman's religious views had much in common with Paine's. His brand of natural theology is a kind of eighteenth-century deism modified by "idealistic" metaphysics of an Emersonian and Hegelian stripe. Whitman agreed with the author of *The Age of Reason* in repudiating revealed religion, though in a much less public and militant fashion. He concluded his notes for lectures on German idealism with the following remark: "It is certain that what is called revealed religion as founded or alleged to be founded on the Old and New Testament, and still taught by the various churches in Europe and America, is not responded to by the highest, devoutest modern mind." [6] On the other hand he agreed with Paine in holding to the belief in God and immortality, and would have subscribed to the passage in which Paine finds the evidences of God in nature.

It is only in the CREATION that all our ideas and conceptions of a *Word of God* can unite. The Creation speaks a universal language, independently of human speech or human language. . . . Do we want to contemplate His power? We see it in the immensity of creation. Do we want to contemplate his wisdom? We see it in the unchangeable order by which the incomprehensible whole is governed. Do we want to contemplate his munificence? . . . In fine, do we want to know what God is? Search not the book called the Scriptures, which any human hand might make, but the Scripture called the creation.[7]

Whitman did not, like Paine, regard the Old and New Testaments as made up of "impositions and forgeries." On the contrary, he considered that "the old prophets and *exaltés*, the spiritual poets and poetry of all lands (as in the Hebrew Bible)" had about them "a living glow, fondness, warmth" not found in "the keenest modern philosophers." [8] But their theology he did not take literally, and the most authentic revelation of the divine he found in the creation itself. In religious feeling Whitman took much after his mother's family, who were Quakers, as Paine's father was a Quaker. But he would have agreed with Paine's sentiment in the following:

The religion that approaches the nearest of all others to true Deism, in the moral and benign part thereof, is that professed by the Quakers; but they have contracted themselves too much by leaving the works of God out of their system. Though I reverence their philanthropy, I cannot help smiling at the conceit that if the taste of a Quaker could have been consulted at the Creation what a silent and drab-colored Creation it would have been! Not a flower would have blossomed its gayeties, nor a bird been permitted to sing.[9]

Idealism

What distinguishes Whitman's conception of nature from Paine's or from that of most eighteenth-century deism and natural theology is his distinct assumption of some form of idealistic metaphysics. Idealism seems to be the key to that trinity of concepts—man, Nature, God. In *Democratic Vistas* (1871) Whitman indicates idealism as the proper guide for New World poets in their interpretation of nature.

Nature, true Nature, and the true idea of Nature, long absent, must, above all, become fully enlarged, and must furnish the pervading atmosphere to poems, and the test of all high literary and esthetic compositions. I do not mean the smooth walks, trimm'd hedges, poseys, and nightingales of the English poets, but the whole orb, with its geologic history, the kosmos, carrying fire and snow, that rolls through the illimitable areas, light as a feather, though weighing billions of tons.

Furthermore, as by what we now partially call Nature is intended, at most only what is entertainable by the physical conscience, the sense of matter, and of good animal health—on these it must be distinctly accumulated, incorporated, that man, comprehending these, has, in towering superaddition, the moral and spiritual consciences, indicating his destination beyond the ostensible, the moral.

To the heights of such estimation of Nature indeed ascending, we proceed to make observations for our Vistas, breathing rarest air. What is I believe called Idealism seems to me to suggest, (guarding against extravagance, and ever modified even by its opposite) the course of inquiry and desert of favor for our New World metaphysics, their foundation of and in literature, giving hue to all.[10]

The most likely place for Whitman to have first encountered idealism is Emerson's *Nature*, his Essays, and many of his poems— all in print long before Whitman began writing the poems included in *Leaves of Grass*. The influence of Emerson on Whitman has been pointed out by many writers.[11] Whitman was especially affected by Emerson's teaching in the essay on "Self-Reliance." [12] There has been some controversy as to the date of Whitman's first acquaintance with Emerson, the period at which this influence began to operate: a controversy having its origin in Whitman's unwillingness, in his later years, to have his debt to Emerson exaggerated. The most recent studies of this question have been made by Professor John B. Moore and Professor Clarence L. F. Gohdes, who are in essential agreement in their conclusions.[13] According to Mr. Moore, "Whitman was more indebted to Emerson than to any other for fundamental ideas in even his earliest *Leaves of Grass*." [14] According to Mr. Gohdes, Whitman certainly "lied about the date of his first acquaintance with Emerson's works." [15] J. T. Trowbridge declared in 1902 that Whitman used to take a volume of Emerson with him along with his dinner pail while working as a carpenter in 1854. "He freely admitted that he could never have written his poems if he had not first 'come to himself,' and that Emerson helped him to 'find himself.' " [16] In a very early poem Whitman shows acquaintance with Emerson as a lecturer. Mr. Gohdes points out the extreme likelihood of his early knowledge of Emerson, on account of his newspaper affiliations, through book reviews and articles on the New England poet. He calls attention to Whitman's review of "Spiritual Laws" in the Brooklyn *Eagle* of December 15, 1847.[17] Further unmistakable evidence of early acquaintance with Emerson's writings is furnished by the enthusiastic paragraph on them found among Whitman's notes.[18] This was written as a note to a magazine article dated May, 1847; Whitman's editor, judging by paper and writing, dates it in the early fifties. Throughout his life Whitman often expressed great admiration for Emerson as a poet and thinker, and he could hardly have failed to be impressed with the Concord seer's doctrine of nature as the externization of thought, his conception of the oneness of all the universe as the changing expression of the "eternal Pan."

Whitman was early aware of the importance of Carlyle, especially as "the introducer of Goethe and the principal German writers from 1827 onward 10 years." [19] At an early period he was reading "Carlyle's criticisms on Goethe"; and in his reading notes he clearly drew on certain of Carlyle's reviews for his outlines of the lives of Goethe and Richter.[20] He knew that Carlyle was influential in introducing German transcendentalism "through the great reviews and magazines—and through his own works and example." [21] I don't know whether he read *Sartor Resartus*. In his old age, he shows some acquaintance with *Heroes and Hero-Worship*, a book in which there is a considerable tincture of "natural supernaturalism." [22] I find no evidence that he had read Carlyle's articles on the "State of German Literature" (1827) and on Novalis (1829), in which he might have found a sketchy account of German idealism, with some particular reference to the views of Kant and Fichte.

But Whitman speaks of the German philosophers in the most explicit terms. There are among his papers two elaborate sets of notes on the German idealists,—the first to be found in his "Preparatory Reading and Thought," specifically labeled "Sunday evening lectures," and probably written in the sixties or early seventies; [23] the second found in *Specimen Days*, printed under the heading "Carlyle from American Points of View," and dated 1882.[24] In each of these sets of notes Whitman refers to Joseph Gostick as the at least partial source of his information on Hegel.[25] An examination of the several books of this Gostick (afterwards Gostwick) in which Hegel is discussed makes it certain that the volume on which Whitman drew was his *German Literature* of

1854.[26] And it is certain that Whitman was indebted to Gostick for some—but not all—of his information about Hegel, Kant, Schelling, as well as about Leibniz and the historian Niebuhr. Gostick refers to several handbooks on German philosophy accessible in English; and Whitman's references to German philosophers are all of a kind to suggest that he enlarged his knowledge of them through such handbooks, through encyclopedias or other compendious sources of information. The importance of establishing Gostick's volume of 1854 as one of the sources lies in the possibility thus revealed that Whitman made his acquaintance with German idealists, such as it was, early enough to have influenced him in writing Leaves of Grass. This possibility is raised to a considerable probability by the internal evidence, which seems to indicate that the ideas of these German philosophers, however slight and superficial was his knowledge of them, influenced him profoundly in his own thinking.

Of Hegel Whitman says that "he probably rendered greater service (in the domain of metaphysics) than any man we know, past or present"; [27] that "only Hegel is fit for America—is large enough and free enough"; [28] that "I rate [Hegel] as Humanity's chiefest teacher and the choicest loved physician of my mind and soul"; [29] and other things in a similar vein. And with Hegel he joins "the name of Kant and perhaps Fichte and Schelling." [30]

Kant, as Whitman explains, makes necessary an idealistic philosophy by "dethroning the laws of sight, touch, weight, etc., making us doubtful of the realities we thought so absolute." [31] He dwells on the subjectiveness of Fichte, which was supplemented and corrected by Schelling's "theory that the human mind and external nature are essentially one." [32]

That which exists in concrete forms etc. in Nature, exists morally and mentally in the human spirit. . . . The chief forte of [Schelling's philosophy]—seeking to counterbalance and restrain Fichte's all-devouring egoism—is the essential identity of the subjective and objective worlds, or, in terms, that which exists as mentality, intelligence, consciousness in man, exists in equal strength and absoluteness in concrete forms, shows and practical laws in material nature—making the latter one with man's intuitions. The same universal spirit manifests itself in the individual Man, in aggregates, in concrete Nature, and in Historic progress.[33]

Whitman dwells on Hegel as a counterpoise both to the pessimism of Carlyle and to the disposition of the times to make too much of Darwinism, "unspeakably precious" as are Darwin's tenets to biology and "henceforth indispensable to a right aim and estimate in study." [34] He seems to regard Hegel's political theory as full of support for American democracy, and his way of linking up politics with ethics and metaphysics as suited to be salutary discipline to us in our great undertaking.[35] He believes that the democratic poets of the future must be—

. . . not only possess'd of the religious fire and abandon of Isaiah, luxuriant in the epic talent of Homer, or for proud characters as in Shakspere, but consistent with the Hegelian formulas, and consistent with modern science. America needs, and the world needs, a class of bards who will, now and ever, so link and tally the rational physical being of man, with the ensemble of time and space, and with this vast and multiform show, Nature, surrounding him, ever tantalizing him, equally a part, and yet not a part of him, as to essentially harmonize, satisfy, and put at rest.[36]

Whitman's admiration for Hegel's philosophy is based on many features which are congenial to his own way of thinking. There is first his spiritual idealism in general, and then his concept of the spiritual evolution of the universe from within, which is a "dialectic" process of creative thought. There is the comprehensiveness of his view, bringing together in a single conspectus all phases of life, science and history. And there is his consequent moral interpretation of the universe, and his attitude toward evil as a transient and necessary expression of the laws of the moral universe.

Penetrating beneath the shows and materials of the objective world we find, according to Hegel . . . that in respect to human cognition of them, all and several are pervaded by *the only absolute substance* which is SPIRIT, endued with the eternal impetus of development, and producing from itself the opposing powers and forces of the universe. A curious triplicate process seems the resultant action; first the Positive, then the Negative, then the product of the mediation between them; from which product the process is repeated and so goes on without end.[37]

According to Hegel the whole earth . . . with its infinite variety, the past, the surroundings of to-day, or what may happen in the future, the contrarieties of material with spiritual, and of natural with artificial, are all, to the eye of the *ensemblist*, but necessary sides and unfoldings, different steps or links, in the endless process of Creative thought, which, amid numberless apparent failures and contradictions, is held together by central and never-broken unity—not contradictions or failures at all, but radiations of one consistent and eternal purpose; the whole mass of everything steadily, unerringly tending and flowing toward the permanent *utile* and *morale*, as rivers to oceans. As life is the whole law and incessant effort of the visible universe, and death only the other or invisible side of the same, so the *utile*, so truth, so health are the continuously immutable laws of the moral universe, and vice and disease, with all their perturbations, are but transient, even if ever so prevalent expressions.[38]

It is evident that what most attracts Whitman in idealism is the importance and centrality it gives to man, whose thoughts are the measure and proper interpreters of the universe. This is clear in the abstract of Schelling given above. Of Hegel he says:

He has given the same clue to the fitness of reason and fitness of things and unending progress, to the universe of moral purposes that the sciences in their spheres, as astronomy and geology, have established in the material purposes, and the last and crowning proof of each is the same, that they fit the mind, and the idea of the all, and are necessary to be so in the nature of things.[39]

This Emersonian thought, "they fit the mind," is variously expressed in Whitman's poems.

Whatever satisfies Souls is true.[40]

. . . .

And that where I am, or you are, this present day, there is the centre
    of all days, all races,
And there is the meaning, to us, of all that has ever come of races and
    days, or ever will come.[41]

. . . .

Ethereal, pervading all [the Spirit], (for without me, what were all?
    what were God?)
Essence of forms—life of the real identities, permanent, positive,
    (namely the unseen,)
Life of the great round world, the sun and stars, and of man—I, the
    general Soul. . . .[42]

This last passage reminds one of Fichte's characterization of nature: "she who only exists for me, and exists not if I am not." [43] This view of the centrality of the "I" is, according to Whitman, a doctrine of Hegel. "The human soul stands in the centre, and all the universes minister to it, and serve it and revolve round it." [44] In the same passage in his notes, the world of things is seen as the mirror of our spirit, and the means of "identifying" it.

As a face in a mirror we see the world of materials, nature with all its objects, processes, shows, reflecting the human spirit and by such reflection formulating, identifying, developing and proving it. [45]

This notion of the human soul as identified, or given individual concrete existence, by material objects, is common in the poems.

You objects that call from diffusion my meanings, and give them
    shape! [46]

.   .   .   .

I too had been struck from the float forever held in solution,
I too had receiv'd identity by my Body. [47]

.   .   .   .

We realize the soul only by you, you faithful solids and fluids. [48]

.   .   .   .

It is not to diffuse you that you were born of your mother and father
    —it is to identify you . . . [49]

It is clear that Whitman was not intimately familiar with the philosophical systems of these German thinkers. He did not pretend to be a systematic philosopher, but regarded himself as a prophet proceeding by inspiration. He was well aware that the ultimate mysteries of the universe cannot be explained, and we certainly can find no close logical sequence in his thinking. But, Quaker-like, he was inclined to hold that men could arrive at essential spiritual truths by direct intuition. In his prose notes he defends the appeal to intuition by reference to Fichte. In his poems he celebrates "the intuitions of men and women" and sings—

Of the conformity of politics, armies, navies, to them and to me,—
Of the shining sun by them— Of the inherent light, greater than the
    rest. . . .[50]

So far as there is any logical starting-point for his thinking, any
original fount from which his conclusions flow, it would seem to
be the conviction, supported by Emerson, Schelling and Hegel,
that the subjective and objective worlds are essentially one.

What is the fusing explanation and tie—what the relation between
the (radical, democratic) Me, the human identity of understanding,
emotions, spirit, etc., on the one side, of and with the (conservative)
Not Me, the whole of the material objective universe and laws, with
what is behind them in time and space, on the other side. . . . Schelling's answer is . . . that the same general and particular intelligence,
passion, even the standards of right and wrong, which exist in a conscious and formulated state in man, exist in an unconscious state, or in
perceptible analogies, throughout the entire universe of external Nature . . . thus making the impalpable human mind, and concrete nature
. . . convertible, and in . . . essence one.[51]

Whitman's enthusiasm for the universe down to its every least
creature and aspect was doubtless native and temperamental; but
it was given intellectual support by his belief that the universe is
rational and moral like man, and that nature and man are alike
parts of a unified coherent scheme, which, however difficult it may
be to understand in detail, is in the large an affair of "great laws
and harmonious combinations." [52] He insists in his poems that one
must never take any person or object separately.

All must have reference to the ensemble of the world, and the com-
    pact truth of the world. . . .[53]

.   .   .

The simple, compact, well-join'd scheme—myself disintegrated, every
    one disintegrated, yet part of the scheme . . .[54]

This view of the universe as harmonious (and benevolent) he
found supported, not merely by the transcendentalists, but also by
Leibniz, another notable "ensemblist." [55] There are many respect-

ful references to Plato in Whitman's notes, but no clear evidence that he was acquainted with Plato's philosophy. It was mainly, it seems, by the new German route that Whitman arrived at the eighteenth-century poetic doctrine of Universal Harmony.

Religious Optimism

Universal Harmony is a mainly religious doctrine. And the poetry of Whitman, however unorthodox, is ostentatiously religious. He sings of the Modern Man, "cheerful—for freest action form'd, under the laws divine." [56] Of himself he says: "Divine am I inside and out, and I make holy whatever I touch or am touch'd from." [57] Everything in the world, he declares, exists for the sake of religion.

Each is not for its own sake;
I say the whole earth, and all the stars in the sky, are for Religion's sake.
I say no man has ever yet been half devout enough;
None has ever yet adored or worship'd half enough;
None has begun to think how divine he himself is, and how certain the future is.
I say that the real and permanent grandeur of These States must be their Religion;
Otherwise there is no real and permanent grandeur . . . [58]

When a child asked him, *What is grass?* he answered, among other things:

Or I guess it is the handkerchief of the Lord,
A scented gift and remembrancer, designedly dropt,
Bearing the owner's name someway in the corners, that we may see and remark, and say, *Whose?* [59]

Whitman is penetrated with the nineteenth-century faith in progress—a faith compacted of religion and a mystical, quasi-scientific evolutionism. He is much concerned with "the procreant urge of the world," which cannot fail to give its push to each one of us.[60] He represents himself as the culmination of a long upward trend.

My feet strike an apex of the apices of the stairs;
On every step bunches of ages, and larger bunches between the steps;
All below duly travel'd, and still I mount and mount.

. . . .

Immense have been the preparations for me,
Faithful and friendly arms that have help'd me.

. . . .

Before I was born out of my mother, generations guided me;
My embryo has never been torpid—nothing could overlay it.

For it the nebula cohered to an orb,
The long low strata piled to rest it on,
Vast vegetables gave it sustenance,
Monstrous sauroids transported it in their mouths.[61]

"Song of the Open Road" is a mystical "ode" in celebration of human life, which is defined in terms of spiritual evolution. It is profoundly religious, but utterly unchristian, in that nothing is said of sin, of discipline, or of faith other than the faith in existence itself.

The Soul travels;
The body does not travel as much as the soul;
The body has just as great a work as the soul, and parts away at last
    for the journeys of the soul.

All parts away for the progress of souls

. . . .

They go! they go! I know that they go, but I know not where they go;
But I know that they go toward the best—toward something great.[62]

The goal of this progress he cannot define; and since it is perpetual, no final goal is ever reached; it is an eternal process of creation, as in Hegel's system, as in Goethe. But that the process is good he has no doubt. This the soul recognizes at every contact with nature.

Now I see the secret of the making of the best persons,
It is to grow in the open air, and to eat and sleep with the earth.

. . . .

Here is the test of wisdom;
Wisdom is not finally tested in schools;
Wisdom cannot be pass'd from one having it, to another not having it;
Wisdom is of the Soul, is not susceptible of proof, is its own proof,
Applies to all stages and objects and qualities, and is content,
Is the certainty of the reality and immortality of things, and the excel-
    lence of things;
Something there is in the float of the sight of things that provokes it
    out of the Soul.[63]

. . . .

Allons! whoever you are, come travel with me!
Traveling with me, you find what never tires.
The earth never tires;
The earth is rude, silent, incomprehensible at first— Nature is rude and
    incomprehensible at first;
Be not discouraged—keep on—there are divine things, well envelop'd;
I swear to you there are divine things more beautiful than words can
    tell.[64]

While there is no prayer-book Christianism about this, no conviction of sin, no call to penitence and absolution, there is yet a
call to activity and struggle, and away from the sluggish apathy
of unawakened life.

My call is the call to battle—I nourish active rebellion;
He going with me must go well arm'd;
He going with me goes often with spare diet, poverty, angry enemies,
    desertions.[65]

And Whitman does describe a state from which men must be
saved.

Behold, through you as bad as the rest,
Through the laughter, dancing, dining, supping, of people,
Inside of dresses and ornaments, inside of those wash'd and trimm'd
    faces,
Behold a secret silent loathing and despair.

. . . .

Smartly attired, countenance smiling, form upright, death under the
    breast-bones, hell under the skull-bones,

Under the broadcloth and gloves, under the ribbons and artificial
    flowers,
Keeping fair with the customs, speaking not a syllable of itself,
Speaking of anything else, but never of itself.[66]

No Christian writer—not St. Augustine—has expressed more
poignantly the sense of tragic futility that comes upon a man without faith. This is a rare moment in Whitman, and corresponds to
the passage in Emerson's "Woodnotes" in which he addresses poor
man as "orphan and defrauded." The answer too is similar to
Emerson's, though less explicit in statement. Man having fallen
into such a state of mind—being thus "lost" to spiritual truth—how
is he to be "saved"?

Behind all of Whitman's poetic enthusiasm lies the implicit faith
in immortality. This faith grew more insistent with the passing of
the years. "I believe in immortality, and by that I mean *identity*." [67]
But there is no specific reference to this subject in the present context. And, in any case, his faith in immortality is a sort of variant
of his faith in existence as such. Immortality is the vaguely conceived continuance *ad infinitum* of the process which Whitman
finds so good.

Whitman's answer seems to be virtually identical with Emerson's. Man is to be saved from his personal despair by being made
to realize that he is a part of the universal process, and that this
universal process is in essence good.

There is something which comes home to one now and perpetually;
It is not what is printed, preach'd, discuss'd—it eludes discussion and
    print;
It is not to be put in a book—it is not in this book;
It is for you whoever you are—it is no farther from you than your
    hearing and sight are from you;
It is hinted by nearest. commonest, readiest—it is ever provoked by
    them.
. . . .

The sun and stars that float in the open air;
The apple-shaped earth, and we upon it—surely the drift of them is
    something grand!

I do not know what it is, except that it is grand, and that it is happiness,
And that the enclosing purport of us here is not a speculation, or bon-
mot, or reconnoissance . . .[68]

. . . .

What will be, will be well—for what is, is well,
To take interest is well, and not to take interest shall be well.

The sky continues beautiful,
The pleasure of men with women shall never be sated, nor the pleasure
of women with men, nor the pleasure from poems,
The domestic joys, the daily housework or business, the building of
houses—these are not phantasms—they have weight, form, location;
Farms, profits, crops, wages, government, are none of them phantasms,
The difference between sin and goodness is no delusion,
The earth is not an echo—man and his life, and all the things of his life
are well-consider'd.

You are not thrown to the winds—you gather certainly and safely
around yourself;
Yourself! yourself! Yourself, forever and ever! [69]

. . . .

Pleasantly and well-suited I walk,
Whither I walk I cannot define, but I know it is good,
The whole universe indicates that it is good,
The past and the present indicate that it is good.

How beautiful and perfect are the animals!
How perfect the earth, and the minutest thing upon it!
What is called good is perfect, and what is called bad is just as perfect,
The vegetables and minerals are all perfect, and the imponderable
fluids are perfect;
Slowly and surely they pass'd on to this, and slowly and surely they
yet pass on.

I swear I think now that everything without exception has an eternal
Soul!
The trees have, rooted in the ground! the weeds of the sea have! the
animals!

I swear I think there is nothing but immortality!
That the exquisite scheme is for it, and the nebulous float is for it, and
   the cohering is for it;
And all preparation is for it! and identity is for it! and life and materials are altogether for it! [70]

In this Psalm of Life, Whitman's conception of immortality is
much too inclusive to appeal to the Christian mind. He is far too
liberal in his bestowal of "eternal souls." He proves too much. No
poet or mystic has ever been more absolute in his acceptance of the
order of things, and the ecstasy with which he declares all things
right.

There was doubtless something in the very mixing of elements
that predisposed Whitman to this universal optimism. But there
was never perhaps a moment in history more favorable to the development of such an attitude. Expanding America before the
Civil War, before it was torn with desperate strife; the great West
still open for pioneers; democracy triumphant and as yet not disenchanted and cynical; industry prospering but not yet conscious of
the class war; mechanical invention moving fast and quite unaware
of the terrors of over-production and unemployment; science advancing confident on every front, not yet caught in the iron grip
of determinism; religion growing mild, and in the deliquescence of
dogma, keeping only what it wanted—immortality, benevolent
providence, the brotherhood of man; and to cap all, a new transcendental philosophy, proceeding with all the fanfare of logic and
metaphysical subtlety to establish an order in which rationality
and purpose were enthroned in the very nature of things, guaranteed by a God who was the creative principle of the universe,
immanent in all.

The Democracy of Nature

If the divine principle is immanent in all things, there is nothing
that is not holy. This logic of transcendentalism Whitman carries
much farther than any philosopher or poet. Being a poet, he carries it over into the concrete; and being somehow free from the
ethical prepossessions of most nature-poets, he can give it a more

complete and startling illustration than they. Moreover, his social democracy is more militant, and this he extends from the human realm to include all creatures and objects of the universe. Like Carlyle and Emerson, he finds that "all the things of the universe are complete miracles, each as profound as any." [71] He rejoices to "peruse manifold objects, no two alike, and every one good." [72]

I believe a leaf of grass is no less than the journey-work of the stars,
And the pismire is equally perfect, and a grain of sand, and the egg of
    the wren. [73]

He retains that sense of wonder whose loss in our day Carlyle considers the cause of our unfaith.

        O such themes! Equalities!
        O amazement of things! O divine average! [74]

Whitman's wonder is equalitarian. His amazement does not stop with the stars. It is equally evoked by the humblest and most familiar objects. The divine Something is "hinted by nearest, commonest, readiest—it is ever provoked by them."

Will you seek afar off? you surely come back at last,
In things best known to you, finding the best, or as good as the best,
In folks nearest to you finding the sweetest, strongest, lovingest . . . [75]

    It is this democratic spirit which leads Whitman to insist on including those most scorned within the embrace of his wonder and affection.

This is the meal equally set—this is the meat for natural hunger;
It is for the wicked just the same as the righteous—I make appointments
    with all;
I will not have a single person slighted or left away . . . [76]
       .   .   .   .

I speak the pass-word primeval—I give the sign of democracy;
By God! I will accept nothing which all cannot have their counterpart
    of on the same terms.

Through me many long dumb voices;
Voices of the interminable generations of slaves;
Voices of prostitutes, and of deform'd persons . . .[77]

. . . .

Here [in the open road] the profound lesson of reception, neither pref-
erence or denial:
The black with his woolly head, the felon, the diseas'd, the illiterate
person, are not denied;
The birth, the hasting after the physician, the beggar's tramp, the
drunkard's stagger, the laughing party of mechanics,
The escaped youth, the rich person's carriage, the fop, the eloping
couple,
The early market-man, the hearse, the moving of furniture into the
town,
They pass—I also pass—anything passes—none can be interdicted;
None but are accepted—none but are dear to me.[78]

The Open Road is a symbol of the universe conceived as a condition for the evolution of souls. All that the universe contains is
part of the sacred process—the procreant Urge of the world. The
Earth is more specifically a symbol of physical nature, and it
teaches the same lesson of reception.

The earth does not argue,
Is not pathetic, has no arrangements,
Does not scream, haste, persuade, threaten, promise,
Makes no discriminations, has no conceivable failures,
Closes nothing, refuses nothing, shuts none out,
Of all the powers, objects, states, it notifies, shuts none out.[79]

It is nature, teaching universal acceptance, who teaches the
reverent acceptance of the body, which is so notable an article of
Whitman's creed. In the prudish age in which he wrote, Whitman
considered it necessary to insist on the equal sacredness of every
organ, and to celebrate the body as the means of continuing that
"procession, with measured and beautiful motion," [80] which the
universe is in Hegelian philosophy. Hence the many passages which
offended the taste of Emerson, and which he regarded as likely to
interfere with Whitman's effectiveness as a teacher, but which

Whitman sturdily refused to give up, and which, in the long run, may prove a chief source of his strength, because of the consistency they show with his general thought. These are found especially in "Walt Whitman" and in the poems included under the heading, "Children of Adam."

The celebration of the sexual impulse is part of a sensual mysticism in which the poet realizes his kinship with the lower orders and the material processes of nature. At times he goes so far as to describe the very genital organs in terms of fond praise. In "Children of Adam" the freedom of nature is sometimes specifically associated with the free life of the sexes; at other times the sense of freedom or escape takes the form of imaginative identification with plants and minerals and beasts, and even with meteorological phenomena—"snow, rain, cold, darkness."

O to be absolv'd from previous ties and conventions—I from mine, and
    you from yours!
O to find a new unthought-of nonchalance with the best of nature! [81]

. . . .

Give me the drench of my passions! Give me life coarse and rank!
To-day, I go consort with nature's darlings—to-night too. . . .[82]

. . . .

Now transmuted, we swiftly escape, as Nature escapes;
We are Nature—long have we been absent, but now we return;
We become plants, leaves, foliage, roots, bark;
We are bedded in the ground—we are rocks. . . . [Etc.] [83]

Whitman's interpretation of sex is comprehensive and philosophical. He realizes that sex, taken broadly, is central to all human experience—the root of the affections and the foundation of government; that the radiating influence of this primary impulse is felt in art and morality.[84] Moreover, his view of sex is metaphysical; sex is a physical symbol of the creative potency of the universe. His cult of sex is consciously religious, phallic.[85]

Whitman does not give the impression, on the whole, of a man morbidly obsessed with sex. On the contrary. So catholic is he in his interest in all human occupations, and especially in the manly and arduous interests, that sexual gratification makes a very minor strain in the total volume of his song. Moreover, he is as capable of celebrating normal married life and chastity [86] as he is the mere sexual impulse. But the mere sexual impulse he feels bound to praise, not simply because of its radical importance, but also in conformity with his principle of universal "acceptance."

> I harbor, for good or bad—I permit to speak, at every hazard,
> Nature now without check, with original energy.[87]

And in accordance with the same principle, he is bound to include death and all evil.

I make the poem of evil also—I commemorate that part also;
I am myself as much evil as good, and my nation is— And I say there
  is in fact no evil;
(Or if there is, I say it is just as important to you, to the land, or to
  me, as anything else.) [88]

Whitman's realism in regard to evil is in line with his equalitarian attitude towards everything in nature, but it is supported by his transcendental view of the entire scheme of things. At times it takes on a striking resemblance to Christian Science doctrine ("and I say there is in fact no evil"); but then he corrects himself and shows a more realistic recognition of hard facts. In the last analysis, he justifies evil, like Hegel, like Pope and Archbishop King, by reference to the universal harmony of things. But these philosophers accept evil only in the abstract; whereas Whitman has a godlike tolerance and affection for evil-doers in the flesh.

His view of death, which he praises in so many of his later and most famous poems, is complicated by his faith in immortality,— a faith supported by transcendental philosophy. But here also operates the democratic motive of universal acceptance. One feels that Whitman, in his high mysticism, would accept death with almost equal enthusiasm merely as a part of the life-process which he so unquestioningly embraces. It is thus that Meredith accepts death—as a phase of life.

"O, Ye Fountains, Meadows, Hills, and Groves"

Thus far, in discussing Whitman's view of nature, we have used the word, and illustrated its use by him, in the sense of the material world in general, often identical with the universe, including its laws and forces and the impulses that come to man from the physical world. In this sense nature includes man and man's life as part of itself, except in so far as he is considered in his spiritual aspect; and this last must indeed be regarded as an artificial distinction, considering the identity of subjective and objective in the transcendental view.

We have had little to say of the scenery and natural history of the out-of-doors. These are amply present in Whitman's poetry, though not so directly treated nor so much for themselves as in Wordsworth or Shelley. They generally appear as the appropriate background for man's life and the means of fostering manly virtues; or else they stand symbolically for the larger nature which includes everything and relates itself to the divine plan.

There is no doubt that Whitman regarded himself as a nature-poet, if only by virtue of his primitiveness and abandon. Thus, in a paragraph of *Specimen Days*, while traveling in the Rocky Mountains in 1868, he noted the affinities of his poetry with wild nature.

"I have found the law of my poems," was the unspoken but more-and-more decided feeling that came to me as I pass'd, hour after hour, amid all this grim yet joyous elemental abandon—this plenitude of material, entire absence of art, untrammel'd play of primitive Nature —the chasm, the gorge, the crystal mountain stream, repeated scores, hundreds of miles—the broad handling and absolute uncrampedness— the fantastic forms. . . .[89]

Whitman's feeling for nature was profound, intense, and intimate. He was a lover of solitary musing and observation. Both as a young man and later as an invalid and broken old man, he was accustomed to make long retreats to wild and secluded places. Many of his poems were written in sea-girt caves and rural dells of Long Island. *Specimen Days* is full of minute and loving notations on bird-life, insect-life, on trees, the seasons and times of day, with their corresponding moods.

In general, however, his poems are too didactic and human in their interest to admit of very much of this sort of thing, though every one remembers the gray-brown bird, the heart-shaped

leaves, and the fallen star of "President Lincoln's Burial Hymn."
The love for nature is everywhere felt.

> The press of my foot to the earth springs a hundred affections;
> They scorn the best I can do to relate them.[90]

But immediately a connection is made with the humanity which he
associates with the out-of-doors.

I am enamour'd of growing out-doors,
Of men that live among cattle, or taste of the ocean or woods.
Of the builders and steerers of ships, and the wielders of axes and
   mauls, and the drivers of horses;
I can eat and sleep with them week in and week out.[91]

Still, there is implied here, and elsewhere more explicitly set
forth, the contrast between artificial man and the non-human
aspects of nature. There is the full nineteenth-century doctrine of
"back to nature." In many passages of *Specimen Days*, in rural re-
tirement, Whitman talks of getting "close to nature." [92] He rejoices
in the freedom of nature—"no talk, no bonds, no dress, no books,
no *manners*"; [93] in the "entire absence of art, books, elegance—so
indescribably comforting, even this winter day." [94] Nature he
represents, like Wordsworth, as a cure for sick humanity and a
counterpoise to morbid books.

> Present literature, while magnificently fulfilling certain popular de-
> mands, with plenteous knowledge and verbal smartness, is profoundly
> sophisticated, insane, and its very joy is morbid. It needs tally and ex-
> press Nature, and the spirit of Nature, and to know and obey the
> standards.[95]

Self-conscious man may learn from contemplating a tree the lesson
of being as opposed to seeming.

> One lesson from affiliating a tree—perhaps the greatest moral lesson
> anyhow from earth, rocks, animals, is that same lesson of inherency,
> of *what is*, without the least regard to what the looker-on (the critic)
> supposes or says, or whether he likes or dislikes. What worse—what
> more general malady pervades each and all of us, our literature, educa-

tion, attitude toward each other, (even toward ourselves,) than a morbid trouble about *seems*, (generally temporarily seems too,) and no
trouble at all, or hardly any, about the sane, slow-growing, perennial,
real parts of character, books, friendship, marriage—humanity's invisible foundations and hold-together? [96]

The most extreme statement of this contrast between "the world"
and nature is the following note:

After you have exhausted what there is in business, politics, conviv-
iality, love, and so on—have found that none of these finally satisfy, or
permanently wear—what remains? Nature remains, to bring out from
their torpid recesses the affinities of a man or woman with the open air,
the trees, fields, the changes of seasons—the sun by day and the stars of
heaven by night. We begin with these convictions. Literature flies so
high and is so hotly spiced, that our notes may seem hardly more than
breaths of common air, or draughts of water to drink. But that is part
of our lesson.[97]

Thus Whitman realizes as vividly as Wordsworth "the affinities
of a man or woman with the open air, trees, fields," etc. He does
not dwell so much on the "forms of beauty" themselves as do
Wordsworth and Shelley; but quite as infallibly as Wordsworth,
even more infallibly than Shelley, he rises from the individual object or scene to a contemplation of the divine order of which it is
a symbol.

Man, so diminutive, dilates beyond the sensible universe, competes
with, outcopes space and time, meditating even one great idea. Thus,
and thus only, does a human being, his spirit, ascend above, and justify,
objective Nature, which, probably nothing in itself, is incredibly and
divinely serviceable, indispensable, real, here.[98]

Lo! Nature (the only complete, actual poem) existing calmly in the
divine scheme, containing all, content, careless of the criticisms of a
day, or these endless and wordy chatterers [writers]. And lo! to
the consciousness of the soul, the permanent identity, the thought, the
something before which the magnitude even of democracy, art, literature, etc., dwindles, becomes partial, measurable—something which fully
satisfies (which those do not).[99]

So it is that nature brings Whitman, as it brought Wordsworth
and Emerson, to the consciousness of the soul. This was accom-

plished, as he believed, by a direct intuition, by the "inherent light." But if he needed a more philosophical justification for his view, he could refer to the demonstration by Schelling and Hegel that, in the "one eternal process of creative thought," [100] subjective and objective are identical, and "the impalpable human mind and concrete nature . . . convertible and in . . . essence one."

This was not a mere abstract formula with Whitman, but something applicable to one's own dealings with the world of sense. As an old and broken man, Whitman could derive spiritual and material benefit from the realization of his personal oneness with that "presence" which the romantic poets called the "spirit of nature." Thus on September 5, 1877, he wrote of his sheltered situation on a day of drizzling rain "pleasantly imprisoned" under a leafy oak tree.

Doubtless there comes a time—perhaps it has come to me—when one feels through his whole being, and pronouncedly the emotional part, *that identity between himself subjectively and Nature objectively which Schelling and Fichte are so fond of pressing.* How it is I know not, but I often realize a presence here—in clear moods I am certain of it, and neither chemistry nor reasoning nor esthetics will give the least explanation. All the past two summers it has been strengthening and nourishing my sick body and soul, as never before. Thanks, invisible physician, for thy silent delicious medicine, thy day and night, thy waters and thy airs, the banks, the grass, the trees, and e'en the weeds! [101]

So it is with Whitman as with Emerson that a sense of oneness with the "eternal Pan" brings atonement and restoration to the "orphan and defrauded" soul.

The End of a Phase

The position of Whitman in relation to other nature-poets is rather peculiar. On the whole he belongs with Coleridge and Emerson by virtue of his transcendentalism. Only his transcendentalism is not theological like Coleridge's; and in metaphysics he is infinitely less acute, systematic and well-informed. But his *rationale* is metaphysical. As for his emotional urge, it is a curious combination of the sensual and the religious. In richness of sensuous outfit, in devotion to the concrete, he is most like Wordsworth and Goethe. And his comprehensive enthusiasm for every variety of man, for every aspect of human experience and every item of life and nature, is supported and suffused by an intuitive religious faith as fundamental and unwavering as Wordsworth's own.

Whitman's democratic passion links him with Wordsworth and Shelley, with Swinburne and Meredith. He is part and parcel of the revolutionary movement, whose watchwords are nature, liberty and brotherhood. His individualism, congenial with Emerson's, at the same time that it is revolutionary, is romantic and mystical. It involves the romantic evaluation of the individual soul, supported by the "formulas" of German idealism.

His relation to naturalism is paradoxical. For all his earthy sensualism, he is less naturalistic than Emerson in the philosophic sense, because he is so much less concerned with the formulations of science. For the same reason he is less naturalistic than Shelley and Wordsworth, and infinitely less so than Goethe. Among the later writers, he is decidedly less naturalistic than Meredith and Hardy.

In his interpretation of nature he stands at the peak of transcendentalism. His evolutionism is more Hegelian than Darwinian. After Whitman transcendentalism plays a small part in naturepoetry. The leading role is played by Darwinian evolution, whether for the glorification of nature or for its dethronement. Whitman represents the end of a phase.

PART THREE

THE VICTORIANS

Change is on the wing to bud
Rose in brain from rose in blood.
— Meredith

*   *   *

CHAPTER XIV

ARNOLD

IT IS well known that Matthew Arnold was strongly under the influence of both Wordsworth and Goethe. He was not averse to philosophical speculation in poetry. And one might expect him to have turned out nature-poetry of high significance. But as a matter of fact his references to nature in the abstract show a certain confusion of attitude. Sometimes they are conventional and admiring; more often perhaps they are critical and disparaging. And throughout they are lacking in the warmth and richness that marked the romantic treatment of nature. This is presumably due to his want of enthusiasm for either science or religion, the two main inspirers of nature-worship. One feels at once, in reading Arnold, that one has reached a period distinctly more "modern" than that of Wordsworth; that the poet no longer makes those religious assumptions in regard to the universe which were latent in Wordsworth's philosophy of nature. He is the least transcendental of English poets; and no German inspirations had come in, as with Emerson and Whitman, to give a new lease of life to nature.

Equally marked is a certain aloofness, in his poems, from the scientific movement of his day. There is very slight reference to evolution. Most of his poems were written before the publication of *The Origin of Species* or before the evolutionary idea had gained wide currency; and he did not have, it seems, the natural bent in the direction of scientific thought which enabled Emerson, Tennyson, and even Browning to anticipate the prevalence of these ideas. He was of course familiar with the materialistic philosophy of Lucretius and Empedocles; but its chief effect on his thought was to emphasize the divorce between man, with his spiritual faculties, and the "universe of things." In the early "In Utrumque Paratus," he admits as one possible hypothesis the self-subsistence of nature, independently of any divine mind; but only to point out that this leaves man, the spiritual king, in shivering isolation, separate from his "brother-world," and to warn man against too great pride in his own existence, which may be a mere phenomenal dream.

Man versus Nature

While Arnold indicates several different lessons to be learned from nature, it is almost invariably the sharp distinction between nature and man which forms the point of his departure. In his early sonnet, "In Harmony with Nature," he points out the absurdity of this phrase, taken from some foolish preacher.

> Know, man hath all which Nature hath, and more,
> And in that *more* lie all his hopes of good.
> Nature is cruel, man is sick of blood;
> Nature is stubborn, man would fain adore;
>
> Nature is fickle, man hath need of rest;
> Nature forgives no debt, and fears no grave;
> Man would be mild, and with safe conscience blest.
>
> Man must begin, know this, where Nature ends;
> Nature and man can never be fast friends.
> Fool, if thou canst not pass her, rest her slave!

The doctrine of this poem, that of the "new humanists," is identical with Goethe's in "Das Göttliche," a poem with which I think it probable that Arnold was familiar. The English and German poems illustrate equally well the ambiguity inherent in the use of the word nature unless it is carefully defined. The two poets are here using this word to designate the "world of things" as opposed to the moral world of man; whereas it is often used to designate the natural order which includes man and his moral world together with the world of things. But Arnold's poem reminds us how hard it is to maintain the distinction. The world of things, which is cruel, evidently includes the lower animals to which man is so close akin; and the cruelty, fickleness, and vengefulness of "nature" are obviously characteristics of man in so far as he shares in the world of things. The division comes within man himself between that which is from his lower "nature," and those godlike traits which we choose to call "human."

The distinction is highly important, of course. But the naturist will at once be moved to ask whence man derives his humanity if not from nature. We have seen that "Das Göttliche" does not represent Goethe in his typical feeling towards nature. From the very beginning he mainly conceived of nature as all-inclusive. "Who sees her not everywhere sees her not aright . . . You obey her laws even when you strive against them; you work with her even when you mean to work against her . . . For everything she is to blame, and to her must credit be given for everything."

The same sharp distinction between nature and man is found in Arnold's sonnet, "Religious Isolation," in which he warns a friend against the desire to make nature share his thoughts, like a child imagining that "some incurious bystander" has a common interest with him. Man must learn to play alone his religious game.

> What though the holy secret, which moulds thee,
> Mould not the solid earth? though never winds
> Have whisper'd it to the complaining sea,
>
> Nature's great law, and law of all men's minds?—
> To its own impulse every creature stirs;
> Live by thy light, and earth will live by hers!

It is as if Arnold were rebuking Wordsworth—or Goethe—for indulging in the pathetic fallacy and reading into inanimate nature thoughts which only man can have. As a matter of fact, one might as readily accuse Arnold of lack of imagination, in not being able to see that whatever consciousness man has comes from unconscious nature. "Men are all within her, and she within all . . . She has no speech nor language; but she creates tongues and hearts, by means of which she feels and talks." Perhaps Arnold does have a glimmering of this thought; otherwise what can he mean by "nature's great law, and law of all men's minds"? The reference of this phrase is hopelessly obscure. At first it seems to refer to the "holy secret" which does *not* mould the solid earth; then it seems to be a grandiloquent label for the truth that "to its own impulse every creature stirs." But in any case it is a considerable concession to the naturalist point of view to talk at all of "Nature's great law," let alone equating it with the "law of all men's minds."

Nature versus Man

At other times Arnold maintains the distinction between nature and man in order to exalt the moral qualities felt in nature above the restlessness of man. Most doubtful humanism! Here indeed Arnold is himself frankly indulging in the pathetic fallacy, attributing to inanimate nature moods and qualities which are lent her by ourselves. They are variously described in different poems. In "Resignation" (1849) he is recommending to his Fausta the stoical character that seems to be impressed on the country scene, or the peace which he feels at the heart of the cosmos—

> That general life, which does not cease,
> Whose secret is not joy, but peace . . .
>   . . . .
> Yet, Fausta, the mute turf we tread,
> The solemn hills around us spread,
> This stream which falls incessantly,
> The strange-scrawl'd rocks, the lonely sky,
> If I might lend their life a voice,
> Seem to bear rather than rejoice.

In "Lines Written in Kensington Gardens," again, it is peace which he reads into general nature.

> Calm soul of all things! make it mine
> To feel, amid the city's jar,
> That there abides a peace of thine,
> Man did not make, and cannot mar.

The calmness and mute endurance, the static character of nature as here felt by Arnold, are in marked contrast with the joyfulness

and animation so often recorded by Wordsworth, and especially
in contrast with the prolific and tumultuous life celebrated by
Goethe—this latter surely the nearest of the three to a literal rendering of what we know of nature from scientific observation.
More of the Wordsworthian or Goethean view appears in the
famous "Self-Dependence"; but even here, there is a suspicion of
coldness and stoicism in the "joy" with which the stars perform
their shining, and the "mighty life" to which the heavenly bodies
attain. And of course the pathetic fallacy is here in full panoply.

> Unaffrighted by the silence round them,
> Undistracted by the sights they see,
> These demand not that the things without them
> Yield them love, amusement, sympathy.
>
> And with joy the stars perform their shining,
> And the sea its long moon-silver'd roll;
> For self-pois'd they live, nor pine with noting
> All the fever of some differing soul.
>
> Bounded by themselves, and unregardful
> In what state God's other works may be,
> In their own tasks all their powers pouring,
> These attain the mighty life you see.

In other poems, Arnold, more conventionally, celebrates the
steadfastness or the greatness of nature. In "The Youth of Nature,"
the poet is rowing on a lake near where Wordsworth lies dead,
and musingly debates the question whether the beauty and inspiration of nature are in nature herself or in the poet who so well
sings her praises. Whereupon she herself replies, assuring him that
loveliness, magic and grace are actually here, are set in the world;
they are the life of the world; the singer is less than his themes,
"Life, and emotion, and I." And she ends her discourse with the
assurance that while race after race of men pass, dreaming that
nature lives but for them, it is she that remains when they are dust.

This theme is pursued in "The Youth of Man." The poet is
observing a man and woman, now old, and he thinks back to the
time when they stood as youthful lovers in this same garden and

made light of the poetic nonsense on the subject of nature. Then he proceeds to show nature after all these years unchanged while the lovers have grown old. They feel now how fair nature had been, and how weary and unprofitable have been their faded, ignoble lives. Whereupon the poet turns to an imaginary young reader and urges him, while it is yet time—

> Yearn to the greatness of Nature!
> Rally the good in the depths of thyself!

This is feeble poetry and perfunctory morality. The poem is highly inadequate either as a criticism of Wordsworthian nature-philosophy or as defense of it—this futile questioning as to whether nature is or isn't there. It exhibits too dim a sense on Arnold's part of the complex and massive implications of the term nature to Wordsworth's generation.

Somewhat more pointed and pertinent is Arnold's "Morality." Here he pictures a light-hearted and debonair Nature puzzling over the moral strenuousness of man, and wondering where he got it from—surely not from her? And then she recollects that she too has once felt "that severe, that earnest air." But where and when was it?

> I knew not yet the gauge of time,
> Nor wore the manacles of space;
> I felt it in some other clime,
> I saw it in some other place.
>   'Twas when the heavenly house I trod,
>   And lay upon the breast of God.

This is indeed neat, and it does suggest, for once, that man's moral being is not completely without relation to the natural order in which it flowers. But it involves, at the same time, the notion of a divine origin of nature—the notion of God, so thin and uncongenial to Arnold. His conception of divinity has none of the richness of Coleridge's, drawn from metaphysics and mystic theology; nor of Wordsworth's, drawn from natural theology and his passion for the earth; nor of Goethe's, drawn from his passion for beauty and his devotion to science. And if there is a hint of Shelley's platonism in

Arnold's imagery, it is but a cold and fleeting glimmer. What we most feel in the whole poem is Arnold's wistful loneliness in this no-man's-land where he wanders, between an old faith weakly grasped and a new faith not yet surmised.

Natural versus Supernatural

If Arnold has little of the positive faith of the nature-poets, he has at least something of the negative and critical, the disciplinary side of that faith. He has not the glow and hopefulness of Words-worth, nor the revolutionary enthusiasm of Shelley. Science does not exalt him as it did Goethe; nor does the concept of evolution lift his heart as it did Goethe and Swinburne and Meredith. What he does share with the nature-poets—and in him it stands out in high relief, owing to the comparative want of the other elements of their faith—is their implicit or explicit disapproval of the super-natural, their espousal of what Swinburne calls "the actual earth's equalities"; their determination to cultivate—

> Knowledge and patience of what must
> And what things may be . . .

This disciplinary aspect of nature-philosophy is set forth in "Empedocles upon Etna" (1852), in the long sermon of the philos-opher to his disciple Pausanias. Empedocles deprecates man's dis-position to struggle and rave against the order of things, his dream that the world exists for his benefit, and that he has a right to happiness. Instead of studying the actualities of things in order to determine the limits within which he is free to move, man invents gods to gratify the dreams of his heart.

> The world's course proves the terms
> On which man wins content;
> Reason the proof confirms—
> We spurn it and invent

A false course for the world, and for ourselves, false powers.

The consequence is that, looking to supernatural powers for aid, we neglect the means we have at our disposal in our own breasts.

We would have inward peace,
Yet will not look within;
We would have misery cease,
Yet will not cease from sin;
We want all pleasant ends, but will use no harsh means.

In this discourse of Empedocles, Arnold rises to a conception of the universal order to which we belong, though we are reluctant to acknowledge it, unwilling to conform to its decrees, and fain instead to invent evil gods, whom we blame for our distresses, and kind gods who may be relied on to bring to fulfilment our feeble undertakings. These verses are rather abstract and prosy; but they must be quoted to set Arnold in his place among poets concerned with the philosophic concept of nature.

All things the world which fill
Of but one stuff are spun,
That we who rail are still,
With what we rail at, one;
One with the o'erlabour'd Power that through the breadth and length

Of earth, and air, and sea,
In men, and plants, and stones,
Hath toil perpetually,
And travails, pants and moans;
Fain would do all things well, but sometimes fails in strength.

.   .   .

This is not what man hates,
Yet he can curse but this.
Harsh Gods and hostile Fates
Are dreams! this only *is*—
Is everywhere; sustains the wise, the foolish elf.

Not only, in the intent
To attach blame elsewhere,
Do we at will invent
Stern Powers who make their care
To embitter human life, malignant Deities;

But, next, we would reverse
The scheme ourselves have spun,
And what we made to curse
We now would lean upon,
And feign kind Gods who perfect what man vainly tries.

Man has an ambition to understand the universe and the secrets
of his own mind. But soon growing discouraged with the enormity
of the task, he gives it up and weakly concludes that the search for
knowledge is a sin, since "man's measures cannot mete the immeasurable All." He abandons to imaginary gods the business of comprehending the universe. And since the world has failed to gratify
his craving for joy, he assumes that the gods will provide a realm
beyond death to make up for this want.

The leading ideas of this discourse of Empedocles will be found
later, in much more splendid poetic garb, in Swinburne and Meredith, combined with more heartening articles of the nature-faith.
Again, Arnold's suspicion of nature as pagan and immoral will be
found vigorously expressed in Tennyson and Hardy. His preference of man's ideal morality to nature's cruelty is echoed by
Tennyson, who conceives of man's ideals in more explicitly religious terms. It is Arnold's anticipation of the sterner and more
critical side of the later poets that constitutes his only significant
contribution to the philosophy of nature in English poetry.

Chapter XV

TENNYSON

Tennyson is anything but a nature-poet in the sense in which this term applies to the romantic poets, Wordsworth and Shelley and Goethe. He is a notable landscape painter. The rich and cultivated English countryside appears in his poems in the form of deliberate pictorial compositions combining in unique fashion melting grace of line with a certain hard objective precision of detail. This rural country may be described at length for its own beauty or serve as setting for his stories and portraits, but is almost invariably stamped with the associations of immemorial social use. It carries accordingly the emotional freight implied in the loved humanity of which it is an expression as well as the pure esthetic appeal of line and color, of composition and nuance.

But Tennyson is the most clear-headed of poets. He indulges very little in unconscious pathetic fallacy. He never confuses the beauty of landscape with a conviction of the benevolence of nature. For him there would be practically no sense in Wordsworth's declaration that—

> Nature never did betray
> The heart that loved her.

Still less is there in his poetry anything like the complete ecstatic self-abandonment to the world-process shown by Goethe in his "Fragment über die Natur." His unromantic common sense and want of sympathy with Wordsworthian effusiveness over nature appear in that one of the "Juvenilia" entitled "Character." It is the satirical portrait of a cold-hearted, self-centered esthete and philosopher who, among other things, adheres to the cult of nature.

The word nature appears in Tennyson with average frequency
but almost the only passage in which it is used in a sense and a
context strongly suggesting Wordsworth is one near the end of
"The Two Voices" (1834). In this poem, written on the death of
Hallam, the still small voice of doubt and disillusion suggests to the
poet that he is so full of misery it were perhaps better not to be.
But the sight of a happy family on their way to church sets speaking in his heart a second more cheerful voice, bringing with it "a
hidden hope." His mood is changed.

> And forth into the fields I went,
> And Nature's living motion lent
> The pulse of hope to discontent.
>
> I wonder'd at the bounteous hours,
> The slow result of winter showers:
> You scarce could see the grass for flowers.

Here, for once in Tennyson, the word nature associates the
beauty of the out-of-doors with the vitality and bountifulness of
the natural process, and links up both of these conceptions with
the spiritual hopes and aspirations of man. But that is as far as the
analogy with Wordsworth holds. Tennyson does not begin with
nature and attribute to her beneficent suggestion the spiritual hope
of man. On the contrary, he begins with the happy family on
their way to church—that is, with religion and the social sanctities
connected with it. It is religion and virtue which reflect their cheerful light upon "Nature's living motion" and thus enable the poet to
associate the beauty of the rural scene with the hopes of his heart.

Opposition of Nature and God

Almost invariably in Tennyson the word nature denotes distinctly either the world of material things which is the subject-
matter of scientific study, or else the natural instincts and impulses
which we share with the lower creatures and which thus bring us,
as animals, under the observation of science. In Wordsworth and
Shelley, as we have seen, these conceptions are likely to underlie
and reinforce the more esthetic and spiritual views of nature. In

Tennyson, it is just the contrary. Generally speaking, there is no association between the concept of nature and the beauty of the world, and still less between nature and the spiritual faculties and aspirations of man which make him akin to the divine. There is most often an implicit or explicit dualism, impelling the poet to a more or less hopeless effort to reconcile the practically irreconcilable claims of nature and God.

Thus in "In Memoriam" (1833–50), we find him asking,

> Are God and Nature then at strife,
> That Nature lends such evil dreams? [1]

We find him listening to the suggestions of his sorrow.

> "The stars," she whispers, "blindly run;
>   A web is wov'n across the sky;
>   From out waste places comes a cry,
> And murmurs from the dying sun:
>
> "And all the phantom, Nature, stands—
>   With all the music in her tone,
>   A hollow echo of my own,—
> A hollow form with empty hands." [2]

Tennyson has emerged from the period dominated by the assumptions of natural theology, in which a Wordsworth could assert—

> Our cheerful faith, that all which we behold
> Is full of blessings.

Tennyson is indeed distinctly in advance of the more popular science and theology of his day. In an earlier chapter I have given some examples of the argument from design, prevalent in the seventeenth and eighteenth centuries,—a type of argument still vigorously flourishing in the Bridgewater treatises of 1833. Probably the best known work of this kind was William Paley's *Natural Theology* (1802). Paley contended that the manifold nice adjustments of organ to function, of organ to organ, of organism to environment, are so many proofs of the reign of purpose in nature, so many demonstrations of the providence of God. Suppose, says Paley, that a traveler should come by chance upon a watch lying on a barren heath. He would be compelled on observing the complicated contrivances of the machine, all for a given end, to conclude that it had been made by some intelligent being for the purposes which it serves. In nature we find innumerable instances of creatures with organs precisely adapted to the ends they serve in the animal economy; and we must conclude, as in the case of a watch, that these creatures were all fashioned by an intelligent being with these specific ends in view.

Such evidences for design are traced in much detail by Paley in the eyes of human beings, of birds and fish; in the wings of birds and fins of fish; in various organs of insects; 's well as in the arrangement of the starry heavens. Similar arguments I have earlier cited from Robert Boyle in regard to the movements and situation of the planets, the wings of bats, and the visual organs of flies. With writers like Boyle and Paley, these instances of adaptation, of "final causes" in nature, were proofs of the existence of God. Not so for Tennyson.

> I found Him not in world or sun,
>   Or eagle's wing, or insect's eye;
>   Nor thro' the questions men may try,
> The petty cobwebs we have spun.[3]

Thus Tennyson anticipates the position of modern-science, which has its own natural way of accounting for the adaptation of organ to function and of organism to environment, without recourse to "final causes" and without reference to the deliberate act of Deity. From the generation of Paley to that of Tennyson was a long step; and already poet, scientist and theologian alike were beginning to doubt the sufficiency of the evidences for divinity brought forward from a study of nature. Thus Newman, in his *Tamworth Reading Room* letters (1841), replies to the claim of Sir Robert Peel that the study of science is itself conducive to religious faith.

When Sir Robert Peel assures us from the Town-hall at Tamworth that physical science must lead to religion, it is no bad compliment to him to say that he is unreal. He speaks of what he knows nothing about. To a religious man like him, Science has ever suggested religious thoughts; he colours the phenomena of physics with his own mind, and mistakes an interpretation for a deduction. "I am sanguine enough to believe," he says, "that that superior sagacity which is most conversant with the course and constitution of Nature will be first to turn a deaf ear to objections and presumptions against Revealed Religion, and to acknowledge the harmony of the Christian Dispensation with all that Reason, assisted by Revelation, tells us of the course and constitution of Nature." Now, considering that we are all of us educated as Christians from infancy, it is not easy to decide at this day whether Science creates Faith, or only confirms it; but we have this remarkable fact in the history of heathen Greece against the former supposition, that her most eminent empirical philosophers were atheists, and that it was their atheism which was the cause of their eminence. "The natural philosophies of Democritus and others," says Lord Bacon, "*who allow no God or mind* in the frame of things, but attribute the structure of the universe to infinite essays and trials of nature, or what they call fate or fortune, and assign the causes of particular things to the necessity of matter, *without any intermixture of final causes*, seem, as far as we can judge from the remains of their philosophy, *much more solid*, and to have *gone deeper into nature*, with regard to physical causes, than the philosophies of Aristotle or Plato: and this only because they *never meddled with final causes*, which the others were perpetually inculcating." [4]

Newman considers at some length "the questions men may try, the petty cobwebs we have spun,"—that is, the operations of inference and reason upon the data of observation. He believes that we are not so constituted as to arrive at religious truth through the unaided operation of the reason. "The heart is commonly reached, not through the reason, but through the imagination, by means of direct impressions, by the testimony of facts and events, by history, by description." Religion is, like life, an affair of action and not of thinking.

Life is not long enough for a religion of inferences; we shall never have done beginning, if we determine to begin with proof. . . . I would rather be bound to defend the reasonableness of assuming that Christianity is true, than to demonstrate a moral governance from the physical world. Life is for action. If we insist on proofs for everything, we shall never come to action; to act you must assume; and that assumption is faith. [5]

In Tennyson, too, we shall find this "assumption" which is "faith." In nature he cannot find that benevolence and perfection which was so largely assumed by the romantic nature-poets. In "The Two Voices" he says of man,

> That type of Perfect in his mind
> In Nature can he nowhere find.

In "In Memoriam" there are many references to the imperfections of nature, "pangs of nature," [6] "Nature, red in tooth and claw." [7] In "Maud" (1855), the doleful speaker of the monologue states distinctly:

> For nature is one with rapine, a harm no preacher can heal;
> The Mayfly is torn by the swallow, the sparrow is spear'd by the shrike,
> And the whole little world where I sit is a world of plunder and prey. [8]

Thus Tennyson clearly anticipates the many utterances of later poets—of Stevenson, of Hardy—on the cruel destructiveness of nature in the "struggle for existence." To this cruelty of nature Tennyson recurs in several later poems,—for example, in "Faith" (published in the posthumous volume of 1892), and in "The Promise of May" (1882). In this latter poem, the self-indulgent hedonist justifies his own irresponsible morality by reference to the cruelty of nature.

> "What are we?" says the blind old man in Lear,
> "As flies to the Gods; they kill us for their sport."
> The Gods! but they, the shadows of ourselves,
> Have past for ever. It is Nature kills,
> And not for *her* sport either. She knows nothing.
> Man only knows, the worse for him! for why
> Cannot he take his pastime like the flies?
> And if my pleasure breed another's pain,
> Well—is not that the course of Nature too,
> From the dim dawn of Being—her main law
> Whereby she grows in beauty—that her flies
> Must massacre each other? this poor Nature! [9]

Tennyson sounds here another characteristic note of the later poets. Nature "knows nothing." She kills but she has no consciousness of what she is doing. She is brutish but brainless. In "Despair" (1885) the speaker is another unbeliever, or man of doubtful faith, inclined to suicide.

O we poor orphans of nothing—alone on that lonely shore—
Born of the brainless Nature who knew not that which she bore!
Trusting no longer that earthly flower would be heavenly fruit—
Come from the brute, poor souls—no souls—and to die with the
     brute. . . .

Here again is Tennyson's third, or perhaps his first and last, count against nature, that she means death for man as for all the rest of her brute creation. Tennyson abhors the thought of regarding—

. . . human love and truth
As dying Nature's earth and lime.[10]

Tennyson's dualism is shown in the many passages in which nature and God are mentioned together as two diverse concepts which we must take into account in order not to miss an essential element of truth. In one of his panegyrics of Hallam, Tennyson mentions the expression of eye which sums up the qualities of the perfect gentleman.

Nor ever narrowness or spite,
   Or villain fancy fleeting by,
   Drew in the expression of the eye,
Where God and Nature met in light.[11]

For Tennyson it was not sufficient, as it might have been for Wordsworth, to describe the natural beauty of the man's expression as an index of his spiritual fineness. To the beauty of nature, expressed in the purely material features, it is necessary to add, in explicit statement, the divine beauty which cannot be referred to material causes. Later on in the same poem Tennyson is speculating on the present status of his dead friend.

What art thou then? I cannot guess;
   But tho' I seem in star and flower
   To feel thee some diffusive power,
I do not therefore love thee less:

My love involves the love before;
   My love is vaster passion now;
   Tho' mixed with God and Nature thou,
I seem to love thee more and more.[12]

Here the natural comparison of Tennyson's thought is with that of
Shelley on the dead Keats. Like Shelley's Keats,

He is made one with Nature; there is heard
His voice in all her music.

But instead of identifying nature with "that Power . . . which
has withdrawn his being to its own," Tennyson feels obliged to
distinguish clearly between those parts of the dead friend which
are mixed with nature (the material universe) and those which
are mixed with God (the spiritual being who guarantees personal
immortality).

Views of Science and Evolution

Since nature is conceived by Tennyson as the world of things
subject to the scrutiny of science, it is particularly interesting to
note the tone in which he refers to science and scientists. In
"Maud" there is a contrast between the scientist and the poet quite
in the spirit of Wordsworth's "A Poet's Epitaph." Wordsworth, it
will be remembered, contrasts the poet with the loveless political
"statist," with the rosy divine, the militant soldier, the moralist—

A reasoning, self-sufficing thing,
An intellectual all-in-all,—

the hard-faced lawyer, and the sensual "physician" (scientist). And
after all these comes the modest poet, "retired as noon-tide dew,"
wise with—

> The harvest of a quiet eye
> That broods and sleeps on his own heart.

> But he is weak; both man and boy,
> Hath been an idler in the land;
> Contented if he might enjoy
> The things which others understand.

Tennyson's contrast between poet and scientist reminds one of Wordsworth's, and his scientist borrows some of the traits of the lawyer and the moralist in Wordsworth.

> The man of science himself is fonder of glory, and vain,
> An eye well-practiced in nature, a spirit bounded and poor;
> The passionate heart of the poet is whirl'd into folly and vice . . .[13]

This man of science is, of course, like Wordsworth's "physician," a philosopher—that is, a *philosophe*, a thinker all absorbed in—

> . . . that false secondary power
> By which we multiply distinctions.

That is, he is one given to dissection and analysis of the living experience, and incapable of the synthesis that restores it to life. For Tennyson that is all that nature demands or offers. But for Wordsworth "the lore of Nature" is something sweeter than can be obtained by the analytic power of science.

> Sweet is the lore which Nature brings;
> Our meddling intellect
> Misshapes the beauteous forms of things:—
> We murder to dissect.

It is, of course, the fatalist creed of his own age that Tennyson is reacting against, as he describes it in "Despair" (1885)—"the new dark ages of the popular press," when "the Sun and the Moon of our science are both of them turn'd into blood . . . for their knowing and know-nothing books are scatter'd from hand to hand."

It is what materialistic science makes of man that arouses the hostility of Wordsworth and Tennyson. Thus Tennyson writes in "In Memoriam":

> I trust I have not wasted breath:
> I think we are not wholly brain,
> Magnetic mockeries; not in vain,
> Like Paul with beasts, I fought with Death;
>
> Not only cunning casts in clay:
> Let Science prove we are, and then
> What matters Science unto men,
> At least to me? I would not stay.
>
> Let him, the wiser man who springs
> Hereafter, up from childhood shape
> His action like the greater ape,
> But I was *born* to other things.[14]

We must not infer, from these references to the conclusions drawn by certain scientists, that Tennyson took no stock in science, or that he shrank from it in the manner of many "artistic" souls that take to poetry. His was a mind singularly open to whatever engaged the intellect of his time. Mr. Lionel Stevenson, in his *Darwin Among the Poets*, has shown that Tennyson was far more interested in science, and far better informed about it, than the average man of letters. When he went to Cambridge as an undergraduate he was already well acquainted with various works of natural history and enthusiastic about astronomy. His interest in science was maintained during his university days, and afterwards. During the period 1833–35, according to a schedule of his studies, he was devoting his afternoons to languages and his mornings to science; one morning each to chemistry, botany, electricity, animal physiology, mechanics. He read Lyell's *Geology* in 1837, and ordered *Vestiges of the Natural History of Creation* as soon as he saw it advertised in 1844.[15] His ordinary conversation with young ladies was likely to run on paleontology—gigantic ferns and ichthyosaurs—or on the nervous system of lower animals.

What is still more remarkable than his interest in science is his early absorption of certain of the general ideas involved in the concept of evolution. On going to Cambridge in 1828, he was already acquainted with two of the special concepts implying evolution,— that of Laplace in astronomy and that of Buffon in geology. He appears even to have gone so far, in some college discussion, as to propound the theory that "the development of the human body might possibly be traced from the radiated, vermicular, molluscous and vertebrate organisms." [16] It is thus clear that at a very early period Tennyson showed a most unusual interest in the concept of evolution. But we should not too hastily assume that he definitely adopted this scientific theory or actually assumed its truth in his poems.

Mr. Stevenson cites many passages from Tennyson's poems, early and late, in which he assumes the nebular hypothesis, refers to prehistoric animal forms, dwells upon Change as a fundamental factor in human life, or makes other more apparent approximations to the specific doctrines of organic evolution. Thus, as early as in "The Palace of Art" (1832), he refers to the prenatal development of man's brain, as an analogy for the development of the soul, and the progressive development in nature from lower to higher forms of being. The soul is speaking:

> "From change to change four times within the womb
>   The brain is moulded," she began,
> "So through all phases of all thought I come
>   Into the perfect man.
>
> "All nature widens upward: evermore
>   The simpler essence lower lies.
> More complex is more perfect, owning more
>   Discourse, more widely wise." [17]

It is worth dwelling a moment on these stanzas, omitted by Tennyson in later versions of the poem. There is here, I think, no evidence that Tennyson held the scientific doctrine of evolution as understood by biologists like Lamarck or Darwin. The fourfold development of the fœtus described in the first stanza was known in 1833 to Lyell, who expressly argued that it had no bearing on the evolutionary hypothesis.

The cerebral hemispheres, then, arrive at the state which we observe in the higher animals only by a series of successive metamorphoses. If we reduce the whole of these evolutions to four periods, we shall see that in the first are born the cerebral lobes of fishes . . . The second period will give us the organization of reptiles; the third, the brain of birds; and the fourth, the complex hemispheres of mammalia. . . . It will be observed, that these curious phenomena disclose, in a highly interesting manner, the unity of plan that runs through the organization of the whole series of vertebrated animals; but they lend no support whatever to the notion of a gradual transmutation of one species into another; least of all of the passage, in the course of many generations, from an animal of a more simple to one of a more complex structure.[18]

In "In Memoriam" there is another reference to the development of the fœtus during the antenatal period. It occurs in the Epilogue, written for a wedding in 1842, and refers to the child that shall be born of this wedding.

> A soul shall draw from out the vast
> And strike his being into bounds,
>
> And, moved thro' life of lower phase,
>   Result in man, be born and think,
>   And act and love, a closer link
> Betwixt us and the crowning race
>
> Of those that, eye to eye, shall look
>   On knowledge; under whose command
>   Is Earth and Earth's, and in their hand
> Is Nature like an open book;
>
> No longer half-akin to brute,
>   For all we thought and loved and did,
>   And hoped and suffer'd, is but seed
> Of what in them is flower and fruit. . . .

Here again the development of the fœtus is made to illustrate the development of the individual soul; and the rising of the human being in the womb through lower to higher phases is a symbol and promise of the spiritual improvement and perfection of the race.

So far as I know, there is no clear statement anywhere in Tennyson of the defining factor of biological evolution, the "gradual transmutation of one species into another,"—let alone the specific Darwinian theory of "natural selection." So far as the evidence of his poems goes, Tennyson may well have assumed, with Lyell, that each separate species in plant and animal life was the result of a special act of creation. I know that Hallam Tennyson explicitly declares: "My father brought 'Evolution' into Poetry. Ever since his Cambridge days he believed in it." [19] This declaration is made in a note to Tennyson's poem "By an Evolutionist," and is supported by a quotation from Andrew Lang to the effect that Tennyson "had brooded from boyhood on these early theories of evolution," and by reference to "a remarkable passage in 'Sea Dreams.'" But a careful reading of "Sea Dreams" brings to light no passage remarkable in relation to evolution except a vague reference to the gradual modification of the earth's surface by geological process—the view propounded by Lyell, who was firmly opposed to the theory of evolution in biology. In his Memoir of the poet his son expresses himself much more cautiously; Tennyson thought that *"evolution in a modified form was partially true."* [20] It is quite possible that the modified form of evolution accepted by Tennyson amounted to little more than the "graduated scale of being" discussed in Chapter XI.

It is true that Tennyson was more imbued than Lyell with the notion of "progressive development," as is shown in the second of the canceled stanzas from "The Palace of Art." This notion turns up frequently in his poems, and is generally the essence of what Mr. Stevenson regards as his evolutionism. In poems like "In Memoriam" and "The Princess" (1847), according to Mr. Stevenson, the evolutionary concept is "clear enough for the initiated, but not so explicit as to force itself on the attention of the orthodox reader as a startling heresy." [21] It is equally probable that the modern student reads into these poems definite evolutionary implications which were not there for the poet.

When *The Origin of Species* was advertised, Tennyson was interested enough to order a copy in advance. But he was disappointed with Darwin's work and spoke slightingly of it. He even tended to fall into the popular notion of Darwinism as deriving man's descent from the ape. If one is at first surprised that Tenny-

son should not have been gratified by the confirmation brought to
his own "evolutionary" views, one finally comes to distinguish
between what may be called sentimental evolutionism and the simple theory of biological descent. What Tennyson held was evidently what Professor Morris Cohen calls the "myth" of evolution.
This is the rather vague and uncritical notion of a steady upward
progress of organized life. It was this notion of upward progress,
falling in with the dominant note of nineteenth-century sentiment,
that attracted Tennyson in the concept of evolution. He regarded
the "life of Nature as a lower stage in the manifestation of a principle which is more fully manifested in the spiritual life of man." [22]
It is this notion that underlies most of Tennyson's references to
change in human society and institutions, such as the famous one
in "Morte d'Arthur,"—"The old order changeth, yielding place to
new." This is no more essentially related to the evolution theory
than Carlyle's clothes-philosophy, or that other famous declaration in "Locksley Hall":

Yet I doubt not through the ages one increasing purpose runs,
And the thoughts of men are widened with the process of the suns.

Mr. Stevenson cites other significant passages from many poems
early and late. The most interesting and significant of all are the
following famous stanzas from "In Memoriam":

> Contemplate all this work of Time,
>   The giant labouring in his youth;
>   Nor dream of human love and truth,
> As dying Nature's earth and lime;
>
> But trust that those we call the dead
>   Are breathers of an ampler day
>   For ever nobler ends. They say,
> The solid earth whereon we tread
>
> In tracts of fluent heat began,
>   And grew to seeming-random forms,
>   The seeming prey of cyclic storms,
> Till at the last arose the man;

Who throve and branch'd from clime to clime,
The herald of a higher race,
And of himself in higher place,
If so he type this work of time

Within himself, from more to more;
Or, crown'd with attributes of woe
Like glories, move his course and show
That life is not as idle ore,

But iron dug from central gloom,
And heated hot with burning fears,
And dipt in baths of hissing tears,
And batter'd with the shocks of doom

To shape and use. Arise and fly
The reeling Faun, the sensual feast;
Move upward, working out the beast,
And let the ape and tiger die.[23]

A careful examination of this passage, in connection with other vaguer statements in "In Memoriam," brings out the following points associated with the scientific theory of evolution. The conception of the earth as beginning "in tracts of fluent heat" suggests the nebular hypothesis, for long the dominant evolutionary way of conceiving cosmic origins, and that and the following lines suggest, more vaguely, the geological concept of the natural evolution of the earth's substance. The late arrival of man on the earth after due geologic preparation, and the implication that man has risen from the "lower" brutish to higher distinctly human or spiritual phases, lend themselves to the evolutionary concept of man as the product of organic evolution. But it is not clear whether any reference is intended to the "origin of species." And we know that Tennyson was definitely opposed to the notion that the mind of man might be regarded as a product of natural evolution.

On the whole, "In Memoriam" gives but doubtful evidence that Tennyson, at the time of its composition, had accepted the scientific theory of organic evolution. All that is clear is that man is a late arrival on the earth—a point acknowledged by Lyell—that he has developed considerably from the original half-brutish state, and is capable, if rightly inspired, of much greater development. What Mr. Cohen calls the "mythical" elements of popular evolutionism come in with the idea of human life as a disciplinary process by which the spirit is refined into an essence freed from brutish elements; the idea of this process as involving the progressive perfecting of the human race; and that of its inevitable tendency towards "one far-off divine event," which is, under God's purposeful direction, the goal of "the whole creation." It was, among other things, the complete absence of these "mythical" elements that repelled Tennyson in Darwin's scientific treatise.

There is one trait in Tennyson's picture which is particularly interesting in connection with Meredith's conception of evolution. The perfecting of man is to be accomplished by his "working out" the brutish elements of his primitive nature.

> Arise and fly
> The reeling Faun, the sensual feast;
> Move upward, working out the beast,
> And let the ape and tiger die.

This image is repeated by Tennyson, in one form or another, in several of his later poems. Thus in "The Ancient Sage":

> An evil thought may soil thy children's blood;
> But curb the beast would cast thee in the mire,
> And leave the hot swamp of voluptuousness . . .

In "Locksley Hall Sixty Years After":

> Earth at last a warless world, a single race, a single tongue.
> I have seen her far away—for is not Earth as yet so young?—
> Every tiger madness muzzled, every serpent passion killed . . .

In "The Dawn" and "The Making of Man":

> . . . . but when shall we lay
> The Ghost of the Brute that is walking and haunting us yet, and be
> free?

. . . .

Where is one that, born of woman, altogether can escape
From the lower world within him, moods of tiger, or of ape?
Man as yet is being made, and ere the crowning Age of ages,
Shall not æon after æon pass and touch him into shape?

This image of the beast to be "worked out" of human nature
appears not infrequently in the poems of Meredith contained in
the volumes, *Poems and Lyrics of the Joy of Earth* (1883), *A
Reading of Earth* (1888), and *A Reading of Life* (1901). Meredith, however, as we shall see, gives a rather different turn to his
moral, and in especial, his conception of man's advance in spirituality is not complicated, like Tennyson's, with the idea of personal
immortality.

Immortality and Faith

It is often difficult to know whether Tennyson is speaking of
the spiritual improvement of the race or of the perfecting of the
individual spirit destined to immortal continuance. The very passage in which Tennyson adjures us to "let the ape and tiger die"
begins with his declaration of belief—

> . . . that those we call the dead
> Are breathers of an ampler day
> For ever nobler ends.

And elsewhere he associates the "eternal process" with a distinct
declaration of the continuance of the spiritual life of the individual
after death.

> I wage not any feud with Death
> For changes wrought on form and face;
> No lower life that earth's embrace
> May breed with him, can fright my faith.

> Eternal process moving on,
> From state to state the spirit walks;
> And these are but the shatter'd stalks,
> Or ruin'd chrysalis of one.

Nor blame I Death, because he bare
The use of virtue out of earth:
I know transplanted human worth
Will bloom to profit, otherwhere.[24]

Tennyson seems here to resort to the notion of reincarnation, which is stated still more distinctly in "De Profundis" (1880), where he thus addresses the spirit of the newborn child:

Live thou! and of the grain and husk, the grape
And ivy-berry, choose; and still depart
From death to death thro' life and life, and find
Nearer and ever nearer Him, who wrought
Not Matter, nor the finite-infinite,
But this main-miracle, that thou art thou,
With power on thine own act and on the world.

Tennyson at no period of his life was content with the positivist notion of the progressive improvement of the race. Over and over again he declares that, unless man survive death, he is—

A monster then, a dream,
A discord. Dragons of the prime,
That tare each other in their slime,
Were mellow music match'd with him.

O life as futile, then, as frail! [25]

And it is precisely because nature gives no assurance of such survival that Tennyson is dissatisfied with it, has for it none of the enthusiasm and trust of a Wordsworth or a Goethe. Nature and evolution do not satisfy him except as they are conducted by a purposeful God, who means well for us in the long run, and guarantees our individual survival. Of earth's hopes he says in "Locksley Hall Sixty Years After,"

Ere she gain her Heavenly-best, a God must mingle with the game:
Nay, there may be those about us whom we neither see nor name,

Felt within us as ourselves, the Powers of Good, the Powers of Ill,
Strowing balm, or shedding poison in the fountains of the Will.

Follow you the Star that lights a desert pathway, yours or mine.
Forward, till you see the highest Human Nature is divine.

Follow Light, and do the Right—for man can half-control his doom—
Till you find the deathless Angel seated in the vacant tomb.

Here is the idea of human progress fused with that of individual immortality, with God, and even with good and evil spirits inspiring our will,—the full panoply of religion.

The faith in immortality, and so in the purposiveness of the eternal process, cannot be had from science, Tennyson frequently lets us know, but is the gift of some mysterious faculty of inner vision. It is what he calls in "The Two Voices," "that heat of inward evidence, by which [Man] doubts against the sense."

> Here sits he shaping wings to fly:
> His heart forebodes a mystery:
> He names the name Eternity.
>
> That type of Perfect in his mind
> In Nature can he nowhere find.
> He sows himself on every wind.
>
> He seems to hear a Heavenly Friend,
> And thro' thick veils to apprehend
> A labour working to an end.

In "In Memoriam" he found not God "in world or sun," etc.; but then, in the chill of doubt—

> A warmth within the breast would melt
>   The freezing reason's colder part,
>   And like a man in wrath the heart
> Stood up and answer'd, 'I have felt.'
>
> No, like a child in doubt and fear:
>   But that blind clamour made me wise;
>   Then was I as a child that cries,
> But, crying, knows his father near;

And what I am beheld again
 What is, and no man understands;
 And out of darkness came the hands
That reach thro' nature, moulding men.[26]

Observation, knowledge, reasoning ("the questions men may try, the petty cobwebs we have spun"), these are inadequate to give us information of God, immortality, freedom of the will, moral obligation. For our information about these we are indebted to a "deeper voice" than nature's, as Tennyson expresses it in his early poem, "On a Mourner." First to the mourner come the cheerful admonitions of nature, bidding the heart beat quicker. And then—

And murmurs of a deeper voice,
 Going before to some far shrine,
Teach that sick heart the stronger choice,
 Till all thy life one way incline
 With one wide Will that closes thine.

Finally to the summons of this deeper voice come Hope and Memory, Faith and Virtue, to complete the spiritual equipment of the man. The opposition of reason and faith as guides to truth was thus expressed by Tennyson in 1869: "Whatever is the object of Faith cannot be the object of Reason. In fine, Faith must be our guide,—*that* Faith which we believe comes to us from a Divine Source." [27]

Tennyson's Metaphysics

Tennyson was from the beginning of a rather mystical bent of mind, pleased with the thought that our personal experience of life may be no more than "the shadow of a dream"; [28] and as he grew older, the difficulty of reconciling nature and God led him to dwell more and more on the superficiality and deceptiveness of the knowledge brought us through our senses. To get at the reality we must dive below the surface of sense-experience and rational knowledge. Thus in "The Ancient Sage,"

If thou would'st hear the Nameless, and wilt dive
Into the Temple-cave of thine own self,
There, brooding by the central altar, thou
May'st haply learn the Nameless hath a voice,
By which thou wilt abide, if thou be wise,
As if thou knewest, tho' thou canst not know;
For knowledge is the swallow on the lake
That sees and stirs the surface-shadow there
But never yet hath dipt into the abysm. . . .

This Nameless, which cannot be known, but which one must assume as if one knew it, reminds one of Herbert Spencer's Unknowable, though Tennyson wishes to base upon it conclusions which Spencer is particularly anxious to avoid. It is the absolute being of idealist metaphysics, not subject to the frailty and delusiveness of phenomenal existence, not conditioned by time, space, and the limitations of human perception. It is the uncaused last term in the chain of causes, to which a certain type of mind is forced by what seems an inevitable logic. It is the God required by Berkeley's system in order to give reality to a universe which is known solely in terms of sense-impressions. Reality, being known only in these terms, would cease to exist apart from the thought which mirrors it. But if we postulate an absolute mind, then we do not have to worry over what becomes of the world in the absence of our individual thought. The same absolute mind which guarantees the reality of our individual thought confirms our knowledge of the external universe.

This Berkeleian conception of the subjective nature of reality is perhaps what lies behind Tennyson's image of "the Temple-cave of thine own self," where, "brooding by the central altar," one may "haply learn the Nameless hath a voice." And it may well be the Berkeleian conception of the necessity of the absolute mind of God to any assurance of external reality, and of the reality of the ego, that leads Tennyson to his statement just below in "The Ancient Sage":

And if the Nameless should withdraw from all
Thy frailty counts most real, all thy world
Might vanish like thy shadow in the dark.

Tennyson's son informs us that soon after his marriage in 1850 the poet took to reading different systems of philosophy (Spinoza, Berkeley, Kant, Schlegel, Fichte, Hegel, Ferrier), but that "none particularly influenced him." [29] Tennyson was, presumably, like all poets, an eclectic in philosophy, taking up here and there phrases and formulations that suited his own need and bent. It is fairly obvious that, with a minimum of the transcendentalism of Emerson and Whitman so far as nature is concerned, he owed more to the German idealists than to the traditional English school of metaphysics.

It is certain that, in his later poems, he labored to patch up a kind of metaphysical system for making intelligible the relation of the individual human spirit with the absolute or eternal world. As a human being man is finite, fleshly, subject to time, change and mortal necessity; as an immortal spirit he is infinite, akin to God, triumphant over death, and a free being, "with power on [his] own act and on the world." His "De Profundis" (begun at the birth of his eldest son in 1852, and published in 1880) represents the human child as developing in two parallel lines, the one mortal and finite, the other infinite and immortal. Like Wordsworth's child in the "Intimations" ode, he comes from God—

> Out of the deep, my child, out of the deep,
> From that great deep, before our world begins,
> Whereon the Spirit of God moves as he will—
> Out of the deep, my child, out of the deep,
> From that true world within the world we see,
> Whereof our world is but the bounding shore.

In his characterization of "this divisible-indivisible world," of "finite-infinite space in finite-infinite time," he reminds one of Schelling in some of his treatises on nature. But there is an even more striking suggestion of the neoplatonic doctrine of the "descent of the soul," found earlier in Shelley.

> O dear Spirit half-lost
> In thine own shadow and this fleshly sign
> That thou art thou—who wailest being born
> And banish'd into mystery, and the pain

Of this divisible-indivisible world
Among the numerable-innumerable
Sun, sun, and sun, thro' finite-infinite space
In finite-infinite Time—our mortal veil
And shatter'd phantom of that infinite One,
Who made thee unconceivably Thyself
Out of His whole World-self and all in all. . . .

Tennyson takes none of Shelley's satisfaction in the thought of
a soul's being made one with nature. He insists more than Shelley
on the pain of banishment into mystery, involved in the fleshly incarnation of the immortal soul. It is true that Shelley refers to
"the eclipsing curse of birth." But the relation of the individual to
the World-self of God, and the metaphysical jargon of divisible-
indivisible, numerable-innumerable, finite-infinite, remind one not
so much of Shelley as of Coleridge, Schelling, Leibniz, or Thomas
Taylor. Certain images, however, are apparently close echoes of
Shelley.

Our mortal veil
And shatter'd phantom of that infinite One

and—

O dear Spirit half-lost
In thine own shadow . . .

remind one inevitably of Shelley's "inmost veil of Heaven," and
the famous figure:

Life, like a dome of many-colored glass,
Stains the white radiance of Eternity,

This figure appears again in "The Higher Pantheism" in slightly
varied form, along with Tennyson's most elaborate effort to explain
the double relation between God and the universe and between
God and man. This poem, written for the first meeting of the
Metaphysical Society, is so clearly definitive of Tennyson's special
non-naturalistic type of pantheism that it is worth quoting entire.

The sun, the moon, the stars, the seas, the hills and the plains—
Are not these, O Soul, the Vision of Him who reigns?

Is not the Vision He? tho' He be not that which He seems?
Dreams are true while they last, and do we not live in dreams?

Earth, these solid stars, this weight of body and limb,
Are they not sign and symbol of thy division from Him?

Dark is the world to thee: thyself art the reason why;
For is He not all but that which has power to feel 'I am I'?

Glory about thee, without thee; and thou fulfillest thy doom
Making Him broken gleams, and a stifled splendour and gloom.

Speak to Him thou for He hears, and Spirit with Spirit can meet—
Closer is He than breathing, and nearer than hands and feet.

God is law, say the wise; O Soul, and let us rejoice,
For if He thunder by law the thunder is yet His voice.

Law is God, say some: no God at all, says the Fool;
For all we have power to see is a straight staff bent in a pool;

And the ear of man cannot hear, and the eye of man cannot see;
And if we could see and hear, this Vision—were it not He?

There is here, beyond a doubt, a certain tincture of pantheism, but anxious and half-hearted. Pantheism, as an interpreter of nature, is the meeting-ground of the older theological and the newer naturalistic philosophy. It is largely a question of main preoccupation and emphasis. Tennyson's main preoccupation is theological and his emphasis, as between nature and God, is upon God. He is a pantheist anxious to guard against a materialistic interpretation of the doctrine.[30] The nature-poet is enthusiastic over nature and her laws. The voice of God he hears in the laws of nature, and his tendency is to reduce God to these laws in which his voice is heard. A more theological pantheist, on the other hand, finds the dignity of natural laws in the fact that one hears in them the voice of God.

So far as man is concerned, the naturalist rejoices in the nature through which man is enabled to find himself and to relate himself to the inner truth of the universe. But the theological-minded

Tennyson is more impressed with the fact that man's spirit is eclipsed and divided from God by the nature in which it finds itself—

> Earth, these solid stars, this weight of body and limb,
> Are they not sign and symbol of thy division from Him?

Nature is indeed a necessary condition of man's mortal existence; but it is a distressful necessity; and Tennyson has anything but a cordial feeling towards an order of things which even temporarily banishes man from the eternal and divine. Accordingly, he could not at any period of his writing have declared himself, like Wordsworth,

> . . . well pleased to recognize
> In nature and the language of the sense
> The anchor of my purest thoughts, the nurse,
> The guide, the guardian of my heart, and soul
> Of all my moral being.

The naturalist is by temperamental bias a monist. He has a craving to reduce all the phenomena of the universe to a single term and therefore to obliterate practically the distinction between objective and subjective. Tennyson was temperamentally a dualist. He wished to maintain the distinction between objective and subjective. Nature was associated in his mind with the objective world; and it gave no sure intimation of God, freedom, immortality. These were to be found only in the realm of the subjective. Hence for him the radical menace of naturalism, of evolutionism, was its growing assumption that man's conscious life was continuous with the natural process and explainable in the same terms. The evolutionary conception, and the nineteenth-century study of physiology and cerebral physiology in particular, tended to favor the materialistic views of the eighteenth-century philosophers such as d'Holbach, quoted in Chapter IV. In my chapter on Goethe I have quoted the statement of Huxley made in 1868 as to the part played by protoplasm in all vital action, concluding with his suggestion that "the thoughts to which I am now giving utterance, and your thoughts regarding them, are the expression of molecular changes in that matter of life which is the source of our other vital phenomena." Many similar statements might be found in various writers during the period of Tennyson's poetic activity, including Herbert Spencer, who sent Tennyson his *Psychology* in 1855 because of its bearing on the problems raised in "The Two Voices."

Evolution and the Spirit

To the subtler type of religious thinker, the offense of evolution did not lie in its views upon the original creation of the universe but in inferences drawn concerning the origin and nature of mind. It was a comparatively easy matter for Tennyson, as it was for orthodox theology, to reinterpret the story of creation in evolutionary terms. Evolution was simply God's method of creation. But the scandal of evolution lay in its pretension to trace intellect itself to the same natural process which directed the evolution of worlds and of animal life, and so to obliterate the distinction between brute and man.

Among the most distinguished of those who sought to combat this tendency was St. George Mivart, a Roman Catholic biologist and professor in the short-lived Catholic University College, London. Mivart's *Genesis of Species* (1871) brought him into the evolutionary controversy, and he continued the argument in *Nature and Thought* (1882) and *The Origin of Human Reason* (1889). Mivart admitted the theory of evolution generally, but denied that it could apply to the human intellect. He believed abstract thought to be absolutely distinct in kind from the sensory life which we have in common with the lower animals and in no sense capable of being derived from it, and that consequently it is impossible to apply the notion of evolutionary origin to man.

My reason shows me that there is this profound difference in nature between man and the lower animals (a difference far greater than that which exists between the gorilla and the tree on which he climbs, or between the gorilla and the soil in which the roots of that tree are embedded), and I infer, therefore, that there was a difference as to the mode and agency of man's origin . . . The Darwinian doctrine not only does not repose upon reason, but it is the absolute negation of reason.

It reposes not on evidence but on ignorance—ignorance of what reason is, and, above all, ignorance of the meaning of the word 'goodness'.[31]

Mivart objects to the Darwinian system, for one thing, because it is connected with the agnostic or "know-nothing" philosophy,—a system of thought "insidiously undermining our rational confidence in human reason, and so weakening the springs of vigorous and healthy action." From the Darwinian belief he anticipates disastrous effects in future thought and action.

Its effects may not show themselves unequivocally in this generation, because its feelings and habits of thought are fully under the influence of anterior beliefs; but nothing can more certainly tend to impoverish all that is most beautiful in human thought and life than a generally accepted belief that man is essentially a beast in origin and nature, his highest feelings of reverence and his deepest tenderness being nothing but a disguised dread of being eaten or a mere animal appetite.[32]

Paul Bourget's novel, Le Disciple (1889), is a striking illustration in story form of how the current doctrine of determinism applied to man's behavior may result in crime and tragedy. And similar illustrations of the evil effects of materialism were given by Tennyson in a number of poems, in "Maud" (1855), "Lucretius" (1868), "The Promise of May" (1882), "Despair" (1885).

Tennyson's dislike for Darwinism has its basis in the same reaction as Mivart's. He did not wish to see this materialistic theory applied to the genesis of man's mind and spirit. As he remarked to Tyndall, "No evolutionist is able to explain the mind of Man or how any possible physiological change of tissue can produce conscious thought."[33] In his early poem, "Love Thou Thy Land," Tennyson compares the action of "change" in the evolution of social forms to its action in the human body. He is impressed with the Carlylean doctrine of perpetual change in society; but he does not wish to see this applied to the essence of the soul itself.

> For Nature also, cold and warm,
>   And moist and dry, devising long,
>   Thro' many agents making strong,
> Matures the individual form.

> Meet is it changes should control
> Our being, lest we rust in ease.
> We all are changed by still degrees,
> All but the basis of the soul.

In this attitude Tennyson was probably more conservative than either the early Wordsworth or the early Shelley, and more so than Goethe at any period of his writing. While neither Wordsworth nor Shelley was considering the matter from the point of view of physiology, and while neither of them had the advantage of the evolutionary concept, Wordsworth did try in his earlier period to view the development of the mind in terms of the associationist psychology, and Shelley took his start from the materialist assumptions of the French philosophers. As for Goethe, there are strong intimations in him of a tendency to explain the higher mental faculties of man as of natural origin, and it is to be presumed that he would have welcomed the speculations based on later studies in cerebral physiology.

But, as we have seen, Tennyson was jealous of the encroachments of nature upon the realm of theology, extremely anxious to define the limits of natural action and subject the findings of science to a theological interpretation. Of the Darwinian hypothesis he hastened to say: "That makes no difference to me, even if the Darwinians did not, as they do, exaggerate Darwinism. To God all is present. He sees present, past, and future as one." [34] And again, in 1863: "Darwinism, Man from Ape, would that really make any difference? . . . Time is nothing, are we not all part of Deity?" [35] When Darwin visited Tennyson, the poet remarked anxiously, "Your theory of evolution does not make against Christianity," and received the comforting assurance, "No, certainly not." [36] This being so on the word of the great scientist himself, Tennyson could afford to take a certain mild satisfaction in Darwinism, providing always that it was interpreted so as to fall in with the assumptions of religion.

Thus we see that Tennyson, while deeply interested in the findings of science, was distinctly an outsider in the naturalistic movement, inclined to regard the concept of nature with a sharply critical eye. The emotional force of naturalism lies in the poet's ability to identify himself as man with nature, to feel behind him and the race the mighty power of universal law. Man is not alone in the universe but partakes in its movement and splendor, as, in religion, man partakes in the glory and power of God. Moreover, in naturalism, man looks to nature for an interpretation of his own faculties and behavior, and for guidance and discipline, taking comfort in the thought that practical wisdom may be learned by a study of her ways. So far as nature was concerned, Tennyson derived emotional impetus mainly from setting himself against her, and combating her claims in the interest of religion. She might be made instrumental towards the ends of religion, but only, as it were, in the initial stages of his progress. And from the very beginning he was before all the child of God, to whom he must look for guidance and discipline and for that divine wisdom by which alone he might attain to his spiritual fulfilment.

Chapter XVI

BROWNING

BROWNING was, if possible, even less of a "naturalist" than Tennyson. By nature he means for the most part, like Tennyson, the world of science. But Mr. Stevenson has shown that he was less well acquainted with science than Tennyson, much less effectually aware of the contemporary implications of science.[1] And he was at least as insistent as Tennyson on the necessity of finding man's destiny and the meaning of the world outside the frame of nature.

It is true that Browning often shows his theoretical interest in scientific studies. Tribute to the joys of scientific research is offered in "Paracelsus"—

> Still seizing fresh pretence
> To turn the knowledge and the rapture wrung
> As an extreme, last boon from destiny,
> Into occasion for new covetings,
> New strifes, new triumphs . . .[2]

This pleasure taken in scientific research is apparent again in certain poems in which Browning refers to the marvelous "mechanics" of natural life. In "Cleon":

> . . . the shell sucks fast the rock,
> The fish strikes through the sea, the snake both swims
> And slides, forth range the beasts, the birds take flight,
> Till life's mechanics can no further go . . .

In "La Saisiaz," he acknowledges—

> . . . that power that went
> To the making of the worm there in yon clod its tenement,

435

and also—

> . . . that which, wise and good,
> Framed the leaf, its plain of pasture, dropped the dew, its fineless food.

In "With Francis Furini," he dwells on the unveiling of nature's marvels:

> Depths on depths to probe
> Of all-inventive artifice, disrobe
> Marvel at hiding under marvel, pluck
> Veil after veil from Nature . . .[3]

These various passages are distinctly reminiscent of the natural theology of the eighteenth century. Each type of animal is perfectly adapted to the element in which it lives. The clod is the ideal tenement of the worm, the leaf its natural plain of pasture, and the dew its "fineless food"! The amphibious snake is adapted both to earth and water, the bird to flight in air, the fish to floating in water. One is reminded of Paley's observations on the purposeful design of wing and fin. And one is prepared for Rupert Brooke's burlesque account of fish theology, and the fish's dream of heaven.

> One may not doubt that, somehow, good
> Shall come of Water and of Mud;
> And, sure, the reverent eye must see
> A Purpose in Liquidity . . .[4]

In "Paracelsus," again, Browning appropriately puts into the mouth of the mystical sixteenth-century philosopher and pioneer of modern scientific methods an enthusiastic account of the pleasure taken by the creator in the varied and progressive manifestations of his power. "Thus climbs pleasure its heights forever and forever." God takes joy in the heaving of the central fire underneath the earth, in the spouting of young volcanoes, and in the foisoning of life under the breath of the spring-wind.

> The grass grows bright, the boughs are swoln with blooms
> Like chrysalids impatient for the air,

The shining dorrs are busy, beetles run
Along the furrows, ants make their ado;
Above, birds fly in merry flocks, the lark
Soars up and up, shivering for very joy;
Afar the ocean sleeps; white fishing-gulls
Flit where the strand is purple with its tribe
Of nested limpets; savage creatures seek
Their loves in wood and plain—and God renews
His ancient rapture. Thus he dwells in all,
From life's minute beginnings, up at last
To man, the consummation of this scheme
Of being, the completion of this sphere
Of life . . .[5]

Here is nature-poetry for the nonce, and poetry more than
usually well supplied with the details of natural history. But considering the date of this poem (1835), the theological emphasis is
far too heavy for it to mark any advance in naturalism. On the
contrary, it seems to mark a recession. The general cast of Browning's nature-poetry is closer to the anxiously theological Coleridge
than to the author of "Tintern Abbey" or the author of the "Hymn
to Intellectual Beauty." He has set out to show—

> . . . how God tastes an infinite joy
> In infinite ways—one everlasting bliss,
> From whom all being emanates, all power
> Proceeds; in whom is life forevermore,
> Yet whom existence in its lowest form
> Includes; where dwells enjoyment there is he . . .[6]

Browning and Evolution

But, it may be asked, does not Browning, in this poem published
long before *The Origin of Species*, set forth the doctrine of evolution? That depends on what is meant by evolution. Evolution, in
its modern scientific form, comprehends the following points:
(1) a steady and continuous process of the physical world by due
degrees from its earlier to its later phases—generally understood to
mean a progress from simpler to more complex, or from more
rudimentary to more highly developed forms; (2) the continuous

evolution of the world of inorganic matter, manifest in the data of astronomy and geology; (3) the derivation of living species from one another; (4) natural selection operating to bring about the derivation and establishment of certain species. In its final logic, evolution seems also to imply: (5) the derivation of organic life from inorganic matter. It is further to be observed that, so far as science is concerned, the evolutionary process is assumed to be natural, brought about by tendencies inherent in the phenomenal world and without the intervention of special creative acts.

Having reference to this definition, I think we may state at once that Browning nowhere rules out the possibility of intervention by supernatural power in the evolutionary process. In a somewhat ambiguous statement of his attitude towards Darwinism, he writes:

When one is taunted . . . with thinking successive acts of creation credible, metaphysics have been stopped short at, however physics may fare: time and space being purely conceptions of our own, wholly inapplicable to intelligence of another kind—with whom, as I made Luria say, there is an everlasting moment of creation, if one at all—past, present, and future, one and the same state. This conception does not affect Darwinism proper to any degree.[7]

For metaphysics it may be true that this conception (an everlasting moment of creation) "does not affect Darwinism proper to any degree." But "physics" cannot conceive Darwinian evolution save in terms of chronological sequence, and with the emergence of each new phase of the universe, the question puts itself: Does this phase mean a new start—a new act of creation—or is it involved in the preceding phase as, in the ordinary sequence of events, consequent is involved in antecedent? This question becomes acute at the point where evolution posits the derivation of one living species from another. Was there a new creation there, or was the later phase involved in the preceding "configuration" according to the natural law of things? To this question, it seems to me, Browning gives no clear answer. He certainly does not take the extreme naturalistic position that the universe is "self-existing and not created." [8] There are many passages in Browning which indicate clearly enough that such a position is nonsense in his eyes, since it leaves out of account the First Cause, which must be regarded as in some sense outside the frame of nature. Thus in "With Francis Furini" he speaks of the secret of nature which continually eludes the scientist, but which—

> Repays his search with still fresh proof—"Externe,
> Not inmost, is the Cause, fool! Look and learn!" [9]

But leaving aside questions of metaphysics, we find that Browning does state rather clearly the first of our listed points of evolutionary doctrine, providing we leave out the words "steady and continuous," which may be thought to beg the question of divine intervention. He represents the world as proceeding by due degrees from its earlier to its later phases, from more rudimentary to more highly developed forms of life, culminating in man. As for the second item, the continuous evolution of the world of inorganic matter, I do not think the case is so clear. Paracelsus gives a vivid picture of the bursting up of molten ore among the rocks and of how "the earth changes like a human face." But there is no reference, I believe, to the distinct geological strata, with their embedded fossils, which to the religious-minded geologist suggested catastrophic destruction, and which by the evolutionist were interpreted in terms of natural and continuous change.

Something more like the idea of evolution comes in with Paracelsus' account of the relation of man to the lower animal forms.

> Thus [God] dwells in all,
> From life's minute beginnings, up at last
> To man—the consummation of this scheme
> Of being, the completion of this sphere
> Of life: whose attributes had here and there
> Been scattered o'er the visible world before,
> Asking to be combined, dim fragments meant
> To be united in some wondrous whole,
> Imperfect qualities without creation,
> Suggesting some one creature yet to make,
> Some point where all those scattered rays should meet
> Convergent in the faculties of man . . .[10]

The human faculties in question are power and love.

> Hints and previsions of which faculties,
> Are strewn confusedly everywhere about
> The inferior natures, and all lead up higher,
> All shape out dimly the superior race,
> The heir of hopes too fair to turn out false,
> And man appears at last. So far the seal
> Is put on life; one stage being complete,
> One scheme wound up: and from the grand result
> A supplementary reflux of light
> Illustrates all the inferior grades, explains
> Each back step in the circle.[11]

In these passages Browning sets forth, through the mouth of Paracelsus, the following ideas: The world has proceeded by due degrees from its earlier to its later phases and from lower to higher forms (point 1). Organized life comes later than inorganic matter; this has bearing on point 5, but there is no suggestion that life was derived from inorganic matter. The culmination of organic evolution is man (point 1 again).

As for the defining features of the Darwinian theory, the derivation of higher forms from lower by natural selection (points 3 and 4), there is no suggestion whatever of the fourth point (natural selection), nor even, I think, any clear suggestion of the third (derivation of one species from another). All that Browning says is that various attributes of the lower creatures are combined in the higher—

> . . . all lead up higher,
> All shape out dimly the superior race . . .

In order to judge what Browning meant here we have to remember how completely his thinking was dominated by teleology—how little he thought in terms of causes and means, how much in terms of ends or "final causes." Even if we do not take him at his word and insist that with God there is but one everlasting moment of creation, we are still dealing here not with the actual chronological process of evolution, in which one phase follows upon another as effect upon cause in the natural world; we are dealing with an ideal scheme or hierarchy of creatures, ranged in ascending order of spiritual dignity, according to a sort of divine logic. We have come back again to Coleridge's "scale of creation." In effect, what Browning says is that, in God's thought, the inorganic comes first, then the lower orders of organized life, and that finally, in God's thought, these lower orders lead up higher and shape out dimly the superior race.

No, not finally; for man is simply starting out on his upward progress to God. "Man is not man as yet." Even when the whole race is perfected on the human plane, man has not yet reached his goal.

> Then shall his long triumphant march begin,
> Thence shall his being date,—thus wholly roused,
> What he achieves shall be set down to him.
> When all the race is perfected alike
> As man, that is; all tended to mankind,
> And, man produced, all has its end thus far:
> But incompleted man begins anew
> A tendency to God.[12]

This is clearly not a scientist's view of evolution, but the ideology of a religious poet, who wishes us to know that, in God's mind, there is a logical sequence from inorganic to organic, from lower life to man, and from man on the human to man on the divine plane. The speculations of science have doubtless had a great deal to do with the general direction taken by this religious speculation. And the scientific speculations that lie back of Browning's thought were such as to lead to the bolder hypotheses of the evolutionists proper. But we have here no definite anticipation of the theories of Darwin.

There is one passage which has been given a mistaken interpretation linking it with evolutionary science. When the life-process has found its culmination in man—

> So far the seal
> Is put on life; one stage being complete,
> One scheme wound up: and from the grand result

A supplementary reflux of light
Illustrates all the inferior grades, explains
Each back step in the circle.[13]

Mr. Stevenson comments:

These last lines apparently mean that the anatomy of man reveals his
relationship to the lower orders through which he has evolved—which
is, of course, one of the scientific demonstrations of evolution.[14]

Here I believe Mr. Stevenson has been betrayed by our natural
tendency to read a pre-evolutionary document in the light of our
post-Darwinian ideas. There is no suggestion of anatomy in the
whole context of this passage. And, moreover, the meaning of this
"reflux of light" is developed at length in the lines which follow,
not at all in the terms of evolutionary science but in terms of old-
fashioned nature-poetry. What Browning goes on to say is that all
nature—winds, landscapes, flowers and birds, sunrise and sunset—is
glorified by the light thrown back by man's imagination on the
world in which he lives. As soon as man is born, he begins to interpret nature in terms of his own moods and fancies. There may be a
touch of anthropology here, but nothing of the anatomical evidences of man's kinship with the lower animal orders.

Of other pre-Darwinian poems of Browning, the one which most
nearly suggests evolutionary views is "Cleon" (1855). The subject
of this poem is the earthly creations of Zeus. First is presented the
perfection of life's mechanics in shell, fish, snake, beast and bird.
These are all very fine, but still mere passive matter, creatures of
the god's shaping fire.

It has them, not they it: and so I choose
For man, thy last premeditated work
(If I might add a glory to the scheme),
That a third thing should stand apart from both,
A quality arise within his soul,
Which, intro-active, made to supervise
And feel the force it has, may view itself,
And so be happy. Man might live at first
The animal life: but is there nothing more?

In due time, let him critically learn
How he lives . . .

Here again, as in "Paracelsus," we have the notion that man's creation follows that of the animals and is meant to supply the deficiencies of the lower orders. And here follows the explicit statement that these deficiencies are supplied in man through his faculty of conscious and critical thought, by which the soul is able to view itself and so be happy. But so far as evolution is concerned, there is nothing here of the scientific conception. There is no hint that man is in any way *derived* from the lower animal orders; and still less that, as posited by philosophers building upon Darwinism, man's thought is a faculty evolved by due degrees from faculties possessed already by mammals, insects, and even plants. The suggestion is that Zeus has caused in man a new quality to "arise within the soul." Apparently this takes place after man has already come into being as a distinct species.

Man might live at first
The animal life: but is there nothing more?
In due time, let him critically learn
How he lives . . .

So far as "Cleon" is concerned, there might be a great gulf fixed between the psychology of the lower animals and that of man, and a new creation with the emergence of man's "soul." It is of course uncritical to lay too much stress on the mere imagery with which a poet clothes his thought; but in the absence of evidence to the contrary, may we not say that Browning's "Cleon," in speaking of the "last premeditated work" of Zeus, shows that the poet still conceives of the creation of man in purely teleological, not to say anthropomorphic, terms? At any rate, there is hardly a hint of the scientific theory of evolution of species by natural selection.

Something like the Darwinian conception of evolution makes its appearance in Browning for the first time in "Prince Hohenstiel-Schwangau" (1871), a dozen years after the publication of *The Origin of Species*. Here the somewhat sophistical apologist for a not-too-ethical line of statesmanship is considering how it comes

about that the higher type of man, while sharing to such a degree
the petty interests and motives of men in general, still "tends to
freedom and divergency in the upward progress." And in this connection, the retired statesman and man of the world deigns to play
with some of the latest theories of science.

> "Will you have why and wherefore, and the fact
> Made plain as pikestaff?" modern Science asks.
> "That mass man sprung from was a jelly-lump
> Once on a time; he kept an after-course
> Through fish and insect, reptile, bird and beast,
> Till he attained to be an ape at last
> Or last but one. And if this doctrine shock
> In aught the natural pride" . . . Friend, banish fear,
> The natural humility replies.
>
> . . . .
>
> God takes time.
> I like the thought he should have lodged me once
> I' the hole, the cave, the hut, the tenement,
> The mansion and the palace; made me learn
> The feel o' the first, before I found myself
> Loftier i' the last, not more emancipate . . .
>
> . . . .
>
> Do I refuse to follow farther yet
> I' the backwardness, repine if tree and flower,
> Mountain or streamlet were my dwelling-place
> Before I gained enlargement, grew mollusc?
> As well account that way for many a thrill
> Of kinship, I confess to, with the powers
> Called Nature: animate, inanimate,
> In parts or in the whole, there's something there
> Man-like that somehow meets the man in me.
>
> . . . .
>
> Yes, I lodged
> In those successive tenements; perchance
> Taste yet the straitness of them while I stretch
> Limb and enjoy new liberty the more.

Here then, at length, Browning does admit tentatively the theory, explicitly defended by Darwin this same year (in *The Descent*

of Man), of the genesis of the human species from lower animal forms as the culmination of a long process of such derivations of more highly organized species from less highly organized ones,—a process traceable all the way back to the "jelly-lump." It should particularly be noted, however, that there is not the remotest suggestion of Darwin's characteristic contribution to evolutionary theory,—the hypothesis of "natural selection" or the notion of the "struggle for existence," which last caused so much distress to Tennyson. On the contrary, the whole discussion is introduced in order to emphasize the teleological view of evolution. It is true that the speculative Prince takes a certain pleasure in recalling the earlier and straiter "tenements" which he has occupied. The remembrance of their "straitness" gives him a vivider sense of his present liberty in a roomier house. Moreover, he is reminded that his own personal identity has been maintained throughout the whole of his progress through "fish and insect, reptile, bird and beast," and the penultimate ape.

> From first to last of lodging, I was I,
> And not at all the place that harbored me.

But then he goes on with an elaborate figure of speech by way of showing that the whole process has been conducted by some purposeful, some deliberately planning mind outside, the "foresight still outside the series." Which is, I take it, a fairly explicit repudiation of the notion of "natural selection."

It is clear, I think, that Browning did not conceive of evolution in the scientific sense before the publication of *The Origin of Species*, and that he never admitted the hypothesis of "natural selection." What then shall we think of Browning's statements in his declaration provoked by the rumor that he was opposed to Darwinism?

In reality, all that seems *proved* in Darwin's scheme was a conception familiar to me from the beginning: see in *Paracelsus* the progressive development from senseless matter to organized until man's appearance. Also in *Cleon* see the order of "life's mechanics"—and I daresay in many passages of my poetry: for how can one look at Nature as a whole and doubt that, whenever there is a gap, a "link" must be "missing"—through the limited power and opportunity of the looker? But to go back and back, as you please, *at* the back, as Mr. Sludge is made to insist, you find (*my* faith is as constant) creative intelligence, acting as matter but not resulting from it. Once set the balls rolling, and ball may hit ball and send any number in any direction over the table; but I believe in the cue pushed by a hand. When one is taunted (as I notice is often an easy method with the un-Darwinized)—taunted with thinking successive acts of creation credible, metaphysics have been stopped short at, however physics may fare: time and space being purely conceptions of our own, wholly inapplicable to intelligence of another kind—with whom, as I made Luria say, there is an everlasting moment of creation, if one at all—past, present, and future, one and the same state. This consideration does not affect Darwinism proper to any degree. But I do not consider his case as to changes in organization, brought about by desire and will in the creature, proved.[15]

In view of what Browning has actually written in "Paracelsus" and "Cleon," it is probable that what he considered *proved* in Darwin's scheme was simply "the progressive development from senseless matter to organized until man's appearance," and that even the phrasing of this statement was somewhat affected by theories which had received great publicity since the writing of those poems. He still does not assert distinctly the *derivation* of life from inorganic (or "senseless") matter, which is often regarded as a corollary of the evolution theory; nor the *derivation* of organic species from one another (though this was tentatively granted in "Prince Hohenstiel-Schwangau"). And, most important of all, he does not assert, or even apparently conceive the notion, of such derivation by *natural selection*. "I do not consider Darwin's case as to changes in organization, brought about by desire and will in the creature, proved." Mr. Stevenson has pointed out that this is not Darwin's view at all, but Lamarck's. And it is indeed a very crude phrasing of Lamarck's theory that "la production d'un nouvel organe dans un corps animal résulte d'un nouveau besoin survenu qui continue de se faire sentir, et d'un nouveau mouvement que ce besoin fait naître et entretient." [16] Browning's confusion here shows that he had not the remotest notion of Darwin's thoroughly unteleological concept of natural selection. Natural evolution in any form, as conceived by science, hardly made any impression on the mind of Browning. He was too thoroughly imbued with the notion of design—of the production of effects in nature by a creative intelligence working deliberately for an end.

Naturalism and Immortality

In his general philosophy, Browning had little of the spirit of naturalism. The distinctive mark of naturalism is submission to the natural order as we apprehend it by natural means: joyous acceptance of our place in this order, reconciliation, or at least a disposition to make the most of it as we find it, without recourse to supernatural inspirations. Whatever reconciliation with nature appears in Browning is based upon the assumption that it includes for men a continued personal existence after death. Over and over Browning makes clear that those are the only terms upon which he will accept life as satisfactory. The balance of good and evil in mortal life is heavily on the side of evil; and, without the assumption of immortality, he cannot believe in—what he thinks we must believe in to be reconciled to life—an all-good, all-wise, all-potent director of the universe.

> I must say—or choke in silence—"Howsoever came my fate,
> Sorrow did and joy did nowise—life well weighed—preponderate.
> By necessity ordained thus? I shall bear as best I can;
> By a cause all-good, all-wise, all-potent? no, as I am man!

This is from "La Saisiaz" (1877), and constitutes the substance of Browning's long argument for immortality in that poem. Mortal life is not good enough to be accepted with any satisfaction; the kind of God we assume cannot have provided such a life for us with nothing further to lead to; consequently, the argument assumes a purposeful universe, and one favorable to man. In another passage of the same poem, he refers to the general wretchedness of life unassured of immortality.

> Can we love but on condition, that the thing we love must die?
> Needs there groan a world in anguish just to teach us sympathy—
> Multitudinously wretched that we, wretched too, may guess
> What a preferable state were universal happiness?

Hardly do I so conceive the outcome of that power that went
To the making of the worm there in yon clod its tenement,
Any more than I distinguish aught of that which, wise and good,
Framed the leaf, its plain of pasture, dropped the dew, its fineless food.

A similar argument is found in "Easter Day" (1850), which presents a vision of the Last Judgment, with an interchange of remarks between the poet and a heavenly voice. The poet finds that he has chosen this world, and he rejoices in its manifold pleasures till reminded by the voice that he has cut himself off from Eden— earth's pleasures are merely "the arras-folds that variegate the earth, God's antechamber." Thus he loses his feeling of satisfaction in the natural things of earth. The poet next proposes to take his joy in art, and then in the pleasures of the intellect; but in each case is made to understand how hollow are the satisfactions involved, and—

> A world of spirit as of sense
> Was plain to him, yet not too plain,
> Which he could traverse, not remain
> A guest in:—else were permanent
> Heaven on the earth, its gleams were meant
> To sting with hunger for full light.[17]

And so the poet, being made aware of the merely provisional attractions of earthly joys, of art and intellect, decides, rather late, to choose "love" and let the world go. The voice explains that he might just as well have done this from the beginning, since all the other lower satisfactions were involved with love, God having "in all his works below made love the basis of the plan." This might be taken by an unwary reader to indicate that Browning regards our earthly life as being acceptable in itself without reference to its continuance beyond the grave, since God's love is the basis of all our mortal satisfactions. But this is clearly not the case, since the vision above outlined is Browning's way of demonstrating immortality. The gratifications of earth (suffused with divine love) are good; but they are not good enough.

In "Cleon" (1855) this line of thought is developed with more subtlety and persuasiveness. The pagan Cleon, discussing the

values of life in a letter to his king, points out how notably Zeus
has endowed man for superior satisfactions by giving him the
faculty of conscious thought. But no, he then reflects, that is just
where man is a failure—through his consciousness. It is this which
makes him aware of possible joys which, by his infirmities—for
example the advance of age—he is incapable of taking advantage
of.

> We struggle, fain to enlarge
> Our bounded physical recipiency,
> Increase our power, supply fresh oil to life,
> Repair the waste of age and sickness: no,
> It skills not! life's inadequate to joy,
> As the soul sees joy, tempting life to take.

Cleon then goes on to develop with somber eloquence the inevitable
failure in the attainment of joy, leading him to hanker after something not quite worthy of a pagan philosopher.

> I dare at times imagine to my need
> Some future state revealed to us by Zeus,
> Unlimited in capability
> For joy, as this is in desire for joy.

And he ends his letter with a reference to "one called Paulus,"
who preaches a doctrine which, as he has gathered from one of
his auditors, "could be held by no sane man." This poem is characterized by a penetrating and pathetic view of human psychology.
But the rather childish hedonism of the pagan here and the mysticism of "Easter Day" are almost equally foreign to the naturalistic
temper of a Meredith.

In "Saul" (1845–55) much higher tribute is paid to the satisfactions of mortal life; but the conclusion is the same. Young
David, in his effort to bring Saul out of his maniacal depression,
begins by celebrating the delightsomeness of pastoral occupations
and ceremonies. He plays various familiar tunes: those for calling
the sheep and the quail, "the help-tune of our reapers," "the glad
chaunt of the marriage," the Levites' chorus going up to the altar.
He then goes on to sing of the mere joys of being alive in "our
manhood's prime vigor"—

How good is man's life, the mere living! how fit to employ
All the heart and the soul and the senses forever in joy! [18]

This last section of the poem is one of the finest things in Browning, with its eloquent review of the varied satisfactions of normal life on the purely human plane—the exhilaration of outdoor exercise, the joys of family life, of labor and contest, ambition and achievement.

But after the publication of the poem in its original form, Browning evidently came to feel that it was incomplete—his recital of the joys of life was inadequate to dispel the gloom of a mad King, symbol of the ailing soul of man. And he added a second and longer part in order to expose the insufficiency of natural life and show the need for supplementing it with religious sentiment. In this second part, David dwells on the dignity and fruitfulness of Saul's life and assures him of posthumous recognition. But even this is not sufficient to restore Saul to himself. And now David lifts the subject of man's life to the plane of religious feeling. He first celebrates the world as a manifestation of divine law. He finds perfection in nature, since—

God is seen
In the star, in the stone, in the flesh, in the soul and the clod.[19]

But with all this, man is anything but perfect, and this brings the psalmist to the necessity for "submission of man's nothing-perfect to God's all-complete." The various satisfactions of human life leave one still with a sense of failure and incompleteness.

These good things being given, to go on, and give one more, the best?
Ay, to save and redeem and restore him, maintain at the height
This perfection,—succeed with life's dayspring, death's minute of night?
Interpose at the difficult minute, snatch Saul the mistake,
Saul the failure, the ruin he seems now,—and bid him awake
From the dream, the probation, the prelude, to find himself set
Clear and safe in new light and new life,—a new harmony yet
To be run, and continued, and ended—who knows?—or endure!
The man taught enough by life's dream, of the rest to make sure;
By the pain-throb, triumphantly winning intensified bliss,
And the next world's reward and repose, by the struggles in this.[20]

The Promise of Imperfection

At this point enters a motif, which is constantly recurring in Browning, a doctrine of his which we might denominate the Promise of Imperfection. When faced at last with the problem of grounding his faith in immortality, the poet solves it very simply by the assertion that man's weakness and inadequacy are themselves proofs of his divine destiny.

> What stops my despair?
> This;—'tis not what man Does which exalts him, but what man Would do!
> . . . .
> 'Tis the weakness in strength, that I cry for! my flesh, that I seek
> In the Godhead! I seek and I find it. O Saul, it shall be
> A Face like my face that receives thee; a Man like to me,
> Thou shalt love and be loved by, forever: a Hand like this hand
> Shall throw open the gates of new life to thee! See the Christ stand! [21]

Thus Browning makes a sudden leap from the thought of man's futility to the assurance of his eternal fulfilment. This way of cutting the Gordian knot is hardly the way of naturalism. Naturalism regards the problem of personal immortality as a question of fact, to be determined, if at all, by the ordinary scientific methods of observation and inference. And modern naturalism is generally inclined, in forming an opinion on this question, to consider man's place in the order of nature, along with the other living creatures with whom he shares so much of his being. Nothing of this sort is ever contemplated by Browning. The mere facts of nature are not what he takes into account in considering the doubts that beset us and the likelihood of our survival. At least he never mentions them specifically or attempts to gauge their force. He is guided exclusively by what we may call ethical considerations. Starting with the assumption of a benevolent and purposeful universe, whose main concern is man's well-being, he cannot long remain in doubt that what is incomplete in our mortal life must be completed somewhere else, being satisfied that religion holds the clue to this teleological problem.

Hence his almost inordinate disposition to prize in our experience the evidences of our incompetency. In "Rabbi Ben Ezra" (1864) he takes comfort from the very fact that we have not faith. The capacity for doubt is the proof of our superiority to the brutes, perhaps the gauge of our infinite destiny.

> Rather I prize the doubt
> Low kinds exist without,
> Finished and finite clods, untroubled by a spark.

Our spiritual failures are the gauge of our spiritual aspirations.

> What I aspired to be,
> And was not, comforts me:
> A brute I might have been, but would not sink i' the scale . . .

We are not to be judged by what we have done but by what we have dreamed of doing.

> Not on the vulgar mass
> Called "work," must sentence pass,
> Things done, that took the eye and had the price;
> O'er which, from level stand,
> The low world laid its hand,
> Found straightway to its mind, could value in a trice:
>
> But all, the world's coarse thumb
> And finger failed to plumb,
> So passed in making up the main account;
> All instincts immature,
> All purposes unsure,
> That weighed not as his work, yet swelled the man's amount:
>
> Thoughts hardly to be packed
> Into a narrow act,
> Fancies that broke through language and escaped;
> All I could never be,
> All, men ignored in me,
> This, I was worth to God, whose wheel the pitcher shaped.

This doctrine takes on a slightly platonic cast in "Abt Vogler" (1864). In some mystical way, the musician knows, whatever is good is eternal, whereas the evil has no real existence.

There shall never be one lost good! What was, shall live as before;
  The evil is null, is naught, is silence implying sound;
What was good shall be good, with, for evil, so much good more;
  On the earth the broken arcs; in the heaven a perfect round.

All we have willed or hoped or dreamed of good shall exist;
  Not its semblance, but itself; no beauty, nor good, nor power
Whose voice has gone forth, but each survives for the melodist
  When eternity affirms the conception of an hour.
The high that proved too high, the heroic for earth too hard,
  The passion that left the ground to lose itself in the sky,
Are music sent up to God by the lover and the bard;
  Enough that he heard it once: we shall hear it by and by.

Browning comes very near in "Abt Vogler" to stating a theory acceptable to naturalism. But here as usual he stops short of that point, confusing the issues (as Meredith would say) with his appeal to the supernatural. So that in the main his thought goes directly counter to the trend of naturalism.

Religious Conception of the Soul

One reason for Browning's failure to arrive at a naturalistic or human system of values is the inveterately religious and individualistic way in which he regards the soul. He is like Newman, forever finding himself alone in the universe face to face with two entities, his own soul and the God with which it is confronted. His start from the religiously conceived soul is a cardinal point with Browning. Thus in "La Saisiaz," in his elaborate discussion of the problem of immortality, after some vague preliminary skirmishings, the poet demands that he shall know the truth "howe'er it strike." And this brings him to the starting-point of his whole argument. His basic assumption is that there are two things he knows with assurance— his soul and God.

I have questioned and am answered. Question, answer presuppose
Two points: that the thing itself which questions, answers,—*is*, it
    knows;
As it also knows the thing perceived outside itself,—a force
Actual ere its own beginning, operative through its course,

Unaffected by its end,—that this thing likewise needs must be;
Call this—God, then, call that—soul, and both—the only facts for me.
Prove them facts? that they o'erpass my power of proving, proves them
    such . . .[22]

Browning makes a great point of giving flesh its due, and protesting that flesh may help soul as soul helps flesh. He also frequently complains of the manner in which flesh frustrates the
needs and aspirations of the soul. And all the while he is talking of
soul as some kind of a theological entity, conceivable apart from
material conditions, and capable of existing independently of them.

> What is he but a brute
> Whose flesh has soul to suit,
> Whose spirit works lest arms and legs want play?
> To man propose this test—
> The body at its best,
> How far can that project thy soul on its lone way.[23]

As for the naturalist view of the soul—or psyche—as the simple
flower of the body, that possibility never occurs to Browning at
all. Browning thinks constantly of the soul as tending to "God."
Naturalism thinks constantly of the human mind and spirit as the
child of nature—of earth—sharing her powers and carrying out her
tendencies.

Chapter XVII

SWINBURNE

With Swinburne we come at length to an English poet in whom the evolutionary ideas have borne fruit in a nature-poetry militantly "naturalistic." His poems all appeared after *The Origin of Species;* the volume in which he grapples most directly with man's place in the universe, *Songs Before Sunrise,* dating from 1871. Here he apparently takes for granted the derivation of man by process of evolution from the substance of the material earth. And so completely has he assimilated the concept of evolution that he does not need to use any of the technical terms of science but has already invented a highly poetical vocabulary in which to render what is for him the spiritual gist of evolution, its bearing upon human conduct and destiny.

Naturalism and the Free Spirit

The volume opens with a "Prelude" in which he represents man as bravely and freely facing the realities of existence, without borrowing comfort from any supernatural illusions. He "seeks not strength from strengthless dreams," but communes with nature and takes cheer in "the actual earth's equalities."

> Then he stood up, and trod to dust
> Fear and desire, mistrust and trust,
>   And dreams of bitter sleep and sweet,
>   And bound for sandals on his feet
> Knowledge and patience of what must
>   And what things may be, in the heat
> And cold of years that rot and rust
>   And alter; and his spirit's meat

Was freedom, and his staff was wrought
Of strength, and his cloak woven of thought.

In this new nature-poetry, one is at once aware of a new, strong voice, of marked individuality. This *is* nature-poetry as we hardly have it in Browning or Tennyson, but as Wordsworth gave it to us. The voice is very different from Wordsworth's, but the appeal to nature is similar. Swinburne is even severer than Wordsworth in his desire to draw from elemental things no false comfort but the strength that comes from fronting actualities. In nature there is no special privilege, no intervention in favor of one creature at the expense of another, but all the elements and creatures are subject alike to "the actual earth's equalities."

Swinburne expressly repudiates the disposition, which he may have found in Wordsworth, to read into nature a spiritual meaning which is not there. Neither does he depend, like Tennyson and Browning, on a faith in something beyond nature, nor bewail his lack of faith, like Clough and Arnold. Supernatural faiths he rejects as born of weakness and fear. He takes a position less merely enduring than the Stoics and less showily "noble." It is with something like enthusiasm that he embraces the world of actuality.

To him the lights of even and morn
Speak no vain things of love or scorn,
   Fancies and passions miscreate
   By men in things dispassionate.
Nor holds he fellowship forlorn
   With souls that pray and hope and hate,
And doubt they had better not been born,
   And fain would lure or scare off fate
And charm their doomsman from their doom
And make fear dig its own false tomb.

He builds not half of doubts and half
Of dreams his own soul's cenotaph,
   Whence hopes and fears with helpless eyes,
   Wrapt loose in cast-off cerecloths, rise
And dance and wring their hands and laugh,
   And weep thin tears and sigh light sighs,

And without living lips would quaff
  The living spring in man that lies,
And drain his soul of faith and strength
It might have lived on a life's length.

He hath given himself and hath not sold
To God for heaven or man for gold,
  Or grief for comfort that it gives,
  Or joy for grief's restoratives.
He hath given himself to time, whose fold
  Shuts in the mortal flock that lives
On its plain pasture's heat and cold
  And the equal year's alternatives.
Earth, heaven, and time, death, life, and he,
Endure while they shall be to be.[1]

This is the boldest utterance in English poetry since Shelley. It is in the interest of strength that Swinburne, like Shelley, repudiates the life of "dreams" and "sighs," since these drain the soul of "faith and strength." Faith in what? Faith in one's own soul's life. Swinburne goes on to ask where *does* lie profit in life? He pays due tribute to pleasure and passion as elements in experience. But these soon fall subject to relentless change and time. The one thing least subject to time is the soul; and the soul is its own pole-star,

Because man's soul is man's God still,
What wind soever waft his will
  Across the waves of day and night
  To port or shipwreck, left or right.
      . . . .
  Save his own soul he hath no star,
  And sinks, except his own soul guide,
  Helmless in middle turn of tide.[2]

Thus Swinburne recognizes the soul as that in man's being which has the most enduring reality and significance. But he does not conceive the soul as an entity capable of existence independently of material conditions, nor (like Browning) as a lover yearning after some supernal object of love. This whole series of poems revolves around the revolutionary ideal, the ideal of "Prometheus Unbound"; and the individual soul has its definition by reference to the cause of humanity and the "lamplit race" of those who forward this cause through the generations. But, while he rejoices in the encouragement we may give one another, this poet lays great stress on the need for any soul that is to serve the cause effectually to be a light unto himself.

It has often been assumed, because of his ardent championship of the claims of the flesh, and his disposition to ignore the traditional tabus of Victorian morality, that Swinburne is a mere hedonist, flabby or frantic. Rightly considered, the sensualism of his first volume of *Poems and Ballads* (1866), the worship of Venus, is but one article in the creed of naturalism—of one who begins with earth as the foundation of his system—as well as being a manifesto in the struggle for freedom. Freedom herself is the goddess whom he worships in *Songs Before Sunrise*, and he praises the serious labors of those who seek to establish her firmly in humanity.

> A little time that we may fill
> Or with such good works or such ill
>   As loose the bonds or make them strong
>   Wherein all manhood suffers wrong.
> By rose-hung river and light-foot rill
>   There are who rest not; who think long
> Till they discern as from a hill
>   At the sun's hour of morning song,
> Known of souls only, and those souls free,
> The sacred spaces of the sea.[3]

Swinburne is in many ways more nearly akin to Shelley than to any other English poet. With him as with Shelley the devotion to political liberty was intimately bound up with his devotion to freedom of the spirit. The bulk of *Songs Before Sunrise* is concerned with the ideal of political liberty and with the contemporary historical events and personages bearing upon this.

Earth and Man

But there are half a dozen poems scattered through the collection which develop the philosophical views and the spiritual attitudes lying back of his political position. Besides the "Prelude" and the "Epilogue," the chief of these are "Hertha" and the "Hymn of Man." Hertha is the name of the earth-goddess in Norse mythology, and it is significant that with Swinburne, as later with Meredith, the word "earth" has practically taken the place of "nature." As the earlier nature-poets were imaginatively dominated by astronomy and the notion of law reigning in the stellar universe, those who came in with evolution were naturally dominated by the concepts of geology and biology, and were mainly taken up with the relation of man to the planet from which he has his origin. Mother Earth comes back again into her full honors. "The grey glad mother" is referred to often by Swinburne—in "On the Downs" and "Hymn of Man"; she is apostrophized and prayed to in "The Litany of Nations"; and she speaks at length to her human children in "Hertha."

In thus choosing to celebrate the earth as the guide and origin of human life, Swinburne is issuing his manifesto in favor of the natural interpretation of man and man's spirit as opposed to the supernatural. It is from earth, from nature, that man derives his being, his mind, his aspirations, his morality. Instead of coming "out of the deep, my child, out of the deep," or "from God, who is our home," man is a parcel of the same vital energy that rolls in the sea, that flies with the bird, that opens with the bud.

> O natural force of spirit and sense, that art
> One thing in all things, fruit of thine own fruit . . .[4]

Swinburne here associates the subjective and objective as growing from the same root, like Shelley in "Mont Blanc" or Wordsworth in "Tintern Abbey"; and like Goethe over and over in his poems, he insists, but with even more metaphysical particularity, that this is a *natural* force in spirit and sense. To this he is constrained by reaction from the religious-mystical terminology of Tennyson and Browning. His earth, his nature, is not so much a goddess indulging in the act of creation as a root-stock out of which spring and blossom the flowers of life; a force animating all activities; a fount out of which flow all streams of energy.

I am that which began;
   Out of me the years roll;
Out of me God and man;
   I am equal and whole;
God changes, and man, and the form of them bodily; I am the soul.

Before ever land was,
   Before ever the sea,
Or soft hair of the grass,
   Or fair limbs of the tree,
Or the flesh-coloured fruit of my branches, I was, and thy soul was in
   me.

First life on my sources
   First drifted and swam;
Out of me are the forces
   That save it or damn;
Out of me man and woman, and wild-beast and bird; before God was,
   I am.

Beside or above me
   Nought is there to go;
Love or unlove me,
   Unknow me or know,
I am that which unloves me and loves; I am stricken, and I am the
   blow.

I the mark that is missed
   And the arrows that miss,
I the mouth that is kissed
   And the breath in the kiss,
The search, and the sought, and the seeker, the soul and the body
   that is.

I am that thing which blesses
   My spirit elate;
That which caresses
   With hands uncreate
My limbs unbegotten that measure the length of the measure of fate.

This curious and seeming-mysterious passage from "Hertha"
is very like Emerson's "Brahma." The verses of Swinburne are at

first glance cryptical and full of paradoxes. But in essence they are a simple repudiation of the dualism of thinkers like Tennyson and Browning, and the assertion of a view of nature at one with Goethe's. Everything is in nature,—good and evil, body and spirit, objective and subjective, the fact and the judgment passed upon the fact, man and man's God.

> But what thing dost thou now,
>   Looking Godward, to cry
> "I am I, thou art thou.
>   I am low, thou art high"?
> I am thou whom thou seekest to find him; find thou but thyself, thou
>   art I.

> I the grain and the furrow,
>   The plough-cloven clod
> And the ploughshare drawn thorough,
>   The germ and the sod,
> The deed and the doer, the seed and the sower, the dust which is God.

The geological background of man's origin is referred to in a style reminding one of Blake and the Book of Job.

> Hast thou known how I fashioned thee,
>   Child, underground?
> Fire that impassioned thee,
>   Iron that bound,
> Dim changes of water, what thing of all these hast thou known of or
>   found?

> Canst thou say in thine heart
>   Thou hast seen with thine eyes
> With what cunning of art
>   Thou wast wrought in what wise,
> By what force of what stuff thou wast shapen, and shown on my
>   breast to the skies?

The spirit of earth is an evolutionary force, whose essential property it is to grow, to evolve. It cannot be stopped, and the evil things that threaten to stop it are themselves a part of it.

> Though sore be my burden
>   And more than ye know,
> And my growth have no guerdon
>   But only to grow,
> Yet I fail not of growing for lightnings above me or deathworms
>   below.

> These too have their part in me,
>   As I too in these;
> Such fire is at heart in me,
>   Such sap is this tree's,
> Which hath in it all sounds and all secrets of infinite lands and of seas.

Earth is here imaged as the tree Ygdrasil, the life-tree of Norse mythology. Note the repudiation of purpose. "And my growth have no guerdon but only to grow." Yet, while earth disclaims the notion of deliberate design, she finds her culmination, her glory, in the spirit of man, the end-product of her growth.

> In the spring-coloured hours
>   When my mind was as May's,
> There brake forth of me flowers
>   By centuries of days,
> Strong blossoms with perfume of manhood, shot out from my spirit
>   as rays.

> And the sound of them springing
>   And smell of their shoots
> Were as warmth and sweet singing
>   And strength to my roots;
> And the lives of my children made perfect with freedom of soul were
>   my fruits.

Attitude towards Religion

Swinburne is as passionately anti-religious as Shelley, and for the same reasons. He hates the political tyranny of the church and the spiritual tyranny of the creeds fostering superstition, obstructing the progress of mind and the perfection of spirit. He therefore embraces the evolutionary concept as supplanting the notion of a creative God, a first cause. He has many ways of expressing the naturalistic view. Hertha says of herself that she is not to be regarded as a creator or god.

> Mother, not maker,
>   Born and not made;
> Though her children forsake her,
>   Allured or afraid,
> Praying prayers to the God of their fashion, she stirs not for all that have prayed.

Earth, the essential energy in things, is neither a creator nor herself created. She is "self-existent."

> One forceful nature uncreate
> That feeds itself with death and fate,
>   Evil and good and change and time,
> That within all men lies at wait
>   Till the hour shall bid them climb
>   And live sublime.[5]

>   . . . .

> Thou the ghost of God, the mother uncreated,
> Soul for whom the fleeting forceless ages waited
> As our forceless fancies wait on thee, O Earth;
> Thou the body and soul, the father-God and mother . . .[6]

>   . . . .

> Ah, did they know, did they dream of it, counting the cost and the worth?
> The ways of her days, did they seem then good to the new-souled earth?
> Did her heart rejoice, and the might of her spirit exult in her then,
> Child yet no child of the night, and motherless mother of men?[7]

Swinburne is of course aware of the philosophical urge to postulate a first cause, a great original. But he deprecates the effort to solve an insoluble riddle, which only results in the invention of an immoral and anthropomorphic God, and the creation of more logical difficulties than it settles.

Before the growth was the grower, and the seed ere the plant was
    sown;
But what was the seed of the sower? and the grain of him, whence
    was it grown?
Foot after foot ye go back and travail and make yourselves mad;
Blind feet that feel for the track where highway is none to be had.
Therefore the god that ye make you is grievous, and gives not aid,
Because it is but for your sake that the God of your making is made.
Thou and I and he are not gods made men for a span,
But God, if a God there be, is the substance of men which is man.[8]

Swinburne rejects the notion of God as a person like a man, because that brings in with it all the corollaries of absolute power and
the slavery of the spirit. He will have no truck with Browning's
personal god, towards whom the individual soul yearns and with
whom he makes his particular compact. If there is to be a god, he
must be the god of mankind, not of individuals with souls to be
saved. I believe that here Swinburne may be influenced by Shelley's chorus in "Prometheus Unbound"—

> Man, oh, not men! a chain of linked thought,
> Of love and might to be divided not
>
> . . . .
>
> Man, one harmonious soul of many a soul,
> Whose nature is its own divine control,
> Where all things flow to all, as rivers to the sea . . .[9]

In Swinburne as in Shelley we have the social, the democratic
ideal extended to spiritual notions and taking the place of the
traditional theology of Browning.

But Swinburne's imagination is too much steeped in literary tradition to give up readily the word God, and he is willing to toy
with it if he may be allowed to define it in the spirit of nature and
the Revolution. He is willing to consider the use of the word God
to describe the growing spiritual ideals of humanity. God is thus
not the origin but the culmination of the world-process. He is in
process of growth, subject to the principle of evolution, having his
roots in earth,—"a God with the world inwound whose clay to his
footsole clings." As man's spiritual ideal he is a child of mother-

earth. "Out of me God and man." (The false god of man's corrupt imagining is equally "out of" earth.) As something growing in the mind of man, he is a part of universal nature and akin to the elements. And since the spirit of nature is one, it is impossible to distinguish in the growing god body from soul. As man's ideal he is not the god of individuals but "the fruit of the whole."

There are two passages in which Swinburne develops these ideas with regard to God, "if a God there be." One is in the poem "On the Downs." Here the poet is demanding of nature whether there is "no God or end at all," and wise "secret earth" replies: "There is no God, O son, if thou be none." And then is heard, out of cliff and heath and sea—

> A multitudinous monotone
> Of dust and flower and seed and stone,
>   In the deep sea-rock's mid-sea sloth,
> In the live water's trembling zone,
>   In all men love and loathe,
>   One God at growth.
>
> One forceful nature uncreate
> That feeds itself with death and fate . . .

The other important passage is in "Hymn of Man," and follows immediately on the lines already quoted from that poem.

Thou and I and he are not gods made men for a span,
But God, if a God there be, is the substance of men which is man.
Our lives are pulses or pores of his manifold body and breath;
As waves of his sea on the shores where birth is the beacon of death.
We men, the multiform features of man, whatsoever we be,
Recreate him of whom we are creatures, and all we only are he.
Not each man of all men is God, but God is the fruit of the whole;
Indivisible spirit and blood, indiscernible body from soul.
Not men's but man's is the glory of godhead, the kingdom of time,
The mountainous ages made hoary with snows for the spirit to climb.
A God with the world inwound whose clay to his footsole clings;
A manifold God fast-bound as with iron of adverse things.
A soul that labours and lives, an emotion, a strenuous breath . . .

Such a notion of God Swinburne will admit, provisionally, in recognition of what good he finds in the concepts of religion. But he most earnestly repudiates the cruel and tyrannical, the crude and childish gods which man has been inventing to cover his ignorance and subject his spirit.

He saith to the ages, Give; and his soul forgoes not her share;
Who are ye that forbid him to live, and would feed him with heaven-
    lier air?
Will ye feed him with poisonous dust, and restore him with hemlock
    for drink,
Till he yield you his soul up in trust, and have heart not to know or
    to think?
He hath stirred him, and found out the flaw in his fetters, and cast
    them behind;
His soul to his soul is a law, and his mind is a light to his mind.

. . . .

His soul is at one with the reason of things that is sap to the roots.
He can hear in their changes a sound as the conscience of consonant
    spheres;
He can see through the years flowing round him the law underlying
    the years.
Who are ye that would bind him with curses and blind him with
    vapour of prayer? [10]

It is in favor of "the reason of things" and "the law underlying the years" that Swinburne invokes the spirit of man. This "Hymn of Man" was written during the 1870 session in Rome of the Œcumenical Council which formulated the doctrine of papal infallibility; and it is Swinburne's anti-clericalism that makes him so vehement in denouncing the gods that constrain men's minds.

It is interesting to set over against Swinburne's utterances Newman's argument in favor of infallibility. It is this very passion of intellectual freedom championed by Swinburne which makes the need, according to Newman, for some authority in the earth "to arrest fierce, wilful human nature in its onward course and bring it into subjection." The Bible is not sufficient for this purpose.

It may be accidentally the means of the conversion of individuals; but a book, after all, cannot make a stand against the wild, living intellect of man, and in this day it begins to testify, as regards its own structure and contents, to the power of that universal solvent which is so successfully acting upon religious establishments. . . . I say, that a power, possessed of infallibility in religious teaching, is happily adapted to be a working instrument, in the course of human affairs, for smiting hard and throwing back the immense energy of the aggressive, capricious, untrustworthy intellect.[11]

So Newman declares himself, with his characteristic courage, clarity, and ruthlessness of logic, and with a vehemence of expression unusual in this sober writer. For the occasion is critical. And so the issue is sharply drawn between the natural and the supernatural interpretations of man's place in the world.

We must not forget the strong political motives inwoven with the philosophical motives in these poems of Swinburne. *Songs Before Sunrise* is one continuous celebration of the European struggle for liberty and particularly the Italian *risorgimento*,—the freeing of Venice from Austrian domination, the liberation of Naples, and the liberation of Rome. The occupation of Rome by the Italian army followed close upon the heels of the proclamation of papal infallibility. So that Swinburne's passion for freedom of thought was strongly reinforced by his passion for political freedom. And his celebration of the downfall of the gods—in "Hymn of Man" and "Hertha"—like Shelley's in "Prometheus Unbound"—was all of a piece with his celebration of the downfall of kings.

The Soul of Man

The one moral quality which Shelley prizes most is freedom of soul. It is this quality which Swinburne's earth-spirit most earnestly inculcates in her pupils—a mother who craves of her children not submission to her commands but the strength that comes of independence.

> A creed is a rod,
>   And a crown is of night;
> But this thing is God,
>   To be man with thy might,
> To grow straight in the strength of thy spirit, and live out thy life as the light.

I am in thee to save thee,
  As my soul in thee saith;
Give thou as I gave thee,
  Thy life-blood and breath,
Green leaves of thy labour, white flowers of thy thought, and red
  fruit of thy death.

Be the ways of thy giving
  As mine were to thee;
The free life of thy living,
  Be the gift of it free;
Not as servant to lord, nor as master to slave, shalt thou give thee to me.

. . . .

I bid you but be;
  I have need not of prayer;
I have need of you free
  As your mouths of mine air;
That my heart may be greater within me, beholding the fruits of me
  fair.

. . . .

For truth only is living,
  Truth only is whole,
And the love of his giving
  Man's polestar and pole;
Man, pulse of my centre, and fruit of my body, and seed of my soul.

One birth of my bosom;
  One beam of mine eye;
One topmost blossom
  That scales the sky;
Man, equal and one with me, man that is made of me, man that is I.[12]

So earth sends forth man with no light but her light in his mind,
no strength but her strength in his spirit, and bids him confront
unsupported the forces of darkness and disillusion. Swinburne is
well aware of the weaknesses to which man is liable, the treacheries and surrenders, the cruelties and futilities which have made
up human history. And he is obliged to summon to his aid
the thought of men like Mazzini and Garibaldi for assurance of the

potential stoutness of the human soul. He is obliged to set up the
ideal of a soul capable of standing indomitable amid the treacheries
of men and the lapse of faiths. It is to this potential strength of
soul in men that he looks for bringing in the dawn of man's hopes,
when he shall be, as in Shelley's vision, "free, boundless, fearless,
perfect, one." If this dawn is never to break, then he is willing that
"Man's world die like worlds of old." But meantime he can only
set up the ideal of liberty as the strengthener of men's souls—of
man's soul. And this free soul of man—

> She only, she since earth began,
> The many-minded soul of man,
>   From one incognizable root
>   That bears such divers-coloured fruit,
> Hath ruled for blessing or for ban
>   The flight of seasons and pursuit;
> She regent, she republican,
>   With wide and equal eyes and wings,
>   Broods on things born and dying things.[13]

And when man is disheartened and cannot see for himself "the
sounds and sights of liberty" he takes courage in the recognition of
souls that conform to this ideal,

> Men who have life and grace to give,
> Men who have seen the soul and live.[14]

CHAPTER XVIII

MEREDITH

MEREDITH takes up the theme of evolutionary naturalism where
Swinburne laid it down, and he carries it much farther. He is
equally insistent that man's spirit is naturally derived from Earth;
but his notion of what is involved in the operations of the spirit
is much more comprehensive, includes more of what is implied in
the term "spirituality." It takes much more into account, or lays
more stress on, the demands of common morality and altruism. His
tone is much less revolutionary, more in line with the constructive
movement of Victorian thought. Moreover, while Swinburne
merely takes for granted the development of our spiritual life out
of the natural process of the world, Meredith has a great deal to
say of the causes and conditions of this development, thus giving
more substance and plausibility to the conception. Meredith is
consequently more persuasive than Swinburne, and more helpful to
earnest readers seeking direction for a spirit freed from the bonds
of orthodox religion. Indeed, Meredith illustrates extremely well the
way in which a view of the world built around the concept of nature may take on much of the religious fervor associated with a
supernatural *Weltansicht*, and constitute practically a substitute
religion.

There are many reasons for supposing that Meredith was inspired
by the work of Swinburne. The two men were for a time closely
associated as joint occupants of Rossetti's house in Chelsea. With
several of the *Songs Before Sunrise* Meredith was acquainted before
the publication of the volume; in 1866 and 1867 he was in correspondence with his friend Swinburne about these poems and
Meredith's novel *Vittoria*, which deals with the revolt in Italy.
Swinburne publicly championed Meredith's *Modern Love* against

a stupid contemporary attack. Meredith declared in the last letter he wrote—on the occasion of Swinburne's death—"He was the greatest of our lyrical poets." In the same letter he refers to "the many times when at the starting of an idea (by Swinburne) the whole town was instantly ablaze with electric light." [1] His friendship with Swinburne and his great admiration for him make it highly probable that he read the *Songs Before Sunrise* with great attention. It is certain that, before the date of its publication (1871), Meredith's nature-poetry had been rather vaguely and thinly Wordsworthian in thought, and lacking any suggestion of the evolutionary concept. The first volume of poems in which his characteristic evolutionary naturalism appears was *Poems and Lyrics of the Joy of Earth* (1883), including "The Woods of Westermain" and "Earth and Man." The latter poem in particular has much to suggest "Hertha," and in these and other poems of the volume the term Earth has almost altogether taken the place of the traditional Nature. The other volumes of Meredith particularly important in relation to the concept of nature are *A Reading of Earth* (1888) and *A Reading of Life* (1901).

Whatever the case may be with regard to the influence of Swinburne upon Meredith, the following facts are evident. Meredith's evolutionism follows Swinburne's by more than ten years. He agrees with Swinburne in laying his stress upon Earth rather than Nature, thus signalizing the transfer of the imagination from the general astronomical field to that of life on our planet. His attitude towards supernatural religion is essentially that of Swinburne (and Arnold) rather than that of the dominant poets, Tennyson and Browning. Like Swinburne he bases this attitude on evolutionary considerations. Like Swinburne he transfers the stress from the individual soul to the race.

Early Nature-Poetry

As for Meredith's earlier nature-poetry, it is sufficient to refer to two poems, "South-West Wind in the Woodland" (1851) and "Ode to the Spirit of Earth in Autumn" (1862). The first of these poems is Meredith's "Ode to the West Wind"; but the concluding passage of philosophical comment is almost sheer Wordsworth.

The voice of nature is abroad
This night; she fills the air with balm;
Her mystery is o'er the land;
And who that hears her now and yields
His being to her yearning tones,
And seats his soul upon her wings,
And broadens o'er the wind-swept world
With her, will gather in the flight
More knowledge of her secret, more
Delight in her beneficence,
Than hours of musing, or the lore
That lives of men could ever give.

Meredith here takes a position very like that of Wordsworth in "Expostulation and Reply" and "The Tables Turned." The poem as a whole and others of the period show that he has emotionally absorbed the Wordsworthian feeling towards nature, including the assumption of nature's "beneficence." But of the general philosophy lying back of Wordsworth's feeling there is little evidence. Meredith offers no suggestion of *why* this yielding to nature's yearning tones should enlighten us in regard to the truth of things.

In the "Ode to the Spirit of Earth in Autumn"—a second try at the same theme—Meredith has taken a step forward, and introduces an idea hardly to be found in Wordsworth. In some respects this poem is more like Shelley's "Ode to the West Wind" than "South-West Wind in the Woodland." A dominant thought of this poem is Shelley's,—that the turbulent autumn winds are a means of preparing the spring.

They swing in the branches, they roll in the moss,
    They blow the seed on the air.
Back to back they stand and blow
The winged seed on the cradling air,
A fountain of leaves over bosom and back.

Meredith's thought has a somewhat different slant from Shelley's. He is dealing essentially with the problem of personal death, and how we may reconcile the thought of death with a belief in nature's goodness. And he takes the position so common in his later

poems that our only way of accepting the fact of personal death is
to lose ourselves in the thought of nature's eternal life.

> And may not men to this attain?
> That the joy of motion, the rapture of being,
> Shall throw strong light when our season is fleeing,
> Nor quicken aged blood in vain,
> At the gates of the vault, on the verge of the plain?
> Life thoroughly lived is a fact in the brain,
>   While eyes are left for seeing.
> Behold, in yon stripped Autumn, shivering grey,
>   Earth knows no desolation.
>   She smells regeneration
>   In the moist breath of decay.

This thought recurs frequently in various forms in Meredith's
later poems; and there, under the stimulus of the evolutionary concept, it takes on greater substance, weight, and emotional force.
For the concept of evolution is associated in Meredith, as in so
many of the Victorian poets, with that of spiritual progress. By
Meredith, as by Swinburne, and less constantly by Tennyson, it is
associated with the thought of the race, of the stake each individual
has in the progress and perfecting of humanity. And in Meredith
it greatly confirms his devotion to nature by making more under-
standable his filial relation to the earth and the means by which
have been developed the mental faculties which he derives from
her.

Earth and Mind

This fact of the derivation of our mental faculties from the sense-
life and so from the material world is central in Meredith; and the
statement of it in him is so much more distinct and uncompromising
than in any earlier English poet that it gives him a place of extreme
importance in the history of poetic naturalism. In "The Woods of
Westermain" (1883) he says we may learn something of earth and
ourselves by looking into the eyes of oxen. We may—

> Read their pool of vision through,
> Back to hours when mind was mud;

> Nigh the knot that did untwine
> Timelessly to drowsy suns;
> Seeing Earth a slimy spine,
> Heaven a space for winging tons.

Thus he refers to the origin of life (and so of mind) in the primeval mud of an early geologic era when the atmosphere of earth was favorable to gigantic flying animals—somewhat telescoping his geologic periods in the swift perspective view. In the same poem and elsewhere he refers to the brain as growing out of our sense life (blood) and the spirit as a further development of brain; and asserts that animal instinct and the human mind grow equally out of the soil of earth.

> Of our Earth they ply the laws,
> Have in Earth their feeding root,
> Mind of man and bent of brute.

In "A Faith on Trial" (1888), he insists that spirit is not a transcendental product, but—

> That from flesh unto spirit man grows
> Even here on the sod under sun.

In "Earth and Man" (1883) he refers to mind as the "issue" of the senses. And other poems in which the same assumptions are made are the sonnets, "Sense and Spirit" and "Earth's Secret" (1883) and "The Test of Manhood" (1901).

It is not by any means in order to belittle man that Meredith dwells upon his earthly origin. On the contrary he takes the view of Goethe that man's mind is the means by which nature is enabled to realize herself. "Sie hat keine Sprache noch Rede; aber sie schafft Zungen und Herzen, durch die sie fühlt und spricht." So Meredith declares,

> He sows for bread, and she in spirit reaps:
> She conscient, she sensitive, in him;
> With him enwound, his brave ambition hers:
> By him humaner made; by his keen spurs
> Pricked to race past the pride in giant limb . . .[2]

That is, it is only through man's mind, her creation, that earth
is enabled to pursue the higher operations of the spirit. In "Earth
and Man" Meredith follows the example of Swinburne in
"Hertha," making Earth rejoice in the spiritual flowering she at-
tains in man. He represents Earth as contemplating her "great venture, Man," and recognizing what she owes to him.

xxiv

She hears him. Him she owes
For half her loveliness a love well won
By work that lights the shapeless and the dun,
Their common foes.

xxv

He builds the soaring spires,
That sing his soul in stone: of her he draws,
Though blind to her, by spelling at her laws,
Her purest fires.

xxvi

Through him hath she exchanged,
For the gold harvest-robes, the mural crown,
Her haggard quarry-features and thick frown
Where monsters ranged.

xxvii

And order, high discourse,
And decency, than which is life less dear,
She has of him: the lyre of language clear,
Love's tongue and source.

The thing works both ways. Earth owes to man whatever is at-
tainable through conscious thought. But man has no thought save
from earth; from her he has the very laws which his thought enables him to formulate; from her, the emotional reactions that
underlie his religion, wrong or right. Even when he is at odds with
her, it is her essence in him that provokes him to this reaction.
Here again we remember Goethe's Nature. "Man gehorcht ihren

Gesetzen, auch wenn man ihnen widerstrebt; man wirkt mit ihr, auch wenn man gegen sie wirken will." So Meredith—

xxix

If he aloft for aid
Imploring storms, her essence is the spur.
His cry to heaven is a cry to her
He would evade.

xxx

Not elsewhere can he tend.
Those are her rules which bid him wash foul sins;
Those her revulsions from the skull that grins
To ape his end.

xxxi

And her desires are those
For happiness, for lastingness, for light.
'Tis she who kindles in his haunting night
The hoped dawn-rose.

However different his poetic idiom, Meredith is here taking sides with Swinburne and Goethe against the dualism of Tennyson and Browning. The passage from "Earth and Man" is the equivalent of that strange series of paradoxes in "Hertha" which I have brought into comparison with Emerson's "Brahma." Meredith is asserting here, as Swinburne asserted in "Hertha".: out of Earth come "God and man." That is, our religious impulses, both those approved by nature, and those upon which she frowns, are an outgrowth of our natural instincts. There is nowhere any separate source of religious inspiration, transcending nature and giving the lie to her. There is not even in man a faculty for supplementing the teaching of nature which is not itself derived from nature— that is, originally from the impulsions of sense.

Science and the "Spiritual Element"

We are here, of course, on very difficult philosophic ground, on which misunderstandings readily occur through want of agree-

ment on definitions, or through—it may be—certain ultimate ambiguities involved in abstract thought. Mr. Stevenson, after sum-
marizing Meredith's philosophy of God and nature, remarks:

> All of this is a logical deduction from the evolutionary principle,
> with the single exception of the assumption that Nature possesses a
> spiritual element. In making this assumption, Meredith passed beyond
> the range of science, and depended, even as Tennyson and Browning
> did, on intuition. But the fact which he asserts by that sanction is more
> easily reconcilable with evolution than their demonstrations of God
> and the immortal soul, and is actually nothing more than a sublimation
> of the laws governing nature in general and evolution in particular.[3]

This is a cautious and conservative statement, and yet I have
the impression that considerable misunderstanding of Meredith
might arise through Stevenson's use of the terms "spiritual" and
"intuition."

It is undoubtedly true that Meredith "passed beyond the range
of science." He was writing as a poet,—that is, as one who deals
with the emotional coloring which the facts of life have for men—
have or may have for us, according to the degree of our intellectual
and imaginative cultivation. He did not always confine himself,
like Swinburne, to strictly poetic language, but allowed himself at
times to indulge in words of more dangerously philosophical connotation like "goodness" and "beneficence." As to nature's possessing a "spiritual element," I think it misleading to say that Meredith
made any such assertion except in the sense that man's mind, which
is itself a part of nature, develops in the direction of spirituality.
And when we analyze the many passages in which this idea is expressed, it grows more and more doubtful whether Meredith's
"spirituality" signifies anything more than a cultivated moral sense,
or what we may call social or cosmic imagination—a disposition to
sink purely individual considerations in the general well-being of
the race. Obviously this is not present in nature before the arrival
of man; for Meredith asserts over and over again that "spirit" or
"soul" is man's contribution to the natural process.

> Earth was not Earth before her sons appeared,
> Nor Beauty Beauty ere young Love was born.[4]

The only sense in which Meredith assumes a spiritual element in nature is this: nature actually involves the evolution of man, who is a creature capable of some measure of altruism; and this altruistic tendency has actually developed in man as a result of his dealings with his environment and in accordance with the "laws"—that is, the observed behavior—of the natural world. In this sense then, Earth—as we review her history—has actually borne certain flowers of spirit—

> She being Spirit in her clods,
> Footway to the God of Gods.[5]

And this flowering of the spirit has been conducted by the natural process of Change—Meredith's poetic term for evolution.

> Change is on the wing to bud
> Rose in brain from rose in blood.[6]

This is certainly going beyond the range of science. For science deals with ponderable facts, with forces susceptible of exact mathematical treatment. It deals with what Mr. Hyman Levy calls "isolates"—that is, very particular and limited "systems" of phenomena, "that can be imagined as isolated from their setting in the universe without appreciably disturbing their structure and the process they present." [7] Such isolates science has thus far been able to find almost exclusively in the world of material objects and movements; and it has, by the nature of things, made extremely slow progress in finding any such systems capable of satisfactory isolation in the realm of human behavior, let alone the subjective accompaniments of human behavior. Nevertheless, common sense recognizes that human beings are capable of greater or less degrees of moral responsibility, of social imagination. It is universally assumed that this ethical or imaginative condition is related to men's thinking processes. And it is one of the distinguishing marks of naturalism that men's thinking processes are classed among the products of evolution, and not as having their origin in some distinct "spiritual" realm. In this matter, Meredith is uncompromisingly on the side of naturalism.

It may be unfortunate, from the point of view of scientific or philosophical precision, that he should have made use of so many terms deeply tinged with religious and philosophical assumptions which he did not share. This is the fault of many circumstances working together: of the paucity of our vocabulary; of Meredith's want of philosophical training; of his conciliatory spirit and his wish not to break too violently with a tradition which had served a useful purpose; and finally of the poet's instinct to use wherever possible a word of emotional coloring rather than a technical term. The words "spirit" and "spiritual" had their origin in ways of thinking quite alien to those prevailing today; and they often lead persons of highly trained intelligence into assumptions quite unjustified by the plain facts, simply by force of obscure associations still clinging to them. In primitive usage, they imply the separateness of the conscious ego from the body with which it is associated in common experience—the separate identity of the "soul" and its capacity for existing and functioning outside of the natural process and unconditioned by it. This conception is still very strong in Tennyson and Browning, however refined and cautious may be the terms in which they express it. And, in less obviously religious philosophies, there is still somehow an implied opposition between the "natural" and the "spiritual," with the spiritual assumed as in some way paramount, more real, more original than the natural.

The word "spirit" is in many languages synonymous with the most commonly used word for "mind"—*Geist, esprit*. And "spiritual" comes more and more to take on the simple meaning of "mental," "intellectual," or "subjective." But still, with our disposition to use words in an "honorific" rather than a severely "descriptive" sense, we often use the term "spiritual" with a flavoring of praise in referring to the operations of scientific, artistic, speculative thought. Again, since religion has been so generally associated in the great civilizations with the ethical ideals prevailing, the word spiritual has come to mean ethical, characterized by a refined and elevated moral sense. Here again it is almost inevitably honorific in flavoring as well as descriptive; and its honorific character derives not merely from the general credit attaching socially to fine moral character, but quite as much, I suppose, from the credit traditionally attaching to religious faith.

Meredith was, like us all, a complex of ideas, notions, emotional reactions of diverse origin. He had been brought up by the Moravian brothers of Neuwied on the Rhine, who combined a fine ethical ideal and a humane manner of life with an orthodox religious faith. It would be strange if, in using words of religious origin, he should quite thoroughly clear them of religious connotations very significant to him in his childhood. It was certainly his aim to do so. He wrote to a friend in 1861: "Our great error has been (the error of all religion, as I fancy) to raise a spiritual system in antagonism to Nature." [8] Again he said in 1888: "I have written always with the perception that there is no life but of the spirit; that the concrete is really the shadowy; yet that the way to spiritual life lies in the complete unfolding of the creature, not in the nipping of his passions." [9] In the first of these statements, he is obviously using the term "spiritual system" for any system which professes to find the essential truth of life outside the frame of nature. In the second statement he is using "spiritual life" to indicate a life given significance by ethical preference, choices, evaluations. It is such ethical evaluations which for him give meaning to life.

The Humane Ideal

It would doubtless make for clearness if, in place of spirit, we should read, in Meredith, "moral ideal." For it is invariably a moral or humane ideal which he has in mind when he talks of spirituality. Meredith, if he is assuming "a spiritual element in nature," is simply assuming that human beings are capable of a humane ideal. They are capable of conceiving it so vividly in their imaginations as to put a constraint upon their selfish impulses in hopes of furthering this ideal on earth.

Let us examine more closely certain passages in which this "spiritual" element is referred to by Meredith. "A Faith on Trial" is a poem written after the death of the poet's wife, in which, in his bereavement, he goes to nature for comfort. And the sole comfort which she gives him—since she will make no concession to his craving for personal immortality—is the sense of union with his race. This is brought to his mind by a ceremonial procession of gay children which tends to put him at one "with the hungers of [his] kind." He is brought to the conception of a Reason born of contact with "the numbers"—a Reason shaped by thought of the common interest. Reason he describes as

> Mirror of Earth, and guide
> To the Holies from sense withheld:
> Reason, man's germinant fruit.
> She wrestles with our old worm
> Self in the narrow and wide:
> Relentless quencher of lies. . . .

It is Earth who is speaking. "The Holies from sense withheld" might be thought to point to some "spiritual element." The context shows it to be what I have described above, an ideal for the race. This ideal is withheld from sense in that, in order to entertain it, one must be capable of seeing beyond the selfish cravings of our senses. It is our reasoning faculty which makes it possible for us to ignore the immediate promptings of sense in the interest of a larger ideal.

As a matter of fact, Meredith is specifically arguing here against what would have been called a "spiritual element" by Tennyson or Browning. He is arguing against the demand for personal immortality, which is made—as he tells us over and over again—not by our spiritual nature but by our sensational nature, which shrinks from the grave and craves more and more sense life. It is our sense that craves a goal, a heavenly guerdon for our earthly strivings, a union beyond death with "a face like thy face." This Meredith calls "the cry of unfaith."

> Spirit raves not for a goal.
> Shapes in man's likeness hewn,
> Desires not; neither desires
> The Sleep or the Glory: it trusts;
> Uses my gifts, yet aspires;
> Dreams of a higher than it. . . .
> . . . .
>
> The dream of the blossom of Good
> Is your banner of battle unrolled. . . .
> . . . .

Hopeful of victory most
When hard is the task to sustain
Assaults of the fearful sense
At a mind in desolate mood
With the Whither, whose echo is Whence;
And humanity's clamour, lost, lost;
And its clasp of the staves that snap;
And evil abroad, as a main
Uproarious, bursting its dyke.
For back do you look, and lo,
Forward the harvest of grain!—
Numbers in council, awake
To love more than things of my lap,
Love me; and to let the types break,
Men be grass, rocks rivers, all flow;
All save the dream sink alike
To the source of my vital in sap;
Their battle, their loss, their ache,
For my pledge of vitality know.
The dream is the thought in the ghost;
The thought sent flying for food;
Eyeless, but sprung of an aim
Supernal of Reason, to find
The great Over-Reason we name
Beneficence: mind seeking Mind.
Dream of the blossom of Good,
In its waver and current and curve,
With the hopes of my offspring enscrolled!
Soon to be seen of a host
The flag of the Master I serve!

Meredith is here calling for an exercise of the imagination by which a man may pass beyond his own individual case and lose himself in the "dream" of nature's perpetual life. At times his conception has almost the pure estheticism of Goethe's vision of nature. "Es ist ein ewiges Leben, Werden und Bewegen in ihr, und doch rückt sie nicht weiter. Sie verwandelt sich ewig, und ist kein Moment Stillestehen in ihr." So Meredith—

> . . . let the types break,
> Men be grass, rocks rivers, all flow;
> All save the dream sink alike
> To the source of my vital in sap.[10]

When I speak of the pure estheticism of Goethe's vision, I refer to the delight taken in the mere thought of nature's inexhaustible energy of self-perpetuation and transformation, as if the pattern which she describes in her progress through time were in itself a value for the mind irrespective of any possible ethical implications. And sometimes, as I say, Meredith seems to share this feeling of Goethe's.

But ever back of his imaginative formulations lies the suggestion that nature's perpetual life, now that man has come on the scene, involves the ethical "dream of the blossom of Good,"—a moral ideal passed on from generation to generation of human dreamers. The ethical implication is made very clear in "The Thrush in February" (1885), Meredith's crabbed and didactic version of "To a Skylark" or the "Ode to a Nightingale." Like Keats's nightingale, Meredith's thrush is an immortal bird, not individually but by virtue of its deathless song.

> Full lasting is the song, though he,
> The singer, passes: lasting too,
> For souls not lent in usury,
> The rapture of the forward view.
>
> With that I bear my senses fraught
> Till what I am fast shoreward drives.
> They are the vessel of the Thought.
> The vessel splits, the Thought survives.
>
> Nought else are we when sailing brave,
> Save husks to raise and bid it burn.
> Glimpse of its livingness will wave
> A light the senses can discern
>
> Across the river of the death,
> Their close. . . .

In this series of strained and mixed figures Meredith gives us his notion of the humane ideal, the dream of the blossom of Good, passed on by those who die to those who succeed them—his version of Swinburne's lamplit race, in which "each from each takes heart of grace." There is really nothing mystical here. It is merely an imaginative expression of a familiar fact of history, the continuous tradition of civilized ideals. It takes on a more mystical cast in "A Faith on Trial," where Meredith speaks of our dream as—

> The thought sent flying for food;
> Eyeless, but sprung of an aim
> Supernal of Reason, to find
> The great Over-Reason we name
> Beneficence: mind seeking Mind.

Nature, Reason, Purpose

We know perfectly well that Meredith had no faith in a conscious intelligence guiding the universe—that when he speaks of the Mind which our mind seeks, he is referring poetically to what we may call the Intelligibility of the universe. There is in the universe a great Over-Reason in the sense that our mind, in its study of nature, is not perpetually baffled by irrationality, but finds, over a wide range of observation, that the objective facts conform to the patterns of classification brought by the mind. This is, in spite of much metaphysical hair-splitting, the prime assumption of all scientific investigation. The element of rationality in nature itself is shown by Mr. Morris Cohen, for example, to be present in the principle of identity found in the terms of any scientific proposition.[11]

A somewhat less technical account of the essential rationality of the phenomena studied by science was given by the biologist C. Lloyd Morgan in *The Interpretation of Nature*, an expansion of his Lowell Lectures of 1905.

Naturalism, interpreting the material universe in terms of mechanism, formulates an ideal construction in terms of causal antecedence and sequence; in this it believes with a faith which is worthy of our admiration, since it is founded on certain selected aspects of experience. When it is modest, which I fear is not always the case, it confesses that its ideal construction cannot as yet always be applied with confidence to the observed facts, but it claims that wherever and whenever, in the existing state of assured knowledge, it can be so applied it fits the actual facts (new facts as well as old) with much accuracy. Let us accept this position and see what follows. The ideal construction of rationalism is admittedly rational and connected. But when this scheme (which is the product of our rational thought) is applied to the data of sensory experience (which are independent of our rational thought and over which our reason has no control) it is found to fit the given changes of configuration. Hence, just in so far as the connections of the ideal scheme coincide with the sequences of sensory experience, may we assume that these sequences have some underlying connection—something that makes them of such a kind that they can be rationally treated.[12]

Morgan goes on to explain that "science ignores . . . the existence of a 'power or force which actuates the whole machine.' " Science as science does not go beyond the assumption that the sequences of sensory experience have "something that makes them of such a kind that they can be rationally treated."

If this is what Meredith means when he refers to the great Over-Reason, he does not pass beyond the range of ordinary scientific assumptions. And I believe that this is partly what he means. But it must be acknowledged that he has passed beyond the range of science when he chooses to name this Over-Reason Beneficence, to identify it with the Good, or to speak—as he does more than once—of Nature's aim, her design, or goal. It is here that Mr. Stevenson is fully justified in his assertion that Meredith assumes the possession of a "spiritual element" by nature. The notion of nature as beneficent is Meredith's heritage from the poetry of the age of Thomson and Wordsworth. And the chief basis for this interpretation of nature is the poets' assumption that nature is purposive, their adoption of the teleological views of natural theology.

It is quite generally agreed today that science as such knows nothing of purpose in nature, and that such notions are likely to vitiate any experiment or hypothesis in physics or biology. There is certainly no teleological element in strictly scientific accounts of organic evolution. But that science rules out of court the philosophical hypothesis of purpose has been denied by many eminent scientists and philosophers. Lloyd Morgan, whose speculation fell within the period of Meredith's writing, is one scientist who declares his own extra-scientific faith in the purposiveness of the universe. And this element he finds precisely in the causality which, on the scientific side, he wishes to restrict to mechanical terms. His reasoning is too complicated to be reproduced here. I can merely state that it has its basis in his assumption that human behavior may be purposive, and the parallel he draws between the relation of antecedent and consequent in ordinary material causation and their relation in conscious human behavior. One consideration which seems to have weighed heavily with Morgan in adopting this postulate is derived from the evolutionary view of cosmic history, and is such as to have appealed strongly to thinkers of Meredith's generation.

Supposing that we grant that determining purpose is a real factor in human thought, then since that thought is, for naturalism, a product of evolution which is essentially one and continuous, it is only the final term of a purpose that has been operative throughout the whole course of that evolution. It is just because I believe that all that science discloses is the manifestation of a continuous purpose that I believe that the manifestation is itself continuous, and that the origin of life and mind are ideally capable of explanation in terms of antecedence; coexistence and sequence.[13]

I am not competent to judge how much weight may be given to this argument, nor for that matter to the general argument of Morgan for purposiveness in the universe. I presume that fault can be found with his reasoning on the grounds of a more critical psychology and metaphysics. What I wish to indicate is that here, in Meredith's own time, is a physical scientist of eminence who, acknowledges that purposiveness cannot be found in nature by science, yet believes that it may be read into nature by philosophical reasonings not in conflict with any of the findings or assumptions of science. Morgan is particularly concerned to establish firmly the position of naturalism before proceeding to supplement it with his theory of purpose. And he is particularly anxious to show "that a belief in purpose as the causal reality of which nature is the expression is not inconsistent with a full and whole-hearted acceptance of the explanations of naturalism, within their own appropriate sphere." [14] He does not even dream of questioning the cogency of the doctrine of determinism, as it has been so boldly questioned in certain recent speculations by eminent scientists.

The teleology of Morgan is much more guarded and modest than that of the eighteenth-century theologians. He does not suggest that the several organs of the body have been specially given a certain conformation so as to behave in such and such ways; that animals have been purposely designed to conform to such and such conditions of climate, or to serve such and such needs of man. He does not fall into any of the gross absurdities of natural theology. He simply insists that in the causal relation "the antecedent idea of the end contains implicitly the sequent attainment of the end." And similarly in Meredith there is no suggestion of the naïve particularity of Wordsworth's ascriptions of design in "The Excursion." If nature is regarded as purposive, it is in its inherent logic and essence.

It is even possible that Meredith does not regard nature as purposive in the strict sense of Morgan's philosophy, but that his images give that impression because of the inveterate ambiguity of certain words like "end" and "goal." End may be the purpose in view, or it may be the terminus of an action, the point at which it arrives. And so with goal; it may be the winning-point or terminus of a race, or it may be the point or end aimed at. In referring to the goal of nature, Meredith may mean the point towards which it tends, which determines its actual direction, whether or not it may be considered as having a conscious aim. And if in his poems Earth's "goal" is interchangeable with Earth's "thought" or "design," this may perhaps be regarded as merely a poetic fiction involved in the personification of Earth. But it is quite possible that Meredith did not know himself how far he meant these terms to be taken literally—that he never squarely faced the ultimate metaphysical consequences of his thought.

The majority of the passages colored by teleology have reference to nature's well-known business of the reproduction of the species. In "The Thrush in February" he speaks of Earth's "thought to speed the race"; in "With the Persuader," of "the pleasures Earth designed to people and beflower the waste." Such expressions one is likely to find even in popular scientific writing, and pass over as being merely figurative.

In some cases it is not quite clear whether references to nature's aim or goal include merely this matter of physical reproduction or involve the added notion of the intellectual and spiritual accompaniments of the process in human life. In "The Test of Manhood" Meredith discusses the higher manifestations of love which come into being in the course of man's effort to conciliate the opposing claims of Artemis and Aphrodite.

> Then knows he Love, that beckons and controls;
> The star of sky upon his footway cast;
> Then match in him who holds his tempters fast,
> The body's love and mind's, whereof the soul's.
> The Earth her man for woman finds at last,
> To speed the pair unto her goal of goals.

In "The Woods of Westermain," Meredith is explaining that our view of nature depends on whether we interpret her through our mind (or spirit) or merely through our selfish hungers.

> Look with spirit past the sense,
> Spirit shines in permanence.
> That is She, the view of whom
> Is the dust within the tomb,
> Is the inner blush above,
> Look to loathe, or look to love;
> Think her Lump, or know her Flame;
> Dread her scourge, or read her aim;
> Shoot your hungers from their nerve;
> Or, in her example, serve.

In the first of these passages, Earth's "goal of goals," judging from the context, means not merely love itself but the highest possible refinement of love in accordance with our ethical ideals. In the second passage, Earth's "aim" is doubtless, to begin with, the continuance of the human race. But here again the context indicates that Meredith has in mind the continuance of a race in which the faculty of intelligence has developed and flowered in the "dream of the blossom of Good." It is not of course respectable, in science, to ascribe to nature an "aim" in evolving intelligence. The most that science can take into account is the conditions surrounding this evolution and the rôle played by this faculty in the life of the organism possessing it. But the poet, representing man in his practical and emotional interests as well as man the scientist, may properly consider what significance the intelligence has for him, what purpose it serves, or may be made to serve, in the life of himself and the race. If intelligence is seen to be the ultimate product of evolution so far as he is concerned, it is natural enough—it is almost inevitable—for him to look upon it as the "goal" of the process, if only because of the double meaning of the word. As a matter of scientific fact, he may not be justified in asserting that this incident to the process is its aim; but in appraising its significance for man, it is very difficult to distinguish the purpose which it serves for him from the purpose which it may be thought to have in the nature of things.

Morgan quotes an eloquent passage from Kant on that general orderliness in the universe which almost compels one to the assumption of design in the whole.

In our appreciation of this striking passage [Morgan comments], we must, however, bear in mind that Kant regarded the notion of design or purpose as regulative and not constitutive. We can go no further than saying that, as regulative, the notion permits us to regard all connection between phenomena *as if* it was the expression of purpose. It is purposive for us; not necessarily purposive in its inner constitution.[15]

Here, as I understand it, Morgan is falling back on his second line of defense, having given up—at least for the moment—his notion of design as "constitutive." Now, I do not suppose that Meredith was a close enough thinker to have consciously drawn the distinction here made. But perhaps we may give him the benefit of this distinction, and understand the purpose he ascribes to nature in the evolution and continuance of human intelligence as belonging to the category of the "regulative" or *as if*.

And one other distinction we must note. His spiritual ideal is for him strictly speaking an *ideal* rather than an accomplished fact.

It is the "dream" of exceptional spirits here and there in the past and present, and the anticipated dream of a larger number in the future. Like Swinburne, he contemplates the possibility that man may never realize the ideal which the imagination of the poet has set for him. Man is Earth's "great venture," which may or may not turn out well, depending on the stoutness of his heart. And the conclusion of "Earth and Man" shows us the mother doubtfully regarding her offspring.

> Meanwhile on him, her chief
> Expression, her great word of life, looks she;
> Twi-minded of him, as the waxing tree,
> Or dated leaf.

The Utilitarian Test: Survival

But now the question arises in regard to this ethical ideal of Meredith's—this dream of the blossom of Good—where does it come from?—what justification of it can be found in nature? To these questions I do not think that Meredith gives any systematic answer or such as would satisfy the demands of a strict philosophy. But if the implications of his writing were drawn out, I think we should find that his inherent system is utilitarian, and of a type of utilitarianism characteristic of a period of evolutionary assumptions. So far as the individual is concerned, this ethical ideal is such that its realization would lead to the fullest and soundest life for him; and at the same time, it is such as to lead to the greatest common welfare of the race. Such is the natural view of a poet who was the intimate friend of men like Leslie Stephen, Edward Clodd, John Morley, and the contemporary of Herbert Spencer and John Fiske. And his assumption seems to be that this ethical ideal is the natural product of the evolutionary process operating in human society. It is a product of the struggle for existence as it manifests itself among men organized socially. In the last analysis the test of value would appear to be the evolutionary test of survival. But it is sometimes left doubtful whether the poet has in mind the survival of the individual or of the race. Perhaps it is assumed that, in the long run, this comes to the same thing.

The statements which most distinctly echo the evolutionary concepts of the struggle for existence and the survival of the fittest are found in "Earth and Man." Earth is here represented as having started man on his race and as now looking on to see how it will come out.

> For he is in the lists
> Contentious with the elements, whose dower
> First sprang him; for fierce vultures to devour
> If he desists.

Man is inclined to quarrel with these hard conditions of his life, but in reality they are what have given him the strength he has, and have been the means of developing his faculties ("by hunger sharply sped to grasp at weapons ere he learns their use"), and compelling him to make use of intelligence.

> She prompts him to rejoice,
> Yet scares him on the threshold with the shroud.
> He deems her cherishing of her best-endowed
> A wanton's choice.

> Albeit thereof he has found
> Firm roadway between lustfulness and pain;
> Has half transferred the battle to his brain,
> From bloody ground.

There are many references to the education by struggle and pain. In "A Faith on Trial," "Wisdom is won of its fight, the combat incessant." And the "roadway between lustfulness and pain" is a recurring motif throughout many years of writing. In "The Thrush in February" it is made the road to civilization.

> Since Pain and Pleasure on each hand
> Led our wild steps from slimy rock
> To yonder sweeps of gardenland . . .

This is the theme of the entire volume, *A Reading of Life*. Here man's life is represented as a constant struggle between the opposing forces within him personified in the goddesses Artemis and

Aphrodite. Artemis symbolizes the strenuous and self-denying life, Aphrodite the life of self-indulgence, and so they bear a rough parallelism with the Pain and Pleasure, the pain and lustfulness of the earlier poems. Meredith celebrates in turn the virtues of the two goddesses. Each is necessary to the good life. But neither should be followed exclusively. Aphrodite furnishes the milk of life, without which we grow shriveled and perverted. Artemis by herself leads to a vicious asceticism. Aphrodite by herself leads to flabbiness and disintegration. Salvation is to be had only by holding them both in mastery and yielding their dues to each. This makes man the battlefield of the contending forces, and from his struggle to keep them in order comes his strength.

> His force to fly, his will to see,
> His heart enlarged beyond its ribbed domain,
> Had come of many a grip in mastery,
> Which held conjoined the hostile rival twain,
> And of his bosom made him lord.[16]

This ceaseless struggle to maintain his equilibrium not only makes man strong, according to Meredith, but develops in him the vision of the ideal.

> This gift of penetration and embrace,
> His prize from tidal battles lost or won,
> Reveals the scheme to animate his race:
> How that it is a warfare but begun;
> Unending; with no Power to interpose;
> No prayer, save for the strength to keep his ground,
> Heard of the Highest; never battle's close,
> The victory complete and victor crowned:
> Nor solace in defeat, save from that sense
> Of strength well spent, which is the strength renewed.
> In manhood must he find his competence;
> In his clear mind the spiritual food:
> God being there while he his fight maintains;
> Throughout his mind the Master Mind being there,
> While he rejects the suicide despair;
> Accepts the spur of explicable pains;

Obedient to Nature, not her slave:
Her lord, if to her rigid laws he bows;
Her dust, if with his conscience he plays knave,
And bids the Passions on the Pleasures browse. . . .[17]

Meredith's Attitude towards Religion

It will at once be observed that the "God" of this poem, the "Highest," and the "Master Mind," are all figurative expressions for the spiritual ideal towards which man tends. They are understood as similar expressions are understood by Swinburne. This terminology is a concession to the religious sentiment of Meredith's time, and does not mean that he accepts the actual religious tenets. This is shown in the present passage by the lines beginning, "no Power to interpose," and over and over again in Meredith's poems by very specific rejection of current dogmas. Indeed, one of the chief forms taken by the Egoism which he deprecates is the system of beliefs which have their origin in what he calls man's "shrinking nerves." This or some equivalent phrase is found in many of his poems—in "The Thrush in February," "Hard Weather," "The Woods of Westermain," "A Faith on Trial," "Earth and Man"—and in every case it is associated with man's fear of death and his recourse to supernatural beliefs to save him from panic—

> The Legends that sweep her aside, (i.e. Earth)
> Crying loud for an opiate boon,
> To comfort the human want,
> From the bosom of magical skies . . .[18]

In one place Meredith concedes that these Legends are "good ships of morality for our crude developing force." But more often he condemns them as "our sensual dreams" or as the product of "sensation insane at a stroke of the terrified nerve." [19]

There are lengthy passages in "The Woods of Westermain" and "A Faith on Trial" in which this view of supernatural religion is presented. But perhaps it is most distinctly characterized in brief in "Earth and Man." Meredith is speaking of man's terror at the thought of death.

xx

Therefore the wretch inclines
Afresh to the Invisible, who, he saith,
Can raise him high: with vows of living faith
For little signs.

xxi

Some signs he must demand,
Some proofs of slaughtered nature; some prized few,
To satisfy the senses it is true,
And in his hand,

xxii

This miracle which saves
Himself, himself doth from extinction clutch,
By virtue of his worth, contrasting much
With brutes and knaves.

There follows the passage already quoted in which Meredith lists
the moral contributions of man to earth's loveliness, and that in
which his religious aspirations are ascribed to natural impulses. He
would already have realized the ideal and have felt "stern joy"
earth's origin, "but that the senses still usurp the station of their
issue mind." With the aid of his mind he will be able to look on
human history as a record of spiritual progress.

xl

His fables of the Above,
And his gapped readings of the crown and sword,
The hell detested and the heaven adored,
The hate, the love,

xli

The bright wing, the black hoof,
He shall peruse, from Reason not disjoined,
And never unfaith clamouring to be coined
To faith by proof.

Meredith's objection to the "Legends" is (like Swinburne's) that they are weakening to the moral fiber and that they divert attention from the central problem of life, which is to make the most of "reality." In 1906 he wrote to a friend: "Never attempt to dissociate your ideas from the real of life. It weakens the soul; and besides it cannot be done—and again it is a cowardly temporary escape into delusion, clouding the mind." [20] Wisdom is only to be found in hard reality.

> Harsh wisdom gives Earth, no more;
> In one the spur and the curb:
> An answer to thoughts or deeds;
> To the Legends an alien look;
> To the Questions a figure of clay.
> Yet we have but to see and hear,
> Crave we her medical herb.
> For the road to her soul is the Real:
> The root of the growth of man. . . .[21]

Here are strongly indicated Meredith's utilitarianism and his agnosticism. Towards the ultimate philosophical questions (Whence and Whither) he takes the same attitude as Swinburne in his "Hymn of Man." These problems are insoluble, and they lead to the invention of legends that, as Swinburne says, "give not aid." Meredith, in his pragmatic way, calls them "the Questions that sow not nor spin." The true answer to the questions is the work we do.

> Our questions are a mortal brood,
> Our work is everlasting.[22]

Meredith's emphasis on work and his use of the word reality are perhaps echoes of his admired Carlyle. But his teaching has a more democratic and humanitarian cast than Carlyle's. Our work is a part of Reality. And in Meredith the work that counts is work for what Swinburne calls the great Republic, that is, for the common well-being of the race. It is "the numbers" (humanity as a whole) that are "Reality's flower." That is, Meredith teaches that

Nature is concerned not for the individual but for the race (or even for life) as a whole, and in order to have significance in nature's order a man must tame and subject that old worm, Self or Egoism.

The poem in which Meredith is chiefly concerned with the education of the old worm is "The Woods of Westermain." These woods are a symbol of the natural order, or life, and Meredith has particularly in mind here the evolutionary process by which man's education is conducted. It is here that Meredith may have been influenced by Tennyson. The reader will remember how Tennyson takes comfort in the thought that, in the process of evolution, man may—

> Move upward, working out the beast,
> And let the ape and tiger die.

In "The Woods of Westermain" Meredith indicates the mind as the ground upon which the egoistic and altruistic impulses may be reconciled.

> Here the ancient battle ends,
> Joining two astonished friends,
> Who the kiss can give and take
> With more warmth than in that world
> Where the tiger claws the snake. . . .

Meredith's main symbol for the egoistic impulse is "the scaly Dragon-fowl," which represents an imaginative synthesis of the dragon suppressed by the hero of medieval romance and the prehistoric monster brought into prominence by paleontology.

The difference between Tennyson and Meredith is that Tennyson wants the beast in man to die and—so to speak—be resurrected as an angel; whereas Meredith wishes to keep him alive and use him for humane ends. He sees in the egoistic impulse not merely its selfishness and cruelty but also the vital energy by which all good results may be accomplished. One is reminded of the leading role played by self-interest in all utilitarian systems of morality and political economy. The dragon-fowl is a force, and—

Oft has he been riven; slain
Is no force in Westermain.
Wait, and we shall forge him curbs,
Put his fangs to uses, tame . . .

. . . .

Him shall Change, transforming late,
Wonderously renovate.

. . . .

Change, the strongest son of Life,
Has the Spirit here to Life.[23]

The evolutionary process in man means the development of brain from "blood," and spirit from brain; and the problem of natural morality is to keep these three necessary forces united in our feeling and action.

Earth that triad is: she hides
Joy from him who that divides.[24]

Perhaps the final test of a true philosophy of nature is for Meredith the "joy" which he here refers to as made possible by keeping intact the triad, blood and brain and spirit. This at any rate seems to be for him the ultimate "value" arrived at in a realistic interpretation of nature. And here again he is at one with the utilitarian moralist. This "joy" is the "pleasure" whose attainment determines the "utilities" involved in a given line of conduct. And like Mill and Bentham, and the utilitarians generally, he extends the meaning of pleasure to include the gratifications of the social imagination, the gratifications of "benevolence" so eloquently celebrated by Godwin. If you rightly interpret nature, Meredith says,

You a larger self will find:
Sweetest fellowship ensues
With the creatures of your kind.
Ay, and Love, if Love it be
Flaming over *I* and *ME*,
Love meet they who do not shove
Cravings in the van of Love.[25]

It will be remembered that, in Hartley's system, the sensations are built up, by the law of association, into several classes of intellectual pleasures (and pains), including the pleasures of the moral sense, which are the culmination of our spiritual life.

The Religious Emotion in Meredith

It can hardly be questioned that some element of the subjective enters into Meredith's appraisal of nature and life. What Meredith contends for is essentially this. It is possible for men of cultivated imagination to conceive of themselves as part of a life-process which moves in the direction of spirituality, and to sink their personal pains and failures in a sense of the larger life of which they are a part. Some other thinker, with all the same facts in mind, might easily reply: The pains and failures involved in the total life-process so greatly outweigh the spiritual gratifications as to make them virtually negligible. And as to the cultivated imagination which enables a man to rise superior to his own personal sufferings and littleness, whether a man can attain to this depends on the accident of his birth and the conditions of his life—on, for example, his health. It may well be that, in the majority of instances, it is a thing impossible of attainment. And how shall we weigh the miseries of the many against the spiritual felicities of the elect? Such an answer we might expect from a writer of Hardy's temperament, and it would be difficult to arbitrate between the two opposed views except on the basis of the temperament which we individually may possess. At most we can say that the two views are on all fours so far as fact and logic go, and that the choice may well be made of that view which promises to conduce most to a happy life. Such a choice is pragmatic and amounts to an act of faith.

There is no doubt that Meredith's presentation of his view has much of the fervor of religious faith. And we may say that his motives for taking this view are religious in the broadest sense of that word. Impressed with the helplessness and inadequacy of man taken individually, he wishes to associate him with some power or movement greater than himself, so that in this association he may "find a larger self." He is unable to accept the notion of a personal God.

He cannot answer the ultimate questions Whence and Whither. But the laws and operations of nature, involving the development of man's spiritual faculties, provide him with a scheme of things consonant with this sober observation of fact, to which he can, in his helplessness, attach himself, an order to which he can give his enthusiastic allegiance. He is thus enabled to exercise the impulse of loyalty which has been ingrained in his nature by traditional religion and by the necessities of social organization, and yet without giving up his right to determine his actions in accordance with the dictates of reason. He is not called upon for obedience to any code not approved by his intelligence. The ideal of an improved humanity is one—at least admitted in the natural order—to which he can attach himself with all the force of his moral feeling and with the reverence traditionally accorded to divine beings. It is conceived in the democratic spirit of Meredith's time and enforced by the emotion of brotherhood. In this way again, socially speaking, he finds a larger self. He is thus not dependent on what he is in himself for his value and significance, but takes on a dignity by reflection from the race to which he belongs and the cosmic order in which his race has its part.

In pursuing this social ideal man is guided by what he can ascertain of the laws of nature, and thus shapes for himself a more or less rational and consistent code of behavior. The felt need for guidance is one of the most powerful motives leading man to religion. But it is not the most powerful, as it is not the most primitive. The most primitive is, I suppose, the need for protection, the need to feel oneself at home in the world. Man never altogether outgrows his childhood. It is not without significance that in nature-poetry the motherhood of nature corresponds to the fatherhood of God in supernatural religion. Essentially the same emotion reigns in naturalism as in traditional religion. In the want of religion man rallies to nature in order not to feel himself an orphan in the universe.

PART FOUR

DISAPPEARANCE OF THE CONCEPT OF NATURE

Unmeasured power, incredible passion, enormous craft:
    no thought apparent but burns darkly
Smothered with its own smoke in the human brain-vault:
    no thought outside: a certain measure in phenomena:
The fountains of the boiling stars, the flowers on the
    foreland, the ever-returning roses of dawn.

—Robinson Jeffers

Chapter XIX

HARDY

THOMAS HARDY heralds the disappearance from English poetry of nature with a capital N. Even more vigorously than Tennyson he denies the benevolence of nature conceived as the unity of things personified or as the sum of natural laws. And since he has no religious power, like Tennyson's God, to set up in contrast to nature, as a guarantee of happiness for spiritual beings, nothing is left in him of the optimistic *Weltansicht* characteristic of the palmy days of nature-poetry. He has neither the naturalism of Wordsworth nor his religion-inspired optimism.

First and last, in his poems and novels, he has many references to what, as he says in "The Dynasts,"

> Men love to dub Dame Nature—that lay-shape
> They use to hang phenomena upon—
> Whose deftest mothering in fairest spheres
> Is girt about by terms inexorable! [1]

But Hardy seems to be clear enough through all his writing that nature is nothing more than a lay-shape, or convenient personification, and that she is strictly conditioned by "terms inexorable" which have no reference to our human notions of goodness and benevolence.

It is true that, especially in his earliest work, he sometimes refers to nature in a conventional way as the course of things which, if it could be left unopposed by artificial human arrangements, would naturally work for good ends. Thus in the earliest dated of his poems in which he uses the term nature, the sonnet "Discouragement":

To see the Mother, naturing Nature, stand
All racked and wrung by her unfaithful lord,
Her hopes dismayed by his defiling hand,
Her passioned plans for bloom and beauty marred:

Where she would mint a perfect mould, an ill;
Where she would don divinest hues, a stain,
Over her purposed genial hour a chill,
Upon her charm of flawless flesh a blain:

Her loves dependent on a feature's trim,
A whole life's circumstance on hap of birth,
A soul's direction on a body's whim,
Eternal Heaven upon a day of Earth,
Is frost to flower of heroism and worth,
And fosterer of visions ghast and grim.[2]

Nature and the "universal harshness"

It is interesting to find Hardy thus referring to the scholastic
natura naturans ("Naturing Nature"), whose passioned plans are
for bloom and beauty, and echoing Wordsworth's complaint of
"what man has made of man." But even here there are suggestions
of flaws inherent in the natural design itself, such that man could
hardly be expected to be happy in following his impulse—"Her
loves dependent on a feature's trim"—"A soul's direction on a
body's whim." In a poem of the same period, Hardy describes a
meeting of two lovers in a church. The man is going to die; the
woman to comfort him protests that she loves him; but struck by
the tragic irony of the case, she could not prize—

A world conditioned thus, or care for breath
Where Nature such dilemmas could devise.[3]

Another poem records the passing of Hardy's illusions in regard to nature. The glory has departed, and the poet looks back
sadly on the time when he—

Wrought thee (nature) for my pleasure,
Planned thee as a measure
  For expounding
  And resounding
Glad things that men treasure.[4]

"In a Wood" (1887–96) records his discovery that the vegetable world is, like the world of men, a scene of fighting and mutual destruction.[5] In "Nature's Questioning" Hardy quite reverses Wordsworth's procedure. Instead of going to "field, flock and tree" for an answer to his own questions about the universe, he represents these natural creatures as coming to him for light on questions that leave them entirely bewildered.[6] In "The Bullfinches," the poet informs the birds that while "all we creatures" are, according to the faeries of Blackmoor Vale, under the care of "the Mother," yet she never tries to protect us from danger, but works on dreaming and heedless.[7] The indifference of "the Matron," or "the Great Dame," to her children's fate is expressed in "At a Bridal"[8] and "To an Orphan Child";[9] her blindness and unconsciousness in "The Lacking Sense,"[10] "Doom and She,"[11] "The Sleep-Worker."[12]

The altered feeling towards Dame Nature is strikingly exhibited in Hardy by the type of landscape, season, weather, which dominates his poetry and prose. The gentle, the sublime, the luxuriant, the cheerful aspects of nature have largely given place to the severe, the sombre, the meagre. An unusually large number of pieces is devoted to aspects of weather hostile to man and beast—"Winter in Durnover Field,"[13] "A Backward Spring,"[14] "A Wet August,"[15] "If It's Ever Spring Again,"[16] "An Unkindly May,"[17] "Snow in the Suburbs," and a whole series of snow pieces.[18] The romantic and picturesque landscapes of "Alastor" and "Endymion" have given place to "Winter's dregs" and "the land's sharp features." The soaring ecstasy of Shelley's skylark and the "shadows and sunny glimmerings" of Wordsworth's green linnet have given place to—

  An aged thrush, frail, gaunt and small,
  In blast-beruffled plume.[19]

The sombre philosophy of Hardy harmonizes with the prevailing sombreness of nature, whether in his poems or novels. And in the reciprocal action of his philosophy and his temperament, gravely musing and saturnine, it is impossible to say which has more affected the other. At any rate, he appears to have a natural preference in taste for aspects of nature which reflect the modified gloom of his intellectual outlook. His own rationale of this is given in a classic passage in his famous description of Egdon Heath.

Indeed, it is a question if the exclusive reign of this orthodox beauty is not approaching its last quarter. The new Vale of Tempe may be a gaunt waste in Thule: human souls may find themselves in closer and closer harmony with external things wearing a sombreness distasteful to our race when it was young. The time seems near, if it has not actually arrived, when the chastened sublimity of a moor, a sea, or a mountain will be all of nature that is absolutely in keeping with the moods of the more thinking among mankind. And ultimately, to the commonest tourist, spots like Iceland may become what the vineyards and myrtle-gardens of South Europe are to him now; and Heidelberg and Baden be passed unheeded as he hastens from the Alps to the sand-dunes of Scheveningen.[20]

In his novels Hardy's references to personified nature exhibit the same general attitude as in his poems. There is this one apparent exception to be noted, that, where there is opposition between natural impulse and the restrictions of law and convention, natural impulse is assumed to be right. This opposition is strongest in *Tess of the D'Urbervilles* (1891) and *Jude the Obscure* (1894–95). Tess, about to bear her illegitimate child in the rural seclusion of Blackmoor, reproached herself for her guilt, as if she were out of harmony with the world. She was terrified without reason by "a cloud of moral hobgoblins."

Walking among the sleeping birds in the hedges, watching the skipping rabbits on a moonlit warren, or standing under a pheasant-laden bough, she looked upon herself as a figure of Guilt intruding into the haunts of Innocence. But all the while she was making a distinction where there was no difference. Feeling herself in antagonism, she was quite in accord. She had been made to break an accepted social law, but no law known to the environment in which she fancied herself such an anomaly.[21]

So in ironic vein the author refers to her short-lived infant as "that bastard gift of shameless nature who respects not the civil law." When Angel Clare made love to her later at the dairy farm, she felt in honor bound to reject his suit, but this was against nature. "Every see-saw of her breath, every wave of her blood, every pulse singing in her ears, was a voice that joined with Nature in revolt against her scrupulousness." [22] Her very instinct not to tell him of her "past" was "her instinct of self-preservation." [23] After their marriage, when she had at length told him, Clare could not bear to go on living with her "while that [other] man lives, he being your husband in the sight of Nature, if not really." [24] But this appeal to nature seems to the author perverse; he suggests on the contrary: "Some might risk the odd paradox that with more animalism he would have been the nobler man."

In *Jude* there is a considerable number of references to nature as running counter to the religious restrictions upon the sex-impulse. Gibbon is quoted on "insulted nature" in reference to the excessive chastity of the early saints.[25] Sue's sticking to her husband, whom she loathes, is by Jude ruled to be wrong, "speaking from experience and unbiassed nature." [26] Of her marriage to himself, Jude declares, "Nature's own marriage it is, unquestionably!" But though they were legally married, Sue, taking the high ecclesiastical point of view, protests that this is not "Heaven's marriage." In the eyes of God she considers herself still married to her first husband.[27] And in this whole debate there is no doubt that Hardy's sympathy is on the side of nature as against the notions of conventional religion. Jude reflects as follows on his frustrated career:

Strange that his first aspiration—towards academical proficiency— had been checked by a woman, and that his second aspiration—towards apostleship—had also been checked by a woman. "Is it," he said, "that the women are to blame; or is it the artificial system of things, under which the normal sex-impulses are turned into devilish domestic gins and springes to noose and hold back those who want to progress?" [28]

And Sue, before she turns religious, reflects thus upon her own dilemma: "It is none of the tragedies of love that's love's usual tragedy in civilized life, but a tragedy artificially manufactured for people who in a natural state would find relief in parting!" [29]

But while Hardy recognizes, like every one else, the distress caused when natural impulse is balked by artificial codes of conduct, none realizes more acutely than he that nature herself is full of cruelty. Social codes are themselves a part of nature; and, beyond all that can be controlled by social codes, are the infinitely complicated lines of circumstance which tend to make impossible the attainment of happiness by any created being.

In the ill-judged execution of the well-judged plan of things, the call seldom produces the comer, the man to love rarely coincides with the hour for loving. Nature does not often say "See!" to a poor creature at a time when seeing can lead to happy doing; or reply "Here!" to a body's cry of "Where?" till the hide-and-seek has become an irksome, outworn game.[30]

Men's harshnesses towards women are but an outgrowth of "the universal harshness . . . the harshness of the position towards the temperament, of the means towards the aims, of to-day towards yesterday, of hereafter towards to-day." [31] Thus in the interplay of human desire and aspiration with the circumstances under which they are to be gratified, there is an inherent want of adjustment which, in many different ways, determines their frustration and disappointment.

The very natural impulses which Hardy champions against the conventions of society bring misery with them. Referring to the half-dozen Durbeyfield children condemned by nature to sail along in one ship with their heedless parents, Hardy remarks:

Some people would like to know whence the poet whose philosophy is in these days deemed as profound and trustworthy as his song is sweet and pure, gets his authority for speaking of "Nature's holy plan." [32]

Referring to the hopeless passion of the dairy maids for Clare, he speaks of "cruel Nature's law." [33] Tess, after making her confession to Clare, still looked absolutely pure, "Nature, in her fantastic trickery, had set such a seal of girlishness upon [her] countenance." [34]

In *Jude* the principal characters are unanimous in finding nature indifferent or hostile to man. Jude often felt "the scorn of Nature for man's finer emotions, and her lack of interest in his aspirations." [35] Phillotson, reflecting on the misery of Sue, declares: "Cruelty is the law pervading all nature and society; and we can't get out of it if we would!" [36] Sue finds that "Nature's law [is] mutual butchery." [37] And the author in his own person, referring to the weakness of women as a sex, declares that they "by no possible exertion of their willing hearts and abilities could be made strong while the inexorable laws of nature remain what they are." [38] Above all, the young Jude is revolted by his realization that, in nature's plan, the lower animals must be the victims of man, through that "flaw in the terrestrial scheme, by which what was good for God's birds was bad for God's gardener." [39]

This idea of a flaw in the terrestrial scheme is everywhere present in Hardy's writing. Thus in *The Return of the Native* (1878), he speaks of the "long line of disillusive centuries" which have permanently displaced the cheerful Hellenic idea of life. "That old-fashioned revelling in the general situation grows less and less possible as we uncover the defects of natural laws, and see the quandary that man is in by their operation." [40]

Other Formulations: God, Chance, Fate

Nature is but one of many alternative terms used by Hardy for designating the unity of process and the directing power in the world. Fate and destiny are words found more often in the mouths of the characters, who reflect the superstitious philosophy of untrained country-people. God and providence are terms they take up from their religious culture. Chance, hap, circumstance are words suggestive of the seeming capriciousness of events, their irrelevance to human aims and direction. None of these terms is to be regarded as indicating that Hardy seriously adhered to the philosophy implied in its use. At no period of his writing did Hardy share the religious views of his characters, and God or the gods, providence, chance, fate, must all be taken in a figurative and dramatic sense, as reflecting the point of view of human beings caught in a web too large and complicated for mortal understanding.

That Hardy was a scientific determinist in his interpretation of how things come about is evident from many passages in the novels. Thus, in *The Mayor of Casterbridge* (1886), he comments as follows on the seeming element of chance in a certain act of Lucetta, involving a striking coincidence.

That she had chosen for her afternoon walk the road along which she had returned to Casterbridge three hours earlier in a carriage was curious—if anything should be called curious in concatenations of phenomena wherein each is known to have its accounting cause.[41]

Again, he comments on Henchard's superstitious notion of the intervention of a sinister intelligence.

Henchard, like all his kind, was superstitious, and he could not help thinking that the concatenation of events this evening had produced was the scheme of some sinister intelligence bent on punishing him. Yet they had developed naturally.[42]

His explanation of how these events came about is immediately followed by reference to the "mockery" of the case and "this ironical sequence of things"; and so we know that the mockery and the irony are not in nature, but simply in the relation of certain natural events to man's intentions, as seen from the point of view of the man himself. So in *The Woodlanders* (1887) a certain fateful letter of Marty South is called "the tiny instrument of a cause deep in nature."[43] Of men's attitude towards a causality which they cannot trace Hardy speaks in the same book.

The petulance that relatives show towards each other is in truth directed against that intangible Causality which has shaped the situation no less for the offenders than the offended, but is too elusive to be discerned and cornered by poor humanity in irritated mood.[44]

In *Tess*, again, Hardy speaks of Tess and Clare balanced on the edge of passion. "All the while they were none the less converging, under the force of irresistible law, as surely as two streams in one vale."[45]

That the doings of individuals form a part of the entire pattern of cause and effect which makes up the universe is a point often emphasized.

Hardly anything could be more isolated or more self-contained than the lives of these two walking here in the lonely antelucan hour, when gray shades, material and mental, are so very gray. And yet, looked at in a certain way, their lonely courses formed no detached design at all, but were part of the pattern in the great web of human doings then weaving in both hemispheres, from the White Sea to Cape Horn.[46]

In this web, since all happens naturally and according to law, nothing comes about capriciously. But in the relation between outward circumstances and the needs and desires of men, there is infinite possibility for what men call accident, chance, fate, destiny, and the irony of circumstances that throw jeering reflections on one another.

That Knight should have been thus constituted: that Elfride's second lover should not have been one of the great mass of bustling mankind . . . was the chance of things. That her throbbing, self-confounding, indiscreet heart should have to defend itself unaided against the keen scrutiny and logical power which Knight . . . would sooner or later be sure to exercise against her, was her misfortune. A miserable incongruity was apparent in the circumstance of a strong mind practising its unerring archery upon a heart which the owner of that mind loved better than his own.[47] . . . Circumstance has, as usual, overpowered her purposes—fragile and delicate as she—liable to be overthrown in a moment by the coarse elements of accident.[48] . . . That waggery of fate which started Clive as a writing clerk, Gay as a linendraper, Keats as a surgeon, and a thousand others in a thousand other odd ways, banished the wild and ascetic heath lad to a trade whose sole concern was with the especial symbols of self-indulgence and vainglory.[49] . . . The next slight touch in the shaping of Clym's destiny occurred a few days after.[50] . . . And then, as a hoop by gentle knocks on this side and on that is made to travel in specific directions, the little touches of circumstance in the life of this young girl shaped the curves of her career.[51] . . . Thus these people with converging destinies went along the road together.[52] . . . Out of which maladroit delay sprang anxieties, disappointments, shocks, catastrophes—and what was called a strange destiny.[53]

By fate or destiny Hardy means the course of a man's life as determined by all the antecedent circumstances in the chain of causality. There is nothing here of the Greek religious conception of fate, or of a destiny or nemesis having us individually in mind.

Fate is not arbitrary, being only another name for natural causality. The seeming arbitrariness of fate is an illusion of men; it overrules our will because, in its large and impersonal working, it has no reference to our will. An accident is a mere crossing of two sets of circumstances, an intersection of two orbits, which registers as an interference. Circumstances are the separate moments in the chain of causation. Circumstance is another name for the conditions under which we carry on our lives—most noted when unfavorable.

Throughout Hardy's work the emphasis is thrown, both by the author and by the characters of his fiction, on those elements in circumstance which are unfavorable to men's hopes.

"There's a back'ard current in the world, and we must do our utmost to advance in order just to bide where we be." [54] . . . "Having found man's life to be a wretchedly conceived scheme, I renounce it." [55] . . . A fancy some people hold, when in a bitter mood, is that inexorable circumstance only tries to prevent what intelligence attempts.[56] . . . So the two forces were at work here as everywhere, the inherent will to enjoy, and the circumstantial will against enjoyment.[57] . . . "There is something external to us which says, 'You shan't!' First it said, 'You shan't learn!' Then it said, 'You shan't labor!' Now it says, 'You shan't love!' " [58]

Too numerous to mention are the instances in the poems of this hostility of circumstance to men's desires and aspirations. Whole volumes are devoted to its exemplification, as indicated by the titles, *Satires of Circumstance, Time's Laughingstocks.* The upshot of volumes of poems is stated in general terms in "Yell'ham-Wood's Story." Yell'ham-Wood is one of Hardy's many impersonations of nature, and the general lesson of nature as stated by the voice of this forest is as follows:

> It says that Life would signify
>   A thwarted purposing:
> That we come to live, and are called to die.
>   Yes, that's the thing
>   In fall, in spring,
>   That Yell'ham says:—
> "Life offers—to deny!" [59]

Hardy does not believe in any God, or gods, or providence having regard for men or other creatures. But he recognizes the anthropomorphic disposition to invent gods and blame them for the ills of life. He expressly declares that his characters are mistaken in doing so; and when he himself uses these terms, it is clear that it is ironically and satirically.

"Providence, whom I had just thanked, seemed a mocking tormentor laughing at me." [60] . . . Even then Boldwood did not recognize that the impersonator of Heaven's persistent irony towards him, who had once before broken in upon his bliss, scourged him, and snatched his delight away, had come to do these things a second time.[61] . . . But Providence is nothing if not coquettish; and no sooner had Eustacia formed this resolve than the opportunity came which, while sought, had been entirely withholden.[62] . . . Yet, instead of blaming herself for the issue she laid the fault upon the shoulders of some indistinct, colossal Prince of the World, who had framed her situation and ruled her lot.[63] . . . But the ingenious machinery contrived by the Gods for reducing human possibilities of amelioration to a minimum—which arranges that wisdom to do shall come *pari passu* with the departure of zest for doing—stood in the way of all that.[64] . . . This consciousness upon which he had intruded was the single opportunity of existence ever vouchsafed to Tess by an unsympathetic First Cause [65] . . . "Justice" was done, and the President of the Immortals (in Æschylean phrase) had ended his sport with Tess.[66]

The Immanent Will

The final term chosen by Hardy for designating the unity and the directing power of the universe is one taken, in all probability, from Schopenhauer,—the Immanent Will. Mr. Ernest Brennecke, in *Thomas Hardy's Universe*, has drawn many parallels between Hardy's philosophy in *The Dynasts* and that of Schopenhauer in *Die Welt als Wille und Vorstellung*; and he and Mr. Stevenson have traced through the poems the gradual replacement of Chance, Circumstance, God, Providence, Nature, and other unsatisfactory terms, by the more satisfactory—but still admittedly tentative and groping term—the Immanent Will. Hardy's characterization of the Immanent Will in *The Dynasts*—in many ways identical with his earlier characterization of God in the poems—will make clear why it was that the sometimes alternative term nature had ceased to have for him the cheerful and mystical significance it had for poets like Wordsworth and Shelley and later for poets like Emerson, Whitman, Swinburne and Meredith—had altogether ceased indeed to be a term to conjure with.

Mr. Brennecke is at some pains to make us understand that Schopenhauer's Will—and more dubiously, Hardy's—implies an idealistic metaphysic. The term will, taken from man's conscious and purposive action, is extended to cover all operations of the organic and inorganic world. But it amounts to no more than an urge in things which gives them the direction and the form which they have. The idealism is found altogether in the formative, the organizing character of this urge, which follows certain patterns vaguely suggestive of the world-patterns of Aristotle and Plato. Whatever may be the case with Hardy, Schopenhauer had a growing aversion to materialistic systems as incapable of explaining the organizing and formative character of this power. The behavior of the universe as a whole and in all its parts is the expression of an inherent, and as we might say, protoplasmic nature, an inner urge, and not merely the result of impulsion from without. In this sense the system of Schopenhauer, and of Hardy after him, is idealistic.

But the idealism of Schopenhauer and Hardy, as I understand it, is distinguished from most idealistic systems by the fact that it does not imply rationality. Hardy, at any rate, does not attribute intelligence to the universal Will, or assume the existence of any intelligent supreme being lying back of or explaining the Will. Intelligence is a late and secondary development, to a large extent a delusion, and at any rate following upon the urge and action of the Will. Consequently the teleology of these men is sharply distinguished from that of most idealists, and in particular from that of writers like Cudworth and the eighteenth-century natural theologians. The Will follows unconsciously a plan inherent in itself, and the universe is purposive in that in every detail it carries out the original plan. But that this original plan implies the special adjustment of each part, of each organ and each organism, to the rôle it is to play in the universe, is certainly not remotely suggested in Hardy's writing; there is no suggestion that living creatures, including man, were destined to happiness under this plan; that it is benevolent in its particular dispositions; or that—as in the favorite

eighteenth-century systems, in Shaftesbury, Pope, Wordsworth—
the particular dispositions, however unsatisfactory by themselves,
may be conceived of as building up in a whole which is harmonious
and good taken altogether.

The word Will in Hardy and Schopenhauer carries for the most
part implications quite the contrary of what it carries for religious
thinkers like Coleridge. It is not the expression of intelligent
thought, of "spirit," but of an unconscious impulse, better described in terms of animal instinct, vegetable irritability, and the in-
sensitive—though formal—operations of inorganic matter, in the
formation of crystals, the phenomena of electricity, etc. The impersonal and automatic working of this Will leaves no place for
freedom in the action of men, so that the system is thoroughly
unmoral and deterministic or necessarian.

Thus the Spirit of the Years describes the working of the will
in human history.

> So the Will heaves through Space, and moulds the times,
> With mortals for Its fingers! We shall see
> Again men's passions, virtues, visions, crimes,
>   Obey resistlessly
> The purposive, unmotived, dominant Thing
> Which sways in brooding dark their wayfaring! [67]

The unconsciousness of the Will is again stated thus:

> In that immense unweeting Mind is shown
> One far above forethinking; purposive,
> Yet superconscious; a Clairvoyancy
> That knows not what It knows, yet works therewith.[68]

Again, of the Immanent Will:

> It works unconsciously, as heretofore,
> Eternal artistries in Circumstance,
> Whose patterns, wrought by rapt æsthetic rote,
> Seem in themselves Its single listless aim,
> And not their consequence.[69]

There is something to remind us of Cudworth's Plastic Nature in this Immanent Will, which works purposively and esthetically but without consciousness of what it does, proceeds like a thinking being but without thought—

> Which thinking on, yet weighing not Its thought,
> Unchecks Its clock-like laws.[70]

But in Cudworth the Plastic Nature is purposive and organizing in character by virtue of the Supreme Intelligence whose agent it is, whereas in Hardy the unconscious and unintelligent Will is the supreme principle of the universe, and—as the Spirit of the Years declares:

> In the Foretime, even to the germ of Being,
> Nothing appears of shape to indicate
> That cognizance has marshalled things terrene,
> Or will (such is my thinking) in my span.
> Better they show that, like a knitter drowsed,
> Whose fingers play in skilled unmindfulness,
> The Will has woven with an absent heed
> Since life first was; and ever will so weave.[71]

The mechanism of this Will and of the human beings and other forms of vitalized matter which form a part of it is figured, poetically, in terms derived from anatomy, as a gigantic brain, more suggestive of materialistic science, it seems to me, than of the vague metaphysical idealism which Mr. Brennecke ascribes to Hardy. It is "a seeming transparency . . . exhibiting as one organism the anatomy of life and movement in all humanity and vitalized matter included in the display." Strange waves pass back and forth along gossamer-like threads.

> These are the Prime Volitions,—fibrils, veins,
> Will-tissues, nerves, and pulses of the Cause,
> That heave throughout the Earth's compositure.
> Their sum is like the lobule of a Brain
> Evolving always that it wots not of;

A Brain whose whole connotes the Everywhere,
And whose procedure may not be discerned
By phantom eyes like ours; the while unguessed
Of those it stirs, who (even as ye do) dream
Their motions free, their orderings supreme . . .[72]

Throughout *The Dynasts* terms are used for designating this Will which emphasize the deterministic character of its action, making mere puppets of men, and its want of consciousness and intelligence. "It is," Mr. Brennecke notes, "the Great Necessitator, the Eternal Urger, the High Influence that sways the English realm with all its homuncules, the Master-Hand that plays the game alone, the Back of Things that hauls the halyards of the world.' " [73] In the After Scene, with which the drama closes, it is called the Great Foresightless, the Inadvertent Mind, and—

> . . . the dreaming, dark, dumb thing
> That turns the handle of this idle show.

It is expressly stated here, and elsewhere, that this Will, being foresightless and inadvertent, has no concern with the sufferings of mortals—though obviously it is responsible for them—and that the entire universe, like the small part of it exhibited in this epic of the Napoleonic wars, is, so far as one can make out by reason, "inutile all." The only hope for souls who would like to think well of the universe is that, as man in the course of the ages has evolved consciousness, so conceivably might the supreme will, with happy results for the creation—

> Consciousness the Will informing, till It fashion all things fair!

This mitigating concession, made virtually without preparation at the end of a uniformly hopeless chronicle, is not to be regarded seriously as an element in Hardy's philosophy. It is radically inconsistent with the general concept of the Immanent Will, which expressly rules out the notion of a spirit external to the universe, being conceived as the mere principle of action inherent in the behavior of things. Altogether the Immanent Will is not a concept to arouse the enthusiasm of mortals like the Christian God or the nature of eighteenth-century poetry. It is nothing more than a metaphysical convenience,—a term for expressing the unity and pattern of existing things.

Evolution

The Darwinian theory of evolution was from the beginning assumed by Hardy, and it underlies all his general speculation. As he wrote in 1876, "the evolution of species seems but a minute and obvious process" in the general world-movement, in which "all things merge into one another—good into evil, generosity into justice, religion into politics, the years into the ages, the world into the universe." [74] But the concept of evolution gave him none of the comfort that it did Meredith—quite the contrary. Mr. Stevenson remarks that certain of Hardy's poems have the air of direct rebuttals to Meredith's hopeful evolutionary teaching. Hardy is, for the most part, doubtful of the possibility of any man's contributing to the progress of the race.[75] Heredity, he finds, works "according to mechanical principles, beyond the control of human will." [76] Nature shows no intention of improving the race by the process of reproduction.[77] Hardy fails to find any general tendency to good in the world.[78] In "Nature's Questioning," [79] field, pool, and tree interrogate the poet on the ruling power of the world, reviewing the various alternatives. Is it some "vast Imbecility," good at building but "impotent to tend"; or an "Automaton unconscious of our pains"; or is there some "high Plan as yet not understood," which involves so much suffering as incident to its operation?

The evolution of thought and sensibility, on which Meredith relies for his hopeful view of man's destiny, and for his entire ethical system, is with Hardy the main evidence of the blundering ineptitude of nature or God. It has occasioned untold suffering in both man and the lower animals. This view is more than once expressed by Hardy in his notebooks at different periods.

Law has produced in man a child who cannot but constantly reproach its parent for doing much and yet not all, and constantly say

to such parent that it would have been better never to have begun
doing than to have *over*done so indecisively; that is, than to have created so far beyond all apparent first intention (on the emotional side)
without mending matters by a second intention and execution, to
eliminate the evils of the blunder of overdoing. The emotions have no
place in a world of defect, and it is a cruel injustice that they should
have developed in it.[80] . . . A woeful fact—that the human race is too
extremely developed for its corporeal conditions, the nerves being
evolved to an activity abnormal in such an environment. Even the
higher animals are in excess in this respect. It may be questioned if Nature, or what we call Nature, so far back as when she crossed the line
from invertebrates to vertebrates, did not exceed her mission. This
planet does not supply the material for happiness to higher existences.
Other planets may, though one can hardly see how.[81]

Hardy's most impressive statement of this view in poetry is in
"The Mother Mourns." [82] Here for the nonce the poet assumes,
what he for the most part denies, that Mother Nature is aware of
the sufferings of her creatures, and he represents her as regretting
her evolutionary experiment, which has given man intelligence
capable of judging and condemning her plan.

> "I had not proposed me a Creature
>   (She soughed) so excelling
> All else of my kingdom in compass
>   And brightness of brain
>
> "As to read my defects with a god-glance,
>   Uncover each vestige
> Of old inadvertence, annunciate
>   Each flaw and each stain
>
>   . . . .
>
> "Why loosened I olden control here
>   To mechanize skywards,
> Undeeming great scope could outshape in
>   A globe of such grain?
>
> "Man's mountings of mind-sight I checked not,
>   Till range of his vision
> Has topped my intent, and found blemish
>   Throughout my domain.

"He holds as inept his own soul-shell—
    My deftest achievement—
Contemns me for fitful inventions
    Ill-timed and inane:

"No more sees my sun as a Sanct-shape,
    My moon as the Night-queen,
My stars as august and sublime ones
    That influences rain:

"Reckons gross and ignoble my teaching,
    Immoral my story,
My love-lights a lure, that my species
    May gather and gain."

This poem, in which the evolution of the mind is represented as
a sheer blunder, is, as Mr. Stevenson suggests, a blasting reply to
Meredith's "Earth and Man." In this one poem, for dramatic purposes, nature is figured as a conscious and planning goddess. But,
in the group of poems printed with it in *Poems of the Past and
Present* ("The Lacking Sense," "Doom and She," "The Sleep-
Worker," "The Bullfinches," "God-Forgotten," "The Bedridden
Peasant to an Unknowing God"), Mother Nature, or the alternative God, is shown as blind and dumb, a mere somnambulist. This
is the price which Hardy pays—like Mill before him—for his supposition that the ruling power is not the deliberate planner of
mortal miseries. The ruler of the universe, as they both hold, cannot be benevolent and omniscient at the same time.

Strictly speaking, in Hardy, the ruling power is neither omniscient nor benevolent. It is blind and indifferent. The Immanent
Will, or Fundamental Energy, is no more than the sum total of
all the activity in the universe. In the development of man's intelligence it works by natural selection, which is carried out by mere
"random sequence" of events.

The cognizance ye mourn, Life's doom to feel,
If I report it meetly, came unmeant,
Emerging with blind gropes from impercipience
By random sequence—luckless, tragic Chance,

If ye will call it so. 'Twas needed not
In the economy of Vitality,
Which might have ever kept a sealed cognition
As doth the Will Itself.[83]

It will be observed what an extremely attenuated version of teleology it is that will consist with this Epicurean-Lucretian notion of
luckless Chance as the conductor of evolution. Nothing remains
of purposiveness but the vague esthetic recognition of unity and
pattern in things. Conscious design, providence, harmony, benevolence have all evaporated from the concept of nature. As a subject for poetic exaltation it no longer has any value; and inevitably
it goes into the discard, together with concepts more strictly
theological. Thomas Hardy sounds the death-knell of the old
nature-poetry.

CHAPTER XX

VICTORIAN AFTERGLOW

DURING the last fifty years there has been little distinguished poetry
in the English language, outside of Hardy's, in which the concept
of nature has held an important place. There have, however, been
a considerable number of poets in whom the theory of evolution
has stirred speculations on the place of man in nature, and others
in whom, with no explicit reference to evolution, there are more
or less vague echoes of certain notes of the great Victorians and
Romantics. For the most part these poets lack the robustness of
Wordsworth, Shelley, Tennyson and Meredith, either in thought
or imagination. They tend, in their want of clear faith, to take
refuge in a kind of soft platonism. A more or less vaguely conceived Beauty comes more and more to take the place of the full-
bodied nature that formerly held sway. It is clear that the sun has
gone down and that only a pinkish afterglow lingers in the sky.

"The Ascent of Man"

Research will doubtless bring to light many references to evolution in poets of second- and third-rate standing within the period in
question. One such is Mathilde Blind, whose *Ascent of Man* was
published in 1889, and again, with an introduction by the great
evolutionist, Alfred Russell Wallace, in 1899. This poet gives a
conscientious account of the emergence, during geologic ages, of
vegetable and animal life, first as a pulse stirring in "the plastic
slime" and then as a force building itself up in myriad forms. She
describes the colossal and amorphous creatures of the primeval
ocean, and the ruthless struggle for existence throughout the animal
world, with a "pessimistic view of the pain and misery thus arising"

522

(according to Wallace) "entirely opposed to that of Darwin and the present writer"! She makes due reference to the advantage given to the anthropoid apes by the possession of "the wonder-working hand"; and shows how man's "fight for life"—

> Sharpens his senses, till within
>   The twilight mazes of his brain,
> Like embryos within the womb,
> Thought pushes feelers through the gloom.[1]

She traces the rise of civilization, and gives a review of history, in which the wars of greed and faith are the dominating and depressing feature.

In the section of her poem entitled "The Leading of Sorrow," the poet visits, under the guidance of a veiled figure, the underseas world, the jungle world, and the world of men. In all these worlds, after a first impression of the luxuriant beauty of life, the frightfulness of the struggle for existence comes to the fore. Finally, the poet asks to be taken to "the pale of some imperial city, where the law rules starlike o'er man's life." But even here, while there is law and order, wealth and luxury, she finds that they are accompanied by the most intense misery—by poverty, crime, and hypocrisy in the social order; and she begs to be taken back to the cruel but natural world of the beasts.

> Better far the plain, carnivorous fashion
>   Which is practised in the lion's den.

She then falls into a state of merciful unconsciousness, from which she wakes to a vision of the starry heavens. A voice comes to her from the stars, challengingly:

> Wilt thou judge me, wilt thou curse me, Creature
>   Whom I raised up from the Ocean slime?

This voice proceeds to review the evolutionary process, with an emphasis on its splendid and marvelous character, and a final appeal to Man, the "youngest Child" of the creation, to justify the whole process by making prevail the higher elements in his nature.

> Oh, redeem me from my tiger rages,
>   Reptile greed, and foul hyaena lust;
> With the hero's deeds, the thoughts of sages,
>   Sow and fructify this passive dust . . .

Finally the veiled figure which has guided the poet in her search reveals itself as indeed the appropriate guide to man in his pilgrimage.

> It was Love himself, Love re-arisen
>   With the Eternal shining through his eyes.

Thus in Mathilde Blind we have a very honest facing of the implications of evolution—more brave and honest than the scientist Wallace could show. As in Hardy's "The Mother Mourns," we have nature replying rather woefully to the indignant challenge of her creature man; but here in a much more pious, hopeful and hortatory tone. As in Meredith, we have God, or the godlike in man, represented as the goal of the natural process rather than its original; and as dependent on the efforts of man for his coming to birth. But the means by which this consummation is to be brought about are left entirely vague; there is no suggestion, such as Meredith offers, as to how this spiritual evolution is related to the natural process of which it is a part. Victorian faith in evolution here displays itself in a brave but attenuated form.

Robert Bridges

It is Robert Bridges who has the most to say of nature, and who, most persistently, develops the Meredithian view of the evolution of man's spiritual life out of natural instinct itself. Bridges was a trained physician; his philosophical poems are full of scientific lore; they are written with a mild, genial idiosyncrasy of thought and expression which makes them highly interesting reading. But these *Poems in Classical Prosody* and *The Testament of Beauty* (likewise in classical metres)—in which his theories are mainly developed—are poetry in form only—and that outlandish and irritating; the complacent Toryism of his sentiment gives him in our day a curiously antediluvian air; and—what is more important for our purpose—he has failed to make a more than plausible synthesis of his evolutionary positivism and his religious-platonic cult of Eternal Essences.

As for his evolutionary positivism, this is displayed at length in the first and second of the *Poems in Classical Prosody*. The main problem here is to reconcile the goodness of nature with man's adverse judgments on her; and his argument might seem like an answer to Hardy's in "The Mother Mourns." The point is, simply, that man's moral ideal, by virtue of which he condemns so much in nature, is itself born of her and to be credited to her; it is a result of the process of natural selection.

> And I see man's discontent as witness asserting
> His moral idēal, that, born of Nature, is heir to
> Her children's titles, which nought may cancel or impugn;
> Not wer' of all her works man least, but ranking among them
> Highly or ev'n as best, he wrongs himself to imagine
> His soul foe to her aim, or from her sanction an outlaw.[2]
>
> . . . .
>
> My parable may serve. What wisdom man hath attain'd to
> Came to him of Nature's goodwill throu' tardy selection:
> Should her teaching accuse herself and her method impugn,
> I may share with her the reproach of approving as artist
> Far other idēals than what seem needful in action.[3]

More explicit in its reference to the means by which man's higher nature has been developed is "To Robert Burns" in *Later Poems*. Here Bridges states more clearly than Wordsworth the doctrine of the ministry of pleasure.

> For Nature did not idly spend
> Pleasure: she ruled it should attend
> On every act that doth amend
>   Our life's condition:
> 'Tis therefore not well-being's end,
>   But its fruition.

Pleasures attend the fulfilment of instinct, and Bridges tells us quite categorically what the instincts are, and which one of them has most conduced to the development of the soul in man.

But Instinct in the beasts that live
Is of three kinds; (Nature did give
To man three shakings in her sieve)—
    The first is Racial,
The second Self-preservative,
    The third is Social.

Without the first no race could be,
So 'tis the strongest of the three;
Nay, of such forceful tyranny
    'Tis hard to attune it,
Because 'twas never made to agree
    To serve the unit.

Art will not picture it, its name
In common talk is utter shame:
And yet hath Reason learn'd to tame
    Its conflagration
Into a sacramental flame
    Of consecration.

Those hundred thousand years, ah me!
Of budding soul! What slow degree,
With aim so dim, so true! We see,
    Now that we know them,
Our humble cave-folk ancestry,
    How much we owe them . . .

The reader can fancy how the Victorian poet applies the moral to Robert Burns, and with what graceful openmindedness he pronounces on the erring Scotch poet his "friendly sentence."

But it is not till "The Testament of Love" (1929) that Bridges formally attacks his problem on all fronts; and his argument comes with a strange effect of archaism in the age of Aldous Huxley and T. S. Eliot. Since Mr. Bridges left express instructions that the reproduction of extracts from this poem was not to be allowed, the best I can do is to give a bald abstract of his discussion. In his introduction he declares, like any Romantic, his faith in the order of nature and its goodness. He has no hesitation in ascribing purpose to nature like a seventeenth-century theologian. He then proceeds to state, with all the vigor of a Meredith, and with far more detail of specification, that all man's higher faculties and intellectual constructions—emotion, imagination, ethics, art, the logic of science, philosophical dialectic, mathematics—have been evolved from inanimate nature. Even man's independent will cannot "separate him off from the impercipient." And conscience is "a natural flower-bud on its vigorous plant specialized to a function."

The second book treats of "selfhood,"—which corresponds to the Self-preservative Instinct of the Burns poem. In this book, which is otherwise largely devoted to a defense of war as based in natural instinct and full of benefits to the spirit, Bridges shows how the self-preservative impulse gives rise to parental instinct, which is the main root of man's "purest affection and of all compassion." In the third book he takes up "Breed," which corresponds to the dominant Racial Instinct. This he regards as, even more than Selfhood, the root of man's spiritual life.

In the fourth book, entitled "Ethick," Bridges traces moral obligation in man back to the "determin'd habit of electrons," with which it is essentially identical, except that in man Necessity has become "conscient." He considers how the positive Ought of lower orders of nature is transformed into the Ought Not of man's moral code, by which at times he is obliged to "oppose the bidding of instinct." He shows that religion and duty are one, and that consequently the compulsions of necessity lead by natural stages to identification of self with God.

Thus Bridges arrives, in the end, at a kind of mystical platonic deism suggestive of some of the eighteenth-century nature-poets. There is often a vagueness in his definitions that enables him to pass so airily from the natural to the spiritual. This is felt particularly in his rather confused concept of beauty, which in man becomes spiritualized, "as in its primal essence it must be conceived." One feels that it is the force of his religious sentiment that makes him wish to graft on to Meredith's genetic, positivistic and utilitarian account of the spirit, the platonic notion of Eternal Essences. These platonic essences he makes equivalent, in the popular manner, with "ideas"; and such "innate" ideas are hard to reconcile with evolutionism.

In the second book, he definitely adopts the platonic system, which he interprets in the modern "idealistic" way as implying that "all existence is expression of Mind." Plato's doctrine, he says, flourishes proudly in the schools because "the absurdity of indefinable forms is less than the denial of existence to thought." He thinks it necessary, however, to find a more unassailable term to take the place of the platonic Ideas, and in so doing introduces a vicious ambiguity into his thought. These Ideas he renames Influences; they are "supreme efficient causes of the thoughts of men." Of all these "occult influences" the most important and fundamental is Beauty, which leads man straight to the wisdom of God.

It is a far cry from a natural influence, which may be observed and studied in action, to an eternal Essence, an abstract entity little subject to empirical control, of the sort that flourishes so rankly in the garden of poetical theology. Something might have been done with a definition of beauty based in observable pleasure and pain; this might have been carried over with some plausibility, in the utilitarian manner, into the realm of social life and social morality. But Bridges abandoned too readily the fruitful concept of pleasure to soar on the filmy wings of an elusive and obliging beauty. It is thus that his scientific intentions were betrayed by the loyalty he felt he owed to poetry.

Watson, Noyes, Binyon, Masefield, Lawrence

William Watson faces more boldly than Bridges the ruthless animality of man's origins and the terrible struggle for existence out of which he has won to his present exalted position. In "The Dream of Man" (1893), he shows us a vision of—

> . . . his base beginnings in the depths of time, his strife
> With beasts and crawling horrors for leave to live.[4]

He makes no attempt to trace the process by which man's spiritual qualities came into being; but rejoices in man's stoutness of heart in the face of so much hostility on the part of nature, and declares, without argument, his faith in the God immanent in all things ("The Unknown God"). It is in virtue of this essentially divine character of the universe that man may take a satisfaction in his life. The entire universe makes a symphonic poem or choral song, in which man is one string, seemingly jarred, but really sounding in harmony with the whole.[5] This is a minor Tennyson, as insistent as Tennyson that nature must be eked out with God, but more humble in his demands on the latter. His God is, if possible, more pantheistic, less personal, than Tennyson's; and he seems content with a form of immortality that does not include the survival of the individual. He envisages the time when—

Man and his littleness perish, erased like an error and cancelled,
Man and his greatness survive, lost in the greatness of God.[6]

Alfred Noyes finds his comfort equally in the sense of man as at one with the universal divine process.

We come from the Loom of the Weaver that weaves the Web of the
    Years.[7]

His God is the same absolute being, "the Container of all things," in whom good and evil are reconciled, who is the End to which the whole world strives, in communion with whom man finds his con-summation.[8] Not satisfied, however, with the thought of union with the Whole, Noyes plays with the theosophic doctrine of re-incarnation (as in "The Progress of Love") . . . Another very minor Tennyson, who expresses himself habitually in terms taken from fairy-lore—

    Glimpses of fair forgotten things
    Beyond the gates of birth.[9]

For the rest, untroubled by anything so serious as the philosophical concept of nature, he professes a fairy-tale version of idealism.

        This outer world is but the pictured scroll
            Of worlds within the soul,
        A coloured chart, a blazoned missal-book
            Whereon who rightly look
        May spell the splendours with their mortal eyes
            And steer to Paradise.[10]

Laurence Binyon is a poet of much greater subtlety, but one in whom the philosophical dilemmas and distresses of his time come in a guise so strained and tenuous as to be scarce recognizable. He almost never refers directly to abstract nature, and when he does, characterizes her, realistically enough, as—

> . . . indifferent Nature, affable
> To all philosophies, of each unknown . . .[11]

Nor does he make much use of the theological term, God. He shares the general sentiment of man's oneness with the universal flow of things.

> There is no longer grief nor joy for me,
> But one infinity of life that flows
> From the deep ocean-heart that no man knows
> Out into these unnumbered semblances
> Of earth and air, mountains and beasts and trees,
> One timeless flood which drives the circling star
> In furthest heaven, and whose weak waves we are,
> Mortal and broken off in sobbing foam,
> Yet ever children of that central home,
> Our Peace, that even as we flee we find . . .[12]

His spiritual struggle is carried on, it seems, more purely within his own soul, without theoretical formulations, and largely without reference to the hard, given facts of nature and life. It is a malady of the human mind to which he is a prey, which makes of Earth an enemy, and which can be thrown off only by some mysterious self-help from within. "Time's heir" gropes in darkness, having wrought his own desolation.

> At a touch
> All's to desolation turned.
> Is it he, or Earth, betrays?
> She that seemed to sting him on
> To possession, once possessed,
> Dispossesses him. Her breast
> Stony grows, and hard her gaze.[13]

Then again, at a touch, in the mystery of dawn, "the cry of desolation turns to praise."

> Spirit of Man, dear spirit, sore opprest
> With self-estrangement, and mis-choosing will,
> And all satiety of gainful skill . . .
> . . . .
>
> O undiscovered world that all about us lies
> When spirit to Spirit surrenders, and like young Love sees
> Heaven with human eyes! [14]

The problem of Binyon is one of spiritual therapeutics, not to be solved by any philosophy of nature.

Masefield's start as a poet was distinctly later than the others, with the exception of Noyes, and his work has a much more realistic tone, more skeptical and agnostic, than the others'. He was for a time associated with poets and theosophists who gave his thought a mystical turn, and in one early poem, "A Creed," declares his faith in reincarnation and the spiritual evolution of a man through successive avatars. But this view does not reappear in the series of philosophical sonnets published in *Good Friday and Other Poems* (1916) and *Lollingdon Downs and Other Poems* (1917). In these sonnets his agnostic spirit is shown by the great variety of hypotheses he entertains in regard to ultimate questions, some of them having a decidedly skeptical or materialistic cast.

> If Beauty be at all, if, beyond sense,
> There be a wisdom piercing into brains . . .[15]
> . . . .
>
> What am I, Life? A thing of watery salt
> Held in cohesion by unresting cells,
> Which work they know not why, which never halt,
> Myself unwitting where their Master dwells.[16]
> . . . .
>
> What is this life which uses living cells
> It knows not how nor why, for no known end,
> This soul of man upon whose fragile shells
> Of blood and brain his very powers depend? [17]
> . . . .

What was the Mind? Was it a mind which thought?
Or chance? Or law? Or conscious law? Or Power?
Or a vast balance by vast clashes wrought?
Or Time at trial with Matter for an hour?

Or is it all a body where the cells
Are living things supporting something strange
Whose mighty heart the singing planet swells
As it shoulders nothing in unending change? [18]

The leit-motiv of Masefield's interpretation is Beauty, and in his account of this universal beauty he vacillates between a Yeatsian platonism and a Meredithian positivism. At times it is—

Eternal beauty's everlasting rose
Which casts this world as shadow as it goes—[19]

which is sheer Yeats. Or it is—

Beauty herself, the universal mind,
Eternal April wandering alone,
The God, the holy ghost, the atoning lord,
Here in the flesh, the never yet explored—[20]

which is not Yeats, but might be if we could imagine Yeats a pantheist and condescending to abstractions like the universal mind. This concept I call "platonic" because it suggests that the "primal essence" of beauty (as Bridges would call it) is original in the universal mind, and nature but its shadow and consequence. What I call the note of Meredithian positivism is found in the suggestion of the gradual growth in time of beauty or of good (God):

Or does the glory gather crumb by crumb
Unseen, within, as coral islands rise,
Till suddenly the apparitions come
Above the surface, looking at the skies? [21]

. . . .

... the good God to whom none calls in vain,
Man's Achieved Good, which, being Life, abides,
The man-made God, that man in happy breath
Makes in despite of Time and dusty death.[22]

It is on the whole the "platonic" fancy that dominates the scene. The constant will of this poet is, by an effort of the imagination, to rise from individual beauties of sense and spirit to the concept of a universal spirit of beauty that pervades all nature and all life. He likes to think that—

> Wherever beauty has been quick in clay
> Some effluence of it lives, a spirit dwells,
> Beauty that death can never take away,
> Mixed with the air that shakes the flower-bells.[23]

For him as a child—

> She was within all Nature, everywhere,
> The breath I breathed, the brook, the flower, the grass . . .[24]

He has given up his childish belief in a personal God, but sometimes retains God as another name for the immanent beauty, in which we all share.

> There is no God, but we who breathe the air
> Are God ourselves and touch God everywhere.[25]

It may seem curious that so rough and blunt a poet as Masefield, the laureate of sport and of all active and uncloistered life, should have taken so Pateresque a muse as beauty: and one sometimes wonders whether it was not in half-conscious compensation for what he lacks that he made this choice, and whether it is not a trifle artificial in him. But there is no doubt of his seriousness. And this reduction of the spiritual meaning of the cosmos to Beauty is indeed symptomatic of the Zeitgeist which he breathes. In this reduction, one perceives how anemic has grown the lusty goddess of nature.

In D. H. Lawrence there is a kind of vestigial trace of romantic nature-worship in the "primitivism" and phallic mysticism which are so strong in some of the novels. In *Sons and Lovers*, for example, Paul Morel and Clara feel that in their love-making they have been made one with the great life-forces manifest in all nature.

It was all so much bigger than themselves that he was hushed. They had met, and included in their meeting the thrust of the manifold grass-stems, the cry of the peewit, the wheel of the stars.[26]

The same feeling is often expressed in *The Rainbow*, and in terms so religious that we are made to recognize in the sexual consummation of married people the mystical marriage of heaven and earth.[27] The very title is associated with the procreative urge, symbolizing the function of woman in the holy progress of life.

There was another child coming, and Anna lapsed into vague content. If she were not the wayfarer to the unknown, if she were arrived now, settled in her builded house, a rich woman, still her doors opened under the arch of the rainbow, her threshold reflected the passing of the sun and moon, the great travellers, her house was full of the echo of journeying.[28]

In *Women in Love* there is a darker, more riddling reference to some "mindless progressive knowledge through the senses." [29] And in *Lady Chatterley's Lover* the phallic cult is so downright and simple that it almost ceases to be mystical. What gives it philosophic significance is the fervent persuasion that a happy sexual consummation has an importance far transcending the individuals concerned.

This phallic mysticism is strongly present in poems like "Red Moonrise" and (I believe) "Resurrection." And in at least one of the earlier poems of Lawrence, there is a much more comprehensive pantheism. The crepuscular landscapes of Corot symbolize for the poet the immanence of God in the process of dawn.

> The subtle, steady rush of the whole
> Grey foam-mist of advancing God,
> As He silently sweeps to His somewhere, his goal,
> Is heard in the grass of the sod.[30]

But all in all, there is very little here of the nature-faith of Wordsworth or Meredith. The word nature I have not noticed in Lawrence, and the philosophic concept of nature is nowhere made explicit. Lawrence is decidedly hostile to the attitude of modern science, and there is in him a curious strain of medieval superstition.[31] He shows nothing of that admiration of nature's law which is so strong in all natural theology. His pantheism, such as it is, is pagan rather than Christian or deistic; perhaps it is hardly more than imaginative. His phallic mysticism, if it were not for its intellectual formulation, might well be African. His philosophy is almost wholly wanting in the ethical implications which are invariably present in the nature-poetry of the two preceding centuries. Even the "purpose" and "goal" of the divine process seem in him void of the connotations these terms would have in Shelley or Tennyson. For the most part he wants both the "naturalism" and the ethical religiosity essential to the standard nature-poetry.

Yeats and AE

The cult of nature seems never to have "taken" in Catholic and fairy-dreaming Ireland. At any rate it scarcely shows its nose in the two great characteristic poets of our day, W. B. Yeats and AE (George W. Russell). The philosophic inspirations of Yeats seem to have been steadily mystical if not orthodox. There is little realism in his moony and symbolistic settings and landscapes, especially in the earlier period of folk-lore and fairy-lore. He is dead set against positive science and the scientific interpretation of life; no truth is to be learned from these. Thus in the early "Song of the Happy Shepherd":

> . . . there is no truth
> Saving in thine own heart. Seek, then,
> No learning from the starry men,
> Who follow with the optic glass
> The whirling ways of stars that pass—
> Seek, then, for this is also sooth,
> No word of theirs—the cold star-bane
> Has cloven and rent their hearts in twain,
> And dead is all their human truth.

Yeats's idealism goes far beyond Plato, even to the point of solipsism, if we are to take seriously his declaration, a whole generation later, in "The Tower":

> And I declare my faith;
> I mock Plotinus' thought
> And cry in Plato's teeth,
> Death and life were not
> Till man made up the whole,
> Made lock, stock and barrel
> Out of his bitter soul,
> Aye, sun and moon and star, all.
> And further add to that
> That, being dead, we rise,
> Dream and so create
> Translunar Paradise.

Yeats's preference for the symbolistic and non-natural is beauti-fully expressed in the late poem, "Sailing to Byzantium," in which he begs the holy sages to consume his heart away with sacred fire, and so gather him "into the artifice of eternity."

> Once out of nature I shall never take
> My bodily form from any natural thing,
> But such a form as Grecian goldsmiths make
> Of hammered gold and gold enamelling
> To keep a drowsy emperor awake . . .

Yeats's conception of essential reality is most characteristically ex-pressed in fanciful theosophic imagery, especially in the image of the rose. His rose is an eternal Idea, beside which all transient and mortal, all natural things, have but a shadowy existence. This meta-phorical rose is, of course, one with the female personification of beauty.

> We and the laboring world are passing by:
> Amid men's souls, that waver and give place,
> Like the pale waters in their wintry race,
> Under the passing stars, foam of the sky,
> Lives on this lonely face.[32]

This sort of thing is more in keeping in Yeats than in Masefield, since in Yeats it is unalloyed by the realism of a scientific age.

In AE, again, there is no inspiration of science, and very little realism in the presentation of natural objects and landscapes. His poems are a glimmering tissue of bright images and suggestions to the soul. He was, they say, learned in oriental philosophy, and that was doubtless the main source of his inspiration. But he was an eclectic in mysticism, and most adept in the imaginative synthesis of "platonic" and pantheistic concepts, whencesoever derived. There is even a touch of nature-mysticism in him, of the worship of earth.

> Who is that goddess to whom men should pray,
> But her from whom their hearts have turned away,
> Out of whose virgin being they were born,
> Whose mother nature they have named with scorn
> Calling its holy substance common clay.[33]

This romantic sanctification of earth is made possible, of course, by the consciousness of the divinity immanent in it, and by the sense that, through identification with it, one is united with the divine.

> I begin through the grass again to be bound to the Lord:
>   I can see, through a face that has faded, the face full of rest
> Of the earth, of the mother, my heart with her heart in accord . . .[34]

For the most part, however, nature and earth have dropped decidedly into the background, and what prevails is the nostalgia of the One, the eternal Beauty, the Oversoul in which human beings and natural elements all exist. There is the usual insistence on the unreality and unsatisfactoriness of all finite beauties in the light of the eternal Idea of which they are but shadows.

> Who would kiss the fading shadow when the flower-face glows above?
> 'Tis the beauty of all Beauty that is calling for your love.[35]

This nostalgia of the eternal Beauty is easily translatable into the nostalgia of the noble Past, the Golden Age, of the Irish "Land of Youth," of the au-delà, the dream-country "beyond the Gateways of the Day." These popular variants of platonism seem more native in the Irish poet than in Noyes, and do less to weaken his effect; but they do make clear the non-naturalistic cast of his mind. And so perhaps does his preoccupation with peace and "home." And so does his heart-whispered assurance that the "unattainable beauty" shall yet be attained.

Two American Poets

In American poetry of this century, the philosophical concept of nature is virtually extinct, and the word very seldom appears. There are three powerful poets who are sufficiently exceptional to be considered in this chapter, though there is very little in them of the faith of Wordsworth, Whitman and Meredith.

The earliest of the three is Edwin Arlington Robinson, whose first poems were a product of the nineties. The word and concept of nature are scarcely to be found in Robinson, and the Victorian note is heard in a very attenuated strain of Browningesque spirituality. In *The Children of the Night* (1897) there is reference to an "onward phrase . . . of some transcendent music I have heard."

> And after time and place are overthrown,
> God's touch will keep its one chord quivering.[36]

In *Captain Craig* (1902), old Archibald assures the boy:

> . . . but there's a light behind the stars
> And we old fellows who have dared to live,
> We see it—and we see the other things,
> The other things . . .[37]

These other things, vaguely cosmic and bravely ethical, are what Captain Craig takes more than eighty pages to see. In the famous title-poem of *The Man Against the Sky* (1916), Robinson has a good deal to say of the general hopelessness of our spiritual state, and expresses the Tennysonian view that unless we survive death there is no point or value to life.

> If there be nothing after Now,
> And we be nothing anyhow,
> And we know that,—why live?
> 'Twere sure but weaklings' vain distress

To suffer dungeons where so many doors
Will open on the cold eternal shores
That look sheer down
To the dark tideless floods of Nothingness
Where all who know may drown.

This can hardly be a consistently held and dogmatic view of Robinson's. The general tone of his writing, at any rate, is such as to suggest that he regards ethical values as having an absolute sanction in the nature of things and as giving its significance to life. And the bulk of his poems—dramatic lyrics and psychological narratives—are devoted to separating the true ore from the slag in his spiritual alembic. The slag is there in overwhelming quantity, but he seldom fails to find at the bottom of the vessel a thin deposit of pure gold. Yet his tests are not pragmatic or utilitarian, and he takes no comfort in science, in evolution, or the progress of the race. In "The Man Against the Sky" he refers superciliously to "infant Science" making a pleasant face and waving "again that hollow toy, the Race." Whether Mr. Robinson took more comfort in the recent religious speculations of physicists and astronomers does not appear in his work. It is essentially the "twists of the heart" that interest this poet.

In Edgar Lee Masters there was, until last year, surprisingly little mention of nature, considering the great volume of his verse, his strongly speculative bent, and his willingness to deal in philosophic abstractions. Among the villagers of the *Spoon River Anthology* (1915) there are inevitably included certain lovers of nature (gardeners, naturalists) who speculate on the necessary conditions of human life and the possibility of subjecting men to cultivation like plants. In *Toward the Gulf*, there is (in "Botanical Gardens") reference to the deadly struggle for existence in plant and animal life, and (in "Neanderthal") the author finds in evolution "prodigal proof of ascending life." In *The Open Sea* there is a poem entitled "Nature," in which, having in mind the miseries and degradation of men, the poet questions nature as to whether life is good or bad. The answer is inconclusive, since nature is an "immeasurable Arc,"

. . . to which our brief existence
Is a point, if relative, not understood.

Since nature is everything, he suggests that there can be nothing outside—

> By which to judge this restless brotherhood
> Of will and water, and to quiet doubt
> That life is good.

The ethereal energy that whirls the atoms expresses itself as will in man; and man's will makes it possible for him to sink lower than the beasts or to rise to a high spiritual life. Man may lay a curse on himself. But the curse—

> That man deems his is not upon the far
> And infinite existence. It could nurse
> No evil in great spaces, sun and star
> As great as man's to man, and not lie down
> To death as man does.[38]

Thus Masters, like a judge well trained in the law, pronounces a tentative Not-Guilty upon the universe. Yet he is far from positively asserting its benevolence, rationality and purposiveness.

But it was only yesterday, as it were, that Masters made his most formal attack on the problem of nature. In 1935 this veteran searcher of the mind of man published a volume (*Invisible Landscapes*) which seems to give the lie direct to any statement that ours is not an age of nature-poetry, since it includes more than half a dozen poems dealing directly with the philosophical concept of nature. It is as if, in the "quiet-colored end" of a long career of writing, this turbulent twentieth-century realist had returned to a tone of philosophical sentiment characteristic of the age in which he was born.

In his "Hymn to the Earth" he reviews sympathetically the nature-philosophy of the ancients.

> For they dreamed of a Life that worked these miracles,
> Which was not Earth, but in Earth as a separate spirit,
> Moving through Earth as a Mind, and in fellowship
> With the motion of matter, the force of fire, and making
> The mind of man with the food of earth by Mind.

In his "Hymn to Nature" he shows "how variously Nature rules."
And yet—

> ... despite these protean moods
> Nature is one idea, one spirit.
> To learn that she is the many in the one
> Is to be at peace with the peace of wisdom.
> For though she changes eternally, and is never at rest
> She is steadfast with changeless laws.

Like Goethe, he dwells on the paradoxes of nature.

> She is imperfect and badly ordered;
> She is perfect and of faultless system;
> She is dual in everything, since she is seen
> In relation to man's imagination.

He brings a wealth of modern scientific lore to the illustration
of the natural process of evolution, so largely anticipated by the
speculative genius of the ancients. Like Meredith, he dwells on the
thought and spirit of man as derived from nature.

> For man is in her, and she is in man,
> Whom she has brought forth with all creatures.
> But above all out of her sacred womb
> Is the miracle, the spirit of man, which is herself,
> Given the eyes of herself with which to see her,
> And flamed with her fire with which to obey her.

In "Ultimate Selection" Masters presents the Darwinian theory,
and insists that this evolutionary process involves the selection of
what is best in man—

> ... the love of lovers,
> The passion for the beautiful, and for justice;
> The courage that will fight for man's uplifting,
> The heroism facing death like bees,
> The high imagination which builds the cities ...

And finally, out of man's spiritual experience and memory, there
comes into being a kind of persisting and platonic "heaven of life."

This stratosphere created by verse and music,
And made another existence and a world,
Lives calm and deathless, and is to flesh and days
The fragrance of the garden. . . .

Like Emerson, Masters holds that man's great agony is to feel separate from nature, and that his salvation lies in recovering a state of communion with her.

Brought to see the insignificance of human strength,
And the vanity of complaint and rebellion,
You will submit to nature, and by submitting
You will become at one with her;
And becoming a part of her you will drift
With the flood of Earth-things.
When you have made yourself destiny with her
There can be nothing but peace for you.

Again, in his sensitive feeling for landscapes, and his sense of their impregnation with the spirit of man and of cosmic nature, Masters has something of the tone of Wordsworth.

Altogether, in this latest volume, if Masters' thought is regarded as representative of our time, we may say that much has been salvaged from the wreck of nineteenth-century nature-poetry, and we may look perhaps for a continuance of romantic nature-worship in a chastened and stoical form. But these poems of Masters do not have the stamp of current fashion. The general attitude of the critics and younger poets suggests that, in this phase, he is in no deep sense representative of our age. If this attitude is justified, we shall have to conclude that the nature-poetry of Masters is more a survival from the past than a characteristic phenomenon of the times. It is extremely interesting for itself, and often deeply moving —the product of a strong and original mind—but it gives no augury of the future.

Robinson Jeffers

The latest of the large voices in American poetry is Robinson Jeffers. In Jeffers nature comes back in all her romantic splendor and sublimity, but accompanied by such a ruthless nihilism, so far as man is concerned, that she would be quite unrecognizable to Wordsworth or Meredith, to Shaftesbury or Thomson. By the eighteenth- and nineteenth-century devotees of nature, she was essentially prized for the comfort she brings to man, the assurance she gives him of his own noble destinies. No such comfort is to be found in Jeffers.

He is perhaps the most completely realistic of all nature-poets. He is the chief heir to that scientific tradition against which Tennyson and Browning struggled. He has never questioned the insignificance of man in the vast evolutionary scheme. And he finds no support for human dignity in an idealistic metaphysics which restores man's thought to the position of creator of reality. In his "Credo" he takes direct issue with the Asiatic philosophy which "believes that nothing is real except as we make it."

The beauty of things was born before eyes and sufficient to itself; the
    heart-breaking beauty
Will remain when there is no heart to break for it.[39]

This "harder mysticism" of the occident is in striking contrast to the soft platonism of Noyes and Watson and Bridges and Yeats.

In Jeffers, man is not so much made noble by his participation in non-human nature as shown, in contrast to it, futile and mean, wanting in steadfastness and dignity, and eaten up with fevers of thought that destroy him.

Uneasy and fractional people, having no center
But in the eyes and mouths that surround them,
Having no function but to serve and support
Civilization, the enemy of man,
No wonder they live insanely, and desire
With their tongues, progress; with their eyes, pleasure; with their
    hearts, death.
                    . . . .
                I remember the farther
Future, and the last man dying
Without succession under the confident eyes of the stars.
It was only a moment's accident,
The race that plagued us; the world resumes the old lonely immortal
Splendor . . .[40]

Such being the character of man—so inveterately decadent—Jeffers is no praiser of life. What he celebrates with greatest unction is the peace that lies in the grave. So great are the sufferings and weariness of men, and indeed of all animated beings, that their profoundest longing is for death. There is something of Freudian suggestion here. The poet even extends his view imaginatively to include the inanimate world—the very stars of heaven.

The striding winter giant Orion shines, and dreams darkness.
And life, the flicker of men and moths and the wolf on the hill,
Though furious for continuance, passionately feeding, passionately
Remaking itself upon its mates, remembers deep inward
The calm mother, the quietness of the womb and the egg,
The primal and the latter silences . . .[41]

But in spite of this dark judgment upon man and life, there is in Jeffers something of the romantic view of nature, of existence. Rising above mortal judgments based on the view of man's destiny, this poet conceives of the whole of nature as in some sense good, and of the cycles of man's life as somehow good, too, inasmuch as they partake of the universal process.

The sea's voice worked into my mood, I thought "No matter
What happens to men . . . the world's well made though." [42]

There is, indeed, some suggestion here of the old religious concept of a universal "scheme of things" which is good in the large, however defective it may seem in the parts and from a limited point of view. But the tone and implications of Jeffers are so utterly different from those of natural theology! The world is not "good" for *man*, either materially or spiritually. And it has no purpose, thought, nor meaning, let alone an ethical significance. This is clear in his most deliberate and considered utterances.

I have seen these ways of God: I know of no reason
For fire and change and torture and the old returnings.
He being sufficient might be still. I think they admit no reason; they
    are the ways of my love.

Unmeasured power, incredible passion, enormous craft: no thought ap-
    parent but burns darkly
Smothered with its own smoke in the human brain-vault: no thought
    outside: a certain measure in phenomena:
The fountains of the boiling stars, the flowers on the foreland, the
    ever-returning roses of dawn.[43]

If Jeffers uses the term God, it is not to bring back the assumptions of religion,—reason, benevolence, providence. God is but a
name for the ways of the universe, which includes all good and
ill in a somehow "beautiful" pattern.

God is here, too, secretly smiling, the beautiful power
That piles up cities for the poem of their fall
And gathers multitude like game to be hunted when the season
    comes.[44]
                    . . . .
Our unkindly all but inhuman God,
Who is very beautiful and too secure to want worshippers . . .
                    . . . .
He includes the flaming stars and pitiable flesh,
And what we call things and what we call nothing.
He is very beautiful . . .[45]
                    . . . .
Still the mind smiles at its own rebellions,
Knowing all the while that civilization and the other evils
That make humanity ridiculous, remain
Beautiful in the whole fabric, excesses that balance each other
Like the paired wings of the flying bird.[46]

One would like to know how this poet justifies in his own mind
his constant judgment that the world is beautiful. He is a trained
and subtle thinker; and I fancy that, if he were challenged, he
would admit that he cannot support this judgment on strictly philosophic grounds—that it is, in the last analysis, an anthropomorphic
view. He tries to rise above the plane of man's judgments, and has
rid himself of many purely human assumptions—emotional, ethical,
religious. But in the end he must fall back on his own instruments
of perception, and his purely esthetic appraisal of the universe is

put in terms of man's physical vision and his intellectual craving for order. The physical world is beautiful in color and form in the eyes of men. The vastness of the sea and of the stellar spaces gratifies his longing for release from petty limits. The relative permanence of certain natural objects is in itself pleasing and somehow reassuring.

> This mountain sea-coast is real,
> For it reaches out far into past and future;
> It is part of the great and timeless excellence of things . . .[47]

Timelessness itself is a feature of great esthetic appeal, and it is the most striking feature of the universe. And along with these aspects of the universe is the pattern which it inevitably forms for the musing thought of man—

Beautiful in the whole fabric, excesses that balance each other . . .

This esthetic vision of the world is the very minimum requirement for poetry. It reminds us of the grave suggestion of Joseph Conrad: since "the ethical view of the universe involves us at last in so many cruel and absurd contradictions . . . I would fondly believe that its object is purely spectacular." [48] Jeffers does not go so far as to suggest that the world is spectacular in *object*, or indeed that it has any object at all. But over and over again he does assert that it *is* a spectacle and an excellent, a beautiful one. And that is all that remains of the diadem of stars with which the earlier poets crowned the world,—beauty, reason, purpose, benevolence.

Chapter XXI

THE VANISHING POINT

In the most typical of contemporary poetry, English and American, the philosophical concept of nature has virtually disappeared altogether. It is as if a great weariness had come over the literary mind, making it loath to grapple with cosmic problems, including the problem of man's place in nature. The "esthetic synthesis" has largely broken down, and natural beauty is no longer intimately associated with the concept of universal nature. Earth and the stars are now regarded as scenery, setting; or they are regarded as objects of scientific study. And scientific study is no longer relied on to impress us with the providential and purposive character of the universe. The progress of our race is no longer thought of by poets as guaranteed by the inherent tendencies of nature. Economists no longer appeal so confidently to a God-given "natural order" in commerce and industry. Religious-minded people have gone back to religion for their faith and solace; and an increasingly large number of intellectuals have reconciled themselves to doing without religion of any kind, including the substitute religion which was supplied by nature.

The fundamental problems of metaphysics remain much what they have always been. Scientific method and the massive data of science continue to exert the same heavy pressure on metaphysical thought as in the days of Locke and Berkeley, or in the days of the Greek Academy. But science and "nature" are no longer synonymous terms; and neither common-sense realism nor transcendental idealism makes appeal, as in the seventeenth and eighteenth centuries, to essentially animistic concepts like Henry More's "spirit of nature" or Berkeley's "world-soul." Above all, it would appear, the assumptions of religion no longer bear so bold and frank a part in determining metaphysical opinion.

And besides, metaphysics has grown increasingly critical, technical and difficult. It is less "popular" than in the time of Pope, or of Shelley, or of Emerson; more beyond the grasp of the poetic mind. The "new physics," which in some quarters is supposed to have had so revolutionary an effect on philosophic thought, has seemingly had no effect at all on poetic philosophy.

These are some of the many reasons for the disappearance of universal nature from poetry. But it is possible that other reasons are equally important. And one of these may well be found in that intangible influence which we call fashion or style. The philosophical concept of nature which prevailed in the poetry of two centuries has gone out of style with many other features of that poetry. Contemporary poets are unwilling to deal in philosophic abstractions, favoring the view that poetry should be "simple, sensuous and passionate." The very beauties of nature are much less interesting to contemporary poets than to the Romantics and Victorians; and when they do come into poetry they are much less charged with philosophic meaning. The poetry of our day is overwhelmingly concerned with men, their dramas and their psychology. It is very little concerned with the mystic kinship of man and nature. And it tends to be either sharply realistic or dreamily romantic—romantic in a vein which would have seemed trifling to Wordsworth or Whitman.

The Georgians

The most cursory examination of the poetry contained in the anthologies of *Georgian Poetry* (1911-24) will serve to establish the unimportance of "nature" for the dominant English poets of the period just before and after the World War. The poems of Masefield and Lawrence included in these volumes are markedly wanting in philosophical character. The most Victorian of these poets is John Drinkwater. In his work one finds reference to "Beauty's bloom and ordered plan";[1] to "man's communion with man," to "God's good year," "the great unshapen age," and "the glory of the years to be."[2] But this is not nature. Neither is John Freeman's talk of the spirit of beauty.[3]

In Lascelles Abercrombie we may read of "the unknown powers within man's nature." [4] Harold Monro beseeches Lake Leman—

> Dwell in me, O thou one
> Sweet natural presence.[5]

W. H. Davies may speak in a perfectly conventional way of "Nature in this month of May," and of butterflies leaping queerly "as though escaped from Nature's hand ere perfect quite." [6] Rupert Brooke, writing from Berlin in 1912, can refer with whimsical fondness to the academic preoccupations of Cambridge men, lumping together classical mythology and Meredithian nature-philosophy.

> Some, it may be, can get in touch
> With Nature there, or Earth, or such.
> And clever modern men have seen
> A Faun a-peeping through the green. . . .[7]

And that is the nearest we come to the massive philosophical structure that underlies the nature-poetry of Wordsworth and his tribe.

The playful fairy-lore of Walter de la Mare may often have overtones of emotional symbolism; but it is quite free from mysticism or cosmic philosophy. This is still more true of James Elroy Flecker's "Golden Journey to Samarkand"; of W. J. Turner's "Romance" and "Magic"; of Ralph Hodgson's fanciful reconstruction of the story of Eve. In many of these a delicate and moony fancifulness is combined with an acute and vivid realism, as in Harold Monro's domestic pieces like "Every Thing." In Monro's "Gravity" the universal power is treated with a familiarity and irreverence quite incompatible with the romantic spirit; imaginatively, but with a sort of homely and scientific realism. Realism, again, is imaginative but unromantic in Gordon Bottomley's "The End of the World." Realism appears in W. W. Gibson in a more matter-of-fact and pedestrian guise. And in the war poems of Gibson, of Sassoon, Nichols, Graves, the desperate and muddy realism is unrelieved by any gleam of cosmic star-shine.

Pound, the Imagists, Sandburg

Still less of cosmical philosophy is to be found in Ezra Pound and the Imagist School which he fathered. Pound's poetry is inspired by curious learning in many languages and idioms; in everything but the language and idiom of nature-poetry. This amazing ventriloquist has written with vivid plausibility in the manner of the Scotch popular ballad, the Provençal love-lyric, the Renaissance Italian sonnet, the Hebrew psalms, and the medieval litany. When he writes in the idiom of today it is mainly to make fun of the bourgeois and impudently to celebrate the spiritual bohemia of artist and poet. His *Cantos XXX* are a brilliant palimpsest, in which Greek myths and legends of the Troubadours are discoverable underneath the military, financial and domestic chronicles of Italian cities of the Renaissance, and over all are scrawled the vulgar intrigues of modern capitalism and the obscene inferno of the Great War. Man's ways and passions are enough for Pound, who loves not abstractions nor the anxious philosophies of modern man.

Pound no doubt had something to do with the program worked out by Amy Lowell and John Gould Fletcher for the Imagists, in which is found the following statement:

> We are not a school of painters, but we believe that poetry should render particulars exactly and not deal in vague generalities, however magnificent and sonorous. It is for this reason that we oppose the cosmic poet, who seems to us to shirk the real difficulties of his art.[8]

While the main lines of the Imagist program are sound enough, what appeals to these poets is apparently the transfer of emphasis from matter to manner in poetry. This seems to suit their mental cast. They are none of them naturally given to intellectual speculation unless it be on esthetic problems. Like the French Symbolists, who so deeply influenced them, they are concerned with the rendering of sensations, of elusive moods and impressions. In spite of their disclaimer, they tend to be painters and impressionists. In style they are subject to many various and exotic influences: Chinese and Japanese (Amy Lowell and Fletcher), Greek (H.D.), late Latin (Richard Aldington), as well as French; and this tendency to be derivative in style, together with their disposition to borrow from the techniques of painting and music, goes along with the effect they have of artificiality. They give the impression of being more concerned with the technique of expression than with what they have to say. They have less effect on the emotions than they intend. And the reader begins to wonder whether after all the thought-content of a poem may not be an important factor in rousing the emotions.

Carl Sandburg has many affinities with the Imagists. But he is more of a realist, more homely and down-to-earth. And he has more to say—of the passions of men, of the shaping conditions of modern life, of human society, actual and ideal. There is in him much of the mysticism of Emerson and Whitman—of their mystical faith in life and man. But with him it is more bodiless, unphrased, instinctive and complexional. It has no metaphysical support. And it makes no more appeal to Earth or Nature than to the Absolute Being of Spinoza or Plato's Eternal Ideas.

Other Representative Americans

Robert Frost is a refined modern agnostic in religion and philosophy, a clear-headed and fastidious realist. He has retained the aura of New England transcendentalism without a trace of its philosophy. In his first volume he pays due homage to "the ritualism of nature,"—praying that a spot thick sown with wild orchises might be spared by the mower's scythe.[9] But his poems show none but conscious and fanciful indulgence in the pathetic fallacy. In A Boy's Will he quietly and bluntly states his persuasion that "there is no oversight of human affairs." [10] No American poet is more feelingly—if quietly—attached to earth as "the right place for love." [11] None has more exquisitely displayed the spiritual refinements possible in human life. None is more acutely aware of the metaphysical dilemmas in which man finds himself—

> At one extreme agreeing with one Greek,
> At the other agreeing with another Greek
> Which may be thought, but only so to speak.
> A baggy figure, equally pathetic
> When sedentary and when peripatetic.[12]

But none of our poets has more steadily declined to formulate his thought in philosophical terms.

His references to "nature" are extremely rare. The most significant is in "West-Running Brook," in a passage worth quoting if only to show how little of the traditional nature-philosophy is left in his use of the word. The married lovers whose charming dialogue is the matter of this poem are discussing a certain white wave in the black brook where part of the water is thrown backward by a sunken rock. This brook with its eternal lapse apparently reminds the man of Heraclitus's brook and his πάντα χωρεῖ, and he, muses finely over the relation men bear to the universal lapse of things.

> It flows between us, over us, and *with* us.
> And it is time, strength, tone, light, life and love—
> And even substance lapsing unsubstantial;
> The universal cataract of death
> That spends to nothingness—and unresisted,
> Save by some strange resistance in itself,
> Not just a swerving, but a throwing back,
> As if regret were in it and were sacred.
> It has this throwing backward on itself
> So that the fall of most of it is always
> Raising a little, sending up a little.
> Our life runs down in sending up the clock.
> The brook runs down in sending up our life.
> The sun runs down in sending up the brook.
> And there is something sending up the sun.
> It is this backward motion toward the source,
> Against the stream, that most we see ourselves in,
> The tribute of the current to the source.
> It is from this in nature we are from.
> It is most us.[13]

So. There is in all nature not merely a tendency to run down but a contrary tendency to "send up a little"; shall we say, the drift to death and the impulse to life? The little wave in the brook is frankly a fanciful symbol for this impulse to life, to resistance of death, which, the poet says, is what man has from nature more than anything else. Surely never was nature invoked in more sober fashion; never was more modest claim made on the Power so awesomely regarded by Shelley and Emerson.

Vachel Lindsay was a happy gospeler with a saxophone. His simple aim was to bring the kingdom of heaven down to the streets of Springfield. His sympathetic fancy played with the more picturesque elements of American Life—the camp-meeting negro, the Chinese laundryman, the Salvation Army, the motor-horns of the Santa Fe Trail. He was content to set to jazz the idealism of common life, and to leave philosophy to the academy.

Conrad Aiken, with subtler harmonies and a more refined orchestra, follows down purple corridors the ebb and flow of erotic feeling; or the more comprehensive wish-fulfilment of split personalities instinctively seeking emotional balance in the kaleidoscope of dreams. He has much of the philosophic and speculative temper; but for the most part he keeps within the moony crepuscular heart of introverted man, and looks not forth on the sunlit world of natural forces.

Edna Millay is the most convincing celebrant of woman's love, unmatched in this for candor and precision, unmatched for realism within her range. Her great gift is for racy homeliness of phrase; though she does not disdain abstractions like Faith and Life, and it is she that pronounced judgment in favor of the essential beauty—

Euclid alone has looked on beauty bare . . .

Natural beauty moves her to the point of pain—

O world, I cannot hold thee close enough!

She does not deal in the philosophic concept of nature. The nearest she has come to this is in her "Renascence," where—

O God, I cried, no dark disguise
Can e'er hereafter hide from me
Thy radiant identity!

The religious emotion of this and other early poems has not appeared in later volumes. Earth does come back in *Wine From These*

Grapes (1934), but it is a mother who "does not understand her child," or a mere "unhappy planet born to die." It is no soul of things nor principle of order.

Elinor Wylie was Edna Millay in Venetian glass. Her more tragic spirit, overwhelmed with her desperate lot as woman, took refuge in an intense cold patrician stoicism. She scorns bourgeois models, and writes with the epigrammatic neatness of the seventeenth century. When she turns metaphysical, in "Angels and Earthly Creatures," it is in the seventeenth-century manner. Her psychology is archaic in the distinction of heart, mind and soul (in "This Corruptible"), her religion palely Christian; and she loves to deal, not with nature, but with the four elements—fire, air, water and earth—in which man has so slight and precarious a tenure. This proud and isolate spirit, one feels, would have found a trifle vulgar the philosophic pabulum of the Romantics and Victorians.

T. S. Eliot

The most influential of living poets is probably T. S. Eliot. While this is no doubt partly owing to the vivid power of his personal genius, we cannot but suppose that there is something about him besides his genius that makes him appeal to the contemporary mind, and that he is in large degree representative of the Zeitgeist.

Neither the word nor the concept of nature survives in him. The word is naturally ruled out by his poetic creed, which abjures abstractions and philosophical statements. That the concept of nature is not present even implicitly is perhaps partly owing to his (apparent) insensibility to the beauty of the world, and this may well be an accident of personal organization. He is seemingly so constituted as to derive little pleasure from the impressions of eye, ear and touch, except such pleasure as he takes in the imaginative rendering of certain effects. If one can judge from his poetry, no sounding cataract ever haunted him like a passion; he was never moved to exclaim, "O world, I cannot hold thee close enough!" But, more than this, it gives him no pleasure to contemplate the stars in their courses, nor to consider the order brought by science into the ways of the universe. In his, at bottom, highly philosophical poetry, there is an intense and aching void, an eloquent vacuum, where science might be looked for.

The ways of the universe are for him simply and solely the ways of man; and the ways of man are mainly symbolized by the obscenities, the meannesses and treacheries of our sex-life, by the futilities and half-heartedness of our sentiment and culture. That Love so much celebrated by the poets is represented in him by the beastly drummer, Apeneck Sweeney, by the anemic gold-diggers, Doris and Dusty, by the classic violation of Philomela and the jaded indifference of the ravished typist in "The Waste Land." Modern society in its commercial aspect is represented by Mr. Eugenides, the Smyrna merchant. Contemporary culture and sentiment are represented by J. Alfred Prufrock and the lady of the "Portrait," who discourses so affectedly of friendship and her lost youth. Death is for Eliot "end of the endless journey to no end." [14]

Thus he comes to moral disenchantment as absolute as St. Augustine's. Our spiritual state is a Waste Land, "thoughts of a dry brain in a dry season"; our only cure is religious—

> Burning burning burning burning
> O Lord thou pluckest me out . . .

Here we have the extreme logic of the "new humanism." Eliot can take no pleasure in our oneness with the universal process. He has learned from Irving Babbitt and Paul Elmer More that we owe to nature nothing but what is beastly in us—animal instinct, the cravings of selfhood. The human in us is what is defined by our power of refraining—by the operation of the "inner check." But Eliot has bettered the instructions of his masters. He cannot be content with this bifurcation of our human nature. He cannot remain thus in intolerable isolation. He must find somewhere the origin and sanction of what is human in us; and nature being forbidden, he has no recourse but to the supernatural. Nature—without order, benevolence, purpose, morality, shorn of all that religion and science bestowed upon her—is too easily shown up by reason for an impotent pretender. What can never be shown up by reason is the intuition of the heart, which is God. This alone is sufficient to drown the memory of Life's insolence.

After Eliot

Looking to the immediate future, we have no reason to expect a return to the Wordsworthian concept of nature, if we may judge by the poets who at the present moment give the greatest promise of power. We need not consider the Sitwells (Edith, Osbert, Sacheverell), in spite of their great reputation. Their extreme artificiality keeps them from representing anything serious in the thought of our time. And even if they did stand for something, it would not have a remote resemblance to the ardent faiths of Victorian or Romantic. These pseudo-Watteau landscapes, these moony puppets and straw-stuffed old ladies bear the least possible relation to the concerns of heart and mind. More significant is the whimsical lightness of Humbert Wolfe, his delicate satire, and the fluid gravity of his more serious pieces—"Iliad," "The High Song," "News of the Devil." But while we find here some attempt to assay the values of human life, there is no reference to the cosmical standards of nature and natural law.

Roughly speaking, nearly all of the most promising poets of the moment may be regarded as stemming from Eliot, Pound or Hopkins, or as having some tincture of the "metaphysical" tendencies of these poets. This is particularly true in England of Herbert Read, C. Day Lewis and W. H. Auden; in America, of Archibald MacLeish, Hart Crane, E. E. Cummings, Horace Gregory and John Peale Bishop; and less obviously perhaps it is true of Stephen Spender in England, and in America of Louise Bogan and Allen Tate. Somewhat apart from these in local and individual quality stand the southern poets of *The Fugitive*—John Crowe Ransom, Merrill Moore, and Robert Penn Warren. But they are for the most part at one with their contemporaries in the intense dry intellectuality which marks the post-War poetry in English-speaking countries, in the irony and indirection, in the preoccupation with death, the stoicism, the absence of Romantic "enthusiasm" and of the cosmical sense that went with the enthusiasm.

If there is romantic enthusiasm anywhere among these poets it is in Hart Crane, who tried so hard to build the vision of America, body and spirit, America mythological, geographical and mechanical—Pocahontas, Rip Van Winkle, Eldorado, the Mississippi, the tramps, Brooklyn Bridge, and the airplane—but who lost hope of making his vision prevail and killed himself in despair.

MacLeish has sung the epic of America in "Conquistador" and "Frescoes for Mr. Rockefeller's City." But with the best of intentions the satirical and elegiac notes dominate his music as they do still more that of Gregory and Bishop, of Bogan and Tate. With the firmest determination to be American, he is yet ridden with the nostalgia of the old world.

> This, this is our land, this is our people,
> This that is neither a land nor a race. We must reap
> The wind here in the grass for our soul's harvest:
> Here we must eat our salt or our bones starve.
> Here we must live or live only as shadows . . .[15]

The nearest approach to the cosmic problems of the Victorians he makes in "Einstein," where a great scientist is shown trying to reduce all experience to mathematical terms, and failing only when he cannot compel his atomic world to include himself.

> Like a foam
> His flesh is withered and his shriveling
> And ashy bones are scattered on the dark.
> But still the dark denies him. Still withstands
> The dust his penetration and flings back
> Himself to answer him.
> Which seems to keep
> Something inviolate. A living something.[16]

A most subtle and fascinating essay in metaphysics—equally poised between realism and idealism—but far from any suggestion of making nature the nurse, or guide, or guardian, of the heart, the soul, or all one's "moral being."

It is clear that the poets here considered are bent on solving the problems of man's moral being within the confines of his own "bone vault," without much appeal to the general laws of the universe. Where they look outside themselves, it is to the facts of human experience, and particularly to the social scene. There is a growing tendency for poets to concern themselves, like writers of fiction and literary criticism, with the political, the economic, the industrial factors of modern life. They voice the growing discontent with a decadent social order and the growing hope for a socialistic state. Mr. MacLeish, while he refuses to capitulate to Marxian ideology, is a stinging critic of the commercial "makers of America," taking his cue from the revolutionary frescoes of Rivera and Orozco. Mr. Gregory makes himself the Cassandra of New York in the age of depression. Mr. Auden depicts the hopeless dilemma of the wealthy in a "world that has had its day." Mr. Spender celebrates—

> . . . the failure of banks
> The failure of cathedrals and the declared insanity of our rulers . . .[17]

and looks hopefully to the new generation to build up a better society on the ruins of the present. Mr. Lewis exposes the soft ideologies and sophistications of the elders and urges his own gen-- eration to "give up toys and go into training."

> Hands off! The dykes are down.
> This is no time for play.
> Hammer is poised and sickle
> Sharpened. I cannot stay.[18]

Thus, where Eliot, in his disenchantment, turns to the Christian religion for his comfort, his followers turn to the social revolution.

The poets of nature too, in their day, looked to the social revolution—Wordsworth and Shelley, Swinburne and Meredith.

> Names are there, Nature's sacred watchwords, they
> Were borne aloft in bright emblazonry;
> The nations thronged around, and cried aloud,
> As with one voice, Truth, Liberty, and Love! [19]

The present-day poets have given up nature, having found it bankrupt. Perhaps they have forgotten the grounds of revolutionary faith. They have forgotten their prophet Marx, whose faith is grounded in the necessity of things; they have forgotten the inspirer of the Marxian dialectic, Hegel—for whom the course of history was determined by the creative process of thought which is one with nature. For present-day poets that is too speculative, too transcendental a notion, not conformable to the sober realism in which they trust.

Like the poets of nature they are overcome with the sense of man as "orphan and defrauded." But their solace lies not in the realization of their oneness with the universal process. More sober, more realistic, they content themselves with the sense of human solidarity, the realization of their oneness with the herd of men. The loneliness of man in nature is expressed by Stephen Spender in his beautiful "Winter Landscape," together with his deep need for communion with men. The poet shuts himself in with his evening fire from the sight of the daffodil West and the sense of "our thin dying souls against Eternity pressed." The thought of gulls hiding breast to breast in clefts of the rock brings him a passionate longing to affirm the gregariousness of his own kind.

> And breast to breast, those swans. Sheep huddle and press
> Close. Each to each. Oh,
> Is there no herd of men like beasts where man may go? [20]

The mind of our day has given up, in weariness and perplexity, the effort to cope with the problems of eternity, and to conceive of "nature's social union"—content to fall back on the hope of a social union among men in a rationally ordered state. This is enough to engage the energies of men for a long time to come. It may be that romantic nature has run its course for good and all, and that other formulas may be expected to take its place in the prophetic utterance of poets. At any rate the poets have need of fresh inspirations. And we may hardly look for a revival of the concept of nature till there shall appear a discoverer as great as Newton or Darwin, a thinker as provocative as Kant or Plato, to offer a new synthesis, and give to nature a new lease of life.

NOTES

CHAPTER I

INTRODUCTION AND CONCLUSION

[1] The nineteenth-century faith in progress was fed, no doubt, by many affluents; and in so large a question it would be rash to make a hasty pronouncement. But it is clear that, among the most influential of writers who contributed to spread this faith, were Godwin, in *Political Justice*, and Condorcet, in his *Esquisse d'un tableau historique des progrès de l'esprit humain*, writers who exerted so great an influence on poets like Shelley. It is equally clear that certain Christian writers, like Newman, failed to share the sanguine views of Tennyson, and looked to religion for the hope denied by history.

[2] My colleague, Professor C. A. Moore, has two sound and illuminating essays on the ethical and philosophical concept of nature in eighteenth-century poets: one on "Shaftesbury and the Ethical Poets in England" (*Publications of the Modern Language Association of America*, XXXI—new series, XXIV, 264-325), and one on "The Return to Nature in English Poetry" (*Studies in Philology*, 1917, 243-291). With regard to the meaning and implications of the word nature in the eighteenth century, particularly in esthetic and ethical criticism, Professor Arthur O. Lovejoy has published a number of authoritative articles: "Optimism and Romanticism," in *Publications of the Modern Language Association*, XLII (1927): 921-945; " 'Nature' as an Esthetic Norm," in *Modern Language Notes*, XLII (1927): 444-450; "The First Gothic Revival and the Return to Nature," in *Modern Language Notes*, XLVII (1932): 419-446. Certain phases of the eighteenth-century Arcadian ideal of the "state of nature" are illustrated by Professor Chauncey B. Tinker in his *Nature's Simple Plan*, Princeton University Press 1922. The "noble savage" convention is followed in all its ramifications through the eighteenth- and nineteenth-century romantics by Professor Hoxie Neale Fairchild in *The Noble Savage*, Columbia University Press 1928. Some eighteenth-century writers, as well as poets of the age of Wordsworth, come in for treatment in Fairchild's *The Romantic Quest*, Columbia University Press 1931. The treatment of rural scenery and country life is the main consideration in Myra Reynolds's *Treatment of Nature in English Poetry from Pope to Wordsworth*, Chicago 1896, and C. E. De Haas's *Nature and the Country in English Poetry of the First Half of the Eighteenth Century*, Amsterdam 1928. Earlier treatments of the general concept of nature in English poetry are those of John Campbell Shairp, *On Poetic Interpretation of Nature*, New York 1878, Roden Noel, *Essays on Poetry & Poets*, London 1886, and Stopford Brooke, *Theology in the English Poets* (1874 ?), tenth ed., London 1907; *Naturalism in English Poetry* (lectures delivered in 1902), New York 1920.

[3] For Lovejoy, see "The Supposed Primitivism of Rousseau's *Discourse on Inequality*," *Modern Philology*, XXI (1923), 185-186; also *Primitivism and Related Ideas in Antiquity* (by Arthur O. Lovejoy and George Boas), Johns Hopkins

Press 1935, pp. 240-242. Lovejoy refers in his footnotes to articles by Raymond D. Havens and Lois Whitney on primitivism in the eighteenth century.

⁴ For the *ordre naturel* in economics, see, e.g., Lewis H. Haney, *History of Economic Thought*, New York 1911; Charles Gide and Charles Rist, *Histoire des doctrines économique depuis les physiocrates jusqu'à nos jours*, 2d ed. Paris 1913.

⁵ Lovejoy and Boas, *op. cit.*, p. 103.

⁶ *Ibid.*, pp. 14-15.

⁷ *Ibid.*, Chap. III.

⁸ *Ibid.*, pp. 111-112. Reprinted by kind permission of the Columbia University Press.

⁹ Fairchild, *The Romantic Quest*, p. 9.

¹⁰ *Ibid.*, 251.

¹¹ *Ibid.*, 325.

¹² *Ibid.*, 107.

¹³ *Ibid.*, 376.

¹⁴ Carl Grabo, *A Newton Among Poets*, University of North Carolina Press 1930; *"Prometheus Unbound": an Interpretation*, University of North Carolina Press 1935.

¹⁵ Alfred North Whitehead, *Science and the Modern World*, New York 1925, Chapter V.

¹⁶ Wordsworth, "The Prelude," Book XIII, ll. 20-22 (1850 version).

¹⁷ "The Tables Turned" (1798).

¹⁸ "To My Sister" (1798).

¹⁹ Solomon Francis Gingerich, *Essays in the Romantic Poets*, New York 1929.

²⁰ Among others, Floyd H. Stovall, *Desire and Restraint in Shelley*, Duke University Press 1931; Benjamin P. Kurtz, *The Pursuit of Death: a Study of Shelley's Poetry*, Oxford University Press 1933; Carl Grabo, *"Prometheus Unbound": an Interpretation*, already mentioned, and *The Meaning of "The Witch of Atlas,"* University of North Carolina Press 1935; and Ellsworth Barnard, *Shelley's Religion* (unpublished doctor's dissertation, University of Minnesota 1935). In most of these writers platonism is, however, merely an incidental topic. In note 2 to Chap. VIII, I mention the earlier, more direct, studies of platonism in Shelley by Lillian Winstanley, Helene Richter, and Richard Ackermann. On the subject of Shelley's thought in general, reference should also be made to the introduction and notes in Newman I. White, *The Best of Shelley*, New York 1932.

CHAPTER II

THE FORMS OF NATURE

¹ William Cowper, "The Task," Book I, l. 152.

² Mark Akenside, "The Pleasures of Imagination," first version, Book I, ll. 134-135.

³ Alfred Biese, *The Development of the Feeling for Nature in the Middle Ages and Modern Times*, English translation, London and New York 1905, p. 291.

⁴ Wordsworth, "The Prelude," Book I, ll. 435-438 in the 1805-06 version; this is here identical, in all but punctuation, with the 1850 version, I, 408-411. Citations from Ernest de Selincourt's edition of "The Prelude," Oxford 1926, in which the two versions are given on parallel pages.

⁵ "The Prelude," XII, 241-244 (1805-06); XIII, 242-245 (1850).

⁶ "These beauteous forms": "Tintern Abbey." Cf. "the forms of Nature": "The Excursion," Book IV, 846 (Nowell Charles Smith's edition of *The Poems of Wordsworth*, London 1908, Vol. III, p. 119).

[7] "The Prelude," III, 110 (1850); the 1805–06 version has (l. 111), "the common countenance of earth and heaven."

[8] "Tintern Abbey."

[9] Coleridge, "The Nightingale."

[10] Byron, "Childe Harold's Pilgrimage," Canto III, Stanza xci.

[11] *Ibid.*, III, lxxii.

[12] *Ibid.*, IV, clxxviii.

[13] *Ibid.*, III, xc.

[14] *Ibid.*, III, xiii.

[15] Fairchild, in *The Noble Savage*, p. 176, refers to the emphasis on this point in Wordsworth's letter to Fox accompanying the second edition of *Lyrical Ballads*.

[16] See, e.g., *The Noble Savage*, pp. 368, 370.

[17] Cowper, "The Task," I, 678-680.

[18] Wordsworth, sonnet "Written in London, September, 1802"—"O friend! I know not which way I must look."

[19] Emile Legouis, *The Early Life of William Wordsworth*, translated by J. W. Matthews, London 1897, p. 295.

[20] James Beattie, "The Minstrel," e.g., Book I, stanza iv.

[21] *Ibid.*, I, xl.

[22] *Ibid.*, II, xxii.

[23] *Ibid.*, II, xxxvi.

[24] *Ibid.*, II, xxix.

[25] Wordsworth, "The Excursion," IV, 1207-17 (Smith's edition, Vol. III, p. 127).

[26] Cowper, "The Task," I, 749-753.

[27] *Ibid.*, III, 675ff.

[28] *Ibid.*, III, 290-291.

[29] *Ibid.*, III, 332-340.

[30] *Ibid.*, II, 1-5.

[31] *Ibid.*, III, 108.

[32] Shelley's Preface to "Prometheus Unbound."

[33] Fairchild, *The Noble Savage*, p. 376. Reprinted by kind permission of the Johns Hopkins University Press.

[34] Edward Young, "Night Thoughts," Night IV, ll. 703-705. Among many other similar passages in Young are Night IX, 843-844: "The grand of Nature is the' Almighty's oath,/ In Reason's court, to silence Unbelief." IX, 1005: "That Nature is the glass reflecting God." IX, 1267: "The course of Nature is the Art of God."

[35] William Lisle Bowles, "On a Landscape by Rubens," ll. 43-45, in the *Poetical Works*, Edinburgh 1855, I, p. 143.

[36] Cowper, "The Task," VI, 118-125, 132-133.

CHAPTER III

THE METAPHYSICAL CONCEPT OF NATURE

[1] William Wordsworth, "The Prelude," Book I, ll. 428-431 in the 1805–06 version; essentially identical in the 1850 version, ll. 401-404. My citations from "The Prelude" are all from the edition of Professor Ernest de Selincourt, Oxford 1926, in which the two versions are given side by side.

[2] *Ibid.*, II, 416-418 (1805–06); essentially identical in 1850, II, 397-399.

[3] *Ibid.*, V, 11-17 (1805-06); the 1850 version is somewhat altered.

[4] *Ibid.*, XI, 138-140 (1805-06); essentially identical in 1850, XII, 93-95.

[5] *Ibid.*, XI, 146-148 (1805-06). The 1850 version (XII, 102-105) gives the passage a more theological cast.

[6] See Note on Wordsworth's Reading following the notes to this chapter.

[7] William Cowper, "Table Talk" (1780), ll. 690ff.

[8] Samuel Taylor Coleridge, "Work without Hope."

[9] Robert Southey, "Joan of Arc," Book III, ll. 427-428.

[10] Percy Bysshe Shelley, "The Revolt of Islam," Canto V, Stanza xi.

[11] Coleridge, "The Destiny of Nations" (1796).

[12] Quoted by Edouard von der Hellen, in Goethe's *Sämmtliche Werke* (Jubiläums-Ausgabe, Vol. II, p. 352).

[13] Shelley, "Mont Blanc" (1816).

[14] Shelley, "Hymn to Intellectual Beauty" (1816).

[15] Wordsworth, "To My Sister" (1798).

[16] Shelley, "Queen Mab," Section VI, ll. 146-149.

[17] Emile Legouis, *The Early Life of William Wordsworth*, English translation by J. W. Matthews, London 1897, p. 326.

[18] Mark Akenside, "The Pleasures of the Imagination," first version, Book II, ll. 312-315.

[19] Charles Lyell, *Principles of Geology*, 3 vols., Boston 1842, Vol. III, p. 11.

[20] Coleridge, *The Friend*, in the *Complete Works*, New York 1871, Vol. II, footnote to p. 446 (in Section II, Essay 9).

[21] Henry Brooke, *Universal Beauty, a Poem*, London 1735, Part III, ll. 206-209.

[22] Pierre Louis Moreau de Maupertuis, *Système de la Nature*, Section VI (*Oeuvres de Maupertuis*, Lyon 1768, II, 141-142).

[23] George Cheyne, *Philosophical Principles of Religion Natural and Revealed*, London 1734, Chap. I, Sect. iii, p. 3.

[23a] Letter to Thelwall, Dec. 31, 1796 (E. H. Coleridge's *Letters of Coleridge*, I, 211). The Monro to whom Coleridge refers is presumably one of three relatives, all named Alexander Monro, who occupied successively the chair of anatomy in the University of Edinburgh.

[24] Ralph Cudworth, *The True Intellectual System of the Universe*, London 1678, Chap. III, Sect. xxxvii, par. 4.

[25] *Ibid.*, III, xxxvii, 26.

[26] *Ibid.*, III, i.

[27] *Ibid.*, III, xxxvii, 24.

[28] *Ibid.*

[29] *Ibid.*, III, xxxvii, 21.

[30] See John Burnet, *Platonism*, University of California Press 1928, p. 117.

[31] Cudworth, *op. cit.*, III, ii.

[32] *Ibid.*, III, v.

[33] *Ibid.*, III, xxxvii, 6.

[34] Henry More, *The Immortality of the Soul*, in *A Collection of Several Philosophical Writings*, London 1712, p. 215 (notes to Book III, Chap. xii, Sect. 1).

[35] *Ibid.*, III, xiii, 9, 10 (both p. 223).

[36] *Ibid.*, III, vi, 7 (p. 187).

[37] *Ibid.*, III, xii, 2 (p. 213).

[38] *Ibid.*, III, xii, 5 (p. 214); III, xiii, 7 (p. 219).

[39] *Ibid.*, III, xii, 5 (pp. 214-215).

[40] See below, Chap. VIII.

[41] More, *op. cit.*, III, xii, 4 (p. 214).

[42] *Ibid.*, III, vi, 7 (p. 187).

[43] *Ibid.*, III, xii, 4 (p. 214).

[44] *Ibid.*, III, xiii, 7 (p. 219).

[45] *Ibid.*, note to III, xiii, 1 (p. 224).

[46] *Ibid.*, note to III, xiii, 7.

[47] Edward Stillingfleet, *Origines Sacrae: Or a Rational Account of the Grounds of Natural and Revealed Religion*, 2 vols., Oxford 1817, Book III (Vol. II), Chap. III, Sect. iii, p. 51.

[48] Sir Matthew Hale, *The Primitive Origination of Mankind, Considered and Examined according to the Light of Nature*, London 1677, Sect. I, Chap. i, p. 34.

[49] *Ibid.*, IV, vi, p. 344.

[50] *Ibid.*, pp. 344-345.

[51] Sir Matthew Hale, *A Discourse of the Knowledge of God, and of Ourselves*, London 1688, Chap. I, p. 5.

[52] *A Free Inquiry into the Vulgar Notion of Nature*, in *The Philosophical Works* of Robert Boyle, abridged, etc., by Peter Shaw, 3 vols., London 1738, Vol. II, Sect. I, p. 107.

[53] *Ibid.*, Sect. II, p. 118.

[54] Coleridge, *Aids to Reflection*, in *Complete Works*, New York 1871, Vol. I, footnote to p. 263 (Aphorisms on Spiritual Religion, Reflections Introductory to Aphorism X). In punctuation, I follow Bohn library ed., footnote to p. 167.

[55] Whether Coleridge had actually read the works cited I cannot say. Stillingfleet and Hale he might have read in Wordsworth's copies, providing they were in Wordsworth's possession at any time before the writing of *Aids to Reflection* (first published 1825). That he had some general knowledge of Boyle, at least as early as *The Friend* (first 1809-1810, enlarged version 1818), is clear from his several references to him in that work. That he considered him not merely in his scientific capacity is clear from his reference to him as being one of the "first-rate philosophers," along with Plato, Kepler, Milton, Newton, Leibniz, and Berkeley (Bohn ed., p. 296, Sect. II, Essay 1). Altogether it is very likely indeed that he had read Boyle's *Free Inquiry*.

[56] Boyle, *op. cit.*, Sect. II, p. 117.

[57] *Ibid.*, III, 141.

[58] Boyle, *An Inquiry into the Final Causes of Natural Things* (in *The Philosophical Works*, Vol. II), Sect. IV, Prop. iii, pp. 181-182.

[59] *Ibid.*, Sect. II, p. 163.

[60] Boyle, *Free Inquiry*, etc., Sect. II, p. 113.

[61] Henry Needler's *Works*, London 1728, p. 125.

[62] *Ibid.*, p. 129.

[63] William Knight, *Lord Monboddo and Some of his Contemporaries*, New York and London 1900, p. 122.

[64] See, e.g., Knight's *Lord Monboddo*, pp. 206-207.

[65] George Berkeley, *Siris: A Chain of Philosophical Reflections..concerning.. Tar Water*, etc., London 1844, Section 341.

[66] *Ibid.*, Sect. 278.

[67] *Ibid.*, e.g., Sections 231, 232, 237, 245, 249.

[68] *Ibid.*, Sect. 231.

[69] *Ibid.*, Sect. 161.

[70] *Ibid.*, Sect. 277.

[71] *Ibid.*, Sect. 229.

[72] *Ibid.*, Sect. 154.

[73] *Ibid.*, Sect. 284.

[74] *Ibid.*, Sect. 287.

[75] *Ibid.*, Sect. 326.

[75a] Since my study was completed and in proof, my attention has been called to an article by S. G. Dunn in the English Association *Essays and Studies* for 1932 (XVIII, 74-109), dealing with the influence of Newton on Wordsworth's metaphysical thought. Mr. Dunn refers to Newton's theory of motion, to his

"active principles"; he associates with them the passages from "Tintern Abbey" and "The Excursion" which I have dwelt on; and he cites also certain passages from "The Prelude" particularly interesting in the light they have to throw on the notion of a "spirit of nature"—an "under soul", an "under-presence" (see especially pp. 96-99). I regret that it is too late to refer to Mr. Dunn's views in my main text.

[76] *Rohault's System of Natural Philosophy, Illustrated with Dr. Samuel Clarke's Notes Taken mostly out of Sir Isaac Newton's Philosophy*, done into English by John Clarke, 2 vols., London 1733, Part I (Vol. I), Chap. X, paragraph 13.

[77] *Ibid.*, footnote to the above. Nearly all this passage is italicized in Clarke's note, and reference given to Newton's *Optics.* Another passage from Newton dealing with the active Principles is given in a footnote to par. 15, Chap. XI.

[78] Richard Bentley, *Sermons Preached at Boyle's Lecture*, etc., London 1838, Sermon VII, pp. 157-158, 162 (in *The Works of Richard Bentley*, ed. Dyce, Vol. III).

[79] *Ibid.*, Newton's third letter to Bentley, pp. 211-212. These letters, according to the 1838 edition of Bentley, were first printed in 1756.

[80] *Rohault's System*, Part I, Chap. XIII, footnote to par. 12. All in italics in the original.

[81] *Ibid.*, Part II (Vol. II), Chap. XXV, footnote to par. 22.

[82] Bentley, *op. cit.*, Sermon VII, pp. 167-168.

[83] Kant, *Kritik der praktischen Vernunft*, in Kant's *Schriften*, Berlin 1908, Vol. V, pp. 161-162: "Zwei Dinge erfüllen das Gemüth mit immer neuer und zunehmender Verwunderung und Ehrfurcht, je öfter und anhaltender sich das Nachdenken damit beschäftigt: der bestirnte Himmel über mir und das moralische Gesetz in mir." Etc. Many scholars have held that Kant's categorical imperative had its influence on Wordsworth in the "Ode to Duty." See, e.g., Max J. Herzberg, in *Publications of the Modern Language Association of America*, XL (1925): 335.

[84] Edwin Arthur Burtt, *The Metaphysical Foundations of Modern Physical Science*, London and New York 1925, p. 292.

[85] James Foster, *Discourses on all the Branches of Natural Religion and Social Virtue*, 2 vols., London 1749 and 1752, Vol. I, Chap. IV, p. 93.

[86] Anthony Ashley Cooper, third Earl of Shaftesbury, *Characteristics of Men, Manners, Opinions, and Times*, Robertson's ed., 2 vols., London 1900, Vol. II, p. 113 (being Part III, Sect. i of *The Moralists, a Philosophical Rhapsody*). The italics are mine.

[87] Berkeley, *Siris*, Sect. 277.

[88] James Thomson, *The Seasons*, "Summer," ll. 32-34.

[89] *Ibid.*, ll. 98-100.

[90] Edward Young, *Night Thoughts*, Night IX, l. 711.

[91] Erasmus Darwin, *The Temple of Nature, or, The Origin of Society*, London 1803, Canto IV, Sect. iii, ll. 457-458.

[92] Henry Brooke, *Universal Beauty*, London 1735, Part I, ll. 113-120.

[93] Stillingfleet, *Origines Sacrae*, Book III (Vol. II), Chap. II, pp. 50-51.

[94] Quoted from Needler's *Works*, Letter 11, p. 124. Needler also discusses this contingency of God's withdrawal, and represents the elements as returning to a state of inanition, in his "Vernal Hymn in Praise of the Creator," *Ibid.*, p. 43.

[95] Bentley, *op. cit.*, Sermon VII, pp. 167, 164.

[96] Samuel Clarke, *A Discourse concerning the Being and Attributes of God*, 2 vols., London 1766, Vol. II, Prop. i, p. 14.

[97] Foster, *op. cit.*, Vol. I, Chap. II, pp. 56-57.

[98] Cheyne, *op. cit.*, Chap. I, p. 5.

[99] Burtt, *op. cit.*, p. 257. The italics are in Burtt.

[100] *Rohault's System*, Part I (Vol. I), Chap. XIII, footnote to par. 12.

[101] Benjamin Jowett, *The Dialogues of Plato*, Clarendon Press 1892, Vol. III, pp. 453 and 455.

[102] Shaftesbury, *Characteristics*, Vol. II, p. 112 (Part III, Sect. i of *The Moralists*).

[103] *Ibid.*, p. 113.

[104] *Ibid.*, p. 97. The Latin verses are: "Spiritus intus alit, totamque infusa per artus/ mens agitat molem et magno se corpore miscet/ inde hominum pecudumque genus . . ." (Aeneid, VI, 726-728).

[105] Berkeley, *Siris*, Sections 206, 210, 280.

[106] Shaftesbury, *op. cit.*, II, 96 (Part III, Sect. i of *The Moralists*).

[107] Jowett, *op. cit.*, p. 453.

[108] *Ibid.*, p. 448.

[109] Shaftesbury, *op. cit.*, II, 112 (Part III, Sect. i of *The Moralists*).

[110] Wordsworth, "The Prelude," VI, 567-572 (1805-06); identical in 1850, ll. 636-640.

[111] Jowett, *op. cit.*, p. 456.

[112] "The Prelude," III, 122-124 (1850). It is to be noted that these lines were added after the completion of the 1805-06 version. This platonic note, along with the more orthodox Christianity, grows stronger with the years.

[113] Wordsworth, "The Excursion," IV, 1141-1147. Citations from Nowell Charles Smith's edition of Wordsworth's poems, London 1908, Vol. III.

[114] Shaftesbury, *op. cit.*, II, 97-98 (Part III, Sect. 1 of *The Moralists*).

[115] Shaftesbury, *op. cit.*; e.g., in *An Inquiry concerning Virtue or Merit*, Book I, Part II, Sect. i; Part III, Sect. iii (Vol. I of the 1900 ed.)

[116] *Ibid.*, Book II, Part I (Vol. I).

[117] *Ibid.*, Book II, Part II, Sect. i (Vol. I).

[118] *Ibid.*, Conclusion (Vol. I).

[119] *Ibid.*, Book I, Part II, Sect. i (Vol. I, p. 20). Cf. *The Moralists* (Vol. II), Part III, Sect. i.

[120] *Characteristics* II, 118 (*The Moralists*, Part III, Sect. i).

[121] *Ibid.*, II, 126, 128 (*The Moralists*, Part III, Sect. ii).

[122] *Ibid.*, 112 (*The Moralists*, Part III, Sect. i).

[123] Thomson, *The Seasons*: "Spring," ll. 556-557.

[124] *Ibid.*, 849-855.

[125] *Ibid.*, "Summer," ll. 1746-1748.

[126] Akenside, "The Pleasures of the Imagination," Book I, first version, ll. 62-73.

[127] *Ibid.*, Book II, first version, 315-322.

[128] Brooke, *op. cit.*, Part I, 205-212; Part III, 1-10.

[129] *Ibid.*, I, 352-357.

[130] Burtt, *op. cit.*, p. 275.

[131] *Ibid.*, p. 280.

[132] Quoted from Newton's *Optics* by Clarke in his notes to *Rohault's System*, Part I, Chap. XI, par. 15.

[133] *The Philosophical Works of John Locke*, ed. by J. A. St. John, Bohn library, II, 387. In the *Essay* the reference is Book IV, Chap. iii (Vol. II, p. 193 in Fraser's ed., Oxford 1894).

[134] *Ibid.*, p. 388.

[135] *Ibid.*, p. 389.

[136] Joseph Priestley, *Disquisitions relating to Matter and Spirit*, 2 vols., second ed., Birmingham 1782, Sect. II, p. 24.

[137] *Ibid.*, Sect. IV, p. 44.

[138] *Ibid.*, p. 51.

[139] *Ibid.*, Sect. IX, p. 108.

[140] *Hartley's Theory of the Human Mind* (Priestley's abbreviated version of David Hartley's *Observations on Man*), second ed., London 1790.

[141] Priestley, in *Hartley's Theory*, p. xxiii.

[142] *Ibid.*

[143] Priestley, *Disquisitions*, etc., Sect. XII, p. 146.

[144] Legouis, *op. cit.*, p. 136.

[145] George McLean Harper, *William Wordsworth: his Life, Works, and Influence*, 2 vols., New York 1923, I, 61.

[146] Erasmus Darwin, *The Botanic Garden*, Part I, Canto II, footnote to line 574 (pp. 122-123 in Vol. I of the 4th ed., London 1799).

[147] Erasmus Darwin, *The Temple of Nature*, note on "The Faculties of the Sensorium," in Additional Notes, referring to Canto I, line 250.

[148] Friedrich W. J. von Schelling, introductory Essay to *Von der Weltseele*, in *Sämmtliche Werke*, Stuttgart und Augsburg 1857, Vol. II, pp. 376-378.

[149] See the bewildered letter of Coleridge's disciple, J. H. Green, given in a footnote to Sara Coleridge's edition of *Biographia Literaria*, in *Complete Works of Coleridge*, New York 1868-71, Vol. III, pp. xxi-xxii.

[150] My citations are from the English translation by Josiah and Katharine Royce in Benjamin Rand's *Modern Classical Philosophers*, Boston 1908, pp. 7-8. The entire treatise of Bruno is accessible in German translation, *Von der Ursache, dem Anfangsgrund, und dem Einem*, Jena 1906.

[151] Newton P. Stallknecht, "Wordsworth and Philosophy," in *Publications of the Modern Language Association of America*, XLIV (1929): 1123 and 1127, footnote.

[152] Spinoza, *Ethic: Demonstrated in Geometrical Order*, etc., translated by W. Hale White, etc., 2d ed., New York 1894; see, e.g., Preface to the Fourth Part, p. 177.

[153] Berkeley, *Siris*, Sect. 354.

[154] Clarke, *op. cit.*, I, 25.

[155] Quoted from Helene Richter, "Zu Shelley's philosophischer weltanschauung," in *Englische Studien*, XXX (1901): 232.

[156] Paul Heinrich Dietrich, Baron d'Holbach, *Système de la Nature*, 2 vols., London 1770, Part II (Vol. II), Chap. VI, p. 171.

[157] The passage in Shelley which suggests these citations to Helene Richter, is found in a letter to Hogg, of Jan. 3, 1811, in which Shelley asks if the word "God" does not imply "the soul of the universe, the intelligent and *necessarily* beneficient (sic), actuating principle." (*The Letters of Shelley*, edited by Roger Ingpen, 2 vols., London 1914, I, 29.)

[158] Thomas Taylor, *Five Books of Plotinus*, London 1794, pp. xlix-li.

[159] Elizabeth P. Ebeling, *Shelley's Imaginative Use of his Sources in "Prometheus Unbound,"* with *Special Reference to Calderon*, an M.A. thesis, 1931, deposited in the University of Minnesota Library, p. 32. Miss Ebeling's findings in regard to Shelley and Paracelsus have been published in the North Carolina *Studies in Philology*, XXXII (1935), 508-525.

[160] "The Prelude," VII, 766-768 (1850). In 1805-06, VI, 737, the third line reads, "Was present as a habit . . ."

[161] Cudworth, *op. cit.*, III, xxxvii, 25.

[162] Berkeley, *Siris*, Sect. 274.

[163] Wordsworth refers to "the Poem of Lucretius" as an example of didactic poetry in the Preface to the 1815 edition of his poems.

[164] "The Prelude," V, 15-18 (1805-06). In the 1850 version, the second of the three lines has been changed to the more neutral and orthodox, "As might appear to the eye of fleeting time."

NOTE ON WORDSWORTH'S READING

Philosophical writers known (or possibly known) to Wordsworth, with much reference to philosophical writers known to Coleridge.

In my discussion of Wordsworth's philosophical views, in this (III) and the two following chapters, I mention many philosophical writers and some poets whom there is no demonstrative evidence that Wordsworth had read. References to these writers are made in hopes of throwing light on his ideas and opinions. (See Chapter I.) Few are mentioned with whom there is not some likelihood that he was acquainted, either directly or by hearsay. There is singularly little direct evidence in regard to what he read during the years most important in his writing of nature-poetry (1795–1814). Our main reliance is on two circumstances,–his friendship with Coleridge, beginning in the year 1795, ripening into great intimacy in 1797, and continuing more or less steadily for a considerable number of years thereafter; and the catalogue of the Rydal Mount library as sold at auction after his death, in 1859 (*Transactions of the Wordsworth Society*, No. 6). It is a reasonable assumption that whatever Coleridge was enthusiastically interested in, especially in the years 1795–1807, would not be entirely unknown to Wordsworth; that if he did not actually read the authors to whom Coleridge referred, he would at least take in, with greater or less exactness of understanding, some of the ideas associated with these authors. There is much more information available in regard to authors read by Coleridge in what was for him and Wordsworth the formative period in their thinking about nature, as well as later. With regard to the books in Wordsworth's library, the presence of any item in this list does not of course prove that Wordsworth possessed these books in the years when he wrote "Tintern Abbey" and "The Prelude." But in a general way this list of books gives a notion of the sort of thing which, over a long course of years, went to make up the intellectual background for his imaginative creation.

If Wordsworth possessed books of his own at the period of his sojourn at Racedown and Alfoxden, it may be a matter of speculation what he did with them during his visit to Germany and up to the time of his settlement at Grasmere. Certain references in the recently published *Early Letters of William and Dorothy Wordsworth* (edited by Ernest de Selincourt, Clarendon Press 1935) suggest that his books may have been left in the care of his brother Richard in Staple Inn. In November, 1801, William writes Richard from Grasmere about a "box which he has never received," which he urges him to send off, including "my books etc. etc." (Letter 124). In February, 1802, Dorothy acknowledges receipt of "the Box you sent containing some books of William's," etc. (Letter 126). In January, 1803, William writes: "Some time before his departure John informed us that he had desired your Clerk to pack up a box for us containing such of my books as were in London, some old clothes," etc. (Letter 145). Again, while it is not likely that, in the early years, Wordsworth owned a large and valuable library, it may be pointed out that he had access to several libraries which may have been well stocked with standard and even rare books. In 1797 he wrote Joseph Cottle from Alfoxden urgently requesting the loan of Darwin's *Zoönomia*. "If it is not in your power to borrow it, I wish you would send to Cote House with my compliments to John Wedgewood, and say that I should be much obliged to him if he would let me have it for ten days, at the end of which time it shall certainly be returned." (Knight, *Letters of the Wordsworth Family*, III, 356; Selincourt, *Early Letters*, No. 62). Wordsworth might also have read books borrowed from the Bristol Library by Coleridge. So that, altogether, it is not difficult to suppose him to have been acquainted, say from 1795 on, with many of the serious books contained later in his Rydal Mount library.

Theological Writers

To begin with the theological writers: Cudworth's *True Intellectual System* was in Wordsworth's library in the original folio edition of 1678 (lot 220 of the catalogue). In this case, too, we know that the book in question was familiar to Coleridge at an early and formative period, when he and Wordsworth were living on terms of great intimacy. In the list of books borrowed by Coleridge from the Bristol Library between the years 1793 and 1798 (Paul Kaufman, "The Reading of Southey and Coleridge," *Modern Philology* XXI: 317-320), Cudworth's work appears twice, near the beginning and near the end of the list. So that it is quite probable that Wordsworth heard some discussion of Cudworth's ideas, if he did not actually read him, and that at the critical period for his nature-poetry.

The case of Henry More is not so good. I do not find any work of his listed in the Rydal Mount catalogue. On the other hand, it is certain that Coleridge was, at one period, well acquainted with some of More's writings. He quotes More several times in *Aids to Reflection*, and he owned and annotated the folio *Theological Works*, London 1708,—which, however, did not apparently include his treatise on the Immortality of the Soul (see Thomas J. Wise, *Two Late Poets: A Catalogue of Printed Books*, etc. *of William Wordsworth and Samuel Taylor Coleridge*, London 1927, p. 133.)

Other works of divinity which were in Wordsworth's library are: Sir Matthew Hale's *Primitive Origination of Mankind* in the original folio of 1677 (lot 241); Archbishop Samuel Parker's *Demonstration of the Divine Authority of the law of Nature*, etc., in the original edition of 1681 (lot 279); Bishop Edward Stillingfleet's *Origines Sacrae*, etc. (1662), in the ed. of 1702 (lot 296); Samuel Clarke's *Discourse concerning the Being and Attributes of God*, or, *A Demonstration of the Being*, etc. (sermons preached in 1704 and 1705), 1728 ed. (lot 309); George Cheyne, M.D., *Philosophical Principles of Religion Natural and Revealed*, in two different editions, 1705 and 1753 (lots 210 and 202); James Foster, *Discourses on All the Principal Branches of Natural Religion*, etc., in the original ed. of 1749-1752 (lot 233). In a letter of Coleridge's in 1807, he refers to his notes to Stillingfleet's *Origines Sacrae*; this work, with Coleridge's notes, is in the British Museum (see Earl Leslie Griggs, *Unpublished Letters of Coleridge*, 2 vols., London 1932, No. 171). Wordsworth refers to Stillingfleet in a note to the second of the "Ecclesiastical Sonnets."

Wordsworth had naturally some knowledge of the work of William Paley, who had been a tutor at Christ's College, Cambridge, and whose lectures, revised and enlarged under the title of *The Principles of Moral and Political Philosophy* (1785), immediately became the text-book of the University. His *Horae Paulinae* was published in 1790, *View of the Evidences of Christianity* in 1794, *Natural Theology, or Evidences of the Existence and Attributes of the Deity*, etc., in 1802. There are references to Wordsworth's approval of Paley in Hazlitt's *Spirit of the Age* and Coleridge's *Anima Poetae*. (See K. Lienemann, *Die Belesenheit von William Wordsworth*, Berlin 1908.)

Newtonian Metaphysics

With regard to the metaphysical speculations of Newton, Wordsworth may have had knowledge of them from many different sources. For aught I know, he may have made acquaintance with both the *Optics* and the *Principia* in the regular course of his studies at Cambridge. Newtonian theories are applied to metaphysical and theological problems in nearly all the works of divinity listed in the last paragraph. More important, perhaps, is Jacques Rohault's *Physica ex illus.*

Is. Newtoni et Sam. Clarke, which Wordsworth possessed in the 1718 ed. (lot 154). This is Dr. Samuel Clarke's Latin translation of Rohault's popular exposition of general scientific theory based on Descartes; and includes many illustrative footnotes taken from Newton's *Optics* and *Principia*, intended as correction or refutation of Rohault. (It was translated into English in 1723 by Samuel Clarke's brother, Dr. John Clarke.) It seems not unlikely that Wordsworth may have had this text-book from the time of his residence in Cambridge. Another equally important source of information about Newton's theories (on the side of theology) was Richard Bentley's *Sermons Preached at Boyle's Lecture* (sermons preached in 1692 and 1696), which Wordsworth possessed in the 1724 ed. (lot 186). The late edition of this work which I have consulted contains, in addition to Bentley's expositions of Newton's view, "Four Letters from Sir Isaac Newton to Dr. Bentley; containing some Arguments in Proof of a Deity." But it is stated that these letters from Newton were first printed in 1756; so that it is not certain whether Wordsworth was acquainted with them, even if he had read Bentley's sermons. Wordsworth was acquainted with Bentley's *Dissertation on the Letters of Phalaris* (*Letters*, III, 151).

Scientist-Philosophers

As for the scientist-philosophers, Robert Boyle and Joseph Priestley: Boyle I mention chiefly as a hostile critic of "the vulgar notion of nature." There is, I think, no external evidence that Wordsworth was acquainted with his *Free Inquiry* or other writings, except *Motives and Incentives to the Love of God*, which he had in his library (lot 223). The evidence for Coleridge's acquaintance with Boyle, however, I mention in a footnote to the discussion of Boyle. Wordsworth refers to Priestley in his "Letter to the Bishop of Landaff" (written in 1793) as "the philosophic Priestley." It is not clear from this reference how well Wordsworth was acquainted with his writings, or to what side of his thinking he applies the word philosophic. The philosophic Priestley may be the distinguished student of chemistry and biology; he may be the author of political writings (e.g., *An Essay on the First Principles of Government*, 1768); the author of ecclesiastical history (e.g., *The History of the Corruptions of Christianity*—is this "Priestley's Corruption of Man," borrowed by Southey and by Coleridge from the Bristol Library at some time between 1793 and 1798?). He may be the author of *Disquisitions relating to Matter and Spirit* (including "The Doctrine of Philosophical Necessity Illustrated"), from which I quote in this chapter. Or he may be the editor of Hartley's Theory of the Human Mind, to which I refer in Chapter IV. This version of Hartley is referred to by Coleridge in *Biographia Literaria* (Bohn, p. 53). Coleridge also refers in *Biographia Literaria* to Priestley's theory of matter (Bohn, p. 64). In *Aids to Reflection*, Coleridge refers several times to the unorthodox religious views of Priestley (Bohn, 139, 239, 270); see also his *Unpublished Letters*, I, 49, for his opinion, in 1796, that Priestley was an atheist.

That Wordsworth was well acquainted with David Hartley's *Observations on Man* (1749), Professor Arthur Beatty has made virtually certain in his elaborate study of Wordsworth's thought (see Chap. IV). But what edition of Hartley Wordsworth may have read is not known. It is at least interesting to suppose that he may have read him in Priestley's abbreviated edition (leaving out the theory of vibrations), together with Priestley's introductory essays relating to Hartley's subject. Hartley's theories are referred to disparagingly by Coleridge in *The Friend* (including the original magazine version), and in *Biographia Literaria* (especially Essays v-viii). In *Unpublished Letters*, favorable references to Hartley are found in I, 74, 183; unfavorable, in I, 401, II, 179.

Rousseau, Shaftesbury, Godwin

Among philosophical writers of a belle-lettristic turn, immensely important for their influence on poets in general, were Shaftesbury and Rousseau. Wordsworth possessed Shaftesbury's *Characteristics of Men, Manners, Opinions, and Times*, in the three vol. ed. of 1723 (lot 430). In the "Essay Supplementary to the Preface" (1815 poems), he refers to Shaftesbury as "an author at present unjustly depreciated." He also had Rousseau's *Émile, ou de l'Éducation*, Franckfort 1762, and his *Confessions*, Geneva 1782 (lot 639).

It is to be noted that, in *Aids to Reflection*, Coleridge refers to Shaftesbury, deprecating, in his "pious Deism," Shaftesbury's ignoring of the Christian doctrine of the fall of man (Bohn, 92), and his preference of "a philosophic Paganism to the morality of the Gospel" (Bohn, 128). As for Rousseau, Coleridge several times refers to him in *The Friend* (even in the early magazine version), as "the crazy Rousseau, the dreamer of love-sick tales, and the spinner of speculative cob-webs" (Bohn, 85); as a thinker the whole groundwork of whose philosophy "ends in a mere nothingism" (Bohn, 105). In 1796, Coleridge was planning an attack upon Godwin for his infidelity; see *Unpublished Letters*, I, 60, 65, fn.

It has generally been assumed by the soberest Wordsworth scholars that the poet was deeply influenced by the thought of Rousseau. Professor Harper declares: "Rousseau it is, far more than any other man of letters, either of antiquity or of modern times, whose works have left their trace in Wordsworth's poetry." (G. M. Harper, *William Wordsworth, his Life, Works and Influence*, 2 vols., New York 1923, I, 127-128.) Mr. Harper cites no definite external evidence of Wordsworth's having read Rousseau. The most striking of such evidence, so far as I know, is the paragraph in his pamphlet on "The Convention of Cintra," quoted in Chapter IV, in which he speaks of "the paradoxical reveries of Rousseau" along with similarly disparaging comments on Condillac and Voltaire. This attitude towards Rousseau in 1809 does not make it impossible that in 1791 or 1798 he was more sympathetic towards his views and sentiments. Mr. Harper suggests that Wordsworth's itinerary in his walking-trip of 1790 was partly arranged so as to visit places made glamorous by Rousseau (I, 91-92). He calls attention to the Rousseauistic sentiments of "Descriptive Sketches" in the characterization of primitive man as "Nature's child" (I, 196). He reminds us that Joseph Fawcett, the preacher whom Wordsworth heard and knew personally in 1793-1795, was an enthusiastic admirer of Rousseau (I, 261-267); that one anonymous reviewer of *Lyrical Ballads* found in that volume a suggestion of the dangerous radicalism of Rousseau (I, 283). Wordsworth's early enthusiasm for the French Revolution has often been associated with a probable knowledge of Rousseau's teachings. Mr. Harper finds in "The Prelude" a marked influence of the educational theories of Rousseau. In his poetry more generally, he finds a kinship to Rousseau in his preference for the diction of common speech, his high esteem for reverie as a mode of thought, his desire to simplify, his individualism, etc. In our discussion, the importance of Rousseau is largely confined to certain parallels between his thought and Wordsworth's on the following points: the psychological distinction between active and passive powers (Chapter IV), Rousseau's distinction between the intellectual and the sensitive reason (IV and V), his attitude towards the doctrine of self-interest (V), his attitude towards natural and bookish learning for young children (V), and (possibly) his conception of "what man has made of man" (V).

There is ample reason for assuming Wordsworth's knowledge of Godwin's *Inquiry Concerning Political Justice*, and a strong influence of it upon his views in the years 1793-1798, especially in the matter of political and moral philosophy. The reasons for this assumption are set forth at length by Legouis, Harper, Beatty, and many other scholars—in Harper, see particularly, I, 212, 222, 229,

Chap. XI *passim*, 300; II, 275. In March, 1796, Wordsworth writes a friend that he has received "Godwyn's second edition" (of *Social Justice*, published in that year), in terms suggesting that he was well acquainted with the work in its first edition (Knight, *Letters*, I, 108; Selincourt, *Early Letters*, No. 54; cf. also No. 55, p. 161). In our study, Godwin is of minor importance, being mentioned chiefly in relation to his necessarianism (IV) and his theory of disinterested benevolence (V).

Philosophers

Coming now to more strictly philosophical writers: Plato's dialogues Wordsworth had in two editions, one of them in the translation of Thomas Taylor, 1793, including the Timaeus, to which I refer in this chapter (lots 408, 409). There are conventional references to Plato in Wordsworth's poems and prose (see Lienemann, *op. cit.*, 213-214). Plato is several times mentioned by Coleridge both in *The Friend* and *Aids to Reflection;* and is more often referred to in *Biographia Literaria* than any other philosopher. Plotinus is also mentioned by Coleridge in each of these books, and as many as four times in *Biographia*. But Plotinus seems to have been a thinker more important to Coleridge and Shelley than to the thoroughly English Wordsworth. Another mystical writer frequently mentioned by Coleridge (in *Aids* and *Biographia*) is the German Boehme (Behmen); and it so happens that in the list of Wordsworth's books are found both Jacob Behmen's *De Signatura Rerum, or the Signature of All Things*, English translation 1651, and Boehme's *Theosophick Philosophy unfolded*, by Edward Taylor, 1691 (lots 192, 193). But here again I find no reason for thinking that Wordsworth's thought was in any appreciable degree affected by Boehme; he spoke "another language."

Coleridge, as I have shown, was an enthusiastic Spinozist in the early days of his acquaintance with Wordsworth. In the early magazine form of *The Friend* he quotes a long passage from Spinoza's political philosophy; in *Biographia* and *Aids*, he is frequently busy with Spinoza and his regrettable pantheism, which at an earlier period he had apparently found more palatable. (See Newton P. Stallknecht, "Wordsworth and Philosophy," in *Publications of the Modern Language Association of America*, XLIV (1929), pp. 1123, 1127 footnote, for review of the evidences of Coleridge's knowledge of Spinoza.) But Wordsworth was not dependent on Coleridge for his knowledge of Spinoza. He might have found references to him in Clarke's *Discourse*, together with considerable citations from the (as Clarke considers him) atheistical author of the *Ethics*.

So far as I know, there is no evidence that Wordsworth was acquainted with Giordano Bruno, unless through Coleridge. In *The Friend* (beginning with the original magazine version), Coleridge quotes a considerable passage from Bruno's Latin, with his own translation, including the following sentence: "We examine and seek for the splendour, the interfusion, and communication of the Divinity and of nature, not in meats or drink, or any yet ignobler matter, with the race of the thunder-stricken; but in the august palace of the Omnipotent, in the illimitable ethereal space, in the infinite power, that creates all things, and is the abiding *being* of all things. . . ." (Bohn, 72-73). Coleridge refers to Bruno also in *Biographia* and *Aids*. As for Leibniz, there is clear internal evidence from the poems of Coleridge that he had an early acquaintance with some of his work, especially the *Monadology*. In 1799 he refers to Leibniz in terms of high laudation in a letter to his wife (*Letters*, edited by E. H. Coleridge, 2 vols., 1895, I, 280; cf. I, 360; II, 735). Later he refers to him more than once in *The Friend* (at least in the second edition, 1818), *Biographia Literaria* (1817), and *Aids to Reflection* (1825).

The work of Berkeley's from which I quote illustrations of the idea of the world-soul is *Siris*, and this was not listed among Wordsworth's books. There was listed, however, *Alciphron, an Apology for the Christian Religion*, 1775 (lot 258), which I take to be Berkeley's *Alciphron, or, The Minute Philosopher. In Seven Dialogues. Containing an Apology for the Christian Religion*. We know of Coleridge's unbounded admiration for Berkeley, whose second son he named after the philosopher in May, 1798. Coleridge quotes from *Siris* in *The Friend* in the original magazine version; a copy of *Siris* with annotations by Coleridge is now in the collection of Professor Tinker (see John Louis Haney, "Coleridge the Commentator," in *Coleridge: Studies by Several Hands*, etc., London 1934, p. 122). In the second edition of *The Friend*, Berkeley is included in a list of seven "first-rate philosophers," along with Plato, Kepler, Milton, Boyle, Newton, and Leibniz (Bohn, 296). In *Aids to Reflection*, Berkeleianism is referred to, along with Spinozism, as an outcome of Cartesianism (Bohn, 268 footnotes). Wordsworth could not have failed to know something of this famous philosopher and champion of Christianity; and he may very well have heard something of his special views in the quaint treatise on tar-water, if he had not read it.

Of Locke, he had in his library the *Letter to the Bishop of Worcester* (Stillingfleet), 1697, with his reply to the Bishop's *Answer*, 1699 (lot 266). In this chapter I make some reference to this correspondence. It seems almost certain, on the face of it, that Wordsworth would know something of the theories of Locke in his *Essay on the Human Understanding*, though this book is not listed in the catalogue of his library. Locke was of course well known to Coleridge, who refers to him in *The Friend* (including the early magazine version), *Biographia* and *Aids*, always in terms acknowledging his genius, but with a clear recognition of his radical error, as Coleridge considered, of "taking half the Truth for a whole Truth." (*Aids*, in Bohn ed., 44. Aphorism vi of Moral and Religious Aphorisms.)

With regard to d'Holbach, mentioned in Chap. IV, the only reason I can give for supposing that Wordsworth may have read him is the following item in the Rydal Mount catalogue: "Quintillian, Système de la Nature, par M. Mirabaud, 2 tomes, Londres 1781." My assumption is that two separate items are here run together, the one being Quintillian, and the other the *Système de la Nature*. This work of d'Holbach's was first published in London in 1770 (two volumes) as "par M. Mirabaud," an author who at that date was dead.

Coming now to the German philosophers, Kant, Fichte, Schelling, etc., it is very well known that Coleridge had a considerable knowledge of Kant before he and Wordsworth went to Germany in the autumn of 1798; and that from the time of this German visit of 1798–1799, Coleridge had a very great knowledge of several of the German philosophers. It is known that he borrowed heavily from Schelling in particular, in *Biographia Literaria* and in *Hints towards the Formation of a more Comprehensive Theory of Life* (first published 1848). I believe it can be shown he borrowed both from Kant and Schelling in the essays on scientific method added to *The Friend* in the second edition. (See Chapter XI below.) The subject of Coleridge's borrowings from German authors has yet to be searched to the bottom; but many considerable studies of this subject have been made. Among them the following should be noted as having some bearing on his knowledge and use of the German philosophers: most important of all, Elisabeth Winkelmann, *Coleridge und die Kantische Philosophie* (*Palaestra* 184, 1933), and René Wellek, *Immanuel Kant in England*, Princeton University Press 1931; and then, in receding order of time, J. H. Muirhead, *Coleridge as Philosopher*, London 1930; F. W. Stokoe, *German Influence in the English Romantic Period*, Cambridge University Press, 1926; Max J. Herzberg, "William Wordsworth and German Literature," in *Publications of the Modern Language Association of America*, XL (1925): 302-345; A. C. Dunstan, "The German Influence on Coleridge," *Modern Language Review*, XVII (1922): 272-281; XVIII (1923): 183-201; Helene

Richter, "Die philosophische Weltanschauung von S. T. Coleridge und ihr Ver-
hältnis zur deutschen Philosophie," *Anglia* XLIV (neue Folge XXXII, 1920):
261-290; 297-424; A. C. Bradley, *English Poetry and German Philosophy in the
Age of Wordsworth*, Manchester 1909; John Louis Haney, *The German Influence on Samuel Taylor Coleridge* (an abridgment of a Ph. D. thesis), Philadelphia 1902. In addition to these books and articles should be mentioned the
Basel thesis of Henri Nidecker and his articles on Coleridge Marginalia in the
Revue de Littérature Comparée, referred to in Chap. XI; the articles of De
Quincey, Ferrier, etc., first pointing out Coleridge's borrowing from German
philosophers; Alice D. Snyder, *Coleridge on Logic and Learning*, New Haven
1929; Sara Coleridge's notes to her edition of *Biographia Literaria* (see *Complete
Works of Coleridge*, Harper 1868–1871, Vol. III); J. Shawcross's edition of
Biographia, Clarendon Press, 1907; several German books and articles mentioned
in Herzberg's article named above, and the views of Professor Herford also
summarized by Herzberg. I hope elsewhere to deal more in detail with this matter of Coleridge's German borrowings than there is here any occasion for, and
need not give further references to the literature of the subject.

There is, then, the usual presumption that Wordsworth would have derived
from the conversation of Coleridge some general notion of the German philosophical ideas. Apart from this, there is very little evidence, either "external" or
"internal," of his knowing the German philosophers or being greatly influenced
by them. Herzberg comes to the conclusion that the only German writers who
appreciably affected Wordsworth were Bürger, Schiller, and Frederika Brun. In
one of the visits of the English poets to Klopstock in the autumn of 1798, Wordsworth asked the German poet what he thought of Kant, and was informed that
"his reputation was much on the decline in Germany" (Herzberg, 306). Several
German scholars have traced the influence of Kant's categorical imperative in the
"Ode to Duty." Bradley points out certain resemblances between Wordsworth's
poetry and the philosophy of Hegel (Herzberg, 335). But I have shown how
many other possible sources—especially English sources—there are for Wordsworth's idea of a "soul of all the worlds." Moreover, the published work of
Hegel is too late in date to have affected any of Wordsworth's significant nature-
poetry except perhaps "The Excursion." It seems likely enough that the title of
Schelling's *Von der Weltseele* might have had some effect on Wordsworth's use
of this phrase. It is also not unlikely that the Kantian distinction of *Verstand* and
Vernunft (somewhat questionably developed by writers like Fichte and Schelling) might, through Coleridge, have confirmed Wordsworth in his feeling of
the insufficiency of the "false secondary power by which we multiply distinctions"; might have led to his stress (in the later books of "The Prelude" and in
"The Excursion") on the transcendental powers of the Imagination, or the
imaginative Will. But even here, the roots of Wordsworth's "mysticism" may be
traced, I think, in English soil (or French), and back to a time when he presumably knew nothing of German philosophy.

Nothing more eloquently proclaims the scantiness of our knowledge of
Wordsworth's reading, especially on philosophical subjects, than the following
circumstances. In William Knight's *Letters of the Wordsworth Family* (3 vols.
1907), the index shows but one single reference to the philosophers or theologians
referred to in this note. And that one exception is constituted by a letter to
William Godwin in 1811 declining to put into verse form the story of "Beauty
and the Beast" and reminding Godwin that Wordsworth had to pay 4/9 over-
charge on the parcel he sent him! (Knight misses, in his index, the reference to
Social Justice mentioned above.) There is not one reference to Plato, Locke or
Berkeley; not one to Cudworth, Bentley, Clarke or Paley; not one to Shaftesbury
or Rousseau. This is equally true of Selincourt's *Early Letters of William Wordsworth*, in which more letters are offered for the period covered, and with fewer

omissions. So far as his correspondence shows, Wordsworth might never have opened the grave folio and octavo volumes with which his shelves were lined.

Poets

With regard to his reading in poetry we are much better informed. Of poets, the only ones I have mentioned who can have any bearing on Wordsworth's philosophy of nature, as having possibly influenced it, are the Romans, Virgil and Lucretius, and the English,—Akenside, Beattie, Blake, Brooke, Coleridge, Cowley, Cowper, Darwin, Needler, Pope, Thomson, Young. The most unmistakable evidence that Wordsworth was acquainted with *De rerum naturae* is his references to Lucretius in the prefaces to *Lyrical Ballads* and the 1815 edition of his Poems. For any serious poet of that day educated in the conventional manner no proof is needed that he was familiar with Virgil. But one may refer to the note to "Lycoris," in which he speaks of his schoolboy preference of Ovid to Virgil; to his references to Virgil in the *Letters*, several of them having reference to his translation of parts of the Aeneid; to the quotation from the Aeneid in the preface to the 1815 poems; and to his having in his library at the time of his death the Georgics in Latin and the works of Virgil in translation (lots 680 and 681)—curiously not the Aeneid in Latin, unless in some miscellaneous lot.

The lines from the Aeneid translated by Shaftesbury (mens agitat molem, etc.) Wordsworth might have found quoted in several of the books of divinity in his library, beginning with Cudworth (Book I, Chap. III, Sect. xxxvii, 24). Indeed, this "spiritus intus alit, totamque infusa per artus" might be the sufficient inspiration for Wordsworth's "something far more deeply interfused."

Of the English poets listed above, we may dismiss Brooke and Needler. In a cursory survey, at least, I find no evidence that Wordsworth was acquainted with them. (Dorothy read Brooke's novel, *The Fool of Quality* in 1796; *Letters*, I, 99.) He was acquainted with Blake's *Songs of Innocence* and *Songs of Experience* and liked them, and had the *Songs of Innocence* in his library (see Lienemann, p. 101). The probability of his having early had some knowledge of Erasmus Darwin if only through his brother Christopher is considerable (see Harper I, 60, 61, 187, 195). In the first edition of his poem "To Enterprise" (1822), Wordsworth acknowledges indebtedness to Darwin. I have referred above to his request for a loan of Darwin's *Zoönomia* in 1797. Akenside, Beattie, Cowley, Cowper, Thomson, Young were all in his library (lots 451, 507, 508, 671, 672, 696). In the footnotes to the original edition of "An Evening Walk," he acknowledged indebtedness for words, phrases or images, to a number of poets, including Beattie, Thomson, and Young (Harper I, 289). There is a reference to Akenside in *Early Letters*, No. 155. I refer in Chap. II to Dorothy Wordsworth's early admiration for Beattie's "Minstrel," and her finding in the person of the minstrel a close resemblance to her brother (see *Letters*, I, 53, letter dating from 1793; *Early Letters*, No. 31). That Wordsworth was very early acquainted with Cowper's poems, at the period when one's taste is formed and one learns poetry by heart, is indicated by some remarks recorded by Crabb Robinson (Harper, II, 397). There are references to Cowper in the *Early Letters* in 1802, 1803 and 1805 (Nos. 130, 155, 212); and later (in the more comprehensive *Letters*) in 1807 and 1841 (I, 288; III, 220). Wordsworth refers to Thomson in letters in 1807, 1811, 1823, 1829 (*Letters*, I, 273, 529; II, 210, 359). His knowledge of Pope is evidenced by his obvious imitation of him in his "Lines written as a School Exercise at Hawkshead, Anno Aetatis 14"; by the frequent and respectful references to him in his letters, in 1791, 1796, 1823, 1829, 1830 (see especially I, 107, and II, 359); and by his statement in later years that he knew by heart many thousand lines of Dryden and Pope (Harper, II, 395). Further references to Cowley, Thomson and Pope are found in the "Essay Supplementary to the Preface" (poems of 1815).

Wordsworth quotes a dozen lines from the seventh book of Young's *Night Thoughts* in a letter in 1805 (*Early Letters*, No. 204). As for Coleridge, it is virtually certain that Wordsworth was familiar, from 1795 on, with his friend's "Religious Musings," his "Eolian Harp" and "Destiny of Nations" (see Legouis, Book III, Chap. ii, especially pp. 239-333), and that he continued, through many years, to keep in close touch with Coleridge's work.

CHAPTER IV

WORDSWORTH'S NATURALISM

[1] "The Prelude," IX, 236-237 (1850). In the 1805–06 version, the phrasing is somewhat different, but the sense is the same.

[2] Cowper, "The Task," III, 164-166.

[3] D. J. Sloss and J. P. R. Wallis, *The Prophetic Writings of William Blake*, 2 vols, Oxford 1926, II, 28, 29.

[4] *Ibid.*, p. 35.

[5] *Ibid.*, p. 39.

[6] "Jerusalem," Chap. II, 49. 21-22, 32-37 (*The Prophetic Writings*, Vol. I, pp. 534, 535).

[7] *Ibid.*, Chap. IV, 90. 64-66 (Vol. I, p. 624).

[8] *Ibid.*, Address to the Deists, prefixed to Chap. III (I, 539).

[9] "The Destiny of Nations," II, 38-48.

[10] "Religious Musings," II, 126-131.

[11] "Fears in Solitude" (1798).

[12] "The Prelude," V, 222 (1805-06). In 1850, l. 221, the reading is identical; but this line is followed by another—"Or his pure Word by miracle revealed"— which intensifies the orthodoxy of the position.

[13] *Ibid.*, V, 16-17 (1805-06). In 1850, the first of these lines has been altered so as to do away with a possible suggestion of unorthodoxy.

[14] In *Characteristics*, London 1900, Vol. II (Part II, Section III of *The Moralists*).

[15] *Ibid.*, Part II, Sect. V (Vol. II).

[16] *Ibid.*, Part II, Sect. V. pp. 92-93 (Vol. II).

[17] Boyle, in the second section of his *Free Inquiry into the Vulgar Notion of Nature*, applies the word "naturist" rather disparagingly to those who talk loosely of nature. See *Philosophical Works*, 3 vols., London 1738, II, 121. D'Holbach, in the second part of his *Système de la Nature*, Chap. XIII, p. 367, applies the term *naturalisme* to the view which he wishes to have prevail.

[18] *The Moralists*, Part II, Sect. V., p. 93 (Vol. II of *Characteristics*).

[19] Paul H. D. Baron d'Holbach, *Système de la Nature*, 2 vols., London 1770, I, 51 (Première Partie, Chap. II, Sect. iv.).

[20] Grosart's edition of *The Prose Works* of Wordsworth, I, 161-162.

[21] D'Holbach, *op. cit.*, I, 2.

[22] Legouis, in *The Early Life of William Wordsworth*, translated by J. W. Matthews, London 1897, p. 266, quotes from Hazlitt's *Spirit of the Age* Wordsworth's advice to a young student in the Temple: "Throw aside your books of chemistry and read Godwin on Necessity." See Godwin's *Political Justice*, Book IV, Chap. VIII, "Inferences from the Doctrine of Necessity."

[23] C-F. Comte de Volney, *Les Ruines*, Chap. XXII, Sect. xv, in *Oeuvres Complètes*, Paris 1821, I, 244. In Volney much of this passage is italicized.

[24] Pierre Bayle, *Pensées diverses sur la comète*, Section XCI, édition critique, 2 vols., Paris 1911.

[25] H. Levy, *The Universe of Science*, New York and London 1933, p. 128.

[26] "The Task," III, 221-222, 235-237.

[27] William Paley, *Natural Theology*, etc., London 1830, Chap. XXIII, p. 284.

[28] *Aids to Reflection*, in the *Complete Works*, New York 1871, I, 263. I quote from the Bohn ed., p. 166.

[29] *Ibid.*, in *Complete Works*, I. 272-273. Cf. sections 37 and 38 of Leibniz's *Monadology*, a work by which Coleridge seems to have been early impressed. Cf. also Leibniz's *Theodicée*, Part I, Sect. 7, and *Principes de la Nature et de la Grace*, Sections 7, 8, 11.

[30] *Aids to Reflection*, in *Complete Works*, I. 154.

[31] Legouis, *op. cit.*, 327.

[32] *Ibid.*, 265.

[33] *Ibid.*, 332.

[34] *Ibid.*, 363.

[35] *Aids to Reflection*, in *Complete Works*, I, 361-362. Coleridge continues the quotation from "Tintern Abbey" to the end of the sentence.

[36] "The Prelude," XII, 23-36 (1805-06); in 1850 (XIII, 19-32), almost identical.

[37] *Ibid.*, VI, 305-316 (1805-06); identical with 1850.

[38] My italics. My citation is from *Specimens of the Table Talk* (first published 1835), entry for July 21, 1832, in *Complete Works*, VI, 403.

[39] In Professor Norman Wilde's brief but excellent survey of "The Development of Coleridge's Thought" (*Philosophical Review*, XXVIII (1919): 147-163), the emphasis is laid on the influence of the seventeenth-century theologians. It is mainly since the date of this essay that a detailed study has been made of the German influences, especially in the works of Wellek, Winkelmann and Nidecker referred to in my Note on Wordsworth's Reading and in notes 13 and 36 to Chap. XI. Even yet it must be said that a thorough study remains to be made of Coleridge's knowledge and use of Schelling, though it is clear that he was well acquainted with more than a dozen separate works of that German philosopher.

[40] Arthur Beatty, *William Wordsworth: his Doctrine and Art in their Historical Relation*, second ed., University of Wisconsin Studies in Language and Literature, No. 24, Madison 1927, p. 108.

[41] "Religious Musings."

[42] Beatty, *op. cit.*, 101-102.

[43] *Ibid.*, 103-104.

[44] In Beatty, see especially Chap. V, Chap. VI, pp. 111-113, Chap. VII, pp. 136-144.

[45] "The Prelude," I, 559-566 (1850); almost identical with 1805-06. The italics are mine.

[46] *Ibid.*, I, 581-610 (1850); almost identical with 1805-06. My italics.

[47] "My Heart Leaps Up When I Behold."

[48] "The Solitary Reaper."

[49] "To My Sister."

[50] "The Prelude," XII, 208-215, 223-225 (1850). The corresponding passage in 1805-06 is XI, 258-265, 273-276.

[51] "The Excursion," IV, 1230-1234 (Nowell Charles Smith's ed. of *The Poems of Wordsworth*, Vol. III, p. 128).

[52] Beatty, *op. cit.*, p. 50. Beatty's reference is to Alison's *Essays on the Nature and Principles of Taste*, 1790, Essay II, Chap. VI, vi.

[53] Beatty, *op. cit.*, p. 103.

[54] H. Littledale, *Wordsworth and Coleridge Lyrical Ballads*, London 1930, p. 226.

[55] See Littledale, p. 228. The italics are mine.

[56] Beatty, *op. cit.*, 165.

[57] Quoted from Beatty, *op. cit.*, 195-205.

[58] *Ibid.*, 205.

[59] Sir Matthew Hale, *A Discourse of the Knowledge of God and of Ourselves*, London 1688, Chap. III, pp. 45-46.

[60] Quoted from Beatty, pp. 136-137. Beatty does not give specific reference to chapter or page in Tucker.

[61] Locke's *Essay*, Book II, Chap. VIII, 8.

[62] *Ibid.*, Book II, Chap. XXIII, 37.

[63] *Ibid.*, Book II, Chap. II, 2 (Vol. I, p. 145 of Fraser's ed., Clarendon Press 1894).

[64] Rousseau, *Émile*, Garnier frères, Paris no date, II, p. 95.

[65] *Ibid.*, III, 219.

[66] *Ibid.*, II, 118.

[67] Beatty, *op. cit.*, 125.

[68] "The Prelude," II, 358-363, 368-370 (1850). The corresponding lines in 1805-06 are virtually identical.

[69] *Ibid.*, XI, 269-273 (1805-06). The corresponding lines in 1850 are XII, 219-223.

[70] *Ibid.*, XI, 326-334 (1805-06); almost identical with 1850, XII, 269-277. My italics.

[71] *Ibid.*, XIII, 446-452 (1805-06); almost identical with 1850, XIV, 448-454.

[72] Wordsworth refers in a footnote to his adaptation from Young.

[73] *Biographia Literaria*, Bohn library ed., London 1905, p. 53 (Chap. VI).

[74] *Ibid.*, p. 58 (Chap. VII).

[75] *Ibid.*, 59 (VII).

[76] *Ibid.*, 59.

[77] *Ibid.*, 63-64 (VIII). That these reasonings were taken from Schelling's *Transcendental Idealism* was first pointed out by Professor Ferrier in *Blackwood's Magazine*, XLVII (1840): 296-297, and later by Sara Coleridge in her edition of *Biographia Literaria* (1847); see *Complete Works*, III, 241-246.

[78] David Hartley, *Observations on Man*, 5th ed., Bath 1810; see, e.g., Chap. I, Sect. iii, p. 88; III, vii, 427.

[79] See Hartley, *op. cit.*, I, i, 34.

[80] E.g., I, i, 32; cf. I, iii, 114.

[81] *Ibid.*, III, ii, 373.

[82] *Ibid.*, III, iii, Prop. lxxxix, pp. 381-382. My italics.

[83] Beatty, *op. cit.*, p. 159.

[84] "The Prelude," I, 544-557 (1850); almost identical with 1805-06, I, 571-585.

[85] Sir Matthew Hale, *The Primitive Origination of Mankind*, London 1677, Chap. I, pp. 20-21.

[86] Dr. George Cheyne had a very curious and individual system of philosophy, in which this "universal principle of Action . . . that runs through all the System of Creatures, must analogically be carried through every individual of *spiritual* Beings." See his *Philosophical Principles of Religion*, etc., Part II, "Containing the Nature and Kinds of Infinites," etc., Chap. I, pp. 3-4 of the London 1734 ed.

[87] "The Prelude," XIII, 375-378 (1850); almost identical with 1805-06, XII, 376-379.

[88] *Ibid.*, XIV, 86-118 (1850).

[89] *Ibid.*, XIII, 84-111 (1805-06).

[90] "The Excursion," IV, 1127-1132 (Smith's ed., III, p. 125).

[91] *Ibid.*, IV, 961-964 (III, p. 122).

[92] Newton P. Stallknecht, "Wordsworth and Philosophy," *Publications of the Modern Language Association of America*, XLIV (1929): 1127-1128.

[93] *Ibid.*, p. 1134.

[94] Beatty, *op. cit.*, p. 192.

[95] Mr. Beatty's discussion of the connection between the two odes is on pp.

81-87. I have corrected what is obviously a slip of the pen on Mr. Beatty's part ("twenty-sixth of March"). Later writers differ from Beatty in several points. Thus Fred Manning Smith, who has made a particularly careful study of the matter, on the basis of both external and internal evidence (*Publications of the Modern Language Association of America*, L: 224-234), concludes that Coleridge, in writing his ode, was acquainted certainly with the first four stanzas of Wordsworth's ode (57 lines), and probably also with the first eight stanzas (128 lines). See, too, John D. Rea, in *Modern Philology*, XXVI, 201ff., and Newton Phelps Stallknecht, in *PMLA*, XLIX, 196-207.

96 "The Prelude," II, 239-275 (1805–06).

97 *The Friend*, in *Complete Works*, II, 459-460 (Section II, Essay 11). My italics.

98 "The Church of San Salvador" (1820–1822).

99 Solomon Francis Gingerich, *Essays in the Romantic Poets*, New York, 1929, "Wordsworth," especially III-V.

100 "The Excursion," V, 293-295 (Smith's ed., III, p. 137).

CHAPTER V

Wordsworth and Nature's Teaching

1 D'Holbach, *Système de la Nature* ("par M. Mirabaud"), 2 vols., London 1770, Première Partie (Vol. I), Chap. IV, p. 51.

2 David Hartley, *Observations on Man*, Bath 1810, Part I, Chap. I, Sect. iii, Corollary to Proposition XXII (Vol. I, pp. 117-118).

3 *Ibid.*, Chap. IV, Sect. iv (I, 486-487).

4 *Ibid.*, Conclusion to Part I (I, 524).

5 William Godwin, *Inquiry concerning Political Justice* (first published 1793), Book IV, Chap. I (in the third ed., 1798, Vol. I, p. 256).

6 Shaftesbury, *Characteristics*, 2 vols., London 1900, Vol. I, p. 286 (Book II, Part I, Sect. iii of *Inquiry concerning Virtue, or Merit*). I have partly kept the punctuation of the 3 vol. 1732 ed.

7 *Ibid.*, I, 293 (II, II, i of *Inquiry*, etc.).

8 *Ibid.*, I, 301-302 (II, II, i of *Inquiry*). I have partly kept the punctuation of the 1732 ed.

9 *Ibid.*, I, 338 (Book II, Part II, Conclusion of *Inquiry*).

10 Jean Jacques Rousseau, *La Nouvelle Éloïse*, cited in *Profession de foi du vicaire savoyard*, in *Collectanea Friburgensia*, Fribourg and Paris 1914, footnote to p. 255.

11 *Ibid.*, p. 231 (Sect. 11 of *Profession de foi*, etc.)

12 *Ibid.*, p. 241.

13 Rousseau, *Emile, ou de l'éducation*, Paris, Garnier frères no date, Book IV, p. 256.

14 Voltaire, "La Loi naturelle," Première Partie.

15 Samuel Parker, *A Demonstration of the Divine Authority of the Law of Nature*, etc., London 1681, Part I, Sect. I.

15ª Samuel Clarke, *Discourse concerning the Being and Attributes of God*, 2 vols., London 1766, Vol. I, Prop. I, p. 57.

16 *Ibid.*, Vol. II, p. 65.

17 *Encyclopaedia Britannica*, 11th ed., Vol. VII, p. 621d.

18 "The Prelude," XIII, 20-22 (1850). 1805–06 has "the very quality and shape," etc.

19 Godwin, *op. cit.*, I, 424-425 (Book IV, Chap. X).

20 *Ibid.*, I, 425.

21 "The Excursion," IV, 427-438 (Nowell Smith ed., III, p. 110).

22 Among similar works used by Paley were William Derham's popular *Artificial Clockmaker* (1696), his *Physico-Theology* (1713) and *Astro-Theology* (1714). For the figure of the watchmaker, cf. Sir Matthew Hale's *Primitive Origination of Mankind*, Sect. IV, Chap. IV, p. 326.

23 Edward Stillingfleet, *Origines Sacrae*, etc., 2 vols., Oxford 1817, I, 265-367 (Book III, Chap. I, Sect. xvi).

24 Robert Boyle, *The Philosophical Works*, London 1738, II, 159-160 (second section of *An Inquiry into the Final Causes of Natural Things*).

25 *Ibid.*, p. 160 footnote.

26 *Ibid.*, p. 186 (Sect. IV, Prop. iii).

27 *Ibid.*, p. 182.

28 *Ibid.*, p. 164 (Sect. II).

29 *Ibid.*, p. 163.

30 Richard Bentley, *Sermons Preached at Boyle's Lecture*, London 1838 (Vol. III of Dyce's ed. of the *Works* of Bentley). This edition includes the Four Letters from Sir Isaac Newton to Doctor Bentley (first printed 1756).

31 Bentley, *loc. cit.*, Sermon III, pp. 57-59.

32 Dyce's footnote to the above passage.

33 Arthur O. Lovejoy, "Optimism and Romanticism," in *Publications of the Modern Language Association of America*, XLII (1927): 921-945.

34 John Locke, *Essay concerning Human Understanding*, Book II, Chap. 23, Sect. 12 (Vol. I, p. 403 in Fraser's ed., Oxford 1894).

35 *Ibid.*, Sect. 13, p. 404.

36 George Cheyne, *Philosophical Principles of Religion Natural and Revealed*, London 1734, Part I, Chap. VI, pp. 342-343.

37 William Paley, *Natural Theology*, London 1830, Chap. III, p. 13.

38 See note 33.

39 William King, *De origine mali*, Edmund Law's translation, 4th ed., 2 vols., Cambridge 1758, Vol. I, Chap. III, footnote to p. 117. In regard to the view that no possible alteration in the system but would bring greater inconveniences, the translator says "innumerable instances of this kind are to be met with," and refers to Bentley, Locke, to Grew's *Cosmologia Sacra*, and to "Boyle, Cheyne, Derham, Newentyt, Ray, Cockburn, Edwards, W. Scott, or Pelling." (I, 146.)

40 Locke, *Essay concerning Human Understanding*, Book IV, Chap. 16, Sect. 12 (II, 380-382 in Fraser's ed.).

41 James Foster, *Discourses on All the Branches of Natural Religion*, etc., 1749-1752, Vol. I, Chap. VI, p. 159. I have restored to roman type all but one phrase from the many italicized in the text.

42 Gottfried Wilhelm Leibniz, *Theodicée: Essais sur la bonté de Dieu*, etc., Part I, Sect. 14 (p. 507 in Erdmann's ed. of the *Opera Philosophica*).

43 Pope, "Essay on Man," Epistle I, ll. 45-46.

44 C. A. Moore, "Shaftesbury and the Ethical Poets in England," in *Publications of the Modern Language Association of America*, XXXI: 297.

45 Akenside, "The Pleasures of Imagination," first version, II, 323-350.

46 See for example, Tucker's Vol. II, Chap. VI, on "Things Providential."

47 "Essay on Man," I, 291-292.

48 Shaftesbury, *Characteristics*, 1732 ed., II, 19-20 (Book I, Part II, Sect. i of *An Inquiry concerning Virtue*), with the spelling modernized; I, 246 of the 1900 ed.

49 In *The Moralists* (Part II, Sect. IV), Shaftesbury treats of it in similar terms.

50 *Characteristics*, 1900 ed., II, 23 (Part I, Sect. III of *The Moralists*).

51 "The Excursion," IX, 99 and 105 (Nowell Smith ed., III, pp. 220 and 221).

52 *Ibid.*, III, 809 (Vol. III, p. 96).

[53] *Ibid.*, VI, 998 (Vol. III, p. 176).

[54] *Ibid.*, IV, 1193ff. and "Tintern Abbey."

[55] "The Excursion," I, 195 (Vol. III, p. 40).

[56] Thomson, *The Seasons:* "Spring," ll. 582-585.

[57] *Ibid.*, 867-872.

[58] *Ibid.*, "Hymn," 111-116.

[59] "The Prelude," XIV, 317-320 (1850); in 1805-06 the same thought more awkwardly expressed.

[60] See, e.g., VIII, 365ff. (1850); 510ff. (1805-06).

[61] II, 376-418 (1850); 396-434 (1805-06).

[62] Erasmus Darwin, *Zoönomia*, Part I, Sect. XIII, ii. Citations from the second American taken from the third London ed., Boston 1803.

[63] *Ibid.*, Sect. XIII, iii.

[64] *Ibid.*, Section XIII, v, 2.

[65] H. Littledale, *Wordsworth and Coleridge Lyrical Ballads*, Oxford 1930 (first ed. 1911), pp. 238-239. This passage is from the part added in the 1802 version of the Preface of 1800.

[66] Littledale, *op. cit.*, p. 239.

[67] It has sometimes been assumed by critics of Wordsworth that in his reference to "what man has made of man," he is echoing the doctrine of Rousseau and Godwin, that man, though naturally good, has been depraved by evil social institutions. (See for example, *Émile*, Book IV, p. 259.) I doubt whether this implication is present in the "Lines Written in Early Spring," or whether it is anywhere a considerable factor in Wordsworth's poetic philosophy. It is true that he was at one time so enthusiastic a republican that he wrote a prose pamphlet urging the adoption of this form of government as suited to the realization of the best conditions for human life. It is also true that, in "The Excursion," he argues that the poor have been prevented by vicious industrial conditions from realizing the happiness and fineness of character possible to them under better conditions. In "Descriptive Sketches" he celebrates in the Swiss mountaineer the virtue possessed by him ("Nature's child") through his independence, and he dedicated many a sonnet to the cause of Liberty. But taking his poems as a whole, they are singularly free from the notion of mere social or political institutions as the main determinant of man's spiritual life. It was Wordsworth himself who insisted, in a sonnet of 1802,

> . . . that by the soul
> Only the Nations shall be great and free.

There is, in *Émile*, a phrase rather strongly suggestive of Wordsworth's "what man has made of man." In the second book, in arguing against instructions too advanced for a child's age, he indicates how all kinds of vicious notions may be instilled into the youthful mind by injudicious teachers.

> A chaque instruction précoce qu'on veut faire entrer dans leur tête, on plante un vice au fond de leur coeur; d'insensés instituteurs pensent faire des merveilles en les rendant méchants pour leur apprendre ce que c'est que bonté; et puis ils nous disent gravement: Tel est l'homme. Oui, *tel est l'homme que vous avez fait.* (II, 74).

I do not see, however, how this passage can be brought into relation to Wordsworth's poem, and it seems most reasonable to suppose that the resemblance is accidental. Wordsworth seems to be simply pointing out the difference between man as he might be if he would follow the admonitions of nature, and man as he has made himself through ignoring nature. Nature means him to be happy, and he has made himself wretched. It is possible to connect this with Rousseau's advice to distinguish between the dispositions that come to us from nature and those that come from opinion—"Distinguons toujours les penchants qui viennent de la nature de ceux qui viennent de l'opinion." (III, p. 172.) There may be implied in Wordsworth's poem some such antithesis between the instructions of nature and the mistaken opinions of men. But it is hardly necessary to refer this to the teachings of any particular writer.

[68] John Stuart Mill, *Three Essays on Religion*, 3d ed., London 1874, p. 8.

[69] *Ibid.*, p. 25.

[70] *Ibid.*, p. 65.

[71] "The Excursion," IV, 489-490 (Vol. III, p. 111).

[72] *Ibid.*, VI, 997-1001 (Vol. III, p. 176).

[73] Rousseau, *Émile*, Book II, pp. 117-118.

[74] *Ibid.*, III, 194.

[75] Wordsworth says in the Advertisement to *Lyrical Ballads* (1798): "The lines entitled Expostulation and Reply, and those which follow, arose out of conversation with a friend who was somewhat unreasonably attached to modern books of moral philosophy." Mr. Littledale surmises, in his ed. of *Lyrical Ballads*, p. 220, that the friend was William Hazlitt, though Wordsworth changes the person in the first of the two poems, "connecting it definitely with his old teacher, (partly drawn from William Taylor, the 'gray-haired man of glee')."

[76] "The Prelude," XI, 297-303 (1850); identical with X, 896-901 (1805-06).

[77] *Ibid.*, XI, 353-354 in 1850 version.

[78] Rousseau, *Profession de foi*, critical ed. of Masson in *Collectanea Friburgensia*, p. 61 (section 3 of the First Part).

[79] *Ibid.*, p. 91 (sect. 4 of First Part).

[80] Rousseau, *Émile*, III, 219.

[81] "Tintern Abbey." My italics.

[82] Rousseau, *Profession de foi*, p. 231 (sect. 11 of First Part).

[83] Here again, I suppose, Professor Stallknecht would find a mean between the "language of the sense" and transcendental Reason in Spinoza's intuition, which is the faculty by which man apprehends the sensible experience and the intellectual rationale at one and the same time (see Chap. IV). But whether Wordsworth was conscious of his dilemma, or had found this Spinozistic solution, in 1798, is a very speculative matter. The general tone and phrasing of "The Tables Turned" and its companion poem seem on the whole more in accord with the "sentimental" approach of Rousseau than with the "rational" approach of Spinoza.

[84] "The Prelude," II, 203-221 (1850); virtually identical in 1805-06.

[85] Littledale, *op. cit.*, p. 240; from the 1802 additions to the 1800 Preface.

[86] "The Excursion," IV, 941-968 (Vol. III, pp. 121-122).

[87] *Ibid.*, I, 252-257, 263-273 (Vol. III, p. 42). The italics are mine.

CHAPTER VI

NATURE IN WORDSWORTH: SUMMARY

[1] H. W. Garrod, *Wordsworth*, Oxford University Press 1923. Herbert Read, *Wordsworth*, New York 1931. C. H. Herford, *Wordsworth*, New York 1930. E. C. Batho, *The Later Wordsworth*, Cambridge University Press 1933. Hugh I'Anson Fausset, *The Lost Leader, a Study of Wordsworth*, London & New York 1933. Willard L. Sperry, *Wordsworth's Anti-Climax*, Harvard University Press 1935.

CHAPTER VII

Shelley's Naturalism

[1] "Queen Mab," Part II, line 76.
[2] *Ibid.*, III, 82-83.
[3] *Ibid.*, VIII, 214-215.
[4] *Ibid.*, III, 214-226.
[5] "The Revolt of Islam," Canto VI, Stanza xl.
[6] "The Cenci," Act I, Scene i, ll. 286-287.
[7] "To the Lord Chancellor" (1817).
[8] "Prometheus Unbound," Act I, line 648.
[9] "Queen Mab," II, 257.
[10] *Ibid.*, IV, 103-105.
[11] *Ibid.*, II, 63, 76, 257.
[12] *Ibid.*, VI, 54-57.
[13] *Ibid.*, VI, 39-43.
[14] Much the most detailed information available on Shelley's reading is to be found in Adolf Droop, *Die Belesenheit P. B. Shelley's* (Jena dissertation), Weimar 1906. Droop's discussion is divided into thirteen sections according to the language of the authors read. Most of the sections are divided into parts dealing with "schöne Literatur" and "wissenschaftliche Literatur." Droop gives exact information as to the period in his life in which Shelley was busied with this and that writer, and as to works of his in which reference is made to various writers. Among Greek philosophers mentioned are Plato, Anaxagoras, Democritus, Epicurus, and the neoplatonists translated by Thomas Taylor; among the Romans Lucretius; among modern Latin writers, Spinoza; among the Germans, Kant and Hegel (though Droop is very doubtful of Shelley's having any real acquaintance with Hegel); among the French, Rousseau, Voltaire, Helvétius, d'Holbach, Condorcet, Volney. The list of English philosophical writers with whom Shelley was more or less well acquainted is very long, and includes Bacon, Locke, Berkeley, Hartley, Reid, Hume, Paine, Paley, Dugald Stewart, Godwin, Mary Wollstonecraft Godwin, Robert Forsyth, and Sir William Drummond.

The most extensive treatment of Shelley's knowledge and use of Spinoza is in Sophie Bernthsen's *Shelley's Spinozismus*, Heidelberg 1900. But this work has been shown to be highly uncritical by Helene Richter in her article, "Zu Shelley's philosophischer Weltanschauung," *Englische Studien*, XXX (1902): 224-265; 383-435. Helene Richter discusses the possible influence of many philosophical writers on Shelley's views, taking them up under ten heads: (1) *Necessity of Atheism;* (2) *Queen Mab;* (3) Pantheism; (4) Intellectual Love; (5) Intellectual Beauty; (6) Necessity and free will; (7) Good and evil; (8) State and society; (9) Millennium (10) Immortality. Under (1), she finds closer parallels with Locke and Sir William Drummond than with Spinoza; under (2), closer parallels with d'Holbach; under (5), with Plato; under (6), with Godwin; under (7), with Godwin, d'Holbach and Drummond; under (8), with Godwin, Volney, Hobbes; under (9), with Godwin; under (10), with d'Holbach and Plato. She makes it seem likely that Shelley's knowledge of Spinoza came through the medium of writers like Drummond and Bayle. Altogether she makes it appear that the following were most important in their influence on Shelley's thought; and in the order named: Godwin, Plato, d'Holbach, Drummond, Volney, Locke. She has no suggestion of the possible influence of Plotinus, which I mention in Chap. VIII.

The influence of Volney's *Ruines* on "Queen Mab" has been exhaustively studied by Leon Kellner in his article in *Englische Studien*, XXII (1896): 9-40. See also

A. Beljame's translation of "Alastor" into French prose, Paris 1895, for further evidence of the influence of Volney on Shelley.

Droop is unable to identify the author of a "*Système de la Nature,* par Mirabaud," 1770, which was read by Shelley. The author was d'Holbach, passing himself off under the name of a dead writer. Shelley was reading d'Holbach in 1812/13, and quotes him in the notes to "Queen Mab." It is there also that he refers to Condorcet's *Esquisse d'un tableau historique des progrès de l'esprit humain.*

Sophie Bernthsen discusses the influence of Pliny on Shelley in *Englische Studien,* XXX (1901): 214-224. She comes to the conclusion that Pliny's *Natural History* had a considerable influence on Shelley's pantheism in his youthful writings, including "Queen Mab."

In Chap. VIII I summarize Droop's information on Shelley's knowledge of Plato, of Hume and Berkeley; I quote Hogg on Shelley's readings in Taylor's translations from the neoplatonists, and suggest a reading of Taylor's Plotinus; and I quote Fairchild on the influence of Drummond.

[15] "Queen Mab," I, 264-277.

[16] *Ibid.,* II, 73-82, 97-108.

[17] The passage from d'Holbach was quoted in Chap. IV. Besides his quotations from d'Holbach in the notes to "Queen Mab," Shelley refers to the *Système de la Nature* in a note to "A Refutation of Deism" as "one of the most eloquent vindications of Atheism." (*Complete Works,* VI, 54).

[18] Baron d'Holbach, *Système de la Nature,* 2 vols., London 1770, Part I (Vol. I), Chap. IV, pp. 49-50.

[19] C-F. Comte de Volney, *Les Ruines, ou Meditation sur les Révolutions des Empires* (first published 1791), in Volney's *Oeuvres Complètes,* Paris 1821, Vol. I, Chap. V, pp. 27-28.

[20] D'Holbach, *op. cit.,* Part I, Chap. IV, pp. 50-51.

[21] Roger Ingpen and W. E. Peck, *Complete Works of Shelley,* 1927, Vol. I, p. 144.

[22] "Queen Mab," VI, 146-198.

[23] Shelley, *Complete Works,* I, p. 143. The passage is taken from the fourth chapter of d'Holbach's *Système,* following closely on those passages from this chapter quoted above, that is, pp. 51-52.

[24] Volney, *op. cit.,* Vol. I, Chap. XIII, p. 83. Cf. Shelley's description of nature, in "Queen Mab," VI, 232-235, as "that wondrous and eternal fane,/ Where pain and pleasure, good and evil join,/ To do the will of strong necessity."

[25] "Queen Mab," VII, 13-26.

[26] Shelley, *Complete Works,* I, 147.

[27] Of Shelley's concept of God and his attitude towards that concept, much more is to be said, of course, than can conveniently be said in the present discussion. It is well known that he did not consistently or long maintain the *simple atheism* of his early pamphlet on "The Necessity of Atheism." Already in "Queen Mab," to the statement in the text, "There is no God," he appends in the footnote the following qualification: "This negation must be understood solely to affect a creative Deity. The hypothesis of a pervading Spirit coeternal with the universe, remains unshaken." (Ingpen and Peck's *Complete Works* of Shelley, I, 146). In the year 1812 he had some conversation with Southey on this subject, recorded in Shelley's letters to Miss Hitchener: "He says I ought not to call myself an atheist, since in reality I believe that the universe is God. I tell him I believe that 'God' is another signification for the Universe. . . . Southey agrees in my idea of Deity —the mass of infinite intelligence. . . . Southey says I am not an Atheist, but a Pantheist." (*The Letters* of Shelley, edited by Roger Ingpen, 2 vols., London 1914, I, 205-210. All these citations from Shelley's letter of Jan. 2, 1812.) Helene Richter, who has brought together a large number of Shelley's statements on the subject of God (*op. cit.,* 224-247), believes that he should be called a pantheist.

It is clear, however, that for the most part his pantheism is much nearer to the atheism of d'Holbach than to the pantheism of Southey or Wordsworth (in the period when they could be called pantheists).

Mr. Peck is hardly justified in his statement that, in the "Essay on Christianity" (1815, 1817? see *Complete Works*, VI, 364), "Shelley departs from his pantheistic conception, and openly calls this Spirit, God." (Peck's Shelley, I 330). Apart from the fact that Shelley is, in the passage referred to, trying simply to interpret Christ's idea of the deity, the terms Shelley uses are still pantheistic enough, and the pantheism is not got rid of by calling the spirit God. In "A Refutation of Deism" (1814), Shelley is still using all his powers of argument and irony to combat the Christian idea of God. The ordinary arguments for a creator would equally justify, he shows, "an infinity of creative and created Gods, each more eminently requiring an intelligent author of his being than the foregoing." (*Complete Works*, VI, 47). "The laws of attraction and repulsion, desire and aversion, suffice to account for every phenomenon of the moral and physical world" (p. 49). All the arguments for design defeat themselves. The various attributes of the deity are either drawn "from the passions and powers of the human mind," or else are negations (p. 54). As for the need for mind to explain the beginning of motion, "It is evident . . . that mind deserves to be considered as the effect, rather than the cause of motion" (p. 56). In short, as Shelley's mouthpiece, Eusebes, sums up the argument, he has "proved, that on the principles of the philosophy to which Epicurus, Lord Bacon, Newton, Locke and Hume were addicted, the existence of God is a chimera" (p. 57). Even in "Prometheus" (1818-1819) Demogorgon explains that, in his account of the creation and governance of the world, he has been using anthropomorphic terms ("I spoke but as ye speak"). I see no reason for not supposing that Shelley continued to hold to the end the position, taken in "A Refutation of Deism" (p. 47), that the universe "has endured from all eternity": which is the position of the ancient philosophers whom English theologians agreed in calling atheists.

Shelley used the word God in these early years, as Barnard points out, as a name for all that is detestable in popular religion. In the preface to "The Revolt of Islam" he writes: "The erroneous and degrading idea which men have conceived of the Supreme Being . . . is spoken against, but not the Supreme Being itself." It is probable that his aversion to the idea of God, in the years 1812-1816, was as much on moral and anti-clerical grounds as on metaphysical. In the speculations and poems of later years, he is much more given to use the word God for "the pervading spirit of the universe." (A. H. Beaven, *James and Horace Smith*, p. 173.) And recent writers on Shelley are more or less agreed that God was likely to be identified in his mind with the impersonal spirit of Good in which he so passionately believed. Thus Gingerich: "Love, like the words Necessity and Power already noted, is a word almost interchangeable with Wisdom, or Nature, or God, and though it has a human side, it is chiefly a cosmic force as impersonal and impalpable as Time, or Nature, or any other of Shelley's abstractions, which live and work in a necessarian spirit almost exclusively independent of the human consciousness." (*Essays in the Romantic Poets*, p. 203.) Stovall: "The Daemon of the World, or the Spirit of Love, becomes in a sense the interpreter of inscrutable Necessity, and stands to Shelley in the same relation that Christ stands to the Christian. . . . Cythna's invocation to Love . . . contains further evidence that the various names employed by Shelley—Love, Spirit of Beauty, Spirit of the Universe, and Mother of the World—all refer to the same being." (*Desire and Restraint in Shelley*, p. 145.) "Since Shelley did not attribute to God the creation of the material universe, but only of the 'living world,' it may be that he (in "Prometheus") identified God and Love" (217). Barnard argues, somewhat unconvincingly, that Shelley's God should be regarded as personal, since his Nature is purposive, implying *will* (*Shelley's Religion*, Chap. II, sect. iii). Barnard, more than any other writer, shows how complicated is Shelley's theology. His God is entirely benevolent, but without omnipotence. Behind God lies "some higher principle, standing above God and Mutability and the element in which they contend." His God, or Spirit of Good, is to him as Christ in the Christian system, a mediator between man and the Absolute (sect. ix).

[28] "The Revolt of Islam," Canto VIII, stanza v.

[29] *Ibid.*, IX, xxxiii.

[30] "The secret power which animates the universe," as it appears in the English translation, Philadelphia 1799.

[31] "The Revolt of Islam," IX, xxvii.

[32] "Alastor," ll. 18-23.

[33] "Adonais," stanza XLIII.

[34] Shelley, *Complete Works*, I, 157.

[35] D'Holbach, *op. cit.*, Part I, Chap. VI, p. 81.

[36] Shelley, *Complete Works*, I, 160.

[37] Leopold Brandl, *Erasmus Darwin's Temple of Nature* (Vol. XVI of *Wiener Beiträge zur Englischen Philologie*), Wien und Leipzig 1902, p. 146.

[38] Darwin, "The Temple of Nature," Canto II, Sect. ii.

[39] *Ibid.*, II, v.

[40] *Ibid.*, III, iii.

[41] *Ibid.*, III, viii.

[42] Newman I. White, "Shelley's Prometheus Unbound, or Every Man his Own Allegorist," in *Publications of the Modern Language Association of America*, XL (1925): 179, refers to the *Examiner*, 1822, pp. 355, 370, 389, for Hunt's interpretation.

[43] W. M. Rossetti, in *Publications of the Shelley Society*, Series I, Part 1, p. 63. Rossetti also calls Asia "the spirit of universal love" in the Shelley Society's *Notebook*, Part I, p. 87.

[44] John Todhunter, *A Study of Shelley*, London, 1880, p. 139.

[45] J. A. Symonds, *Shelley*, New York 1878, p. 122.

[46] Translation of H. A. J. Munro, 4th ed., in the London 1907 reprint. The Latin is: "Alma Venus, caeli subter labentia signa/ quae mare navigerum, quae terras frugiferentis/ concelebras, per te quoniam genus omne animantum/ concipitur visitque exortum lumina solis." (I, 2-5).

[47] Unde omnis natura creet res auctet alatque (1. 56).

[48] Quae quoniam rerum naturam sola gubernas/ nec sine te quicquam dias in luminis oras/ exoritur neque fit laetum neque amabile quicquam,/ te sociam studeo scribendis versibus esse/ quos ego de rerum natura pangere conor . . . (21-25).

[49] Darwin, "The Botanic Garden," Part I, Canto II, ll. 1147-1154.

[50] "The Temple of Nature," Canto I, Sect. V, ll. 295-302.

[51] *Ibid.*, 371-378.

[52] Carl Grabo, *A Newton among Poets*, Chapel Hill, N. C., 1930, p. 46.

[53] "Prometheus Unbound," III, iv, 17-19.

[54] Grabo, *op. cit.*, p. 133.

[55] *Ibid.*, 141.

[56] *Ibid.*, 142.

[57] *Ibid.*, 143. The passage is found in Shelley's *Complete Works*, VI, 50.

[58] Grabo, *op. cit.*, Chap. IX.

[59] Note to "Queen Mab," VI, 45-46. See *Complete Works*, I, 143.

[60] Grabo, p. 26.

[61] *Ibid.*, 185.

[62] *Ibid.*, 185-190.

[63] "Prometheus Unbound," III, iv, 78.

[64] *Ibid.*, III, iii, 90-97.

[65] See Joseph Gostwick's *German Culture and Christianity*, London 1882, Chap. XV.

[66] Elizabeth Pierce Ebeling, *Shelley's Imaginative Use of his Sources in "Prometheus Unbound,"* a manuscript thesis deposited in the University of Minnesota library. The portions of this thesis pertinent to our discussion have been printed, with some alteration, under the title, "A Probable Paracelsian Element in Shelley," in North Carolina *Studies in Philology*, XXXII (1935), 508-525.

[67] Ebeling, *op. cit.*, pp. 32-33; corresponding passage in *Studies in Philology*, 514.

[68] *Ibid.*, pp. 38-39; *Studies in Philology*, 515.

[69] *Ibid.*, p. 36; *Studies in Philology*, 513.

[70] *Ibid.*, p. 29; *Studies in Philology*, 509. Miss Ebeling here quotes a letter of Shelley's to Godwin, June 3, 1812; Shelley's *Letters*, ed. Roger Ingpen, New York 1909, I, 314.

CHAPTER VIII

SHELLEY'S "PLATONISM"

[1] W. L. Renwick, editor, *Daphnaïda and Other Poems* by Edmund Spenser, London 1929. The commentary on the "Fowre Hymnes" is pp. 209-224.

[2] The following are among the most important studies: Lillian Winstanley, "Platonism in Shelley," in *English Association Essays*, Vol. IV (Oxford 1913); Helene Richter, "Zu Shelley's philosophischer Weltanschauung," in *Englische Studien*, XXX (1901): 224-265, 383-435, especially sections III, V, X; Richard Ackermann, *Quellen, Vorbilder, Stoffe zu Shelley's Poetischen Werken*, Erlangen und Leipzig 1890 (especially good for the many reminiscences of Plato in "Epipsychidion"). More recently there are the Shelley studies of Stovall, Kurtz, Grabo and Barnard listed in note 20 to Chapter I.

[3] Adolf Droop, *Die Belesenheit Shelley's*, Weimar 1906.

[4] Thomas Jefferson Hogg, *The Life of Shelley*, 2 vols., New York and London 1933, Vol. I, p. 121.

[5] *The Complete Works* of Shelley (Ingpen and Peck), VII, 206. The passage in which Shelley uses the term "intellectual beauty" is in the Greek (Symposium 28): 'αλλ' επὶ τὸ πολὺ πέλαγος τετραμμένος τόῦ καλοῦ. Helene Richter remarks: "Platon's gedanken sind so sehr seine eigenen, dass er sie in den Ausdruck kleidet, den er selbst für seinen höchsten schönheitsbegriff gewählt: *Intellectual Beauty*." (*Eng. Stud.* XXX: 254).

[6] "Prometheus Unbound," I, 648-651.

[7] *Plotinus on The Divine Mind: Being the Treatises of the Fifth Ennead*. Translated from the Greek by Stephen Mackenna, Medici Society 1926 (Vol. IV), Book viii, Sections 3 and 5.

[8] *Ibid.*, Section 12.

[9] *An Essay on the Beautiful* (from the Greek of Plotinus), translated by Thomas Taylor, London 1917. See, e.g., pp. 10-11 in Taylor's Introduction.

[10] *Ibid.*, pp. 25 and 29. *Plotinus, the Ethical Treatises: Being the Treatises of the First Ennead*, etc., translated by Mackenna, Medici Society 1917 (Vol. I), Book vi, Sections 5 and 6.

[11] Taylor, *op. cit.*, p. 34; Mackenna, *op. cit.*, Section 8.

[12] Taylor, pp. 19-20; Mackenna, Section 2.

[13] Taylor, p. 19; Mackenna, Section 2.

[14] Taylor, p. 34; Mackenna, Section 8.

[15] Taylor, p. 42.

[16] "The Witch of Atlas," stanza 12. The platonism of "The Witch of Atlas" has recently received elaborate study at the hands of Professor Grabo, in *The Meaning of "The Witch of Atlas,"* 1935.

[17] "Prometheus Unbound," II, v, 66-67.

[18] Ebeling, *op. cit.*, pp. 40-41; *Studies in Philology*, XXXII, 517. Grabo, *"Prometheus Unbound": An Interpretation*, pp. 25-27.

[19] "Prometheus Unbound," I, 195-202.

[20] "The Witch of Atlas," stanza 63.

[21] Letter of Shelley to Horace Smith, Apr. 11, 1822, in *The Letters*, ed. Ingpen, II, 959-960. Cf. Shelley's "Essay on Life": "The shocking absurdities of the popular philosophy of mind and matter, its fatal consequences in morals, and their violent dogmatism concerning the source of all things, had early conducted me to materialism. This materialism is a seducing system to young and superficial minds. It allows its disciples to talk and dispenses them from thinking. But I was discontented with such a view of things as it afforded; man is a being of high aspirations, 'looking before and after,' whose 'thoughts wander through eternity,' disclaiming alliance with transience and decay." This is quoted from the *Complete Works*, VI, 194. The "Essay on Life" probably dates from 1815 (*ibid.*, p. 360). Shelley goes on to say that high contemplations on man's life are forbidden alike by materialism and the popular philosophy; "they are only consistent with the intellectual system." And he gives a sketch of a guarded form of idealism, referring to Sir William Drummond's *Academical Questions* as giving "perhaps the most clear and vigorous statement of the intellectual system."

[22] "Prometheus Unbound," II, iv, 119-120.

[23] Shelley's translation in *Prose Works*, II, 83.

[24] Cited by Droop in his discussion of Shelley's readings in Berkeley.

[25] This statement I take from Droop. The best authority for this view is the statement of Mrs. Shelley in her collection of Shelley's *Essays, Letters from Abroad* (1840), referring to the Essay "On Life": "Shelley was a disciple of the Immaterial Philosophy of Berkeley. This theory gave unity and grandeur to his ideas, while it opened a wide field to his imagination." Etc. (See *Complete Works*, VI, 360.) The best *loci* for studying Shelley's "Berkeleianism" are the Essay "On Life" (esp. pp. 195-197 in *Complete Works*, VI) and the fourth one of the fragmentary "Speculations on Metaphysics" (*ibid.*, VII, 65). In the second of these passages he speaks of the verbal disputes which have arisen from the distinction made between external and internal reality. "This is merely an affair of words, and as the dispute deserves, to say, that when speaking of the objects of thought, we indeed only describe one of the forms of thought—or that, speaking of thought, we only apprehend one of the operations of the universal system [of beings]." In the Essay "On Life" Shelley is evidently trying to avoid some of the extreme idealistic (and religious) assumptions of the "intellectual system." "Yet, that the basis of all things cannot be, as the popular philosophy alleges, mind, is sufficiently evident. Mind, as far as we have any experience of its properties, and beyond that experience how vain is argument! cannot create, it can only perceive . . . It is infinitely improbable that the cause of mind, that is, of existence, is similar to mind." Shelley, then, seems to have adopted the Berkeleian analysis of objective reality in terms of thought, but to have balked at Berkeley's view of active mind (or God) as the spring of the universe. He was, I should say, trying to maintain his non-theistic position. Shelley's reference, by the way, is not to Berkeley but to Drummond as the exponent of the "intellectual system."

[26] Hoxie Neale Fairchild, *The Romantic Quest*, New York 1931, pp. 382-384.

[27] *Ibid.*, pp. 389-390. Another study of the influence of Berkeley and Drummond on Shelley is that of G. S. Brett in *Studies in English*, Toronto University Press 1931, pp. 170-202.

[28] See Shelley's discussion of necessity and free will in notes to "Queen Mab,"

Complete Works, I, 144-146. In Helene Richter's numerous citations from Shelley under the head of "Nothwendigkeit und Willensfreiheit" (*op. cit.*, pp. 258-265), it would appear that: (1) Shelley clung to the notion of necessity for two reasons, (a) because it maintained moral phenomena within the chain of natural cause and effect; (b) because it enabled the moral philosopher to regard the actions of men with more humane indulgence and understanding, and gave hope that moral education might be effective as operating within the chain of natural causes. (2) He often insisted on man's freedom of action—if he would but have faith in it—because that made possible his program of reform and amelioration. All this is in marked contrast with Coleridge's concern for freedom of the will as insuring man's moral and religious responsibility. The emphasis with which Shelley insisted on necessity or on freedom depended on whether at the time he was more impressed with the need for order and regularity in the natural world or with the need for human initiative in the improvement of human conditions. In neither case was he primarily concerned, like Coleridge, with man's obligation to a being to whom he is morally subject, or with virtuous action as an end in itself.

29 See my citation from his "Speculations on Metaphysics" in footnote 25 above.

30 "Mont Blanc."

31 *Letters*, I, 70-71.

32 *Complete Works*, VII, 64.

33 Mary Shelley, *Valperga; or, The Life and Adventures of Castruccio, Prince of Lucca*, 3 vols., London 1823, II, 99-102.

34 We need not suppose that Shelley was trying to give a precise interpretation of Plato's cave of the mind or Porphyry's cave of the nymphs. Indeed, it is possible that he had more immediately in mind not so much Plato as Bacon. In his "Essay on Christianity" he says: "Every human mind has, what Lord Bacon calls its 'idola specus,' peculiar images which reside in the inner cave of thought." (*Complete Works*, VI, 241.) This essay dates from about the same period as "Mont Blanc."

35 Walter Edwin Peck, *Shelley: His Life and Work*, 2 vols., Boston and New York 1927, I, 469.

36 "O May I Join the Choir Invisible."

37 *Five Books of Plotinus*, translated from the Greek by Thomas Taylor, London 1794, pp. 239-240 (treatise on Nature, Contemplation, and the One).

38 Charles Lamb, "Christ's Hospital Five and Thirty Years Ago."

39 *Five Books of Plotinus*, pp. 263-264. This notion of "an occult fire or light or spirit diffused throughout the universe" is the subject of much discussion by Berkeley in his *Siris* (e.g., sections 153, 156, 161, 206, 207, 229, 277, 280, 291), together with several other features of Shelley's universal spirit, and his notion of the world as seeing itself, expressed in "Hymn of Apollo" (see note 12 to Chap. IX; also section, *Anima Mundi: Berkeley* in Chap. III).

40 *Five Books of Plotinus*, p. 261.

41 *Ibid.*, pp. lxiv-lxvi. The italics are mine.

42 *Ibid.*, p. 104 (The Nature and Origin of Evil).

43 *Ibid.*, p. 244 (Nature, Contemplation, and the One).

44 There is considerable ambiguity or inconsistency in Shelley's various statements in regard to the soul's status after death. A large number of these statements have been assembled by Helene Richter (under the head of Unsterblichkeit, *op. cit.*, 428-435). In his letters to Miss Hitchener in 1811, there are several declarations of a belief in immortality. For the most part, in later years, when not expressing himself in "platonic" terms, his declarations are in the form of clear denial of this belief (as in his essay "On a Future State," in "Alastor," "The Revolt of Islam," IV, viii, "The Cenci," V, iv, 115). What I call "platonic" terms are those in which he attempts to express the idea that virtue (for example) or thought survives the death of the person in whom it is incarnate (as in "The Re-

volt of Islam," XX, xxxvii, IX, xxx: "That virtue, though obscured on Earth, not less/ Survives all mortal change in lasting loveliness"). In the essay "On Christianity" he states the Christian doctrine of immortality, not as a believer but as a sympathizer; and not seldom in his poems he gives poetic expression to sentiments proper to the situation without intent to declare belief. There are also passages in which he suggests the continued existence of the soul not individually but as part of "the vast sum of action and thought which disposes and animates the universe" ("Punishment of Death"); and other passages in which he expresses the notion of the spirit's being made one with nature. Of Shelley's writings as a whole, I think we may say, as of "Adonais," that his "platonism" only served to confuse the issues involved in the question of immortality.

Shelley's attitude toward immortality has recently been discussed with great thoroughness by Kurtz in *The Pursuit of Death* (see especially Chap. III, sect. iv, and Chap. VI, sect. i), and by Barnard in *Shelley's Religion* (especially Chap. V). Both Kurtz and Barnard illustrate the elusive and protean character of Shelley's speculations; but the upshot of both their discussions is to rule out the idea of personal survival, owing to Shelley's disposition to get rid of personality altogether in his ideal state. Thus Kurtz: "His idealistic utterances in *On Life* are connected with a persuasion that personality is a sort of fallacy; and the suggestion that survival must be in an inconceivable mode of being negatives, by implication at least, the definite concept of separate entity" (p. 134). "And what is it, this final statement [in 'Adonais']? What but the clear demotion of the antithesis of life and death under a superior synthesis? The key-phrase changes. No longer is it: I change but I cannot die. It becomes: I live *and* I die, the many change and pass; but the One remains, and the individual in losing his worldly personality by becoming one with the eternal achieves the perfection of self" (288). Such is the mystical paradox involved in the "definition of the aesthetic moment" adapted by Kurtz from James Mark Baldwin, and made the basis of his whole discussion of Shelley. "The higher reality is the mystical faith that annihilates the difference between fact and the dream" (121). Whether Shelley would have subscribed to this doctrine in just this form is a matter of doubt; but it must be acknowledged that it has been made to throw light on the confusions of his thought in relation to immortality. Barnard makes no use of this theory, but his findings, on the basis of a still more thorough examination of the evidence, agree essentially with Kurtz's so far as the personal survival of death is concerned. "There is to be found in none of his speculations about reincarnation or ultimate union with the 'one Spirit' any assertion that the soul remains conscious of any past existence . . . Shelley is at one with the adherents of Buddhism, Brahmanism, and other Eastern faiths, in regarding the human personality as something to be got rid of or transcended; and so is in direct opposition to the main tendency of European religious thought . . . In the end, according to Shelley, personality certainly *is* to be extinguished; for in his eyes it is a source of pain and error, a limitation to be transcended." (Chap. V, sect. v.)

[45] Browning, "Abt Vogler."
[46] Grabo, *"Prometheus Unbound": an Interpretation*, pp. 60, 67, 69-70, 139.
[47] *Ibid.*, 65, 68, 72, 89, 92, 128, 139.
[48] *Ibid.*, 15, 30.
[49] "Prometheus Unbound," III, iv, 196-201.
[50] *Ibid.*, III, i, 52.
[51] *Ibid.*, IV, 14.
[52] *Ibid.*, III, i, 81.
[53] Grabo, *op. cit.*, p. 50.
[54] *Ibid.*, 173.
[55] *Ibid.*, 169.
[56] "Queen Mab," IV, 139-147.

[57] Mr. Grabo considers that "there is clear evidence that Shelley subscribed to the evolutionary theory of man's ascent from lower forms of life" (p. 143); and that he probably "subscribed to the theory of Helvetius that man was descended from a tribe of monkeys which had learned the use of their thumbs" (p. 183). He bases his opinion on a passage in "Prometheus" (IV, 287-318), in which reference is made to "prehistoric races destroyed by some cataclysm of nature." He believes that Shelley took over the evolutionary theory in part from Erasmus Darwin. The passage in "Prometheus" almost certainly shows that Shelley had some knowledge of paleontology. But the notion of prehistoric races destroyed by a cataclysm does not necessarily carry with it the theory of organic evolution. This theory is, I should say, strikingly unimportant in Shelley's writing, if it is there at all. And his psychology and theory of knowledge were singularly unaffected by evolutionism.

CHAPTER IX

GOETHE

[1] Max Morris, Einleitung to Vol. XXXIX of the *Sämtliche Werke* (Jubiläums-Ausgabe), Stuttgart und Berlin (first vol. 1902), p. viii.

[2] *Sämtliche Werke*, XXXIX, pp. 3-6, give the German from which I translate.

[3] Thomas Henry Huxley, in his essay on "A Liberal Education."

[4] Morris, *op. cit.*, p. xiv.

[5] Baron d'Holbach, author's preface to the *Système de la Nature*.

[6] Morris, *op. cit.*, xi.

[7] *Ibid.*

[8] *Ibid.*, viii.

[9] First published in 1808. This song is translated by Carlyle in *Sartor Resartus*, Book I, Chap. viii.

[10] *Sämtliche Werke*, II, 352-353.

[11] The general thought round which Goethe's mind is playing in these stanzas from "Vermächtnis" and "Das Göttliche," and which is so well phrased in the title of "Dauer im Wechsel," as well as in many lines of that poem, is a commonplace in philosophical speculation; and it would be vain to attempt to trace it to particular sources. Still, it may not be without significance that, in Schelling's *Von der Weltseele* (1798), a treatise which very probably suggested to Goethe the title of his poem, "Weltseele," there are many striking passages in which the same thought (in many of its aspects) is given an expression highly technical, to be sure, but still not without close likeness to Goethe's in one point or another. I will quote one or two of these. My references are to Schelling's *Sämtliche Werke*, Stuttgart und Augsburg 1857, Vol. II. "Aber ebenso unmittelbar gegenwärtig und in jedem Theil erkennbar ist das All in Einem, wie es überall das Leben aufschliesst und im Vergänglichem selbst die Blume der Ewigkeit entfaltet" (p. 377). "Dasselbe Principium ist in jener allgemeinen Seele erkennbar, welche die Zeit durchdringt, das Zukünftige voraussieht, ahndet in den Thieren, das Gegenwärtige mit dem Vergangenen in Uebereinstimmung setzt, und jene lose Verknüpfung der Dinge in der Zeit völlig aufhebt ... die allgemeine und allzeitige Weisheit und königliche Seele des Ganzen ..." (p. 370). "So also lebt das Wesen in sich geschlossen, das Einzelne zeugend, wandelnd, um im Zeitlichen die Ewigkeit abzuspiegeln, indess es selbst, aller Formen Kraft, Inhalt und Organismus, die Zeit in sich als Ewigkeit setzt und von keinem Wechsel berührt wird" (373-374). "Das *Unwandelbare* in diesem Produkt ist allerdings nur der Begriff, den es ausdrückt ..." (516). "Die Endlichkeit des Dings, d. h. des Verbundenen, ist, dass

es nur daure und von der Allmacht der Copula überwältiget vergehe. Aber seine Ewigkeit ist, dass es zum Ganzen gehört, und dass sein Daseyn, so kurz oder lang es gedauert haben mag, in dem Ganzen als ein ewiges aufbewahrt ist" (365).

[12] In considering possible suggestions for Shelley's imagery in his reading, we should perhaps take into account certain speculations referred to by Berkeley in his *Siris*. "Marcilius Ficinus also, observing it to be a doctrine in the Timaeus of Plato, that there is an occult fire or light or spirit diffused throughout the universe, intimates that this same occult invisible fire or light is, as it were, *the sight of the mundane soul*. And Plotinus, in his fourth Ennead, sheweth it to be his opinion, that *the world seeth itself and all its parts*." (Sect. 207; my italics.)

[13] Morris, *op. cit.*, pp. l-lii. Cf. Henry Fairfield Osborn, *From the Greeks to Darwin*, pp. 183-184.

[14] Morris, *op. cit.*, pp. xix-xx.

[15] *Ibid.*, viii.

[16] Two of Coleridge's recorded opinions on this subject are given by George R. Potter in his article on "Coleridge and the Idea of Evolution," in *Publications of the Modern Language Association of America*, XL (1925): 379-397. Another, still more striking than these, is given by J. H. Muirhead in his *Coleridge as a Philosopher*, London 1930, pp. 132-133. Another disparaging reference to "the Ourang Outang theology of the origin of the human race" is found in Coleridge's *On the Constitution of the Church and State* (*Complete Works* of Coleridge, New York 1868-71, VI, 65). Still another reference, equally disparaging, is found in *Specimens of the Table Talk*, entry for July 1, 1833 (*Complete Works*, VI, 463). This passage I quote in Chap. XI.

[17] For Coleridge's view, see, e.g., *Hints towards the Formation of a More Comprehensive Theory of Life*, London and Philadelphia 1848 (to be found in *Complete Works*, as Appendix to *Aids to Reflection*, Vol. I; also in the Bohn ed. of *Miscellanies, Aesthetic and Literary*). After a long account of the successive stages in "the advance of Nature," Coleridge comes to "that last work, in which Nature did not [but?] assist as handmaid under the eye of her sovereign Master, who made Man in his own image, by superadding self-consciousness with self-government, and breathed into him a living soul." (*Complete Works*, I. 411.) For Lyell, see, e.g., in *Principles of Geology*, 3 vols., Boston 1842, Book I (Vol. I), Chap. IX, pp. 252, 259-260.

[18] Morris, *op. cit.*, xxxiii.

[19] Osborn, *op. cit.*, 187.

[20] Morris, *op. cit.*, xxvi.

[21] *Ibid.*, xxviii.

[22] *Ibid.*, x.

[23] *Ibid.*, xxxiv-xxxv. Cf. Osborn, op. cit., 184-185.

[24] Morris, *op. cit.*, xxxviii.

[25] *Ibid.*, xlv.

[26] *Ibid.*

[27] *Ibid.*, xlvi.

[28] Ruskin, *Fors Clavigera*, Letter 5.

[29] Morris, *op. cit.*, ix.

CHAPTER X

CARLYLE

[1] *Sartor Resartus*, Book II, Chap. vi. In the Centenary edition of *The Works* of Carlyle, Vol. I, p. 123. This passage is an almost literal reproduction of a page

in Carlyle's early fragmentary romance, *Wotton Reinfred;* see *The Last Words of Thomas Carlyle,* New York 1892, p. 168.

[2] The characterization of Kant's philosophy in Carlyle's *Life of Schiller* (1825) is extremely vague, with the stress laid on its "air of mysticism" and its association with heterodoxy. Centenary edition of *Works,* XXV, 108-114.

[3] Professor Hill Shine, who has made a very thorough study of the evidences of Carlyle's reading in German philosophy during his formative period, seems to think that at that time he was acquainted with no work of Fichte's but *Ueber das Wesen des Gelehrten.* See his "Carlyle and the German Philosophy Problem during the year 1826-1827," in *Publications of the Modern Language Association,* L (1935), 807-827. Professor Charles Frederick Harrold is inclined to think that Carlyle was influenced by several other works of Fichte, including *Die Bestimmung des Menschen.* "That he never cited these works—assuming that he read them—may be explained by Carlyle's habit of acknowledging only those sources which he either translated or closely paraphrased." (*Carlyle and German Thought 1819-1934,* New Haven 1934, p. 14.) Harrold has made use, in his comprehensive study, of the findings of many earlier scholars, including Margaret Storr, *The Relation of Carlyle to Kant and Fichte,* Bryn Mawr 1929.

[4] Essay on Novalis, in *Works,* XXVII, 28.

[5] *Ibid.,* 33.

[6] *Ibid.,* 34-35.

[7] *Ibid.,* 29.

[8] *Ibid.,* 39, 40.

[9] *Ibid.,* 23. The Term "Kantism" is applied, in *Wotton Reinfred,* to the teaching of Dalbrook (Coleridge); see *Last Words,* p. 84.

[10] Essay on Novalis, in *Works,* XXVII, 10, 23, 36.

[11] *Ibid.,* 25-26.

[12] *Ibid.,* 27. This pseudo-Kantian distinction is developed at length in *Wotton Reinfred* by a character apparently modeled on Coleridge; see *Last Words,* 83-87.

[13] Essay on Novalis, in *Works,* XXVII, 24-25.

[14] *Ibid.,* 25.

[15] Essay on the State of German Literature, in *Works,* XXVI, 58.

[16] *Sartor Resartus,* Book I, Chap. viii, in *Works,* I, 43.

[17] *Ibid.,* Book I, Chap. xi (Vol. I, 57).

[18] *Ibid.,* I, x, 52.

[19] *On Heroes, Hero-Worship,* etc., Lecture I; in *Works,* V, 36.

[20] *The French Revolution,* Book I, Chap. ii; in *Works,* II, 6.

[21] *Sartor Resartus,* e.g., I, viii, 42-43; III, viii, 207-210.

[22] *Ibid.,* I, viii, 43.

[23] *Heroes, Hero-Worship,* etc., Lecture II, in *Works* V, 69.

[24] *Sartor Resartus,* I, viii, 41.

[25] Charles Frederick Harrold, *Carlyle and German Thought: 1819-1834,* p. 124.

[26] *Ibid.,* p. 96.

[27] *Ibid.,* 98.

[28] *Ibid.,* 86.

[29] *Ibid.,* 93.

[30] *Ibid.,* 76.

[31] *Ibid.,* 104.

[32] *Ibid.,* 106-107.

[33] Note the ironic reference to a Rational University, *Sartor Resartus,* II, iii, 90.

[34] Second essay on Richter, *Works,* XXVII, 155; *Sartor Resartus,* I, v, 28.

[35] *Sartor Resartus,* I, xi, 54-55; III, vii, 200-201.

[36] *Ibid.,* II, iii, 90.

[37] Second essay on Richter, *Works,* XXVII, 155. It is characteristic of Carlyle

that Nature herself is represented as repudiating atheism, and that atheism is another name for the selfish social theory of "the Bentham-Radical set." Thus he says of them, in a letter to Sterling in 1839: "Nature abhors a *vacuum:* worthy old girl, she will not make a wretched, scraggy Atheism and Egoism fruitful in her world; but answers to it: Enough, thou scraggy Atheism; go thy ways, wilt thou!" (*New Letters of Thomas Carlyle*, ed. Alexander Carlyle, 2 vols., London 1904, I, 175.)

[38] *Sartor Resartus*, III, vii, 200-201.

[39] Essay on the Death of Goethe, *Works*, XXVII, 377; *On Heroes, Hero-Worship*, etc., Lecture I, 29-30 (*Works*, Vol. V).

[40] Essay on Goethe's Works, in *Works*, XXVII, 437.

[41] *Sartor Resartus*, III, viii.

[42] *Ibid.*, III, viii, 206.

[43] *Ibid.*, 210.

[44] *Heroes, Hero-Worship*, etc., Lecture I, 8-9; cf. 11.

[45] *Sartor Resartus*, I, x, 53.

[46] Newman, *The Tamworth Reading Room*, in *Discussions and Arguments on Various Subjects*, London 1918, p. 302. One sentence I have italicized.

[47] *Last Words*, p. 137.

[48] *Chartism*, Chap. III, in *Works*, XXIX, 132. *Heroes*, Lecture II, in *Works*, V, 69. *Latter-Day Pamphlets*, No. I, in *Works*, XX, 15; No. II, pp. 55, 71.

[49] *Past and Present* (in *Works*, Vol. X), Book III, Chap. i, p. 137.

[50] *Ibid.*, III, v, 158.

[51] *Ibid.*, III, xi, 196.

[52] *Latter-Day Pamphlets* (Vol. XX), I, 15.

[53] *Chartism* (Vol. IV), Chap. IV, p. 137. *Heroes*, II, 55, 64; VI, 232.

[54] *Chartism*, VIII, 179, *Latter-Day Pamphlets*, II, 75; V, 203.

[55] *Past and Present* (Vol. X), III, iv, 152; xi, 196.

[56] *Heroes*, II, 64.

[57] *Chartism*, III, 132.

[58] *Heroes*, VI, 238-240.

[59] *Ibid.*, VI, 243.

[60] *History of Frederick the Second*, etc. (*Works*, Vol. XII), Book IV, Chap. iii, p. 340.

[61] *Heroes*, VI, 204.

[62] *Chartism*, V, 149.

[63] *Heroes*, VI, 203.

[64] *Ibid.*, VI, 232.

[65] *Chartism*, X, 65.

[66] Harrold, *op. cit.*, p. 81.

[67] *Ibid.*, 85.

[68] *Heroes*, II, 63.

[69] Matthew Arnold, *Culture and Anarchy*, New York 1907, Chap. I, p. 34.

[70] *Ibid.*, IV, 126-127.

[71] *Ibid.*, p. 293 (being in Letter X of *Friendship's Garland*).

[72] Arnold's lecture on "Literature and Science," in *Discourses in America*, London 1912, p. 135.

[73] Arnold, Preface to *God and the Bible*, New York 1883, p. xxxvii.

[74] *Latter-Day Pamphlets*, I, 17.

[75] Preface to *God and the Bible*, p. xli.

CHAPTER XI

COLERIDGE, EMERSON, AND NATURALISM

[1] *Emerson's Journals*, with annotations by Edward Waldo Emerson and Waldo Emerson Forbes, Boston 1909–14, Vol. III, p. 163.

[2] Some study of "Emerson's Indebtedness to Coleridge" has been made by Frank T. Thompson. See his article with that title in *Studies in Philology*, XXIII (1926): 55-76. In his article on "Emerson and Carlyle," *Studies in Philology*, XXIV (1927): 438-453, Mr. Thompson refers to a fuller study of the influence of Coleridge on Emerson to be found in his doctoral dissertation entitled *Emerson's Debt to Coleridge, Carlyle, and Wordsworth*, University of North Carolina 1925.

I have myself noted references to Coleridge, and probable echoes of him, throughout the Journals, as well as in his published writings, much too numerous to be listed here, which I hope to put together in a separate article. I might mention briefly certain points in this connection. In October 1829 (*Journals* II, 268), Emerson has a list of eight "book memoranda," all referring to books mentioned in *Aids to Reflection*, which Emerson wishes to look up. In reference, apparently, to one of these items, Emerson gives the page number in his edition of Coleridge's *Aids*. Many of these books which he found mentioned in Coleridge he certainly did look up, as it was his custom to do with Coleridge's references.

The next work of Coleridge's which he read was *The Friend*. In December of 1829, Emerson writes his aunt of the great interest and sympathy with which he is reading that book (*Journals* II, 277-279). In 1834 there are pages of reflection evidently inspired by *The Friend*, as well as in his published writings, much too numerous 326-327). In the same year he refers to Coleridge among other educators as having joined the cry for a systematic Moral Education (III, 348). He evidently shared the views of James Marsh, president of the University of Vermont, who edited, with an introduction, the first American edition of *Aids to Reflection*, published in Burlington, Vermont, in 1829, and who (apparently) inspired the first American edition of *The Friend*, likewise published at Burlington, in 1831. See Miss Marjorie Nicolson's interesting article on the educational aspect of Coleridge's influence in America, entitled "James Marsh and the New England Transcendentalists," *Philosophical Review*, XXXIV (1925): 28-50. For a general account of Coleridge as an encyclopedist and educator, see Alice D. Snyder, *Coleridge on Logic and Learning*, Yale University Press 1929. Besides the various suggestions taken by Emerson from *The Friend* referred to in the text, there are a large number of probable echoes in Emerson's phrasing of the "idealistic" philosophy, as well as references to a number of authors whom Emerson was probably led to look up by finding them mentioned here by Coleridge.

Coleridge's treatise *On the Constitution of the Church and State* was apparently the third one of his prose works read by Emerson. There are references to, and quotations from, this work in 1834 and 1835 (*Journals* III, 371, 383, 488); and Emerson refers to it in his lecture on contemporary English writers in November 1835, along with *Biographia Literaria* and *The Friend*, as among the best of Coleridge's works. (Cabot's *Memoir* of Emerson, II, 723-724). There are several possible traces of Emerson's reading of this book in the Journals and the Essays.

In June 1835 Emerson had been reading *Specimens of the Table Talk* (first edition, in London and New York, that same year), as shown by a quotation (III, 494). In 1838 is another reference (V, 140), having to do with Giotto's frescoes at Pisa. Other remarks of Coleridge in *Table Talk* which were probably followed up by Emerson had to do with several writers in whom he later showed an unusual interest.

Biographia Literaria seems to have been the fifth one of Coleridge's prose works to be read by Emerson. The first definite allusion to this which I have noted is in June 1835 (III, 503). Later in the year Emerson refers to it in connection with Coleridge's death (III, 540); and in his lecture at the end of the year, he speaks of *Biographia Literaria* as "the best book of criticism in the English language" (Cabot, II, 723). This book must be regarded, I think, as particularly stimulating to Emerson's studies in philosophy. Wherever Emerson may have come first on the term "transcendental" for characterizing the "idealistic" philosophy, the *Biographia Literaria* must be regarded as an important *locus* for its use. Emerson must have been impressed with Coleridge's references to Kant and Schelling, as well as to Paley, Spinoza, Boehme; and it is at least possible that references in this book may have been the starting point of Emerson's interest in certain of the neoplatonists, etc.

The last book of Coleridge's to be read by Emerson was his *Literary Remains in Prose and Verse* (including the Shakespeare lectures), from which Emerson quotes in 1838 (V, 119).

³ The *Treatise on Method* has recently been reprinted, with an admirable historical introduction, by Professor Alice D. Snyder, London 1934. In her footnotes Miss Snyder indicates all the main points of correspondence between the *Treatise* and *The Friend*. The references to Plato, Bacon, Linnaeus and John Hunter may easily be found by consulting her index. The distinction between Idea and mere hypothesis is found on p. 19 (Sect. I, par. 8), and more elaborately developed on pp. 58-59 (Sect. III, pars. 16 and 17). In the *Treatise*, as in *The Friend*, Coleridge's thought is much more philosophical than Emerson's in *Nature*. But I humbly opine that his use of the term Idea is vague and ambiguous, the more so as he applies it to a wider and wider range of subjects—the physical sciences (mixed sciences, as he calls them), and then, poetry, logic, grammar, moral philosophy, metaphysics, theology. But the discovery of these ambiguities I must leave to some one better trained in philosophy and dialectic.

⁴ The *Complete Works* of Coleridge, Harper 1868-71, 7 vols., Vol. II, p. 420.

⁵ Emerson, *Nature, Addresses and Lectures*, in Centenary Edition of Emerson (1904), Vol. I, p. 55.

⁶ *Kritik der reinen Vernunft*, first edition, p. 307, second edition, p. 364, Kant's *Gesammelte Schriften*, Berlin 1911, IV, 196 and III, 242.

⁷ Translation by Norman Kemp Smith, Macmillan 1929, p. 306.

⁸ The passage in *Aids to Reflection* occurs in Aphorism VIII, in the inserted essay "On the Difference in Kind of Reason and the Understanding," particularly pp. 247-253 in *Complete Works*, Vol. I, including the footnote to p. 251ff. The passage in Kant from which I suppose Coleridge to have taken his suggestion for much of this exposition is found in the Preface to the second edition of the *Kritik* (1787), pp. xi-xvi; see *Gesammelte Schriften*, Berlin 1911, III, 9-12. The sentences which seem to me most pertinent in connection with Coleridge's essays on scientific method in *The Friend* are these: "Denn er [Thales in his study of the isosceles triangle] fand, dass er nicht dem, was er in der Figur sah, oder auch dem blossen Begriffe derselben nachspüren und gleichsam davon ihre Eigenschaften ablernen, sondern durch das, was er nach Begriffen selbst *a priori* hineindachte und darstellte, (durch Construktion) hervorbringen *müsse*, und dass er, um sicher etwas *a priori* zu wissen, der Sache nicht beilegen *müsse*, als was aus dem nothwendig folgte, was er seinem Begriffe gemäss selbst in sie gelegt hat." "Sie begriffen [scientists in the Renaissance], dass die Vernunft nur das einsieht, was sie selbst nach ihrem Entwurfe hervorbringt, dass sie mit Principien ihrer Urtheile nach beständigen Gesetzen vorangehen und die Natur nöthigen müsse auf ihre Fragen zu antworten, nicht aber sich von ihr allein gleichsam am Leitbande gängeln lassen müsse . . ."

⁸ᵃ In the *Treatise on Method*, Coleridge quotes a number of passages from the

Novum Organum having to do with well and ill conceived experiments, with the importance in experiment of the *prudens quaestio,* and the distinction between true ideas and the false idols of the mind. But he gives it all his own special idealistic twist, and mingles with it many phrases drawn from German metaphysic not at all in keeping with Bacon's cast of mind and his general emphasis on inductive method. And this applies even more strongly to his treatment of Bacon in *The Friend.*

⁹ *The Friend,* in *Complete Works,* II, 449-450. This note is not found in the Bohn edition.

¹⁰ *Aids to Reflection,* in *Complete Works,* I, 219, fn. In the Bohn edition, p. 119, fn. I have kept the "pointing" of Coleridge as found in the Bohn ed.

¹¹ *The Friend,* in *Works,* II, pp. 421, 422 (Essay V), 428 (Essay VI) and 435, fn. (Essay VII). The Emerson phrases are (1) from his paper "On the Uses of Natural History," in J. E. Cabot's *Memoir of Emerson* (2 vols. Boston and New York, 1888), I, 227; (2) from *Nature* in Centenary ed., I, 29 (Chap. IV); (3) from *Nature,* p. 68 (Chap. VIII).

¹² Friedrich W. J. von Schelling, *Ideen zu einer Philosophie der Natur* (1797), in his *Sämmtliche Werke,* Stuttgart und Augsburg 1857, Vol. II, p. 55. For Coleridge's acquaintance with the *Ideen,* see Note 36.

¹³ Schelling, *Einleitung zu einem Entwurf eines Systems der Naturphilosophie* (1799), in *Sämmtliche Werke,* Vol. III (1858), pp. 279-280. The passage concludes with the statement that "speculative physics (the soul of true experiment) has heretofore been the mother of all great discoveries in nature." That Coleridge was acquainted with the *Einleitung* there is no external evidence that I know of. But the years bring certainty of his acquaintance with an ever increasing number of Schelling's works. Elizabeth Winkelmann lists twelve works which he is known to have read (*Coleridge und die Kantische Philosophie,* pp. 124-125). But neither she nor Wellek (*Immanuel Kant in England*) mentions either the *Allgemeine Deduktion* nor the *Erstes Entwurf,* which Nidecker shows that Coleridge had read (see Note 36): and they confine their attention curiously to certain early works of Schelling which contain his criticism of Kant.

¹⁴ Emerson, *Nature, Addresses, and Lectures,* in Centenary ed., I, 27-28 (Chap. IV of *Nature*).

¹⁵ *Ibid.,* 67, 69-70, 75 (all Chap. VIII). For another of Emerson's variations on this theme of the pregnant idea, see the lecture on Poetry and Imagination, in *Letters and Social Aims,* Centenary ed., VIII, 24; also the essay on "Nature" in *Essays,* Centenary ed., III, 183.

¹⁶ James Elliot Cabot, *A Memoir of Ralph Waldo Emerson,* Boston 1888, I, 227. Cf. "The American Scholar," in Centenary ed., I, 85-86.

¹⁷ *The Friend,* in *Works,* II, 432.

¹⁸ *Nature,* in Centenary ed., I, 56.

¹⁹ *The Friend,* in *Works,* II, 430-431; also footnote to 446-447. Cf. *Aids to Reflection,* in *Works,* I, 357. References to Hunter are found in Emerson's *Journals,* I, 363; II, 473; III, 343; IV, 113; VIII, 546; X, 265, 364. Emerson's dynamic theory of life is expressed in his essay on "The Over-Soul" (Centenary ed., II, 270); in "The Method of Nature" (I, 200). A striking argument for this way of regarding life is found in *Aids to Reflection* in *Works,* I, 357-359. Cf. *Kant's Metaphysische Anfangsgründe* (with which Coleridge was acquainted), in *Schriften,* IV, 532-534, and 544.

²⁰ Centenary ed., III, 176, 179.

²¹ In a footnote to p. 449 (Essay X), Coleridge distinguishes between *vis naturans* and *natura naturata.* This passage has many points of likeness to certain paragraphs in Schelling's *Einleitung zu dem Entwurf eines Systems der Naturphilosophie,* in his *Werke,* III, 284. Schelling in his discussion combines (like Coleridge) the notion of "the productive power," the distinction of object and

subject, and the identity of the two, the distinction of *natura naturans* and *natura naturata*, and reflections on the purposiveness in nature. Another footnote of Coleridge's to p. 424 of *The Friend* (Essay VI), distinguishes between nature in the two senses of *forma formans* and *forma formata*. This entire paragraph, except for the Latin terms, is a literal and unacknowledged borrowing from the opening sentences of Kant's *Metaphysische Anfangsgründe der Naturwissenschaft*, together with the accompanying footnote of Kant's (*Gesammelte Schriften*, IV, 467). The distinction between the two aspects of nature (*natura materialiter spectata* and *natura formaliter spectata*) is also found in Kant's *Kritik der reinen Vernunft*, second ed., pp. 163 and 165 (in *Schriften*, III, 126, 127).

[22] *The Friend*, in *Works*, II, 449-450 (Essay X of Section II).

[23] *Ibid.*, II, 448 (Essay IX).

[24] *Ibid.*, II, 460 (Essay XI). The italics are mine.

[25] *Ibid.*, II, 461-462. My italics.

[26] *Nature*, in Centenary ed., I, 75-76.

[27] "The Method of Nature," in Centenary ed., I, 197.

[28] "Poetry and Imagination," in *Letters and Social Aims*, Centenary ed., VIII, 16, 20, 23.

[29] "Nature," in *Essays*, Centenary ed., III, 196.

[30] "The Poet," in *Essays*, III, 14.

[31] *Nature*, in Centenary ed., I, 49, 52, 59 (all Chap. VI).

[32] Of the development of Emerson's views on evolution, and the books that influenced him, I give a somewhat fuller account in an article in the *University of Toronto Quarterly*, III (1934): 474-497. This subject is touched on by Harry Hayden Clark in an interesting article on "Emerson and Science" in *Philological Quarterly*, X (1931), 225-260. Mr. Clark refers in a footnote to several nineteenth-century books and articles in which the subject is discussed.

[33] *Aids to Reflection*, in *Works*, I, 180-181.

[34] Charles Lyell, *Principles of Geology*, 3 vols., Boston 1842, III, 82 (Book III, Chap. iv).

[35] See my Chapter XV.

[36] M. Nidecker has given a résumé of his doctoral thesis in the *Bericht der philologisch-historischen Abteilung der philosophischen Fakultät*, Basel 1927. He has also made many of his findings more accessible in a series of articles, dealing with Coleridge's marginal notes on works of several German philosophers, published in the *Revue de littérature comparée*. The articles on the Steffens marginalia are in XI (1931): 274-285, and XII (1932): 856-871; and indicate in detail the innumerable borrowings of Coleridge from these two works. The passages taken from Schelling are found in Coleridge's *Complete Works*, I, 413-415; in Schelling's *Sämmtliche Werke*, IV, 15-19, being sections 21 and 22 of the *Allgemeine Deduktion*.

Coleridge's copy of Schelling's *Ideen* is in the British Museum. Nidecker transcribes his marginal notes in *Rev. de litt. comp.*, VII (1927), 530-534. Nidecker is of opinion that Chap. VI of the *Ideen* influenced the *Theory of Life*. One apparent borrowing, which Nidecker does not there mention, is the footnote to p. 392 (on three kinds of motion), taken from the *Ideen*, *Werke*, II, 28-29. In connection with the marginalia to Steffens's *Grundzüge* (*Revue*, XI, 274-285), Nidecker cites a note showing that Coleridge was probably acquainted with the *Erster Entwurf*, which formed the basis for much of Steffens's theory in both the *Grundzüge* and the *Beiträge*. Evidence of Coleridge's acquaintance with *Von der Weltseele* is less demonstrative, but strongly presumptive in view of his habit of reading everything of Schelling's he could lay his hands on and borrowing his ideas without acknowledgment.

[37] Coleridge uses the word "evolution" in his *Theory of Life*, in *Works*, I, 401; in his "Monologue on Life," published in *Fraser's Magazine*, XII (1835): 5; and

in the "Dialogue between Demosius and Mystes," appended to the volume *On the Constitution of the Church and State*, in *Works*, VI, 140. Schelling uses the word "evolution" in his *Erster Entwurf eines Systems der Naturphilosophie*, in *Werke*, III, 206-207, 258, 262, 263-264, 267. Steffens speaks interchangeably of "die Stuffen (sic) der Evolution" and "die Stuffen der Entwicklung," in *Beiträge zur innern Naturgeschichte der Erde*, Freyberg 1801, pp. 271 and 267.

38 It is true that all three of them occasionally dwell on the gradual character of the transitions in the natural process. And Schelling does in one place at least consider not unfavorably the *possibility* of an "Umgestaltung" and "Uebergang einer Form oder Art in die andere." (*Von der Weltseele*, in *Werke*, II, 348-349.) But this idea of an actual "transmutation of species" is a hypothesis vaguely entertained and mentioned incidentally in the course of interminable metaphysical disquisitions; it is in no way essential to the concept of evolution held by these men—and was, as I have shown, several times expressly repudiated by Coleridge.

39 Steffens, *Anthropologie*, II, 18.

40 Schelling, *Erster Entwurf*, in *Werke*, III, 196-197.

41 *Letters of Samuel Taylor Coleridge*, edited by Ernest Hartley Coleridge, 2 vols., London 1895, II, 648.

42 Henry Fairfield Osborn, *From the Greeks to Darwin*, New York 1905, p. 143. In *Zoönomia*, the more pertinent passages are to be found in Part I, Sect. XXXIX, "Of Generation," especially in sub-section iv (pp. 387-401 of the Boston 1803 ed., Vol. I). In *The Temple of Nature*, the most important passages are found in footnotes, such as the notes to I, 283, 314, 327, 417; to II, 122, 302; IV, 147; and in certain of the "Additional Notes," such as that on "Spontaneous Vitality of Microscopic Animals" and "The Faculties of the Sensorium."

43 *Sämmtliche Werke*, V, 286-287 (achte Vorlesung).

44 Lyell, *op. cit.*, I, 252.

45 The whole passage is quoted by J. H. Muirhead in his *Coleridge as a Philosopher*, London 1930, pp. 132-133.

46 *Table Talk*, in *Works*, VI, 463 (July 1, 1833).

47 Emerson, *Journals*, II, 352.

48 John Abernethy, *Physiological Lectures* (Vol. II), in *The Surgical and Physiological Works*, 2 vols., London and Hartford 1825, Lecture I of the 1814 series, pp. 6 and 17; Lectures II and VII of the 1817 series, pp. 29, 35, 125.

49 *Journals*, II, 329-330.

50 Cabot, *Memoir*, I, 223-224. Cf. *Nature*, Centenary ed., I, 43. Bell's want of sympathy with the evolution view is shown, e.g., pp. 144-145, 221, 223. Reference to the progressive system, etc., pp. 106, 225-226. The comparison of man's hand to the flipper of the saurian and the fin of the fish, pp. 225-226, 104-106 and footnote.

51 *Journals*, III, 299-300.

52 *Ibid.*, IV, 129-130. The mention of Saint-Hilaire on p. 113 was probably suggested by a reading of Lyell. Cabot's summary account of Emerson's lecture is given in his *Memoir*, II, 725.

53 *Journals*, IV, 116-117. The corresponding passage in Lyell's account of Lamarck's theory is found in *Principles*, III, 16 (Book III, Chap. I).

54 *Philological Quarterly*, X (1931): 225-260. This article is full of most valuable information in spite of the uncritical attitude on this subject.

55 *Journals*, VII, 51-52; cf. also 69.

56 *Ibid.*, VII, 104.

57 Stallo's book is mentioned in *Journals*, X, 423, as having been published in 1849. Emerson quotes Stallo in that entry and also in that of December, 1849 (VIII, 76-78), in which he mentions together Schelling, Oken, Hegel, Saint-Hilaire.

58 *Journals*, VIII, 77. I do not find this exact formulation in Stallo; but it would

appear to be a kind of summary of the discussion by Stallo on pp. 6-7 beginning: "The doctrine was that an original, chaotic, all-pervading mass was gradually arranged, organized itself in successive concretions, and advanced to a complete formalization, to the perfect transparency of law." The reference to geology follows. It is here, by the way, that Stallo comes nearest to a statement of the Lamarckian theory of evolution.

[59] *Journals*, VIII, 77. This appears in Stallo, p. 16, in exactly these words, and italicized.

[60] *Journals*, X, 423.

[61] "Poetry and Imagination," in *Letters and Social Aims*, Centenary ed., VIII, pp. 4-8.

[62] See *Nature, Addresses* and *Lectures*, Centenary ed., I, xxix.

[63] *Journals*, VII, 69.

[64] Emerson may have read of the *Urschleim* theory and of the spherules with a liquid content in Stallo, pp. 256-258.

[65] *Journals*, VIII, 9.

[66] *Ibid.*, VIII, 78.

[67] *Ibid.*, VIII, 477. My italics.

[68] *Ibid.*, X, 459-462.

CHAPTER XII

EMERSON'S NATURE-POETRY

[1] There are reminders of Coleridge's "Religious Musings" and "Eolian Harp," and of Goethe's "Weltseele." Emerson refers more than once to Goethe's poem in the *Journals* (IV, 30; VI, 400); his reference to "my speculations on the All in Each in nature" suggests an acquaintance with the "Eins und Alles."

[2] Frederic Ives Carpenter, *Emerson and Asia*, Harvard University Press 1930, pp. 109-121.

[3] *Journals*, II, 344. This is, as the context shows, a part of the notes made by Emerson on De Gerando's *Histoire Comparée des Systèmes de Philosophie*.

[4] *Ibid.*, IV, 247.

[5] *Ibid.*, V, 179.

[6] Emerson's *Poems*, in Centenary ed., IX, 420.

[7] *Nature, Addresses, and Lectures*, in Centenary ed., I (1904), p. 43 (Chap. V).

[8] Schelling, *Von der Weltseele*, in *Sämmtliche Werke*, 1857, II, 359. If we miss here the word "microcosm," we may find it not far distant in the same introductory essay to the *Von der Weltseele* (p. 374). I do not mean to assert that Emerson had found this notion in Schelling's German; there are too many intermediaries through whom it might have come to him. Indeed he did find virtually the same thought in Goethe (*Journals*, IV, 28).

[9] *Nature*, etc., p. 55 (Chap. VI). There is always the possible influence of Carlyle to be taken account of. Emerson's "solid seeming block of matter" reminds one of Carlyle's "this so solid-looking material world" and "this so solid-seeming world" quoted from *Sartor Resartus* in Chap. X. The thought of the entire passages quoted from Carlyle has a resemblance to that of Emerson here.

[10] *Von der Weltseele*, in *Werke*, II, 364.

[11] *Nature*, etc., pp. 10, 27.

[12] *Von der Weltseele*, in *Werke*, II, 569: "die gemeinschaftliche Seele der Natur."

[13] See Note 2, Chap. XI.

[14] "The Over-Soul," in *Essays*, Centenary ed., II, 269.

[15] "The Poet," in *Essays*, Centenary ed., III, 13. Cf. *Journals* V, 497.

[16] *Journals*, V, 206.

[17] Henrik Steffens, *Grundzüge der philosophischen Naturwissenschaft*, Berlin 1806, p. xiii.

[18] *Ibid.*, xix-xx. My translation not guaranteed!

[19] Schelling, *Ideen zu einer Philosophie der Natur*, in *Sämmtliche Werke*, II, 13-14.

[20] *Ibid.*, 47.

[21] References to Cousin are found in *Journals*, III, 439 (Jan. 13, 1835) and IV, 404.

[22] *Sartor Resartus* (in *Works*, Vol. I), Book II, Chap. VII, p. 133. Cf. the metaphors used by Carlyle in giving his interpretation of Novalis's nature-philosophy, Chap. X. Cf. Fichte's *Werke*, II, 317.

[23] "State of German Literature" (in *Works*, Vol. XIV), p. 56.

[24] J. G. Fichte, *Die Bestimmung des Menschen*, in *Werke*, Berlin 1845, II, 246-247. I have given the translation of William Smith from his *Fichte's Popular Works*, London 1889, I, 404.

[25] Fichte, *Werke*, II, 315. Smith's translation, I, 474.

[26] Fichte, *Werke*, II, 258. Smith's translation, I, 415-416.

[27] *Sartor Resartus* (in *Works*, Vol. I), Book II, Chap. IX, p. 153.

[28] Frederick B. Wahr, *Emerson and Goethe*, Ann Arbor 1915, pp. 126-127.

[29] *Letters of George Meredith*, 2 vols., New York 1912, I, 173.

[30] "Michael."

CHAPTER XIII

WHITMAN

[1] *The Complete Writings of Walt Whitman*, (Camden ed.) New York and London 1902, Vol. IX, pp. 80-81. These notes of Whitman were taken preparatory to writing his poetry, or to writing the lectures which seem to have been the original form intended by him for publishing his ideas. See Editor's Preface to this Vol. IX of the Camden ed., p. xvi.

[2] *Specimen Days*, in *Complete Writings*, IV, 168-171.

[3] *Common Sense*, in *Life and Works of Thomas Paine*, New Rochelle, New York, 1925, Vol. II, p. 101.

[4] *Ibid.*, 102.

[5] *Ibid.*, 108.

[6] *Complete Writings*, IX, 185-186.

[7] *The Age of Reason*, in *Life and Works*, VIII, 43-44. This passage, all but the first two sentences, is also found in Paine's address on "The Existence of God," given in Vol. IX, pp. 2-3.

[8] *Specimen Days*, in *Complete Writings*, IV, 323.

[9] *The Age of Reason*, in *Life and Works*, VIII, 73.

[10] *Democratic Vistas*, in *Complete Writings*, V, 135-136. This and all other excerpts from the prose of Whitman are reprinted by kind permission of G. P. Putnam's Sons.

[11] See, e.g., the articles of Gohdes, Moore, Riethmüller referred to in notes to this chapter.

[12] See Richard Riethmüller, "Walt Whitman and the Germans," in *German American Annals*, IV (1906): 81.

[13] John B. Moore, "The Master of Whitman," in North Carolina *Studies in Philology*, XXIII (1926): 77-89. Clarence L. F. Gohdes, "Whitman and Emerson," *Sewanee Review*, XXXVII (1929): 79-93.

[14] Moore, *op. cit.*, p. 77.

[15] *Gohdes, op. cit.,* p. 92.

[16] *Ibid.,* 81.

[17] *Ibid.,* 83. See *Uncollected Poetry and Prose of Walt Whitman,* ed. Holloway, Vol. I, p. 243, footnote.

[18] "Preparatory Reading and Thought," in *Complete Writings,* IX, 159-160.

[19] *Ibid.,* IX, 111; cf. IX, 123, 229, 230.

[20] *Ibid.,* IX, 110-111, should be compared with Carlyle's essay on "Goethe's Works" (in *Works,* Vol. XXVII), pp. 427-428, for similarities in the account of Goethe's life, showing unmistakably that this was an authority consulted by Whitman. For Richter the similar passages are in Whitman, IX, 121-122, and in Carlyle, XXVII (his second essay on Richter), 119-120 and 141. There is also some slight trace of Whitman's use of Carlyle's earlier essay on Richter.

[21] *Complete Writings,* IX, 123.

[22] There are references to Carlyle in Whitman's *Complete Writings,* III, 59; V, 71, 76, 211, 270; VI, 103; VIII, 11, in addition to those already given; but no conclusive evidence of what he had read except *Heroes* and "Shooting Niagara." In *November Boughs* (1888) he quotes a paragraph on John Knox from *Heroes and Hero-Worship* (VI, 270).

[23] See editor's note, IX, 166.

[24] Whitman's statement, IV, 318.

[25] IX, 171; IV, 321.

[26] Riethmüller, *op. cit.,* p. 90, says that it was from Gostwick's *German Culture and Christianity* (1882) that Whitman derived his knowledge of Hegel's theology; but this seems to have been a guess on Riethmüller's part. I have carefully examined this later volume of Gostwick's, but cannot find any statement about the German philosophers similar enough to Whitman's to justify the assumption that he was using it for his notes. On the other hand, Whitman was undoubtedly indebted to Gostick's *German Literature* for information about Schlegel and Niebuhr as well as the philosophical writers. In his account of Niebuhr (IX, 116) he refers to "pages 249-50-51 *German Literature*"; this is the correct page reference for Gostick's treatment of Niebuhr, which includes all the facts given by Whitman. The passages concerned with Schlegel are, in Whitman, IX, 120-121; in Gostick, 278-279. The passages concerned with the German philosophers are, in Whitman, IX, 171-172, 176, 180; in Gostick, all p. 269. Gostick's contributions include the position of Locke, etc., "there is nothing in the understanding which has not arrived there through the senses," and Leibniz's reply, "Yes, there is the understanding itself"; the statement as to how Schelling answers the questions left over by Kant; and the summary of the doctrine of Hegel beginning "The heavens and the earth," which Whitman puts in quotation marks and explicitly refers to Gostick. There is also a trace of Gostick in Whitman's statement about Leibniz, p. 184 (Gostick, p. 107). It will be observed, too, that in both of his references to him, Whitman uses the spelling Gostick, which is that of *German Literature,* and not Gostwick, which was the spelling of the name in *German Culture and Christianity.* A number of parallels between the thought of Hegel and Whitman are noted in an article in *University of Texas Studies in English,* No. 9, 134-150, by Moady C. Boatright, who before me reached the conclusion that it was Gostick's 1854 *German Literature* with which Whitman was familiar.

[27] *Complete Writings,* IX, 168.

[28] *Ibid.,* 170.

[29] *Ibid.,* 172.

[30] *Ibid.,* 184.

[31] *Ibid.,* 178.

[32] *Ibid.,* 179-180.

[33] *Ibid.,* 180-181.

[34] *Ibid.,* IV, 322.

[35] *Ibid.,* e.g., IV, 322.

[36] *Ibid.,* V, 141-142 (*Democratic Vistas*).

[37] *Ibid.,* IX, 172-173.

[38] *Ibid.,* IV, 320.

[39] *Ibid.,* IX, 173.

[40] "Manhattan's Streets I saunter'd, pondering," in *Leaves of Grass*, David McKay, Philadelphia, copyright 1900, p. 288.

[41] "With Antecedents," *Leaves of Grass*, p. 189.

[42] "Chanting the Square Deific," *Leaves of Grass*, p. 394.

[43] "Sie, die bloss für mich, und um meinetwillen da ist, und nicht ist, wenn ich nicht bin." (*Sämmtliche Werke*, Berlin 1845, II, 318; Smith's *Popular Works* of Fichte, I, 477.)

[44] *Complete Writings*, IX, 171.

[45] *Ibid.*

[46] "Song of the Open Road," strophe 3, in *Leaves of Grass*, 170.

[47] "Crossing Brooklyn Ferry," 6, in *Leaves*, 184.

[48] *Ibid.,* 12, p. 187.

[49] "To Think of Time," 7, *ibid.,* 389.

[50] "Thoughts," *ibid.,* 324.

[51] *Complete Writings*, IV, 318-319. This is followed by a reference to Hegel's "fuller statement of the matter."

[52] "Carol of Occupations," 4, in *Leaves of Grass*, p. 201.

[53] "Laws for Creations," *ibid.,* 93.

[54] "Crossing Brooklyn Ferry," 2, *ibid.,* 181.

[55] *Complete Writings*, IX, 184.

[56] "One's-Self I Sing," in *Leaves of Grass*, 11.

[57] "Walt Whitman," 24, *ibid.,* 55.

[58] "Starting from Paumanok," 8, *ibid.,* 21.

[59] "Walt Whitman," 6, *ibid.,* 35.

[60] "Walt Whitman," *ibid.,* 33 and 83.

[61] "Walt Whitman," 44, *ibid.,* 84-85. Cf. "Starting from Paumanok," p. 16, "Carol of Words," pp. 219, 220.

[62] "Song of the Open Road," 14, *ibid.,* 177.

[63] "Song of the Open Road," 6, *ibid.,* 172.

[64] *Ibid.,* 174.

[65] *Ibid.,* 178-179.

[66] *Ibid.,* 178.

[67] Riethmüller, *op. cit.,* p. 79, refers to *Century Magazine*, LXXI (old series), p. 85.

[68] "Carol of Occupations," 3 and 4, in *Leaves of Grass*, pp. 200-201.

[69] "To Think of Time," 6, *ibid.,* 388-389.

[70] "To Think of Time," 10 and 11, *ibid.,* 391-392.

[71] "Starting from Paumanok," 13, *ibid.,* 24. Cf. Carlyle's "Natural Supernaturalism" in *Sartor Resartus;* in Emerson, cf., e.g., the Divinity School address (1838).

[72] "Walt Whitman," 7, in *Leaves of Grass*, 37.

[73] "Walt Whitman," 31, *ibid.,* 62.

[74] "Starting from Paumanok," 11, *ibid.,* 23.

[75] "Carol of Occupations," 7, *ibid.,* 209.

[76] "Walt Whitman," 19, *ibid.,* 49.

[77] "Walt Whitman," 24, *ibid.,* 55.

[78] "Song of the Open Road," 2, *ibid.,* 169-170.

[79] "Carol of Words," 4, *ibid.,* 221.

[80] "I Sing the Body Electric," 6, *ibid.,* 103.

[81] "One Hour to Madness and Joy," *ibid.,* 111.

[82] "Native Moments," *ibid.,* 113.

[83] "We Two—How Long We Were Fool'd," *ibid.*, 112.

[84] See, e.g., "A Woman Waits for Me," *ibid.*, 107.

[85] See, e.g., "Ages and Ages, Returning at Intervals," *ibid.*, 115.

[86] See, e.g., "So Long!" *ibid.*, 343.

[87] "Starting from Paumanok," 4, *ibid.*, 18.

[88] "Starting from Paumanok," 8, *ibid.*, 20.

[89] *Complete Writings*, IV, 259.

[90] "Walt Whitman," 14, in *Leaves of Grass*, 42.

[91] *Ibid.*, 43.

[92] *Complete Writings*, IV, 183.

[93] *Ibid.*, 182.

[94] *Ibid.*, 166-7.

[95] *Democratic Vistas*, in *Complete Writings*, V, 134. Cf. *Specimen Days*, *ibid.*, 42-43.

[96] *Complete Writings*, IV, 157-158.

[97] *Ibid.*, IV, 143-144. Cf. IV, 184, in " the inner never-lost rapport we hold with earth, light air, trees, etc."

[98] *Democratic Vistas*, in *Complete Writings*, V, 138.

[99] *Ibid.*, 140.

[100] *Complete Writings*, IX, 172.

[101] *Ibid.*, IV, 187.

CHAPTER XV

TENNYSON

[1] "In Memoriam," LV.

[2] *Ibid.*, III.

[3] *Ibid.*, CXXIV. Cf. Hallam Tennyson's *Memoir* of his father, I, 44: A question discussed by the Apostles was, "Is an intelligible First Cause deducible from the phenomena of the Universe?" Tennyson voted "No."

[4] Cardinal Newman, *The Tamworth Reading Room* (1841), Letter 7, in *Discussions and Arguments on Various Subjects*, London 1918, pp. 298-299.

[5] *Ibid.*, 414-415.

[6] "In Memoriam," LIV.

[7] *Ibid.*, LVI.

[8] "Maud," IV, iv.

[9] "The Promise of May," Act I.

[10] "In Memoriam," CXVIII.

[11] *Ibid.*, CXI.

[12] *Ibid.*, CXXX.

[13] "Maud," IV, vii.

[14] "In Memoriam," CXX.

[15] Lionel Stevenson, *Darwin among the Poets*, Chicago 1932, p. 60.

[16] Hallam Tennyson, *Tennyson, a Memoir*, 2 vols., London 1897, Vol. I, p. 44.

[17] Stevenson, *op. cit.*, p. 67.

[18] Charles Lyell, *Principles of Geology*, 3 vols., Boston 1842, Vol. III, Book III, Chap. IV, pp. 81-82. It is true that the author of *Vestiges of the Natural History of Creation* interprets these same facts as favoring the theory of evolution (see the London 1845 ed., pp. 205-207).

[19] Note to "By an Evolutionist" in Eversley ed. of *The Works of Tennyson*, New York 1908, IV, 599.

[20] Hallam Tennyson, *Tennyson, a Memoir*, II, 167.

[21] Stevenson, *op. cit.*, p. 72.
[22] *Tennyson, a Memoir*, I, 323.
[23] "In Memoriam," CXVIII.
[24] *Ibid.*, LXXXII.
[25] *Ibid.*, LVI.
[26] *Ibid.*, CXXIV.
[27] *Tennyson, a Memoir*, II, 68-69.
[28] "The Princess," III.
[29] *Tennyson, a Memoir*, I, 308.
[30] Cf. *Tennyson, a Memoir*, II, 424: "Matter is a greater mystery than mind. What such a thing as a spirit is apart from God and man I have never been able to conceive. Spirit seems to me to be the reality of the world." cf. Hallam Tennyson's note to a passage in "Idylls of the King": "As far back as 1839 my father had written to my mother: 'Annihilate within yourself these two dreams of Space and Time.' 'I think,' he said, 'matter is merely the shadow of something greater than itself, which we poor short-sighted creatures cannot see.'" Cf. *Tennyson, a Memoir*, II, 69, 151, 170, 469.
[31] St. George Mivart, *Nature and Thought*, London 1882, p. 168.
[32] *Ibid.*, 174.
[33] *Tennyson, a Memoir*, I, 323.
[34] *Ibid.*, I, 322.
[35] Stevenson, *op. cit.*, 95.
[36] *Tennyson, a Memoir*, II, 57.

CHAPTER XVI

BROWNING

[1] Lionel Stevenson, *Darwin among the Poets*, pp. 118-122.
[2] "Paracelsus," V.
[3] "With Francis Furini," X.
[4] Rupert Brooke, "Heaven."
[5] "Paracelsus," V.
[6] *Ibid.*
[7] W. Hall Griffin, *The Life of Robert Browning*, New York 1910, p. 295.
[8] This phrase is used in a recent manifesto of certain American professors of philosophy endeavoring to formulate a religious creed for "naturalists."
[9] "With Francis Furini," X.
[10] "Paracelsus," V.
[11] *Ibid.*
[12] *Ibid.*
[13] *Ibid.*
[14] Stevenson, *op. cit.*, 124.
[15] Griffin, *op. cit.*, p. 295. Reprinted by kind permission of the Macmillan Co.
[16] Quoted as a part of the "four well-known propositions" of Lamarck by Henry Fairfield Osborn, in *From the Greeks to Darwin*, p. 167.
[17] "Easter-Day," XXVIII.
[18] "Saul," IX.
[19] *Ibid.*, XVII.
[20] *Ibid.*
[21] *Ibid.*, XVIII.
[22] "La Saisiaz."
[23] "Rabbi Ben Ezra."

CHAPTER XVII

SWINBURNE

[1] "Prelude" to *Songs before Sunrise*, in *Swinburne's Poems*, 6 vols., London 1905, II, 4-5.
[2] *Ibid.*, 7-8.
[3] *Ibid.*, 9.
[4] "The Eve of Revolution," stanza 25, *ibid.*, II, 24.
[5] "On the Downs," *ibid.*, 195.
[6] "The Litany of Nations," *ibid.*, 65.
[7] "Hymn of Man," *ibid.*, 94.
[8] *Ibid.*, 95.
[9] "Prometheus Unbound," Act IV, ll. 394-5, 400-402.
[10] "Hymn of Man," *ibid.*, 101-102.
[11] Newman, *Apologia pro Vita Sua*, Longmans Green 1905, Chap. V, pp. 245-246.
[12] "Hertha," in *Swinburne's Poems*, II, 75, 78, 79-80.
[13] "Epilogue" to *Songs before Sunrise*, *ibid.*, 232.
[14] *Ibid.*, 233.

CHAPTER XVIII

MEREDITH

[1] *The Letters of George Meredith*, 2 vols., New York 1912, II, 634.
[2] "The Test of Manhood."
[3] Lionel Stevenson, *Darwin among the Poets*, Chicago 1932, p. 223.
[4] "Appreciation" (1883).
[5] "The Woods of Westermain."
[6] *Ibid.*
[7] H. Levy, *The Universe of Science*, New York and London 1933.
[8] *Letters*, I, 33.
[9] *Ibid.*, II, 409.
[10] Meredith's reference to the breaking of the types is perhaps an echo of Tennyson's wistful complaint.

> 'So careful of the type?' but no,
> From scarped cliff and quarried stone
> She cries, 'A thousand types are gone:
> I care for nothing, all shall go.' ("In Memoriam," lxi)

Again we remember Goethe: "Sie scheint alles auf Individualität angelegt zu haben und macht sich nichts aus den Individuum. Sie baut immer und zerstört immer, und ihre Werkstätte ist unzugänglich." ("Fragment über die Natur"). But Goethe and Meredith both seem to imply that there is something in nature which makes her worthy of trust. "Sie hat mich hereingestellt, sie wird mich herausführen. Ich vertraue mich ihr. Sie mag mir schalten. Sie wird ihr Werk nicht hassen."

[11] Morris R. Cohen, *Reason and Nature, an Essay on the Meaning of Scientific Method*, New York 1931, p. 157.

[12] C. Lloyd Morgan, *The Interpretation of Nature*, New York 1906, pp. 76-77. This and all other excerpts from Morgan reprinted with kind permission of G. P. Putnam's Sons.

[13] *Ibid.*, 175-176.

[14] *Ibid.*, 185.

[15] *Ibid.*, 173.

[16] "The Test of Manhood" (1901). This and the following excerpt reprinted, with kind permission of Charles Scribner's Sons, from *The Poetical Works of George Meredith* (1912), pp. 543-544.

[17] *Ibid.*

[18] "A Faith on Trial" (1888).

[19] *Ibid.*

[20] *Letters*, II, 582.

[21] "A Faith on Trial."

[22] "The Question Whither."

[23] "The Woods of Westermain."

[24] *Ibid.*

[25] *Ibid.*

CHAPTER XIX

HARDY

[1] "The Dynasts," Part First (1904), Act. I, Scene vi, p. 54. All excerpts from Hardy's poems reprinted with kind permission of the Macmillan Co.

[2] "Discouragement" (1863-67), in *Human Shows and Far Fantasies* (1925), p. 275.

[3] "Her Dilemma" (1866), in *Wessex Poems and Other Verses* (1898), p. 22.

[4] "To Outer Nature," *ibid.*, 150.

[5] *Ibid.*, 158.

[6] *Ibid.*, 165.

[7] *Poems of the Past and Present* (1901), p. 97.

[8] "At a Bridal" (1866), in *Wessex Poems*, etc., p. 11.

[9] *Ibid.*, 163.

[10] *Poems of the Past and Present*, p. 82.

[11] *Ibid.*, 88.

[12] *Ibid.*, 95.

[13] *Ibid.*, 165.

[14] *Moments of Vision* (1st ed. 1917), p. 143.

[15] *Late Lyrics and Earlier* (1922), p. 35.

[16] *Ibid.*, 67.

[17] *Winter Words* (1928), p. 15.

[18] *Human Shows, Far Fantasies.*

[19] "The Darkling Thrush," in *Poems of the Past and Present*, p. 170.

[20] *The Return of the Native*, Chap. I.

[21] *Tess of the D'Urbervilles*, Chap. XIII.

[22] *Ibid.*, XXVIII.

[23] *Ibid.*, XXX.

[24] *Ibid.*, XXXVI.

[25] *Jude the Obscure*, Part III, Chap. x.

[26] *Ibid.*, IV, ii.

[27] *Ibid.*, VI, iii.

[28] *Ibid.*, IV, iii.

[29] *Ibid.*, IV, ii.
[30] *Tess of the D'Urbervilles*, Chap. V.
[31] *Ibid.*, XLIX.
[32] *Ibid.*, III.
[33] *Ibid.*, XXIII.
[34] *Ibid.*, XXXVI.
[35] *Jude the Obscure*, III, viii.
[36] *Ibid.*, V, viii.
[37] *Ibid.*, V, vi.
[38] *Ibid.*, III, iii.
[39] *Ibid.*, I, ii.
[40] *The Return of the Native*, Book III, Chap. i.
[41] *The Mayor of Casterbridge*, Chap. XXIX.
[42] *Ibid.*, XIX.
[43] *The Woodlanders*, Chap. XLV.
[44] *Ibid.*, XI.
[45] *Tess of the D'Urbervilles*, XX.
[46] *The Woodlanders*, III.
[47] *A Pair of Blue Eyes*, XXX.
[48] *Ibid.*, XL.
[49] *The Return of the Native*, III, i.
[50] *Ibid.*, III, iii.
[51] *The Woodlanders*, XI.
[52] *Ibid.*, VI.
[53] *Tess*, V.
[54] *Desperate Remedies*, Chap. XXI, Section i.
[55] *Ibid.*
[56] *A Pair of Blue Eyes*, XXII.
[57] *Tess*, XLIII.
[58] *Jude the Obscure*, VI, ii.
[59] "Yell'ham-Wood's Story," in *Time's Laughingstocks* (first ed. 1909), p. 207.
[60] *Desperate Remedies*, XXI, i.
[61] *Far from the Madding Crowd*, LIII.
[62] *The Return of the Native*, II, iii.
[63] *Ibid.*, IV, viii.
[64] *The Mayor of Casterbridge*, XLIV.
[65] *Tess*, XXV.
[66] *Ibid.*, LIX.
[67] *The Dynasts*, Part Second, Act II, Scene iii.
[68] *Ibid.*, First, V, iv.
[69] *Ibid.*, Fore Scene.
[70] *Ibid.*
[71] *Ibid.*
[72] *Ibid.*
[73] Ernest Brennecke, Jr., *Thomas Hardy's Universe*, Boston 1924, p. 97. The references are to Part First, VI, iii; I, iii; Second II, iv; Third, VIII, vii.
[74] Lionel Stevenson, *op. cit.*, pp. 240-241.
[75] *Ibid.*, 255-257.
[76] *Ibid.*, 258.
[77] "At a Bridal."
[78] Stevenson, pp. 261-263, refers to "The Farm Woman's Winter," "In a Wood," "A Meeting with Despair," "To Life," "On a Fine Morning."
[79] *Wessex Poems*, etc., p. 165.
[80] Florence Emily Hardy, *The Early Life of Thomas Hardy*, New York 1928, p. 192 (May, 1881). Reprinted by kind permission of the Macmillan Co.

81 *Ibid.*, pp. 285-286 (April, 1889). Reprinted by kind permission of the Macmillan Co.

82 *Poems of the Past and Present*, p. 69.

83 *The Dynasts*, Part First, V, iv.

CHAPTER XX

Victorian Afterglow

1 Mathilde Blind, *The Ascent of Man*, London 1899, Part I, Section ii.

2 Robert Bridges, *Poems in Classical Prosody*, Epistle I, lines 212-217. Quoted, by kind permission of the publishers, from *The Poetical Works of Robert Bridges*, Oxford University Press 1912.

3 *Ibid.*, Epistle II, 418-422. This, and the following passage from "To Robert Burns", quoted, by kind permission of the Oxford University Press, from *The Poetical Works of Robert Bridges*.

4 *The Poems of William Watson*, London and New York 1905, I, 205.

5 "Vita Nuova," *ibid.*, p. 106.

6 "Hymn to the Sea," *ibid.*, p. 40.

7 Alfred Noyes, "The Loom of Years," in *Collected Poems*, Stokes 1913, Vol. I, p. 2.

8 See, e.g., "The Paradox," *ibid.*, I, 91.

9 "On the Downs," *ibid.*, II, 50.

10 Reprinted by permission from "The Two Worlds," in *Collected Poems*, Vol. II, p. 66, by Alfred Noyes. Copyright, 1910, by Frederick A. Stokes Co.

11 Laurence Binyon, "Nature," in *Collected Poems*, London 1931, I, 54. This and the other quotations from Laurence Binyon made by kind permission of the publishers, the Macmillan Co.

12 "The Renewal," *ibid.*, I, 40.

13 "The Sirens, an Ode," *ibid.*, I, 344.

14 *Ibid.*, I, 349.

15 John Masefield, *Good Friday and Other Poems*, New York 1916, p. 107. This and the other quotations from John Masefield made by kind permission of the publishers, the Macmillan Co.

16 *Ibid.*, 80.

17 Masefield, *Lollingdon Downs and Other Poems*, New York 1917, p. 17.

18 *Ibid.*, 13.

19 *Good Friday*, p. 87.

20 *Ibid.*, 72.

21 *Ibid.*, 74.

22 *Lollingdon Downs*, p. 10.

23 *Good Friday*, p. 101.

24 *Ibid.*, 67.

25 *Ibid.*, 99.

26 D. H. Lawrence, *Sons and Lovers*, Chap. XIII.

27 *The Rainbow*, at the end of Chap. III.

28 *Ibid.*, at the end of Chap. VI.

29 *Women in Love*, Chap XIX.

30 "Corot," in *Love Poems and Others*, New York 1913, p. xxxiii.

31 See Aldous Huxley's illuminating introduction to *The Letters of D. H. Lawrence*, New York 1932, e.g., p. xx.

32 W. B. Yeats, "The Rose of the World," in *Poetical Works*, 2 vols., New

York 1915, I, 170. This and the earlier quotations from W. B. Yeats made with kind permission of the publishers, the Macmillan Co.

³³ George W. Russell ("AE"), "The Virgin Mother," to be found in G. DeW. Sanders and J. H. Nelson, *Chief Modern Poets of England and America*, New York 1929, p. 114. This and other quotations from AE made by kind permission of this poet's publishers, the Macmillan Co.

³⁴ "Reconciliation," *ibid.*, p. 125.

³⁵ "Carrowmore," *ibid.*, p. 117.

³⁶ Edwin Arlington Robinson, "L'Envoi," in *The Children of the Night* (1897), New York 1914, p. 121.

³⁷ "Issac and Archibald," in *Captain Craig* (1902), New York 1915, p. 95. This and the following quotation from "The Man Against the Sky" made by kind permission of Mr. Robinson's publishers, the Macmillan Co.

³⁸ Edgar Lee Masters, "Nature," in *The Open Sea*, New York 1921, p. 302. These excerpts from "Nature" and those below from several poems in *Invisible Landscapes* (Macmillan 1935), are all reproduced by special permission of Mr. Masters, to whom I wish to express my thanks for his courtesy.

³⁹ Robinson Jeffers, "Credo," in *Roan Stallion, Tamar, and Other Poems*, Modern Library ed., p. 295. Reprinted by courtesy of Random House, New York.

⁴⁰ Jeffers, "The Broken Balance," in *Dear Judas*, New York 1929, pp. 117, 118. Reprinted by courtesy of Random House, New York.

⁴¹ "Night," in *Roan Stallion, Tamar, and Other Poems*, New York 1925, p. 84. Reprinted by courtesy of Random House, New York.

⁴² "Autumn Evening," *ibid.*, 94. Reprinted by courtesy of Random House, New York. Cf. "Shine, Perishing Republic," *ibid.*, 95.

⁴³ "Apology for Bad Dreams," *Roan Stallion*, etc., Modern Library ed. p. 278. Reprinted by courtesy of Random House, New York.

⁴⁴ "A Little Scraping," in *Give Your Heart to the Hawks*, New York 1933, p. 112. This and the three following excerpts from this volume reprinted by courtesy of Random House, New York.

⁴⁵ "Intellectuals," *ibid.*, 113.

⁴⁶ "Still the Mind Smiles," *ibid.*, 115.

⁴⁷ "A Little Scraping," *ibid.*, 111.

⁴⁸ Joseph Conrad, *A Personal Record*, in *Complete Works*, New York 1925, Vol. VI, p. 92.

CHAPTER XXI

THE VANISHING POINT

¹ *Georgian Poetry 1911–1912*, p. 81.

² *Ibid.*, 81, 80, 82.

³ *Georgian Poetry 1918–1919*, p. 63.

⁴ *Georgian Poetry 1911–1912*, p. 20.

⁵ *Ibid.*, 134.

⁶ *Ibid.*, 60, 61.

⁷ *Ibid.*, 34.

⁸ *Some Imagist Poems, an Anthology*, Boston 1915, p. vii.

⁹ *A Boy's Will*, New York 1915, pp. viii and 25.

¹⁰ *Ibid.*, vii and 18.

¹¹ "Birches," in *Mountain Interval*, New York 1916, p. 39.

¹² "The Bear," in *West-Running Brook*, New York 1828, p. 64. This and the

following excerpt reprinted by kind permission of the publishers, Henry Holt and Co.

13 "West-Running Brook," *ibid.*, 37.

14 "Salutation," in Drinkwater, Canby, and Benét's *Twentieth-Century Poetry*, Cambridge 1929, p. 373.

15 "American Letter," in *Poems 1924–1933*, p. 164. The excerpts from this poem and from "Einstein" reprinted by kind permission of the publishers, Houghton Mifflin Co.

16 "Einstein," *ibid.*, 75.

17 "After They Have Tired," in Stephen Spender's *Poems*, New York 1934, p. 48.

18 C. Day Lewis, "The Magnetic Mountain," Section 18, in *Collected Poems*, New York 1935.

19 "Prometheus Unbound," Act I, ll. 648-651.

20 "Winter Landscape," in Louis Untermeyer's *Modern British Poetry*, third revised edition, pp. 769-770. Quoted by special permission of Mr. Spender.

INDEX

Roman numerals refer to chapters in which the author is treated as a main subject. Mere book and page references in the Notes are not listed in this Index, except in the case of editors and scholars whose names would not otherwise appear.